# Sociolinguistics and Language Teaching

THE CAMBRIDGE APPLIED LINGUISTICS SERIES

Series editors: Michael H. Long and Jack C. Richards

This series presents the findings of recent work in applied linguistics which are of direct relevance to language teaching and learning and of particular interest to applied linguists, researchers, language teachers, and teacher trainers.

*In this series:*

**Interactive Approaches to Second Language Reading** *edited by Patricia L. Carrell, Joanne Devine, and David E. Eskey*

**Second Language Classrooms** – Research on teaching and learning *by Craig Chaudron*

**Language Learning and Deafness** *edited by Michael Strong*

**The Learner-Centered Curriculum** *by David Nunan*

**Language Transfer** – Cross-linguistic influence in language learning *by Terence Odlin*

**Linguistic Perspectives on Second Language Acquisition** *edited by Susan M. Gass and Jaquelyn Schachter*

**Learning Strategies in Second Language Acquisition** *by J. Michael O'Malley and Anna Uhl Chamot*

**The Development of Second Language Proficiency** *edited by Birgit Harley, Patrick Allen, Jim Cummins and Merrill Swain*

**Second Language Writing** – Research insights for the classroom *edited by Barbara Kroll*

**Genre Analysis** – English in academic and research settings *by John M. Swales*

**Evaluating Second Language Education** *edited by J. Charles Alderson and Alan Beretta*

**Perspectives on Pedagogical Grammar** *edited by Terence Odlin*

**Academic Listening** *edited by John Flowerdew*

**Power and Inequality in Language Education** *edited by James W. Tollefson*

**Language Program Evaluation** –Theory and practice *by Brian K. Lynch*

**Sociolinguistics and Language Teaching** *edited by Sandra Lee McKay and Nancy H. Hornberger*

**Contrastive Rhetoric** – Cross-cultural aspects of second language writing *by Ulla Connor*

**Teacher Cognition in Language Teaching** *by Devon Woods*

**Second Language Vocabulary Acquisition** *edited by James Coady and Thomas Huckin*

**Text, Role, and Context** – Developing Academic Literacies *by Ann M. Johns*

**Immersion Education: International Perspectives** *edited by Robert Keith Johnson and Merrill Swain*

**Focus on Form in Classroom Second Language Acquisition** *edited by Catherine Doughty and Jessica Williams*

**Interfaces Between Second Language Acquisition and Language Testing Research** *edited by Lyle F. Bachman and Andrew D. Cohen*

**Culture in Second Language Teaching and Learning** *edited by Eli Hinkel*

**Network-based Language Teaching** – Concepts and Practice *edited by Mark Warschauer and Richard Kern*

# Sociolinguistics and Language Teaching

Edited by

*Sandra Lee McKay*

San Francisco State University

*Nancy H. Hornberger*

University of Pennsylvania

CAMBRIDGE UNIVERSITY PRESS

PUBLISHED BY THE PRESS SYNDICATE OF THE UNIVERSITY OF CAMBRIDGE
The Pitt Building, Trumpington Street, Cambridge, United Kingdom

CAMBRIDGE UNIVERSITY PRESS
The Edinburgh Building, Cambridge CB2 2RU, UK
40 West 20th Street, New York, NY 10011–4211, USA
10 Stamford Road, Oakleigh, Melbourne 3166, Australia
Ruiz de Alarcón 13, 28014 Madrid, Spain

http://www.cup.cam.ac.uk
http://www.cup.org



First published 1996
Fifth printing 2000

Printed in the United States of America

Typeset in Sabon

*Library of Congress Cataloging-in-Publication Data*
Sociolinguistics and language teaching / edited by Sandra Lee McKay, Nancy H. Hornberger.
p. cm. – (Cambridge applied linguistics series)
Includes bibliographical references.
ISBN 0-521-48205-4 (hardback. – ISBN 0-521-48434-0 (paperback).
1. Language and languages – Study and teaching – Social aspects.
2. Sociolinguistics. I. McKay, Sandra. II. Hornberger, Nancy H.
III. Series.
P53.8.S63 1996
306.4′4 – dc20 95-748
CIP

A catalog record for this book is available from the British Library.

ISBN 0 521 48205 4 hardback
ISBN 0 521 48434 0 paperback

# Contents

List of contributors vii
Series editors' preface viii
Preface ix
Acknowledgments xii

I LANGUAGE AND SOCIETY 1

Chapter 1 *Language attitudes, motivation, and standards* 3
Mary McGroarty

Chapter 2 *Societal multilingualism* 47
Kamal K. Sridhar

Chapter 3 *World Englishes* 71
Braj B. Kachru and Cecil L. Nelson

Chapter 4 *Language planning and policy* 103
Terrence G. Wiley

II LANGUAGE AND VARIATION 149

Chapter 5 *Regional and social variation* 151
John R. Rickford

Chapter 6 *Pidgins and creoles* 195
Patricia C. Nichols

Chapter 7 *Language and gender* 218
Rebecca Freeman and Bonnie McElhinny

III LANGUAGE AND INTERACTION 281

Chapter 8 *Ethnographic microanalysis* 283
Frederick Erickson

Chapter 9 *Interactional sociolinguistics* 307
Deborah Schiffrin

Chapter 10 *Intercultural communication* 329
J. Keith Chick

IV LANGUAGE AND CULTURE 349

Chapter 11 *The ethnography of communication* 351
Muriel Saville-Troike

Chapter 12 *Speech acts* 383
Andrew D. Cohen

Chapter 13 *Literacy and literacies* 421
Sandra Lee McKay

CONCLUSION 447

Chapter 14 *Language and education* 449
Nancy H. Hornberger

Index 474

# *Contributors*

J. Keith Chick, University of Natal, South Africa
Andrew D. Cohen, University of Minnesota
Frederick Erickson, University of Pennsylvania
Rebecca Freeman, University of Pennsylvania
Nancy H. Hornberger, University of Pennsylvania
Braj B. Kachru, University of Illinois, Urbana
Mary McGroarty, Northern Arizona University
Bonnie McElhinny, University of Toronto
Sandra Lee McKay, San Francisco State University
Cecil L. Nelson, Indiana State University
Patricia C. Nichols, San Jose State University, California
John R. Rickford, Stanford University, California
Muriel Saville-Troike, University of Arizona
Deborah Schiffrin, Georgetown University, Washington, D.C.
Kamal K. Sridhar, State University of New York, Stonybrook
Terrence G. Wiley, California State University, Long Beach

# *Series editors' preface*

While there are a number of useful introductions to sociolinguistics, this book is unique in that it presents a coherent overview of the field of sociolinguistics for second language teachers, focusing in particular on issues likely to be of interest to language teachers and others interested in the educational implications of sociolinguistic research. The editors have employed a useful framework to elucidate the different levels of interaction that are relevant in examining social dimensions of language and language learning, one which contrasts macro and micro dimensions of language use in contexts which range from international to national, community, interpersonal, and personal.

Throughout the book, the contributors seek to broaden our understanding of how second language teaching and learning is related to a broad range of factors including societal, political, cultural, psychological, and interpersonal issues. These are shown to influence our conception of language, attitudes toward languages and their users, notions of standards, appropriacy and politeness, and motivation to learn languages, as well as the choices we make when we communicate with different people. Each chapter focuses on one important aspect of sociolinguistic inquiry, examining the assumptions behind a particular approach, the research methods it makes use of, and the findings that have emerged from it, and then explores implications for second language teaching.

While sociolinguistics is not a field which seeks to inform classroom methodology in language teaching directly, it plays a central role in helping define the nature of language itself and, hence, in clarifying what communicative competence in a second language entails. This collection of papers will therefore be a valuable reference source for teachers, teacher educators, graduate students, and others interested in the relationship between the social context of language learning and success in learning a second or third language.

Michael H. Long
Jack C. Richards

# Preface

In many countries today, classrooms reflect a rich diversity of linguistic backgrounds. Students bring to the classroom not only other languages but also different varieties of English and culturally learned ways of using English. It is against this backdrop that teachers in general, and language teachers specifically, face the challenging task of respecting linguistic diversity while promoting common standards. Central to fulfilling this task is an understanding of the relationship between language and society, for it is the social context that both provides the conditions for linguistic diversity and reinforces the conventions necessary to maintain linguistic standards. The purpose of this book is to help language teachers and teachers of linguistically diverse and multicultural classes gain an understanding of the many ways in which language and society interact. It is addressed to pre-service and in-service teachers, primarily teachers in ESL/EFL and bilingual classrooms, teachers of linguistically and culturally diverse classes, and foreign language teachers.

Deciding how to present a text dealing with the relationship between language and society is problematic because some scholars in the field emphasize the manner in which social and political forces influence language use, often referred to as the *sociology of language*, whereas others focus on how language and language use reflect the larger society, at times referred to as *sociolinguistics*. In large part, the distinction rests on whether one emphasizes the society or the language. In addition, some researchers emphasize the macrolevel of analysis, for example, societal patterns of bilingualism, and others focus on the microlevel, for example, forms of address in face-to-face interaction.

A major assumption of this text is that both perspectives and both levels of analysis are critical for an understanding of the interaction between language and society. In fact, we believe that it is helpful to define the different areas of work in sociolinguistics by the intersection of these perspectives and levels. That is, we suggest that it is useful to distinguish between a macrolevel and a microlevel of social analysis and a macrolevel and a microlevel of linguistic analysis. In dealing with the social context, one can focus either on the larger context, like nations and communities, or on the more limited context of a particular social situation, with domains or communities of practice bridging macro to micro. In dealing with linguistic concerns, one can examine larger issues, like the choice of one language over another, or more specific items, like the choice of one phonological feature over another, with pragmatics or discourses bridging macro to micro. These distinctions between perspectives and levels of analysis provide the basis for the four major sections of the book, as shown below and described in the following paragraphs.

Levels of Social Analysis

| Levels of Linguistic Analysis | | Macro | Micro |
|---|---|---|---|
| | Macro | *Language and society* (Part 1)<br>Language attitudes, motivation, and standard<br>Societal multilingualism<br>World Englishes<br>Language planning and policy | *Language and culture* (Part 4)<br>Ethnography of communication<br>Speech acts<br>Literacy and literacies |
| | Micro | *Language and variation* (Part 2)<br>Regional and social variation<br>Pidgins and creoles<br>Language and gender | *Language and interaction* (Part 3)<br>Ethnograpic microanalysis<br>Interactional sociolinguistics<br>Intercultural communication |

The chapters in Part 1, "Language and Society," deal with the manner in which the larger social and political context affects language use at a macrolevel. In general, language use is analyzed on a macrolevel, with some of the issues being why a country might select one language over another for its official language, what factors contribute to language prestige, or what the emergence of a standard language implies for other related varieties. The chapters in Part 2, "Language and Variation," move to the microlevel of linguistic analysis and focus on how the larger social context affects the particular linguistic forms that an individual uses. One chapter, for example, examines how geographical region and social class influence the phonological, structural, and lexical features of the language used, and another asks to what extent societal norms are reflected in gender differences in discourse patterns and interactional style.

In Part 3, "Language and Interaction," the focus moves to the micro-level of social as well as linguistic analysis. The chapters in this part deal with how a specific social situation or role relationship influences both verbal and nonverbal communication and vice versa. In Part 4, "Language and Culture," the social level of analysis continues on the microlevel, focusing on specific social situations and role relationships, but the level of linguistic analysis is more macro, focusing on generalizations about the ways particular cultures and communities use and value language. One emphasis of this part, for example, is on examining how children in particular communities are socialized to use language and literacy; another is on the range of linguistic, interactional, and cultural knowledge language users must have in order to communicate appropriately in particular contexts. The concluding chapter of the volume, "Language and Education," attempts to draw together all the foregoing chapters by examining how language, in all its societal, variational, interactional, and cultural diversity, both influences and is influenced by education.

Each part of the book begins with a brief introduction which discusses the focus of the part and relates it to other parts of the text. Each chapter, written by a specialist in the area, provides an overview of the issues addressed in the field and discusses typical methodological approaches. Because this text is concerned with how sociolinguistic research affects language teaching and the linguistically diverse classroom, each chapter also includes a section that discusses the pedagogical implications of the issues discussed. Throughout, international as well as national (i.e., United States) cases are cited in order to emphasize the relevance of these issues for all global contexts. Finally, each chapter closes with lists of suggestions for further reading and references.

We wish to thank all the contributors to this volume, who devoted many hours to polishing their chapters, clearly demonstrating how the research and major issues in their field have implications for the teaching of English. Without their careful work and insights, this book would not have been possible.

Sandra Lee McKay
Nancy H. Hornberger

# Acknowledgments

The authors and publisher wish to thank the following for permission to reproduce copyrighted material:

**Figure 1,** page 156: Reprinted from Kurath, H. (1949). *A Word Geography of the Eastern United States,* Fig. 125. Ann Arbor: University of Michigan Press. In Reed, C. E. (1977). *Dialects of American English,* p. 99. Amherst, University of Massachusetts Press. **Figure 2,** page 157: Reprinted by permission of the publishers from *Dictionary of American Regional English,* Vol. I, Introduction and A–C, edited by Frederic G. Cassidy, Cambridge, Mass.: The Belknaps Press of Harvard University Press, Copyright © 1985 by the President and Fellows of Harvard College. **Figure 3,** page 158, and **Figure 4,** page 159: Reprinted from Kurath, H. (1949). *A Word Geography of the Eastern United States,* Figs. 42 and 3. Ann Arbor: University of Michigan Press, © by the University of Michigan, 1949, 1977. **Figure 5,** page 160: Reprinted from Hughes, A., and Trudgill, P. (1979). *English Accents and Dialects,* p. 33. London: Edward Arnold (Publishers) Ltd. **Figure 6,** page 161: Reprinted from Agar, D. E. (1990). *Sociolinguistics and Contemporary French,* p. 23. Cambridge: Cambridge University Press. **Figure 7,** page 162: Reprinted from Barbour, S., and Stevenson, P. (1990). *Variations in German,* p. 71. Cambridge: Cambridge University Press. **Figure 8,** page 164: Reprinted from Wolfram, W. (1991). *Dialects and American English,* p. 87. Englewood Cliffs, N.J.: Prentice Hall. Based on Labov, W. (1991). "The Three Dialects of English," in Eckert, P. (ed.). *New Ways of Analyzing Sound Change.* Orlando, Fla.: Academic Press. **Figure 9,** page 168: Reprinted from Labov, W. (1972). *Language in the Inner City.* Philadelphia: University of Pennsylvania Press. Originally in Labov, W. (1966). *The Social Stratification of English in New York City.* Washington, D.C.: Center for Applied Linguistics. **Table 1,** page 169, and **Figure 10,** page 170: Reprinted from Holmes, J. (1992). *An Introduction to Sociolinguistics.* Essex, England: Longman Group. **Figure 11,** page 171: Reprinted from *Language and Communication,* Vol. 6, no. 3, John R. Rickford, "The Need for New Approaches to Social Class Analysis in Sociolinguistics," pp. 215–221, Copyright 1986, with kind permission from Elsevier Science Ltd., The Boulevard, Langford Lane, Kidlington, OX5 1GB, UK. **Figure 1,** page 220: Reprinted from Fairclough, N. (1989). *Language and Power* (Language in Social Life Series), p. 25, Essex, England: Longman Group. **Figure 1,** page 453: In Hornberger, N. (1989). "Continua of Biliteracy," *Review of Educational Research 59* (3). Copyright 1989 by the American Educational Research Association. Reprinted by permission of the publisher. **Table 1,** page 462, and **Figure 2,** page 463: Reprinted from Hornberger, N. (1991). "Extending Enrichment Bilingual Education: Revisiting Typologies and Redirecting Policy." In Garcia, O. (ed.). *Focus on Bilingual Education. Essays in Honor of Joshua A. Fishman,* Vol. 1. Philadelphia: John Benjamins.

# PART I: LANGUAGE AND SOCIETY

The chapters in this part explore how the larger social and political context can affect social attitudes toward particular languages and language varieties, as well as individual motivation to learn a language. This part also examines the manner in which the social and political context influences language use on a macrolevel as, for example, in the designation of an official language or a bilingual's choice of language. Taken together, all the chapters in Part I employ a macrolevel social and linguistic analysis as they describe such concepts as linguistic standards, diglossia, language transfer, and corpus and status planning. We begin with a focus on language attitudes, since it is here that the social and individual factors of language use dramatically affect one another.

In the first chapter, "Language Attitudes, Motivation, and Standards," Mary McGroarty examines how social factors influence an individual's attitude and motivation toward learning a language and how social attitudes create and legitimize language standards. In this chapter, McGroarty provides a definition of attitudes and motivation and surveys early research of these constructs. She then discusses current theoretical approaches to studying language attitudes and motivation, emphasizing the research done in school settings and on teacher, student, and parent attitudes. Next, McGroarty discusses how language attitudes influence the creation of norms and standards as well as the formation of language policies. She ends the chapter by elaborating on the ways in which language teachers can promote individual motivation to learn a language; she also emphasizes how language teachers must be aware of the complex relationship between language attitudes and standards and must work to develop language policies that value linguistic diversity.

In Chapter 2, "Societal Multilingualism," Kamal Sridhar examines contexts and uses of multilingualism and exemplifies the manner in which societies allocate different uses for the languages widely spoken in a society. She also examines the reasons why bilinguals switch from the use of one language to another and explores the patterns and functions of that switching. In closing, Sridhar discusses the implications of multilingualism for language teachers, emphasizing the need for teachers to value bilingualism and to determine goals and standards for language teaching in light of the larger social and political context.

In the third chapter, "World Englishes," Braj Kachru and Cecil Nelson focus on the use of English in a global context and delineate the uses and users of English internationally in terms of three concentric circles: the Inner, Outer, and Expanding Circles. The authors provide examples of the structural, lexical, discourse, and literary characteristics of Outer Circle varieties of English and examine issues surrounding the existence of these varieties such as linguistic norms and standards and bilingual creativity. The chapter closes with a listing of specific areas of language teaching in which the study and teaching of world Englishes have particular relevance.

The final chapter of this part, "Language Planning and Policy," explores the manner in which societies make decisions to solve what are perceived of as communication problems. Terrence Wiley reviews three types of language planning – corpus planning, status planning, and language acquisition planning. He points out that language planning decisions can be undertaken by government officials as well as by influential individuals and be either explicitly or implicitly stated. Next, Wiley delineates two major approaches toward language planning, the neoclassical and historical-structural, and summarizes the work of three influential language theorists who exemplify aspects of these approaches. This discussion is followed by an examination of the kinds of linguistic, political, and economic goals language planning often sets out to achieve. In the final section, Wiley discusses language in education planning, examining the manner in which the U.S. courts, linguists, and classroom teachers participate in language planning decisions.

# 1 *Language attitudes, motivation, and standards*

Mary McGroarty

So, if you really want to hurt me, talk badly about my language. Ethnic identity is twin skin to linguistic identity – I am my language. Until I can take pride in my language, I cannot take pride in myself.

(Anzaldúa, 1987, p. 59)

Language is an intimate part of social identity. Anzaldúa testifies to the deeply felt bond between language and selfhood, a bond demanding that any language variety used by speakers during natural communication take its place as a legitimate form of expression. For teachers, her words suggest that respect for all forms of language used in the communities in which they teach is essential. At the same time, in all school settings, language is always the medium and sometimes the object of formal study. Often, teachers have a particular responsibility for certain aspects of language instruction, whether they be acquisition of native language literacy skills or skills in a second language. How can teachers carry out their charge while respecting the languages and language varieties that students bring to school and using existing language skills to build new ones? How can teachers enable students to achieve the linguistic mastery that will allow them access to both further opportunities and personal satisfaction, if students so desire?

Teachers have long asked themselves why some students excel in a subject but others, generally similar in background, academic preparation, and experience, struggle with or ignore it. When the subject is language instruction, whether in a native or a second language, a host of factors come into play. This chapter addresses one set of factors related to success in the language classroom: the attitudes and motivation of those who participate, both students and teachers. Although these factors are not the only ones that account for differences in classroom processes and student outcomes, they shape the environment for instruction and individual efforts of teachers and students in important ways.

The discussion in this chapter has benefited from the comments and suggestions of Bill Grabe, Nancy Hornberger, Sandra McKay, Suzanne Scott, and Keith Walters at various stages of manuscript preparation, and I am grateful for their insights and assistance.

What, precisely, are the relationships between an individual's attitudes and motivation, the social context of learning, and success in language learning? This question has driven many recent investigations, and it cannot be answered quickly or easily. Current theory and research have provided clear indications that the relationships between a person's prior linguistic and academic experience, the social context of instruction, and the results of formal language instruction have complex and reciprocal connections with each other. Positive attitudes about language and language learning may be as much the result of success as the cause. Furthermore, students with positive general attitudes may not be particularly successful if these attitudes are not linked with effective strategies that enable them to take advantage of instructional opportunities presented to them. In addition, students are affected by the attitudes and examples of their peers, teachers, and parents, with respect to language study, and by social and institutional language policies as reflected in, for example, required courses of language study, both first and second, in schools. The status of a language in a society, whether native or second language, further shapes the social climate for language study; in the case of English, language diffusion and the nativization of English around the world mean that distinctions such as second language or foreign language are increasingly hard to draw, because varieties of English and norms for use emerge in response to local communicative needs (Cheshire, 1991; Kachru & Nelson, this volume). Finally, attitudes and motivation affect learners and teachers in ways that, though perhaps powerful, are often unconscious; thus it is difficult to identify their influence readily or unambiguously.

Educators who want to gain a better grasp of the many influences of attitudes and motivation on language teaching need to understand the multiple and sometimes conflicting facets of these influences in order to see how they contribute to the processes and results of language instruction. This chapter surveys this complex topic by providing, first, the definitions of attitudes and motivations used in earlier studies and, then, a discussion of how attitudes have been measured directly and indirectly in past research. Then a theoretical approach used in some current investigations, accommodation theory, is summarized, and how it has been used to illuminate certain aspects of speakers' behavior during interaction explained. Issues and research related to language attitudes, particularly those of teachers, parents, and students in educational settings, are presented next. Then, an explanation is given of the central, though often unacknowledged, role of language norms and standards in language instruction, a role operative in both native and second language settings; in addition, some of the tensions surrounding normative issues are discussed. The dual function of language policy as a constraint on and expression of attitudes and values about language is addressed next. The chapter closes with an identification of the pedagogical implications related to attitudes and motivation in four principal areas: promoting positive motivation, discovering the forms of language relevant for instruction, creating classroom opportunities to use and explore different language forms, and influencing language policies at a variety of levels. The general goal of this chapter is to offer readers an informed overview of the most current approaches to language attitudes and motivation, to note current sources for further information in each area, and to illuminate the sociolinguistic and educational significance of the topics included here and in the other chapters in this volume.

## Definitions

Much early work in the study of language attitudes traces both basic conceptualization and form of measurement to the work of Gardner and Lambert (1972), psychologists interested in the language attitudes of Anglophone and Francophone Canadians, adults and children, toward English and French. Gardner has continued this line of inquiry and built it into a comprehensive model of second language acquisition in school settings, and his definitions continue to influence current work. In this frame of reference, *attitude* has cognitive, affective, and conative components (i.e., it involves beliefs, emotional reactions, and behavioral tendencies related to the object of the attitude) and consists, in broad terms, of an underlying psychological predisposition to act or evaluate behavior in a certain way (Gardner, 1985). Attitude is thus linked to a person's values and beliefs and promotes or discourages the choices made in all realms of activity, whether academic or informal. In this framework, *motivation* refers to the combination of desire and effort made to achieve a goal; it links the individual's rationale for any activity such as language learning with the range of behaviors and degree of effort employed in achieving goals (Gardner, 1985).

## Measurement of attitude and motivation

### *Early work*

The classic direct measures of individual attitudes and motivation used by Gardner and Lambert (1959, 1972) were extensive self-report questionnaires given to persons involved in second language study or bilingual situations, mainly in Canada, where the salience of skills in both French and English was high. Items on these questionnaires appeared in the form of statements about the language, the person or group using the target language, and the reasons for studying a particular language or languages in general; the respondent was asked to mark individual opinions on a Likert-type scale of 5 to 7 points. In one of the early studies of pupils in French immersion programs, for example, pupils were asked to rate their reactions to English-Canadians, French-Canadians, and French people from France according to these scales:

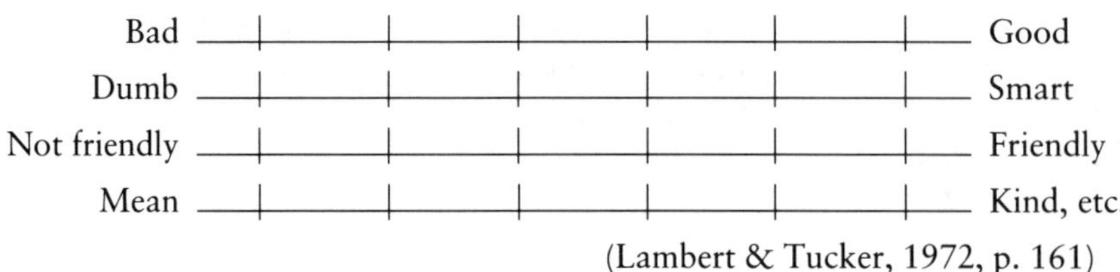


(Lambert & Tucker, 1972, p. 161)

Note that in this example the sample rating scale contains only polar adjectives, not definitions, so that respondents bring their own ideas about what the descriptors mean to the exercise. The use of global adjectives related to general personality characteristics, not specifically to language forms or linguistic features, was typical of such research. Responses were then analyzed statistically to determine patterns of correlation between a respondent's replies to various items and other measures such as participation in immersion programs.

An additional measure of attitude toward speakers of the language, as contrasted with opinions about language study, was the matched guise technique developed by Lambert. In the *matched guise technique,* people listened to taped samples of individuals speaking French and English and rated the speakers on affective and cognitive qualities, like those in the Likert-type scale, such as their relative strength, good humor, or intelligence using semantic differential scales based on Osgood, Suci, and Tannenbaum (1957). The scales, like the Likert scales, were based on a semantic differential consisting of polar adjectives ranged along a 5- to 7-point continuum; respondents were asked to rate speakers or speech samples by quickly selecting the point on the continuum which corresponded to their feelings or opinions. The poles on any continuum were never defined; therefore, respondents brought to bear their own meanings of the statements as they rated the stimulus. Results generally indicated that respondents perceived the cognitive and affective traits of the speakers differently depending on which language was spoken, even though, in the original stimulus tapes, all the speakers were bilinguals using each of their languages in different speech samples; thus the variation in response was interpreted as a result of respondents' own attitudes about these two languages rather than any genuine difference in the traits of the speakers, who were the same individuals. This technique has also been applied to language varieties such as regional dialects (see the discussion in Luhman's 1990 study of Appalachian English) and has enriched the understanding of language evaluation by showing that, even when listeners may downgrade the prestige or likelihood of achievement by speakers of a nonstandard form, they may evaluate the same speakers very highly in terms of friendliness, honesty, or integrity; to some degree, then, these solidarity-related factors contribute to covert prestige, which to some extent counteracts the view that the standard prestige form is the only possible target for use.

Among the many additional and influential contributions of the studies of Gardner, Lambert, and their colleagues to the definition of motivation was the development of the *orientation index* to second language study. This index sought to identify the types of motivation associated with success in language. It adapted the initial distinction, still widely used in psychology, between *intrinsic motivation*, based within the individual, and *extrinsic motivation*, based on an individual's perception of external rewards that will accrue from some action. The usual procedure was to ask respondents to rate their degree of agreement or disagreement with several statements about possible reasons for learning a language, as in the following:

The study of French could be important to me because:

It would help me better understand the French people and their way of life.

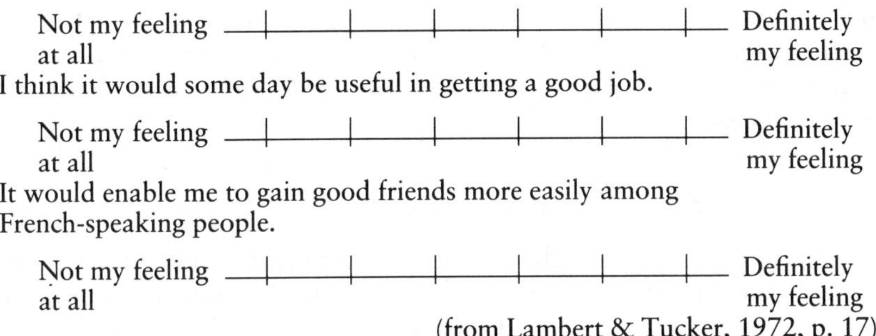

Not my feeling at all ⊢—⊢—⊢—⊢—⊢—⊢ Definitely my feeling

I think it would some day be useful in getting a good job.

Not my feeling at all ⊢—⊢—⊢—⊢—⊢—⊢ Definitely my feeling

It would enable me to gain good friends more easily among French-speaking people.

Not my feeling at all ⊢—⊢—⊢—⊢—⊢—⊢ Definitely my feeling

(from Lambert & Tucker, 1972, p. 17)

Largely on the basis of results of similar self-report questionnaires done with Anglophone Canadian students of French and their parents, Gardner and Lambert proposed two overarching constructs governing motivation to learn a language, which they later labeled *orientations* (Gardner, 1985): integrative motivation, the desire to be like and interact with speakers of the target language, and *instrumental motivation*, the desire to learn a language in order to achieve some other goal such as academic or occupational success. Integrative motivation was found to be more strongly linked with success in second language study for a school-age population, but later studies (e.g., Lukmani, 1972; Oller, Baca, & Vigil, 1977) indicated that the relative contribution of one or the other type of motivation varied according to setting and level of students investigated. For adults interested in job success, instrumental motivation could be just as or even more powerful than integrative motivation (Gardner & MacIntyre, 1991). Indeed, later work on motivation using Gardner-Lambert–type questionnaires suggests that orientation is an indirect rather than a direct influence on achievement (Gardner, 1985); that is, along with other factors, it operates in combination to affect language learning. Recent research using multiple indicators of attitude, including gender, age, language background, type of school attended, and local youth culture, has shown that these variables together shape attitudes, which in turn affect and are simultaneously influenced by ability in a language (Baker, 1992, Chap. 3). Furthermore, it is not so much the type but the intensity of motivation that makes a difference in successful outcomes of second language study (Snow, Padilla, & Campbell, 1988), confirming the experience of teachers who see that students with many distinct motivational profiles can learn a language. Instructional obstacles come about not because students have different types of motivation but because some students are relatively less motivated by any combination of integrative, instrumental, or other orientations. Having no clear purpose and no strongly felt reason to learn another language, such students are unlikely to expend the effort required. The social context of instruction sets some of the parameters of language learning that affect the presence and intensity of different types of motivation: for students in a foreign language setting, the idea of integrating with the host culture may be remote for all but a few, whereas the need to learn a language for clearly defined job activities may be stronger.

## *Limitations of the classic approach*

The psychometric approaches to the definition and measurement of attitudes and motivation have established a well-grounded theoretical model for second language acquisition in educational settings, but the model has had limited impact on classroom practice for several reasons. Many of these limitations are discussed in more detail by Crookes and Schmidt (1991), who note that the definitions of motivation used in sociopsychological research have been too narrow and too remote from pedagogical issues to provide direction for teachers, who usually use the term *motivation* more inclusively to capture aspects of student behavior they find relevant to success or failure in formal instruction. Sociopsychological approaches also present theoretical problems.

First comes the matter of causality. Because it is not clear whether instrumental motivation is the cause or, just as likely, the result of successful efforts to acquire a second language (Strong, 1984), it would be unwise to ask teachers to devote efforts to encouraging this type of motivation rather than working directly through specific classroom techniques to ensure greater success in language learning. Second, even researchers skilled in these investigations note that results depend on how each construct is measured (Gardner & MacIntyre, 1993); changes in questionnaire content can affect results in ways that belie the underlying constructs, for example, by altering the item clusters used to define the constructs. Third, because the methodology and analysis for studying attitudes and motivation have been derived mainly from the discipline of experimental psychology and have been used largely to build models of language acquisition, the classroom is treated generically; that is, a differentiated picture of the classroom processes and interactions that might shape an individual's access to the language studied is not available.

Some recent studies (see Ely, 1986a, b) have augmented the more abstract models of attitude and motivation by correlating the results of the questionnaires with self-reported risk taking as indicated, for example, by volunteering answers or raising one's hand in the classroom. In selecting only the visible aspects of student behavior, these studies too are limited in their applicability to the full range of classroom issues that teachers face in designing instruction, but these efforts add behavioral specificity to earlier models of the motivational factors that affect language instruction.

Other recent commentators have questioned the possibility that success in second, as compared with foreign, language learning must necessarily reflect similar motivational profiles, since foreign language learners are less likely than second language learners to have detailed knowledge about the target culture (Dörnyei, 1990). The experimental or quasi-experimental framework of such studies is thus useful in constructing an ex post facto picture of language learning but does not provide specific methodological guidance for those interested in planning classroom-level interventions to affect either language learning or language attitudes in many situations (Crookes & Schmidt, 1991; Roberts, Davies, & Jupp, 1992).

Finally, the parameters of motivational investigations in L2 settings have often been drawn narrowly rather than broadly, so that they have focused on the L2 learner or even the L2 classroom in relative isolation. Even researchers skilled in this paradigm admit that it has limited the usefulness of the ensuing theoretical models; L2 motivation must be integrated into a more complete picture of personality and of the interaction between person and situation, taking into account such traits as generalized need to achieve and anxiety, which affect many kinds of learning (Gardner, 1991; Horwitz, Horwitz, & Cope, 1991).

Thus more recent studies have often sought to situate language learning aptitude and motivation within a broader account of the human personality, on the one hand, and the social context of instruction, on the other. Individual personality factors studied include more global psychosocial tendencies such as general personality type, assessed by such indicators as, for example, the Meyers-Briggs type indicator (MBTI; see Ehrman, 1990; Oxford & Ehrman, 1988) or the relative strength of ego boundaries, which determine the degrees of flexibility or rigidity individuals show in the face of new situations or emotionally laden situations (Ehrman, 1994). Moreover, the relationship between other general psychological factors and language learning success is not completely straightforward, for in some cases, it appears that the absence of facilitating factors is a greater disadvantage than the presence of factors thought to promote success (Ehrman, 1993). In addition, other recent commentators on L2 motivation note that earlier motivational models neglected potentially valuable additions from other areas of psychology such as general educational, industrial-occupational, and social learning theory, all of which can contribute useful insights for second language learners and teachers (Oxford & Shearin, 1994). Common to this more recent work, whether done to better describe a single construct such as anxiety, better elucidate the relationships between general personality traits and success at language learning, or apply insights from other areas of psychology to language learning, is the realization that there is no single pattern of motivation that guarantees success or failure in all language learning situations.

Many empirical studies suggest that much depends on the interaction between the person, the nature of instruction received, and the broader language learning context (Baker, 1992). Because the social context of instruction is specifically related to which language is being taught to whom and because classrooms differ in the nature of instruction offered, it is reasonable for teachers to expect that interrelationships between these factors will change according to who is studying which language, in what social setting, and with what kind of classroom instruction. In a large-scale study of elementary-level foreign language learners, McGroarty (1988) found that learners in first-year Spanish and first-year Japanese classes who persisted and succeeded through a year of second language instruction showed some overlaps and some differences. For both groups, motivational factors representing overall interest in languages, the particular language chosen for study, and perception of parental and social support for second language study were associated with proficiency and achievement indicators, and distinctive factors representing a positive attitude toward language classroom instruction (for Spanish) and perceived instrumental value of learning the second language (for Japanese) differentiated the students of these two languages. As Crookes and Schmidt (1991) remark, differences in findings are to be expected in studies which use the standard sociopsychological approach, because the factor analytic procedures used to identify various motivational influences generally result in items being sorted differently in different samples.[1] In the ensuing analyses, the procedures may then confuse differences within the student group with differences in instructional settings and social contexts of L2 instruction; this complicates both interpretation and matters of justifiable pedagogical suggestions.

Moreover, the issue of motivational profiles related to the overall educational experience specific to certain age levels and groups of students deserves more detailed investigation, as Anderman and Maehr (1994) show with respect to middle school levels and Graham (1994) demonstrates in her discussion of motivation in African-American students. When membership in a specific linguistic or ethnic group has relevance for language study as a part of the curriculum, it is important to examine group as well as individual motivations which contribute to initial choice, persistence, and success in language study. Once more, the intergroup relationships characteristic of the social context of language instruction (or language repression; see Hurtado & Rodríguez, 1989) are likely to affect the success of various groups of students differentially, and such effects need more specific documentation. Recent theories in social sciences have indicated renewed interest in the role of affective factors as they shape cognition (see, e.g., Denzin, 1984), and this trend too suggests that comprehensive theories of motivation for all areas of human activity, language learning included, must integrate emotional influences along with the traditionally studied cognitive factors in accounting for achievement (Weiner, 1992).

## Connections with behavior: Accommodation theory

Also grounded in social psychology, work on *accommodation theory* by Giles and colleagues (1979, 1991) has helped to connect attitudes and motivation to language behavior during social interaction. Originally developed to account for style shifting and speech evaluation of speakers within a native-speaking British-English context, the theory

1 The mathematical underpinnings for this observation are outside the scope of this chapter. Briefly, though, the differences stem from the differences both of range and in instructional context found in the various samples of students studied. The factor structure derives from the degree to which different items are intercorrelated, and this, in turn, depends on the range of traits found in the sample of the population studied. In addition, the responses of students studying a foreign language who have very limited access to the language outside their classes may be very different from the responses of students studying a language widely available in the environment outside the classroom. Thus it is reasonable that different samples should show differing factor structures even when the items used to examine them are the same or similar.

posits that attitudinal factors related to feelings of solidarity or distinctiveness encourage an individual to modify speech in the direction of a superior social reference group through increased frequency of use of prestige or standard variants (*convergent accommodation*), or, in some settings, to use socially marked features to emphasize a distinctive social identity (*divergent accommodation*). Beebe (1988) provides a succinct historical summary of the various analytic streams contributing to this approach to analysis of oral interactions; most relevant to the current discussion is that accommodation theory includes aspects of attributions speakers make about each other (see also Hewstone, 1983) and their desire to increase, decrease, or maintain the sense of intergroup distinctiveness created through interaction. Beebe and Zuengler (1983) have applied this theoretical approach to second language acquisition. They note that accommodation theory, in its emphasis on performance data, enables researchers to examine actual interaction rather than psychological constructs; at the same time, they caution against an automatic application of sociolinguistic findings from first language settings to second language data: speakers operating in a second language work from a base of variable language proficiency, particularly while learning the language, and this unstable proficiency affects their ability to accommodate interlocutors in speech because they cannot consistently use features they have not yet fully acquired. The following example shows how a second language speaker not yet in full control of English phonology eventually resolved the potential misunderstanding of the native speaker interlocutor:

NNS: And they have the chwach there
NS: The what?
NNS: The chwach . . . I know someone that . . .
NS: What does it mean?
NNS: Like um like American people they always go there every Sunday, you know . . . every morning that
NS: Yes?
NNS: There pr-that -the American people get dressed up to go to um chwach
NS: Oh to church . . I see

(data from Pica, 1988, cited in Gass & Varonis, 1991, p. 140)

Gass and Varonis (1991) provide numerous examples of the types of miscommunication that can occur and descriptions of the means speakers use to resolve misunderstandings in spoken interactions. Most relevant to this chapter is the notion that, when accommodation theory is considered with respect to second language learners, the learner's proficiency level in the language of interaction is a critical variable. For native speakers, notions of the presence (or absence) of willingness to accommodate presume control of the forms or features which could mark convergence or divergence from the interlocutor; for second language users, this is not a given. Gass and Varonis provide a useful theoretical and practical complement to the research on language anxiety discussed previously. Communication anxiety for second language learners includes worry about the kind of judgments that will be made about them (Horwitz, Horwitz, & Cope, 1991), and it is likely that incomplete control of the language would cause learners anxiety about others' opinions of them.

However, even when nonnative speakers have mastered certain features, whether or not they will use them during interaction depends on several additional social and contextual factors, such as who their interlocutors are and the reasons for, and perceived consequences of, any interaction. Zuengler's recent work (1993; Zuengler & Bent, 1991) illustrates the interesting role of expertise: When fluent, advanced-level ESL male university students interacted with native-speaking partners in conversations about a general topic and about their mutual major field, the person who was the relative expert, regardless of native speaker status, dominated the conversation. When expertise was equal, there was no consistent pattern of domination by one group or the other revealed by amount of speech or number of interruptions. Clearly, then, the social and personal valence of any interaction between native and nonnative speakers, including, crucially, the knowledge each has about the topic under discussion, affects the degree to which they are likely to accommodate to each other during communication. This line of research on the combined effects of proficiency level in the L2 and the level of expertise in the topic of interaction is important in several applied settings such as communication between international teaching assistants (ITAs) and native speaker students or between nonnative medical personnel and native speaker patients.

## Research on language attitudes as reflected in speaker behavior

Sociolinguistic research, particularly research conducted within the variationist paradigm (see Beebe, 1988, for an overview of this paradigm and related L2 research), has provided some general indicators of the influences of speakers' attitudes on language behavior in a wide variety of settings. This research has shown the power of community norms, particularly those related to peer group membership, that shape the choices made by speakers. Labov's classic study of adolescent males in Harlem indicated that those best integrated into a coherent social group or gang outside the school setting showed the highest use of distinctive features of black English vernacular,[2] whereas those young men who were not part of the group did not command the same verbal repertoire; in terms of mastery of vernacular forms, they were "lames" (Labov, 1972, 1973). In a study of 28 male teenagers, all native speakers of Spanish who had lived in the greater New York area for an average of 3 years, Goldstein (1987) found that extensive contact with black English speakers was a necessary but not sufficient condition for using two features of black English, distributive *be* and negative concord, in one's own speech; however, even the participants who had had extensive contact with African-Americans did not use these features categorically (as would be true in black English) but, rather, variably.

Reports on the kinds of dialectal features found in native American communities also indicate that some features such as freely variable plural markers (e.g., "Some plywoods blew out of my pickup," "I have lots of friend") or variable verb agreement ("My parents wants you to go," "My favorite things is my friends and my hobbies"; all examples from Beck & Foster, 1989) are common in the English of more traditional people with relatively less exposure to education. Many times, though not always, such speakers are also those who know the tribal language. In some communities, this leads younger speakers whose English is closer to the mainstream to apply various disparaging nicknames (e.g., Navajo "Johns" or "Johnnies") to those who use the tribal language or whose style of speaking in English is not proficient (Beck, 1992; Beck & Foster, 1989). Teenagers' use of such within-group nicknames indicates the linguistic insecurity, ambivalence, and tension surrounding native language use and local varieties of English (Holm, 1994). Much of the research on native American varieties of English has dealt mainly with discrete linguistic features of phonology, morphology, and lexis.

More recent research examines, in addition, larger units such as speech acts and genre definitions which vary according to subgroup membership. Differences at the discoursal as well as discrete linguistic feature level evoke interlocutor reactions related to notions of communicative norms regarding, for example, what constitutes appropriate organization and coherence strategies within a text (Leap, 1993), an acceptable response to a compliment (see Chick, this volume; Cohen, this volume), a reasonable factual account of a past event (Heath, 1983), or an adequate answer to a question during an employment interview (Akinnaso & Ajirotutu, 1982). As sociolinguistics has begun to identify discourse-based conditioning of the choice of discrete linguis-

2 In this chapter, the terms *black English Vernacular* and *black* are used where they appeared in the original studies to denote what would now be termed *African-American Vernacular English* and *African-American* (see Rickford, this volume).

tic forms, investigators have become more aware of the power of differing definitions of competent performance in apparently comparable speech situations and the need to identify and sometimes modify conventional discourse patterns related to educationally relevant settings such as classrooms or reading groups (McGroarty, 1991; Sato, 1989). Moreover, commentators tracing the history of discussion of dialect differences in the United States have pointed out that past scholarship itself often reflects the implicit prejudices of its social context (see Smitherman-Donaldson, 1988), rendering it essential that researchers and teachers both take a fresh look at contemporary patterns of language variation.

Research on speaker and interlocutor attitudes toward varieties of language use often reveals patterns differentiated by gender. Typically, though not always, women are found to use prestige variants more frequently when discrete linguistic items are analyzed; their use of speech act and discoursal features comes closer to reflecting the overt prestige forms of their communities. Furthermore, women often overestimate their own level of adherence to standards, whereas men tend to underestimate theirs (Luhman, 1990). Recent investigators have noted the problematic nature of gender-divided findings, pointing out that they may be the artifact of other equally crucial but less easily measured social indicators such as women's uncertain social status in many communities as social and economic conditions change (see Freeman & McElhinny, this volume; Uchida, 1992; Williams, 1992) and the relative undervaluing (particularly in academic or professional contexts) of the language forms and styles associated with women's activities such as nurturance, socialization, and play (Pratt, 1987). Whatever the reasons for such findings, they provide strong evidence that true norms for language use must reflect the behavior and reactions of women as well as men if they are to be comprehensive.

## Attitudes toward language in educational settings

Like sociolinguistic research generally, studies of attitudes in educational settings have moved from studies of the effect of discrete linguistic features to consideration of larger units of discourse as they shape and reflect the actions, interactions, and reactions of participants, including teachers, students, and parents (McGroarty, 1991). Also, rather than being studied as the single determinative factor in linguistic outcomes, language attitudes are now more often linked with other factors such as perceived competence and personal and academic self-esteem (see Cabazón, Lambert, & Hall, 1993), or beliefs about the ethnolinguistic vitality of the community which uses whatever language is to be learned or retained (e.g., Allard & Landry, 1992; Kraemer & Olshtain, 1989), or patterns of actual language use in the home and other settings (Hakuta & D'Andrea, 1992) to generate comprehensive models of language learning or retention. Increasingly sophisticated statistical procedures such as path analysis have been used to explore the direction, magnitude, and significance of multiple affective factors such as attitudes and demographic and contextual influences on language learning and use.

## *Teacher attitudes*

The pioneering work in language attitudes of teachers done by Williams and his collaborators in the 1970s examined teacher reaction to students speaking different varieties of American English (Williams, 1973, 1976). Initial studies used samples of black and white children, matched for socioeconomic status and gender, talking about similar topics; the audiotapes were rated on a semantic differential by groups of black and white teachers who taught in inner-city schools in Chicago and Memphis. Factor analyses of teacher judgments revealed two factors accounting for evaluations: one reflected confidence and eagerness to communicate, as indicated by amount of speech, sentence length, and perceived enthusiasm and lack of hesitation; the other embodied an "ethnicity/nonstandardness" dimension related to the number of nonstandard features typical of black English Vernacular (e.g., redundant pronoun reference, deviations from standard pronunciation in word-final [$-s$] or [$-z$]; Williams, 1976). Generally, both black and white teachers rated children who were high on the first factor as likely to succeed in language arts; white teachers showed a tendency to stereotype children based on the second factor, while black teachers, showed more differentiated (i.e., less stereotyped) ratings of children whose speech samples included nonstandard features. Later investigations expanded these groupings by including Mexican-American along with black and white children, all of either middle- or lower-class socioeconomic status, as subjects and used an additional, visual source of information, the videotape rather than just the audiotape. The tapes were rated by black and white teachers in central Texas. Teacher ratings in this study showed that the confidence or eagerness dimension had no correlation with stereotyping for children of middle-class status and had a small but significant correlation with stereotyping for lower-class children; the nonstandard dimension, though, was moderately correlated with stereotyped ratings for both middle- and lower-class children, making it the more influential aspect of teacher judgments in this experimental situation (Williams, 1976).

Ford (1984) added an element of quality of academic work to an investigation of teacher attitudes toward students who did or did not show elements of Spanish language influence in their speech. She created "composite children" at the fourth-grade level by pairing six compositions rated at similar levels (two average, and two each above and below average for their grade level) with audiotapes of six children, three of them using Spanish-influenced English, and three not. Forty teachers in the southwestern United States rated the tapes and compositions. Results showed that, regardless of the comparable quality of student compositions and regardless of the length of their own teaching experience, teachers gave a lower rating to the compositions of the children whose English showed Spanish features. Although teachers' experience and their own ethnicity (whether Hispanic or non-Hispanic) did not counteract the tendency to stereotype students, teachers' first language background did: Ratings from teachers whose first language was Spanish (a small number, unfortunately but predictably) showed a much smaller gap in their predictions of social status about students who did and did not show Spanish influence in their English, thus indicating that a teacher's first language can attenuate stereotypical negative expectations of a group that might otherwise be stigmatized in a school setting.

Some of the earlier experimental studies of teacher attitudes have been criticized for using decontextualized speech samples and intentionally vague instruments such as semantic differentials to elicit judgments about learning potential and instructional success, two traits that, more recent research indicates, are both highly contextualized. Thus researchers have turned to more naturalistic methods such as ethnographic observation and teacher interviews to explore implicit language attitudes that control interaction. It is notable that these studies, too, generally reveal that teachers and other high-status evaluators, particularly those who do not share the linguistic or ethnic background of their students, often perceive essential connections between oral and literate language abilities without realizing that various features and styles of oral discourse do not have a direct bearing on potential for success in literacy skills (see McKay, this volume).

Often, teachers unconsciously draw on their own language socialization background in their classroom discourse styles (Poole, 1992), even with learners whose socialization has been different from the teachers'. In a study of black and white first-graders' performances during the daily oral sharing time, Michaels (1986) found that the white teacher could more successfully scaffold the performance of the white children with whom she shared discourse conventions related to the "topic-centered" style, as contrasted with the "topic-associating" style more typical of black children (see Rickford, this volume, for further discussion). Shared discourse conventions in this classroom led to more synchronous interaction between the child teller and the teacher as chief interlocutor; throughout the year, the teacher persisted in trying to shape children's discourse toward a topic-centered norm because of her belief that this was central to success in literacy, even though at least one child who consistently favored a topic-associating style was, in fact, already one of the best readers in the class (Michaels, 1986).

Furthermore, ethnographic research helps to reveal important interactions of participant attitudes toward school and literacy events with other crucial sociodemographic variables such as gender. Ethnographic research shows that school, particularly elementary school, is often perceived as a feminine setting, thus promoting a positive orientation to literacy activities for girls and implicitly expecting different types of performance (and relatively less success) from boys (Solsken, 1993). Researchers doing such studies typically do not measure attitudes specifically but, following ethnographic tradition, infer attitudes from behaviors and comments of participants in a setting of interest (see Saville-Troike, this volume, for more details on ethnographic studies of communication). Such efforts are an essential complement to experimentally manipulated studies of language attitude because they add an essential component of ecological validity to quantitative experimental work and reveal how attitudes unconsciously shape repeated interactions in critical instructional settings and thus create conditions that promote success for some students but inadvertently discourage others from mastering aspects of literacy.

## *Student and parent attitudes*

The attitudes of students and parents are particularly shaped by the personal experiences of schooling and by the specific learning context. Thus it cannot be expected that all second language students, whether immigrants or refugees, share similar attitudes toward learning a new language or that native speaker students adding control of a mainstream variant to their native dialects are comparable to second language learners. The educational situations of first-language students adding prestige variants or acquiring literacy in their native language and those of second language students working to develop oral language proficiency and often literacy too are not necessarily comparable, although they may overlap. Generally, research done in American Vernacular English settings such as the situation of creole speakers discussed by Nichols (this volume) demonstrates that native-speaking students who use a nonmainstream dialect comprehend mainstream speakers quite well by the time they have had 4 to 5 years of formal schooling, but teachers who are monodialectal mainstream speakers frequently misunderstand students who use other dialects. In such cases, teachers need to develop the same kind of receptive competence in local dialect features that is expected of their students with respect to mainstream language if they wish to ensure an accurate understanding of their students, particularly during the initial years of school experience.

Learners of English as a second language are in a rather different situation: their level of comprehension of the standard or any dialect is influenced by amount of exposure to the language. As learners increase in second language proficiency, typically but not always after ever-longer periods of residence in an environment in which the second language is widely used, they become more knowledgeable about and sensitive to dialectal and contextual variation in language. Goldstein's study (1987) of the teenage Spanish speakers' use of black English features in their relatively advanced English showed that choice of a black or white reference group, determined through a 5-point rating scale applied to ideal self, blacks, and whites, indicated no relationship between personal reference group and linguistic behavior. She suggests that linguistic behavior, especially in advanced-level students, is a product of many factors in addition to choice of personal reference group; learners may well choose to use prestige variants, even if their close friends are not from the mainstream prestige dialect community, if they sense that using such forms makes a difference in achieving their goals.

The attitudes of parents reflect personal histories, including their responses to the wider cultural themes framing their own experiences. Thus parents who believe that they may have been stigmatized because of their own language are particularly eager to have their children acquire a standard language; they may value their home dialect in certain contexts but insist that their children have ample opportunity to develop skill in the prestige standard. A recent study of parents from several different ethnic groups in the Detroit area has indicated that parents, whether immigrant or second-generation residents in the United States, believed that children must develop strong English skills and retain and develop their home language as well (Lambert & Taylor, 1987). Many of them having achieved bilingual skills in their own lives, they saw no contradiction between these two goals and perceived both as vital for their children's educational and personal development. Similarly, Spanish-speaking parents of children in bilingual programs endorse the value of bilingual instruction, including maintenance of the home language and age-appropriate attainment in English literacy skills (Torres, 1988). Another study of parents whose children attended a Spanish immersion program has shown that even parents who are not themselves bilingual or members of highly cohesive ethnic communities support the opportunity for their children to become bilingual (Craig,

1994), seeing participation in such a program as an avenue toward not only development of dual-language mastery but, equally important to them, ability to survive in an increasingly multicultural environment.

Attitudes toward school instruction in which a community dialect is used and attitudes toward school situations in which another language is the medium of instruction[3] show some interesting contrasts in terms of the pattern of support for bilingualism as an educational goal to be attained through formal instruction which uses both language forms in the classroom. Parents who use a community variety such as African-American Vernacular English may well oppose the use of such language for literacy instruction even when they reveal a detailed knowledge of and loyalty to this variety (see Rickford, this volume, for further discussion). Note that, in such cases, bidialectal skills still figure as an important goal of education; in this situation, it is simply assumed that the home dialect need not be taught in school, which is the place for formal instruction in and practice of the standard language. Indeed, well-educated bidialectal speakers of African-American English show considerable diversity in their attitudes toward this variety; they are by no means unanimous in supporting or opposing its widespread use by African-Americans either in or out of school (Speicher & McMahon, 1992). In some ways, such findings parallel those related to parent and community members in bilingual communities where a long-established home language, such as Quechua, has thrived for centuries in communities where the school is seen as an exclusively Spanish-speaking environment (Hornberger, 1987). In such cases the attitudes of parents and community members may well reflect the historical experiences of groups which have been marginalized and oppressed.

On the other hand, the use of some aspects of a community dialect, such as commonly used lexical items, in instruction may actually improve student comprehension, as has been the case with some vernacular Spanish materials discussed by Morales (1991). Hence, from a linguistic perspective, it is clear that blanket prohibitions of a community dialect in school whether as a medium for student-to-student or teacher-to-student communication are not justified; decisions about the contextual appropriateness of various language forms should instead reflect the student's age and proficiency level as well as the intent of any particular instructional interaction.

Furthermore, regardless of which language or dialect appears in in-

3 The line between a language and a dialect is not always clear and reflects historical, political, and economic factors as well as considerations of linguistic structures (see Crystal, 1987, Secs. 2, 47, 51, and 52). Contemporary social evaluations of language forms, as well as educational history and traditions, help in judging the appropriateness of a particular language variety or dialect for classroom use in oral and written domains.

structional materials, it is clear that teachers would do well to understand the variety their students use. Bilingual and bidialectal students have often borne the sole responsibility for increasing their communicative repertoires through mastery of the dominant school or mainstream language variety, but goals of two-way communicative accuracy between teachers and students suggest that, at the very least, teachers would benefit from developing receptive competence in the language varieties used by the major groups of students in their classrooms so as to avoid misunderstanding. Discussing the situation of bilingual students in the United States during the early 1980s, Politzer observed that "students whose total language competence is indeed a composite of two languages should, at least in their initial contacts with school, have contact with teachers who can utilize this total competence" (1981, p. 15). The same is true for students who use a dialect different from that found in school settings.

Much of the aforementioned research identifies general attitudes toward language varieties or target groups who use a language variety, constructs which have been termed *distal* factors in their influence on achievement in a language class (Crookes & Schmidt, 1991, p. 478). Some recent studies seek to link these distant and indirect influences on learning with classroom participants and conditions, describing, for instance, student profiles before (e.g., Roberts, 1992) and after second language instructional programs of varying degrees of length and intensity (e.g., Baldauf & Lawrence, 1990; Holmquist, 1993; Mantle-Bromley & Miller, 1991; Lambert, 1987; Lambert & Tucker, 1972; Snow, Padilla, & Campbell, 1988). Procedures from attitudinal research have been applied directly to classroom activities (see, e.g., Green, 1993) to provide a sense of the activities students enjoy and find helpful. When students have never before engaged in language study, they may well become discouraged, initially at any rate, to discover that a second language is not mastered in a matter of months or even a year or two.

When effects of instruction have been studied, it is important to note that formal second language study does not necessarily improve general social attitudes toward either the language or the target group; such effects depend greatly on the duration and quality of teaching and on the social context of instruction. The issue of general attitudes toward the target language group is an intriguing one; overall, the results of attitude studies demonstrate some arresting parallels with studies of cross-cultural attitude change showing that contact between different groups (the *contact hypothesis;* see Hewstone & Brown, 1986) is insufficient to bring about positive feelings toward another group. In considering the possibility for attitudinal change through language study, we cannot forget that attitudes and motivation for study are not only cognitive but have strong affective components, so that emotional concomitants of second language study must be addressed explicitly to make the learning experience a positive one.

## Creation and legitimation of norms and standards

### *Descriptive versus prescriptive norms*

The matter of norms for language teaching is problematic, reflecting the tensions between descriptive and prescriptive approaches to language and the tensions between public attitudes and expectations regarding language education, which often embody idealized visions of "proper" language use, and the complexities and variation of actual language behavior. A *descriptive norm,* as used by sociolinguists, is a statement of the form or feature of language that most speakers use most of the time; it is thus a statement of statistical probability and one which admits variation. A *prescriptive norm,* in contrast, is a formally stated rule meant to apply to all language uses in all settings; it is the stuff of which grammar and spelling handbooks are constituted.

Sociolinguists note that linguistic norms are typically differentiated by mode of communication, with oral language generally showing greater variability than written language and with different situations also demanding different linguistic forms and styles. As used by social psychologists, furthermore, the term *norms* includes not just the actual forms of language used but the expectations of speakers regarding the appropriate tone and stance conveyed by language in different situations; thus the research of social psychologists often reflects attention to the cognitive and affective expectations of participants in an interaction as realized through speech (see Gallois & Callan, 1991), reminding us that in some disciplines, as well as often in the public understanding of the term norms, affective factors operate, often unconsciously, to shape the evaluation of language forms used. Furthermore, native speakers of a language often have strongly felt opinions regarding where the "best" varieties of their language are spoken (though their opinions do not always coincide; see Preston, 1986), and their perceptions contribute to public attitudes related to appropriate language use and language instruction. Nonnative speakers may come to share some of these perspectives as they learn the language (Alford & Strother, 1990). Considered from an inclusive perspective, then, linguistic norms include probabilistic statements about what forms or features occur most often; codified rules appearing in reference works, usually phrased as invariant recommendations (though not always, for some arbiters of language such as textbook writers and editors become more sophisticated); and the expectations of those who use the language regarding the suitability of different linguistic features and styles according to different modes and communicative situations. As Bartsch (1987) notes, "Norms count as reason for certain behavior and as reason for criticism and correction of other behavior" (p. 173).

Linguists use *norm* in a neutral sense to describe the most frequently used language form, but, as used by members of the public, the term norms includes an element of positive valuation as well, and the tension between linguists' use of the term and public understanding of language norms affects both educational discourse and pedagogical techniques. Coulmas (1989) notes that professional linguists have, particularly in this century, taken a position of "prescriptive abstinence" (p. 177) which requires them to remain neutral on matters related to evaluation of good or proper language. He explains that this intellectual neutrality, related to the concept of linguistic relativism, often frustrates members of the educated public, who, in this age of specialization, want language specialists to offer definitive statements regarding appropriate language. Similarly, Lo Bianco (1989) identifies a "cultural gap between linguists and the public" (p. 182) in the Australian setting, caused in part by the relative invisibility of language issues in a society where the dominance of English monolingualism has, until very recently, obscured the validity of even identifying language as a possible target of public policy.

## *Standards and schooling*

The tension between the professional linguist's use of the term norms and that of the general public also figures in consideration of language standards. The notion of *standard* strongly connotes attention to written language; as linguists note, "a standard language variety is one which has undergone the lengthy process of standardization" (Finegan & Besnier, 1989, p. 496), which includes four stages: selection of a norm, elaboration for different uses, restriction of diversity, and codification in grammar or dictionaries (see Wiley, this volume). A standard language is thus the end result of this historical process. Public discussions of language standards, heard mainly in the context of laments about declines in school-related skills or achievement measures, nearly always present the linguistic uniformity embodied in a standard as evidence of felicity and appropriateness in expression, threatened by incorrect use, or as evidence of moral superiority and accurate thinking, which has been, presumably, threatened by changes or by variant forms. This is by no means only a contemporary phenomenon; as Milroy and Milroy (1985) explain, the "complaint tradition" in English has existed since the end of the seventeenth century and arose at approximately the time that written English became widely disseminated through inexpensive texts made possible by improved printing technology. Codification and prescription, focused as they were (and are) on writing, thus took "the norms of formal registers of standard English rather than the norms of everyday spoken English" (p. 37) as the appropriate models for authoritative reference works on the language. The actual magnitude and extent of change in language standards (which occur continuously, though more slowly than in speech because written reference works and codified rules constrain allowable variation) may, in the public mind, be overshadowed by the emotional reactions accompanying the perceptions of change. Simply put, to many public audiences, change in language standards equals decline, and a decline not just in linguistic mastery but in some ineffable moral attributes, too.

Because one of the main objectives of formal schooling is to teach reading and writing, schools are one of the central arenas for the promotion of prescriptive norms of written language (see Wiley, this volume). Historically, school systems have played a central role in creating and standardizing a national written language, not only in the United States (Baron, 1982) and Britain (Milroy & Milroy, 1985) but in other countries such as France and Germany (Resnick, 1991). Schools are certainly not the only institutions which shape language norms; in various societies, religious or governmental institutions and media, both print and electronic, contribute to the creation, maintenance, and change of language norms, as do age-related trends in language use. In schools, emphasis on propriety in writing, interpreted once more as adherence to the most formal registers of the language, is often even greater than in other institutional settings. The prescriptive norm usually reigns supreme; teachers are often regarded (and may regard themselves) as preeminently enforcers of prescriptive linguistic norms (grammar, spelling, or punctuation "police").[4] This, too, is neither a novel nor a fading theme of public opinion; Farr and Daniels (1986) observe that "the idea of propriety in speech is still firmly rooted

4 Many teachers have experienced the power of such public attitudes regarding the appropriate role of language teachers when, upon first telling another person of their occupation, they are met with a grimace and the half-kidding but telling remark, "Oh! An English teacher. I'd better watch my grammar." That such attitudes remain widespread even among well-educated groups attests to the tenacity of the view of teachers as guardians of conservative linguistic tradition.

Furthermore, the interaction of gender-based social expectations regarding language use (Luhman, 1990; Uchida, 1992) with the demographic fact of the predominantly female teaching staff, found particularly at the early levels of language and literacy instruction in many countries (Apple, 1993), very likely increases both public demand for and teachers' own expectations of the emphasis on prestige language forms in education. This topic deserves much further research as educators try to determine optimal instructional approaches which respect the diverse social identities of both teachers and students.

in American public education and in the professional culture of its teachers" (p. 49).

Along with community members such as learners and parents, teachers may view their principal linguistic responsibility as one of inculcating "correct language" without realizing that, even for educated native speakers, natural and correct language includes a variety of language forms, not a single variant (Beebe, 1988; Milroy & Milroy, 1985). With a firmer understanding and appreciation of the multiplicity of language forms and functions, each chosen according to communicative context, situation, audience, and purpose, teachers can become developers of sensitivity toward many varieties of language rather than pedantic linguistic enforcers. Valdman (1988) notes that there are multiple pedagogical norms for language teaching and that the choice of the range of norms to be used during instruction is conditioned by learners' proficiency level in the second language and general linguistic sophistication. The same is true for speakers of dialects different from the standard.

Besides sensitizing students and themselves to language variability, though, educators are also charged with developing learners' active mastery of the standard language in oral and written modes. This is a pedagogical as well as a social and political challenge. Pedagogically, it requires teachers to design and implement methods, materials, and activities which allow repeated use of many language varieties, including but not necessarily limited to the standard, in different communicative contexts; this diversification of opportunities to produce appropriate language forms and functions is equally important in second language (see Swain, 1993; Swain & Lapkin, 1994) and native language literacy settings (see Farr & Daniels, 1986; Heath, 1983), though it translates into different activities according to students' proficiency levels, background, and the broader school context of instruction. Socially, this means that teachers need to have a good understanding of the local social context which may, for example, promote certain types of language or literacy activities for some groups (see Tharp & Yamauchi, 1994) or for one gender (see Solsken, 1993) but de-emphasize them for others. Politically, it demands that teachers be sensitive to the many currents of language-related opinions and evaluations in their communities; they must thus pay attention to student and parent attitudes and expectations regarding language instruction, including the sometimes tacit evaluation of different language forms and the tensions between emphasis on the prestige forms and the solidarity-related aspects of language which establish covert prestige forms. Moreover, teachers need to be aware that, for some members of the public, the presence of language forms considered vulgar or obscene, even if such forms occur in literature considered to be classic, can lead to protests regarding curricular content (DelFattore, 1992).[5] If such protests occur, teachers must be prepared to defend their choices by responding to both literal concerns about language forms and the symbolic dimensions of the fears of parents or other community members that a language form such as a mild expletive, even if commonly used in speech, should not appear in any text that students might encounter. Here, again, sensitivity to language variation and sound professional judgment regarding choice of materials can help teachers make reasonable instructional decisions.

## *Sociopolitical influences on choice of norms and standards*

At present, any discussion of pedagogical norms and standards must also acknowledge the lively debate around the conservative versus critical study of education and the related discussions about changing the relationships between students and teachers in more egalitarian directions (see Apple, 1993; Aronowitz & Giroux, 1991; Giroux, 1992; Shor, 1992). Although this topic is well beyond the scope of discussion here, it is essential to emphasize that issues of language norms and standards for instruction are bound up with matters of wider relationships which may express the overt or covert domination of one group by another (see Chick, this volume; Fairclough, 1989; Villanueva, 1993). Furthermore, educational institutions typically resist change on many levels (Sarason, 1971, 1990); schools and the individual classrooms which constitute them are more likely to be places where existing social relationships, including inequities, are ratified and reinforced than places which enable personal or social transformation along any but socially sanctioned lines. Choice of a particular language or linguistic variant either as object or medium of instruction is thus never neutral but an indicator of the power relationships and social domains ascribed to language or language varieties in any society. Because this is evident in cases of classic diglossia (see Sridhar, this volume) but equally perti-

5 Although the topic of censorship of school materials, particularly textbooks and other assigned readings, is well beyond the scope of this chapter, it is prudent for language teachers who work in United States elementary and secondary schools to be prepared to respond to concerns of community members who may object to the discrete forms used or the content of language instruction. As DelFattore (1992) shows, such protests have risen sharply since 1980 and have led large commercial publishers to alter teaching materials. Although language forms considered vulgar or profane (e.g., *damn*) are frequently the overt targets for proposed restriction, supporters of censorship see them as red flags which indicate the presence of what they believe to be subversive value positions. Interestingly, among the topics to which putative censors have reacted most strongly are presentations which imply that language is gradually developed and amenable to various interpretations, depending on circumstances of use, both foundations of contemporary sociolinguistic thought (see DelFattore, 1992, especially Chaps. 3 and 7).

nent to any society in which more than one dialect is potentially available for use in education, the issue of choice of instructional norms is relevant to nearly every contemporary instructional context.

The growth and changing distribution of English around the world (Cheshire, 1991; Kachru & Nelson, this volume) make the issue of norms for English language instruction a far more complex matter than the simple dichotomy between British and American grammar and pronunciation that animated discussion in the English language teaching profession during the 1940s, 1950s, and 1960s (Phillipson, 1992). The choice of norms for English language teaching is no longer (if it ever was) simply British versus American. All available descriptive research indicates that there are multiple national standards and often a range of acceptable local variants in phonology, lexis, grammar, and discourse patterns for English emerging in the many places where English is used (Kachru, 1992; Kachru & Nelson, this volume; Sato, 1989; Smith, 1987). Multiple and emerging norms are typical of all languages linked with more than one demographic center and of languages in long-term contact with one another. As Spanish has become more widely spoken in the United States, for example, lexical and grammatical forms and frequencies are changing in response to long-standing contact with English (Silva-Corvalán, 1994). History, geography, and political and commercial relationships all help to determine appropriate choices and models for teaching.

## Language policies as channels and expressions of public attitudes

*Language policies,* or the official and institutional practices related to language and language instruction, embody and shape attitudes toward language. They affect several aspects of language education, including decisions related to the time allotted for language instruction, to the language and language varieties chosen as models and media for instruction, to the choice of materials, and to teacher certification, to name just a few. (For more detail on the ramifications of language policy in education, see Wiley; McKay, this volume.) The distribution of effort as illustrated by curricular time allocated to literacy instruction in the first language as compared to second language instruction is one indication of the social importance accorded to language, and it is sometimes a flash point during periods of social change (Smith, 1993). Similarly, the importance accorded to the provision of qualified teachers and appropriate materials, as indicated by related legislation or board of education policies (Phillips, 1994), is another indicator of public attitudes regarding language instruction, native or second language. Even with good-quality curriculum and trained teachers, successful formal second language study may not bring about full bilingualism if the larger social context renders it irrelevant in many important daily contexts (as Resnick, 1993, contends is the case for English instruction in Puerto Rico) or characteristic of marginal social identity (see Sridhar, this volume).[6] Furthermore, participants in formal language study programs may view efforts to change their language behavior as assertions of undue power on the part of institutions or employers (see Gowen, 1992, on the attitudes of participants in a job training program) and thus resist efforts to alter their usual style and range of language and literacy behavior. Such feelings also have important consequences for educational practice, for the affective overtones of the educational experience of teachers, learners, and parents often outlast the memories of particular topics of instruction (Jackson, 1992).

Language policies in education are not, however, merely manifestations of attitudes toward language or toward speakers of a particular language or language variety. They include these dimensions, but they also reflect too often ignored attitudes toward larger issues such as the role of government in the provision of human services, including education; appropriate levels of public expenditures; and expressions of local leadership styles. In studying the attitudes of a random sample of adults from selected areas of the United States toward bilingual education, Huddy and Sears (1990) found that attitude toward bilingual education was connected with other political attitudes toward, for ex-

6 The relative value accorded first and second language skills for certain students in a particular socioeducational setting is a significant subtext in the evaluation of second language programs. Part of the reason for the perception of the great success of students in Canadian-French immersion programs is that, for the most part, results for immersion students have been compared to results of second language learning for students receiving instruction in French as a foreign language, not to native speakers of French. Immersion students unquestionably show greater functional control of French than do French as a foreign language students, though they are not generally equal to native speakers, particularly in the areas of productive skills of speaking and writing (see Harley, Allen, Cummins, & Swain, 1990).

In part, immersion programs are viewed favorably because they produce functional bilinguals at no cost to native language educational development and thus, in the Canadian context, represent additive bilingualism (Lambert, 1984). In the United States, in sharp contrast, program designs tend to be different (Genesee, 1984) and the achievement of students in bilingual programs is nearly always compared to that of native speakers of English or to students of the same language group who have already learned enough English to have left the bilingual program; thus the value of native language skills, if those skills are in a language other than English, is often deemphasized in large-scale programmatic evaluations (Cziko, 1992; Ramírez, 1992), attesting to a subtractive rather than additive model of bilingualism. The emphasis on regular systematic evaluation of skills in two languages rather than one is a useful indicator of the valorization of bilingualism in any society.

ample, appropriateness of government involvement in social services and fiscal constraints on government. Most respondents supported bilingual education when it was defined as a means of assisting students to master English, but many fewer felt that government support for native language maintenance was warranted. Such research suggests that the symbolic dimensions of language attitudes as related to education cannot be ignored; these are a product not only of narrowly linguistic concerns but also of more general social and political orientations. Even in a country such as the United States, where language is not a primary public issue, political assumptions about language shape public discourse related to language use and language education (Sonntag & Pool, 1987).

The attitudes toward language and language instruction held by elite groups in a society are particularly influential in determining educational policies. American legislators, a particularly powerful group (as is the case for legislators in any political entity where they control the resources for education), show varying levels of support for language learning, maintenance, and retention, depending on general political preference, relative costs or perceived benefits of any language intervention, regional loyalties, and the salience of language issues to their home constituencies (Judd, 1989). Hence, the general political orientations, including the "assumptive worlds" of policymakers (Marshall, Mitchell, & Wirt, 1989) and the symbolic referents of a policy, must be considered in understanding approaches to language and language education.

Local constellations of political power and leadership also play central roles in educational systems where local levels of governance, as opposed to national governance through a ministry of education, bear the main responsibility for planning and supporting education. The more decentralized and localized the decision making, the greater the scope for different local leadership styles to affect educational decisions. In the United States, each state presents a particular configuration of historically generous or relatively lesser support, both monetary and symbolic, for education; a more or less developed infrastructure of expertise and physical resources to support educational efforts; and reliance on appointed versus elected leaders; all these factors affect decisions related to education (Marshall, Mitchell, & Wirt, 1989). States differ greatly in these characteristics; therefore, it is no surprise that levels of support for and expertise in language and literacy education also vary.

Further, most members of state boards of education are appointed or elected because of political factors, of which expertise in education is not always the principal or even a major criterion (Phillips, 1994); thus individuals who do not have backgrounds in the profession of education are placed in influential decision-making positions. Legislators and members of boards of education typically draw their legitimacy from the political system, not from any particular professional expertise in education; thus their assumptions regarding language and language learning are much more likely to reflect "folk linguistic" theories or commonsense understandings about language which are, in fact, erroneous in light of substantial current research (Cummins, 1980; see McLaughlin, 1992). Because teachers are at once members of the public and professionals charged with the main responsibility for language and literacy attainment within the educational system, this situation creates conflicts for them in resolving matters of language pedagogy.

The more decentralized and truly democratic the decision making, the greater the potential for conflict and the greater the need for the educational system to address conflict openly and resolve it creatively. Skills in identification and resolution of conflict, whether over linguistic matters, cultural differences, or general educational policy, have not been part of the training of many language educators, but current educational realities imply that such abilities are central to the effectiveness of teachers who work in multilingual, multiethnic settings, and thus these abilities must be actively developed so that teachers can be prepared for their professional roles. Milk (1994) has described one such innovative program, which combines leadership training and opportunities to develop skills in conflict resolution with the linguistic and cultural experiences more traditionally used to prepare bilingual teachers.

## Educational implications: Arenas for pedagogical action

### *Promoting individual, classroom, and schoolwide motivation*

*Motivation,* which can be defined as a desire to learn plus a willingness to expend effort in doing so, affects mastery in many subjects, not only language, and the field of educational psychology abounds in discussions of motivation. Though much early research on language attitudes and motivation was purely descriptive and does not warrant direct pedagogical application, the accumulating research findings do offer guidance. First, it is wise for teachers not to base their work on a priori assumptions about student interests, individual predilections, motivation, and background without making efforts to discover the many possible factors which shape motivation in the specific situation in which they work. The growing and more differentiated body of research on language learning motivation has revealed that there is no single model that accounts for all cases of language learning; consequently, there is no universal prescription for improving student and teacher attitudes or increasing student motivation (Oxford & Shearin, 1994). Work in general educational psychology (see Corno & Kanfer, 1993) also reminds us that motivation to pursue and persist in any activity is a result of a whole set of interrelated factors, none of which is, by itself, individually determinative of effort or outcome. Nonetheless, the absence of universal prescriptions does not mean that instructors are powerless; there are several specific paths open to them to aid them in identifying the attitudinal and motivational factors relevant to their instructional situation and to help them provide the kind of instruction that might enable more students to be more successful in their pursuit of second language proficiency and high-level literacy skills. Hence each teacher must take steps to identify the variety of goals, interests, and predispositions about language that students bring to the second language classroom and capitalize on them (Oxford & Shearin, 1994). Further, working with other teachers where appropriate, instructors can take steps to identify effective ways to diversify instruction and make students more aware of their own learning processes and the rewards of language study, both intrinsic and extrinsic. Such awareness can improve a whole school's learning environment and decrease the strong influence of extrinsic rewards (i.e., grades or public display of competitive achievements on an honor roll), which hamper students' willingness to take risks in facing a challenging subject such as language instruction, particularly as they get older (Anderman & Maehr, 1994).

Acquisition of literacy skills in a native language remains a great focus of concern for educators virtually everywhere, and it is an area where student attitude and motivation play an important though not always immediately obvious role. Weighing the importance of extrinsic and intrinsic motivation in acquisition of literacy and other complex symbol systems, the educational psychologist Csikszentmihalyi (1990) observes that both types of motivation are required to induce people to learn. He notes that acquisition of literacy has, for centuries, been associated with ability to manipulate economic power, giving rulers and governments substantial incentives to develop a cadre of literacy specialists. However, in today's postindustrial economy the economic advantages of universal literacy are less direct, though still consequential. Far too often neglected, he argues, are the intrinsic rewards of literacy, the possibilities for deriving personal satisfaction from reading and writing activities carried on in any sphere of life, job-related or not (1990). Although teachers have little control over the external rewards for literate skills in the larger society, they can both model and promote activities that lead students into the enjoyment as well as the employment of the many literacies relevant for their lives. Addressing the situation of secondary-level students who use nonmainstream dialects, Farr and Daniels (1986) provide a well-rationalized set of fifteen principles related to writing instruction; many of their suggestions, such as giving student writers frequent and consistent practice in a variety of writing forms for different audiences, allowing students to develop their own topics, having positive expectations of student progress, and integrating a variety of interesting reading materials with writing, accord with principles of good instruction for any group of developing writers and are well within the power of most teachers to implement.

## *Discovering the language relevant for instruction*

What forms of language and literacy are relevant in the lives of students and their parents? This question has multiple answers that depend on different instructional settings, and this is one of the main challenges to language educators: to discover what functions and forms of language and which language varieties (and what forms of knowledge; see Moll, 1992) matter in the communities in which they work, in terms of both present activities and future aspirations. Providing detailed, accurate, and specific answers is one way to create a learning environment that enhances motivation. Many recent commentators (see Corson, 1991; Pease-Alvarez & Vásquez, 1994) offer educators useful guidelines for gathering information about the varieties and functions of language that figure in home, community, and school settings. Such information, often gathered by the students themselves, can become a resource in efforts to expand the understanding and active mastery of additional language varieties, and it can increase the language awareness of teachers as well as their students. Indeed, trained language teachers, even more than teachers of other subjects, can focus their professional knowledge of linguistics and current models of reciprocal language pedagogy on increasing the language awareness of everyone in their classrooms, including themselves, thereby expanding the recognition and control of the variety of pedagogical norms (Valdman, 1988) appropriate for their students.

The fact that multiple standards exist is a crucial insight for teachers and students of language, and it suggests that teaching materials and practices ought to make them explicit. Further, students developing bilingual capabilities will need to know about the norms governing oral and written modes in each of their languages (Hornberger, 1989). Even if students aim for production abilities in one national standard, such as Canadian or Australian English, they may find it useful to recognize variants of pronunciation, grammar, lexicon, or discourse style characteristic of other standards. On a more abstract level, learning that the very notion of standards is a socially constructed one and that language users create and modify forms of language according to contexts of use can be a signal insight for students and teachers. Moreover, this approach allows them to connect the study and development of language with achievement of power and prestige in the social spheres in which they participate (Lemke, 1989; Villanueva, 1993; Walsh, 1991).

## *Expanding opportunities to use multiple forms of language*

The intimate connection between language and social identity means that learners need the chance to build social identities which include the mastery of a socially effective range of the oral and literate behaviors. This is a great challenge to educational systems and to norms of classroom discourse, which often provide only an idealized (and reductionist) view of language forms worthy of emulation and restrict student participation in frequency and format to faint echoes of a teacher's voice (Pratt, 1987).

Studies of classroom discourse (e.g., Cazden, 1986) have repeatedly shown that language classrooms, whether second or native language settings, severely constrain the oral and literate range of language behaviors in which students are required or allowed to participate. In addition, investigations of instructional practices such as group work, first developed to expand participation opportunities, have shown that preexisting attitudes regarding status and capability influence participation in groups; students perceived to have low levels of relevant academic skills are often left out of group interactions, thus further limiting their access to knowledge (Cohen, 1994). This research, considered in conjunction with the research on language-specific attitude and motivation considered in this chapter, suggests that, to improve both student attitude and motivation, teachers need to recognize a wide variety of language behaviors and to be able to distinguish dialectal variation, whether regional or social, from errors in speech behavior. Teachers must also realize that their own and their students' preexisting attitudes toward language skills and literacy abilities will affect student participation, and they must find ways to recognize multiple abilities and use them as a springboard in developing better language and literacy skills (Cohen, 1994). Teachers must create in their classrooms a range of participation opportunities so that students can experience a wide variety of language forms and functions, oral and literate, including those that will provide for success in the public arena in their societies.

Recent educational research conducted in and out of classrooms offers numerous specific suggestions for accomplishing these aims. Much recent work in native language literacy growth indicates that developing multiple opportunities for readers at different skill levels to interact around text in both reading and writing expands students' literacy capabilities (Cole & Griffin, 1986). Optimal styles of interaction must be discovered for each classroom; here again, there is no foolproof recipe for conducting a class, but language teachers can draw on their awareness of discourse patterns to see how best to adapt classroom presentation and discussion techniques to their students. Tharp and Yamauchi (1994) describe the adaptation of typical classroom discourse patterns to the preferred modes of interaction of native American students and set out some of the questions teachers can ask themselves as they seek to create a setting for consistently effective instructional conversations in their classrooms. Although, for good reason, teachers focus on the classroom as the place where language skills are to be developed, it is essential not to ignore the possibilities available to students through other avenues such as youth clubs or community organizations. A recent examination of successful alternative organizations for adolescents in four United States cities shows that giving young people, including young people who may not be strongly oriented to school activities, successful experiences in public speaking and dramatic performance pushes them to develop the individual and public presentation styles they can later call upon in other contexts when needed (Heath & McLaughlin, 1993). Knowing this, teachers can encourage their students (and students' parents, if it is appropriate to do so) to pursue and persist in any activities, school-based or not, which require that they develop and practice multiple styles of speaking and literacy uses.

More controversial is the recommendation that teachers promote language and literacy to transform their students' lives and possibilities. National literacy campaigns, often linked with political and social transformation, express this most clearly.[7] Yet, even if teachers do not work in a system explicitly dedicated to social transformation of an entire society, they can have some impact on the practices related to the construction and implementation of curriculum, community involvement, and assessment that provide advantages or disadvantages to the students they face each day (Cummins, 1986) and thus work to empower rather than to disadvantage students; in this way they can generate transformative practices that apply to themselves and to their stu-

7 Often, national literacy campaigns do not use trained teachers as the main literacy promoters, sometimes because of the severe shortage of trained teachers, sometimes because of other factors such as the desire to involve an influential segment of the population such as university students in literacy campaigns rather than other activities which might promote diverse or opposing political perspectives (see Cooper, 1989, on the role of university students in the Ethiopian literacy campaign of 1974–1976; see also McKay, 1993, on national literacy campaigns). Hence educators interested in mass literacy campaigns as models for intervention must be alert to the underlying social and political context and the multiple political goals which animate such efforts in evaluating their applicability to different instructional settings. Related to the matter of social transformation is the debate regarding the role of the teacher as an intellectual who can operate in either a traditional or a transformative mode (Giroux, 1992; see Villanueva, 1993, Chap. 7).

dents. Although teachers must be realistic about the constraints of the institutional and national systems within which they work (Tollefson, 1991), they generally have some discretion related to instructional practices and procedures in their classrooms. Their control of choice of materials and assessment methods depends greatly on the particular instructional setting.

## *Influencing language policies*

At the local school or district level, individual teachers interested in promoting better language instruction can sometimes affect decisions through their participation in informal or formally designated committees charged with developing curriculum or making recommendations related to instructional practice, materials, or assessment. Through the group efforts of professional associations, teachers can sometimes find new ways to disseminate effective instructional and assessment practices by participating in the legislative process, if it is feasible to do so within their governmental system (see McGroarty, in press), or in executive oversight activities such as those conducted by ministries of education. Effective participation in the policy process demands a proactive rather than reactive stance; teachers must contribute at the time of policy formulation and not wait until implementation or evaluation if they want to help determine pedagogical directions. Because educational policies inevitably change as they are implemented, teachers need to be willing to share their experiences at various stages of a program with relevant audiences of fellow professionals and interested members of the public. Such information sharing can take several forms: Individuals or groups within a school or a district can meet periodically to monitor their concerns and exchange ideas; local, state, or national authorities or professional organizations can provide a forum for discussion; professional organizations for teachers can appoint or elect individuals or committees to investigate relevant issues and take a leadership role for the organization, if warranted, in public debates and decision-making processes.

In their efforts to affect policy, teachers need to be aware of the power of factors in the wider climate of opinion with respect to second language and forms of literacy as reflected in the language policies, official and unofficial, at play in their schools, local and state communities, and nations (see Wiley, this volume). With their professional expertise, teachers can help disabuse policymakers of some of the erroneous ideas about language learning which abound in the world of folk linguistics. Teachers can provide accurate current information or can press educational oversight agencies to collect such data, they can describe promising practices, and they can promote the widespread societal commitment needed to establish and maintain high-quality instructional programs. Hence teachers must pay attention to public attitudes regarding languages and language learning, "proper" forms and uses of language, and appropriate spheres for language learning activities; they must recognize how the study of language fits within the more general attitudes related to education in the surrounding society. Such awareness coupled with a willingness to act together with other constituencies such as teachers of other languages and ethnic communities can enable teachers to contribute to setting the public agenda for language-related questions, legitimizing discussion of language issues by bringing their expertise and experience to bear, and broadening the scope of public language policy, where warranted (Lo Bianco, 1989).

## Now what? Final reflections on motivation

Raising the language awareness of all participants is a place to start, but increased awareness must be coupled with increased opportunity for the practice and development of valued forms and functions of language. Tensions related to choice of norms and forms for language education will continue; educators need to know how to recognize the tensions surrounding language use and language teaching and how to address these tensions with realism and creativity. The great challenge to teachers of first and second languages is to provide students with the opportunity to expand their linguistic repertoires in speech and in writing in ways that will enhance their abilities to participate effectively in their societies (see Hornberger, 1989). This presumes that teachers have a professionally appropriate level of knowledge and some awareness of the appropriate means for carrying out needs analyses related to language, to language variation, to their students, and to the goals and contexts of language instruction. Having such awareness and professional skills, teachers are better equipped to plan and implement language instruction which promotes a variety of participation opportunities, intensity of exposure and instruction in language, and multiple possibilities for success in the various aspects of language and literacy use which have personal and societal consequences for them and for their students.

### Suggestions for further reading

Baker, C. (1992). *Attitudes and language.* Clevedon, England: Multilingual Matters Ltd.

This book seeks to update the considerations of the roles of attitudes in language learning by placing research on language attitudes in the wider context of other attitudinal research. The first three chapters offer a concise overview of the theoretical importance, content, and procedures used in research on language attitudes to date. The remaining three chapters and the appendixes focus on the author's extensive survey of attitudes toward Welsh and English in Wales analyzed via path analysis to construct a model of attitudes toward Welsh on the part of the young people surveyed. The most interesting theoretical contribution of this study is the author's contention that attitudes toward bilingualism itself may be different from separate attitudes toward either of the languages involved, requiring investigators to look specifically at constructs related to bilingualism in a holistic sense. Furthermore, the Welsh-English data indicate that the local youth culture is a particularly strong influence on young people's attitudes toward language use and language instruction and ought not to be ignored in developing models of language attitude.

Crookes, G., & Schmidt, R. W. (1991). Motivation: Reopening the research agenda. *Language Learning, 41*(4), 469–512.

This article provides a thoughtful critique of the exclusive reliance on models of attitudinal research based solely on social psychology and points out that most teachers rely, implicitly or explicitly, on concepts of motivation that are much broader than those studied by most L2 researchers to date. The authors argue that both theory and practice demand an expansion of the definitions of and procedures used to study language learning motivation, and that much can be learned from existing studies of motivation in education, where factors such as student effort, engagement, and persistence have been studied in relation to various classroom factors such as teachers' previewing of information, the availability of interesting materials, and different types of rewards. They conclude with an outline of a research agenda that emphasizes more systematic and detailed attention to instructional, individual student, and contextual factors in working toward a fuller understanding of the nature and effect of motivation on second language learning.

Gardner, R. C. (1985). *Social psychology and second language learning: The role of attitudes and motivation.* London: Edward Arnold.

This volume is a comprehensive and careful account of the entire field of sociopsychological language attitude studies since Lambert and Gardner's seminal work of the 1960s and 1970s. It presents attitudinal and motivational factors as one important source of individual differences in language learning behaviors and outcomes, with particularly close investigation of the integrative pattern of motivation. The research summarized centers on formal second language learners in the North American context, with the principal focus on the many Canadian projects involving Anglophone students at various levels learning French. The reciprocal influence between attitudes and successful (or unsuccessful) language learning experiences is explored, as is the influence of parental attitudes on language learning, a signal factor in some school settings. Gardner concludes by presenting his own socioeducational view of language learning which merits attention because of its differentiated view of the multiple influences on successful language acquisition in formal and informal settings. The book provides a detailed account of the theories and empirical procedures used to study language attitudes and motivation within the framework of social psychology.

Giles, H., Coupland, J., & Coupland, N. (Eds.) (1991). *Contexts of accommodation: Developments in applied sociolinguistics.* Cambridge: Cambridge University Press.

The nine papers in this collection address different aspects of communication accommodation theory (CAT) and provide a representative sample of its application to various communicative settings, including mass media, medical and psychotherapeutic consultations, and courtroom discourse. Of greatest interest to those interested in second language issues are Chapter 1, by the editors, with its succinct presentation of CAT; Chapter 7, by Zuengler, on developing better explanatory models of what happens in native-nonnative interaction; Chapter 8, by Gallois and Callan, on the concept of communicative norms as they affect reactions to target language speech used by immigrant groups; and Chapter 9, by Bourhis, on the links between the communicative environment of organizations and individual linguistic choice, with special attention to bilingual contexts.

Oxford, R., & Shearin, J. (1994). Language learning motivation: Expanding the theoretical framework. *The Modern Language Journal, 78*(1), 12–28.

This excellent and optimistic article shows that studies of language learning motivation and related pedagogical recommendations would benefit greatly from incorporating recent insights from branches of psychology such as personality and industrial or occupational psychology as they relate to learning generally and to language learning specifically. The authors recognize the signal importance of work done in educational psychology and emphasize that other branches of psychology also have much to offer both students and teachers in their quest for effective language learning and instruction. They conclude with several practical suggestions directly bearing on what learners and teachers can do to enhance possibilities for success. This article, together with that by Crookes and Schmidt (1991), constitutes a good point of departure for readers interested in an overview of current developments in the study of language learning motivation.

Shuy, R. W., & Fasold, R. W. (Eds.) (1973). *Language attitudes: Current trends and prospects.* Washington, DC: Georgetown University Press.

The twelve papers in this classic collection present mainly variants of the matched guise technique used in several different linguistic contexts, including French-Canadians in Quebec; Mexican-Americans, African-Americans, and Puerto Ricans in the United States; and Spanish-Quechua bilinguals in Peru. Together, the papers exemplify the substantive focus on discrete linguistic features and modes of analysis characteristic of sociolinguistics in the 1970s. The book is a useful point of departure for those wishing to see how the early studies of language attitude have continued to influence current investigations; many of the variables used in these earlier studies have been expanded and incorporated into the more complex models accounts now in use. The substantive concerns regarding interethnic tensions, gender differences, and attitudes toward socially dominant and subordinate language and dialect groups remain current, although the methodology used to investigate them has grown more sophisticated.

## References

Akinnaso, F. N., & Ajirotutu, C. S. (1982). Performance and ethnic style in job interviews. In J. J. Gumperz (Ed.), *Language and social identity* (pp. 119–144). Cambridge: Cambridge University Press.

Alford, R. L., & Strother, J. B. (1990). Attitudes of native and non-native speakers towards selected regional accents of U.S. English. *TESOL Quarterly, 24*(3), 479–495.

Allard, R., & Landry, R. (1992). Ethnolinguistic vitality beliefs and language maintenance and loss. In W. Fase, K. Jaspaert, & S. Kroon (Eds.), *Maintenance and loss of minority languages* (pp. 171–195). Amsterdam: John Benjamins.

Anderman, E., & Maehr, M. (1994). Motivation and schooling in the middle grades. *Review of Educational Research, 64*(2), 287–309.

Anzaldúa, G. (1987). *Borderlands/La frontera: The new mestiza.* San Francisco: Spinsters/Aunt Lute Book Co.

Apple, M. W. (1993). *Official knowledge: Democratic education in a conservative age.* New York: Routledge.

Aronowitz, S., & Giroux, H. (1991). *Postmodern education: Politics, culture, & social criticism.* Minneapolis: University of Minnesota Press.

Baker, C. (1992). *Attitudes and language.* Clevedon, England: Multilingual Matters Ltd.

Baldauf, R. B., & Lawrence, H. (1990). Student characteristics and affective domain effects on LOTE retention rates. *Language and Education, 4*(4), 225–248.

Baron, D. E. (1982). *Grammar and good taste: Reforming the American language.* New Haven, CT: Yale University Press.

Bartsch, R. (1987). *Norms of language.* London: Longman.

Beck, A. (1992, October). "I'll be there until . . .": Some thoughts on the origins of Navajo English. Paper presented at Faculty-Student Symposium on Columbus and the New World Order, Northern Arizona University, Flagstaff, AZ.

Beck, A., & Foster, S. (1989). Navajo English as nativized dialect. Paper presented at Second Language Research Forum, University of California, Los Angeles.

Beebe, L. (1988). Five sociolinguistic approaches to second language acquisition. In L. Beebe (Ed.), *Issues in second language acquistion: Multiple perspectives* (pp. 41–77). New York: Newbury House/Harper and Row.

Beebe, L., & Zuengler, J. (1983). Accommodation theory: An explanation for style shifting in second language dialects. In N. Wolfson & E. Judd (Eds.), *Sociolinguistics and second language acquisition* (pp. 195–213). Rowley, MA: Newbury House.

Cabazón, M., Lambert, W., & Hall, G. (1993). Two-way bilingual education: A progress report on the Amigos Program. Research report no. 7. University of California at Santa Cruz: National Center for Research on Cultural Diversity and Second Language Learning.

Cazden, C. (1986). *Classroom discourse: The language of teaching and learning.* Portsmouth, NH: Heinemann.

Cheshire, J. (1991). Introduction: Sociolinguistics and English around the world. In J. Cheshire (Ed.), *English around the world* (pp. 1–12). Cambridge: Cambridge University Press.

Cohen, E. G. (1994). *Designing groupwork: Strategies for the heterogeneous classroom* (2nd ed.). New York: Teachers College Press.

Cole, M., & Griffin, P. (1986). A sociohistorical approach to remediation. In S. de Castell, A. Luke, & K. Egan (Eds.), *Literacy, society, and schooling* (pp. 110–131). Cambridge: Cambridge University Press.

Cooper, R. L. (1989). *Language planning and social change.* Cambridge: Cambridge University Press.

Corno, L., & Kanfer, R. (1993). The role of volition in learning and performance. In L. Darling-Hammond (Ed.), *Review of research in education* (pp. 301–341). Washington, DC: American Educational Research Association.

Corson, D. (1991). Realities of teaching in a multiethnic school. *International Review of Education, 37*(1), 7–31.

Coulmas, F. (1989). Democracy and the crisis of normative linguistics. In F. Coulmas (Ed.), *Language adaptation* (pp. 177–193). Cambridge: Cambridge University Press.

Craig, B. (1994). American attitudes toward bilingualism: Implications for language acquisition planning. Paper presented at American Association of Applied Linguistics Conference, Baltimore, MD.

Crookes, G., & Schmidt, R. W. (1991). Motivation: Reopening the research agenda. *Language Learning, 41*(4), 469–512.

Crystal, D. (1987). *The Cambridge encyclopedia of language.* Cambridge: Cambridge University Press.

Csikszentmihalyi, M. (1990). Literacy and intrinsic motivation. *Daedalus, 119*(115–140).

Cummins, J. (1980). Mother tongue maintenance for minority children: Some common misconceptions. Unpublished manuscript. Ontario: Modern Language Centre, Ontario Institute for Studies in Education.

Cummins, J. (1986). Empowering minority students. *Harvard Educational Review, 56* (18–36).

Cziko, G. A. (1992). The evaluation of bilingual education: From necessity and probability to possibility. *Educational Researcher, 21*(2), 10–15.

DelFattore, J. (1992). *What Johnny shouldn't read: Textbook censorship in America.* New Haven, CT: Yale University Press.

Denzin, N. K. (1984). *On understanding emotion.* San Francisco, CA: Jossey-Bass.

Dörnyei, Z. (1990). Conceptualizing motivation in foreign-language learning. *Language Learning, 40*(45–78).

Ehrman, M. (1990). Owls and doves: Cognition, personality, and learning success. In J. E. Alatis (Ed.), *Georgetown University roundtable on languages and linguistics 1990* (pp. 413–437). Washington, DC: Georgetown University Press.

Ehrman, M. (1993). Ego boundaries revisited: Toward a model of personality and learning. In J. E. Alatis (Ed.), *Strategic interaction and language acquisition,* (pp. 331–362). Washington, DC: Georgetown University Press.

Ehrman, M. (1994, March). Ego boundaries and a view of language aptitude. Paper presented at TESOL Convention, Baltimore, MD.

Ehrman, M., & Oxford, R. (1995). Cognition plus: Correlates of language learning success. *The Modern Language Journal, 79*(1), 67–89.

Ely, C. (1986a). An analysis of discomfort, risktaking, sociability, and motivation in the L2 classroom. *Language Learning, 36*, 1–25.

Ely, C. (1986b). Language learning motivation: A descriptive and causal analysis. *Modern Language Journal, 70*, 28–35.

Fairclough, N. (1989). *Language and power*. New York: Longman.

Farr, M., & Daniels, H. (1986). *Language diversity and writing instruction*. New York: ERIC Clearinghouse on Urban Education, Institute for Urban and Minority Education.

Finegan, E., & Besnier, N. (1989). *Language: Its structure and use*. Orlando, FL: Harcourt Brace Jovanovich.

Ford, C. (1984). The influence of speech variety on teachers' evaluation of students with comparable academic ability. *TESOL Quarterly, 18*(1), 25–40.

Gallois, C., & Callan, V. J. (1991). Interethnic accommodation: The role of norms. In H. Giles, N. Coupland, & J. Coupland (Eds.), *Contexts of accommodation* (pp. 245–269). Cambridge: Cambridge University Press.

Gardner, R. C. (1985). *Social psychology and second language learning: The role of attitudes and motivation*. London: Edward Arnold.

Gardner, R. C. (1991). Foreword. In E. K. Horwitz & D. J. Young (Eds.), *Language anxiety: From theory and research to classroom implications* (pp. vii–viii). Englewood Cliffs, NJ: Prentice Hall.

Gardner, R. C. & Lambert, W. E. (1959). Motivational variables in second language acquisition. *Canadian Journal of Psychology, 13*, 266–272.

Gardner, R. C., Lalonde, R. M., & Moorcroft, R. (1985). The role of attitudes and motivation in second language learning: Correlational and experimental considerations. *Language Learning, 35*(2), 207–227.

Gardner, R. C., & Lambert, W. E. (1972). *Attitudes and motivation in second language learning*. Rowley, MA: Newbury House.

Gardner, R. C., & MacIntyre, P. D. (1991). An instrumental motivation in language study: Who says it isn't effective? *Studies in Second Language Acquisition, 13*, 57–72.

Gardner, R. C., & MacIntyre, P. D. (1993). On the measurement of affective variables in second language learning. *Language Learning, 43*(2), 157–194.

Gass, S. M., & Varonis, E. M. (1991). Miscommunication in nonnative speaker discourse. In N. Coupland, H. Giles, & J. Wiemann (Eds.), *"Miscommunication" and problematic talk* (pp. 121–145). Newbury Park, CA: Sage Publications.

Genesee, F. (1984). Historical and theoretical foundations of immersion education. In California State Department of Education, *Studies in immersion education: A collection for United States educators* (pp. 32–53). Sacramento, CA.

Giles, H., Coupland, J., & Coupland, N. (Eds.). (1991). *Contexts of accommodation: Developments in applied sociolinguistics*. Cambridge: Cambridge University Press.

Giles, H., & St. Clair, R. (Eds.). (1979). *Language and social psychology*. Baltimore, MD: University Park Press.

Giroux, H. (1992). *Border crossings: Cultural workers and the politics of education*. New York: Routledge.
Goldstein, L. M. (1987). Standard English: The only target for nonnative speakers of English? *TESOL Quarterly, 21*(3), 417–436.
Gowen, S. G. (1992). *The politics of workplace literacy: A case study*. New York: Teachers College Press.
Graham, S. (1994). Motivation in African Americans. *Review of Educational Research, 64*(1), 55–117.
Green, J. M. (1993). Student attitudes toward communicative and non-communicative activities: Do enjoyment and effectiveness go together? *Modern Language Journal, 77*(1), 1–10.
Hakuta, K., & D'Andrea, D. (1992). Some properties of bilingual maintenance and loss in Mexican background high school students. *Applied Linguistics, 13*(1), 72–99.
Harley, B., Allen, P., Cummins, J., & Swain, M. (1990). *The development of second language proficiency*. Cambridge: Cambridge University Press.
Heath, S. B. (1983). *Ways with words*. Cambridge: Cambridge University Press.
Heath, S. B., & McLaughlin, M. (Eds.). (1993). *Language and social identity: Beyond ethnicity and gender*. New York: Teachers College Press.
Hewstone, M. (Ed.). (1983). *Attribution theory: Social and functional extensions*. Oxford: Basil Blackwell.
Hewstone, M., & Brown, R. (1986). Contact is not enough: An intergroup perspective on the 'contact hypothesis.' In M. Hewstone & R. Brown (Eds.), *Contact and conflict in intergroup attitudes* (pp. 1–44). Oxford: Basil Blackwell.
Holm, W. (1994, January). Navajo language shift and retention and other matters. Lecture presented at Northern Arizona University, Flagstaff, AZ.
Holmquist, J. C. (1993). Social and psychological correlates of achievement: Spanish at Temple University. *Modern Language Journal, 77*(1), 34–44.
Hornberger, N. (1987). Bilingual education success, but policy failure. *Language in Society, 16*, 205–226.
Hornberger, N. (1989). Continua of biliteracy. *Review of Educational Research, 59*(3), 271–296.
Horwitz, E., Horwitz, M., & Cope, J. (1991). Foreign language classroom anxiety. In E. K. Horwitz & D. J. Young (Eds.), *Language anxiety: From theory and research to classroom implications*. Englewood Cliffs, NJ: Prentice Hall.
Huddy, L., & Sears, D. O. (1990). Qualified public support for bilingual education: Some policy implications. *Annals of the American Academy of Political and Social Sciences, 508*, 119–134.
Hurtado, A., & Rodríguez, R. (1989). Language as a social problem: The repression of Spanish in south Texas. *Journal of Multilingual and Multicultural Development, 10*(5), 401–419.
Jackson, P. W. (1992). *Untaught lessons*. New York: Teachers College Press.
Judd, E. (1989, April). Language policy and the 100th Congress. Paper presented at the 23rd TESOL Convention, San Antonio, TX.
Kachru, B. (Ed.). (1992). *The other tongue: English across cultures*, 2nd ed. Urbana: University of Illinois Press.
Kraemer, R., & Olshtain, E. (1989). Perceived ethnolinguistic vitality and

language attitudes: The Israeli setting. *Journal of Multilingual and Multicultural Development, 10*(3), 197–212.
Labov, W. (1972). *Language in the inner city: Studies in black English vernacular.* Philadelphia: University of Pennsylvania Press.
Labov, W. (1973). The linguistic consequences of being a lame. *Language in society, 2*(1), 81–115.
Lambert, W. E. (1972). *Language, psychology, and culture: Essays by Wallace E. Lambert.* (A. S. Dil, Ed.). Stanford, CA: Stanford University Press.
Lambert, W. E. (1984). An overview of issues in immersion education. In California State Department of Education, *Studies on immersion education: A collection for United States educators* (pp. 8–30). Sacramento, CA.
Lambert, W. E. (1987). The effects of bilingual and bicultural experiences on children's attitudes and social perspectives. In P. Homel, M. Palij, & D. Anderson (Eds.), *Childhood bilingualism* (pp. 197–221). Hillsdale, NJ: Lawrence Erlbaum.
Lambert, W. E., & Taylor, D. M. (1987). Language minorities in the United States: Conflicts around assimilation and proposed modes of accommodation. In W. A. Van Horne & T. V. Tonnesen (Eds.), *Ethnicity and language* (pp. 58–89). Milwaukee: University of Wisconsin System Institute on Race and Ethnicity.
Lambert, W. E., & Tucker, G. R. (1972). *Bilingual education of children: The St. Lambert experiment.* Rowley, MA: Newbury House.
Leap, W. (1993). Written Navajo English: Texture, construction, and point of view. *Journal of Navajo Education, 11*(1), 41–48.
Lemke, J. L. (1989). Social semiotics: A new model for literacy education. In D. Bloome (Ed.), *Classrooms and literacy* (pp. 289–309). Norwood, NJ: Ablex.
Lo Bianco, J. (1989). Science or values: The role of professionals in language policymaking. In C. Candlin & T. McNamara (Eds.), *Language, learning and community* (pp. 173–191). Sydney: National Centre for English Language Teaching and Research, Maquarie University.
Luhman, R. (1990). Language attitudes in Kentucky. *Language in society, 19,* 349–377.
Lukmani, Y. M. (1972). Motivation to learn and learning proficiency. *Language Learning, 22,* 261–273.
Mantle-Bromley, C., & Miller, R. B. (1991). Effect of multicultural lessons on attitudes of students of Spanish. *Modern Language Journal, 75*(4), 418–425.
Marshall, C., Mitchell, D., & Wirt, F. (1989). *Culture and education policy in the American states.* London: Falmer Press.
McGroarty, M. (1988). University foreign language learning: Spanish and Japanese. Technical report no. 10. University of California, Los Angeles: Center for Language Education and Research.
McGroarty, M. (1991). English instruction for linguistic minority groups: Different structures, different styles. In M. Celce-Murcia (Ed.), *Teaching English as a second or foreign language,* 2d ed. (pp. 372–385). New York: Newbury House.
McGroarty, M. (in press). Language policy in the U.S.: National values, local loyalties, pragmatic pressures. In W. Eggington (Ed.), *English et al.: Lan-*

*guage and language-in-education policies in English dominant nations.* Amsterdam: John Benjamins.

McKay, S. (1993). *Agendas for second language literacy.* New York: Cambridge University Press.

McLaughlin, B. (1992). Myths and misconceptions about second language learning: What every teacher needs to unlearn. Educational practice report no. 5. Santa Cruz, CA: National Center for Research on Cultural Diversity and Second Language Learning.

Michaels, S. (1986). Narrative presentations: An oral preparation for literacy with first graders. In J. Cook-Gumperz (Ed.), *The social construction of literacy* (pp. 94–116). Cambridge: Cambridge University Press.

Milk, R. D. (1994, March). Bicultural training for bilingual teachers. Paper presented at Colloquium on the Roles of Culture in Teacher Training, 28th TESOL International Convention, Baltimore, MD.

Milroy, J., & Milroy, L. (1985). *Authority in language: Investigating language prescription and standardisation.* London: Routledge & Kegan Paul.

Moll, L. (1992). Bilingual classroom studies and community analysis: Some recent trends. *Educational Researcher, 21*(2), 20–24.

Morales, F. (1991). The role of Spanish language varieties in the bilingual classroom. In M. McGroarty & C. Faltis (Eds.), *Languages in school and society: Policy and pedagogy* (pp. 293–315). Berlin: Mouton de Gruyter.

Oller, J. W., Jr., Baca, L., & Vigil, F. (1977). Attitudes and attained proficiency in ESL: A sociolinguistic study of Mexican Americans in the Southwest. *TESOL Quarterly, 11,* 173–182.

Osgood, C. E., Suci, G. J., & Tannenbaum, P. H. (1957). *The measurement of meaning.* Urbana: University of Illinois Press.

Oxford, R., & Ehrman, M. (1988). Psychological type and adult language learning strategies: A pilot study. *Journal of Psychological Type, 16,* 22–32.

Oxford, R., and Shearin, J. (1994). Language learning motivation: Expanding the theoretical framework. *The Modern Language Journal, 78*(1), 12–28.

Pease-Alvarez, C., & Vásquez, O. (1994). Language socialization in ethnic minority communities. In F. Genesee (Ed.), *Educating second language children* (pp. 82–102). New York: Cambridge University Press.

Phillips, J. K. (1994). State and local policy on the study of world languages. *Annals of the American Academy of Political and Social Science, 532,* 88–98.

Phillipson, R. (1992). *Linguistic imperialism.* Oxford: Oxford University Press.

Politzer, R. L. (1981). Social class and bilingual education: Issues and contradictions. *Bilingual Education Paper Series, 5*(2). Los Angeles: Evaluation, Dissemination, and Assessment Center, California State University, Los Angeles.

Poole, D. (1992). Language socialization in the second language classroom. *Language Learning, 42*(4), 593–616.

Pratt, M. L. (1987). Linguistic utopias. In N. Fabb, D. Attridge, A. Durant, & C. MacCabe (Eds.), *The linguistics of writing: Arguments between language and literature* (pp. 48–66). New York: Methuen.

Preston, D. R. (1986). Five visions of America. *Language in society, 15,* 221–240.

Ramírez, J. D. (1992). Executive summary. *Bilingual Research Journal, 16*(1 & 2), 1–62.

Resnick, D. P. (1991). Historical perspectives on literacy and schooling. In S. R. Graubard (Ed.), *Literacy* (pp. 15–32). New York: Hill and Wang.

Resnick, M. (1993). ESL and language planning in Puerto Rican education. *TESOL Quarterly, 27*(2), 259–275.

Roberts, C., Davics, E., & Jupp, T. (1992). *Language and discrimination: A study of communication in multi-ethnic workplaces.* London: Longman.

Roberts, L. P. (1992). Attitudes of entering university freshmen toward foreign language study: A descriptive analysis. *Modern Language Journal, 76*(3), 275–283.

Sarason, S. (1971). *The culture of the school and the problem of change.* Boston, MA: Allyn and Bacon.

Sarason, S. (1990). *The predictable failure of educational reform.* San Francisco, CA: Jossey-Bass.

Sato, C. (1989). A nonstandard approach to standard English. *TESOL Quarterly, 23*(2), 259–282.

Sears, D. O., & Huddy, L. (1989). Language conflict as symbolic politics: The role of symbolic meaning. Unpublished manuscript, University of California, Los Angeles.

Shor, I. (1992). *Empowering education: Critical teaching for social change.* Chicago: University of Chicago Press.

Silva-Corvalán, C. (1994). *Language contact and change: Spanish in Los Angeles.* New York: Cambridge University Press.

Smith, F. (1993). *Whose language? What power? A universal conflict in a South African setting.* New York: Teachers College Press.

Smith, L. E. (Ed.) (1987). *Discourse across cultures: Strategies in world Englishes.* New York: Prentice Hall.

Smitherman-Donaldson, G. (1988). Discriminatory discourse on Afro-American speech. In G. Smitherman-Donaldson & T. van Dijk (Eds.), *Discourse and discrimination* (pp. 144–220). Detroit, MI: Wayne State University Press.

Snow, M. A., Padilla, A. M. & Campbell, R. N. (1988). Patterns of second language retention of graduates of a Spanish immersion program. *Applied Linguistics, 9*(2), 182–197.

Solsken, J. W. (1993). *Literacy, gender, and work in families and in school.* Norwood, NJ: Ablex.

Sonntag, S., & Pool, J. (1987). Linguistic denial and linguistic self-denial: American ideologies of language. *Language Problems and Language Planning, 11*(1), 46–65.

Speicher, B., & McMahon, S. (1992). Some African-American perspectives on black English Vernacular. *Language in Society, 21,* 383–407.

Strong, M. (1984). Integrative motivation: Cause or result of successful second language acquisition. *Language Learning, 34*(3), 1–14.

Swain, M. (1993). The output hypothesis: Just speaking and writing aren't enough. *Canadian Modern Language Review/La revue canadienne des langues vivantes, 50*(1), 158–164.

Swain, M., & Lapkin, S. (1994). Problems in output and the cognitive processes they generate: A step towards second language learning. Unpublished manuscript, Ontario Institute for Studies in Education.

Tharp, R. G., & Yamauchi, L. (1994). Effective instructional conversation in native American classrooms. Educational practice report no. 10. Santa Cruz, CA: National Center for Research on Cultural Diversity and Second Language Learning.

Tollefson, J. W. (1991). *Planning language, planning inequality.* New York: Longman.

Torres, M. (1988). Attitudes of bilingual education parents towards language learning and curriculum and instruction. *NABE Journal, 12*(2), 171–185.

Uchida, A. (1992). When "difference" is "dominance": A critique of the "anti-power-based" cultural approach to sex differences. *Language in Society, 21,* 547–568.

Valdman, A. (1988). Classroom foreign language learning and language variation: The notion of pedagogical norms. *World Englishes, 7*(2), 221–236.

Villanueva, V. (1993). *Bootstraps: From an American academic of color.* Urbana, IL: National Council of Teachers of English.

Walsh, C. (Ed.). (1991), *Literacy as praxis: Culture, language, and pedagogy.* Norwood, NJ: Ablex.

Weiner, B. (1992). *Human motivation: Metaphors, theories, and research.* Newbury Park, CA: Sage.

Williams, F. (1973). Some research notes on dialect attitudes and stereotypes. In R. Shuy and R. Fasold (Eds.), *Language attitudes: Current trends and prospects.* Washington, DC: Georgetown University Press.

Williams, F. (1976). *Explorations in the linguistic attitudes of teachers.* Rowley, MA: Newbury House.

Williams, G. (1992). *Sociolinguistics: A sociological critique.* London: Routledge.

Zuengler, J. (1993). Encouraging learners' conversational participation: The effect of content knowledge. *Language Learning, 43*(3), 403–432.

Zuengler, J., & Bent, B. (1991). Relative knowledge of content domain: An influence on native-non-native conversations. *Applied Linguistics, 12*(4), 397–415.

# 2 *Societal multilingualism*

Kamal K. Sridhar

## Introduction

The terms *bilingualism* and *multilingualism* have been used interchangeably in the literature to refer to the knowledge or use of more than one language by an individual or a community. This practice will be continued here, but we must allow for the possibility that multilingualism may be more than just a magnified version of bilingualism. Multilingualism can be, and has been, studied both as an individual and as a societal phenomenon. When it is viewed as an individual phenomenon, issues such as how one acquires two or more languages in childhood or later, how these languages are represented in the mind, and how they are accessed for speaking and writing and for comprehension become central. When it is viewed as a societal phenomenon, one is concerned with its institutional dimensions, that is, with issues such as the status and roles of the languages in a given society, attitudes toward languages, determinants of language choice, the symbolic and practical uses of the languages, and the correlations between language use and social factors such as ethnicity, religion, and class. In this chapter, selected aspects of multilingualism as a societal phenomenon and their implications for language teaching are discussed.

Bilingualism is a worldwide phenomenon. Most nations have speakers of more than one language. Hundreds of millions of people the world over routinely make use of two or three or four languages in their daily lives. Furthermore, even so-called monolinguals also routinely switch from one language variety – a regional dialect, the standard language, a specialized technical register, a formal or informal style, and so on – to another in the course of their daily interactions. According to one influential theory (Gumperz, 1971), a multilingual's facility in moving from one language to another as the occasion demands is but an extension of the monolingual's capacity to shift registers and styles (p. 3). The study of multilingualism, therefore, not only focuses on one of the most significant types of language use but also has the potential to shed light on language behavior in general.

There are several types of societal multilingualism. The most common type occurs when a country or region consists of several language groups, each of which is primarily monolingual. Canada is a good example. In such a case, the nation as a whole is multilingual but not all individuals are necessarily multilingual. This situation has been referred to as the *territorial principle of multilingualism* (Grosjean, 1982, pp. 12–13). On the other hand, multilingualism can be based on the *personality principle* (Grosjean, 1982, pp. 12–13); that is, where bilingualism is the official policy of a country and most individuals are multilingual. India and several countries in East and West Africa are good examples of this type. In reality, most multilingual nations exhibit a combination of these two types.

### *Reasons for multilingualism*

How do societies become multilingual? There are many reasons. The most obvious factor leading to societal multilingualism is migration. When speakers of one language settle in an area where another language is used and over the years continue to maintain their own language, the result is multilingualism. Spanish in the United States is a good example of this. Another cause of societal multilingualism is cultural contact. When a society imports and assimilates the cultural institutions (e.g., religion or literature) of another society, over the years multilingualism may result. The use of Arabic and Western European languages, for example, English, French, Portuguese, Spanish, and Dutch in Asia, Africa, and Latin America bear testimony to this phenomenon. A third reason is annexation, as in the case of the French- and Spanish-speaking parts of the United States, and colonialism, as in many parts of Latin America, Asia, and Africa, where colonial languages such as Spanish, French, and especially English became entrenched and continue to play crucial roles long after the cessation of colonial rule. Other reasons include the commercial, scientific, and technological dependence of the speakers of certain languages on the speakers of other languages.

## Speech communities

In the study of societal multilingualism, it becomes evident that certain types of approaches to the study of language are more relevant and useful than others. *Generative grammar,* the dominant theoretical model in linguistics during the past three decades, has little to say about societal multilingualism or even about individual multilingualism. This is because this paradigm is focused on the structure of language and not its communicative function or context. What is needed is a theory of language in which the study of the internal structure of language is complemented and, to the extent possible, explained by its being situated in a communicative (interactional) matrix. In various functional approaches to language, particularly those of Ferguson (1959), Fishman (1972a), Gumperz (1971), Halliday (1973), and Hymes (1974), considerable attention has been paid to the social use of language. Through such approaches it is possible to learn about the interaction of language and society, the contribution of social context to linguistic meaning, the social functions of language, and the use of language as a major social institution.

It need hardly be stressed that communication is skilled work. Generally, individuals are versed in the norms and patterns of interaction in their societies. A conglomeration of individuals who share these same norms about communication is referred to as a speech community. A *speech community* is defined as a community sharing a knowledge of the rules for the conduct and interpretation of speech. Such sharing consists of knowledge of at least one form of speech and knowledge also of its patterns of use. Labov (1972) emphasizes the importance of shared attitudes and shared norms: "The speech community is not defined by any marked agreement in the use of language elements, so much as by participation in a set of shared norms . . ." (p. 120). Hymes (1974) stresses the fact that members of a speech community are unified by norms about uses of language. Bolinger (1975) points to a great diversity of speech communities: "There is no limit to the ways in which human beings league themselves together for self-identification, security, gain, amusement, worship, or any of the other purposes that are held in common; consequently there is no limit to the number and variety of speech communities that are to be found in society" (p. 333). Bolinger's definition allows for the possibility of more than one speech community within any geographical area. The group that one chooses to identify with does not always remain constant. At one point, the determining factor might be language, at another point religion, and at yet another point caste or ethnicity. This perspective of shifting, overlapping, intersecting, and complementing identities is particularly suited to the characterization of multilingual speech communities. In the case of monolinguals, the norms may establish when to speak or interrupt a speaker, how to compliment or thank someone, how to request something politely, and so on. In the case of multilinguals, the norms will include all of the above, plus considerations such as which language to use on what occasion and with whom.

## Verbal repertoire

The notion of verbal repertoire is central to the discussion of multilingualism, both in the individual and in a society. *Verbal repertoire* refers to the total range of linguistic resources available to an individual or a community. For monolingual speakers, this includes the range of regional, social, functional, and stylistic varieties that they command, either productively (i.e., in speaking or writing) or receptively (i.e., in reading or understanding spoken language). In the case of a multilingual individual or society, the verbal repertoire is obviously more complex in the sense that it encompasses not only varieties of the same language but also entirely different languages. It is important to keep in mind that each language in the repertoire brings with it its own set of grammatical, lexical, pragmatic, and sociolinguistic rules and conventions (norms).

Pandit's (1972) illustration of a day in the linguistic life of a spice merchant in India is a classic example of a multilingual's verbal repertoire:

> A Gujarati spice merchant in Bombay uses Kathiawadi (his dialect of Gujarati) with his family, Marathi (the local language) in the vegetable market, Kacchi and Konkani in trading circles, Hindi or Hindustani with the milkman and at the train station, and even English on formal occasions. Such a person may not be highly educated or well versed in linguistic rules, but knows enough to be able to use the language(s) for his purposes. (p. 79)

An important characteristic of multilingualism pointed out by Pandit's example is the fact that multilinguals do not necessarily have a perfect or nativelike command of *all* the languages (or *codes,* as these languages or language varieties have come to be called) in their verbal repertoires. Multilingualism involving balanced, nativelike command of all the languages in the repertoire is rather uncommon. Typically, multilinguals have varying degrees of command of the different languages in their repertoires. The differences in competence in the various languages might range from command of a few lexical items, formulaic expressions such as greetings, and rudimentary conversational skills all the way to excellent command of the grammar and vocabulary and specialized registers and styles.

Another major characteristic of multilingual competence might be called *selective functionality.* Multilinguals develop competence in each of the codes to the extent that they need it and for the contexts in which each of the languages is used. For example, a multilingual might have an excellent reading, writing, speaking, and comprehending knowledge of one or two languages but might be more comfortable using one language for academic or professional purposes and another for intimate or emotional expression. This is in part a function of differential command of registers (functional varieties) but also of habitual associations between languages and contexts.

Thus, a multilingual's linguistic competence is a composite of many partial competences which complement one another to yield a rich and complex resource adequate for fulfilling all the life functions (Grosjean, 1982). It follows that in judging the adequacy of the multilingual's linguistic competence one must keep in mind the composite nature of the repertoire. It is neither necessary nor common to find native or near-native competence in all the languages of a multilingual's repertoire. This phenomenon has important implications for language teaching, as we will see in the final section of this chapter.

## *Language choice*

As a discipline, sociolinguistics provides the methodology for analysis and description of the interactional contexts: Who uses what language with whom and for what purposes? It provides frameworks with which to analyze the linguistic choices available to the multilinguals and their reasons for choosing one code from among the several that are available to them. One of the basic assumptions in sociolinguistics involving multilingual speech communities is that, as stated by Elias-Olivares (1979):

> In a heterogeneous speech community, with varying degrees of linguistic diversity and social complexity, speakers interact using different speech varieties drawn from a repertoire of choices which for the most part are not random. On the contrary, the distribution of usage of these choices is determined by several factors in the social communicative system of the community. (p. 121)

Given the existence of different languages in the repertoire of a society or of a multilingual individual, how and when are the languages used? To answer this question, the notion of domains is very important. *Domains,* according to Fishman (1972b), explore "who speaks what language to whom and when in those speech communities that are characterized by widespread and relatively stable multilingualism" (437).

Barber (1952) has formulated domains at the sociopsychological level. He groups the domains as intimate (family), formal (religious-ceremonial), informal (neighborhood), and intergroup (economic and recreational activities as well as interactions with governmental-legal authority). In the research on domains by Fishman and associates (Rubin, 1968; see also Fishman, 1978), language choice is discussed in terms of the following domains: the family, the playground and street, the school, the church, literature, the press, the military, the courts, and governmental administration (Fishman 1972b, p. 441). In investigating multilingual societies, subsequent researchers have either added to or reduced the numbers of domains.

An examination of how the languages of a multilingual community are used reveals a highly sophisticated and efficient pattern. All the languages are not used in all the domains. It is believed that certain languages are particularly suited to certain domains. There is an enormous body of research investigating language use in different domains; for example, language use in intimate (e.g., family, friends, neighborhood) versus utilitarian (e.g., place of work, government offices, banks) domains has been investigated by many researchers. Rubin (1968) presents the case of Guarani and Spanish in Paraguay, where Spanish is used in the government, in business transactions, and with foreigners, whereas Guarani is preferred with friends, family, and servants. In Indonesia, the Javanese language has two speech levels, the formal style, known as *kromo* (used with older and higher-status people), and the intimate style, known as *ngoko* (used with peers and with people of lower status). Speakers choose the level depending on their relationship with others in the group (Alip, 1993). K. K. Sridhar (1982) demonstrates that speakers in urban centers in South India employ a triple-layered distribution in which English, the regional language Kannada, and Hindi (the official language of the country) play different roles, depending on intimacy, status, and power.

## Patterns of use

All the languages in the repertoire of a multilingual community are not equally distributed in terms of power, prestige, vitality, or attitude. In other words, some languages are more valued than others. This phenomenon can be referred to as the *asymmetric principle of multilingualism*. The languages in a multilingual community can be viewed as being arranged on a hierarchy (Kachru & Sridhar, 1978). The position of a given language on this hierarchy is determined by very pragmatic considerations. The larger the number of desired roles a language enables its speakers to play in a given society, the higher its place on the hierarchy. The more restricted the range of valued roles a language provides, the lower its place on the hierarchy. This principle can be illustrated with some examples from India. In the Indian society, the repertoire of an educated multilingual may consist of a large number of languages or codes. An individual might speak a rural and/or a caste dialect at home with members of the family and people from an extended kinship and/or what may be called *native place network*. Here, this dialect or minority language serves essentially to establish an ethnic identity; it may have no written literature or even a script. For example, the Brahman dialect of Tulu, a Dravidian language, is spoken in the coastal areas of the state of Karnataka in South India. It differs considerably from the non-Brahman dialect. Neither the non-Brahman nor the Brahman dialect is used for writing. Although it is spoken by about two million persons, the Tulu language is restricted in its functional range.

All Tulu speakers are bilingual in the local state language, Kannada, which serves as their medium of instruction through the secondary school. Kannada has a wider range of roles, as the language of education, administration, commerce, media, and literature. Kannada therefore gives the Tulu speaker regional identity and statewide mobility. However, even Kannada is restricted relative to certain desired roles. In addition to learning Kannada, Tulu speakers will learn English at the postprimary school level, further widening their linguistic resources. English empowers the speaker to gain access to higher technical education, to communicate on an interstate (pan-Indian) and international level, and to participate in the influential national press and media, and it provides national and international mobility as a job candidate. As a marker of sophistication, modern knowledge, and access to power, English also bestows a tangible competitive advantage and a certain intangible glamour or prestige value. However, the Tulu speaker will also study or informally learn Hindi, which is the chief medium of popular Indian movies, a useful *lingua franca* (a common language used by speakers of different language backgrounds) for communications with North Indian states, and increasingly the official language of the federal government. Still, there are roles that none of these languages individually, or all of them together, can play satisfactorily. The Tulu speaker might also learn the classical language Sanskrit to access, preserve, and symbolize the classical lore of India in an enormous range of fields from religion through medicine. Nor is this all. Depending on lifestyle and networks of business and personal interactions, an individual might also learn one or more regional languages, such as Tamil, Telugu, or Marathi, which she or he will use with varying degrees of proficiency. Thus, in a multilingual's verbal repertoire each language uniquely fulfills certain roles and represents distinct identities, and all of them complement one another to serve the complex communicative demands of a pluralistic society.

As the preceding discussion reveals, the languages of a multilingual community are differentially evaluated on the basis of the habitual associations between the languages and the domains of their use. If the domains in which a language is used are highly valued, then that language is perceived to be highly valued (and conversely). For example, the habitual use of Sanskrit in ritualistic and intellectual contexts by the most prestigious group in the Indian social system over thousands of years has given the language the status of a sacred, intellectual language. (But this association also sometimes works to its disadvantage: Sanskrit is perceived to be too orthodox, difficult, and old-fashioned for everyday purposes.) English, on the other hand, because of the colonial history and association with currently valued domains of higher administration, science and technology, international commerce, Western culture and pop entertainment, is perceived as all-powerful and as a ticket to upward mobility. However, it is important to keep in mind that evaluation of languages in multilingual societies is not always based on materialistic criteria. The revival of Hebrew in Israel, the struggle to reestablish Catalan and Basque in Spain, the movement to revitalize Sanskrit in India, and the continued maintenance of home languages by many groups of migrants over several centuries are reminders that factors such as tribal, caste, ethnic, and national identities are also powerful forces in the use, maintenance, revival, and regulation of languages (S. N. Sridhar, 1987). Movements, often quite successful, now exist in many parts of the world aimed at gaining recognition and status for indigenous languages sidelined or oppressed during colonial and postcolonial regimes (e.g., in Malaysia, the Philippines, Ecuador, Bolivia, and Peru). These movements typically take the form of a demand for extending the functional range of indigenous languages to include domains of power, authority, and prestige by their use in, for example, education, administration, and the legal system. Concomitantly, there are efforts to prevent hegemonic languages from usurping smaller languages by restricting the domains of use of the more prevalent languages. The dynamics of language in a multilingual society reflect the evolution of power in that society. Thus, the languages of a multilingual society exist in a state of organic tension with one another that involves small but cumulatively perceptible shifts in functional range.

## *Diglossia*

A rigid form of functional specialization is seen in the phenomenon referred to as diglossia in Ferguson (1959). At the outset, it should be made clear that Ferguson's concept referred to the specialization of two varieties of the same language. Fishman (1972a) extended this concept to functional specialization of two or more languages within a community. We will first review Ferguson's notion and then its extension. *Diglossia* (Ferguson, 1972) is defined as

> [A] relatively stable language situation in which, in addition to the primary dialects of the language (which may include a standard or regional standards), there is a very divergent, highly codified (often grammatically more complex) superposed variety, the vehicle of a large and respected body of written literature, either of an earlier period or in another speech community, which is learned largely by formal education and is used for most written and formal spoken purposes but is not used by any sector of the community for ordinary conversation. (p. 245)

A diglossic situation exists in a speech community where two codes perform two separate sets of functions. Referring to the superposed variety as high (H) and the other varieties (standard or dialects) as low (L), Ferguson cites the following as examples: classical Arabic (H) and colloquial Arabic (L), standard German (H) and Swiss German (L) in Switzerland, Katharevousa (H) and Demotiki (L) in Greece, and standard French (H) and Haitian Creole (L) in Haiti. Ferguson (1972) states, "One of the most important features of diglossia is the specialization of function for (H) and (L). In one of the situations only (H) is appropriate and in another only (L), with the two sets overlapping only very slightly" (pp. 235–236). Taking the example of Arabic, he shows that the H variety is used in church and mosque sermons, political speeches, university lectures, news broadcasts, newspaper editorials, and poetry. The L variety is used for giving instructions to waiters, servants, and clerks, in personal letters, in conversations with friends and family, in radio soap operas, in captions on political cartoons, and in folk literature. Ferguson (1972) identifies three conditions in a speech community that lead to diglossia. The first is the existence of a large body of literature in a language that is similar to or the same as the indigenous language. This literature must embody some of the fundamental values of the community. Second, literacy in the community is usually restricted to a small elite. Third, a long period of time, even centuries, is involved in establishing the first and second conditions (p. 247).

The speakers of all the languages mentioned above regard H as superior to L in many respects. Attitudinally, some speakers are very strongly in favor of the H variety, so much so that they deny the existence of L by stating that speakers of the L variety are merely speaking the language incorrectly. This is true in the case of Arabic speakers (p. 237). Educated Arabs deny using the L variety of Arabic, as do Haitian Creole speakers, who claim to use only French. Often, the speakers believe that the H variety is more logical, more beautiful, and better able to express important thoughts. Subsequent research shows that several other communities such as Tamil in South India exhibit diglossic characteristics. (For an up-to-date bibliographic review on diglossia, see Hudson, 1992.)

Fishman (1972a) has generalized the concept of diglossia to bilingual communities. He notes that a hierarchical evaluation of languages as high and low is found in bilingual communities as well. For example, in Zaire, French is reserved for prestige domains such as higher education, law, and administration and thus functions as a high language relative to Lingala and other indigenous languages which are used in less prestigious domains and thus function like low languages. This extension of diglossia to bilingual communities works in most cases, except that there are many communities in which the high language is also a mother tongue and not necessarily one that is learned only in school.

Furthermore, diglossia is generally interpreted as implying a rather rigid complementarity or exclusivity of functions; that is, where one variety is appropriate, the other is never used. However, as will be seen later in this chapter, in many bilingual or multilingual situations one encounters not only a complementarity of languages but also a type of use which is best described as *overlapping* or *intermeshing*. Also, in a bilingual (as opposed to the diglossic) situation, the codes in question may not be so sharply differentiated into high or low codes in terms of prestige. These differences mean that the application of diglossia to bilingualism cannot be precise.

Recent empirical research on diglossia in Greece, the Arab world, and elsewhere suggests that the dichotomy may be giving way to intermediate varieties; that is, in contexts which were previously thought to be the exclusive domain of the high varieties, the use of less formal varieties which incorporate some elements of the low variety is seen.

## *Code switching*

When two or more languages exist in a community, speakers frequently switch from one language to another. This phenomenon, known as *code switching,* has attracted a great deal of research attention in the last two decades. Scholars have investigated the structural patterns, functional determinants, social correlates, and psycholinguistic processes of code switching in diverse communities such as Norway, Kenya, India, and the United States to name just a few. Blom and Gumperz (1972) distinguish between two types of code switching. In *situational code switching,* the switch is in response to a change in situation, for example, when a new participant enters the scene, or to a change in the topic of conversation or the setting. A case in point would occur at the end of an official transaction, when a speaker might switch from the standard language to the local dialect to inquire about family matters. In *metaphorical code switching,* the switch has a stylistic or textual function, for example, to signal a quotation, to mark emphasis, to indicate the punch line of a joke, or to signal a change in tone from the serious to the comic. Code switching is thus not random but functionally motivated. In order to explain code switching, we need a theory of language that considers not only the structure of sentences but the structure of conversations, a theory that addresses not only grammaticality of sentences but also their acceptability with reference to the functions of language and the contexts in which it is used. In a series of insightful studies of multilingualism in East Africa, Carol Myers-Scotton (1993a) explains code switching in terms of a theory of rights and obligations. According to her, members of a multilingual speech community are aware of the range of codes that would be appropriate for a particular type of conventionalized exchange and they assign meanings to choices based on such expectations. Any deviation from the neutral or unmarked choice conveys symbolic social messages regarding the identity and attitudes of the speaker. In this sense, code switching is governed by a "grammar of consequences" (Scotton, 1988).

In this context, one might point out the difference between diglossia and code switching. Simply put, diglossia occurs across domain boundaries, and code switching occurs within domains. In diglossic situations, people can be quite aware that they have switched from H to L or vice versa, whereas code switching appears to be quite unconscious. As Tay (1989) says, "On the functional plane, it should be stressed that the typical code switcher or mixer is usually not aware of why he/she switches codes at certain points of the discourse . . ." (p. 412). She recommends that more research be carried out to determine the communicative intent and the attitudes of bilingual and multilingual speakers. As noted, diglossia involves little overlapping of codes; code switching, as will be seen shortly, involves quite a bit of overlap. Finally, the codes in a code switching situation are not necessarily sharply separated in terms of how they are attitudinally evaluated relative to one another.

## *Code mixing*

A common mode of code switching is the switching of languages within sentences, which some researchers (Bhatia & Ritchie, 1989; Bokamba, 1988; Kachru, 1992a; Sridhar & Sridhar, 1980), refer to as *code mixing*. This example, from Kachru in Hindi-English (1992a, p. 185), is illustrative: "Bhai, khana khao ("Brother, eat up"), and let us go." Consider also this example from Edo (a language spoken in Nigeria) and English (Kamwangamalu, 1989):

> DIRECTOR: Dial *enumber naa, n'uniform'en* Mr. Oseni *ighe a* approve *encontracti nii ne*. But *khamaa ren ighe o gha ye* necessary *n'o* submit-e photostat copies *oghe* estimate *n'o ka ya* apply *a ke* pay *ere*. You understand?
>
> (Dial this number, and inform Mr. Oseni that we approved the contract already. But tell him that it will still be necessary for him to submit photostat copies of estimate that he first applied with before we pay him. You understand?) (pp. 328–329)

The distinction between code switching and code mixing is important because code mixing raises several issues involving grammar. For example, what kinds of morphemes, words, or phrases can be mixed from one language into another? Is this mixture governed by the grammar of the *host* or *matrix* language or the *guest* or *embedded* language? Are there any universal constraints on the structure of such bilingual mixing? What are the implications of mixing for theories of mental processing of languages in bilinguals? What textual, stylistic, or literary functions are served by such mixing? These and related questions have been studied extensively since the mid-1970s, making code mixing one of the hottest topics in the research on bilingualism. (See Myers-Scotton, 1993a, for a bibliography.)

Code mixing is distinguished from borrowing on the following grounds (Sridhar & Sridhar, 1980): (1) Borrowing may occasionally involve a few set phrases but is usually restricted to single lexical items. Code mixing, however, involves every level of lexical and syntactic structure, including words, phrases, clauses, and sentences. (2) Borrowed words can occur even in the speech of monolinguals, whereas code mixing presupposes a certain degree of bilingual competence. (3) The set of borrowed expressions in a language typically represents semantic fields outside the experience of the borrowing language, whereas the expressions that occur in code mixing may duplicate existing expressions – in other words, code mixing is not always used to fill lexical gaps. (4) Borrowings represent a restricted set of expressions, with some creativity in the margins, whereas code mixing draws creatively upon practically the whole of the vocabulary and grammar of another language. (5) Borrowings represent mostly nouns and, marginally, a few adjectives and other categories, whereas code mixing draws on every category and constituent type in grammar.

Certain types of code mixing are regarded as acceptable, whereas certain other types are rejected by code mixers as ungrammatical. It is arguable that the felicitous use of code mixing, therefore, implies a more sophisticated linguistic competence than monolingual language use: it presupposes the ability to integrate grammatical units from two different language systems into a more complex linguistic structure.

Although it makes a rather liberal use of the guest language resources, code mixing is not a random or "free-for-all" phenomenon. Several researchers have shown that code mixing is rule governed or subject to several grammatical constraints, some of which have been claimed to be universal. Among the more widely discussed constraints are the *free morpheme constraint* and the *equivalence constraint* proposed by Poplack (1980; see updated discussion in Poplack & Sankoff, 1988) and the *dual structure principle* (Sridhar & Sridhar, 1980). Recently, Myers-Scotton (1993b) has proposed a comprehensive and integrated *matrix language frame* model which aims to address grammatical, psycholinguistic, and sociolinguistic considerations in code mixing.

Code mixing and code switching serve the same functions. Among the more prominent functions is *identity marking*. A speaker may use a particular code to signal a specific type of identity, for example, English or French for modernity, sophistication, or authority, in many parts of the world (Kachru, 1978; Myers-Scotton, 1993a; Pandit, 1978; S. N. Sridhar, 1978); Sanskrit for nationalistic and traditionalistic image in India (Kachru, 1978); Arabic and Persian for Islamic identity; Hindi-Urdu to signal a "macho" image in South India (S. N. Sridhar, 1978); French (as opposed to Russian) for a sophisticated, diplomatic, courtly image in czarist Russia, as depicted in Tolstoy's *War and Peace;* and local languages (as opposed to Swahili or English) for ethnic or tribal solidarity in East Africa (Myers-Scotton, 1993a). Other functions, according to Myers-Scotton (1993a), include the following: Mixing can be employed as a strategy of neutrality when the use of any one language in the repertoire might suggest the wrong message, such as "talking down" to somebody or suggesting an uncultivated persona (p. 70). Code mixing is also used for stylistic function, for example, to signal a transition to the sublime or the ridiculous as in the choice of Latinate or Yiddish diction in Milton's epics and Yiddish stand-up comedies, respectively. (For a detailed discussion of the functions of code switching and code mixing, see Myers-Scotton, 1993a.)

Code mixing has often been regarded negatively by teachers, prescriptive usage legislators, and even by the speakers themselves (see Gumperz & Hernandez-Chavez, 1972; Haugen, 1969; Mkilifi, 1978, for a discussion of such attitudes; see also McGroarty, this volume, on attitudes). Code mixing has been regarded as a sign of laziness or mental sloppiness and inadequate command of language. It has been claimed to be detrimental to the health of the language. The traditional pedagogical resistance to code mixing stems from a combination of puristic attitudes and the use of a monolingual paradigm of language. These attitudes distort and devalue many aspects of multilingual behavior. Recent research has demonstrated that code mixing is quite common in multilingual societies around the world and is often used by speakers who are highly proficient in all the languages being mixed. Code mixing serves important sociocultural and textual functions as an expression of certain types of complex personalities and communities. It is a versatile and appropriate vehicle, especially for the expression of multicultural communities. It is not surprising, therefore, to find that many creative writers have used code mixing as a powerful expressive resource to convey multicultural experiences. As increased communication brings greater linguistic and cultural contact among nations, an increasing use of code mixing can be found in many multilingual societies around the world (see Bhatia & Ritchie, 1989; Bokamba, 1988; Desai, 1982; Kamwangamalu, 1989; Mkilifi, 1978).

Contrary to what is often claimed, code mixing is not confined to speech; it is also found in formal writing. Yau (1993) demonstrates that in Hong Kong, where ninety-five percent of the population speaks Chinese, a variety of Chinese code mixed with English is very much in use in Chinese written materials. The written materials he analyzed included Chinese textbooks covering fourteen different subject areas, ten Chinese magazines, and twenty-seven popular entertainment books. At times, the code-mixed items in English were as high as fifty-seven percent of the text. Yau concludes that English is used very commonly, especially in topics dealing with science and technology and business and commerce. Code mixing with English also occurs in the written media. In the case of Singapore, Tay (1989) demonstrates that often two or three dialects of Chinese are mixed with English, as in:

Everyday, you know *kao tiam* (Hokkien for "nine o'clock") *li khi a* (Teochew for "you go"), everybody /wa/ (nonverbal gesture for reading books).

(Everyday at 9 o'clock you go to find everybody reading books.) (p. 416)

Obviously, such writing presupposes multilingual competence on the part of the readers.

A number of studies have focused on code mixing and code switching in the United States, particularly between Spanish and English. Torres (1989) found that in the New York Puerto Rican community she investigated, the first- and second-generation members were familiar with three codes: English, Spanish, and a mixed code. Each generation had its preferred codes for informal discussions between family members. Although the first generation tended to interact in Spanish with some code mixing, the younger generation used more English. Although the Spanish the younger generation spoke was influenced by English, they nevertheless used a lot of Spanish. Similar findings have been reported by Poplack (1980) and others. Elias-Olivares (1979) remarks that the task in describing the language situation of Chicano speech communities is not so much describing the referential function of language varieties the speakers command and use but describing the socioexpressive functions of these varieties. This would enable us to see whether they convey seriousness or joking, distance or relationship, and so on, between the structure of language and the structure of speaking (p. 132).

## Patterns in structure

### *Convergence*

An extreme effect of language contact is *linguistic convergence,* or the extensive structural modification of the languages of a geographic area in the direction of one another, even though the languages may belong to different language families. Cases of extensive mutual adaptation are relatively rare and come about because of centuries, if not millennia, of intensive and extensive societal multilingualism. However, the process is attested quite widely. Convergence is distinguished from the more common phenomenon of borrowing by the fact that the usually conservative areas of morphology and syntax may also be affected, in addition to the phonology and the lexicon. Convergence results in the formation of a *Sprachbund* (a term introduced by Trubetzkoy, discussed in Emeneau 1956, p. 3), or a linguistic area in which the languages come to resemble each other structurally more than do their siblings from their own genetic stock. The best-known example of a linguistic area is South Asia, where languages from four language families have converged (see Emeneau, 1956; Gumperz & Wilson, 1971; Masica, 1976; S. N. Sridhar, 1981; Thomason & Kaufman, 1988).

In their classic paper "Convergence and Creolization: A Case from the Indo-Aryan/Dravidian Border in India," Gumperz and Wilson (1971) discuss how language contact has led to linguistic diffusion in Kupwar, a small village in Maharashtra, India. Describing this community, they say:

> There is every indication that the Kannada-speaking Jain cultivators and the Marathi-speaking service castes have both been in the region for more than six centuries. The Urdu-speaking Muslims date from the days of the Mogul domination three or four centuries ago. (p. 153)

The languages spoken in this area belong to two different language families – Marathi and Urdu belong to the Indo-European family, and Kannada and Telugu to the Dravidian family. Because they all live in the same village, most members are bilingual or trilingual. Gumperz and Wilson have analyzed a large number of morphological and syntactic structures in the languages of the area to show that the adaptations have been far reaching and multilateral. Each language has adopted some features of the others. Commenting on the significance of these data for a theory of language change, Gumperz and Wilson (1971) remark:

> The need for constant code-switching and for mutual adaptation within a situation in which home languages are maintained has led to reduction and adaptation in linguistic structure. Historically viewed, moreover, where one is used to thinking of grammar as most persistent, lexicon as most changeable, in the normal development of a language, in Kupwar it is grammar that has been adaptable, lexical shape most persistent. (p. 166)

## *Transfer*

Convergence is only a clear and dramatic example of a phenomenon that is found in all language contact situations, namely, adaptation and assimilation of the structure of one language by another. The central mechanism involved here is *language transfer,* which is a powerful force in language change, acquisition, and use in multilingual communities.

It is important that the psycholinguistic and sociolinguistic significance of language transfer is understood. This concept has suffered neglect and distortion because of its erroneous identification with a behaviorist theory of (second) language acquisition, according to which transfer is a mechanical product of habits from the first language (Dulay & Burt, 1974). However, recent research has shown that transfer is compatible with a cognitive view of language acquisition as well (Odlin, 1989; S. N. Sridhar, 1980). In this view, transfer is an efficient and economical psycholinguistic process in which the tried and tested rules of the first language are used as hypotheses in mastering a second language. Transfer reduces cognitive dissonance and contributes to processing economy.

Sociolinguistically also, transfer plays a positive role in multilingual communication. The objection to mixing and transfer is based on the claim that such processes interfere with intelligibility. However, when the interlocutors share the same languages, transfer from one to the other enhances the expressive resources of each language without causing interference or reducing intelligibility. Communication in multilingual societies often presupposes this multilingual competence (see K. K. Sridhar, 1989; S. N. Sridhar, 1992, for details).

This and related research on language interaction in multilingual communities make it clear that multilingualism cannot be regarded as simply an extension of language variation but poses special challenges and holds special promises for the construction of a theory of language.

## Implications for language teaching

The foregoing sections on what multilingualism is, how it works, and its distinctive features and consequences have several implications for language teaching professionals in the United States and worldwide. In this section we shall outline some implications of a realistic, cross-cultural understanding of societal multilingualism for second language teaching in the United States and other Anglophone countries (cf. Kachru, 1992b; Kachru & Nelson, this volume), with some reference to EFL and ESL teaching worldwide. ESL teachers in the United States (at all levels – grade school, high school, college, and adult populations) deal with students from different countries and with different sociocultural backgrounds. Classes in the United States are becoming increasingly heterogeneous. The 1990 U.S. Census showed that, of 248 million people, 31.8 million foreign language speakers communicate in 329 different languages (Usdansky, 1993). The trend in the United States is toward some sort of maintenance rather than complete assimilation (Fishman, Nahirny, Hoffman, & Hayde, 1966). The American tendency to expect immigrant languages to fade away and to then expect students to enroll and do well in foreign language courses is a paradox. Clearly, there is a need for a fresh approach to second language teaching in the United States. After all, the goal of second language teaching is to create bilinguals. A clear understanding of how bilingualism works should be a cardinal prerequisite in the preparation for language teaching in the United States and other Anglophone countries.

The preceding discussion of societal bilingualism suggests the following implications for second language teaching:

1. Language teachers need to revise their attitudes with regard to the status and value of bilingualism. Because of earlier dubious research (reviewed ably by Hakuta, 1986), bilingualism has come to be identified with a low level of intelligence, poor educational performance, and socioeconomic stagnation. People have begun to recognize that this perception is wrong and that bilingualism is independent of intelligence and consistent with the highest educational and socioeconomic achievement (McGroarty, this volume).
2. The role of English vis-à-vis other languages in the learner's and the community's verbal repertoire should be reassessed. Teachers need to recognize the fact that English, despite its undoubted importance, may be only one of the languages in a learner's repertoire. The learner's other languages have distinctive and valued roles to play in the learner's community. Ignoring the existence of these languages or negating their values by insisting on a maximal or exclusive use of English even in the home domain (as many teachers routinely advise anxious immigrant parents to do) runs contrary to the dynamics of multilingualism and is detrimental to the learner's self-respect and cultural identity. Teachers need to recognize that children and adults are capable of adding languages to their existing repertoires. In other words, what is called for is an additive model of bilingualism (Lambert, 1978, p. 217), not a replacive one.
3. The functional complementarity of languages also implies that it may be unnecessary and unrealistic to expect complete and nativelike competence in the entire range of registers, styles, and functions of English. Expectations regarding how much English and what kind of English learners need to learn should take into account the contributions of the learners' other languages as well as English. This implication is particularly relevant in the case of English language teaching overseas.
4. It is also clear that teachers need to be familiar with the other

languages in the learners' repertoires. Such familiarity can prevent situations such as the one in New York City, where teachers assumed that Jamaican Creole speakers were speakers of African-American Vernacular English (Pratt-Johnson, 1993; see also Rickford, this volume).

Another set of implications follows from the dynamics of language contact. As noted earlier, code switching and code mixing are widely attested, natural manifestations of language contact, and they are functionally and formally systematic behaviors.

5. Language teachers trained in a monolingual, monocultural paradigm have often been needlessly harsh toward minority students who switch and mix languages. An enlightened and informed approach to language teaching would foster a tolerant and relativistic attitude rather than the current exclusionary one. From this perspective, a mixed code is as appropriate for in-group, bicultural communication as a monolingual code would be for communicating with monolingual interlocutors.
6. The preceding discussion of language contact shows that multilingualism involves not only a division of labor but also a great deal of give and take between languages. This suggests that it is unrealistic for the language teacher to expect learners to keep their languages compartmentalized and thus avoid code switching and, especially, code mixing. On the contrary, varying amounts of influence of one language over another at all levels is to be expected. Such transfer need not necessarily be regarded as interference. Although some types of transfer can lead to loss of intelligibility and pragmatic failure, other types can actually enhance the communicative resources of the target language, besides adding color, charm, and variety to the language. For example, the semantic formulas for the performance of speech acts such as requesting or complimenting vary from one speech community to another, and transfer of such conventions can often be enriching (cf. Cohen, this volume). In the literature on second language acquisition (see Kachru, 1986; Sridhar & Sridhar, 1992), this positive role of transfer in bilingual communication has received much less attention than the negative "interference" role. Such a relaxed, open-minded, or tolerant attitude to language variation is characteristic of traditionally multilingual societies and contributes to the promotion of cultural pluralism. After all, nativelike performance is not an end in itself but one statement of the real goal of language teaching, namely, communicative effectiveness.

Since English is the most widely learned second language in the world today, some implications of societal multilingualism specifically for the teaching of English might be identified. First of these is the recognition of the wide range of variation in the use of English around the world. Besides the native varieties such as British and American English, there are a number of extensively used nonnative varieties such as Indian, Filipino, Singaporean, or Nigerian English, which differ considerably from native varieties (Kachru, 1992b; Kachru & Nelson, this volume; Smith & Sridhar, 1993). The nonnative varieties have acquired their distinctive characteristics because of their use as a second language by people with different mother tongues and for the expression of different sociocultural content. These varieties are not acquisitionally deficient or fossilized interlanguages but functionally viable varieties which follow different but productive formal processes of grammar and usage (Sridhar & Sridhar, 1986). These facts need to be kept in mind when placement and proficiency tests for incoming international students are devised and evaluated (Kenkel & Tucker, 1989).

As an international language, English is being used increasingly in nonnative contexts. Among these contexts are groups of nonnative users communicating with one another (for example, an Israeli software engineer communicating with his or her Brazilian counterpart) and native speakers communicating with nonnative speakers (for example, a salesperson from the U.S. Caterpillar Company negotiating with Japanese buyers). Thus, the traditional prototype paradigm of second language teaching, which assumed that a nonnative learner learned English in order to communicate with a native speaker of English, no longer represents the primary context of the use of English in the world today (Smith & Sridhar, 1993). A teacher of English, therefore, must be aware of this change and tailor the curriculum accordingly. In particular, this involves sensitivity to the variations in lexical, pragmatic, and other norms resulting from the fact that users of the English language interact with an enormous range of verbal repertoires and cultural contexts around the world.

How can we bring about the change of perspective just described? The ideal starting place is in teacher training programs. The multilingual research paradigm needs to be incorporated into such core courses as Methods and Materials for Teaching English, the Structure of English, Contrastive Linguistics and Error Analysis, and Language Testing. In addition, it would be appropriate to introduce a required course in sociolinguistics, with a strong component on societal bilingualism, for teacher trainees. An awareness and an understanding of societal multilingualism are crucial to any program in second language teaching and bilingual education.

## Suggestions for further reading

Fasold, R. (1984). *The sociolinguistics of society.* Oxford: Basil Blackwell.
A good critical presentation of the major issues and methods of sociolinguistics, especially from the point of view of multilingualism. The discussion of diglossia, language choice, language attitudes, and empirical methods is particularly good.

Fishman, J. A. (Ed.). (1978). *Advances in the study of societal multilingualism.* The Hague: Mouton.
The papers in this extensive collection deal with societal multilingualism all over the world. The focus is on interactions between linguistic and sociocultural, political, economic, educational, and other factors that determine the functional allocation of roles for the different language(s) in a multilingual's repertoire.

Grosjean, F. (1982). *Life with two languages.* Cambridge, MA: Harvard University Press.
This is an excellent source as a general and comprehensive introduction to bilingualism, including topics such as bilingualism in the world and the United States, bilingualism in society, the bilingual child and the bilingual adult, and bilingual speech and language.

Myers-Scotton, C. (1993). *Social motivations for codeswitching.* Oxford: Oxford University Press.
This is one of the first books that focuses on code switching as a type of skilled performance and not an alternative strategy used by deficient bilinguals, as has been historically believed. Using data from multilingual communities in Africa (mostly Kenya), Myers-Scotton demonstrates that bilingual and multilingual speakers have an additional style at their command which they use only with other bilinguals who share the same codes.

Preston, D. (1989). *Sociolinguistics and second language acquisition.* Oxford: Basil Blackwell.
This informative book focuses on research in sociolinguistics and second language acquisition and successfully demonstrates how the contributions of one group of researchers can enrich the other. The crucial role(s) played by a variety of interactional factors (sociolinguistics) and individual learner characteristics (second language acquisition) are brought together in this volume.

Pride, J. B. & Holmes, J. (1972). *Sociolinguistics.* Harmondsworth, United Kingdom: Penguin Books.
The rich collection of articles in this text cover a wide range of topics related to multilingualism, using data from different countries. Discussions on language standardization, domains, language use, and dialectical and stylistic variation are particularly good.

Wolfson, N. (1989). *Perspectives: Sociolinguistics and TESOL.* Rowley, MA: Newbury House.
This text, written for the nonspecialist, explores issues such as bilingual education, multilingualism, the rapid spread of English among nonnative speakers, and other related issues to demonstrate the growing impact of sociolinguistics on the TESOL profession. In addition, Wolfson offers a critical review of methods used in sociolinguistic research.

Wolfson, N., & Judd, E. (Eds.). (1983). *Sociolinguistics and language acquisition*. Rowley, MA: Newbury House.
In this collection of papers, second language acquisition is viewed from a sociolinguistic perspective. In addition to describing sociolinguistic findings in situations in which different languages are used in a variety of speech communities, several studies report on a single speech act or event in the context of its use within an English-speaking community.

## References


Alip, F. B. (1993). Language planning in Indonesia. Unpublished Ph.D. dissertation. Stony Brook, NY: State University of New York.

Barber, C. (1952). *Trilingualism in Pasqua: Social functions of language in an Arizona Yaqui village*. Unpublished master's thesis. Tucson: University of Arizona.

Bhatia, T. K., & Ritchie, W. C. (Eds.) (1989). *Code-mixing: English across languages*. Special issue, *World Englishes, 8*(3).

Blom, J. P. & Gumperz, J. J. (1972). Social meaning in linguistic structure: Code-switching in Norway. In J. J. Gumperz & D. Hymes (Eds.), *Directions in sociolinguistics* (pp. 407–434). New York: Holt, Rinehart and Winston.

Bokamba, E. (1988). Code-mixing, language variation, and linguistic theory: Evidence from Bantu languages. *Lingua, 76*, 21–62.

Bolinger, D. L. (1975). *Aspects of language* (2nd ed.). New York: Harcourt Brace Jovanovich.

Desai, B. T. (1982). A linguistic study of the English elements in Kannada-English code-switching. Unpublished doctoral dissertation. Hyderabad: Central Institute of English and Foreign Languages.

Dulay, H. C., & Burt, M. K. (1974). You can't learn without goofing. In J. C. Richards (Ed.), *Error analysis: Perspectives on second language acquisition* (pp. 95–123). London: Longman.

Elias-Olivares, L. (1979). Language use in a Chicano community: A sociolinguistic approach. In J. B. Pride (Ed.), *Sociolinguistic aspects of language learning and teaching* (pp. 120–134). Oxford: Oxford University Press.

Emeneau, M. B. (1956). India as a linguistic area. *Language, 32*, 3–16.

Ferguson, C. A. (1959). Diglossia. *Word, 15*, 325–340.

Ferguson, C. A. (1972). *Language structure and language use*. Stanford, CA: Stanford University Press.

Fishman, J. A. (1972a). *The sociology of language*. Rowley, MA: Newbury House.

Fishman, J. A. (1972b). Domains and the relationship between micro- and macro- sociolinguistics. In J. J. Gumperz & D. Hymes. (Eds.), *Directions in sociolinguistics* (pp. 435–453). New York: Holt, Rinehart and Winston.

Fishman, J. A., Nahirny, V. C., Hoffman, J. E., & Hayde, R. G. (Eds.). (1966). *Language loyalty in the United States*. The Hague: Mouton.

Fishman, J. A. (Ed.). (1978). *Advances in the study of societal multilingualism*. The Hague: Mouton.

Greenfield, L. (1972). Situational measures of normative language views in relation to person, place, and topic among Puerto Rican bilinguals. In

J. A. Fishman (Ed.), *Advances in the sociology of language* (Vol. 2, pp. 17–35). The Hague: Mouton.

Grosjean, F. (1982). *Life with two languages.* Cambridge, MA: Harvard University Press.

Gumperz, J. J. (1971). *Language in social groups.* Stanford, CA: Stanford University Press.

Gumperz, J. J., & Hernandez-Chavez, E. (1972). Bilingualism, bidialectalism, and classroom interaction. In J. J. Gumperz (Anwar Dil, Ed.). *Language in social groups* (pp. 312–339). Stanford, CA: Stanford University Press.

Gumperz, J. J., & Wilson, R. (1971). Convergence and creolization: A case from the Indo-Aryan/Dravidian border. In D. Hymes (Ed.), *Pidginization and creolization of languages* (pp. 151–167). London: Cambridge University Press.

Hakuta, K. (1986). *The mirror of language: The debate on bilingualism.* New York: Basic Books.

Halliday, M. A. K. (1973). *Explorations in the functions of language.* London: Edward Arnold.

Haugen, E. (1969). *The Norwegian language in America: A study in bilingual behavior.* Bloomington: Indiana University Press.

Hudson, A. (1992). Diglossia: A bibliographic review. *Language in society, 21,* 611–674.

Hymes, D. (1974). *Foundations in sociolinguistics: An ethnographic approach.* Philadelphia: University of Pennsylvania Press.

Kachru, B. B. (1978). Toward code-mixing: An Indian perspective. In B. B. Kachru & S. N. Sridhar (Eds.), *Aspects of sociolinguistics in South Asia.* Special issue of *International Journal of the Sociology of Language, 16,* 27–44.

Kachru, B. B. (1986). *The alchemy of English.* Oxford: Pergamon Press.

Kachru, B. B. (Ed.). (1992b). *The other tongue: English across cultures* (2nd ed.). Urbana: University of Illinois Press.

Kachru, B. B. (1992a). Multilingualism and multiculturalism. In W. Bright (Ed.), *International encyclopedia of linguistics* (Vol. 1, pp. 182–186). Oxford: Oxford University Press.

Kachru, B. B., & Sridhar, S. N. (Eds.). (1978). *Aspects of sociolinguistics in South Asia.* Special issue of *International Journal of the Sociology of Language, 16,* 27–44.

Kamwangamalu, N. M. (1989). A selected bibliography of studies on code-mixing and code-switching (1970–1988). *World Englishes, 8*(3), 433–439.

Kenkel, J., & Tucker, G. R. (1989). Evaluation of institutionalized varieties of English and its implications for placement and pedagogy. *World Englishes, 8*(2), 201–214.

Labov, W. (1972). *Sociolinguistic patterns.* Philadelphia: University of Pennsylvania Press.

Lambert, W. E. (1978). Some cognitive and sociocultural consequences of being bilingual. In J. E. Alatis (Ed.), *Georgetown University roundtable on languages and linguistics* (pp. 214–229). Washington, DC: Georgetown University Press.

Masica, C. P. (1976). *Defining a linguistic area: South Asia.* Chicago: University of Chicago Press.

Mkilifi, M. (1978). Triglossia and Swahili-English bilingualism in Tanzania. In J. A. Fishman (Ed.), *Advances in the study of societal multilingualism*. The Hague: Mouton.

Myers-Scotton, C. (1993a). *Social motivations for code-switching: Evidence from Africa*. Oxford: Oxford University Press.

Myers-Scotton, C. (1993b). *Duelling languages: Grammatical structures in code-switching*. Oxford: Oxford University Press.

Odlin, T. (1989). *Language transfer*. Cambridge: Cambridge University Press.

Pandit, P. B. (1972). *India as a socio-linguistic area*. Poona: Poona University Press.

Pandit, P. B. (1978). Language and identity: The Punjabi language in Delhi. In B. B. Kachru & S. N. Sridhar (Eds.), *Aspects of sociolinguistics in South Asia*. Special issue of *International Journal of the Sociology of Language, 16*, 98–108.

Poplack, S. (1980). "Sometimes I'll start a sentence in Spanish y termino en espanol": Toward a typology of code-switching. *Linguistics, 26*, 47–104.

Poplack, S., & Sankoff, D. (1988). Codeswitching. In A. Ulrich et al. (Eds.), *Sociolinguistics/Soziolinguistik* (pp. 1174–1180). Berlin: Mouton de Gruyter.

Pratt-Johnson, Y. (1993). Curriculum for Jamaican creole-speaking students in New York City. *World Englishes, 12*(2), 257–264.

Rubin, J. (1968). *National bilingualism in Paraguay*. The Hague: Mouton.

Scotton, C. M. (1988). Code-switching as indexical of social negotiations. In M. Heller (Ed.), Codeswitching: Anthropological and sociolinguistic perspectives (pp. 151–186). Berlin: Mouton de Gruyter.

Smith, L., & Sridhar, S. N. (Eds.) (1993). *The Extended family: English in global bilingualism*. Special issue of *World Englishes, 11*, 2–3.

Sridhar, K. K. (1982). English in South Indian urban context. In B. B. Kachru (Ed.), *The other tongue*, (141–153). Urbana: University of Illinois Press.

Sridhar, K. K. (1988). Language maintenance and language shift among Asian Indians: Kannadigas in the New York area. *International Journal of the Sociology of Language, 69*, 73–87.

Sridhar, K. K. (1989). *English in Indian bilingualism*. New Delhi: Manohar.

Sridhar, K. K., & Sridhar, S. N. (1986). Bridging the paradigm gap: Second language acquisition research and indigenized varieties of English. *World Englishes, 5*(1), 3–14.

Sridhar, S. N. (1978). On the functions of code-mixing in Kannada. In B. B. Kachru & S. N. Sridhar (Eds.), *Aspects of sociolinguistics in South Asia*. Special issue of the *International Journal of the Sociology of Language, 16*, 109–117.

Sridhar, S. N. (1980). Contrastive analysis, error analysis, and interlanguage: Three phases of one goal. In K. Croft (Ed.), *Readings on English as a second language for teachers and teacher trainers* (pp. 91–119). Boston: Winthrop.

Sridhar, S. N. (1981). Linguistic convergence: Indo-Aryanization of Dravidian languages. *Lingua, 53*, 199–220.

Sridhar, S. N. (1987). Language variation, attitudes, and rivalry: The spread of Hindi in India. In P. H. Lowenberg (Ed.), *Language spread and language policy* (pp. 300–319). Washington, DC: Georgetown University Press.

Sridhar, S. N. (1992). The ecology of bilingual competence: Language interaction in the syntax of indigenized varieties of English. *World Englishes, 11*(1–2), 141–150.

Sridhar, S. N. & Sridhar, K. K. (1980). The syntax and psycholinguistics of bilingual code-mixing. *Canadian Journal of Psychology, 34*(4), 409–416.

Sridhar, S. N., & Sridhar, K. K. (1992). The Empire speaks back: English as a non-native language. In P. H. Nelde (Ed.), *It's easy to mingle when you are bilingual.* Special issue of *Plurilingua* (Bilingualism and Contact Linguistics), *13*, 187–198.

Tay, M. W. J. (1989). Code switching and code mixing as a communicative strategy in multilingual discourse. *World Englishes, 8*(3), 407–417.

Thomason, S. G., & Kaufman, T. (1988). *Language contact, creolization, and general linguistics.* Berkeley: University of California Press.

Torres, L. (1989). Code-mixing and borrowing in a New York Puerto Rican community: A cross-generational study. *World Englishes, 8*(3), 419–432.

Usdansky, M. L. (1993, April). Census: Languages not foreign at home. *USA Today,* p. 1.

Yau, M. S. (1993). Functions of two codes in Hong Kong Chinese. *World Englishes, 12*(1), 25–33.

# 3 *World Englishes*

Braj B. Kachru
and Cecil L. Nelson

## Introduction

This chapter provides an overview of the topics and relationships of sociolinguistics, world Englishes, and language teaching. Although the more specific TESL cannot be equated with the more general enterprise of language teaching, still there is undoubtedly more international teaching, materials production, and published thought in TESL than in any language of wider communication, such as Arabic, French, Hindi, or Spanish. Language teachers can readily generalize from research in and hypotheses about TESL. And similarly, although no one would want to make a comparison between what is going on with and what is studied about English and the field of sociolinguistics, the language has rightly been called "the great laboratory of today's sociolinguist" (Kahane & Kahane, 1986, p. 495). That is, what applies to global English is most often found to apply to other language situations involving languages of wider communication.

In this chapter, then, we will usually refer to *world Englishes* and the *teaching of English;* it should, however, be understood that the observations and analyses here will have relevance to sociolinguistics and to teachers of languages of wider communication. All these languages (e.g., Arabic, French, Hindi, or Spanish) have more than one accepted standard and set of norms for creativity, and thus are termed *pluricentric languages.* Because the term world Englishes, and its meaning, may not be familiar or transparent, its sources and features will be briefly described.

## The global spread of English

There is little question that English is the most widely taught, read, and spoken language that the world has ever known. It may seem strange, on some moments' reflection, that the native language of a relatively small island nation could have developed and spread to this status. Its path was foreseen, however, by John Adams, who, in the late eighteenth century, made the following insightful prophesy (cited by B. Kachru, 1992a, p. 2):

> English will be the most respectable language in the world and the most universally read and spoken in the next century, if not before the close of this one.

The global spread of English has been viewed as two diasporas (see, e.g., B. Kachru, 1992d). The first diaspora involved migrations of substantial numbers of English speakers from the present British Isles to, for example, Australia, New Zealand, and North America. Those English users who left the old country for new ones brought with them the resource of language and its potentials for change which are always with us, though we are not often called upon to contemplate them explicitly. The language that they brought with them changed over time, to be sure, but no more or less substantially or rapidly than the language "at home," for all languages evolve in the natural course of time and use.[1]

The second diaspora of English, in the colonial contexts of Asia and Africa, entailed transportation of the language, but only to a small extent transportation of English-speaking people. Thus, the language was brought into new sociocultural contexts by a very small number of users; nevertheless, English became extremely important and useful to the much larger local populations, who have continued to expand the roles of English, often with greater vigor in postcolonial times.

Along with the mere numbers, it is important to note that these language-contact situations involved English and genetically unrelated and widely divergent Asian and African languages and, concomitantly, their cultures, both of which were far removed from the experience and common presuppositions of the native English speakers. These contact situations have had striking and lasting effects on English in these regions, so that although these contemporary Englishes have much in common, they are also unique in their grammatical innovations and tolerances, lexis, pronunciations, idioms, and discourse.[2]

## Characteristics of world Englishes

Everyone is cognizant of the notion of *dialects* of languages, including English. Dialects are characterized by identifiable differences vis-à-vis other dialects, in pronunciation, lexical choice or usage, grammar, and so on; we speak easily of *southern English, New England English, American English,* and *British English* (see Rickford, this volume).

1 See B. Kachru 1992d, p. 231.

2 For more information on the historical-chronological aspects of the diasporas of English, see B. Kachru, 1992d, for a quick digest; 1965 and 1966 for early treatments; and (1994) for a recent summation.

These are all dialects: types of English that are identified with the residents of particular places. There are also age, gender, and other sorts of group-related dialects – as is so often the case with language-involved issues, the label depends upon the question that is being addressed. Any speaker can be said to speak various dialects, depending upon the circumstances of a discussion: In terms of geography, one of the authors grew up speaking southern American English; in terms of profession and education, both authors speak standard English; and so on.

The well-known national dialects are not usually referred to as such, for the term *dialect* has acquired various sorts of stigmatized baggage over the years. In some speakers' minds, to say that people speak a dialect is tantamount to saying that they are provincial, perhaps not well educated – though this is neither a necessary nor a proper connotation of dialect in its technical meaning. However, because of these negative associations, most people nowadays – especially in the United States – use *variety* to refer to a subtype of a language, for example, the American and British varieties of English.

Still, the substitution of one term for another is just that, and "my variety versus yours" can still be a point of contention. The implications for attitudes about control of the language are extremely hard to overcome. The concept *standard English* has been defined in various ways, as exemplified in the writing of the major scholars described in the next passages (see also McGroarty, this volume).

The British phonetician David Abercrombie (1951) wrote of the social barrier (in this case, "bar") represented by *Received Pronunciation* (RP), the variety traditionally used at and associated with the universities of Oxford and Cambridge in Britain:

> [V]ery often the first judgement made on a stranger's speech is the answer to the question: which side of the accent-bar is he? . . . The accent-bar is a little like a colour-bar – to many people, on the right side of the bar, it appears eminently reasonable. It is very difficult to believe, if you talk R.P. yourself, that it is not intrinsically superior to other accents. (p. 15)

Abercrombie's association of language-based prejudice with racial prejudice clearly makes the point that such language attitudes are undemocratic. He points out that RP speakers are "outnumbered these days by the undoubtedly educated people who do not talk RP" (p. 15). In fact, as McArthur (1992) notes, "It has always been a minority accent, unlikely ever to have been spoken by more than 3–4% of the British population" (p. 851). In this position of minority presence but widespread and important influence, RP constituted a kind of attitudinal despotism, not unlike the cross-cultural one which allows users of native varieties of English to look down on users of nonnative varieties.

Strevens (1983) made a cogent and useful distinction between *dialect*, "differences of grammar and vocabulary," and *accent,* "differences of pronunciation" (p. 88). Strevens notes that we expect to find a consistent pairing of dialect and accent in any given area, and he points out that "[s]ince dialect + accent pairs co-exist in this way it is not surprising that most nonspecialists, and even many teachers of English, habitually confuse the terms *dialect* and *accent,* and observe no distinction between them" (p. 89).

One key point, then, is the following: "[I]n fact, the only cases where this strict pairing [of dialect and accent] does not operate are precisely in relation to Standard English" (Strevens, 1983, p. 89). This is why, for example, we are not at all surprised when standard English is spoken with various accents in the United States by network news anchors and by international politicians on both sides of the Atlantic. We recognize fundamental sorts of structural and semantic sameness, and are aware of but do not put a high value on differences of pronunciation. Strevens's analysis would strip the attitudinal goodness away from standard English – this is not the same as saying that he would take away its attributions of utility: "[I]n this analysis *every* user of English uses one dialect or another, and one accent or another. Standard English is one particular dialect among many hundred" (Strevens, 1983, p. 88).

Commonly accepted varieties of English today include American and British, of course, and also Australian, Canadian, and New Zealand. No one would argue with the first two. The last three might cause some controversy in certain quarters; this matter will not be discussed here. There are many national varieties of English in the world today; a sense of their extent and distribution can be gained by reviewing a list of countries in which English is an official language. Refer to Table 1, which is not intended to be an exhaustive list. English may be a co-official language, or it may be, as in the United States, the official language in fact though not in law. A more comprehensive list of "territories for which English is a significant language" is given in McArthur (1992, pp. xxviii–xxix).

When you hear someone speak, you perhaps first identify their variety in terms of their pronunciation or accent. American speakers say "path" and British speakers say "pahth," Americans say "Jag-uar" and "Nicara-gua," and British say "Jag-u-ar" and "Nicarag-u-a," and so on.

In assessing written text, one can notice word choice or *lexis,* preferred word combinations or *collocations,* and grammar.[3] If a text contains the subject-verb combination *the public are . . .* , for example,

3 Discourse characteristics are, of course, also markers of national and regional varieties. By its nature, discourse requires longer passages for exemplification, and so will not be treated here. See the subsequent discussion, and also Larry Smith (Ed.). (1987) *Discourse across cultures: Strategies in world Englishes.*

TABLE 1. COUNTRIES IN WHICH ENGLISH HAS OFFICIAL STATUS

| | | |
|---|---|---|
| Antigua and Barbuda | Irish Republic | St. Vincent and the Grenadines |
| Australia | Jamaica | Seychelles |
| Bahamas | Kenya | Sierra Leone |
| Barbados | Lesotho | Singapore |
| Botswana | Liberia | Tamil |
| Brunei | Malawi | South Africa |
| Cameroon | Malta | Surinam |
| Canada | Mauritius | Swaziland |
| Dominica | New Zealand | Tanzania |
| Fiji | Nigeria | Trinidad and Tobago |
| Gambia | Papua New Guinea | Uganda |
| Ghana | Philippines | United Kingdom |
| Grenada | Puerto Rico | United States of America |
| Guyana | St. Christopher and Nevis | Zambia |
| India | St. Lucia | Zimbabwe |

*Source:* Adapted from Crystal, 1987, p. 357.

we can guess that it is probably British; if it refers to parts of a car as *hood* and *trunk,* it is probably American, for the British would be *bonnet* and *boot.* Current BBC usage allows use of the verb *agree* without a preposition (*on* or *upon*), as in "a trade pact has been agreed between the two parties"; informal polls of students indicate that this usage is not widely current in the United States. One can make great lists of lexical and other differences between such major varieties, to say nothing of regional differences within each variety (evident in the various readily available dialect atlases), but when all that is said, it is still apparent that American and British speakers watch each others' movies and news broadcasts and read each others' newspapers and novels without any serious impediments.

If you glance at the front pages of, say, *The New York Times,* the London *Times, The Times of India,* and Singapore's *The Straits Times,* you will probably notice more similarities than differences; that is, you will have little trouble reading and understanding the headlines and news stories before you. In fact, the front pages of major English-language dailies in other parts of the world bear striking resemblances to one another, although close reading may reveal some unfamiliar features, depending upon the reader's origin. Consider, then, the following sample, taken more or less at random, from the front page of *The Nation* (January 6, 1989), an English-language daily newspaper published in Lahore, Pakistan:

Islamabad, Jan. 5: Yuli [sic] Vorontsov, the Soviet Deputy Foreign Minister, currently shuttling in the region to find a solution to the Afghan problem, met Sahabzada Yaqub Khan this morning for about 45 minutes. . . . [S]ources at

Pakistan's Foreign Office are adamantly evasive to comment on the progress made so far. . . .

Implying that it must pressurise the Seven-Party Alliance to withdraw some of their demands blocking the inclusion of Afghan Communists . . .

At a glance, the text is in English; any reader of this chapter can make out the information in the passage. At the same time, there are features that mark it as not American and not British. In lexis, the American or British reader will be struck by *adamantly* as a modifier of *evasive,* requiring some extension of the adverb's meaning, and by the use of *pressurise* (in its apparently intended sense) instead of *pressure.* In grammar, the use of *shuttling* without something like *back and forth between* may seem unusual, and *evasive to comment* will probably not be considered happily parallel to, say, *eager to comment.*

If one turns from the front pages and editorial pages of such global dailies, the national or regional character of the publication is likely to be even more apparent. (It should be said that this is certainly also true if one compares, say, *The New York Times* with a small-town daily in the United States.) Consider, for example, this excerpt from the same edition of *The Nation,* on an inside page (p. 4):

Karachi, Jan. 5: Goods worth more than Rs one crore were gutted when a major fire broke out in a godown in Raheedabad SITE area this morning, fire brigade sources said . . .

At least 25 KMC fire tenders rushed to the scene and controlled the raging fire in more than seven hours . . .

This passage contains the Indian currency abbreviation *Rs,* for rupees; the Hindi-Urdu number-word *crore,* a unit of 10 million; and *godown,* common in Asian contexts for "warehouse." In grammar and usage, the term *gutted* does not have its American meaning (structures, not goods, are destroyed, specifically from the inside out); and the positive-sounding *controlled the raging fire* does not, from the writers' point of view, accord very well with the negative *in more than seven hours;* American usage would probably be something like *it took over seven hours to control the blaze.* These features of national lexis and usage do not interfere substantially with transmission of message; they do mark the text as something other than American or British, or Australian or Canadian. There may, of course, be deeper linguistic and cultural differences; these details will not be explored here (see B. Kachru, 1992b, for an examination of such considerations).

It is imperative that teachers and students be aware of the sort of presence that English has in the world today, in order to keep the divergences among the extant varieties in a reasonable context. That is, that there are differences does not automatically imply that someone is wrong. The concept of a monolithic English as the exponent of culture and communication in all-English-using countries has been a convenient working fiction that is now becoming harder and harder to maintain. What we now have in reality is English language*s* and English literature*s* – a much more insightful posture for research. And we believe that this insight has theoretical and pedagogical significance, for both describing and teaching varieties of English and their literatures. To understand the pluralism of English, it is therefore vital to see its spread, uses, and users in sociolinguistic contexts.

## Issues

It is now generally recognized that, for purposes of rational analysis, descriptive characterizations of language provide the most positive opportunities for cogent insight into the way language actually works, as opposed to prescriptive declarations of the way one or another group or individual wishes language to work. Descriptive analyses of linguistic phenomena can even inform our notions of *standard* and *model,* allowing us to see clearly what are traditional, learned conventions (which certainly have their place in standard usage, recognized genres of writing such as the short essay, and so on).

In the same spirit, the descriptive approach should be applied to world Englishes. No other language even comes close to English in terms of the extent of its usage. What might be seen as a weakness in the sense there are many varieties of English is actually a clear indication of the importance and status of English in the world today. There is a great range of proficiency evidenced by the users of English in every country, from Asia to the New World. Even people who have very little proficiency in English use it in their daily business or personal lives; for comparison, we might ask what American person who has had 4 years of high school French ever tries (or needs) to use it for anything? The answer, of course, is that virtually no one does – quite the opposite in the case of English in the countries where it has become a utility language.

### *Types of variation and types of users*

The uses and users of English internationally have been discussed profitably in terms of three concentric circles.[4] Briefly, the circles model captures the global situation of English in the following way.

The *Inner Circle* comprises the old-variety English-using countries, where English is the first or dominant language: the United States,

4 See B. Kachru, 1985, 1992d, 1994.

Britain, Canada, Australia, and New Zealand. In these countries, though other languages surely are spoken, there is seldom if ever a question of any language other than English being used in an extensive sense in any public discourse (e.g., in media, government, education, and creative writing). It may be significant that in the United States, for example, the Constitution does not even bother to mention an official language. That such a statutory status has been deemed unnecessary is probably a silent testament to the assumed sway of English. Such questions have had to be addressed in other, multilingual countries, such as India, Nigeria, and Singapore.

The *Outer Circle* comprises countries where English has a long history of institutionalized functions and standing as a language of wide and important roles in education, governance, literary creativity, and popular culture, such as India, Nigeria, Pakistan, Singapore, South Africa, and Zambia. India has the third-largest English-using population in the world, after the United States and Britain, and Nigeria and the Philippines closely follow India.

The *Expanding Circle* countries are those in which English has various roles and is widely studied but for more specific purposes than in the Outer Circle, including (but certainly not limited to) reading knowledge for scientific and technical purposes; such countries currently include China, Indonesia, Iran, Japan, Korea, and Nepal. However, it must be remembered that languages have life cycles, particularly in multilingual societies, and thus the status of a language is not necessarily permanent.

This concentric-circle schematization is not merely a heuristic comparison or metaphor. Some examination of the various situations and case studies of English around the world, and of the history of the spread of English, will convince the reader that the circles model is valid in the senses of earlier historical and political contexts, the dynamic diachronic advance of English around the world, and the functions and standards to which its users relate English in its many current global incarnations.

It is telling, for example, that English is the associate official language or an official language in India, Nigeria, and various other countries of the Outer Circle (see Table 1). The sheer numbers of English users worldwide are almost unimaginable to the monolingual, monocultural English teacher. But it is difficult to define an English user in terms of either amount of use or degree of proficiency. Freshman composition students at United States universities, for example, may be monolingual speakers of English, yet it is not uncommon – indeed, it is quite usual – to hear their professors complaining that they "can't write," "have limited vocabularies," "have no sense of idiom," and so on. Indeed, a number of committees and commissions have been set up in the United States and Britain to address precisely these sorts of concerns. Being labeled a native speaker is of no particular a priori significance, in terms of measuring facility with the language.[5]

Thus, we believe that deciding who will be labeled an English user is not so straightforward as might be imagined. However, accepting even cautious estimates, there must be at least three nonnative users of English for every old-country native user. At the other end of the caution scale, perhaps a third of the world knows and uses English; see Crystal (1985), who concluded, "I am happy to settle for a billion [English-users world-wide]" (p. 9). Such considerations should arouse some interest in a reexamination of our axioms and postulates regarding the basic matter of our English language teaching.

The concept of English in its Inner, Outer, and Expanding Circles is only superficially equivalent to *native, ESL,* and *EFL.* In thinking of a country as an ESL country or of a person as an ESL speaker, for example, we perpetuate the dichotomy of native versus nonnative, "us versus them."

When we say "English as a second (or even third or fourth) language," we must do so with reference to something, and that standard of measure must, given the nature of the label, be English as someone's first language. This automatically creates attitudinal problems, for it is almost unavoidable that anyone would take "second" as less worthy, in the sense, for example, that coming in second in a race is not as good as coming in first. It is of the utmost importance that professionals in English-language teaching recognize the great variety of users and uses of English today. (This is much less difficult for multilinguals in their many cultural settings to understand than it may be for people in, say, the United States and Britain, who perceive themselves as essentially monolinguals.)

## *Interlanguage and World Englishes*

It has been claimed (see Selinker, 1972, 1992) that the concept of *interlanguage* accounts for the observable differences between varieties of English in the Outer as compared with the Inner Circle. The concept

5 It must be said that overtones of racism, explicit or implied, conscious or unintentional, may intrude into such attitudinally loaded areas. We may recall, for illustration, the ugly words of Pap Finn's infamous "I'll never vote ag'in" speech (Mark Twain, *The Adventures of Huckleberry Finn,* 1985, p. 30): "There was a free nigger there from Ohio . . . , most as white as a white man. . . . And what do you think? They said he was a p'fessor in a college, and could talk all kinds of languages, and knowed everything. . . . [W]hy, he wouldn't a give me the road if I hadn't shoved him out o' the way. . . ." It may be that judgments other than linguistic or educational overshadow assessments of "good" or "poor" English. It is this sort of attitude that has allowed the condoning of various sorts of linguistic imperialism, the devaluing of other languages in favor of English, in different global contexts. It is our responsibility as teachers in this multicultural area to be on the alert for less overt but just as poisonous attitudes in writing and in speech.

has had a wide appeal, and may even be said to constitute a school of thought, with numerous adherents. The *inter*-prefix refers to the notion that the linguistic system that any given learner or community of learners or users has at any particular moment is quantitatively and conceptually somewhere between the first language and the target. A number of discussions have pointed out the weaknesses and fallacies of such a view (see B. Kachru 1994; Y. Kachru, 1993; Sridhar & Sridhar, 1986).

The validity of an interlanguage concept of Outer Circle Englishes would hinge crucially on two elements: the desire of learners of English to emulate one or another Inner Circle English model, and the availability of such models in accessible materials, not only in the classroom but also in broader social and cultural interactions. Neither of these conditions can be shown to obtain in broad ways in the Outer Circle. To be sure, one could find individuals in, say, India who actively seek to speak British English and who evaluate their own and others' productions with this model in mind. One could probably find many more people who think that they speak British English, and in countries such as India, Nigeria, and Singapore one often meets such people. There is thus a confusion between the perception of use and the linguistic reality.

## *Range and depth*

An important first step toward being able to discuss English in its global context is to overcome a quite natural or intuitive (i.e., a priori and unexamined) concept of the ownership of language. Hymes (1967) wrote that we have always typically thought of any given social group as:

> [A]n "ethnolinguistic" unit, that is, the boundaries of a language, a culture, and a people were seen as identical. One spoke typically of one people, one culture, and one language by one name: the Crow, Crow culture, the Crow language. (pp. 4–5)

In contrast to this "mono" view, over the years we have been obliged to broaden our associations of people and places with English, from the British Isles to the new worlds of North America and Australia. But we did not, perhaps, conceptualize those forms as different in kind; we still think of these native English speakers as Anglo-Saxon in some sense. (For example, the term *Anglo* is used, in various contexts and sorts of reference, to apply to white Americans.) This association of language and peoples cannot be fruitfully examined merely in terms of form (i.e., in terms of words and grammatical rules). It is necessary, therefore, to establish a relationship between a language or language variety and its functions.

The term *range* refers to the contexts or domains in which English functions (law, education, business, and popular culture), and *depth* refers to the extent of use of English in the various levels of society. For example, in India or Singapore, use of English ranges from personal domains, with or without mixing, to business, education, administration, creative writing, and journalism. The result is that English has social penetration, that is, depth, that varies in its manifestations from educated to mixed varieties and to what is locally called *basilect*. In Nigeria, the situation is essentially the same, with the locally marked variety termed *Nigerian pidgin*. These situations contrast with that in Egypt or Japan, where the use of English is highly restricted as to range, and so it has not attained a similar degree of depth.

## *The native speaker*

The often-mentioned term *native speaker* is usually taken to refer to someone who learned a language in a natural setting from childhood as first or sole language. This casual labeling, which used to be so comfortably available as a demarcation line between this and that type or group of users of English, must now be called into serious question (see Paikeday, 1985). It cannot be overemphasized that both attitudes toward English and the degree and types of input that learners receive may vary significantly from place to place. *Input* is used here to refer not only to English as it is taught to people in formal schooling but also as it is available in media such as newspapers and in elements of popular culture such as creative writing.

Attitudes toward varieties in the two diaspora areas can be quite distinct. Standard British and American users, on the whole, are expected to be rather tolerant of each others' English but are likely to be intolerant of the usage of South Asians, Southeast Asians, West Africans, or East Africans. On the other hand, it is likely that users of the second diaspora area will look up to the usage of someone from Britain or North America, without ever considering whether that variety is actually very much used or usable in their own contexts. The attitudinal situation is complicated in Outer Circle countries by the inescapable fact that English is a colonial legacy that has prompted continual cries for the minimization or elimination of its use in favor of the promotion of an indigenous language. Often, English is settled on in an uneasy compromise, for it is no one's first language and thus confers no real or imagined advantage to one group over another.

Part of the unease stems from the fact that, by and large, these countries have always looked to external reference points (i.e., British and, to a lesser extent, American) for their norms, so that, for example, in Singapore, where English has been used as the language of industry and business for a long time, British English continues to be looked upon by many as the standard of good use. Such attitudinal schizophrenia is yet another cause of complexities in the larger English-using world.

## *Speech community*

A vital sociolinguistic concept relevant to English teaching is that of the *speech community,* the body of speakers who share a language as well as its interrelated social rules of use, its standards and its norms. (see McGroarty, this volume; Sridhar, this volume).

Without tracing its origins to the Germanic languages on the European continent, we can agree that English originated (as English) in the British Isles and that its standard form arose from the usage of educated people – basically, those who could read and write and were close to the royal court (see B. Kachru, 1992c). In the absence of any official policy, the standard was largely a matter of loose convention. The lack of official blessing did not, however, lessen its reality as a concept, a shibboleth, a marker of the "right sort of person." When English spread to the New World, beginning in the sixteenth century, those at home in England – still the seat of religious, educational, and legal authority – clearly thought of the language as remaining the same in its various geographical incarnations. Differences were attributed to improper learning and regarded as errors.

The long-standing debate, even now not wholly laid to rest, over which language is better, that of Britain or of the United States, has had all sorts of effects over the decades, from establishment of literary canon to what pronunciations and usages are correct and should, therefore, be taught. The publication of Mencken's revolutionary *The American Language* was a sharp rejoinder to pro-British, "anti-other" claims of superiority, a pointed assertion that the English of the New World was as vibrant and worthwhile as that of the Old. Indeed, by the time of the publication of the fourth edition, Mencken (1936) wrote:

> [T]he American form of the English language was plainly departing from the parent stem, and it seemed at least likely that the differences between American and English would go on increasing. This was what I argued in my first three editions. (p. vi)

Mencken goes on, in the fourth edition, to make the following prophetic statement:

> But since 1923 the pull of America has become so powerful that it has begun to drag English with it, and in consequence some of the differences once visible have tended to disappear. . . . [T]he Englishman, of late, has yielded so much to American example, in vocabulary, in idiom, in spelling and even in pronunciation, that what he speaks promises to become, on some not too remote to-

morrow, a kind of dialect of American, just as the language spoken by the American was once a dialect of English. (p. vi)

(See B. Kachru, 1986, for a detailed discussion of the impact of American English.)

As English spread across many borders and people began to worry about differences in forms of English, some way of accommodating the differences had to be found, to maintain the convenient fiction that we all speak the same language. Such attempts were mostly rather unconvincing, consisting mainly of passing off differences as "minor," "insignificant," or "just a matter of vocabulary." At times, of course, this position has been attacked, as by Bernard Shaw's famous depiction of the United States and Britain as "two peoples separated by a common language." But basically, there have been two groups or schools of thought: one that underemphasized the differences between American and British English, and one that overemphasized them. If one takes a balanced view of the differences and the trends of change, however, it seems that Mencken's assessment has, on the whole, been proved correct.

## *Standards and codification*

It is worth noting that English-using countries in the Inner Circle have never had any sort of codifier, like the French Academy, which was founded in 1635 with the express purpose "to labour with all possible care and diligence to give definite rules to our language, and to render it pure, eloquent, and capable of treating the arts and sciences" (Crystal, 1987, p. 4). One might well wonder, then, what the codifying agencies of English have been. The codification has been a matter of convention, and perpetuation of convention, through dictionaries, grammars, rhetoric handbooks, and pressures of various other types – the makers of all of these being unwilling to stretch very far beyond the reach of their immediate predecessors in what they deemed acceptable form and usage – and through the newspapers and other widely disseminated popular media that use those sources for their style sheets and usage manuals. Further, to these tangible influences the extremely powerful agencies of social and psychological pressures of various sorts must certainly be added (see McGroarty, this volume). This codification has taken place almost exclusively in the Inner Circle countries; this has made it necessary for the Outer and Expanding Circles to look to these sources when in need of citable authority, and it has functioned as a deterrent to their setting up authorities of their own.

There are certainly relationships between use and many facets of language, all of them the topic of much previous discussion and all warranting further investigation. Among them are the relationships (possibly also differences) between use and acceptance, standard, institutionalization (in grammars and dictionaries, for example), and normative reference points in education and in society at large.

Observing the different attitudes toward possible norms of English around the world prompts the notion of *pluralistic* centers of reference for norms and standards; if there are two – the United States and Britain – why not three? If three, why not a dozen? It is all too easy to step back from the world and pronounce upon this or that as "should be done otherwise." To return to Mencken (1936): "[A]fter 1850 the chief licks at the American dialect were delivered, not by English travelers, . . . but by English pedants who did not stir from their cloisters" (p. 27). The sort of pseudotheory that Mencken refers to, practiced by "cloistered" scholars and having no grounding in real-world data and experience, is especially to be avoided in an endeavor which is essentially sociolinguistic and therefore gets at the heart of communicative ability among and between people.

## *Monolingual attitudes and bilinguals' creativity*

Though it has until relatively recently gone unnoticed by "mainstream" English studies, bodies of literature in English have existed in West and East Africa and in South and East Asia for almost a hundred years. A key observation in an examination of global English literature is that English is used by writers who are multilingual and who do not belong culturally to what may be broadly termed the *Judeo-Christian tradition*. Clearly, English is used in a complete range of interactional contexts across entire cultures, including spoken and written media. The question has been raised: What are the linguistic, cultural, and social characteristics reflected in the writings of such users of English? Defining these characteristics leads to an examination of the concept of the *bilinguals' creativity*. Such creativity is clearly demonstrated in the many works by writers such as Wole Soyinka of West Africa, who won the Nobel Prize for Literature in 1986, and Anita Desai and Raja Rao of India.

A short example such as the following, from Mukherjee's *Jasmine* (1989), illustrates this point:

> The next morning I packed my brothers' tiffin carriers more indulgently than usual – extra dal, extra chapatis . . . – and slipped in my most important question: "The friend who came over, not the Sardarji, does he speak English?" I couldn't marry a man who didn't speak English. To want English was to want more than you had been given at birth. (p. 68)

This passage contains not only variety-specific lexical items *(tiffin carriers, dal, chapatis, Sardarji)* but also the culturally defined family interaction (the narrator packs her brothers' lunches for them) and, not incidentally for our topic, a direct reference to the importance of English in the Outer Circle, at least to some people: "To want English was to want more than you had been given at birth."

Language teachers can use such examples to illustrate bilingual writers' creativity in English, including paradigm examples of stylistic experimentation, mixing of codes, and acculturation of English in various other cultural settings. Interpretations of such literary work that is based in the old canons as reference points and in old paradigms as analytical devices cannot account for the great cultural and social diversities that readers will encounter in these literatures. To dismiss them because they do not fit the old paradigms is, to say the least, unscientific.[6]

English has certainly earned its keep as a language of literary creativity in all parts of the world to which it has been transplanted. With the growing body of works available and the growing number of authors writing in English, new canons have developed, not yet recognized all over the world but making their presence felt, nonetheless. The shelves of libraries and bookstores are beginning to feel more and more weight of productions from writers of the Outer Circle.[7]

Such creative writing must employ various strategies (including that of "no strategy" – leaving the readers on their own) to make context and action comprehensible and interpretable to readers. Another example can be taken from Mukherjee's *Jasmine* (1989):

> In Hasnapur wives used only pronouns to address their husbands. The first months, eager and obedient as I was, I still had a hard time calling him Prakash. I'd cough to get his attention, or start with "Are you listening?" Every time I coughed he'd say, "Do I hear a crow trying human speech?" Prakash, I had to practice and practice . . . so I could say the name without gagging and blushing in front of his friends. . . . His friends were like him: disrupters and rebuilders, idealists. (p. 77)

This brief passage, a narration by a newly married Indian woman, is constructed in such a way that the reader is let in on the cultural context – for example, traditional wives do not call their husbands by name. The use of the new, "disruptive" speech act form is correlated with the new generations' ideals and aims, with which the husband, at any rate, wishes to associate himself. Such examples can be found in many texts from Outer Circle authors.

Y. Kachru (1991) argues convincingly that:

6 See, for example, the papers in the *Symposium on Speech Acts in World Englishes,* edited by Y. Kachru (1991) including "Speech Acts in World Englishes: Toward a Framework for Research" by Y. Kachru, "Discourse Markers in Indian English" by T. Valentine, and "Multi-ethnic Literature in the Classroom: Whose Standards?" by S. Tawake.

7 See Loh and Ong (Eds.) (1993), and Ashcroft, Griffiths, and Tiffin (1989).

> [L]iterary sources provide valuable data for identifying culture-specific speech act effects such as the role of blessings in leave-taking, and the effect of using kinship terms as terms of address for showing deference or solidarity in South Asia. These data are perfectly authentic in that they were not specifically produced for speech act research. They were reproduced in writing because, in the judgement of the authors, they simulate actual conversations in real-life situations. (p. 304)

Any area of investigation that is valid in our current conceptions of the fields of discourse and literary analysis may be pursued in world Englishes. (See, e.g., Valentine, 1985, 1988, on issues of gender-related aspects of new-English discourses.)

In the same way that Inner Circle writers have available to them a range of speech and speaker types, from dialectal-informal (e.g., southern American "y'all") to standard formal, so Outer Circle creative writers have access to a broad range of English usages, including restricted pidgin or basilect, localized forms (which may or may not be mixed varieties), and acrolectal forms that would be considered nonlocalized international standard English. Certainly many authors may choose to write in a nonregional or nonnational idiom in one work, whereas in another they may cast their characters in markedly local voices (compare, for example, Raja Rao, 1988 with 1963). This versatility available to the multilingual user of English may include sorts of options that are not available to the American or British creative writer.

D'souza (1991) categorized Indian English writers as minimizers, nativizers, and synthesizers (p. 308), in terms of their degree of "Indianness" in speech act types and features. She discusses, for example, nativizers such as Mulk Raj Anand, who "seek to recreate within the text the speech acts that they see as salient within the Indian context" (p. 309). She cites this example from Anand:

> "Basheshwar!" the Pathan iterated, grinding his words first softly, then hard. . . . Basheshwar Singh, the son of a dog! . . . The seed of a donkey!"
>
> "You remember him then Khan?" Dhanu asked thinking that the Pathan was abusing Basheshwar affectionately, as is the custom among intimate friends in Hindustan. (p. 309)

Inner Circle English users will note the forms of abuse, which are quite different from the conventional formulaic expressions in American or British contexts. In terms of use, we might say that, although it is not uncommon for "intimate friends to abuse one another affectionately" in Inner Circle contexts (as, perhaps, roommate to roommate, when one has pulled off a coup of some sort – "You dog, you"; or when one has confessed to an error or failing – "You jerk!"), the extent, coupled with the more literal-sounding form of the examples in the passage, marks it as not Inner Circle in its form and its function. We note also in passing that, through the courtesy of the narrator, we are given to understand that members of this speech community, like those of any other, have to stay alert for proper interpretation and be prepared to switch interpretations as new data come in. (See B. Kachru, 1994, for a discussion of the concepts surrounding literary canons in Inner and Outer Circle literatures.)

## *Power and ideology*

It is rightly claimed that English has created a culture for itself wherever it has assumed importance in business, education, and so on, across the countries of the Outer and Expanding Circles. As the medium of expression of various sorts of overt power, for example, the power of the law or of educational gatekeepers, language may become identified with power and take on a power of its own. This is exactly what has happened with English in its many geographical and national contexts.[8]

Like any sort of power, linguistic power may be positive or negative, beneficial or exploitative. One group or faction within an Outer Circle country may view English as an exponent and tool of national identity (as opposed, say, to fragmentary regional identities), whereas an opposing view may hold that English is a colonial remnant and, as such, has no place in the national culture. The power of English globally shows in many ways, including its very spread and its giving access to modernity in terms of technology and many forms of knowledge, as well as a certain connoted liberalism and progressiveness (for detailed discussions, see B. Kachru, 1986; Kandiah, 1984; and Phillipson, 1992).

One unchallenged manifestation of this power of English derives from its great range of *functions* (from business and science and technology to more interpersonal ones), which give it its importance in and across so many contemporary societies. The choice of English over a traditionally indigenous language, or vice versa, has various implications in a multilingual society. For example, if you choose to address me in English, you may in so doing imply an elevated regard for my standing as an educated, modern person, but you may at the same time devalue me as a compatriot. Such choices may be little understood by the monolingual English user.

The functional range of English is unprecedented. Earlier languages

8 See B. Kachru (1986): "[T]he study of linguistic power is not exactly of the same type as is the study of the use of power by the state, in the legal system, for religious commands, and so on. Linguistic power has to be understood essentially through symbols and manipulation of the symbols" (p. 123). It involves the addition of a language or language variety to the already available codes of a society, or the elevation of a variety to the detriment of another.

of wider communication were mainly restricted to religion as they spread beyond their original homelands, for example, Arabic in South Asia and Sanskrit in South-East Asia, but English is used for virtually any imaginable function in its various twentieth-century homes. Sridhar and Sridhar (1986) write that "[T]here is empirical evidence to show that the functions of English not only complement but overlap those of the local languages in a number of domains, such as friendship, correspondence, transactions[,] etc."[9] (p. 7).

If users in the Outer and Expanding Circle countries believe, as does Abbas (1993), that "[W]e do need English to be members of the 'world community', . . . 'the world of nations' " (p. 155), then English automatically has power. It is also a symbol, which can be manipulated to the aggrandizement of some and the detriment of others.

In earlier days, it was taken for granted (at least in academic circles) that English was something that belonged to "us" and was to be made available to "them." This notion gave the Inner Circle countries a great deal of real and imagined power over the users and use of English. However, it has come to be the case that many, many nonnative users of English employ it as a common language to communicate with other nonnatives, while the interactional contexts in which nonnative and native speakers use English with each other are fast shrinking. This is true at every level, including that of acquisition, which may be the hardest notion to relinquish.

## *Teaching English across the world: Types of input*

Monolingual English teachers with little if any cross-cultural experience may have to stop and think about the situations in which English is acquired across the world. In most cases, it is taught to nonnative speakers by nonnative speakers, neither teachers nor students (who themselves become the next generation of teachers) ever having any contact with a native user. The Nigerian linguist Bamgbose (1982), for example, draws our attention to this point when he writes that:

9 Sridhar and Sridhar (1986) add that "Code-switching and code-mixing are formal manifestations of this overlap" (p. 7). This fact does not detract from the force of the observation, or from the place that English holds in a multilingual society, such as India. It may be true that "mixing" with English is frequent and that English is not used in all the domains that it would be in a linguistically restricted society, such as the United States, or for all users in a given society. For example, Crystal says (in Paikeday, 1985, p. 68): "I know several foreigners whose command of English I could not fault, but they themselves deny they are native speakers. When pressed on this point, they draw attention to such matters as . . . their lack of awareness of childhood associations, their limited passive knowledge of varieties, the fact that there are some topics which they are more 'comfortable' discussing in their first language. 'I couldn't make love in English,' said one man to me."

> One noticeable effect of the refusal to accept the existence of a Nigerian English is the perpetuation of the myth that the English taught in Nigerian schools is just the same as, say, British English; . . . In our teaching and examinations we concentrate on drilling and testing out of existence forms of speech that even the teachers will use freely when they do not have their textbooks open before them. (pp. 99–100)

That is, people do not always speak the way they think they do, and linguistic insecurity is perhaps one of the chief motivations for linguistic prescriptivism. What Bamgbose has written about Nigerian English can be said, with appropriate adjustments of references to language and setting, about any institutionalized variety of English.

This issue of the types of input available to learners in the Outer and Expanding Circles is at the core of any pragmatic view of models and standards of English for users in the included countries. It may be seen as bound up with another issue, that of identity: If a typical American has no wish to speak like or be labeled as a British user of English, why should a Nigerian, an Indian, or a Singaporean user feel any differently?

In terms of identity, it is probably a truism to point out that people's language affiliations are a significant part of themselves, and of their images of themselves. Crystal (1987) notes: "More than anything else, language shows we 'belong'; providing the most natural badge, or symbol, of public and private identity" (p. 18). In more specific terms, he says that "language can become . . . a source of pleasure, pride, anxiety, offence, anger, and even violence." Compare also the preceding discussion on available English input: Nigerians teach Nigerians and Indians teach Indians, just as North Americans teach North Americans. There is no a priori reason to think that the development of one variety is any stranger than the other. In any case, most learners of English in Outer Circle and Expanding Circle contexts never have any serious contact with an Inner Circle speaker; and, as anyone who has ever tried it can testify, it is not possible, in any complete and active sense, to learn a language from a book.

## *Communicative competence*

The substantive issue of language identity becomes bound up with the new pairing of a language and a culture that yields a distinctive communicative competence for the speakers of, for example, a new English.

It is confusing sometimes, because of the broad concept that "we all speak English," but it is nonetheless true that the rules of speaking change with time and place – just as they might be expected to do, if we think about the development of any language (see Saville-Troike, this volume). If we take a comparative stance, then we construe differences as mistakes in the variety that we are investigating (see Nelson, 1992).

In terms of teaching methodology, the concerns and discussion in this chapter make it clear that range and depth can best be explained if a *functional* view of language is adopted. Such a view will provide a theoretical backdrop for both the learner and the teacher of English. In this volume, Saville-Troike has discussed the *ethnography of communication* in detail (with reference to Hymes's use of the term). That, of course, is one functional approach. Another functional approach worth exploring is that of M. A. K. Halliday, applications of which occur in several studies done on world Englishes.[10]

The main point that Halliday's research emphasizes is the functional nature of language. His interpretation of language function is that every text created by a language user involves interpersonal, ideational, and textual functions (see, e.g., Halliday, 1970). These functions have to do, respectively, with social relationships and individual identity, meaning potential (what the speaker can say in a situation), and the ability to construct recognizable and situationally appropriate discourse. Halliday puts these functional components of the underlying language system at the heart of the interpretation of how language works.

Language usage by a group or by an individual is not innate – rather, it is brought about and formed over time by its very use. As discussed throughout this chapter, if this is true within a variety, and easily seen across major varieties such as American and British English, then there is no reason to suppose that it is or should be otherwise across varieties that include newer ones, as in India and Nigeria. No one can deny that a part of learning different American dialects and registers, say, is the learning of the social rules of when to speak and to be silent, and so forth. To use the example of silence, it is easily shown that the role of silence as a speech act varies from culture to culture. In response to a direct question, silence in Hindi or in Japanese at least borders on acceptance, but in English it most often indicates uncertainty (see Crystal 1987, p. 172). Like word boundaries and other junctures that are not segmentally a sensible part of the language, silence is a real and necessary component of the entire system.

The key element in communicative competence is just these sorts of considerations of *appropriateness* in all facets of language, including rate of speech and level or register of lexis. It is easily understood that what is appropriate for a situation in one culture may not be so in another; indeed, it is important to recognize the different sorts of situations that exist across cultures, which, although they may be similar in

10 See, for example, Halliday, 1970, 1973, 1975.

terms of kind and function to situations in other cultures, are yet unique.

Such cultural-situational distinctiveness is evident in examples in the literature of cross-cultural English studies. In a study of simple request behavior, for example, it has been shown that 76 percent of Indian speakers (of various first languages) "used indirect questions involving permission, ability, or willingness, much like native speakers would use. . . . However, as many as [20 percent] used imperatives or desideratives, reflecting Indian language conventions" (Sridhar, 1989, pp. 104–105).

Simple greeting exchanges in world Englishes can provide readily accessible examples. "I see you've put on weight" may be the equivalent of "You're looking well," an interpretation quite different from the one a typical American speaker would assign to the statement, as has been shown in Berns's (1990, pp. 35–36) report and analysis of her encounter with a Zambian English speaker. One must be familiar with the context in which the utterances are produced – not merely the immediate conversational context but the broader sociocultural context underlying it. It is not reasonable to think that English, or any pluricentric language, can in itself have such force as to establish identical situational interpretations across cultural boundaries.

These sociolinguistic considerations cannot but change the perceptions of one who has been operating with the notions of deficit linguistics as background. Either we admit to creating and accepting a linguistic caste system, under which a person is born into one or another group and can never really rise out of it (or fall, for that matter), whether by effort, marriage, or emigration, or we must agree that the old speech community notions are no longer relevant. As long as the old-fashioned English speech community continues to be the paradigm of reference, a monolingual, monocultural way of looking at the linguistic world is unavoidable. For all that it sounds egalitarian and inclusive, it continues, for the sorts of reasons outlined, to be oppressive and divisive. "Black" or "Hispanic" – any labeled English – is only with difficulty seen as merely nonstandard, with no attendant negative judgments of correctness, worth, and goodness.

These sorts of considerations have wide implications, both in terms of theory and of application. They open the door to almost endless series of questions about how people perceive themselves and others in terms of and by means of language. In applied terms, more and more questions are arising in areas such as language policy and planning. Should the United States officially adopt English as its single language of government and law? What should the statutory place of English be in highly multilingual settings such as South Asia and West Africa? Matters of personal and literary style are natural connections to investigations of language identity. All these areas are cast into new light in view of the unique geographical and cultural spread of world Englishes.

## Intelligibility

A major fear expressed by those concerned with standards and correctness has been that English is crumbling at its edges, becoming less and less English in the mouths – and from the pens – of those who (it is claimed) do not so much use it as abuse it. Drawing on the concept that is the source of a definition of *dialect* versus *language,* namely that dialects are mutually intelligible variants of a given language, speakers and writers have voiced the fear that the varieties of English will become mutually unintelligible, and so undeserving of the label *English*.

These concerns about the decay of English must be studied, analyzed, and contrasted by any teacher of English. An abundance of insights that aid in understanding sociolinguistic attitudes, notions of correctness, and linguistic control can be found in the body of literature discussing this topic. A good example is Quirk (1985), who writes of "the diaspora of English into several mutually incomprehensible languages" (p. 3). In the face of the large quantity of well-attested scholarly literature showing large ranges and depths for the use of English, Quirk asserts that "the relatively narrow range of purposes for which the non-native needs to use English . . . is arguably well catered for by a single monochrome standard form that looks as good on paper as it sounds in speech" (p. 6). He wants all English-using countries to accede to "a form of English that is both understood and respected in every corner of the globe where any knowledge of any variety of English exists" (p. 6). Although Quirk never says explicitly that we should all be learning British standard English, his very lack of identification of the "single monochrome standard form" leaves the reader in little doubt of what his choice would be.[11]

The best responses to this notion of "dissolution" have been articulated with clear empirical support by Larry Smith, in his own work and with coauthors (see, e.g., Smith, 1988; Smith & Nelson, 1985; Smith & Rafiqzad, 1983). First, Smith points out that the most common situation of English use in the Outer Circle is that of nonnatives using it to communicate with nonnatives, as already mentioned in this chapter. Further, Smith proposes the idea that any text is received by a reader or

11 Graeme Kennedy, as a commentator for Quirk's paper (Quirk & Widdowson, 1985), writes: "There is a delicious irony in Professor Quirk's . . . paper . . . [It] reflects, in many respects, the position Prator [1968] advocated, namely the desirability of a global standard. However, since the orthodoxy has changed, it might be argued that Professor Quirk articulates a new British heresy. You simply cannot win." (p. 7)

hearer on three levels – intelligibility, comprehensibility, and interpretability. Each level is more comprehensive than the preceding one and may comprise its information, although it does not necessarily rely upon it. Briefly, the levels can be described as follows.

In its narrow sense, *intelligibility* consists of word-level recognition. If you recognize that you are hearing (or reading) English, then the language is intelligible to you, according to this technical definition of the term. Smith and Rafiqzad (1983), for example, asked subjects to fill in the blanks in a written cloze passage matching an audiotaped reading of the passage by English speakers from various countries. To the degree that the subjects were successful, the passage was judged as more or less intelligible to them.

Interpretation of this sort of data – as indeed of any linguistic interaction – absolutely requires consideration of both the producer and the receiver of the text in question and, in any broader, real-world test, would require consideration of the circumstances under which the text was produced – what J. R. Firth called the *context of situation* (see B. Kachru, 1986, p. 106).

To the degree that a recipient finds a text meaningful, it has *comprehensibility*. If someone says, "Please open the door," and if the words are intelligible to you and you can assign referential meaning to them (you understand *please* as a polite request opener, *open* as referring to a particular activity, *door* as having a certain concrete referent in the immediate environment, and so on), then that bit of text is comprehensible to you. Further, if you interpret the utterance "Please open the door" as a request for a particular activity which you may carry out, ignore, object to, or otherwise react to in ways that will, in their turn, elicit another round of interpretation and response from the other participants in the situation, it is comprehensible to you.

Although the preceding example seems straightforward, it is easy to find examples of English text that are not readily intelligible or comprehensible to a receiver. For instance, consider Indian matrimonial advertisements such as the following (cited in B. Kachru, 1992b, p. 311). The first, from the English-language daily *The Hindu* (Madras, India), contains, within its English matrix, terms that would be transparently obvious to the readers of the newspaper but which are probably opaque to most of the readers of this chapter:

> Non-Koundanya well qualified prospective bridegroom . . . for graduate Iyangar girl. . . . Mirugaservsham. No dosham. Average complexion. Reply with horoscope.

The code-mixed items (e.g., *Mirugaservsham,* "birth star," and *dosham,* "a flaw in one's horoscope," are not italicized or otherwise specially marked; they are an integral part of the text for the intended readership, who will recognize their meanings, uses, and importance.

Texts such as the next example may contain only "English" elements, and so pass the test of intelligibility, but may be false cognates, not comprehensible to the monolingual Inner Circle reader:

Matrimonial correspondence invited . . . for my son . . . clean shaven.

In this example, *clean shaven* is not just an assertion of good grooming habits; it is included in the advertisement to indicate that the prospective bridegroom is not a traditional Sikh. The comprehensibility of such elements requires a cultural awareness that tends to exclude Inner Circle English users; comprehension of the texts demands multilingual and multicultural competence. (For code mixing and switching, see, e.g., Bhatia & Ritchie, 1989; see especially Kamwangamalu, 1989.)

*Interpretability* refers to the apprehension of intent, purpose, or meaning behind an utterance. It is the capacity to take "Gee, it's hot in here" as the equivalent, as far as appropriate response is concerned, of the direct request "Please open the window." Smith (1988) points out very insightfully that, contrary to what we might think initially, certainly contrary to what we teach students from grammar textbooks, "interpretability is at the core of communication and is more important than mere intelligibility or comprehensibility" (p. 274). A few moments' consideration will bear out this observation. What makes grunts, sighs, and nonreferential word utterances such as "Well . . . ," and "Rats!" so communicatively effective is their contextual interpretability.

Perhaps the most startling point that emerges from the evidence of Smith's investigations concerns the role of native speakers and the relationship of Inner Circle English to other Englishes; as Smith and Rafiqzad (1983) write:

[T]he native speaker was always found to be among the least intelligible speakers [in the study], . . . (average of 55 per cent [only the speaker from Hong Kong was lower, at 44%]). (p. 52)

Although the focus at the time was intelligibility, the same may be said for Inner Circle vis-à-vis Outer Circle speakers at the levels of comprehensibility and interpretability as well. (This finding of the nonprimacy of native-variety English worldwide has been replicated; see, e.g., Smith, 1988.)

Startling may be too mild a word for the effect of this discovery on the practice and practitioners of English teaching. It has always been an axiom that native-speaker English was the best, therefore certainly the most widely usable in any circumstance, and if people couldn't understand you, it was their fault (the value judgment inescapable), because their English wasn't "good enough." This conceptualization of English on its own terms in its various contexts is quite different from the monomodel, a priori importance that many have attached to Inner

Circle English in the past; it is more explanatorily powerful, and it is empirically verifiable.

## World Englishes in the classroom

The study and teaching of world Englishes can be employed in very positive ways in any number of areas in language teaching – not only in teaching English to Outer or Expanding Circle learners. Some aspects of pedagogical inquiry that might be addressed using world Englishes as data or their study as theoretical basis are described in the following passages.

### *Scientific thought and method*

In perhaps the first place, pragmatic examination of the facts and issues of world Englishes leads one – teacher and student alike – to come to grips with observed phenomena and inferred hypotheses, as opposed to defending closely held beliefs blindly. One can defend to the death the notion of "one model and standard" (or two, or perhaps three) for all would-be English users, but that will not stop the wide world from using English for conversing, bargaining, studying, and trading.

### *English as medium of multiculturalism*

Our concern with multiculturalism is a result of the relatively recent recognition by the educational community (and other communities) that models need to be found which will accommodate the facts of population trends and interactions today. And one of the important, if not most important, versatile, and expanding vehicles of implementing and experiencing multiculturalism is English, in its many multicultural incarnations. It is the vehicle of cross-cultural awareness that can be used not only to teach but to learn, in bidirectional ways, multicultural literatures, customs, and acceptance. If teacher trainees are not exposed to multicultural ideas and examples, they go out into the world in very much the same state of mind as a certain zealous sort of religious missionary who seeks to show "the lost" the error of their ways – without knowing anything about their ways.

Leading students (or leading teachers to lead students) to discover language differences as a way of laying a foundation for examining the differences and their importance should not be difficult. It is likely that major American and British newspapers are available at school and public libraries. News magazines, popular magazines, and fiction are also ready sources of language data. An easy first exercise might be to gather lists of unfamiliar lexical items; teacher trainees in the United States, for example, could be directed to examine texts produced in Britain to find non-American lexis and usage and to bring in lists of American equivalents that they have intuited or researched. Once it was established that differences exist among Inner Circle varieties, their next assignment would be to extend the search into texts from the Outer Circle. The class could read a novel, for example, or groups could be responsible for examining parts of a large text.

The immediate benefits of such exercises would be (1) that the students would move beyond an abstract belief in the existence of world Englishes to a hands-on, if limited, familiarity with them, and (2) that they would overcome a reluctance to approach another variety once they found that the texts in these other varieties were accessible to them.

## *International business and English for special purposes*

As the cross-cultural medium of choice in the latter years of the twentieth century, English has become – or at least is perceived as – indispensable in many areas of international business and for such special purposes as air and sea traffic control. Englishes for special purposes (ESP), including aviation English (Airspeak) and Seaspeak, have been extensively discussed and analyzed; for brief characterizations and examples, see the relevant entries in McArthur (1992). Students might be led to examine the functional advantages and disadvantages of such limited forms of English and the rationales and methodologies for constructing them.

## *Sociolinguistic profiles of Englishes and their users*

In the largely monolingual cultures of the old-variety English-using nations, references to the multilingual (and multicultural) conditions obtaining in foreign places may go unheeded because they are so far from the experience of the users. Explorations of world Englishes have the potential, then, of opening the eyes of English users to the great array of cultures in the world.

## *New-English literatures*

The old canons of literature no longer even come close to exhausting the scope and depth of available topics, devices, and genres available in today's literary world. Because literature draws on all aspects of human life and communication, this is a comprehensive area to delve into with students, opening their awareness to a broader world – without their having to learn a new language but just learning to become open to new forms and uses of their own language. As B. Kachru (1994) writes in the conclusion of "The Speaking Tree": "[W]e are depriving ourselves – as teachers and students – of an immense resource of cross-cultural perspectives and strategies of multilinguals' creativity, if world Englishes are viewed exclusively from Judeo-Christian and monolingual perspectives" (p. 15). For a discussion of this issue, see also Thumboo (1992).

## *Discourse pragmatics*

One can readily examine new-English discourses for their speech act features, as has been done for American and British Englishes. The new cultures in which English has been or is in the process of being nativized have their own necessities for politeness, apology, persuasive strategies, and so on. In studying the different sorts and manifestations of these features, we can know better what to look for, just as the study of languages is the basis of the linguist's study of language. Y. Kachru (1991) writes in this regard that "In order to account for the socially-realistic use of the English language [(B.) Kachru, 1981], a richer theory incorporating the notions of speech act, conversational analysis, sociolinguistics, and ethnography of communication is needed to study the illocutionary force and perlocutionary effect of locutionary acts" (p. 304). This "richer theory" will take into account a much broader range of data than is available from looking at only one variety or a limited set of varieties. After all, it is a well-established tenet of scientific inquiry that one cannot adequately describe an object from inside it. We are all bound by our assumptions: It is our job as educated people and educators to make our assumptions as broadly based as possible.

Again, it would be relatively easy to design hands-on experience tasks for students and teacher trainees. They could be asked to identify and discuss the conversational discourse markers in fiction or to compare items like the Indian matrimonial advertisements discussed earlier or obituary notices from American, British, and Outer Circle newspapers.

## *Standardized tests of English*

It has been shown that "in language testing, an implicit (and frequently explicit) assumption has long been that the criteria for measuring proficiency in English around the world should be candidates' use of particular features of English which are used and accepted as norms by highly educated native speakers of English" (Lowenberg, 1993, p. 95). This is so, as Lowenberg points out, despite the fact that native (i.e., Inner Circle) English users are less and less involved in interactions in English around the world. Lowenberg notes that "several items [included in his study] on actual tests and in test preparation materials do not reflect usage norms in the non-native varieties and are therefore not entirely valid indicators of proficiency in English as a world language" (pp. 95–96).

## Conclusion

We believe that world Englishes provide paradigm examples of the relationships between linguistic and language-teaching theory, methodology, and application. The preceding sections have shown that anecdotal statements regarding the global spread of English are not empirically sound or functionally valid. The spread of English provides a language teacher with an abundance of data for relating second language issues to pedagogical concerns. This can be done in several ways: through the study of variation, the pragmatics of variation, varieties and culture, and varieties and creativity. These assumptions reflect at least three most powerful sets of pedagogical tools: curriculum, testing, and resource materials.

For achieving positive goals, however, it is most important in teacher training to create teacher awareness of the status and functions of Englishes in the world today and in the future.

### Suggestions for further reading

An extensive updated bibliography on a variety of topics related to world Englishes is B. Glauser, E. W. Schnwider, and M. Görlach (Eds.) *A New Bibliography of Writings on Varieties of English 1984–1992/1993*. (1993). Amsterdam and Philadelphia: John Benjamins. B. Kachru in *The Other Tongue* ((1992) includes major references for approaches, issues, and resources on world Englishes. Two other important resources are L. Smith (Ed.) (1987). *Discourse across Cultures: Strategies in World Englishes*. London: Prentice Hall, and *World Englishes in Contact and Convergence*, special issue of *World Englishes 13*(2) (1994).

The following works listed in the References section are useful for understanding the spread of English, the profiles of various English-using countries, the implications of the spread, and current controversies: Bailey and Gorlach, (Eds.) 1982; Cheshire (Ed.) 1991; B. Kachru (Ed.) 1982, 1992; B. Kachru, 1986; Platt, Weber, & Lian, 1984; Smith & Nelson, 1985; Tickoo, 1988.

An indispensable reference volume is T. McArthur (Ed.) (1992). *The*

*Oxford Companion to the English Language*. London and New York: Oxford University Press, which includes invited entries on areas related to the English language from major English-using countries.

Another valuable resource for advanced students is the *Cambridge History of the English Language* (6 vols.). Cambridge and New York: Cambridge University Press; Vol. 5, edited by Robert Birchfield (1994), will be of special interest to students of world Englishes.

Four journals focus on world Englishes: *English World-wide: A Journal of Varieties of English* (1980–; Amsterdam & Philadelphia: John Benjamins); *World Englishes: Journal of English as an International and Intranational Language* (1985–; Oxford: Blackwell); *English Today* (1985–; Cambridge: Cambridge University Press); and *World Literature Written in English* (WLWE) (1961–; Guelph, Ontario, Canada: University of Guelph).

## References


Abbas, Shemeem (1993). The power of English in Pakistan. *World Englishes, 12*(2), 147–156.

Abercrombie, David (1951). R. P. and local accent. *The Listener,* 6. (Reprinted in D. Abercrombie, *Studies in phonetics and linguistics*. London: Oxford University Press.)

Ashcroft, B., Griffiths, G., & Tiffin H. (1989). *The empire writes back: Theory and practice in post-colonial literatures*. New York: Routledge.

Bailey, R. W., & Gorlach M. (Eds.) (1982). *English as a world language*. Ann Arbor: University of Michigan Press.

Bamgbose, A. (1982). Standard Nigerian English: Issues of identification. In B. Kachru (Ed.) (1992). *The other tongue: English across cultures* (2nd ed., pp. 99–111). Urbana: University of Illinois Press.

Berns, M. (1990). *Contexts of competence: Social and cultural considerations in communicative language teaching*. New York: Plenum Press.

Bhatia, T. K., & Ritchie, W. (Eds.) (1989). *Code-mixing: English across languages*. [Special issue.] *World Englishes 8*(3).

Cheshire, J. (Ed.) (1991). *English around the world: Sociolinguistic perspectives*. Cambridge: Cambridge University Press.

Crystal, D. (1985). How many millions? The statistics of English today. *English Today, 1*, 7–9.

Crystal, D. (1987). *The Cambridge encyclopedia of language*. Cambridge: Cambridge University Press.

D'souza, J. (1991). Speech acts in Indian English fiction. *World Englishes, 10*(3), 307–316.

Halliday, M. A. K. (1970). Language structure and language function. In J. Lyons (Ed.), *New horizons in linguistics*. Harmondsworth: Penguin Books.

Halliday, M. A. K. (1973). *Explorations in the functions of language*. London: Edward Arnold.

Halliday, M. A. K. (1975). *Learning how to mean*. London: Edward Arnold.

Hymes, D. (1967). The anthropology of communication. In F. E. X. Dance

(Ed.), *Human communication theory: Original Essays*. New York: Holt, Rinehart and Winston.

Kachru, B. B. (1965). The *Indianness* in Indian English. *Word, 21*, 391–410. [Revised version in B. Kachru (1983). *The Indianization of English: The English Language in India* (pp. 128–144). Delhi: Oxford University Press.]

Kachru, B. B. (1966). Indian English: A study in contextualization. In C. E. Bazell, J. C. Catford, M. A. K. Halliday, and R. H. Robins (Eds.), *In memory of J. R. Firth*. London: Longman. [Revised version in Kachru (1983). *The Indianization of English: The English Language in India* (pp. 99–127). Delhi: Oxford University Press.]

Kachru, B. B. (1981). Socially realistic linguistics: The Firthian tradition. *International Journal of the Sociology of Language 31*, 65–89.

Kachru, B. B. (1983). *The Indianization of English: The English language in India*. Delhi: Oxford University Press.

Kachru, B. B. (1985). Standards, codification, and sociolinguistic realism: The English language in the outer circle. In R. Quirk and H. Widdowson (Eds.), *English in the World: Teaching and learning the language and literatures* (pp. 11–30). Cambridge: Cambridge University Press.

Kachru, B. B. (1986). *The alchemy of English: The spread, functions and models of non-native Englishes*. Oxford: Pergamon Press.

Kachru, B. B. (1992a). Introduction: The other side of English. In B. Kachru (Ed.) *The other tongue: English across cultures* (pp. 1–15). Urbana: University of Illinois Press.

Kachru, B. B. (1992b). Meaning in deviation: Toward understanding non-native English texts. In B. Kachru (Ed.) *The other tongue: English across cultures* (pp. 301–326). Urbana: University of Illinois Press.

Kachru, B. B. (1992c). Models for non-native Englishes. In B. Kachru (Ed.) *The other tongue: English across cultures* (pp. 48–74). Urbana: University of Illinois Press.

Kachru, B. B. (1992d). The second diaspora of English. In T. W. Machan & C. T. Scott (Eds.), *English in its social contexts: Essays in historical sociolinguistics* (pp. 230–252). New York: Oxford University Press.

Kachru, B. B. (1994). The paradigms of marginality. Plenary address at International TESOL. Baltimore, MD.

Kachru, B. B. (1994). The speaking tree: A medium of plural canons. In J. E. Alatis (Ed.), *Educational linguistics, cross-cultural communication and global interdependence* (pp. 1–17). Georgetown University Roundtable, 1994. Washington, DC: Georgetown University Press.

Kachru, B. B. (Ed.) (1992). *The other tongue: English across cultures* (2nd ed.). Urbana: University of Illinois Press.

Kachru, Y. (Ed.) (1991). Symposium on speech acts in world Englishes. *World Englishes 10*(3), 295–304.

Kachru, Y. (1993). Interlanguage and language acquisition research. [Review of L. Selinker, *Rediscovering interlanguage*. London: Longman.] *World Englishes 12*(2), 265–268.

Kahane, H., & Kahane, R. (1986). A typology of the prestige language. *Language, 62*, 495–508.

Kamwangamalu, N. (1989). A selected bibliography of studies on code-mixing and code-switching (1970–1988). *World Englishes 8*(3), 433–440.

Kandiah, T. (1984). 'Kaduva': Power and the English language weapon in Sri

Lanka. In P. Colin-Thome & A. Halpe (Eds.), *Honouring EFC Ludowyk: Felicitation Essays* (pp. 117–154). Dehiwela: Tisara Prakasakayo Ltd.

Kennedy, G. (1985). Commentator 1. In R. Quirk & H. Widdowson (Eds.) (1985). *English in the world: Teaching and Learning the Language and Literatures* (pp. 7–8). Cambridge: Cambridge University Press.

Loh, C. Y., & I. K. Ong (Eds.) (1993). *South East Asia writes back!* London: Skoob Books.

Lowenberg, P. H. (1993). Issues of validity in tests of English as a world language: Whose standards? *World Englishes, 12*(1), 95–106.

McArthur, T. (Ed.) (1992). *The Oxford companion to the English language.* Oxford: Oxford University Press.

Mencken, H. L. (1936). *The American language: An inquiry into the development of English in the United States* (4th ed.). New York: Knopf.

Mukherjee, B. (1989). *Jasmine.* New York: Grove Weidenfeld.

Nelson, C. L. (1992). Bilingual writing for the monolingual reader: Blowing up the canon. *World Englishes, 11*(2/3), 271–275.

Paikeday, T. M. (1985). *The native speaker is dead!* Toronto: Paikeday Publications.

Phillipson, R. (1992). Linguistic imperialism. London: Oxford University Press.

Platt, J., Weber H., & Lian, H. M. (1984). *The New Englishes.* London: Routledge.

Quirk, R. (1985). *The English language in a global context.* In R. Quirk & H. Widdowson (Eds.). (1985). *English in the world: Teaching and Learning the Language and Literature* (pp. 1–6). Cambridge: Cambridge University Press.

Quirk, R., & Widdowson, H. (Eds.) (1985). *English in the world: Teaching and learning the language and literatures.* Cambridge: Cambridge University Press.

Rao, R. (1963). *Kanthapura.* London: Allen and Unwin. [Originally published in 1938.]

Rao, R. (1988). *The chessmaster and his moves.* New Delhi: Vision Books.

Selinker, L. (1972). Interlanguage. *International Review of Applied Linguistics, 10,* 209–231.

Selinker, L. (1992). *Rediscovering interlanguage.* London: Longman. [Series on applied linguistics and language study.]

Smith, L. E. (1988). Language spread and issues of intelligibility. In P. Lowenberg (Ed.), *Language spread and language policy: Issues, implications, and case studies* (pp. 265–282). Georgetown University Roundtable on Languages and Linguistics 1987. Washington, DC: Georgetown University Press.

Smith, L. E., & Rafiqzad, K. (1983). English for cross-cultural communication: The question of intelligibility. In L. Smith (Ed.). *Readings in English as an international language.* (pp. 49–58). Oxford: Pergamon.

Smith, L. E., & Nelson, C. L. (1985). International intelligibility of English: Directions and resources. *World Englishes, 4*(3), 333–342.

Smith, L. E. (Ed.) (1983). *Readings in English as an international language.* Oxford: Pergamon.

Smith, L. E. (Ed.) (1987). *Discourse across cultures: Strategies in world Englishes.* London: Prentice Hall.

Sridhar, K. K. (1989). *English in Indian bilingualism.* New Delhi: Manohar.

Sridhar, K. K., & Sridhar, S. N. (1986). Bridging the paradigm gap: Second language acquisition theories and indigenized varieties of English. *World Englishes, 5*(1), 3–14.

Strevens, P. (1983). What is "Standard English"? In L. Smith (Ed.). *Readings in English as an international language.* (pp. 87–93). Oxford: Pergamon.

Thumboo, E. (1992). The literary dimension of the spread of English. In B. Kachru (Ed.) *The other tongue: English across cultures* (pp. 255–282). Urbana: University of Illinois Press.

Tickoo, M. L. (1988). In search of appropriateness in EF(S)L teaching materials. *RELC Journal, 19*(2).

Twain, M. (1985 [1885]). *The adventures of Huckleberry Finn.* London: Penguin Books.

Valentine, T. (1985). Cross-sex conversation in Indian English fiction. *World Englishes, 4*(3), 319–332.

Valentine, T. (1988). Developing discourse types in nonnative English: Strategies of gender in Hindi and Indian English. *World Englishes,* 7(2), 143–158.

# 4 *Language planning and policy*

Terrence G. Wiley

## Introduction

This chapter provides a brief introduction to the fields of language planning and language policy. It is divided into five major sections: The introduction addresses basic issues and assumptions which underlie and influence the direction of the study of language planning and policy. The second section discusses key definitions, describes various levels and types of language planning, and identifies those who are officially and unofficially involved in it. The third part contrasts influential scholarly orientations and approaches toward language planning and policy analysis and briefly reviews the work of several authorities in terms of their approaches. The next section describes and analyzes major goals for language planning, that is, language goals, political goals, and economic goals. The fifth section focuses on language in education planning and deals with two important legal challenges to established policies and practices. It also revisits a contentious debate over appropriate instruction for language minorities and considers issues of professional responsibility for linguists and language teachers. Next, it examines the impact of negative institutional language policies and practices and provides examples of positive steps that educators can take in promoting education for language minorities. In the discussion of issues, an attempt is made to maintain a critical stance toward controversial matters in order to avoid glossing over some of the underlying conflicts and tensions within the field. A brief conclusion completes the chapter.

Language planning is relatively young as a field of formal academic study, dating roughly from the 1960s. Much of its literature has been concerned with language issues in "developing" countries and in countries undergoing major processes of social, economic, or political change. Despite its recency as an academic field, language planning and policy analysis have long existed as activities of states and empires, though not always explicitly under these labels. In the absence of formal policies, language decisions have long figured in the agendas of powerful commercial interests, of modernizers, and of writers and stylists. Official language decisions are imposed as explicit policies handed down by governments. Unofficial policies, which also have influence, result from the pronouncements of language academies or flow from the works of "great" writers or various "authorities" such as lexicographers, influential publishers, or religious reformers. The stated reasons for promoting language change often sound noble and frequently cite the greater good that will result from the change. However, there is usually more at issue than just language, because decisions about language often lead to benefits for some and loss of privilege, status, and rights for others (Leibowitz, 1971, 1974). Since language becomes a focal point in social, political, and economic struggles, it is important for applied linguists and language educators to reflect on their roles as active participants in these struggles.

Before an attempt is made to define language planning and to discuss its relevance for applied linguists and language teachers, it is useful to make explicit several issues which underlie this discussion by addressing some basic questions. The first is: How do general assumptions about the study of language influence the study of language planning and language policy? This issue relates to how we conceive of language since that will determine how we study and analyze it. Broadly speaking, language can be seen both as a code and as social behavior. As a conventionalized code, it is a rule-governed system composed of subsystems. As codes, all languages and varieties of languages are adequate in allowing their speakers to attribute meaning, to represent logical thought processes, and generally to communicate among themselves. But language is more than just a code; it also involves social behavior. As social behavior, language enters a realm in which there are norms for behavior either based upon a consensus regarding what appropriate linguistic behavior is or based upon the ability of some individuals to impose their standard on others. Those doing the imposing may believe that there is an "inherent" superiority in their language norms and practices over those of others. Such beliefs, however, confuse the adequacy of language as a code with social rules of appropriateness. They confuse grammar with language etiquette. (See Wolfram & Fasold, 1974, for an elaboration of this distinction. See also Labov, 1982, for a discussion of the logical adequacy of nonstandard varieties of language.)

Even when it is studied as a social phenomenon, language is often described in neutral, technical-sounding terms as a "means of communication" for "social intercourse." Leibowitz (1974), however, maintains that language is more aptly viewed as a means of social control. From this perspective, language planning and policy must consider the social, economic, political, and educational contexts in which groups with unequal power and resources contend with one another. As an instrument of social control, language often becomes a surrogate for other factors underlying the language conflict (cf. Mullard, 1989; Phillipson, 1989, 1992).

Another basic question that may be asked is: How does attributing higher status to some varieties of language over others through language planning affect the status of the speakers of each variety? The attribution of status to the language varieties can become a subtle means of social control. The term *dialect,* for example, in popular usage often carries a connotation of substandard. Linguists usually approach dialects in descriptively neutral terms, seeing them as regionally or socially distinct varieties of a language that are mutually intelligible with other varieties. Although some linguists object to the term *dialect* for technical reasons, most believe that it is applicable to all varieties of languages including the standard (Crystal, 1987). However, as Roy (1987) explains, "[L]anguage varieties that coexist within the same environment may have different social values, particularly if one variety is used as a medium of wider communication. The language variety that has the higher social value is called a 'Language', and the language variety with the lower social value is called a 'dialect'. It has been said with only slight flippancy that a language is a dialect with an army" (p. 234). As we shall see, the label applied in both popular and scholarly usage can have great significance, not only for the status of the language variety, but also for its speakers (see Rickford, this volume; Sridhar, this volume).

Motivations to use language as an instrument of social control are influenced by scholarly and popular attitudes toward language variation and multilingualism. In this regard it is useful to ask: What attitudes do scholars and laypeople have toward language diversity? The image of Babel (see Crawford, 1992a; Haugen, 1973, 1992), that is, of a fall from a state of unified linguistic grace into a condition of linguistic chaos is frequently evoked in countries where there are deeper majoritarian – or dominant group – fears and prejudices directed at other groups. In societies where the majority of the population is monolingual, as in many Anglophone countries including the United States, there is often an underlying assumption that monolingualism – especially in English – represents an ideal natural state, whereas multilingualism represents a temporarily abnormal condition. Bhatia (1984), however, counters that monolingualism, even in monolingual majority societies, is never absolute, "because no speech community is either linguistically homogeneous or free from variation" (p. 24). Many people nonetheless see multilingualism as a "normal" condition. From their perspective, the imposition of one-language-only policies is more of a problem than a solution. There is a need to be aware of the underlying language ideologies of both scholars and laypersons, for their beliefs will affect the policies they support or oppose (cf. Fishman, 1978,

1981). It is easy to overemphasize language attitudes and by so doing fail to see how they relate to – or act as surrogates for – other social attitudes toward race, ethnicity, religion, or economic status (Mullard, 1989; Pattanayak, 1989).

Although language planning frequently attempts to solve conflicts over language, it can also result in creating conflicts. Thus, we may ask: What is the relationship between language planning and various types of conflicts – social, legal, economic, political, educational? Language planning affects speakers of regional and social varieties within the language, immigrants who do not speak the standard or majority language, and indigenous conquered peoples and colonized peoples who speak languages other than the dominant one. In struggles for power and dominance between groups, language is often the surface focal point for deeper conflicts. Applied linguists and language teachers are not immune from these conflicts but must consider how their skills and work relate to them.

There are a great number of areas in which conflicts arise over language (Crawford, 1992a; Weinstein, 1983). Language planning can be a factor either in solving communication problems or in causing them. Some of the more common causes of conflicts occur during periods of rapid social and demographic change. People who had previously enjoyed privilege and high status feel threatened by a newly mobilized language minority[1] group. Fearing the loss of their position, the elite argue for a "unifying" official language – theirs, of course. They may also point to a literacy crisis and call for the promotion of language and literacy skills – naturally in their language. Meanwhile, the language minority people become frustrated in their attempts to improve their social, political, or economic positions, for they suddenly find themselves blocked by their purported lack of "proper" language skills – a situation caused by the imposition of new language policy barriers.[2] Language minorities begin to realize that the language ante for participation has been raised too high and surmise that language requirements may have hidden purpose. They might try to promote their own language as equal to or superior to the dominant language. In this case, elites might then seek to mobilize the dominant group to

1 The label *language minority* is problematic, since it may refer either to a numerical minority or to lesser power among speakers who constitute a numerical majority but speak a nondominant language. Recently, some investigators have suggested dropping the term, since it can also be seen as ascribing a lower status to the people to which it refers. In analysis of language conflict situations between groups with unequal power and resources, the term *minority* is probably no less ascriptive than *nondominant*.

2 Examples include designating a specific language for public use and oral language and literacy requirements related to, for example, immigration and voting, admission to higher education, employment and promotion, and establishing business and conducting business (cf. Crawford, 1992b; Leibowitz, 1969).

"defend" its language – calling it the *common language* – and claim that one language is needed as a means of promoting national unity. Elites are thereby using language as a means of deflecting a "class-based" challenge to their position. They recast class antagonisms as "threats from another ethnic or national group, thereby promoting cultural solidarity over and above class" (Weinstein, 1983, p. 121).

Attacks on language can be more fundamentally related to attempts to deprive people of access, status, and power. In the extreme, struggles that supposedly originated over language can lead to resistance, widespread interethnic conflict, and even civil war. Ethnic cleansing is not far removed from, or unrelated to, "linguistic cleansing."[3] The outcome of such conflicts may result in the redrawing of "administrative districts within a country to ensure autonomy" or in the creation of "independent states with language as the rallying point of identity" (Weinstein, 1983, p. 121).

A final question that can be asked is: What are some of the major assumptions about language rights? Macías (1979) made two important distinctions concerning language rights which help to explain the contexts in which a commitment to language rights is exercised:

> There are here two kinds of rights: (1) the right to freedom from discrimination on the basis of language(s); and (2) the right to use one's language in the activities of communal life. There is no right to choice of language, of governmental service for example, except as it flows from these two rights above in combination with other rights, such as due process, equal enforcement of the laws, and so on. But, the identifiability and legal standing of a class based on language is recognized throughout the international community. (p. 41–42)

Macías also notes that the focal point for human rights in much of the Western, that is, European and American, discussion is located in the individual rather than in the group. Marxists and many leaders from other parts of the world take a collective view of rights (p. 42). Framing language rights issues from the perspective of either the individual or the group as the locus of rights has implications for how we approach language planning, since individual protections can either supersede or be overruled by those of the group.

## Key definitions used within the field

### *Corpus, status, and language acquisition planning*

Language planning is generally seen as entailing the formation and implementation of a policy designed to prescribe, or influence, the language(s) and varieties of language that will be used and the purposes

3 I owe this phrase to my colleague Professor Robert Berdan of California State University at Long Beach.

for which they will be used. The *International Encyclopedia of Linguistics* offers the following definition of *language planning:*

> [A] deliberate, systematic, and theory-based *attempt to solve the communication problems* of a community by studying the various languages or dialects it uses, and developing a policy concerning their selection and use; also sometimes called language engineering or language treatment. *Corpus planning* deals with norm selection and codification, as in the writing of grammars and the standardization of spelling; *status planning* deals with initial choice of language, including attitudes toward alternative languages and the political implications of various choices. (Bright, 1992, Vol. 4, pp. 310–311; emphasis added)

According to this definition, *language planning* involves two interrelated components: corpus planning and status planning (this distinction was originally proposed by Heinz Kloss, 1969). *Corpus planning* involves "activities such as coining new terms, reforming spelling, and adopting a new script. It refers, in short, to the creation of new forms, the modification of old ones, or the selection from alternative forms in a spoken or written code" (Cooper, 1989, p. 31). It entails efforts to change the body or corpus of a language. Corpus planning may include attempts to define or reform the standard language by changing or introducing forms in spelling, pronunciation, vocabulary, and grammar. It may include orthography planning, which involves the creation and reform of alphabets, syllabaries, and ideographic writing systems. Examples of corpus planning include the reforms of Hebrew, Norwegian, and Turkish and, in the case of Chinese, the promotion of a common spoken form, *Putónghuà* (in the People's Republic of China), and a provision for a romanized written form, *Pinyin*. Efforts to rid languages of gender bias are also examples of corpus planning.

*Status planning* has several dimensions. It has been linked to the official recognition which national governments attach to various languages, especially in the case of minority languages, and to authoritative attempts to extend or restrict language use in various contexts (Cooper, 1989, p. 32). (See also Kloss, 1971, 1977; Leibowitz, 1971, 1982, for an extended discussion of these issues.) Status planning issues include, for example, the designation of the language(s) of instruction in schools and decisions regarding whether (and in which languages) bilingual ballots may be used. In these cases, status planning concerns the relationship between languages rather than changes within them. However, status planning is also concerned with the position of different varieties of a single language. In this case, status planning becomes a function of corpus planning. Historically, the creation of a standard language often begins with the selection of a regional or social variety – usually a written variety – that provides a base language for grammatical refinement and vocabulary. This initial language choice confers privilege upon those whose speech and writing most closely conform to the newly selected standard. It inevitably elevates one variety of language over other varieties. Here, again, corpus planning determines status planning, since the process of standardization results in what is usually called the *proper* or *correct* variety or is sometimes called the *preferred* or *power* variety. All these terms indicate that the standard is more valued than other varieties (see also Williams, 1992).

Cooper (1989) proposes a third major type of language planning, *language acquisition planning,* which follows from this definition: "Language policy-making involves decisions concerning the teaching and use of language, and their careful formulation by those empowered to do so, for the guidance of others" (p. 31). He contends that this additional category is needed because considerable planning energy is directed toward language spread, especially through education. Technically, status planning relates to increasing or restricting the *uses* of a language but not to increasing the number of its *speakers.* Thus Cooper argues for acquisition planning as a separate major category of language planning. *Language spread* can be thought of as promoting the acquisition of a new language or as promoting a variety of a particular language as the standard.

Other definitions help us to grasp the purported motivations underlying language planning and help to identify those who do planning. According to Jahr (1992; cf. Fishman, 1974), language planning (LP) involves:

> [O]rganized activity (*private* or *official*) which *attempts to solve language problems* within a given society, usually at the national level. Through LP, attempts are made to *direct, change,* or *preserve* the linguistic norm or the social status (and communicative function) of a given written or spoken language variety of a language. LP is usually conducted according to a declared program or a defined set of criteria, and with a deliberate goal by *officially appointed committees* or bodies, by *private organizations,* or by *prescriptive linguists working on behalf of official authorities.* Its object is to establish norms (*primarily written*) which are *validated by high social status;* oral norms connected with these written standards follow. (pp. 12–13; emphasis added)

Here, as in the first definition of *language planning* in this section, a claim is made that language planning attempts to solve communication or language problems. In pursuing these ends, language planning appears to be a practical activity that attempts to produce socially beneficial results. However, additional issues may be raised. For example, who defines *language problems?* How do they become problems? For whom are they a problem? And, perhaps most important, does language planning itself ever cause language and communication problems? In other words, how do we reconcile the benevolent-sounding attempt to solve communication problems with the fact that the attempt can impose a form of social control? (cf. Fairclough, 1989; Tollefson, 1991).

There is much more that could be said on the subject of definitions and many more definitions that could be considered. Cooper (1989), for example, has identified twelve definitions and then offers his own:

> Language planning refers to deliberate efforts to influence the behavior of others with respect to the acquisition, structure, or functional allocation of their language codes. (p. 45)

This definition has a number of virtues, which are succinctly stated in Cooper's own defense of his definition:

> This definition neither restricts the planners to authoritative agencies, nor restricts the type of target group, nor specifies an ideal type of planning. Further it is couched in behavioral rather than problem-solving terms. Finally, it implies *influence* rather than change inasmuch as the former includes the maintenance or preservation of current behavior, a plausible goal of language planning, as well as the change of current behavior. (p. 45; emphasis in the original)

The use of *influence* suggests that planning is not limited to those who have official power or have armies at their disposal. It should also be noted, however, that influence often functions within a context of ideological control. Change may be explicitly forced, but influence operates in a wider domain wherein consent can be manufactured rather than coerced (cf. Fairclough, 1989; see Tollefson, 1991).

## *Government planning and language strategists*

In addition to technical definitions regarding language policy, there are also definitional issues related to the level at which language planning occurs and concerning just who language planners are. In some countries, such as Australia, language policy formation is more centralized than in the United States. Language planning in the United States has the appearance of being more open. Policies may be derived from de facto planners, such as state educational agencies, or from tradition more broadly (McKay, 1993, see especially Chap. 2). The principal questions in both centralized and decentralized contexts are: How are language decisions made, and by whom? Weinstein (1979, 1983) contends that there are two major forces in determining societal language choices: (1) governmental planning, which he sees explicitly as planning, and (2) individual, that is, influential individuals, whom he calls *language strategists*. In this regard, Tollefson (1991) makes an important distinction between government and state. "*Government* implies a group of individuals sharing equally in the exercise of power, whereas *state* refers to the apparatus by which dominant groups maintain their power" (p. 10; emphasis in the original). Language policies are one tool by which the state can solidify and expand its power and thereby the power of those who control the state. Historically, the emerging modern European nation-states promoted "national" vernaculars as a means of creating "imagined communities" that would have a sense of national unity and loyalty among their peoples (Anderson, 1991; see also Hobsbawm, 1992). (Although I do not wish to belabor this issue here, Tollefson's point is well taken. In this chapter, the use of the term *government* should be seen as embodying Tollefson's sense of the term *state.*) This division is somewhat heuristic, however, since individual strategists can influence policy making or in some cases can play the role of leader of state and of language strategist. King Alfonso X (r. 1252–1284) of Spain is probably the best example, for he was both king and a lexicographer who replaced Latin and Arabic technical terms with Castilian equivalents (Weinstein, 1983, p. 63).

From Weinstein's perspective, language choices are involved in both formal language policies and in the promotion of informal (or market-related) language strategies. Both can result in language decisions which either expand or constrain the language choices of most people. Language decisions in decentralized contexts – such as in the United States – appear to be more open because the lines of influence and authority are not clearly drawn. Heath (1976) suggests using the framework of a language policy configuration to explain the various forces which converge to shape policies. A *language policy configuration* includes a focus on unofficial, but influential, practices which come to have the force of policy (see also Tollefson, 1981).

When prescriptive linguists or applied linguists are employed by the state to help solve communication problems, or when language teachers (working in state-supported institutions) attempt to promote the standard, or when they teach a second language, they work within a political context. Also, private organizations that retain linguists and language teachers have agendas of their own. Regardless of whether language decisions are initiated by official governmental language planners or through the influence of language strategists, the decisions have social and political impact. As Weinstein (1983) notes:

> [P]lanning of any kind is dynamic, which is to say that it is the instrument of leaders who desire to change society; it implies a skepticism about the efficacy of "natural" forces and aims at "change by means of rationally coordinated state actions." Specifically, language structure and usage become a communication problem when they present a barrier to the nonlinguistic changes that the government is promoting. (p. 37)

This observation underscores Leibowitz's position on language policies as instruments of social control and the stance taken in the structural-historical approach (discussed later in this chapter). When the state decides to act on a communication problem, it has nonlinguistic agendas. Weinstein (1979, 1983) is also keen to observe that there are other influential players in language planning and in the formation of language policy; that is, the language strategists:

> Writers, translators, poets, missionaries, publishers, and dictionary makers can shape language for political and economic purposes; their effectiveness may be greater than government. These cultural elites have the power to transform language into a symbol for new community frontiers and interests which are defined and defended by political and economic elites with whom they are allied. Attaching a positive value to a variety of language transforms it into a form of capital, useful for gaining entry into a community or for claiming economic benefits. Not all writers wish to intervene in language matters, and many writers who innovate do so for aesthetic reasons. Those who innovate linguistically in order to promote political, social or economic interests should be called "language strategists." [1983, p. 62)

Historically, there are many well-known language strategists, among them Chaucer, who broke with Norman French in favor of English and expanded the use of English, and Dante, who created some of his greatest work in his native Tuscan (which he claimed was dialect-free). There was Nebrija of Spain, who sought to purify Castilian and defend it against the "corruption" of vernaculars; Martin Luther, who convinced others that God could speak languages other than Latin; and Noah Webster, who "labored" to rid American English of the British *labour*. Rabrindranath Tagore promoted Bengali, and Lu Xun chose vernacular over classical Chinese. More recently, influential advocates of antiracist and antisexist[4] discourse can also be seen as language strategists who recognize the power of words to ascribe status. Their opponents attempt to trivialize their prescriptions for nonracist and nonsexist terminology efforts with the *PC* ("politically correct") label. By so doing, influential spokes*persons* of the anti-PC movement are also language strategists who attempt to maintain the linguistic status quo.

Both governmental language planners and language strategists are involved in the "deliberate" attempt to make or even impose language decisions. Contrary to much of the field of linguistics, which prides itself on its detached descriptivism, language planning strives to *prescribe* policy for the stated purpose of solving "communication problems," which it often does. Again, however, communication problems can also result from the imposition of language policies by one group upon another.

4 See Frank & Anshen (1983) for a detailed proposal for nonsexist language. See also Freeman & McElhinny, this volume for a review of issues in language and gender.

## *Explicit versus implicit language planning*

Finally, in defining language policies there is also a need to distinguish between *explicit* or *official* policies and those which are *implicit* or even *tacit,* embedded in institutional practices (cf. Baldauf, 1994, regarding "unplanned" language policy and planning). For example, although the U.S. government has never specified English as the official language, English is required in most of its operations. English is the language of courtrooms. Applications for federal grants, for example, carry a requirement that they be submitted in English. Many job announcements carry requirements that applicants speak English. Historically, English language and literacy requirements have served a gatekeeping function in immigration (McKay & Weinstein-Shr, 1993) and have provided "legal sanction" for discrimination (Leibowitz, 1969).

Implicit language policies have been equated with accidental policies, as in the case of the English-only policies that the U.S. Bureau of Indian Affairs imposed on Native-American children (Kaplan, 1991, p. 153). This is, however, a dubious example of an "accidental" policy, since the plain purpose of the policy was language eradication and cultural dominance. According to Norgren and Nanda (1988):

> The aim [of Indian boarding schools] was not merely to teach children the dominant language and culture, but to wrench them completely away from their native cultures and estrange them from their parents and the influence of their tribes. In these schools there was an absolute prohibition on Native American children speaking their own languages, and those that did were humiliated, beaten, and had their mouths washed with lye soap. Though most children were forced to stay in schools, some parents, despite great obstacles, did remove their children when they realized the unswerving intent of officials to use the schools to destroy their cultures and languages. (p. 186; see also Leibowitz, 1971)

Implicit or tacit policies can become hegemonic. *Hegemony* refers to the ability of dominant groups to maintain and exercise power either through coercion or by the manufacture of consent; that is, through their ability "to gain consent for existing power relationships from those in subordinate positions" (Tollefson, 1991, p. 11). Linguistic hegemony is achieved when dominant groups create a consensus by convincing others to accept their language norms and usage as standard or paradigmatic. Hegemony is ensured when they can convince those who fail to meet those standards to view their failure as being the result of the inadequacy of their own language (cf. J. Collins, 1991). Schools have been the principal instruments in promoting a consensus regarding the alleged superiority of standardized languages.

## Scholarly orientations and approaches toward language planning

One reason why there are so many definitions of language planning is the fact that language policy theorists and planners adopt markedly different perspectives toward language planning. Consideration of the major orientations is important, since "Clearly what language planners seek to do will derive largely from how they perceive language change" (G. Williams, 1992, p. 123). Ruíz (1984) provides an important analysis of the two dominant orientations toward language planning, *language as problem* and *language as right,* and proposes a third, *language as resource.* In Ruíz's sense, *orientation* refers to:

> [A] *complex of dispositions toward language and its role, and toward languages and their role in society.* These dispositions may be largely unconscious and pre-rational because they are at the most fundamental level of arguments about language. . . . Orientations are basic to language planning in that they . . . determine the basic questions we ask, the conclusions we draw from the data, and even the data themselves. . . . In short, orientations determine what is thinkable about language in society. (p. 16, emphasis in original)

Ruíz contends that the majority of the work done by language planners "has been focused on the identification of language problems" (p. 18). He attributes this emphasis to the fact that language planning is seen either as an instrument for national development or as a remedy for social problems that are presumed to result from the linguistic mismatch between language minorities and the dominant society. Ruíz identifies a number of difficulties associated with this orientation, the most salient of which is its outlook on cultural and social diversity as "problems."

Ruíz also identifies the source of the language as right orientation. The rise of this orientation follows from the recognition that "since language touches many aspects of social life, any comprehensive statement about language rights cannot confine itself to merely linguistic considerations" (p. 22). Ruiz observes that "[b]y extension, this means that discrimination as to language has important effects in many other areas" (p. 22; cf. Leibowitz, 1969, 1971, 1974). Ruíz further notes that there are many unresolved problems and technical issues associated with this orientation, especially since language planners who have this orientation enter into confrontation, activism, and advocacy.

Based upon what he sees as limitations of the first two orientations, Ruíz suggests – within the context of language planning in the United States – that the language as resource orientation resolves some of the difficulties of the other two. He contends that

> A closer look at the idea of language-as-resource could reveal some promise for alleviating some of the conflicts emerging out of the other two orientations:

it can have a direct impact on enhancing the language status of subordinate languages; it can help to ease tensions between majority and minority communities; it can serve as a more consistent way of viewing the role of non-English languages in U.S. society; and it highlights the importance of cooperative language planning. (pp. 25–26)

In recent years, many scholars and language teachers have embraced language as a resource as a basic tenet of their fields.

## *Neoclassical versus historical-structural approach*

Other scholars have focused on the notion of approaches to language planning. Tollefson (1991), for example, contrasts two broad approaches: (1) the *neoclassical approach* and (2) the *historical-structural approach*. The notion of an *approach*, as it is used here, refers to how language planning is done, that is, to the methods employed, the manner in which it is undertaken, and the way in which issues are framed. Approaches are influenced by *orientations* in the sense that Ruíz uses the term. Tollefson (1991, p. 31) describes the major differences between the neoclassical and historical-structural approaches as involving:

1. The unit of analysis each employs (the neoclassical emphasizes individual choices, whereas the historical-structural considers the influence of sociohistorical factors on language use)
2. The role of the historical perspective (the neoclassical approach tends to focus more on the current language situation; the historical-structural approach considers the past relationships between groups)
3. Criteria for evaluating plans and policies (i.e., the neoclassical approach often presents its evaluations in ahistorical and amoral terms, whereas the historical-structural approach is concerned with issues of class dominance and oppression)
4. The role of the social scientist (the neoclassical model typically assumes that the field of applied linguistics and teachers are apolitical; the historical-structural approach concludes that a political stance is inescapable, for those who avoid political questions inadvertently support the status quo)

Tollefson's analysis strongly parallels Street's (1984, 1993; cf. Hornberger, 1994b; see also McKay's discussion of Street, this volume) analysis of underlying models in the study of literacy and literacy policies. The inclusion of literacy policy is warranted here, because much – though not all, by any means – that falls under the heading of language planning policy involves literacy. Much of the activity in corpus planning is focused on attempts to standardize the written language. Street uses the terms *autonomous* and *ideological models*, which are roughly parallel to Tollefson's *neoclassical* and *historical-structural approaches,* respectively. Both authors have made significant critical contributions within their respective areas. Taken together, they demonstrate a strikingly parallel approach to underlying assumptions in the fields of language and literacy planning, policy, and instruction. Both authors maintain that the neoclassical-autonomous camp has generally been dominant, and both conclude that this approach has been limited by its lack of concern with social, historical, and ideological contexts. Their conclusions can be characterized as revisionist insofar as they have broken with prior dominant paradigms within the field. From the perspective of Ruíz's orientations, the historical-structural and ideological approaches can essentially be placed in both the language as right and the language as resource orientations because language planners adhering to them frequently become advocates for language rights and also try to promote the maintenance and/or development of minority languages as social, cultural, and political resources.

The appeal of the neoclassical-autonomous approach arises from its formal neatness and alleged neutrality. Because it focuses on the formal properties of language and the structural characteristics of language varieties, analysis is tidy; that is, it is relatively uncontaminated by the complexity and inequality of the real world. Applied to corpus planning, this approach tends to focus on the formal properties of language to the exclusion of their use within social contexts. From the standpoint of status planning, language communities are characterized in terms of the "structural characteristics of language varieties and the degrees of multilingualism" (Tollefson, 1991, p. 29). Concerning acquisition theory, the success of the learner in acquiring a new language is seen as correlating with individual psychological factors such as motivation to assimilate into the dominant society. The approach ignores the historical and social context within which individuals live; that is, it overlooks differential power between groups. It neglects the way in which the dominant group treats minority groups, and by so doing, it ignores the factors that affect individual motivation to learn or to be assimilated. Nor does it question assimilation as a goal or consider alternatives to assimilation.

When focused on the study of literacy, the neoclassical-autonomous approach sees the invention and utilization of print as having "cognitive consequences" for individuals and for whole societies. These alleged cognitive consequences are viewed as resulting more from print as a technology than from the social practices in which it is used (see McKay, this volume; Street, 1984, 1993; Wiley, in press). Thus, language planning as a factor in promoting mass literacy in "developing" countries is approached largely as a technical problem, rather than as a sociohistorical and political one. "It does not include analysis of the forces that lead to the adoption of the planning approach . . ." (Tollefson, 1991, p. 28; cf. G. Williams, 1992).

The historical-structural and ideological approach views language planning and literacy issues differently. It sees language and literacy development and language reform in terms of how they relate to social, economic, and political purposes which enable people to direct their own lives in ways they find meaningful. This approach also sees societal planning and policy as largely resulting from the dominant social and political institutions in which they are embedded. They cannot be treated as separate, autonomous things unto themselves. Similarly, "language problems" are seen to result from social stratification, that is, from the differential power and resources of groups. Institutions and social relationships between groups are seen as being rooted in history. Thus, the history of institutions and group relationships must be analyzed if the sources of conflict that lead to language problems are to be understood. Finally, this approach assumes that language and literacy policies are more likely to be accepted when they build upon the linguistic resources that people already have.

Examples of each of these approaches can be seen in the works of several scholars, which are briefly described in the following passages. The classification scheme used here is analytic; it does not necessarily represent how these scholars would categorize the approach of their own work. It is also necessary to point out that the totality of the work of each writer does not always fall neatly into only one category or the other.

## *Neoclassical-autonomous aspects of Einar Haugen's approach toward language planning*

Einar Haugen is widely regarded as one of the pioneers and more influential theorists in language planning (see Haugen, 1966, 1973/1992, 1983). His contributions include the development of a major theoretical framework in which he outlines four phases of language planning. On the whole, Haugen's work demonstrates aspects of both the neoclassical and the historical-structural approaches. His discussion of the notion of *linguistic racism* (1973/1992), for example, anticipated more recent analyses representative of the historical-structural approach (e.g., Mullard, 1988; Phillipson, 1988, 1992). Nevertheless, Haugen's phases of language planning provide an example of the neoclassical approach and can be outlined as follows:

1. The selection of a language variety or varieties that provide the basis for a new norm; the language chosen may be an indigenous language variety (typically a regionally or socially prestigious one)

2. Codification, through the choice of script, the determination of phonology and its correspondence to an orthography, and of morphology and rules of word formation (this involves issues of corpus planning and sometimes orthographic planning)
3. Implementation, which pertains to initial diffusion of the new codified norm throughout society (usually by means of schools and official and/or religious and commercial agencies)
4. Elaboration and modernization, which involve ongoing efforts to spread the norm and to extend its ability to meet various communication needs of the society (adapted from Jahr, 1992, pp. 13–14; cf. Crystal, 1987, p. 364.)

Haugen's approach here is to view language planning as a largely technocratic process concerned with systematizing and cultivating a standardized language code in an effort to solve communication problems. He emphasizes the importance of the written standard over the spoken:

> It will be quite impossible even to enter upon the subject if we maintain the usual position of linguists . . . that writing is 'merely a way of recording [oral] language by means of visible marks.' . . . [I]n the study of LP we shall have to reverse this relationship. (1972/1966, p. 163)

Haugen observed that linguistic norms are based upon a taught, written standard. He notes that dialects are commonly considered, at best, charming nuisances which can only be "tolerated":

> It seems to me that all the activities of rhetoricians and normative grammarians, from Samuel Johnson to the lowliest school-marm in American rural schools, need to be reevaluated in terms of this model. *Dialects, whether regional or social, have their charms, but they hamper communication by calling attention to features which either are or ought to be irrelevant to the message.* They label their man by his social history, and their maintenance is often advocated precisely by those who wish to maintain a snobbish distinction of class. *If dialects are to be tolerated,* the teaching of tolerance must begin with other and more basic features of inequality in society than the purely linguistic one. (1972/1962, p. 253; emphasis added)

As Haugen was aware, language planning cannot avoid the historical relationships between groups; nor can it avoid the political, ethnic, racial, social, and economic issues that are involved in defining their current relationships. His appeal to teach tolerance by focusing on the "more basic features of inequality" is well taken; however, from a historical-structural view, the more germane point would be to demonstrate how language prejudices and discriminatory language policies function in conjunction with them.

Despite his concern for equality *among* standard languages, he saw "nonstandard" variation *within* languages as problematic, as the following illustrates:

> It would be nice if we could persuade polite society to accept Eliza Doolittle as she is, but in our heart of hearts most of us would prefer to associate with her after Dr. Higgins has straightened out her aiches. (1972/1962, p. 154)

Here, Haugen, yields to the dominance of literate, standardized forms of language over the irregularity of dialects as a cure for the problems associated with the disease of linguistic variation. He valued diversity among languages, that is, among taught, standardized varieties; however, the existence of competing varieties within a language posed a problem from the standpoint of language planning. A language was to be defined only in terms of its literary, standardized form.

## *Heinz Kloss: A middle ground between the approaches*

Heinz Kloss is a major contributor to the literature on the history of language policy formation and its implications for language rights (see Kloss, 1971, 1977). His work establishes the importance of the state in creating policies toward immigrant majority languages that can (1) promote, (2) accommodate, (3) tolerate, or (4) suppress them. In the case of U.S. history, Kloss asserts that immigrant language minorities existed in a climate of toleration-oriented rights in which they were left to their own devices and energies to maintain their native language.

> As our study shows . . . the non-English ethnic groups in the United States were Anglicized not *because of* nationality laws which were *unfavorable* toward their languages but *in spite of* nationality laws which were relatively *favorable* to them. Not by legal provisions and measures of authorities, not by governmental coercion did the nationalities become assimilated, but rather by the absorbing power of the highly developed American society. (1977, p. 283; emphasis in original)

For Kloss, linguistic assimilation was voluntary, given the opportunities offered by the society as a whole. He contends that voluntary linguistic assimilation was possible, given the openness of the U.S. society, and because many immigrants saw opportunities in the United States as being superior to those in their countries of origin. In drawing these conclusions, Kloss is functioning from within a European – if not mostly Western European – immigrant paradigm. He seems to equate linguistic assimilation with economic and political assimilation. Kloss tends to understate the differences between the experiences of Western European immigrants and those of immigrants from Asia and Latin America, not to mention those of indigenous and colonized peoples. Kloss does acknowledge instances of discrimination:

> [D]iscrimination [in voting] consequently prevented the Mexicans from developing into a genuine national minority which possesses the citizenship of the host country. 'If you become a citizen but are treated as a foreigner, what have you gained?' was a typical complaint. . . . *It should not be overlooked, however, that naturalization is frequently not coveted because the immigrant, following his Mexican and Latin tradition, considers problems of government and the community as something that has to be cared for by officials who are paid to do this.* . . . Authorities, on the other hand, often treat even members of the second generation as aliens. (1977, p. 51, emphasis added)

Kloss's ambivalence is demonstrated here. On the one hand, he notes the disincentive toward assimilation based upon discrimination; on the other hand, he finds fault with "Mexican and 'Latin' tradition." Kloss does, however, offer examples of when the United States has accommodated minority languages and admits to one major exception to this pattern, that is, the case of the outright suppression of German-Americans during World War I (see later discussion in this chapter). Kloss's ideas move in the direction of the historical-structural approach because he recognizes the importance of the state's policies toward minority languages, as the following illustrates:

> The withholding of political rights is incidentally subject to the same considerations as that of human rights: the Mexicans are affected by such withholding not because they speak a foreign language but because they have a different color of skin. (1977, p. 51)

Again, however, he downplays more systematic institutional racism and language discrimination, as the following indicates:

> There were only isolated instances of an oppressive state policy aiming at the elimination of non-English languages. There were, however, a great many instances in which individuals (including public school teachers) and groups exerted unofficial moral pressure upon members of the minority groups, especially children, so as to make them feel that to stick to a "foreign" tongue meant being backward or even un-American. (1977, p. 284)

Kloss's framing of language discrimination as a problem of individuals is typical of the neoclassical approach. There is no systematic analysis of the attitudes and practices of the host society across a broad field of social practices (cf. Leibowitz, 1969, 1971, 1974). In fact, social practices are relegated to a position of secondary importance, as the following passage illustrates:

> In individual cases knowledge of the English language was made a prerequisite for ordinary vocational positions which were in no way connected with politics. An 1897 Pennsylvania law required that laborers occupied in mines who intended to become miners had to take an examination during which they . . . had to prove their command of English; this was designed to keep out Slavic workers. . . . Much more frequent than is evident from such isolated state regulation were cases of actual discrimination against members of non-English

groups in the open labor market. But in such cases *society, and not the state, discriminated; such discrimination is not directly related to the legal status of linguistic minorities.* (1977, p. 51, emphasis added)

Kloss tended to avoid looking at how language policies function in conjunction with institutional racism (see Haas, 1992; Weinberg, 1990a) and other forms of social discrimination that often underlie the imposition of restrictive language practices. There is a considerable body of evidence that the "unofficial moral pressure" occurred across a broad range of social and institutional contexts (see Leibowitz, 1969, 1971, 1974; Luebke, 1980; Weinberg, 1977). By focusing on formal statutes rather than on the sociopolitical climate in which minority language groups must function, we avoid confronting the tacit policies which are often at odds with official policies.

## *Arnold Leibowitz's historical-structural–ideological approach*

Arnold Leibowitz concentrates on the imposition of English language requirements for access to and participation in a variety of contexts: political, legal, economic, and educational (see Leibowitz, 1969, 1971, 1974, 1980, 1982, 1984). He looks at the experiences of immigrants of European origin, such as German-Americans, but then turns to those of Japanese and Chinese immigrants, to Native Americans (indigenous-language minorities), to people of Mexican origin (both immigrants and colonized peoples), and to Puerto Rican Americans (as colonized peoples). By focusing on language as an instrument of social control, Leibowitz departs from the immigrant language policy concern that preoccupies much of the literature on language policy in the United States.

For example, he notes that English literacy requirements were used by the Massachusetts and Connecticut legislatures to exclude English-speaking Irish Catholics from voting during the 1850s (1974). During the same time period that English language and literacy requirements were being imposed on European immigrants, English literacy requirements were being used to exclude African-Americans from voting. Leibowitz concludes that the motivation to impose English language and literacy requirements has been based upon the "degree of hostility" of the majority toward the language minority group "usually because of race, color, or religion" (1971, p. 4). Thus, language restriction is not something that has occurred in isolation from other forms of discrimination. He notes that attacks on language have always clearly signaled to the groups affected that there was more involved, since the act of imposing language requirements or restrictions itself often takes on more significance than its substantive effects.

Leibowitz suggests that, if language is viewed as a means of social control, a variety of disciplines can converge in an effort to understand not just "communication problems" but the sources of deep societal conflicts that result from differential power among groups (1974). He can reach these conclusions only because he casts his net more widely across sociopolitical and sociohistorical contexts than neoclassical scholars do. Leibowitz's analyses of a variety of social, political, economic, and educational contexts in his earlier work (1969, 1971, 1974) seems to have anticipated the more overtly historical-structural–ideological approach of more recent scholars (e.g., Fairclough, 1989; Grillo, 1989; Lippi-Green, 1994; Phillipson, 1992; Roberts, Davis, & Jupp, 1992; Tollefson, 1991; G. Williams, 1992).

## Goals of language planning

### *Language goals*

Whether language policies are implicit or explicit, they involve goals. On the surface these goals may be seen as either (1) language-related (wherein language issues appear to be the major focus as an end in themselves) or (2) politically and economically motivated (wherein language appears to be a means to an end). Upon closer inspection, however, even goals that appear to be mostly language related are generally not without political or economic connection and impact. Among language-related goals, three broad types of policies can be identified: (1) language shift policy, (2) language maintenance policy, and (3) language enrichment policy. How language diversity is seen has a major bearing on the agendas for language policy. As noted above, Ruíz (1984) contends that language diversity can either be seen as a problem, a right, or a resource (see also Crawford, 1992a; Hornberger, 1994a; McKay & Wong, 1988).

Historically, given the many contexts for contact between peoples (e.g., nation formation, migration, trade, wars, conquest and colonization, religious proselytization, intermarriage), language shift is a relatively common occurrence. Language shift can occur as a gradual process, or it can be explicitly planned. When language diversity is seen as a problem, language shift policy is a goal for language acquisition planning, whether explicit or implicit. Bright (1992) describes language shift as "The gradual or sudden move from the use of one language to another, either by an individual or a group" (Vol. 4, p. 311). Assuming its inevitability, some scholars have attempted to determine the rate of language shift among immigrant groups. In the case of the United States, Veltman's analysis of census data (1983) determined the rate of shift to be roughly a three generational one (from native language monolingualism to English monolingualism). However, several of Veltman's assumptions have been questioned. Most curious is his exclusion of bilingualism as a circumstance equal to monolingualism. If bilingualism is not considered, language shift is seen as an either-or phenomenon toward a *language* rather than toward *multilingualism* (Wiley, 1990–1991, in press).

Fishman (1981) notes that a considerable degree of language shift has occurred in the United States although there has been neither a constitutional mandate nor a subsequent legal declaration that English be the official language. Rather, the shift has resulted from an implicit policy fostered by "a complex web of customs, institutions, and programs [which] has long fostered well-nigh exclusive reliance upon English in public life" (p. 517). In the absence of an explicit policy, for two centuries "literally hundreds of millions of Americans have been led, cajoled, persuaded, embarrassed into, and forced to forget, forego and even deny languages that were either their mother tongues, their communal languages, or their personal or communal additional tongues" (p. 517).

Despite implicit language shift policies and intergenerational drifts toward dominant languages, there are numerous reasons why many individuals who have a minority language status do not shift but remain loyal to their native languages (Fishman, 1966). *Language loyalty* refers to the attachment to one's native language. It has been defined as "A concern to preserve the use of a language or the traditional form of a language, when that language is perceived to be under threat" (Bright, 1992, Vol. 4, p. 310). According to Fishman (1981), language loyalty is based upon the persistent attempt to preserve ethnic identity in the face of linguistic and cultural dominance. In education, policies that promote native language maintenance are seen as providing both a cognitive foundation for the transfer of literacy skills from a student's native language to his or her second language (i.e., the dominant language of instruction) and a means of fostering the self-confidence and sense of a self-worth deemed essential for promoting academic success (Crawford, 1991; Cummins, 1981, 1984a, 1984b, 1985). Fishman (1981) observes that in the United States, policies to promote language maintenance have not been considered (by powerful elites) in the public's (i.e., the dominant group's) interest. He concludes: "Until it can be so considered, it must be freed from the suspicion of divisiveness and incompatibility with progress, modernity, and efficiency" (p. 522). The major attempts to promote language maintenance policy have been in connection with bilingual education. Although initially embraced with enthusiasm as "a major effort to Anglify the last 'unfortunates' " (p. 519), bilingual education has been steadily attacked, especially since the early 1980s, allegedly out of Anglophone majoritarian fears that maintenance promotes separatism. The idea that societal bilingualism could be a goal in its own right is lost amid fears of linguistic balkanization (see Crawford, 1992a; Simon, 1988).

Probably more than any other scholar, Fishman (e.g., 1981, 1991) has drawn attention to what he terms *language enrichment policy* by exploring ways to reverse language shift. His position is analogous to that of environmentalists who try to preserve endangered species in the face of imminent species extinction. Fishman pursues ways to maintain endangered languages in the face of imminent "linguicide." He attempts to find ways to provide practical and theoretical assistance "to communities whose native languages are threatened because their intergenerational continuity is proceeding negatively" (Fishman, 1991, p. 1). His goal is to extend promotion-oriented rights to the world's "endangered" languages. This issue is tied to the larger theme, identified by Tucker (1994), of *ethnic revitalization.* (See Haacke, 1994; Hornberger, 1994a; Kaplan, 1994; & Patthey-Chavez, 1994, for related discussions in various international contexts.) As the discussion now moves to goals other than language, it is important to realize that many of these goals are mutually exclusive (see also Coulmas, 1994).

## Political goals

Among the more explicitly political goals of language planning are those that attempt to use language as a means to promote *nation building*. Historically, language planning played a major role in the development of the modern European nation-state. It played this role partly because of the invention of the printing press and the expansion of vernacular literacy (Anderson, 1991).

> It remains only to emphasize that in their origins, the fixing of print-languages and the differentiation of status between them were largely unselfconscious processes resulting from the explosive interaction between capitalism, technology and human diversity. But as with much else in the history of nationalism, once 'there', they could become formal models to be imitated, and, where expedient, consciously exploited in a Machiavellian spirit. (p. 45)

Taking its cue from the historical role of language in promoting national unification, language planning has taken on considerable importance in the creation of new nations from former colonies. Often the geographical boundaries of such states are more political than linguistic. They often correspond more to the former imperial boundaries than to language, ethnic, or religious distribution. Language planning in such countries, then, is not only important as a means of solving communication problems amid linguistic diversity; it is a means of unifying people whose primary common attribute is that they were formerly dominated by a foreign power. Language planning offers them the opportunity to continue their relationship under a new national (i.e., state) authority in the absence of their former colonial masters. The plan, however, does not always work. Consider how "well" the Tamils have identified with Sri Lanka. And, for those who believe that one language is a requisite for national unity, note the language situation in India, the world's second-most-populous country and its largest democracy:

> [T]here are 1,652 mother tongues. Depending on how people count, there are between 200 and 700 languages. . . . These languages belong to four language families. There are eight major script systems not counting Roman and Arabic. All these eight belong to a single script family and are derived from Brahmi. (Pattanayak, 1989, p. 379)

In response to the question of whether such linguistic diversity leads to national disintegration, Pattanayak responds:

> No. Many languages are like petals of a lotus. Many languages form a national mosaic. If some petals wither and fall off or some chips are displaced from the mosaic, then the lotus and the mosaic look ugly. With the death of languages the country will be poorer. (p. 379)

A number of European states and postcolonial states, however, have used linguistic unification as a means of promoting national unification. When a single language is used to help define a nation, it operates on horizontal and vertical axes. Along the horizontal axis the promotion of a normative, "standard" variety – among mutually intelligible varieties – allows the state to expand its influence among speakers and to convince them that they are one people. The promotion of a standard is thus an inclusive language policy, for it seeks to unite speakers of a so-called common language. First, however, they must be convinced that it is their common language. To do this, a standard must be developed or selected. The selection of a standard often involves choosing a regional variety that is associated with centers of power and cultural prestige (see Grillo, 1989). Its selection may involve an attempt to disguise the regional bias under the guise of its "transnationalism." Sometimes, speakers of a closely related oral language, Serbs and Croats during the nineteenth century, for example, are separated by the lack of a common script (Weinstein, 1983). Orthography planning provided a means for trying to bring together groups who perceived themselves as different. Conversely, Turks in the early twentieth century created a romanized script to distance their people from Arabs (Weinstein, 1983).

Furthermore, established as the standard, the "national" language lends itself to defining a vertical social hierarchy. Along the vertical axis, language proficiency in the standard functions as a means of enhancing and reinforcing stratification among speakers of the same language. Thus, the standard may be used as a gatekeeping mechanism to limit upward mobility to those who have acquired it. Schools play a critical role because they teach the standard and promote continued academic learning through it. Instruction in the literature written by "great writers" (language strategists) of the standard adds status legitimacy to the standard. High-status varieties are associated with the educated, who, through privilege, have access to schools and to the "national" literature canonized therein. In Europe, the bourgeoisie tended to rally behind the standard. In such cases, acquisition planning can be seen as a divisive force along a vertical axis (between classes), since all groups do not have equal access to acquiring the standard through an extended elite education.

Just as an analysis of language planning and language policies is important in the study of nationalism, so too it is significant in the study of imperialism. Phillipson (1992; see also Tollefson, 1991) has undertaken a sweeping analysis of linguistic imperialism. Following Galtung (1980, p. 107), Phillipson defines imperialism as "a relationship where one society . . . can dominate another" (p. 52). He notes that "Galtung's *imperialism theory* posits six mutually interlocking types of imperialism: *economic, political, military, communicative, . . . cultural, and social*" (p. 52). Phillipson identifies linguistic imperialism as a subtype of cultural imperialism.

## *Economic goals*

Language planning often pursues economically motivated goals, such as those pertaining to communication and marketing in international trade (Simon, 1988). Australia has attempted to promote foreign language instruction to improve communication with trading partners who speak Chinese, Indonesian, Japanese, and Korean (Kaplan, 1991). Among other issues are communication and language discrimination in the workplace (Roberts et al., 1992) and language rights in the workplace, just to mention a few. There are also costs associated with changes in language policies and with language. It is estimated that Quebec's promotion of French costs Can$ 100 million annually (Coulmas, 1992). Companies may overtly impose language requirements on workers and applicants. Often, however, implicit or tacit policies are operative:

> For example, in Germany no one can become a branch director of a bank without being accepted by the Federal Office of the Supervision of the Banking Business in Berlin. Although its examination focuses on contents rather than on language, it forces non-German-speaking applicants to be proficient in German, since no allowances are made for limited German proficiency. Hence, even though the management of a foreign bank may not share the conviction that German language proficiency is indispensable for heading a branch office in Germany, it cannot but comply with this requirement. (Coulmas, 1992, p. 134)

Lack of language and literacy skills in the dominant language is frequently cited as if it were the cause of poor economic performance, trade deficits, and low productivity, and as if it were responsible for the social "costs" of crime. For example, Kaplan (1991) contends:

> There is evidence that the highest arrest rates and conviction rates lie among certain linguistic minorities, and there is also evidence that the greatest draw upon social-welfare services *originates* in those same linguistic minorities. In order to reduce the societal costs imposed on the welfare system and criminal-justice system, certain linguistic minorities need to receive linguistic help; i.e., to have greater access to majority-language functions. (p. 163, emphasis added)

Here, as Brodkey (1991) notes, language problems are depicted as a "personal misery" with "public consequences" that can be abrogated only through the intervention of language planning programs (p. 164). In this description, the language minority status of certain (unspecified) groups appears to be their most important attribute, since no other attributes are mentioned. But is language background really the salient factor associated with these social costs? Are wealthy language minorities also disproportionately represented in criminal and social welfare statistics? Are the poor generally, regardless of language background, more likely to be represented in such statistics? Framing "social cost" issues solely in terms of language reflects a majoritarian or dominant group perspective. It imputes agency to "certain" language minority groups who "impose" their costs on the dominant society. The remedy for reducing these societal costs is apparently solely linguistic, involving providing "greater access to majority language functions." Yet historical evidence regarding how best to reduce social costs among immigrant and language minority groups suggests that language or literacy problems are not the cause of social ills but result from them. In the United States, for example, economic and social gains among immigrant language minorities "have been more the results of long-term organized efforts to win better working conditions and benefits than of the acquisition of English language and literacy" (Weinberg; cited in Wiley, 1993). Many of these gains occurred as a result of the great expansion of unionism during the 1930s, and many of the new unionists were from the "undesirable" groups (Wiley, in press). Even with the intervention of mass literacy campaigns, social problems persisted (Graff, 1979). Graff (1987) concludes:

> Criminal prosecution, and probably apprehension as well, derived from the facts of inequality. Punishment, stratification, and illiteracy too were rooted in the social structure; pervasive structures of inequality which emanated from the ethnic and sexual ascription ordered groups and individuals. . . . Achievement of literacy [i.e., in the standard language] or education had little impact upon these structures, and in many cases only reinforced them. (p. 210)

Why should this be so? As language minorities with lower socioeconomic status (SES) make educational gains, the rest of society makes gains too. If a scarcity of "good" jobs persists, the result is what R. Collins (1979) calls *credential inflation,* that is, for example, as lower SES language minorities increase their years of schooling and language skills, their gains are negated as job requirements call for advanced degrees and professional credentials – all of which demand higher levels of language proficiency – that often are not really needed to do the job. To acknowledge credential inflation is not to argue against language in education planning. Rather, credential inflation demonstrates that language planning alone cannot be seen as a cure for deeper societal ills related to social stratification and job scarcity. To make it so is to blame the victim, for the image of remedy (i.e., more schooling and language instruction) is provided without the substance of remedy (economic mobility through better jobs and benefits).

Language planning, especially as it relates to literacy, is commonly seen as having a positive impact on the national economy in technological societies. For example, Vargas (1986) contends that "the need for the nation's work force to be continuously replenished by adequately trained and functionally literate workers becomes increasingly important" (p. 9). However, the causality between national economic well-being and language and literacy planning may be overestimated. Coulmas (1992) notes that during a Nicaraguan literacy campaign of the 1980s there were no "immediate or medium-term consequences for the development of social wealth in that country" despite a 10 percent increase in the literacy rate (p. 211). He concludes that "the socioeconomic value of literacy cannot be measured on a scale with linear progress" (p. 211).

There are also a number of social contexts in local communities where language planning goals are pursued. Many local language planning initiatives are linked to immigration. According to U.N. estimates, as many as a hundred million people may now be trying to migrate voluntarily or involuntarily, fleeing war, genocide, or extreme poverty. Although immigration issues are usually framed as issues of national policy, it is often at the local level where decisions are made that affect accommodation for language differences. In the absence of a stated governmental policy, local community agencies often create their own. Many policies related to access to housing, jobs, schooling, and other social services could be cited, but the case of health care will suffice.

In many communities, health care agencies are staffed by medical personnel who speak the dominant language; some workers, however, may be native speakers of other languages. In California, for example, a nursing shortage (not unrelated to low wages and benefits) resulted in the "importing" of well-trained native speakers of Korean, Illocano, and Tagalog from Korea and the Philippines. All these occupational immigrants, however, are required to speak and have literacy skills in English. Yet, in many local California communities large numbers of patients may speak Vietnamese, Hmong, Khmer, or Spanish. Kaplan (1991) sees this type of situation as being typical of the kind of communication problem which may be addressed through language planning:

> [A] severe social problem can be created by differences between the language in which certain services can be delivered and the language of the population most in need of services. This is most likely to occur in relation to medical services; it is often the case that medical practitioners are trained in a world language, but deliver medical services to populations who do not speak the language in which medical practitioners were trained. (p. 163)

A number of questions can be raised here, for example: How should we analyze and solve the communication problems in this case? Should this case be framed merely as an example of a mismatch of the languages of the medical service providers and the populations they serve? Should the health care agency be required to provide translators or bilingual doctors and nurses if many of its clients cannot understand the language spoken by those who provide the health care? Or does it raise questions regarding the role of language between groups with differential status, resources, and power? In the provision of medical services, for whom is the inability to communicate more of a problem: doctors, nurses, or their patients? For whom do the doctors and nurses work: primarily for the hospital or department of public health or for their patients? In terms of paying for public health, should the taxpayers have the final say regarding whether interpreters will be provided? Whom do we have in mind when we appeal to the taxpayers, only members of the majority or dominant group? If translators are utilized, for whom do they work? For the doctors and nurses? Or for the patients? Or for the taxpayers? If translators recognize a cultural conflict between the doctors and nurses and the patients, what should they do?: Should they attempt to mediate as cross-cultural referees? Should they take the side of the health care provider or of the patient? Should the translators be highly paid because of their bilingual skills? Should the health care agency be required to recruit bilingual personnel to fill the ranks of its "regular" personnel (i.e., its doctors, nurses, clerks, custodians, and laboratory personnel) so that the agency begins to look like the community it serves? If the answer to the last question is yes, should it be yes for both public and private health care agencies? Obviously, the communication problem is related to many other problems which must be considered as part of the language planning process (see Wiley, 1986).

## Language in education planning

In modern societies, education provides one of the major means of promoting language acquisition planning and language shift policy. *Language in education planning* is the primary form of language acquisition planning.[5] Like other forms of language planning, it cannot be discussed in isolation from sociopolitical issues, since it is related to a broader purpose in education, namely, socialization, and since it is an extension of overall governmental policy (Judd, 1991, p. 170). Although schools play an important role in community-based language planning, they also play a major role in promoting national standard languages and thereby help to extend the influence of the state along its horizontal axis across groups. The standard must be explicitly taught as opposed to acquired. There is some irony here, since native speakers of language *X* must go to school to learn the language they supposedly already speak. Illich (1979) offers a provocative critique here as he protests:

> We first allow standard language to degrade ethnic, black, or hillbilly language, and then spend money to teach their counterfeits [i.e. the standardized school languages] as academic subjects. Administrators and entertainers, admen and newsmen, ethnic politicians and 'radical' professionals, form powerful interest groups, each fighting for a larger slice of the language pie. (p. 55)

Although many people hold the rather simplistic notion that writing is merely speech encoded in print, there is more at work. As Haugen understood, schooling facilitates the imposition of the norms of the written or formal standard upon oral varieties of language. Language in education policies also include designating the language(s) of instruction; recruiting teachers based on their language and literacy backgrounds; providing for first, second, and foreign language instruction; and developing curricula, syllabi, and materials that are sensitive to the language and cultural backgrounds of the students (cf. Corson, 1989; Ingram, 1990, 1991).

In the United States, conflicts over language in education have tended to parallel the majority's disposition toward language minority groups in other spheres. Not all groups were treated equally or afforded equal access or resources. Some groups were vigorously discriminated against (Leibowitz, 1971, 1974). Language policies affecting various language minority groups reflected the prejudice or tolerance toward each group's race, ethnicity, and religion (see Kaplan, 1994, p. 157, regard-

5 See Paulston and McLaughlin (1994) for a discussion of language in education planning in international contexts.

ing "vestigial racism" in New Zealand). The issue is not whether U.S. educational language policies have been successful or unsuccessful, but for whom, and under what circumstances, they have been successful or unsuccessful. It is only by looking at the experience of specific groups in schools and elsewhere that we can conclude that language planning can be said to have solved communication problems or promoted social control. Language minority "language problems" have, for the most part, been defined by the majority and its institutions, and the absence of a minority voice in these institutions is a problem. Foremost among language-related cases in the United States that have found their way to the courts are *Meyer v. Nebraska* (1923), *Lau v. Nichols* (1974), and *Martin Luther King Jr. Elementary School Children v. Ann Arbor Board of Education* (1979). The Lau decision has received considerable attention in the literature (e.g., Crawford, 1991, 1992a, 1992b); therefore, attention here will be concentrated on the other two cases, which demonstrate the responses of U.S. courts to language policies and practices.

*Meyer v. Nebraska,* 262 U.S. 390 (1923), involved the attempt to restrict all forms of instruction in the United States to the English language. Meyer taught in a parochial school in Nebraska and used a German Bible history book as a text for reading. He was fined according to a 1919 Nebraska statute that forbade teaching in any language other than English. The Supreme Court decided that the Nebraska law was an unconstitutional violation of the due process clause of the Fourteenth Amendment by a 7 to 2 margin (Murphy, 1992, p. 543). The significant factor in this case, which regarded language rights in educational contexts, is that the court viewed its decision as a defense of other individual liberties. Language was important not in its own right but only in association with other liberties. Oliver Wendell Holmes's dissent was most telling in that he argued that all citizens of the United States should be required to speak a common tongue (Murphy, 1992). The Court's majority did not dispute that position; rather, it affirmed it: "The power of the state to compel attendance at some school and to make reasonable regulations for all schools, *including a requirement that they shall give instructions in English is not questioned*" (cited in Norgren & Nanda, 1988, p. 188, emphasis added; see also Crawford, 1992b).

What is particularly fascinating about this case is the social and political climate that preceded it. The World War I era and the first Red Scare period that followed it were marked by extremism and intolerance. The period from 1880 to 1920 experienced the highest levels of immigration (as a percentage of total population) of any period in the history of the United States. Nativism was in full force; there were recurring attempts to restrict immigration. The Americanization movement sought to promote the English language and social assimilation. Racial minorities, such as African-Americans, continued to be perennial targets of racism and discrimination. In 1917 the United States entered the war against Germany, and intolerance was pursued along linguistic lines as well. German was the second-most commonly spoken language in the United States. Its position was analogous to that of Spanish in the United States today. With the war, xenophobia reached its high-water mark with a frontal assault on all things German, especially the language. Across the country, communities banned German books and instruction. Edicts were passed against public use of German. In the Midwest alone, 18,000 citations were issued for language violations (Crawford, 1991), and an anti-German mob spirit took over in many communities (Luebke, 1980, pp. 9–10).

Where did educators stand in all of this? Luebke (1980) notes that "Many educators lent their authority to the war on German-language instruction in the schools" (p. 5). The attack on German was devastating, and German usage never recovered. Despite *Meyer,* the effect of a popular ideology, fanned by World War I, resulted in the removal of German from the school curriculum. If we were to concentrate only on formal policies in legal statutes, we could not explain how, in just 7 years, German language instruction in high schools went from a high in 1915 of 324,000 students to fewer than 14,000 students of German in 1922. Nor could we explain how, between 1915 and 1948, the percentage of high school students studying German had dropped from 25 percent to less than 1 percent (Leibowitz, 1971). To explain these events, a historical-structural analysis is necessary. Clearly, the fate of German in the United States illustrates that language teachers are not immune from the sociohistorical contexts in which they teach. Similarly, political upheavals in, for example, the former Soviet Union and former Yugoslavia have led to significant changes in official language policies that have also affected designated languages of instruction. Teachers in these societies have likewise not been unscathed by the linguistic reversals of fortune under their new governments.

In the United States since the early 1960s, controversy has surrounded the status of African-American varieties of language and the extent to which there is a need for specialized training for teachers of African-American children. Another hotly debated issue has been whether, and to what extent, they should receive formal instruction in African-American language (see Dillard, 1972). Adding to the controversy is the fact that many of the prescriptions for the education of African-American children have been put forth by white social scientists (e.g., Baratz, 1973; Stewart, 1964; Wolfram & Fasold, 1973), whose intentions and prescriptions have been severely criticized by some commentators (e.g., Sledd, 1969, 1973).[6]

African-American parents have been divided over issues involving language in education, but they have been united in a desire for their children to have access to quality education. In 1979, in Michigan, plaintiffs acting on behalf of African-American children sued the Ann Arbor Board of Education, under the Equal Opportunities Act, for failing to overcome language barriers which obstructed the equal participation of African-American students. The suit resulted in a landmark case, *Martin Luther King Jr. Elementary School Children v. Ann Arbor Board of Education* (henceforth referred to as *Ann Arbor*). One of the most complicated issues in the case dealt with whether African-American children should be given special educational treatment because their language variety was sufficiently different from standard English to pose a barrier to their educational progress (Crawford, 1992b; Norgren & Nanda, 1988). Linguists figured prominently in the case as expert witnesses. Central to the prosecution's case was the contention that the linguistic differences between African-American speech and standard English were significant enough to pose an instructional barrier, especially for basic reading instruction. Judge Joiner, who presided in the case, defined the plaintiff's position:

> This case is not an effort on the part of the plaintiffs to require that they be taught "black English," or that a dual language program be provided. . . . It is a straightforward effort to require the court to intervene on the children's behalf to require the defendant School District Board to take appropriate action to teach them to read in standard English of the school, the commercial world, the arts, the science and professions. This action is a cry for help in opening the doors to the establishment . . . to keep another generation from becoming functionally illiterate. (cited in Norgren & Nanda, 1988, p. 190)

Judge Joiner sided with the plaintiffs. Since the time of the decision, it is not clear that language differences among African-American children in the United States have been accommodated in any systematic way. Moreover, the decision bypassed the more controversial issue, which had been acrimoniously debated during the 1960s and early 1970s, of whether students should be taught in "black English." Nevertheless, applied linguists have continued to be involved in prescribing remedies for intervention in teacher education and in educational practice for African-American children in the wake of the decision (see Rickford, this volume; see also Whiteman, 1980). In recent years, there have again been sporadic calls for instruction in African-American lan-

6 See also O'Neil's (1973) criticism of bidialectal instruction, Shuy's (1980) reflection on the controversy during the 1960s and 1970s, Wolfram's (1994) recent reassessment, and Wiley's discussion (in press).

guage coming from some African-American linguists and educators (see Smith, 1993; S. Williams, 1991), and the issue remains controversial.

## *Issues of professional responsibility*

During the early 1980s, Labov (1982)[7] reviewed the role of linguists in *Ann Arbor* and raised important issues of professional responsibility that remain worthy of consideration by linguists and language teachers today. For social scientists, his primary question is: "How can we reconcile the objectivity we need for scientific research with the social commitment we need to apply our knowledge in the social world?" (p. 194; cf. Shuy, 1993, for a related discussion). For teachers, a similar question can be raised: How can we provide appropriate instruction for all our students, given both historical and contemporary inequities in the education of many language minority students? Labov (1982) offers four principles to guide professional involvement (and suggests a fifth, which is also given here):

The first is called the *principle of error correction*:

> A scientist who becomes aware of a widespread idea or social practice with important consequences that is invalidated by his own data is obligated to bring this error to the attention of the widest possible audience. (p. 172)

The second is the *principle of debt incurred*:

> An investigator who has obtained linguistic data from members of a speech community has an obligation to use the knowledge based on that data for the benefit of the community, when it has need of it. (p. 173)

The third is the *principle of linguistic democracy*:

> Linguists support the use of a standard dialect in so far as it is an instrument of wider communication for the general population, but oppose its use as a barrier to social mobility. (p. 186)

The fourth is the *principle of linguistic autonomy*:

> The choice of what language or dialect is to be used in a given domain of a speech community is reserved to members of that community. (p. 186)

In discussing how a consensus was formed in *Ann Arbor* among linguists regarding the uniqueness of the language spoken by African-Americans, Labov points to the importance of the entrance of black linguists into the field. This suggests a fifth principle:
The *principle of representation in the field*:

> Every field that is dominated by members of one group, who study and prescribe remedies for the "problems" of another, needs to ensure representation

7 Labov has also had his share of critics; again, see Sledd (1969, 1973) regarding Labov's earlier work.

> from the target group in order to guarantee that its voice and insights are not excluded and that assumptions and perspectives of the dominant group are not imposed on it.

This could also be stated as a principle that attempts to ensure the integrity of the field by means of opening it to multiple perspectives. Such a principle helps to avoid either the appearance or the actuality of imposing – even if unintentionally – the biases of the dominant group in the field upon others. Moreover, it allows the profession to begin to look more like (i.e., to be representative of) the people whose needs they are attempting to address. To support this principle is not to advocate a so-called quota system; rather, it is to acknowledge that it is always a good idea to include members of a target population when members of one group are attempting to educate or solve the problems of another.

With slight modification, Labov's principles appear to be equally relevant for language teachers. The principle of error correction might be modified as follows:

> Any language teacher who becomes aware of a widespread language in education policy or practice which has detrimental consequences for his or her students has an obligation to bring this policy or practice to the attention of appropriate audiences (e.g., colleagues, administrators, and parents).

The principle of debt incurred, as it applies to language teachers, could be modified as:

> Since students are teacher's clients, teachers have a responsibility to learn as much as possible about them regarding their linguistic, cultural, and class backgrounds in order to provide appropriate instruction.

The remaining principles need no modification, for they are equally relevant for linguistics and teachers alike.

Labov's principles provide a basis upon which to begin the dialogue on professional responsibility, but questions remain for both linguists and language teachers. In *Ann Arbor,* for example, the contribution of linguists was limited mostly to establishing the existence of a distinct variety of African-American language. The judge and the plaintiff steered clear of the controversial language planning and policy questions such as: Given the distinctiveness of African-American language, what should the language in education policies be? Should they involve only accommodation, as the court decreed? Or should they involve language enrichment policy, as some Afro-centrists have recently argued? In the years since *Ann Arbor,* how much has the educational achievement of African-Americans in the United States improved? Is the persistence of educational underachievement a result of the failure of a language accommodation policy, or is it the result of the failure to implement that policy? In terms of representation, how many African-

American language planners have entered the field since Labov made his observations? To what extent are these issues related to the persistence of more fundamental societal problems such as racism and lack of economic opportunity? (See Kozol, 1991, for a discussion of larger societal inequities which go well beyond those solely focused on language.)

## *Language policies and practices in institutional contexts*

In order to apply Labov's principles, it is useful to examine the institutional contexts in which policies are carried out. As noted earlier in this chapter, language policies can either be implicit or explicit. Many educational language policies tend to be implicit because they result more from institutional practices than official policies. Haas (1992) has examined such practices in terms of how they relate to institutional racism. *Institutional racism* refers to *systematic* institutional practices which have the effect of advantaging some groups and disadvantaging others – regardless of whether they were intended to do so. In an analysis of the state of Hawaii, he identifies a number of instances in institutional practices involving language which have adversely affected language minorities (both speakers of languages other than English and speakers of "nonstandard" varieties of English). For example, after 1924 a test of oral English was used to segregate nonstandard English–speaking children into separate schools from those with mainland (i.e., standard) accents. "Many of the brightest immigrant children went to nonstandard schools, whereas less intelligent native-English speaking students went to standard schools, so both standard and nonstandard schools enrolled students heterogeneous in abilities" according to other measures of aptitude (Haas, 1992, p. 191). In other words, language assessment was used to separate children largely on the basis of race. Haas notes that this practice was abolished only after many children of color acquired "mainland sounding accents" (p. 191). Among forty-four specific examples of institutional racism documented by Haas, six were related to institutional language policies. Although these referred specifically to the case of Hawaii, they are broadly applicable.

1. Insufficient use of minority languages in communicating with parents
2. Unequal grade distributions by race, ethnicity, or language background
3. Underidentification of students in need of language assistance
4. Underserving of students needing language assistance
5. Inappropriate staff composition to provide language assistance to LEP/NELP students

6. Discriminatory requirements for language certification (adapted from pp. 191–214)

Other practices, in addition to those identified by Haas, could be added to the list, for example:

7. Segregation into separate educational tracks based upon language background
8. Unequal access to core academic curricula based upon language background
9. Unequal expectations for success based upon language background
10. Failure to provide members of a speech community with a choice of the language or dialect of instruction

As discussed, several principles related to the professional responsibility of teachers are relevant to redressing these discriminatory institutional practices. For example, the principle of error correction applies to items 1 to 3 and 5 to 9, for these policies and practices need to be exposed and corrected. The principle of representation in the field relates to item 4. Item 10 involves the principle of linguistic autonomy.

Among the more persistent institutional practices that need scrutiny is the use of language tests as one of the primary means of sorting children into special language classifications. Such classifications result in segregated programs within otherwise integrated schools. In the United States, these include non-English proficient (NEP), limited English proficient (LEP), and fluent English proficient (FEP). Classifications such as these were intended to identify students so that they could receive appropriate educational treatment. Nevertheless, they are based solely on proficiency in the socially dominant language, English. Any other linguistic abilities that the children have are ignored (see Macías, 1993). Such language classifications can have the force of racial labeling or act as a surrogate for it (Wiley, in press). Related to this issue is the question of whether language minority children receive appropriate treatment once assessed, classified, and tracked. If appropriate instruction is being provided, why are many children initially classified as LEP, but subsequently reclassified as "learning disabled" several years later? (see Trueba, 1988; Trueba, Jacobs, & Kirton, 1990).

Fortunately, educational language planning can contribute to solving some of these problems when the principles of professional responsibility are used as a guide. Recommendations from the New Zealand Department of Education (1988; cited by Cummins, 1989, p. 61) provide examples of ways in which schools can incorporate minority languages and thereby elevate the status of those languages in the eyes of their speakers. Elevating the status of the students' native languages helps enhance their positive self-identity and promotes *additive bilin-*

*gualism* (oral and academic ability in two languages). The specific recommendations are to:

1. Reflect the various cultural groups in the school district by providing signs in the main office and elsewhere that welcome people in different languages
2. Encourage students to use their L1 (native language) around the school
3. Provide opportunities for students from the same ethnic group to communicate with one another in their L1 where possible (e.g., in cooperative learning groups on at least several occasions)
4. Recruit people who can tutor students in their L1
5. Provide books written in various languages in both classrooms and the school library
6. Incorporate greetings and information in the various languages in newsletters and other official school communications
7. Provide bilingual and/or multilingual signs
8. Display pictures and objects of the various cultures represented at the school
9. Create units of work that incorporate other languages in addition to the school language
10. Provide opportunities for students to study their L1 in elective subjects and/or in extracurricular clubs
11. Encourage parents to help in the classroom, library, playground, and clubs
12. Invite second language learners to use their L1 during assemblies, prize givings, and other official functions
13. Invite people from ethnic minority communities to act as resource people and to speak to students in both formal and informal settings

This list can be evaluated in terms of how it relates to principles of professional responsibility and to language policy and planning more generally. Items 1 and 2 involve the principle of debt incurred; items 4 and 13 relate to the principle of representation in the field; and all the items can be linked to the principle of linguistic democracy.

What can this list tell us about the New Zealand Department of Education's approach to language policy and planning more generally? First, note that some of these recommendations can be seen as institutional efforts as status planning by improving the visibility of minority languages and their speakers. Items 4, 5, 11, and 13 tend to improve language resources when there is a lack of materials and trained personnel, but in any case, they draw upon the linguistic and cultural resources of the language minority community by involving parents and other members of the community in the expanding language resources.

Despite their positive features, blanket recommendations such as these can rarely be implemented without an assessment of the local situation and negotiation with those affected; that is, information about the school and the community is needed before they can be implemented as policies. For example, the relationship between the language minority community and the school should be understood. To what extent does the school personnel reflect the community it serves? If there is a serious mismatch, is it because the language minority population has only recently arrived? Or has the population been there long enough so that the lack of representation in the schools signals that there are more fundamental historical inequities between the groups? Will the recommendations be negotiated with adequate representation from the surrounding community? Will all major constituencies have some voice in discussing these recommendations? Can some opposition be expected from more dominant groups? If they see the implementation of the recommendations as pandering to minorities, what is the best strategy to use in dealing with their fears or prejudices? Does the language minority community see these steps as solutions or as token gestures?

In the absence of any previous attempts to incorporate minority languages and cultures, these suggestions are positive steps to promote the status of previously ignored languages and cultures. They do not, however, elevate minority languages to positions of equality. To do this, other educational language plans such as two-way bilingual programs are more beneficial. Individual programs can be guided by a commitment to general principles involving language rights, by what we know about effective language minority instruction generally. Since local contexts vary, it is necessary to gather as much data as possible in collaboration with the members of the communities to be served. Because many countries have large numbers of both indigenous and immigrant language minorities, language in education planning must be adaptable to meet the needs of students within their school and community contexts (Edelsky & Hudelson, 1991) and must be based upon explicit, adequately funded policies that reflect both local and international varieties of language (see Stubbs, 1994).

## Conclusion

Promoting language change or language preservation is not merely a technical question of determining which language, when, and in what variety. Similarly, providing appropriate language instruction for all students involves more than assessment based upon the dominant language. How we view issues related to language change, language preservation, and language in education planning is influenced by (as Ruíz, 1984, and others have noted) whether we see language diversity as a problem or as a resource. When language diversity is seen as a problem, in the society as a whole and in its schools, minority languages tend to be suppressed, ignored, or, at best, accommodated. When language diversity is seen as a resource, minority languages are protected and nurtured. As applied linguists and language teachers, we can play a role in promoting such a view, or we can reinforce what Fishman (1980) called the "ethnicity versus the anti-ethnicity treadmill" (p. 544), in which language policies function as a "bar" rather than as a "door" (Hornberger, 1994b). As Labov (1982) recommends, a commitment to promoting languages and equitable education for language minorities is needed in teaching, given the persistence of social dominance and inequality.

## Suggestions for further reading

Corson, D. (1989). *Language policy across the curriculum.* Philadelphia, PA: Multilingual Matters.

This study surveys a broad range of topics related to language policy across the school curriculum. It details policymaking at the school site level and at the national level. Examples are provided from a variety of nations including Canada, Australia, New Zealand, and the former Soviet Union. The book addresses policy issues related to bilingual education and foreign language instruction. It also addresses social justice issues related to language policy.

Crawford, J. (1991). *Bilingual education: History, politics, theory, and practice* (2nd ed.). Los Angeles: Bilingual Education Series.

This introductory work is highly accessible for the new reader to the field; yet it is well documented and contains important background information that demonstrates the importance of the sociopolitical and sociohistorical contexts of language planning and policy formation related to bilingual education in the United States.

Crawford, J. (1992). *Hold your tongue: Bilingualism and the politics of "English only."* Reading, MA: Addison-Wesley.

This highly readable but mature work provides a critical history of the push behind the "English only" movement. It demonstrates the role of language strategists on both sides of the debate.

Leibowitz, A. H. (1971). *Educational policy and political acceptance: The imposition of English as the language of instruction in American schools.* ERIC ED 047 321.

This unpublished piece has largely been overlooked. It contains a major thesis regarding the reasons for the imposition of English as the language of instruction and the consequences for various language minority groups. This work is being reprinted in a collection of Leibowitz's work being prepared by the California State University at Long Beach and expected to appear in 1995.

Phillipson, R. (1992). *Linguistic imperialism.* Oxford: Oxford University Press.

This work investigates the dominance of English as a world language. It traces the ascendancy of English historically and its influence as a language of dominance in Third World countries. The book also analyzes the relationship between the English teaching profession and the dominance of English as a world language.

Tollefson, J. (1991). *Planning language, planning inequality: Language policy in the community*. New York: Longman.

Tollefson critiques the neoclassical orientation. He looks at language policies in several international contexts and at the ideologies promoting English as a world language. He provides practical examples and raises provocative ethical questions regarding the role of teachers in the language planning process.

## References

Anderson, B. (1991). *Imagined communities: Reflections on the origin and spread of nationalism*. London: Verso.

Baldauf, R. B., Jr. (1994). "Unplanned" language policy and planning. In W. Grabe (Ed.), *Annual Review of Applied Linguistics, 14,* 82–89. Cambridge University Press.

Baratz, J. C. (1973). Teaching reading in an urban Negro school system. In R. H. Bentley, & S. D. Crawford (Eds.), *Black language reader* (pp. 154–171). Glenview, IL: Scott Foresman.

Bright, W. (Ed.) (1992). *International encyclopedia of linguistics,* vols. 1–4. New York: Oxford University Press.

Bhatia, T. K. (1984). Literacy in monolingual societies. In R. B. Kaplan (Ed.). *Annual Review of Applied Linguistics, 1983* 23–38.

Brodkey, L. (1991). Tropics of literacy. In C. Mitchell & K. Weiler (Eds.), *Rewriting literacy: Culture and the discourse of the other* (pp. 161–168). New York: Bergin & Garvey.

Collins, J. (1991). Hegemonic practice: Literacy and standard language in public education. In C. Mitchell & K. Weiler (Eds.), *Rewriting literacy: Culture and the discourse of the other* (pp. 229–253). New York: Bergin & Garvey.

Collins, R. (1979). *The credential society: A historical sociology of education and stratification*. New York: Academic Press.

Cooper, R. L. (1989). *Language planning and social change*. Cambridge: Cambridge University Press.

Corson, D. (1989). *Language policy across the curriculum*. Philadelphia, PA: Multilingual Matters.

Coulmas, F. (1992). *Language and economy*. Oxford: Blackwell.

Coulmas, F. (1994). Language policy and planning: Political perspectives. In W. Grabe (Ed.) *Annual Review of Applied Linguistics, 14*:34–52. Cambridge University Press.

Crawford, J. (1991). *Bilingual education: History, politics, theory, and practice* (2nd ed.). Los Angeles: Bilingual Education Services.

Crawford, J. (1992a). *Hold your tongue: Bilingualism and the politics of "English only."* Reading, MA: Addison-Wesley.

Crawford, J. (1992b). *Language loyalties: A source book on the official English controversy*. Chicago: University of Chicago Press.

Crystal, D. (1987). *The Cambridge encyclopedia of language*. Cambridge: Cambridge University Press.

Cummins, J. (1981). The role of primary language development in promoting educational success for language minority students. In Office of Bilingual Education, California State Department of Education (Ed.), *Schooling and language minority students: A theoretical framework* (pp. 3–49). Los Angeles: Evaluation, Dissemination and Assessment Center, California State University at Los Angeles.

Cummins, J. (1984a). Wanted: A theoretical framework for relating language proficiency to academic achievement among bilingual students. In C. Rivera (Ed.), *Language proficiency and academic achievement* (pp. 2–19). Avon, England: Multilingual Matters.

Cummins, J. (1984b). Language proficiency and academic achievement revisited: A response. In C. Rivera (Ed.), *Language proficiency and academic achievement* (pp. 71–76). Avon, England: Multilingual Matters.

Cummins, J. (1985). *Bilingualism and special education: Issues in assessment and pedagogy*. San Diego, CA: College-Hill Press.

Cummins, J. (1989). *Empowering minority students*. Sacramento: California Association for Bilingual Education (CABE).

Dillard, J. L. (1972). *Black English: Its history and usage in the United States*. New York: Vintage/Random House.

Edelsky, C., & Hudelson, S. (1991). Contextual complexities: Written language policies for bilingual programs. In S. Benesch (Ed.), *ESL in America: Myths and possibilities* (pp. 75–90). Portsmouth, NH: Boyton/Cook, Heinemann.

Fairclough, N. (1989). *Language and power*. New York: Longman.

Fishman, J. A. (Ed.) (1966). *Language loyalty in the United States*. The Hague: Mouton.

Fishman, J. A. (Ed.) (1974). *Advances in language planning*. The Hague: Mouton.

Fishman, J. A. (1978). Positive bilingualism: Some overlooked rationales and forefathers. In J. E. Alatis (Ed.), *Georgetown University Roundtable on Languages and Linguistics,* Washington, DC: Georgetown University Press.

Fishman, J. A. (1980). Language maintenance. In S. T. Thernstrom, A. Orlov, & O. Handlin (Eds.), *Harvard encyclopedia of American ethnic groups* (pp. 629–638). Cambridge, MA: The Belknap Press of Harvard University Press.

Fishman, J. A. (1981). Language policy: Past, present, and future. In C. A. Ferguson & S. B. Heath (Eds.), *Language in the U.S.A.* (pp. 516–526). Cambridge: Cambridge University Press.

Fishman, J. A. (1991). *Reversing language shift: Theoretical and empirical foundations of assistance to threatened languages*. Philadelphia: Multilingual Matters.

Frank, F., & Anshen, F. (1983). *Language and the sexes*. Albany, NY: State University Press.

Galtung, J. (1980). *The true worlds. A transnational perspective*. New York: The Free Press.

Gibbons, J. (1991). Sociology of language. In W. Bright (Ed.), *International encyclopedia of linguistics* (vol. 4, pp. 22–25). New York: Oxford University Press.

Graff, H. J. (1979). *The literacy myth: Literacy and social structure in the nineteenth century city*. New York: Academic Press.

Graff, H. J. (1987). Illiteracy and criminality in the nineteenth century. In H. J. Graff (Ed.), *The labyrinths of literacy: Reflections on literacy past and present* (pp. 187–213). London: The Falmer Press.

Grillo, R. D. (1989). *Dominant languages: Language and hierarchy in Britain and France.* Cambridge: Cambridge University Press.

Haacke, W. (1994). Language policy and planning in Namibia. In W. Grabe (Ed.), *Annual Review of Applied Linguistics, 14,* 240–253. New York: Cambridge University Press.

Haas, M. (1992). *Institutional racism: The case of Hawai'i.* Westport, CN: Praeger.

Haugen, E. (1966). *Language conflict and language planning: The case of modern Norwegian.* Cambridge, MA: Harvard University Press.

Haugen, E. (1972/1962). Schizoglossia and the linguistic norm. In A. S. Dil (Selected), *The ecology of language: Essays by Einar Haugen* (pp. 148–189). Stanford, CA: Stanford University Press.

Haugen, E. (1972/1966). Linguistics and language planning. In A. S. Dil (Selected), *The ecology of language: Essays by Einar Haugen* (pp. 159–190.) Stanford, CA: Stanford University Press. Originally published in W. Bright (Ed.) (1966), *Sociolinguistics* (pp. 50–70). The Hague: Mouton.

Haugen, E. (1973/1992). The curse of Babel. In J. Crawford (Ed.), *Language loyalties: A source book on the official English controversy* (pp. 309–409). Chicago: University of Chicago Press. Reprinted from *Daedalus, 102* (Summer, 1973), 47–57.

Haugen, E. (1983). The implementation of corpus planning: Theory and practice. In J. Cobarrubias & J. A. Fishman (Eds.), *Progress in language planning* (pp. 269–289). The Hague: Mouton.

Heath, S. B. (1976). Colonial language status achievement: Mexico, Peru, and the United States. In A. Verdoodt & R. Kjolseth (Eds.), *Language and sociology.* Louvin: Peeters.

Hobsbawn, E. J. (1992). *Nations and nationalism since 1780: Programme, myth, reality* (2nd ed.). Cambridge: Cambridge University Press.

Hornberger, N. H. (1994a). Language policy and planning in South America. In W. Grabe (Ed.), *Annual Review of Applied Linguistics, 14,* 220–239. Cambridge University Press.

Hornberger, N. H. (1994b). Literacy and language planning. *Language and Education. 8:*(1–2), 75–86.

Illich, I. (1979). Vernacular values and education. *Teacher's College Record, 81*(1), 31–75.

Ingram, D. E. (1990). Language-in-education planning. In R. B. Kaplan (Ed.), *Annual Review of Applied Linguistics, 1989.* New York: Cambridge University Press.

Ingram, D. E. (1991). Language-in-education planning. In W. Bright (Ed.), *International encyclopedia of linguistics,* vol. 2, pp. 302–305. New York: Oxford University Press.

Jahr, E. H. (1992). Sociolinguistics: Minorities and sociolinguistics. In W. Bright (Ed.), *International encyclopedia of linguistics* (Vol. 4, pp. 12–15). New York: Oxford University Press.

Judd, E. (1991). Language-in-education policy and planning. In W. Grabe and R. Kaplan (Eds.), *Introduction to applied linguistics* (pp. 169–188). Reading, MA: Addison-Wesley.

Kaplan, R. B. (1991). Applied linguistics and language policy and planning. In

W. Grabe and R. Kaplan (Eds.), *Introduction to applied linguistics* (pp. 143–168). Reading, MA: Addison-Wesley.

Kaplan, R. B. (1994). Language policy and planning in New Zealand. In W. Grabe (Ed.), *Annual Review of Applied Linguistics, 14*:156–173. Cambridge University Press.

Kloss, H. (1969). *Research possibilities on group bilingualism: A report.* Quebec: International Center for Research on Bilingualism.

Kloss, H. (1971). Language rights of immigrant groups. *International Migration Review, 5*, 250–268.

Kloss, H. (1977). *The American bilingual tradition.* Rowley, MA: Newbury House.

Kozol, J. (1991). *Savage inequalities: Children in America's schools.* New York: Crown Publishers.

Labov, W. (1982). Objectivity and commitment in linguistic science: The case of the Black English trial in Ann Arbor. *Language in Society, 11*, 165–201.

Leibowitz, A. H. (1969). English literacy: Legal sanction for discrimination. *Notre Dame Lawyer, 25* (1), 7–66.

Leibowitz, A. H. (1971). *Educational policy and political acceptance: The imposition of English as the language of instruction in American schools.* ERIC No. ED 047 321.

Leibowitz, A. H. (1974, August). Language as a means of social control. Paper presented at the VIII World Congress of Sociology, University of Toronto, Toronto, Canada.

Leibowitz, A. H. (1980). *The Bilingual Education Act: A legislative analysis.* Rosslyn, VA: National Clearinghouse on Bilingual Education.

Leibowitz, A. H. (1982). *Federal recognition of the rights of minority language groups.* Rosslyn, VA: National Clearinghouse on Bilingual Education.

Leibowitz, A. H. (1984). The official character of language in the United States: Literacy requirements for citizenship, and entrance requirements into American life. *Aztlan, 15*(1), 25–70.

Lippi-Green, R. (1994). Accent, standard language ideology, and discriminatory pretext in courts. *Language in Society, 23*, 163–198.

Luebke, F. C. (1980). Legal restrictions on foreign languages in the Great Plains states, 1917–1923. In P. Schach (Ed.), *Languages in conflict: Linguistic acculturation on the Great Plains* (pp. 1–19). Lincoln: University of Nebraska Press.

Macías, R. F. (1979). Choice of language as a human right – Public policy implications in the United States. In R. V. Padilla (Ed.), *Bilingual education and public policy in the United States. Ethnoperspectives in bilingual education research* (Vol. 1, (pp. 39–75). Ypsilanti: Eastern Michigan University.

Macías, R. F. (1993, May). Language and ethnic classification of language minorities: Chicano and Latino students in the 1990s. *Hispanic Journal of Behavioral Sciences, 15*(2), 230–257.

McKay, S. L. (1993). *Agendas for second language literacy.* Cambridge: Cambridge University Press.

McKay, S. L., & Weinstein-Shr, G. (1993, Autumn). English literacy in the U.S.: National policies, personal consequences. *TESOL Quarterly, 27*(3), 399–419.

McKay, S. L., & Wong, S. C. (Eds.) (1988). *Language diversity: Resource or problem? A social and educational perspective on language minorities in the United States.* Cambridge: Newbury House.

Mullard, C. (1988). Racism, ethnicism and etharchy or not? The principles of progressive control and transformative change. In T. Skutnabb-Kangas & J. Cummins (Eds.), *Minority education: From shame to struggle* (pp. 359–378). London: Multilingual Matters.

Murphy, P. L. (1992). *Meyer v. Nebraska.* In K. L. Hall (Ed.), *The Oxford companion to the Supreme Court of the United States* (pp. 543–544). New York: Oxford University Press.

Norgren, J., & Nanda, S. (1988). *American cultural pluralism and the law* (Language, culture, and the courts, Chap. 10 pp. 185–199). New York: Praeger.

O'Neil, W. (1973). The politics of bidialectism. In R. H. Bentley & S. D. Crawford (Eds.), *Black language reader* (pp. 184–191). Glenview, IL: Scott Foresman.

Pattanayak, D. P. (1989). Monolingual myopia and the petals of the Indian lotus. In T. Skutnabb-Kangas & J. Cummins (Eds.), *Minority education: From shame to struggle* (pp. 379–389). London: Multilingual Matters.

Patthey-Chavez, G. G. (1994). Language policy and planning in Mexico: Indigenous language policy. In W. Grabe (Ed.), *Annual Review of Applied Linguistics, 14,* 200–219. Cambridge University Press.

Paulston, C. B., & McLaughlin, S. (1994). Language-in-education policy and planning. In W. Grabe (Ed.), *Annual Review of Applied Linguistics, 14,* 53–81. Cambridge University Press.

Phillipson, R. (1988). Linguicism: Structures and ideologies in linguistic imperialism. In T. Skutnabb-Kangas & J. Cummins (Eds.), *Minority education: From shame to struggle* (pp. 339–358). London: Multilingual Matters.

Phillipson, R. (1992). *Linguistic imperialism.* Oxford: Oxford University Press.

Ray, S. R. (1968). Language standardization. In J. A. Fishman (Ed.), *Readings in the sociology of language* (pp. 754–765). New York: Mouton.

Roberts, C., Davis, E., & Jupp, T. (1992). *Language and discrimination: A study of communication in multi-ethnic workplaces.* New York: Longman.

Roy, J. D. (1987). The linguistic and sociolinguistic position of black English and the issue of bidialectism in education. In P. Homel, M. Palij, & D. Aaronson (Eds.), *Childhood bilingualism: Aspects of linguistic, cognitive, and social development* (pp. 231–242). Hillsdale, NJ: Lawrence Erlbaum Associates.

Ruíz, R. (1984). Orientations in language planning. *NABE Journal, 8*(2), 15–34.

Shuy, R. (1980). Vernacular Black English: Setting the issues in time. In M. Farr Whiteman (Ed.), *Reactions to Ann Arbor: Vernacular Black English and education* (pp. 1–9). Arlington, VA: Center for Applied Linguistics.

Shuy, R. (1993). *Language crimes: The use and abuse of language evidence in the courtroom.* Oxford: Blackwell.

Simon, P. (1988). *The tongue-tied American: Confronting the foreign language crisis* (2nd ed.). New York: Continuum.

Sledd, J. (1969). Bi-dialectism: The linguistics of white supremacy. *English Journal, 58,* 1307–1315, 1329.

Sledd, J. (1973). Doublespeak: Dialectology in the service of Big Brother. In

R. H. Bentley & S. D. Crawford (Eds.), *Black language reader* (pp. 191–214). Glenview, IL: Scott Foresman.

Smith, E. A. (1993). The black child in the schools: Ebonics and its implications for the transformation of American education. In Antonia Darder (Ed.), *Bicultural studies in education: The struggle for educational justice* (pp. 58–76). Claremont, CA: Institute for Education in Transformation, the Claremont Graduate School.

Stewart, W. (1964). Foreign language teaching methods in quasi-foreign language situations. In W. (Ed.), *Non-standard speech and the teaching of English.* Washington, DC: Center for Applied Linguistics.

Street, B. (1984). *Literacy in theory and practice.* Cambridge: Cambridge University Press.

Street, B. V. (Ed.) (1993). *Cross-cultural approaches to literacy.* Cambridge: Cambridge University Press.

Stubbs, M. (1994). Educational language planning in England and Wales: Multicultural rhetoric and assimilationist assumptions. In J. Maybin (Ed.), *Language and literacy in social practice* (pp. 193–214). Philadelphia, PA: Multilingual Matters and the Open University.

Tollefson, J. W. (1981). Centralized and decentralized language planning. *Language Problems and Language Planning, 5,* 175–188.

Tollefson, J. W. (1991). *Planning language, planning inequality: Language policy in the community.* New York: Longman.

Trueba, H. T. (1988). English literacy acquisition: From cultural trauma to learning disabilities in minority students. *Linguistics and Education, 1,* 125–152.

Trueba, H. T., Jacobs, L., & Kirton, E. (1990). *Cultural conflict and adaptation: The case of Hmong children in American society.* New York: The Falmer Press.

Tucker, G. R. (1994). Concluding thoughts: Language planning issues for the coming decade. In W. Grabe (Ed.), *Annual Review of Applied Linguistics, 14,* 277–286. New York: Cambridge University Press.

Vargas, A. (1986). Illiteracy in the Hispanic community. Washington, DC: National Council of La Raza.

Veltman, F. (1983). *Language shift in the United States.* Berlin: Mouton.

Weinberg, M. (1990a). *A chance to learn: A history of race and education in the United States.* Cambridge: Cambridge University Press.

Weinberg, M. (1990b). *Racism in the United States.* West Port, CT: Greenwood Press.

Weinstein, B. (1979). Language strategists: Redefining political frontiers on the basis of linguistic choices. *World Politics, 31*(3) 344–364.

Weinstein, B. (1983). *The civic tongue: Political consequences of language choices.* New York: Longman.

Whiteman, M. Farr (Ed.) (1980). *Reactions to Ann Arbor: Vernacular Black English and education.* Arlington, VA: Center for Applied Linguistics.

Wiley, T. G. (1986). The significance of language and cultural barriers for the Euro-American elderly. In C. L. Hayes, R. A. Kalish, & D. Guttman (Eds.), *European-American elderly: A guide for practice* (pp. 35–50). New York: Springer.

Wiley, T. (1990–1991). Disembedding Chicano literacy: The need for a group-specific focus on adult literacy. *Journal of the School of Education, CSU Stanislaus, 8*(1), 49–54.

Wiley, T. G. (1993, Autumn). Discussion of Klassen & Burnaby and McKay & Weinstein-Shr: Beyond assimilationist literacy policies. *TESOL Quarterly, 27*(3):421–430.

Wiley, T. G. (in press). *Literacy and language diversity in the United States. Language in Education: Theory and Practice.* McHerny, IL: Center for Applied Linguistics and Delta Systems.

Williams, G. (1992). *Sociolinguistics: A sociological critique.* London: Routledge.

Williams, S. W. (1991). Classroom use of African American language: Educational tool or social weapon? In C. E. Sleeter (Ed.), *Empowerment through multicultural education* (pp. 199–215). New York: SUNY Press.

Wolfram, W. (1994). Bidialectal literacy in the United States. In D. Spener (Ed.), *Adult Biliteracy in the United States* (pp. 71–88). *Language in Education: Theory and Practice, 83.* McHerny, IL: Center for Applied Linguistics and Delta Systems.

Wolfram, W., & Fasold, R. W. (1973). Toward reading materials for speakers of Black English: Three linguistically appropriate passages. In R. H. Bentley & S. D. Crawford (Eds.), *Black language reader* (pp. 172–184). Glenview, IL: Scott Foresman.

Wolfram, W., & Fasold, R. W. (1974). *The study of social dialects in American English.* Englewood Cliffs, NJ: Prentice Hall.

# PART II: LANGUAGE AND VARIATION

The chapters in this part, which focus on how the larger social context affects an individual's use of particular linguistic forms, illustrate a macrolevel of social analysis and a microlevel of linguistic analysis. The authors of Part II demonstrate how geographical location, ethnic background, social class, and gender can all influence an individual's use of particular phonological, structural, lexical, and discourse features of English. At the same time, the chapters illustrate how these linguistic features can serve to define speech communities and perpetuate existing social relationships. Taken together, the next three chapters exemplify the tremendous variation that can exist in the use of English in Anglophone countries.

In Chapter 5, John Rickford examines how geographical region, social class, and ethnic background can affect the linguistic features an individual uses. To begin, Rickford discusses typical methods for studying regional variation and points out the reasons for the development of regional dialects, including geography, settlement patterns, and migration routes. He goes on to define such terms as *dialect areas, isoglosses,* and *relic areas.* This discussion is followed by an examination of language variation due to age and social class and network in which Rickford introduces such concepts as age grading, the principle of accountability, and sociolinguistic markers and indicators. Finally, he discusses the manner in which race and ethnicity can influence language use and summarizes the major phonological and grammatical features of African-American Vernacular English. Throughout the chapter, Rickford notes the implications of regional, social, and ethnic linguistic variation for the classroom language teacher.

In the second chapter, "Pidgins and Creoles," Patricia Nichols discusses how new language varieties can be created out of existing languages and what this means for individuals who speak these varieties. The chapter opens with a summary of typical attitudes toward pidgins and creoles and a discussion of their origins and development. Next, Nichols describes typical research approaches to pidgins and creoles, emphasizing the theoretical and methodological limitations of this research that arise, for example, from studying these varieties in isolation rather than comparatively. She also examines the structure and function of creoles, using Gullah as the basis for this review. The chapter ends with a discussion of the ways in which classroom teachers can use pidgins and creoles as a resource in the classroom and with a call for more study on the discourse-level characteristics of pidgins and creoles.

In the final chapter of this part, "Language and Gender," Rebecca Freeman and Bonnie McElhinny discuss how the use of gender-differentiated language both reflects and can help to perpetuate the subordinate status of women in society. A central goal of the chapter is to increase awareness of how language shapes our understanding of the social world, our relationships with one another, and our social identities. Freeman and McElhinny begin the chapter by discussing sexism in language and suggesting alternatives to sexist practices in naming and representation. Next, they examine two prevalent models for approaching gender-differentiated language: the dominance model, which stresses men's dominance over women, and the difference, or dual-culture model, which stresses men's and women's cultural differences. In place of these models, the authors argue for highly contextualized and localized studies of interaction, and they review several studies which exemplify such an approach. The authors then examine language and gender around the world, looking specifically at language and gender as they relate to genre, multilingualism, politics, the ESL context, and cultures in the United States. The chapter ends with an examination of language and gender in the classroom in which the authors encourage teachers to incorporate the methods of ethnography of communication in their classroom and to promote critical discourse analysis.

# 5 *Regional and social variation*

John R. Rickford

## Introduction

"In the United States of America (or England, or India, or Australia), they speak English." Although this statement is true, it is only a half truth, and understanding the other half of the truth is essential for any language arts teacher. Part of what this statement omits is that other languages besides English are spoken – Spanish, Gujerati, and Vietnamese, for instance – and that students' competence in and attitudes toward these languages, relative to English, can have a big impact on their success in and attitudes toward school. But part of what it omits is also that "English" is not a single entity but, like any other living language, something that varies considerably depending on one's regional background, social class and network, ethnicity, gender, age, and style, to name only the most salient dimensions. Understanding and recognizing such variation is essential for language arts and second and foreign language teachers.

### *Reasons for studying dialects*

But "Why?" you might ask. One reason is to better prepare our students for the vernacular varieties of a foreign language which they can expect to find its native speakers using if and when they have the opportunity to travel abroad. Understanding the variability in our own language and that of our students is also very important for L1 and L2 teachers, because the regional and social dialects that teachers and children speak can have a big impact on students' success at school (see also Nichols, this volume). For instance, if a teacher and student come from different dialect backgrounds, a teacher might have trouble understanding what

It is a pleasure to thank the following individuals for their assistance with this chapter: Renée Blake, Sandra Lee McKay, Geneviève Broderson, Nancy Hornberger, Angela E. Rickford, and Keith Walters. Responsibility for any errors or infelicities is, of course, my own.

a student says, or vice versa. Or a teacher might try to model the pronunciation of a certain vowel by saying that it is similar to the vowel in a model word which turns out to be quite different in the child's dialect. For instance, if the teacher pronounces *bite* with a diphthongal [*ai*], and the student pronounces it with a long monophthongal [*a*:], the child might keep producing [*ba:t*] while trying to imitate the teacher's [*bait*] and might never learn the model pronunciation through this putative model word. Or a teacher might be under the mistaken impression that a student who reads *John walks home* as *John walk home* had failed to see and register the semantic significance of the third present *-s* suffix; the student, however, might have read and understood it perfectly but converted the sentence to the regularities of her native variety of African-American Vernacular English (AAVE) in reproducing it for her teacher. Similarly, an intelligence test which included items involving third present *-s* might discriminate against English dialect speakers whose dialects systematically omitted this form. Finally, both teachers and students could have negative attitudes toward each other depending on the dialects they speak, with those attitudes in turn affecting their ability to work effectively with each other and ultimately limiting their performance as teachers and learners (see McGroarty, this volume).[1]

On the positive side, an increased awareness of regional and social variation can significantly enhance teachers' and students' mutual understanding and appreciation, and can offer teachers additional tools with which to enhance their students' appreciation of literature, their ability to write and use a variety of styles, and their sensitivity to the diversity and richness of the speech communities in which their languages are used.

## *Quiz*

Let us try a brief quiz, involving American English, to illustrate the concepts of regional and social variation, and the challenges they can pose for communication:

1 For the relationship between dialect usage, teachers' attitudes and expectations, and pupils' performance, see Rosenthal and Jacobson, 1968 (which helped to establish the correlation between teachers' expectations and pupils' performance), Williams, 1970 (which reported that pupils perceived as speaking in less standard English were also perceived as being less confident and eager), and Smitherman, 1981 (p. 19, reporting Justice Joiner's opinion in the 1979 case of *Martin Luther King Jr. Elementary School Children v. Ann Arbor Board of Education* that negative attitudes toward African-American Vernacular English had served as a barrier to the equal educational opportunity of AAVE-speaking children).

1. Frank: How is Bob?
   Mary: Bob worries a lot *anymore.*
   What do you think Mary meant? (a) Bob doesn't worry a lot anymore; (b) Bob still worries a lot; (c) Bob worries a lot nowadays; (d) Other: ________.
2. Tabitha: Is she married?
   Jamal: She *BIN* married. (*BIN* is emphatic, heavily stressed)
   What do you think Jamal meant? (a) She's been married before but isn't now; (b) She's married now and has been for a long time; (c) Other: ________.

Among speakers of Mary's Midwestern dialect, the positive *anymore* in example 1 conventionally means "nowadays," indicating that a situation that did not exist in the past now does, but many speakers from other dialect areas think that it means "still" – that a situation that existed in the past still does (Labov, 1973, pp. 65–76). For Jamal, and for other speakers of AAVE, the stressed *BIN* in example 2 has the interpretation of item (b), but speakers unfamiliar with AAVE typically give item (a) as their answer (Labov, 1973, pp. 62–65; Rickford, 1975).[2] Although example (1) shows regional variation and example (2) shows social variation, in both cases the answers offered by speakers unfamiliar with the dialect are quite different from what the speaker intended. Note, too, that although these examples, like many others in this chapter, are from varieties of English in the United States, the comments here apply to other countries and to other languages. Language teachers in non-English and non-American situations will undoubtedly be able to supply comparable examples from their own classrooms and communities. Discovering and discussing such examples should present excellent opportunities for research and pedagogy.

## *Preliminaries*

Three other general points remain to be made before regional and social variation is considered in more detail. The first is that when we speak of *accents* (as distinct from *varieties* or *dialects*), we are referring to features of pronunciation alone – the phones, or individual sound segments in a word, as well as suprasegmental features like accent, tempo, and intonation. The second is that dialects can differ not only *qualitatively* – in the fact that dialect A has feature *X* whereas dialect B

2 Note that understanding and use of *BIN* is not limited to working-class African-Americans. One African-American judge whom I interviewed in Philadelphia was surprised to discover that he was immediately distinguished from his European-American friends by his ability to provide the correct remote phase interpretation to example 2 in the quiz.

has feature *Y* – but also *quantitatively* – in the sense that although both dialects A and B use features *X* and *Y*, feature *X* is used significantly more often in dialect A than in dialect B. Quantitative variation is particularly important in differentiating social dialects, and we will return to this issue when we consider social variation. The third general point to be made is that, contrary to popular perception, dialect differences are usually regular and systematic and should not be regarded as the result of carelessness, laziness, and so on. Although some dialects may command more prestige than others in some circles, they do so usually as the result of external social and political factors. The dialects themselves are natural outgrowths of differences in history, geography, and social interaction. As linguists use the term, there is no negative connotation to *dialect,* which is simply a neutral word describing a variety of a language used by a particular set of people. Everyone speaks a dialect – at least one.

## Regional variation

The study of *regional dialects* – varieties of a language which are spoken in different geographical areas – is among the oldest traditions in the systematic study of intralanguage variation; its roots are in the study of nineteenth-century historical-comparative linguistics. In 1876, in order to corroborate the neogrammarian claim that sound laws operate without exception – for example, that a change from [p] to [f] will occur in *every word* which originally contained a [p] – George Wenker began mailing a dialect questionnaire to thousands of schoolmasters in the north of Germany. As it turned out, Wenker's findings revealed more variability in pronunciation than the neogrammarians predicted (see Chambers & Trudgill, 1980, pp. 37–38, 174 ff.; Davis, 1983, p. 18, for further discussion). However, interest in the systematic study of regional dialects had taken root, and in subsequent years regional dialect surveys were undertaken in a number of countries. In 1896 Jules Gilliéron sent a trained field-worker (Edmond Edmont) into different parts of France to complete dialect questionnaires in person, rather than depending on mailed responses from correspondents whose accuracy in hearing and recording dialect features was unknown. This fieldwork method was basically the one used in later dialect surveys of other countries, including Italy and southern Switzerland (Jaberg & Jud, 1928–1940) and the United States (Cassidy, 1985; Kurath et al., 1939–1943), although in the United States, because of its geographical size, dialect surveys required the use of many field-workers rather than one or two. Cassidy's *Dictionary of American Regional English,* for example, drew on the usage of 2,777 informants from 1,002 communities, who were interviewed by 72 field-workers (Cassidy, 1985, pp. v, xii, xiv).

## *Methods*

If you were to attempt to carry out a regional dialect survey in your classroom or community (assuming that the people therein came from different regions), you would soon run into some of the methodological problems which the earliest dialect geographers faced. For instance, in attempting to elicit a local word or pronunciation, you might simply give what you think is the most general or standard equivalent and ask your respondents how they say it in their dialect, for example:

3. How do you refer to *cottage cheese* in your dialect? Do you have a special word for it?

The advantage of this *direct* method, the one used by Wenker and Edmont, is its expeditiousness. Its disadvantage, however, is that the form used as a prompt might influence the informants' response, causing them to give a different word or pronunciation than they would normally employ. Accordingly, it is more common to use a variant of the *indirect* approach, adopted by Jaberg and Jud and most subsequent dialectologists. For instance, you might ask informants to name an item (cottage cheese) on the basis of a picture or a verbal description, as in:

4. Lumpy white cheese . . . made from sour milk . . . (Cassidy, 1985, p. 883)

Another issue which might arise in your community study is what kinds of informants to select for your survey. One strategy that many dialect surveys in the United States and Europe have used is to select older people who were born and raised in the community and have not moved around much. This makes sense from the point of view of trying to capture distinctive local traditions, but other aspects of much regional dialect research – overrepresenting male respondents, underrepresenting modern (as opposed to traditional) usage, and not making use of socioeconomically stratified random samples – have been the subject of sharp criticism (see Chambers & Trudgill, 1980, pp. 24–36; Pickford, 1956).

## *Dialect maps and isoglosses*

Assuming that you avoided the pitfalls of informant selection and succeeded in conducting a revealing dialect survey, the next issue would be how to display your results. One way would be to list the different

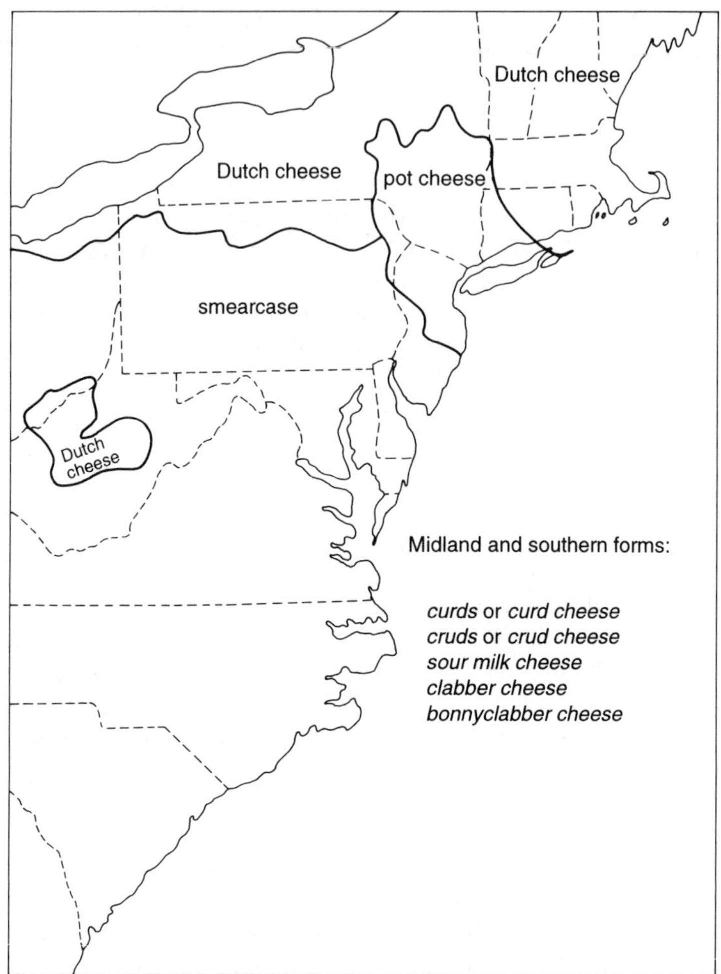


*Figure 1. (In Reed, 1977, p. 99; from Kurath, 1949.)*

responses you received, with an indication of where they seemed to be most prevalent. But a more graphic way of showing the results would be to chart the distribution of the variants on a dialect atlas or map, as Reed (1977, p. 99; drawing on data in Kurath, 1949, Fig. 125) did for the northeastern variants of *cottage cheese* in the United States (see Figure 1). The lines separating the areas in which each variant is used (*Dutch cheese, pot cheese* and *smearcase*) are called *isoglosses* (see Chambers & Trudgill, 1980, p. 103, for further discussion of this term).

A related way of displaying your results (usually, in fact, as a prelimi-

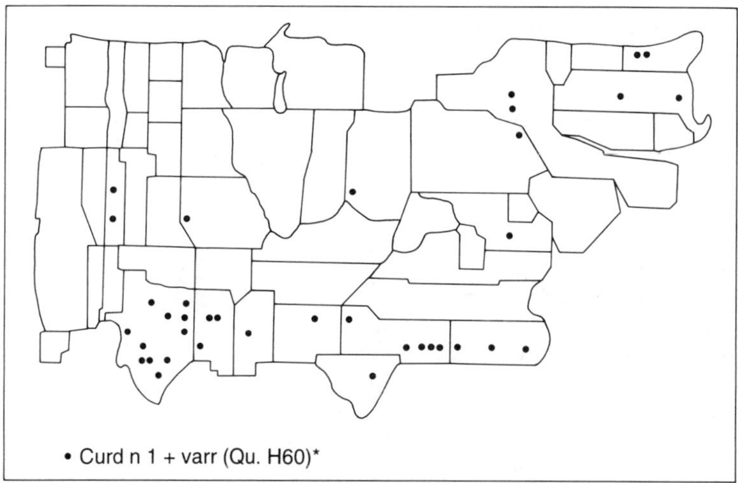


*The dots indicate the location of informants who gave *curd* or its variants (*curds, curd cheese*) in response to question H60 on the DARE questionnaire: "[What do you call] the lumpy white cheese that is made from sour milk?"

*Figure 2. (From Cassidy, 1985.)*

nary to drawing isoglosses) is to use a symbol for every location on a map in which a certain variant was attested, as in Figure 2 (from Cassidy, 1985, p. 883), which shows where in the United States the noun *curd,* "freq. pl, also *curd cheese,*" was offered in response to the description in example 4.[3] The distribution here is primarily southern, providing partial confirmation for the indication in Figure 1 (from research nearly five decades earlier) that *curds* and *curd cheese* are "midland and southern forms."

## Dialect areas

When different isoglosses bundle or run together, they may be taken to define a *dialect area.* In Figure 3, for instance (from Kurath, 1949, Fig. 42), the isoglosses separate the northern dialect area, in which *pail, faucet, skunk,* and *merry Christmas!* are used, from the Midland and South dialect areas, in which *bucket, spicket, polecat,* and *Christmas gift!* are used, respectively. Figure 4 (from Kurath, 1949, Fig. 3) further separates the North, Midland, and South dialect areas of the eastern United States, and their subdivisions, without indicating the specific

3 The DARE maps of the United States differ from conventional maps because they display population density rather than land area (Carver, 1985, p. xxiii).

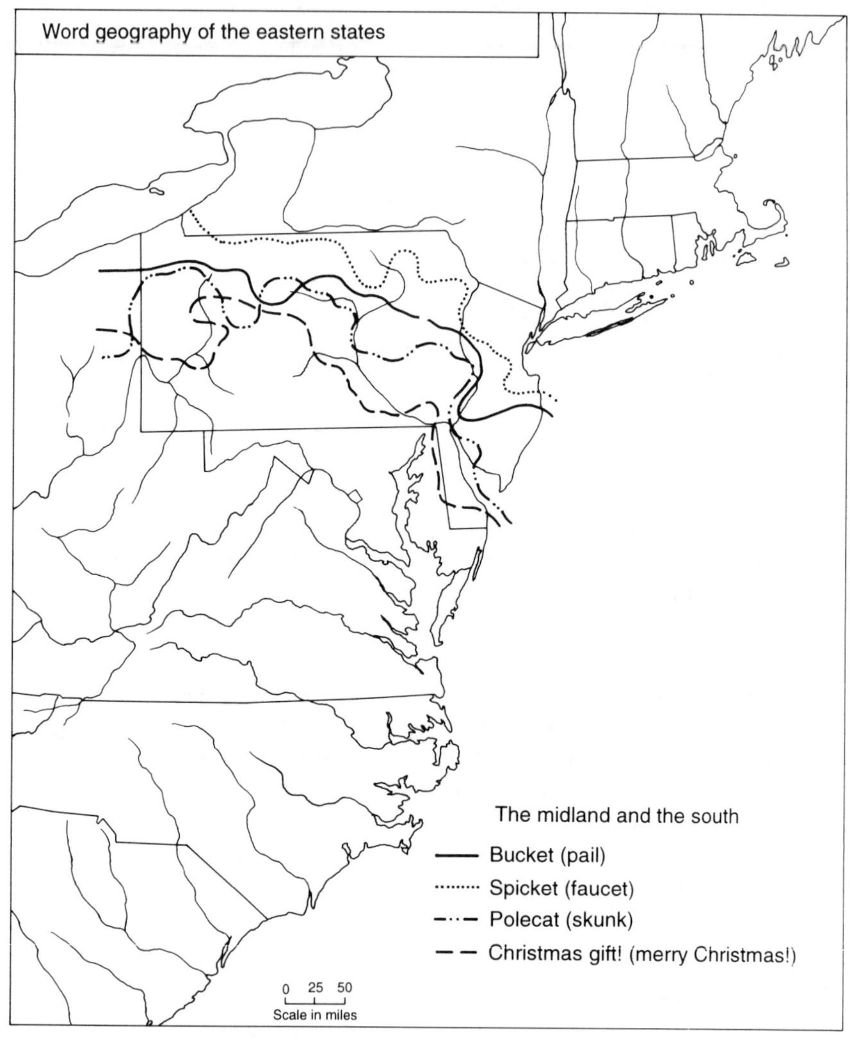


*Figure 3. (From Kurath, 1949.)*

features (primarily lexical; Reed, 1977, p. 23) upon which the divisions are based.

## *Phonological isoglosses*

All the isoglosses discussed so far involve lexical features, or words. But dialects can be distinguished by their phonological features or

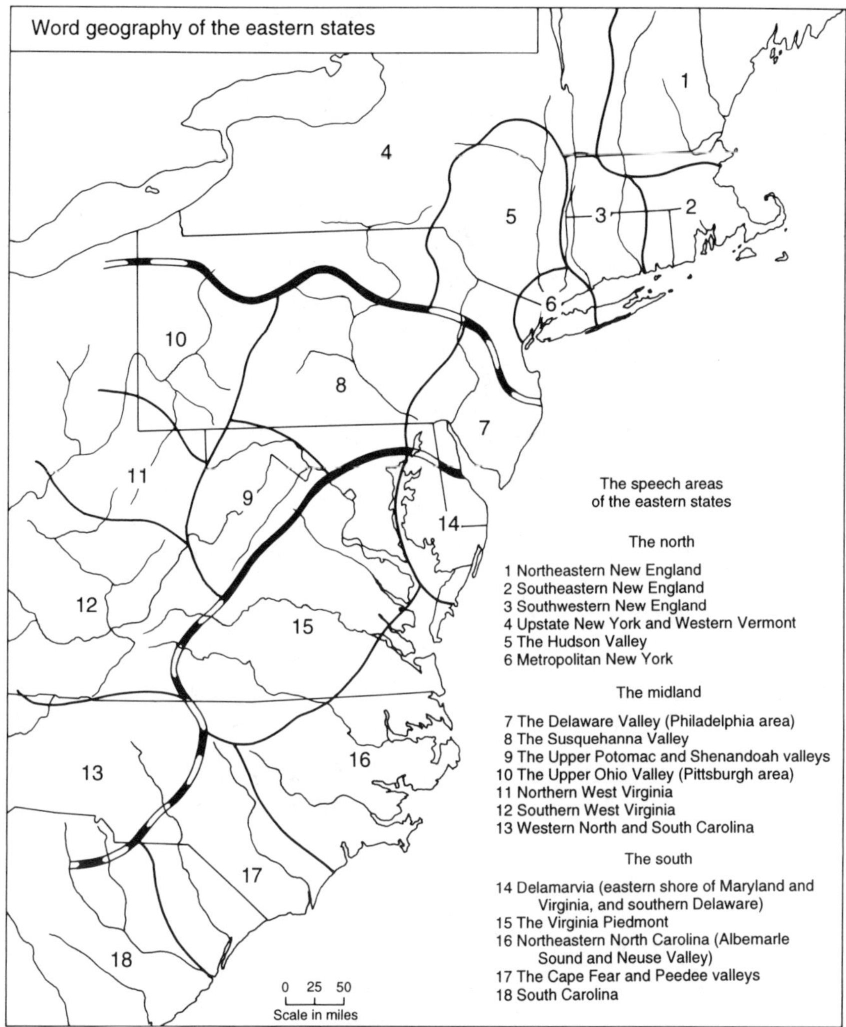


*Figure 4. (From Kurath, 1949.)*

pronunciations too. Figure 5 shows the distribution of postvocalic /r/ – the pronunciation of /r/ after a vowel, as in *bark* – in Britain. Speakers in the areas labeled A – including Ireland, Scotland, southwestern England, and a small area near Liverpool – pronounce their /r/s in this position, but speakers in the B area – basically the rest of England and Wales, including the city of London – do not. As Chambers and Trudgill (1980, p. 10) note, the discontinuous distribution of the *r*-

*Figure 5. (From Hughes & Trudgill, 1979.)*

pronouncing areas indicates that these are *relic areas* – remnants of an earlier time when *r*-pronunciation was more widespread; subsequently this usage was displaced by an *r*-less innovation. Interestingly, in the prestigious Received Pronunciation (RP) of those in "the upper reaches of the social scale" (Hughes & Trudgill, 1979, p. 2), the *r*-less pronunciation is the norm, in contrast with New York City English, in which *r*-lessness is most characteristic of the lower and working classes (Labov,

1966, p. 240). This is an excellent illustration of the sociolinguistic generalization that linguistic features do not have social significance in and of themselves but only in terms of the social groups that use them. In England, it is prestigious to "drop your *r*'s"; in New York City, it is not.

## *Combinations of features*

Of course, dialect areas are often distinguished not just by lexical isoglosses or by phonological ones but by combinations of lexical, phonological, and grammatical features. For instance, the Wallon (Wal-

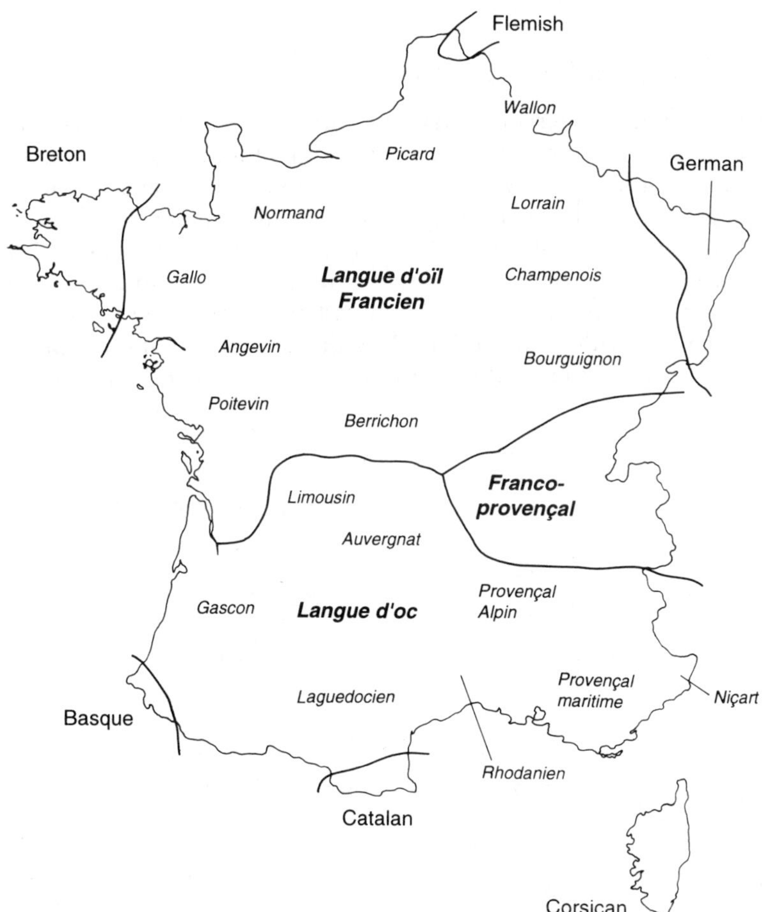


*Figure 6. French regional languages and dialects. (From Ager, 1990.)*

loon) dialect in the northeast of France – adjacent to Belgium and part of the larger *Langue d'oïl* region (see Figure 6) – is distinguished from standard French by the following features, among others (Ager, 1990, p. 20):

5. Pronunciation: The /r/ is pronounced gutturally

   Lexis: The numerals *septante and nonante* correspond to French *soixante-dix* ("seventy") *quatre-vingts* ("eighty")

   Syntax: *Avoir* is followed by an adjective as in *avoir bon de faire quelquechose* (or *facile, difficile, dur,* etc.), in the sense of *trouver bon de faire quelquechose* ("find it good to do something," or easy, difficult, hard, etc.)

## *Why do regional dialects arise?*

Regional dialect differences arise for various reasons. One factor is the influence of geography itself. A river, a mountain range, or an expanse of barren land can serve to keep two populations apart, and since languages are constantly undergoing change (although we seldom notice it happening), the dialects of the two separated populations will, over time, drift apart. Conversely, a river can help to spread an innovative feature, if populations up and down its banks are in contact with each other. This is evident in the East Middle German situation depicted in Figure 7, where the southern form *hinten,* "behind," has made its

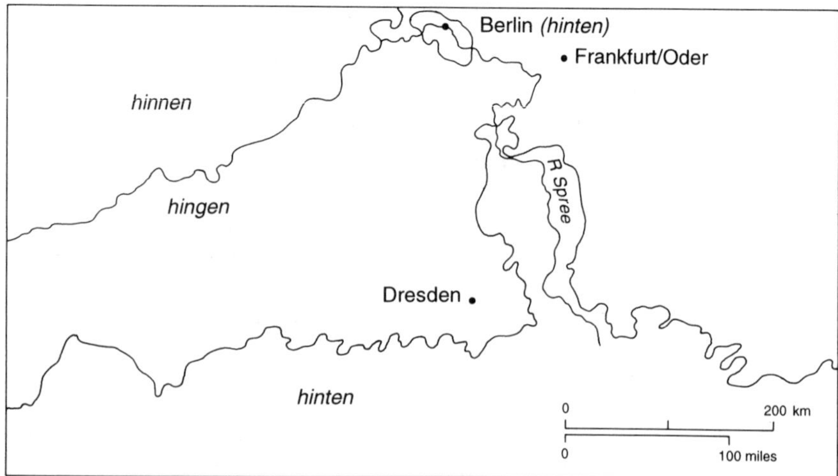


*Figure 7. Variants of* hinten *in East Middle German. (From Barbour & Stevenson, 1990.)*

greatest penetration into *hingen* territory along the course of the river Spree (Barbour & Stevenson, 1990, p. 71). Moreover, in accord with a pattern of urban diffusion to which Peter Trudgill has most forcefully drawn our attention (see Chambers & Trudgill, 1980, p. 189 ff.), the innovation has already jumped ahead to the urban center of Berlin.

Other factors besides geography that help to create regional dialects include political boundaries, settlement patterns, migration and immigration routes, territorial conquest, and language contact. (See Davis, 1983, pp. 4–5; Wolfram, 1991, pp. 22–26, for further discussion.) In Texas, for instance, contact with Louisiana French in the eastern part of the state has led to loans like *jambalaya,* "rice stew," and *bayou,* "inlet," and contact with Mexican Spanish along the southern border has yielded loans like *mesa,* "dry plateau," and *lariat,* "rope with a noose" (Reed, 1977, p. 52).

Contrary to what many people might think, television has not been a significant force in spreading dialect patterns or obliterating dialect differences, particularly in the more highly structured domains of phonology and grammar (see Trudgill, 1983, p. 61). This appears to be because television is a noninteractive medium; watchers do not talk back to it and get judged or responded to on the basis of their dialect use, as they do in face-to-face verbal interaction.

## *Classroom implications and exercises involving regional dialects*

Teachers of foreign languages might try to do some research on regional dialect differences in the countries where the languages they are teaching are spoken, partly as a way of preparing students for the regional vernaculars they are likely to encounter if they visit the countries themselves and partly as a way of enriching their students' classroom experience (allowing them to move away from the class text for a while, making them more sensitive to the ubiquity of variation in language more generally, and so on). For L1 and L2 teachers (e.g., teachers of English as a native or second language in the United States), regional differences in phonology and grammar are more likely to be a challenge in the classroom than are differences in lexicon or word use. If, for instance, a child uses *jambalaya,* a Louisiana word meaning "spicy rice stew," teachers who are unfamiliar with it are likely to notice it and ask what it means, and they may be quite willing to accept such regionalisms in writing for the local color they convey. But the mergers and near mergers of vowels produced by the kinds of *chain shifts* (sequenced changes in a set of vowels) which are currently taking place in the United States might be more problematic. Figure 8 (from Wolfram,

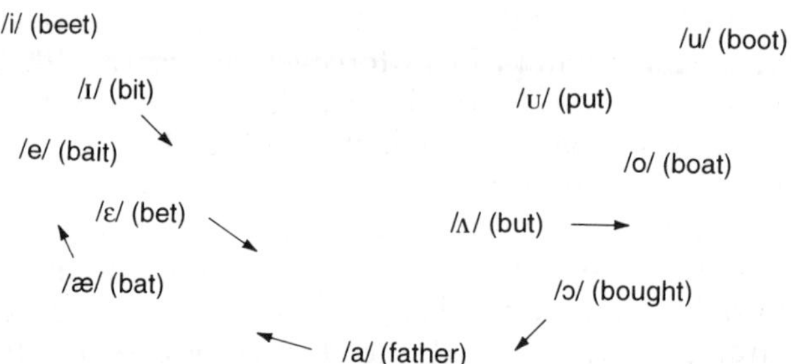


*Figure 8. Vowel rotation in northern cities chain shift. (From Wolfram 1991; based on Labov, 1991.)*

1991, p. 87, based on Labov, 1991, p. 25) shows the northern cities chain shift that is taking place in cities like Buffalo, Cleveland, Detroit, and Chicago; for teachers not from these areas, a student's pronunciation of *bat* might be mistaken for *bet,* and his or her pronunciation of *bet* for *but.* Labov and colleagues at the University of Pennsylvania (see Labov, 1988) have begun to investigate the effects of these vowel differences on oral comprehension. The extent to which they affect reading and writing is as yet unknown.

Interesting classroom exercises for language arts and foreign language teachers to do with their classes include viewing and discussing films which discuss or exemplify regional dialect differences (e.g., *American Tongues* and *Yeah, You Rite!* for American dialects[4] and *The Story of English* [McCrum et al., 1986] for English dialect differences worldwide), investigating dialect differences in the classroom and the surrounding community (for example, with the checklists in Cassidy with Duckert, 1970; Wolfram, 1991, pp. 278–297), and noting regional variants encountered in literature or in travel to other regions.

## Social variation

When we turn from regional variation to social variation, things get somewhat more complicated but also more interesting. For whereas individuals may grow up exclusively or primarily in one region – unless their parents are engaged in occupations that require them to move often (like the military or foreign service) – they typically belong to

4 *American Tongues* was released by the Center for New American Media, and the International Production Center (New York, New York) in 1986. *Yeah, You Rite!* was released by the Center for American Media (New Orleans, Louisiana) in 1984 and is distributed by Côte Blanche Productions (Cut-off, Louisiana). Both video recordings were produced and directed by Louis Alvarez and Andrew Kolker.

many social groups simultaneously and their speech patterns reflect the intersections of their social experiences, categories and roles (e.g., the speech of young upper-middle-class white female "jocks" from the Chicago area, as discussed in Eckert, 1989). Furthermore, whereas regional dialects are often distinguished *qualitatively,* for example, by the fact that speakers in one town use a different word or pronunciation than speakers in another, social dialects are often distinguished *quantitatively,* for example, by the fact that speakers of one ethnic group use a particular feature more frequently than another. And because social dialects may be subject to more stigmatization, social comment, and (attempts at) conscious suppression than regional dialects, the linguists who study social dialects (sociolinguists) usually attempt to obtain samples of *spontaneous or casual speech,* the way people speak when they are most relaxed and least conscious that their speech is being observed. Although our knowledge of regional dialects is largely based on the results of formal questionnaire elicitation, our knowledge of social dialects is largely based on the results of recorded interviews in which people were indirectly encouraged to speak more animatedly because of the topic (e.g., childhood games and customs) or audience (e.g., including close friends or peer group members or both).[5]

Social variation in language might be considered from the perspective of differences between speakers in a variety of dimensions, including (1) age, (2) social class and network, (3) race or ethnicity, and (4) gender. The first three dimensions will be the focus here, because the fourth is covered in another chapter (see Freeman & McElhinny, this volume).

## *Age*

Variation in language according to age may reflect either age grading or change in progress. *Age grading* involves features associated with specific age groups as a developmental or social stage, as in the two-word utterances of children around 18 months of age ("Mommy sock," "Drink soup" – Moskowitz, 1985, p. 55), or the in-group slang of teenagers (*rad,* "cool," *gnarly,* "gross" or "cool" – T. Labov, 1992, p. 350). Normally, speakers abandon the features associated with a particular stage as they grow older, and they begin to speak pretty much like the members of the age group above them as they mature. In the case of *change in progress,* however, age differences reflect an actual change in community norms. When Labov (1966, p. 344 ff.) reported that upper-middle-class New York City speakers in the 20- to 29- and 30- to 39-

5 See Labov (1972a), Bell (1984), and Rickford and McNair-Knox (1993) for a discussion of the effects of topic and audience in sociolinguistic interviews, and also Rickford (1987) for a reminder of the value of elicited intuitions in helping to gauge the full extent of an individual's sociolinguistic competence.

year-old age groups were pronouncing their *r*s in words like *fourth* and *floor* much more often than comparable speakers in the 40- to 49- and 50- to 75-year-old age groups did, this was not just a stage, which the under-40 speakers would abandon as they grew older. On the contrary, they represented the vanguard of a change in community norms with respect to (r) pronunciation – from a basically *r*-less norm to a basically *r*-full norm. Over time, one would expect the newer norm in a change in progress to become established as the norm for all age groups and subpopulations. The study of age differences is thus important for the study of language change ("change in apparent time" – Bailey et al., 1991), but it can sometimes be difficult to tell whether stable age grading or change in progress is going on (see Labov, 1981; Rickford et al., 1991, pp. 127–128).

The kind of age-related language variation which teachers are most likely to notice in school is the use of slang, which, as noted above, is a variety of age grading. Teachers interested in deciphering the slang of their adolescent or teenage students might consult general dictionaries of slang like Partridge (1984), but since slang is often so ephemeral – its value as an in-group marker depends on its being inaccessible to older people and outsiders – dictionaries of this type run the risk of being out of date even before they are printed. One study which is somewhat more than a dictionary is Foster (1986), which concentrates on the "jive lexicon" of African-American and other inner-city teenagers, as well as their characteristic speech events like "ribbin" and "woofin." Drawing on his own teaching experiences, Foster argues that age, race, and class differences between teachers and inner-city youth often make teachers incapable of understanding what their students say and unable to appreciate and control the interactional dynamics in their classrooms (cf. Kochman, 1986, on this point). Another valuable recent work is Teresa Labov's study (1992) of adolescent slang. It provides definitions for about two dozen common adolescent slang items (e.g., *veg out, space cadet, to book, hit the big wazoo*), but more important, it analyzes the relative familiarity of these and other terms among different segments of the adolescent population. The variables examined include geographical background (*guidos* is primarily East Coast, *rad* primarily West Coast), race (*bummer* is more familiar to whites, *bougie* to African-Americans), and gender (*clutch* is somewhat better known among males, and *trashed* somewhat better known among females, although neither of these differences is statistically significant). Since the questionnaire which provided the data for this study is included in an appendix to Teresa Labov's article, teachers may use it in their classrooms, making it the basis of a lively discussion of variation in language and its geographical and social correlates.

Another aspect of adolescent speech which American teachers may have noticed is the use of *go, be like,* and *be all* instead of *say* to introduce quotations in speech ("He's *like,* 'I'm not gonna do that,' and I'*m all,* 'Yes you will!' "). The *be all* form is primarily a California–West Coast innovation. Both *be all* and *be like* occur in contracted rather than full form ("He's all, '. . . ' " rather than "He is all, '. . .' ") and are more frequent with pronoun subjects than full noun phrases ("He's all, '. . .' " rather than "The old lady's all, '. . . ' "). The rise of these two forms may represent change in progress rather than age grading, since neither appears to have been characteristic of older generations in earlier times (see Blyth et al., 1990, for a discussion of *be like*); but only time will tell whether they will become established as new community norms.

## *Social class and network*

Variation in language according to social class is, like variation according to age or ethnicity, a subcategory of variation according to *user* (the differences between groups of speakers in various dimensions), as distinct from variation according to *use* in different styles or registers.[6] Social class variation in language has attracted the most attention and yielded some of the most striking regularities within quantitative sociolinguistics.

The best-known work in this area is Labov's study (1966) of variation in New York City English. In this study, Labov introduced the concept of a sociolinguistic *variable,* a linguistic feature which varies in form and has social significance (p. 49), and established the importance of adhering to a *principle of accountability* in studying such variables – reporting how often they occurred in recorded samples as a proportion of all the cases in which they could have occurred. In Figure 9, for instance, the variable is (*ing*), the realization of the suffix in words like *fishing,* and what is shown is the percentage of the time that speakers "dropped their *g*s" (more accurately, used an alveolar instead of a velar nasal – [ɪn] instead of [ɪŋ]) in all words with such suffixes in their recorded samples.[7] For this study, Labov drew on a random sample of New Yorkers from the Lower East Side, stratified on the basis of occupation, education, and income into the four primary socioeconomic classes shown in Figure 9: lower working class (SEC index nos. 0 to 2), upper working class (3 to 6), lower middle class (7 and 8), and upper

6 This distinction was introduced by Halliday (1964).

7 The convention is to use parentheses to represent the variable, as an abstraction, but to use square brackets or diagonals to represent the phonetic or phonemic variants which realize it in actual speech. It is usually the relative frequency of a particular variant which is represented in the displays of quantitative sociolinguistics (as in Figure 9 and Table 1).

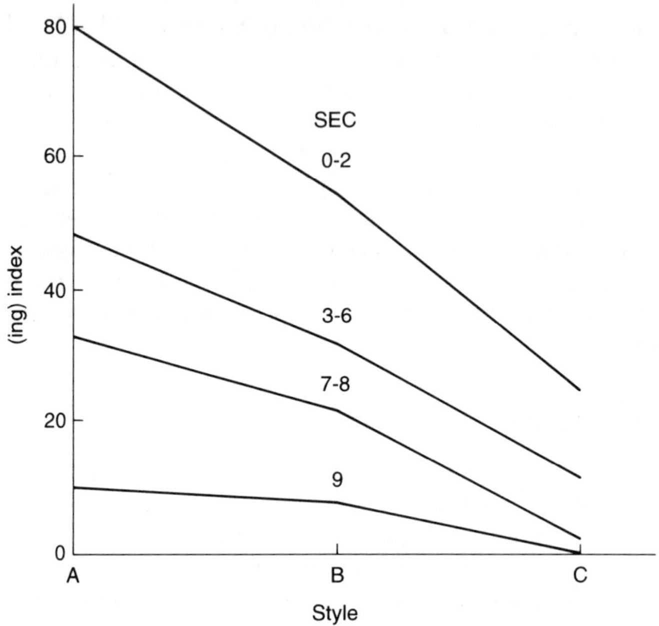


*Figure 9. Class and style stratification of* -ing *in* working, living, *and so on, for white New York City adults. Socioeconomic class scale: 0 to 2, 3 to 6, 7 and 8, and 9. A = casual speech, B = careful speech, C = reading style. (From Labov, 1972b; originally in Labov, 1966.)*

middle class (9). For example, in style A, casual speech, the classes are neatly separated with respect to this variable, with the lower-working-class speakers using [ɪn] most often, and the upper middle class using it least often. What Figure 9 also reveals, however, is that although the social classes are differentiated by their frequencies of [ɪn] in each style, they are similar to each other insofar as they all show lower frequencies of [ɪn] in more formal styles (B, careful speech, and C, reading style).

Variables like (*ing*), which vary simultaneously by social group membership and style, are called sociolinguistic *markers,* in contrast with *indicators,* which are correlated with geographic region or social group membership only. This particular variable is actually a *stable* sociolinguistic marker, because variation in its use does not reflect an ongoing change in New York City English; it is part of a stable pattern which has been observed in several other communities. For instance, Fischer (1958), in an early quantitative sociolinguistic study of (*ing*) among 24 children in a New England village, reported "a slight tendency for the [ɪŋ] variant to be associated with higher socio-economic status" (p. 309) and a strong tendency for its frequency to increase as the context

TABLE 1. PERCENTAGE OF VERNACULAR [ɪn] PRONUNCIATION FOR FOUR SOCIAL GROUPS IN SPEECH COMMUNITIES IN BRITAIN, THE UNITED STATES, AND AUSTRALIA[1]

| Social group | *1* | 2 | 3 | 4 |
|---|---|---|---|---|
| Norwich | 31 | 42 | 91 | 100 |
| West Yorkshire | 5 | 34 | 61 | 83 |
| New York | 7 | 32 | 45 | 75 |
| Brisbane | 17 | 31 | 49 | 63 |

[1]The Norwich data are adapted from Trudgill (1974); the West Yorkshire, from Petyt (1985); the New York City, from Labov (1966), and the Brisbane, from Lee (1989). In Table 1, the number 1 indicates upper middle class or its equivalent, and the number 4 indicates lower working class or its equivalent. Numbers 2 and 3 represent intermediate social classes.
*Source:* Holmes, 1992, p. 153; adapted from various sources.

became more formal.[8] And Wolfram (1991, p. 194), drawing on earlier data from Shuy, Wolfram, and Riley (1967), reported the following mean percentages of [ɪn] in Detroit: upper middle class, 19.4; lower middle class, 39.1; upper working class, 50.5; and lower working class, 78.9. Not only are these figures parallel to the statistics in Figure 9, but they are also parallel to those in Table 1, from Holmes (1992), which includes data from Norwich and West Yorkshire, England, and Brisbane, Australia, as well as New York City. As Holmes observes (1992, p. 152), "[T]here are regional variations between communities, but the regularity of the sociolinguistic pattern in all four communities is quite clear. . . . [P]eople from lower social groups use more of the vernacular [ɪn] variant than those from higher groups." (p. 152)

In order to demonstrate that social class differences can be reflected in patterns of grammar as well as pronunciation, we will draw once again on Holmes (1992, p. 159), whose Figure 10 shows the percentage of unmarked or vernacular third person singular present tense forms (*he walk* instead of *he walks*) in Norwich and Detroit. The stratification here is even sharper than it was for (*ing*) in Table 1 and Figure 9, with the middle-class groups almost never "dropping their *s*," whereas the working-class groups do so quite often. As Holmes notes (1992, p. 159), in a generalization that may be familiar to teachers from their

8 The style distinction was statistically significant, but the socioeconomic differences were not, partly because the sample was small and because this small semirural community did not have marked socioeconomic class divisions. Fischer also found that girls favored the [ɪŋ] variant more than boys did, and that it was more common with "formal" verbs like *criticizing* than with "informal" ones like *punchin*. For a more recent and comprehensive study of internal linguistic constraints on variation between [ɪŋ] and [ɪn], see Houston (1991).

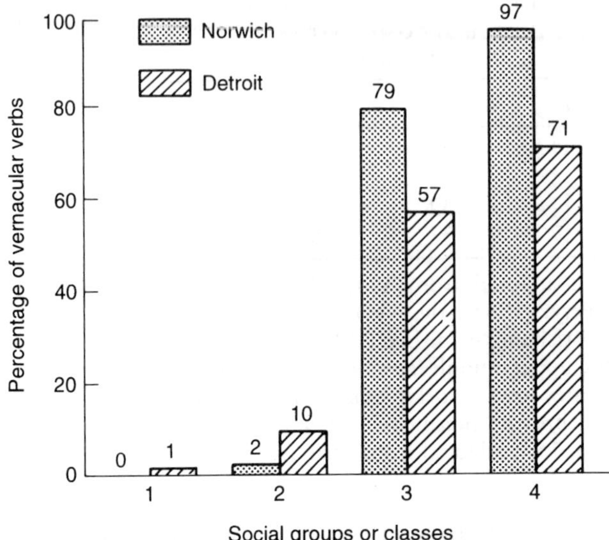


*Figure 10. Vernacular present-tense verb form (third person singular:* she walk*) in Norwich and Detroit. (From Holmes, 1992, p. 159.)*

own classroom experience: "People are often more aware of the social significance of vernacular grammatical forms, and this is reflected in the lower incidence of vernacular forms among middle class speakers in particular." (p. 159). This is reflected too in the sharp difference which Eckert (1989, p. 68) reports between Belten high school "jocks" and "burnouts" with respect to use of multiple negation (as in "He *didn't* eat *none*"). In this Detroit suburb, as in many other communities across the United States, the jocks are more middle class in their orientation and more institutionally identified with the high school (as athletes, club officers, and the like), and not surprisingly, they are much less likely to use this stigmatized grammatical feature (probability = .280) than the "counterculture" burnouts (probability = .720; the difference is significant at the .006 level).[9]

For another example of how dramatically grammatical variables can

9 The probabilities or feature weights which Eckert reports for multiple negation are based on frequency differences observed in speech but represent the output of the variable rule computer program introduced by Cedergren and Sankoff (1974) for the analysis of variable linguistic data. One of the many advantages which the probabilities computed by this program have over observed frequencies is that they provide a multivariate analysis, taking into account the simultaneous effect of other factors (e.g., internal linguistic factors) considered in the analysis of the variable. For a recent discussion of variable rule analysis in linguistics, see Sankoff (1988).

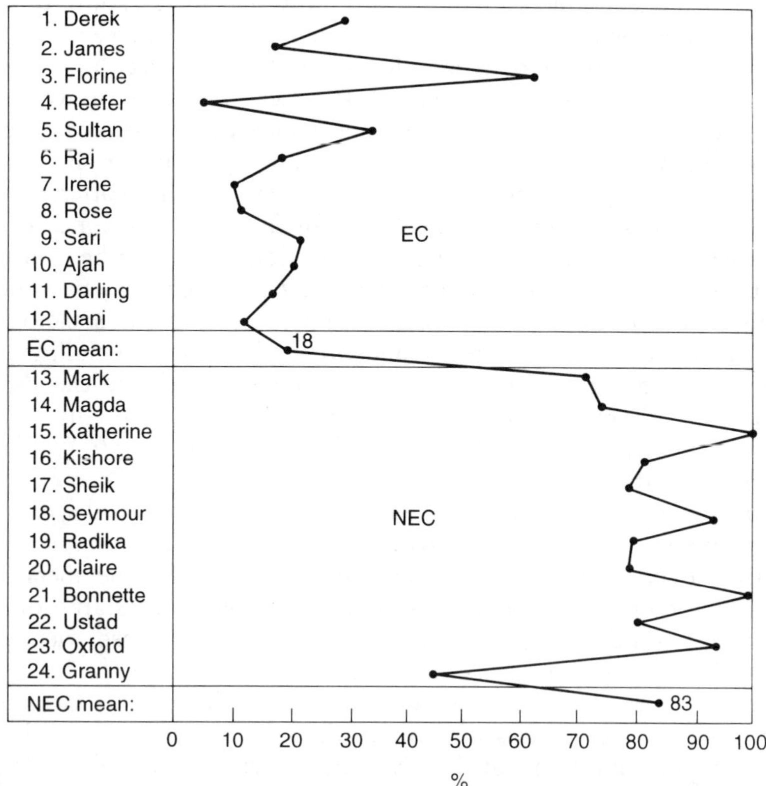


*Figure 11. Relative frequencies of standard English (acrolectal) variants in singular pronoun subcategories among twenty-four residents of Cane Walk. (From Rickford, 1986.)*

stratify a speech community, consider the data in Figure 11, from Rickford (1986). The linguistic variable is the relative frequency with which acrolectal or standard English variants were used in nine singular pronoun categories (acrolectal "*I* see *it*" versus basilectal or creole "*Me* see *um*") in Cane Walk (pseudonym), a rural community in Guyana, South America. The social variable is membership in the two major social classes in the community: estate class (EC), whose members work as weeders or cane cutters and in other field-labor positions on the sugar estate behind the village, and nonestate class (NEC), whose members either hold supervisory positions like field foreman on the sugar estate or who work as shop owners, clerks, or teachers and in other capacities outside the sugar estate. With the exception of Florine and Granny, to whom we will return later in this chapter, the acrolectal pronoun usage frequencies of EC and NEC members simply do not overlap, and their group means – 18 percent and 83 percent, respectively – are as far apart as middle-class versus working-class present tense *-s* usage in Detroit (see Figure 10). One difference, however, is that the decision about how many and which classes to recognize in Cane Walk was done on the basis of an ethnographic approach, considering community members' "subjective" views on the matter, rather than on the basis of an "objective" multi-index sociological measure.[10] Another is that the EC-NEC distinction in Cane Walk can be fruitfully interpreted in terms of sociological *conflict* paradigms, as two social groups with fundamentally different values, whereas the sociological paradigm implicit in Figures 9 and 10, and in most sociolinguistic analysis to date, is a *functional-order* model in which the classes are assumed to share a consensus on norms and values. (See Guy, 1988; Kerbo, 1983, pp. 90–91; Rickford, 1986; Williams, 1992; Woolard, 1985, for further discussion.)

Another aspect of social differentiation which can accord with, but sometimes subdivide or cut across, class groupings is social *network,* a measure of the extent to which and the ways in which members of a community interact with each other. The exceptional status of EC member Florine in Figure 11 is due in part to her close friendship network with NEC members, in particular Mark and Magda, her next-door neighbors. And the exceptional status of NEC member Granny is due in part to her occupational network – the fact that she works all day in a rum shop frequented by EC cane cutters. It was Milroy (1980) who first demonstrated, on the basis of data from Belfast English, that networks which were *dense* (close-knit, in the sense that each member of the network knew one another) and *multiplex* (with members knowing and interacting with one another in multiple capacities, e.g., as friends, coworkers, and family members) could help to maintain local vernacular norms, such as the dropping of the *th* in such words as *mother*. More recently, Edwards (1992) has shown the relevance of network analysis to the use of African-American Vernacular English in Detroit, and Milroy and Milroy (1992) have proposed a theoretical integration of social class and network analysis in sociolinguistics.

## *Race and ethnicity: Focusing on African-American Vernacular English*

In addition to observing language differences related to children's networks and social class backgrounds, teachers may also notice differ-

10 As shown in Rickford (1979), the two social classes can also be distinguished on multi-index measures, but the point is that their identification is done in the first instance on the basis of ethnographically valid community norms.

ences in the English of students from different racial and ethnic backgrounds. They may notice, for instance, that some Mexican-American or Punjabi children have a distinctive accent, that some African-American children speak a different variety of English from that of children from European or Caucasian backgrounds, and that even among the European-Americans, the children from German backgrounds sound slightly different than the ones from French or Polish backgrounds.

Some of these race- and ethnicity-correlated differences in language use reflect the effects of bilingualism in the children's home and/or in the community – the influence on the child's English of another language which they or their parents learned natively. For instance, the fact that in some varieties of Mexican-American English voiced [z] is replaced by voiceless [s] (so that speakers say "soo" for "zoo") may be attributed to transfer or interference from Spanish (Valdés, 1988, p. 130), which does not have voiced [z] in word-initial or word-final position. Similarly, Koreans learning English often have difficulty with English articles (e.g., *a* and *the*), since Korean has no similar forms; conversely, Koreans may feel uncomfortable with the fact that English does not encode the complex honorific distinctions between addressees which are expressed by Korean verbs (Kim, 1988, p. 262).

Foreign language influences of this type are more likely the more recently one's family or ethnic group immigrated – for instance, the children of Vietnamese who immigrated to the United States in the early 1980s are more likely to show such influences than are the grandchildren of Germans who immigrated to the United States in the 1950s. But ethnic varieties of English do not merely reflect passive inheritance from a parental or ancestral language. On the contrary, ethnic varieties are often actively maintained or developed to express the distinctive ethnic identity of their users (LePage & Tabouret-Keller, 1985). That this is so is clear from the fact that African-American Vernacular English remains a distinctive variety in the United States 300 or 400 years after Africans were first brought to the United States and long after direct transfer from African languages was a factor. AAVE is actually an excellent variety to concentrate on in this section, since it is perhaps more different from standard English than any other American English dialect[11] and it has been the focus of considerable description and controversy within linguistics during the past quarter century, often in relation to

11 One variety which is even more different from SE than AAVE is Gullah, or Sea Island Creole, a creole spoken by African-Americans on the islands off the coasts of South Carolina and Georgia (Jones-Jackson, 1987). See Rickford (1974) for arguments and evidence that Gullah's isolation has merely preserved features that may have been more general in African-American English in earlier centuries. See Nichols (this volume) for more on Gullah.

educational issues. AAVE is also one of the features of their students' usage which inner-city teachers most often ask about, so it is especially important for us to consider it in a volume intended for language arts teachers.[12]

## PHONOLOGICAL AND GRAMMATICAL FEATURES OF AAVE

Table 2 identifies the primary phonological and grammatical features of AAVE. Although it is impossible in a chapter of this length to add all the qualifying details about each feature that would be ideal (but see the accompanying footnotes and references), two general comments should be made, one about the frequency with which these features occur among African-American speakers, and the other about their distinctiveness vis-à-vis the colloquial or vernacular English of white Americans.

Not every African-American speaks AAVE, and no one uses the features in Table 2 100 percent of the time. Although it is often said that 80 percent of African-Americans speak AAVE (Dillard, 1972, p. 229), this is a guesstimate rather than a systematic empirical finding. In general, AAVE features are used most often by young lower and working class speakers in urban areas and in informal styles, but how often depends on the feature in question. Wolfram's study of Detroit (1969) remains the most comprehensive source of information on class stratification in AAVE,[13] and Table 3 summarizes some of the systematic class effects it revealed for several features. Note that the lower-working-class (LWC) speakers' usage of these features ranged from a high of 84 percent for consonant cluster simplification to a low of 6 percent for plural *-s* absence, and that although the middle-class speakers used consonant cluster simplification at least half the time, they used the other features very infrequently, in some cases not at all. Investigations of AAVE also show the systematic effects of style, age, sex, and linguistic environment. For instance, Foxy Boston, a teenager from East Palo Alto, California, deleted *is* and *are* 70 percent of the time in one interview with an African-American with whom she was familiar, but

12 AAVE has parallels in Canada and England as well. For the former, see Poplack and Tagliamonte (1991). The distinctive varieties of English spoken by black children in England – influenced to a considerable extent by the Caribbean creole English of older immigrants – has also been the focus of linguistic description and pedagogical discussion over the past 2 decades. For further information, see Sutcliffe (1982), Sutcliffe and Wong (1986), Sutcliffe with Figueroa (1992), and Edwards (1986).

13 Wolfram's sample included twelve representatives of each socieconomic class. The classes themselves were differentiated using an adapted version of Hollingshead and Redlich's (1958) scale, combining scales of education, occupation, and residency (Wolfram, 1969, pp. 32ff.). Since most African-Americans in Detroit at that time were working class, Wolfram suggested (p. 36) that the speech patterns described for the LWC and UWC in his study would be characteristic of the "vast majority" of African-Americans in Detroit.

TABLE 2. SOME MAIN FEATURES OF AAVE AND THEIR SE EQUIVALENTS

*Phonology (pronunciation)*

1. Simplification of word-final consonant clusters, e.g., *han'* for SE "hand," *des'* for SE "desk," *pos'* for SE "post," and *pass'* for SE "passed" (note that the *-ed* suffix in this last example is pronounced as [t]).[a]
2. Realization of final *ng* as *n* in gerunds and participles, e.g., *walkin'* for SE "walking."[b]

3a. Realization of voiceless *th* [Θ] as *t* or *f*, as in *tin* for SE "thin" and *baf* for SE "bath."[c]

3b. Realization of voiced *th* [ð] as *d* or *v*, as in *den* for SE "then" and *bruvver* for SE "brother."

4. Deletion or vocalization (pronounciation as a weak neutral vowel) of *l* and *r* after vowels, as in *he'p* for SE "help" and *sistuh* for SE "sister."
5. Monophthongal pronunciations of *ay* and *oy*, as in *ah* for SE "I" and *boah* for SE "boy."[d]
6. Stress on first rather than second syllable, as in *pólice* instead of SE "políce" and *hótel* instead of SE *hotél.*[e]
7. Deletion of initial *d* and *g* in certain tense-aspect auxiliaries, as in "ah *'on* know" for SE "I *don't* know" and "ah'm *'a* do it" for SE "I'm gonna do it" (Rickford, 1974, p. 109).

*Grammar*

8. The verb phrase (markers of tense, mood, and aspect)

8a. Absence of copula/auxiliary *is* and *are* for present tense states and actions, as in "He Ø tall" for SE "He'*s* tall" or "They Ø running" for SE "They *are* running."[f]

---

[a]The systemic nature of AAVE is shown by the fact that this rule operates only when both members of the consonant cluster are either voiceless, involving no vibration of the vocal cords (as in po<u>st</u>, a<u>sk</u>, and a<u>pt</u>), or voiced, with the vocal cords vibrating (as in *po<u>sed</u>* [*zd*], *ha<u>nd</u>*, and o<u>ld</u>). When one member of the cluster is voiceless and the other voiced (as in *ju<u>mp</u>* or *tha<u>nk</u>*) the cluster cannot be simplified, except in negative forms like *ain'* and *don'*. See Fasold and Wolfram (1978, p. 52) for further discussion.

[b]This is popularly known as "dropping your *g*s," but it doesn't actually involve any *g* dropping at all. What actually happens, in phonetic terms, is that one kind of nasal (an alveolar nasal – with the tongue touching the alveolar ridge right behind the top front teeth) is substituted for another one (a velar nasal – with the tongue touching the velar or upper back region of the roof of the mouth).

[c]As Fasold and Wolfram (1978, pp. 55–56) point out, voiceless *th* is more often realized as *t* at the beginnings of words, and as *f* at the ends of words. Similarly, *d* realizations of voiced *dh* are more common word-initally and *v* realizations are more common word-finally.

[d]As Fasold and Wolfram (1978, p. 61) point out, this feature is common among both blacks and whites in the south, and occurs much more frequently before voiced sounds or pause (as in *side, I*) than before voiceless sounds (as in *site*).

[e]According to Fasold and Wolfram (1978, p. 61), this affects only a small subset of words such as *pólice, hótel,* and *Júly.*

[f]In the grammatical examples, <u>Ø</u> is used to mark the point at which a grammatical form or inflection would occur in equivalent SE examples. This is compara-

TABLE 2 (*cont.*)

8b. Absence of third person present tense *-s*, as in "He walkØ" for SE "He walks" or "He doØn't sing" for SE "He doesn't sing" (Fasold, 1972, pp. 121–149).
8c. Use of invariant *be* to express habitual aspect, as in "He *be* walkin" (usually, regularly, as against "He Ø walkin" right now) for SE "He is usually walking/usually walks" (Fasold, 1972, pp. 150–184).
8d. Use of stressed *BIN* to express remote phase, as in "She *BIN* married" for SE "She has been married for a long time (and still is)" or "He *BIN* ate it" for SE "He ate it a long time ago" (Baugh, 1983, pp. 80–82; Rickford, 1975).
8e. Use of *done* to emphasize the completed nature of an action, as in "He *done did* it" for SE "He's already done it" (Baugh, 1983, pp. 74–77; Labov, 1972c, pp. 53–57).
8f. Use of *be done* to express resultatives or the future or conditional perfect, as in "She *be done had* her baby" for SE "She *will have had* her baby" (Baugh, 1983, pp. 77–80).
8g. Use of *finna* (derived from "fixin' to") to mark the immediate future, as in "He's *finna* go" for SE "He's about to go."[g]
8h. Use of *steady* as an intensified continuative marker (to mark actions that occur consistently and/or persistently), as in "Ricky Bell be *steady* steppin in them number nines" (Baugh, 1983, p. 86).
8i. Use of *come* to express the speaker's indignation about an action or event, as in "He *come* walkin in here like he owned the damn place" (Spears, 1982, p. 852).
8j. Use of *had* to mark the simple past (primarily among preadolescents) as in "then we *had* went outside" for SE "then we went outside" (Theberge & Rickford, 1989).
9. Negation
9a. Use of *ain'(t)* as a general preverbal negator, for SE "am not," "isn't," "aren't," "hasn't," "haven't," and "didn't," as in "He ain' here" for SE "He isn't here" or "He *ain'* do it" for SE "He didn't do it."
9b. Multiple negation or negative concord (i.e., negating the auxiliary verb and all indefinites in the sentence), as in "He *don'* do *nothin*" for SE "He doesn't do anything" (Labov, 1972c, pp. 130–196).
9c. Negative inversion in emphatic statements (inversion of the auxiliary and indefinite pronoun subject), as in "Can't nobody do it" for SE "Nobody can do it" (Sells, Rickford, & Wasow, 1995).
10. Other grammatical features
10a. Absence of possessive *-s*, as in "JohnØ house" for SE "John's house."
10b. Absence of plural *-s* (fairly infrequent), as in "two boyØ" for SE "two boys."
10c. Appositive or pleonastic pronouns, as in "That teacher, *she* yell at the kids" (Fasold & Wolfram, 1978, p. 80) for SE "That teacher Ø yells at the kids."

ble to the use of an apostrophe in phonological examples (e.g., *he'p*) to mark the point at which a consonant or vowel occurs in equivalent SE forms.
[g]There is no published discussion of the use of *finna* in AAVE, but see Ching (1987) for a discussion of its probable source – *fixin to* – in the South.

TABLE 2 *(cont.)*

10d. Auxiliary inversion in embedded questions (without *if* or *whether*), as in "I asked him *could* he go with me" for SE "I asked him whether he could go with me."
10e. Use of *here* go as a static locative or presentational form, as in "*Here go* my own" (said by a 12-year-old girl from East Palo Alto, California, as she showed me her artwork) for SE "Here is my own."

TABLE 3. USE OF SELECTED AAVE FEATURES IN DETROIT, BY SOCIAL CLASS

| Feature | *LWC* % | *UWC* % | *LMC* % | *UMC* % |
|---|---|---|---|---|
| Consonant cluster simplification *not* in past tense (p. 60) | 84 | 79 | 66 | 51 |
| Voiceless *th* Θ → *f*, *t*, or Ø (p. 84) | 71 | 59 | 17 | 12 |
| Multiple negation (p. 156) | 78 | 55 | 12 | 8 |
| Absence of copula/auxiliary *is, are* (p. 169) | 57 | 37 | 11 | 5 |
| Absence of third person present tense *-s* (p. 136) | 71 | 57 | 10 | 1 |
| Absence of possessive *-s* (p. 141) | 27 | 25 | 6 | 0 |
| Absence of plural *-s* (p. 143) | 6 | 4 | 1 | 0 |

LWC = lower working class; UWC = upper working class; LMC = lower middle class; UMC = upper middle class. Numbers are percentage amounts.
*Source:* Wolfram, 1969.

only 40 percent of the time in another interview with a European-American whom she had not met before (Rickford & McNair-Knox, 1993, p. 247). The members of the Cobras street gang in New York City deleted *is* more often when it had a pronoun subject (e.g., *He*) than when it had a noun phrase subject (e.g., *The man*), and more often when recorded with their peer group than when interviewed individually (Labov, 1972c, p. 84). Wolfram (1969, p. 179) reported that the 14- to 17-year-old subjects in his Detroit sample deleted *is* and *are* 68 percent of the time, but the adults did so only 38 percent of the time. In a sample from East Palo Alto, 15-year-old Tinky Gates deleted *is* and *are* 81 percent of the time, her 38-year-old mother, Paula Gates, did so 35 percent of the time, and 76-year-old Penelope Johnson did so only 15 percent of the time. Finally, males are generally reported as using AAVE features more often than females, but this may be partly because the interviewers in most studies are male. For instance, Wolfram (1969, p. 136) reports that the lower-working-class males in Detroit deleted third present *-s* 74 percent of the time compared to 69 percent for lower-working-class females. But Foxy Boston and Tinky Gates, in interviews conducted in East Palo Alto by a female field-worker (Faye

McNair-Knox), showed even higher rates of third present *-s* absence – 97 percent and 96 percent, respectively (Rickford, 1991).

The features of AAVE that appear to be distinctive to this variety (or nearly so) are primarily grammatical. Wolfram (1991, p. 108) lists eight such features, and six of them (including stressed *BIN,* invariant *be,* and *is* absence) are grammatical. Many phonological features of AAVE (e.g., nos. 1, 2, and 4 in Table 2), and some of its grammatical features too (e.g., no. 9b in Table 2), also occur in the colloquial English of white Americans, especially those from the working class, and some of them (like nos. 5 and 8e in Table 2) are characteristic of southern speech (see Feagin, 1979). But, in general, the features which AAVE shares with other American vernaculars occur more frequently in AAVE and/or in a wider range of linguistic environments. For instance, consonant cluster simplification appears to be more common in the AAVE of working-class African-Americans than in white working-class speech, and it occurs in AAVE even when the next word begins with a vowel (e.g., *pos' office*), a position in which many other dialects retain the final consonant (Wolfram, 1991, p. 109).[14] For some AAVE speakers, words like *des'* do not have an underlying final *k,* and the plural form is *desses* according to the same rule that applies to words ending in a final sibilant (e.g., *rose-roses, boss-bosses, church-churches*).

## THE CREOLE ORIGINS AND DIVERGENCE ISSUES

One source of controversy in the study of AAVE is whether the dialect was once more different from standard English and white vernacular dialects than it is now, in particular, whether it was a creole language similar to the creole English spoken in Jamaica, other parts of the West Indies, and elsewhere in the world (e.g., Hawaii and Sierra Leone).[15] Although this issue can be pursued quite independently of educational considerations, there is a potential connection between the historical and educational issues, as noted by Stewart (1970). Stewart pointed out (p. 362) that if educators realized that AAVE came from creole roots and resulted from a very normal and widespread process of historical development rather than from carelessness or ignorance, they might be more willing to recognize the distinctness and validity of the dialect and to take it into account in their language arts pedagogy.

In favor of the creolist view, Stewart (1970) and Dillard (1972, 1992)

14 In other words, speakers of such dialects will say "pos' five letters," deleting the final *t* before a consonant, but "post office," retaining the final *t* before a vowel. Similarly, some AAVE speakers delete or vocalize postvocalic *r* before a vowel, even within the same word (so that "Carol" sounds like "Ca'ol"), but speakers of white vernaculars do not (Labov, 1972c, p. 40).

15 See Nichols, this volume, for definitions of pidgin and creole languages.

have observed that textual attestations of the language of African-Americans from the eighteenth and nineteenth century are even more similar to Caribbean creole English than is modern AAVE. In addition, these authors and others (including Bailey, 1965; Baugh, 1980; Holm, 1984; Rickford, 1977; Rickford & Blake, 1990; Winford 1992) have suggested that when copula absence and other features of modern AAVE are examined carefully and quantitatively, the creole resemblances and origins of AAVE become much clearer. On the other hand, skepticism about the creole origins hypothesis has come from Poplack and Sankoff (1987), who, examining copula absence in the English of the descendants of early nineteenth-century African-American migrants to Samaná, Dominican Republic, conclude that the language of those migrants "was no more creolized than modern ABE [i.e., AAVE], and . . . bore no more resemblance to English-based West Indian creoles than modern ABE, and indeed less."[16] Tagliamonte and Poplack (1988), on the basis of their analysis of past tense marking in Samaná, reach a similar conclusion. In response to the latter paper, Winford (1992) has shown that there exist close parallels between past marking in Trinidadian creole and AAVE, but debate on the creole origins of AAVE is likely to continue.

A more recent and perhaps equally unresolved issue is whether AAVE is currently diverging from white vernaculars, becoming more different from them than it was, say, a quarter of a century ago. This hypothesis was first advanced by Labov and Harris (1986), who argued that, as a result of increasing racial and economic segregation, sound changes in the white community had not diffused to the black community, and grammatical innovations in the black community had not diffused to the white community. To their data from Philadelphia, Bailey and Maynor (1987) added data from the Brazos Valley, Texas, which suggested that the AAVE of urban children had become more different from that of older African-Americans and from white vernaculars. Skepticism about the divergence hypothesis has, however, been raised by some of the contributors in Fasold et al. (1987), by Butters (1989), and by Rickford (1991). One difficulty is that, although the AAVE of the youngest generation shows divergence from white vernaculars with respect to some features, it shows convergence with respect to others. Also, it is unclear whether modern AAVE appears to be diverging simply because more truly vernacular data exist than did twenty-five years ago (Farr & Daniels 1986, p. 34). (See also Bailey, 1993; Bailey & Maynor, 1989; Butters, 1989, for further discussion.)

16 Besides Samaná English, a source of new data for arguments about the creole hypothesis is the set of recordings of former slaves transcribed and analyzed in Bailey, Maynor, and Cukor-Avila (1991).

## ATTITUDES TOWARD AAVE

How people feel about AAVE and people who speak AAVE is an important issue for educators, for at least two reasons. First, teachers often have unjustifiably negative attitudes toward students who speak AAVE (Labov, 1970), and such negative attitudes may lead them to have low expectations of such students, to assign them inappropriately to learning disabled or special education classes, and to otherwise stunt their academic performance (Rosenthal & Jacobson, 1968; Smitherman, 1981, p. 19). Second, teachers trying to decide whether and how to take AAVE into account in their classroom pedagogy might benefit from understanding what the attitudes of students, parents, employers, and other teachers are toward this variety (see McGroarty, this volume).

As it turns out, such attitudes are not uniform. Although educational psychologists such as Bereiter and Engelmann (1966) and Farrell (1983) have berated the use of AAVE structures by young children and have seen them as reflecting or creating cognitive deficits, their conclusions have been persuasively rebutted by linguists (Labov, 1970, and Baugh, 1988, respectively). Leading African-American writers (e.g., Baldwin, 1979, Jordan, 1985) have defended the legitimacy and expressiveness of AAVE, and inner-city African-American teenagers sometimes reject the standard and endorse the vernacular in opposition to mainstream white culture and values (Fordham & Ogbu, 1986, p. 182). At the same time, parents have expressed concern that if their children were limited to the vernacular, this would negatively affect their chances of getting good jobs and going on to college (Hoover, 1978, p. 85), and the validity of this concern has been demonstrated in empirical research by Terrell and Terrell (1983). However, even those parents who prefer the standard for job interviews, for reading and writing, and for schools and formal contexts, accept the vernacular for listening and speaking, particularly in the home and in informal settings, and some have endorsed it for purposes of solidarity maintenance and culture preservation (Hoover, 1978, pp. 78–79).[17] This ambivalence about AAVE is part of a larger "push-pull" dynamic in African-American history (Smitherman, 1986, p. 170), but it is not limited to African-Americans. Taylor's survey (1973) of 422 teachers of various races throughout the country revealed that, although 40 percent expressed negative opinions about the structure and usefulness of AAVE and other vernacular varieties, 40 percent expressed positive opinions (p. 183). Moreover, their

17 Hoover (1978) interviewed eighty California parents, sixty-four from East Palo Alto and sixteen from Oakland. The "standard" and "vernacular" varieties about which they were asked were African-American varieties, spoken by African-American interviewers, and sharing AAVE prosodic and phonological patterns while differing primarily in grammar.

attitudes could not be characterized simply as positive or negative; they varied depending on the aspect of dialect use under discussion, length of teaching experience (those who had been teaching for 3 to 5 years were most positive), and other factors.

Most teachers, parents, and linguists agree, regardless of their attitudes toward AAVE, that children should be taught to read and write fluently as a basis for success in the entire curriculum. Many also believe that students should be assisted in developing bidialectal competence in AAVE and standard English.[18] Linguists have consistently suggested that the goal of being competent in AAVE and Standard English would be better achieved if the structural, rhetorical, and expressive characteristics of African-American vernacular language were taken into account. In the next section we will consider some of their observations and suggestions.

### IMPLICATIONS FOR TEACHING LANGUAGE ARTS TO SPEAKERS OF AAVE

Reading, the subject which parents in Hoover's study (1978, p. 82) ranked as the most important item in the elementary school curriculum, was the first subject to attract the interest of sociolinguists working on AAVE. Labov (1972c, pp. 33–34) observed that, because of the homonyms produced by regular AAVE rules (e.g., *Ruth* = *roof, pass* = *passed*), it might be difficult for teachers to know when they are dealing with a mistake in reading or a difference in pronunciation. For instance, the child who reads "He passed by both of them" as *he pass' by bof of dem* may have decoded the past tense meaning and every other semantic component of the original correctly but simply pronounced the sentence according to the rules of his or her own vernacular. The teaching strategy in this case would be very different from that for a child who had not recognized or understood the significance of the *-ed* suffix. Labov suggested (p. 34) that teachers in the early grades accept the existence of a different set of homonyms in the speech of African-American children to preserve their confidence in the phonic code and facilitate their learning to read.

An alternative strategy, advocated by Baratz (1969), Stewart (1969), and Smitherman (1986), among others, was to introduce AAVE speakers to reading through "dialect readers," which minimize the differences between the printed word and the child's vernacular, and allow the child to concentrate on decoding and comprehension without the additional burden of simultaneously learning a second dialect. Simpkins, Holt, and Simpkins (1977) created the most comprehensive set of dialect materials, a series of *Bridge* readers written in AAVE, a transitional

18 See Sledd (1969) for demurral on this point.

variety, and standard English, as exemplified in these brief excerpts (Simpkins & Simpkins, 1981, p. 232):

6. AAVE: He couldn't find no dictionary, so he split on down to the library. . . . He ask the lady there 'bout books to help him learn some big words like redundancy.

   Transition: He didn't have a dictionary so he went down to the public library. . . . He asked (the librarian) for a book to help him.

   Standard English: He explained to the librarian that he wanted to increase his vocabulary.

The *Bridge* reading program was field-tested with 540 students from the seventh through the twelfth grades, and the students' progress after several months of instruction was "extremely promising," as measured by scores on the Iowa Test of Basic Skills in Reading (Simpkins & Simpkins, 1981, p. 237).[19] Despite these early successes, the series was not retained, and dialect readers have not been widely adopted, for a variety of political, philosophical, and practical reasons, including negative reactions from parents, educators, and community leaders (see Labov, in press; Rickford & Rickford, in press; Wolfram, 1991, pp. 255–266; Wolfram & Fasold, 1969, pp. 142–143).

Another teaching strategy that was proposed a quarter century ago but is less popular these days is the use of drills that focus attention on differences between AAVE and SE and aim to help children develop competence in switching smoothly between them. Here are some examples of translation drills from Feigenbaum (1970, p. 92):

| 7. *Direction* | *Teacher stimulus* | *Student response* |
|---|---|---|
| SE→AAVE | Paula likes leather coats | Paula like leather coats |
| AAVE→SE | He prefer movies | He prefers movies |

One virtue of this method is that it recognized and promoted the integrity of both AAVE and SE. Another is that it made use of second language teaching techniques, in accord with Stewart's suggestion (1964) that SE be taught to AAVE speakers as a "quasi-foreign language." However, the drills were boring and assumed to a certain extent that the teacher spoke AAVE or had some knowledge of it (Keith Walters, personal communication). Moreover, their value was called

19 Simpkins and Simpkins (1981, p. 238) reported that the 540 children using the *Bridge* series showed "significantly larger gains" than a control group of 123 students who did not – an average gain of "6.2 months for four months of instruction compared to only an average gain of 1.6 months for students in their regular scheduled classroom reading activities."

into question by theoretical developments in second language acquisition (Wolfram, 1991, p. 225).[20]

One educational implication of AAVE research which was noted early and continues to be emphasized today is that many standard intelligence tests are biased against speakers of AAVE and similar dialects insofar as they include items which involve differences between AAVE and SE but give credit only for the SE response (see Hoover & Taylor, 1987; Labov, 1976; Smitherman, 1986, pp. 239–241; Vaughn-Cooke, 1983; Wolfram 1976, 1986, 1991). One example is the Illinois Test of Psycholinguistic Abilities (ITPA) grammatical closure subtest, which includes this item:

8. Here is a dog. Here are two ________. (SE *dogs* is correct; AAVE *dog* is "wrong.")

In response to this evidence of bias, some linguists have urged that creators and users of such tests increase their knowledge of the speech of the communities they serve and field-test them with dialect speakers (Wolfram, 1991, pp. 244–247), and others have called for "a national moratorium on all testing until valid measures are devised" (Smitherman, 1986, p. 239).

With respect to writing, a number of useful suggestions have been made by linguists. Farr and Daniels (1986) have isolated fifteen factors associated with effective writing instruction for dialect speakers, including an appreciation of children's native linguistic competence and moderate marking of surface errors (pp. 45–46). In a similar vein, Smitherman (1986, p. 213 ff.) urges that, in their responses to students' writing, teachers concentrate on organization, content, and rhetorical power rather than on superficial errors caused by the transfer of grammatical patterns of AAVE. Ball (1992) has drawn attention to special circumlocution, narrative interspersion, and recursion styles which occur in the expository discourse of African-American students, perhaps reflecting the models of African-American sermons and other expressive oral genres. This line of research is similar in some respects to the work of Michaels (1981) and Taylor and Matsuda (1988), who report that African-American children often use in oral narratives a "topic associating" style, involving "a series of associated segments . . . linked implicitly" rather than a "topic-centered" style involving "tightly structured discourse on a single topic." The teacher who does not recognize this topic-associating style, illustrated in example 9, may prematurely interrupt or curtail students' expressive productions.

20 However, Taylor (1989) has used similar drills quite successfully with college-level students and cites other research in which "the audio-lingual methods, applied to the teaching of Black students, has proved to be a successful tool" (p. 108).

9. A topic-associating narrative: I went to the beach Sunday / and to McDonald's / and to the park / and I got this for my birthday / (holds up purse) my mother bought it for me / and I had two dollars for my birthday / and I put it in here / and I went to where my friend / named Gigi / I went over to my grandmother's house with her / and she was on my back . . . (from Michaels & Cazden, 1986)

A number of researchers have made other suggestions for adapting language arts instruction to the language and culture of African-American youth, advocating, for instance, an increased use of call and response and tonal semantics in classroom exercises (Smitherman, 1986, p. 220), the use of lyrics from popular songs and rap music to develop poetry appreciation, spelling, vocabulary, and sentence structure (Baugh, 1981; Hoover, 1991), and a cultural linguistic approach including increased use of the language experience method, in which children create and read their own thoughts and experiences (Starks, 1983).[21]

Finally, Kochman (1986), Foster (1986), and Morgan (1991) have drawn attention to linguistic and cultural differences between African-Americans and white Americans – for instance, with respect to turn-taking and discussion style. Understanding these differences may improve the teacher's ability to communicate and function effectively in the classroom.

## *Classroom implications and exercises involving social dialects*

Many of the specific suggestions made in the preceding section in relation to AAVE can be applied to social dialects more generally. The overarching need is that teachers recognize the regularity and integrity of the social dialects which children and adolescents employ in the classroom and in the schoolyard, that they appreciate the powerful attachment to such dialects which students often have – sometimes as a vital part of their social identity – and that they build on such dialects, where possible, in language arts and second language and foreign language instruction.

One action teachers might take to increase awareness of and sensitivity to social variation is to show and discuss films and videotapes in which distinctive social dialects are exemplified and/or play a significant role. The list might include the following, but the possibilities are virtually unlimited: *My Fair Lady* (based on George Bernard Shaw's *Pygmalion*), the PBS television series *The Story of English* (with accompanying text by McCrum et al., 1986), the November 19, 1987, discus-

21 See also Heath (1983) and the papers in Brooks (1985).

sion of black English on the Oprah Winfrey Show,[22] and *Daughters of the Dust* (see Dash, 1992, for screenplay and discussion). Literature which exemplifies similar variation may offer even richer possibilities for reflection and analysis. As examples of the many references that might be consulted on this issue, note Holton's (1984) analysis of the use of AAVE in African-American fiction; Brathwaite (1984), Dabydeen and Wilson-Tagoe (1988), and Chamberlain (1993) on Caribbean and Afro-British literature; Lal and Raghavendra (1960) on poetry in Indian English, and James (1986) on third world literature more generally. Recordings of third world poets and authors reading their works in their native varieties of English (e.g., Kay, Agard, D'Aguiar, & Berry, 1990) constitute another valuable classroom resource.

Finally, teachers might elicit from students examples of age-, class-, gender-, and ethnicity-related differences in language use which they have encountered in their own experience, encourage them to exploit such differences creatively to represent various characters in drama and composition, and engage them in discussion of what these differences reflect about social relations and imply for schooling and careers. The results should be dynamic and richly instructive, for teachers and students alike.

## Summary

This chapter has attempted to focus on some of the ways in which English, like other languages, varies in its pronunciation, grammar, vocabulary, and use according to both regional and social factors. Such variation has tremendous implications for all teachers who deal with language instruction, whether as L1, L2, or foreign language instructors. Sometimes such variation poses additional problems and challenges for language teachers, but it is part of the multicultural richness which characterizes most modern societies and should be considered a rich resource for classroom discussion, the development of literacy skills, the enhancement of individual and social identities, and the improvement of intercultural relations and understanding.

### Suggestions for further reading

Brooks, Charlotte K. (Ed.). (1985). *Tapping potential: English and language arts for the black learner.* Urbana, IL: National Council of Teachers of English.

22 The videotape is available from Harpo Productions, Chicago, Illinois. However, as Keith Walters (personal communication) has suggested, it might be most fruitful to show and discuss this videotape after students have learned about the systematicity of AAVE and other dialects and after they understand some of the factors which influence people's attitudes toward such dialects.

This book represents an attempt by a variety of linguists and language practitioners to apply general linguistics principles and research on specific varieties to the education of speakers of those varieties. Reading, writing, and literature are covered in separate sections.

Chambers, J. K., & Trudgill, Peter (1980). *Dialectology*. Cambridge: Cambridge University Press.

This remains one of the best introductions to regional and social dialectology, clarifying key terms and concepts in dialect geography, urban dialectology, sociolinguistics, and variation theory.

Cheshire, Jenny (Ed.) (1991). *English around the world: Sociolinguistic perspectives*. Cambridge: Cambridge University Press.

Although some of the articles in this book are relatively technical, they provide more comprehensive and up-to-date coverage of varieties of English worldwide than is available in any other volume. Among the countries or regions covered are Britain, the United States, Ireland, Canada, New Zealand, Australia, Southeast Asia and Hong Kong, South Asia, southern, East, and West Africa, the Caribbean, and the Pacific.

Holmes, Janet (1992). *An introduction to sociolinguistics*. London and New York: Longman.

This is the most recent and most accessible introduction to the study of language in society currently available. It includes data on multilingualism and social and stylistic variation from speech communities all over the world.

Labov, William (1970). *The study of nonstandard English*. Champaign, IL: National Council of Teachers of English, by special arrangement with the Center for Applied Linguistics.

This is somewhat dated now, and may be difficult to find, but it is an excellent introduction to sociolinguistics and vernacular dialects for teachers, with useful suggestions for doing original research in the classroom.

Wolfram, Walt, & Christian, Donna (1989). *Dialects and education: Issues and answers*. Englewood Cliffs, NJ: Prentice Hall.

This book uses a question-answer format to provide a stimulating introduction to regional and social dialects and the kinds of issues which many language arts, L1, and L2 teachers raise. Although the focus is on American English dialects, the questions and answers are relevant to language teachers everywhere.

## References

Ager, D. E. (1990). *Sociolinguistics and contemporary French*. Cambridge: Cambridge University Press.

Bailey, Beryl (1965). Toward a new perspective in negro English dialectology. *American Speech, 40*(3), 171–177.

Bailey, Guy (1993). A perspective on African American English. In Dennis R. Preston (Ed.), *American dialect research* (pp. 287–318). Amsterdam and Philadelphia: John Benjamins.

Bailey, Guy, & Maynor, Natalie (1987). Decreolization? *Language in Society, 16*, 449–473.

Bailey, Guy, & Maynor, Natalie (1989). The divergence controversy. *American Speech, 64*(1), 12–39.

Bailey, Guy, Maynor, Natalie, & Patricia Cukor-Avila (Eds.). (1991). *The emergence of black English*. Amsterdam and Philadelphia: John Benjamins.

Bailey, Guy, Wikle, T., Tillery, J. & Sand, L. (1991). The apparent time construct. *Language Variation and Change, 3*(3), 241–264.

Baldwin, James (1979). If black English isn't a language, then tell me, what is? *The New York Times,* Sunday, July 29, 1979. [Reprinted in Geneva Smitherman (Ed.). (1981). Introduction: Black English and the education of black children and youth. *Proceedings of the National invitational symposium on the King discussion* (pp. 390–392). Detroit: Center for Black Studies, Wayne State University.]

Ball, Arnetha F. (1992). Cultural preference and the expository writing of African American adolescents. *Written Communication, 9*(4), 501–532.

Baratz, Joan C. (1969). Teaching reading in an urban Negro school system. In Joan C. Baratz & Roger W. Shuy (Eds.), *Teaching black children to read.* (pp. 92–116). Washington, DC: Center for Applied Linguistics.

Barbour, Stephen, & Stevenson, Patrick (1990). *Variation in German: A critical approach to German sociolinguistics*. Cambridge: Cambridge University Press.

Baugh, John (1980). A re-examination of the black English copula. In William Labov (Ed.), *Locating language in time and space* (pp. 83–106). New York: Academic Press.

Baugh, John (1981). Design and implementation of language arts programs for speakers of nonstandard English: Perspectives for a national neighborhood literacy program. In Bruce Cronell (Ed.), *The linguistic needs of linguistically different children* (pp. 17–43). Los Alamitos, CA: South West Regional Laboratory (SWRL).

Baugh, John (1983). *Black street speech: Its history, structure and survival.* Austin: University of Texas Press.

Baugh, John (1988). Language and race: Some implications for linguistic science. In Frederick J. Newmeyer (Ed.), *Linguistics: The Cambridge survey.* (Vol. 4: *Language: The sociocultural context*). (pp. 64–75). Cambridge: Cambridge University Press.

Bell, Allan (1984). Language style as audience design. *Language in Society, 13,* 145–204.

Bereiter, Carl, Engelmann, Siegfried (1966). *Teaching disadvantaged children in the pre-school.* Englewood Cliffs, NJ: Prentice Hall.

Blyth, Carl, Jr., Recktenwald, Sigrid & Wang, Jenny (1990). I'm like, "Say What?!": A new quotative in American oral narrative. *American Speech 65*(3), 215–227.

Brathwaite, Edward (1984). *History of the voice: The development of nation language in Anglophone Caribbean poetry*. London: New Beacon Books.

Brooks, Charlotte K. (Ed.) (1985). *Tapping potential: English and language arts for the black learner*. Urbana, IL: National Council of Teachers of English.

Butters, Ronald K. (1989). *The death of black English: Divergence and controversy in black and white vernaculars*. Frankfurt: Peter Lang.

Carver, Craig M. (1985). The DARE map and regional labels. In Frederic G. Cassidy (Ed.), *Dictionary of American regional English*. (Vol. 1: *Introduction and A–C*). (pp. xxiii–xxxv). Cambridge, MA: Belknap.

Cassidy, Frederic G. (1985). *Dictionary of American regional English* (Vol. 1: *Introduction and A–C*). Cambridge, MA: Belknap.

Cassidy, Frederic G., with Duckert, Audrey R. (1970). *A method for collecting dialect*. American Dialect Society, Publication no. 20. University, AL: University of Alabama Press.

Cedergen, Henrietta J., & Sankoff, David (1974). Variable rules: Performance as a statistical reflection of competence. *Language, 50*(2), 333–355.

Chamberlain, J. Edward (1993). *Come back to me my language: Poetry and the West Indies*. Urbana and Chicago: University of Illinois Press.

Chambers, J. K., & Trudgill, Peter (1980). *Dialectology*. Cambridge: Cambridge University Press.

Ching, Marvin K. L. (1987). How fixed is *fixin' to? American Speech, 62*(4), 332–345.

Dabydeen, David, & Wilson-Tagoe, Nava (1988). *A reader's guide to West Indian and black British literature*. London: Hansib.

Dash, Julie (1992). *Daughters of the dust: The making of an African American woman's film*. New York: The New Press.

Davis, Lawrence M. (1983). *English dialectology: An introduction*. University, AL: The University of Alabama Press.

Dillard, J. L. (1972). *Black English: Its history and usage in the United States*. New York: Random House.

Dillard, J. L. (1992). *A history of American English*. New York: Longman.

Eckert, Penelope (1989). *Jocks and burnouts: Social identity in the high school*. New York: Teachers College Press.

Edwards, Viv (1979). *The West Indian language issue in British schools*. London: Routledge and Kegan Paul.

Edwards, Viv (1986). *Language in a black community*. Clevedon: Multilingual Matters.

Edwards, Walter F. (1992). Sociolinguistic behavior in a Detroit inner-city black neighborhood. *Language in Society, 21*(1), 93–115.

Farr, Marcia, & Daniels, Harvey (1986). *Language diversity and writing instruction*. New York: ERIC Clearinghouse on Urban Education and National Council of Teachers of English.

Farrell, T. J. (1983). IQ and Standard English. *College Composition and Communication, 34*, 470–484.

Fasold, Ralph W. (1972). *Tense marking in Black English: A linguistic and social analysis*. Arlington, VA: Center for Applied Linguistics.

Fasold, Ralph W., & Walt Wolfram (1978). Some linguistic features of Negro dialect. In P. Stoller (Ed.), *Black American English* (pp. 49–83). New York: Delta.

Fasold, Ralph W., Labou, William, Vaughn-Cooke, Fay Boy, Bailey, Guy, Wolfram, Walt, Spears, Arthur & Rickford, John (1987). Are black and white vernaculars diverging? (Papers from the NWAVE-XVI panel discussion). *American Speech, 62*(1), 3–80.

Feagin, Crawford (1979). *Variation and change in Alabama English*. Washington, DC: Georgetown University Press.

Feigenbaum, Irwin (1970). Use of nonstandard in teaching standard: contrast and comparison. In Ralph W. Fasold & Roger W. Shuy (Eds.), *Teaching standard English in the inner city* (pp. 87–104). Washington, DC: Center for Applied Linguistics.

Fischer, John L. (1958). Social influences on the choice of a linguistic variant. *Word, 14,* 47–56.

Fordham, Signithia, & Ogbu, John U. (1986). Black students' school success: Coping with the "burden of 'acting white'." *The Urban Review, 18*(3), 176–206.

Foster, Herbert L. (1986). *Ribbin', jivin', and playin' the dozens: The persistent dilemma in our schools.* Cambridge, MA: Ballinger.

Guy, Gregory R. (1988). Language and social class. In Frederick J. Newmeyer (Ed.), *Linguistics: The Cambridge survey.* (Vol. 4: *Language: The sociocultural context*) (pp. 37–63). Cambridge: Cambridge University Press.

Halliday, M. A. K. (1964). The users and uses of language. In M. A. K. Halliday, A. McIntosh, & P. Stevens (Eds.), *The linguistic sciences and language teaching* (pp. 75–110). London: Longmans.

Heath, Shirley Brice (1983). *Ways with words: Language, life and work in communities and classrooms.* New York: Cambridge University Press.

Hollingshead, August B., & Redlich F. C., (1958). *Social class and mental illness: A community study.* New York: John Wiley.

Holm, John (1984). Variability of the copula in Black English and its creole kin. *American Speech, 59*(4), 291–309.

Holmes, Janet (1992). *An introduction to sociolinguistics.* London and New York: Longman.

Holton, Sylvia Wallace (1984). *Down home and uptown: The representation of black speech in American fiction.* Rutherford, NJ: Fairleigh Dickinson University Press.

Hoover, Mary (1978). Community attitudes toward black English. *Language in Society, 7*(1), 65–87.

Hoover, Mary (1991). Using the ethnography of African-American communications in teaching composition to bidialectcal students. In Mary E. McGroarty & Christian J. Faltis (Eds.), *Languages in schools and society: Policy and pedagogy* (pp. 465–485). Berlin: Walter de Gruyter.

Hoover, Mary, & Taylor, Orlando (1987). Bias in reading tests for Black language speakers: A sociolinguistic perspective. *The Negro Educational Review, 38*(2–3) 81–98.

Houston, Ann (1991). A grammatical continuum for (ING). In Peter Trudgill & J. K. Chambers (Eds.), *Dialects of English: Studies in grammatical variation* (pp. 241–257). London and New York: Longman.

Hughes, Arthur, & Trudgill, Peter (1979). *English accents and dialects: An introduction to social and regional varieties of British English.* London: Edward Arnold.

Jaberg, K., & Jud, J. (1928–1940). *Sprach- und Sachatlas des Italiens und der Südschweiz.* Ringier: Zoofinger.

James, Trevor (1986). *English literature from the third world.* Essex: Longman; Beirut: York Press.

Jones-Jackson, Patricia (1987). *When roots die: Endangered traditions on the Sea Islands.* Athens: University of Georgia Press.

Jordan, June (1985). Nobody mean more to me than you and the future life of Willie Jordan. In *On call: Political essays.* Boston: South End Press.

Kay, J., Agard, J., D'Aguiar, F., & Berry, J. (1990). [Cassette recording of Jackie Kay, John Agard, Fred D'Aguiar, and James Berry reading their own poetry]. London: Bluefoot Cassettes and the British Library National Sound Archive.

Kerbo, Harold (1983). *Social stratification and inequality.* New York: McGraw-Hill.

Kim, Bok-Lim (1988). The language situation of Korean Americans. In Sandra Lee McKay and Sau-ling Cynthia Wong (Eds.), *Language diversity: Problem or resource?* (pp 252–275). New York: Newbury House.

Kochman, Thomas (1986). *Black and white styles in conflict.* Chicago: The University of Chicago Press.

Kurath, Hans (1949). *A word geography of the eastern United States.* Ann Arbor: University of Michigan Press.

Kurath, Hans, Hanley, Miles L., Bloch, Bernard, & Lowman, Guy S., Jr. (1939–1943). *Linguistic Atlas of New England.* (3 Vols.). Providence, RI: Brown University Press.

Labov, Teresa (1992). Social and language boundaries among adolescents. *American Speech,* 67(4), 339–366.

Labov, William (1966). *The social stratification of English in New York City.* Washington, DC: Center for Applied Linguistics.

Labov, William (1970). The logic of nonstandard English. In Frederick Williams (Ed.), *Language and poverty: Perspectives on a theme.* (pp. 153–189). Chicago: Markham.

Labov, William (1972a). Some principles of linguistic methodology. *Language in Society,* 1, 97–120.

Labov, William (1972b). *Sociolinguistic patterns.* Philadelphia: University of Pennsylvania Press.

Labov, William (1972c). *Language in the inner city: Studies in the black English vernacular.* Philadelphia: University of Pennsylvania Press.

Labov, William (1973). Where do grammars stop? In Roger W. Shuy (Ed.), *Sociolinguistics: Current trends and prospects* (pp. 43–88). Report of the twenty-third annual roundtable meeting on linguistics and language studies. Washington, DC: Georgetown University Press.

Labov, William (1976). Systematically misleading data from test questions. *Urban Review, 9,* 146–169.

Labov, William (1981). What can be learned about change in progress from synchronic descriptions? In David Sankoff & Henrietta Cedergren (Eds.), *Variation omnibus* (pp. 177–199). Carbondale and Edmonton: Linguistic Research.

Labov, William (1988). Introduction to studies of cross dialectal comprehension. Paper presented at the seventeenth annual conference on New ways of analyzing variation (NWAVE-XVII). Quebec: Université de Montréal.

Labov, William (1991). The three dialects of English. In Penelope Eckert (Ed.), *New ways of analyzing sound change* (pp. 1–44). New York: Academic Press.

Labov, William (in press). Can reading failure be reversed? A linguistic approach to the question. In V. Gadsden & D. Wagner (Eds.), *Literacy among African American youth.* Creskill, NJ: Hampton Press.

Labov, William, & Harris, Wendell A. (1986). De facto segregation of black and white vernaculars. In David Sankoff (Ed.), *Diversity and diachrony* (pp. 1–24). Amsterdam: John Benjamins.

Lal, P., & Raghavendra, Rao K. (Eds.). (1960). *Modern Indo Anglian poetry: An anthology and a credo*. Calcutta: Writers' Workshop.

Le Page, Robert, & Tabouret-Keller, Andrée (1985). *Acts of identity: Creole-based approaches to language and ethnicity*. Cambridge: Cambridge University Press.

Lee, David (1989). Sociolinguistic variation in the speech of Brisbanc adolescents. *Australian Journal of Linguistics, 9,* 51–72.

McCrum, Robert, Cran, William, & MacNeil, Robert (1986). *The story of English*. London and Boston: Faber and Faber, BBC Publications; New York: Viking. [Videocassettes available from Films Incorporated, Chicago, IL.]

Michaels, Sarah (1981). "Sharing time": Children's narrative styles and differential access to literacy. *Language in Society, 10,* 423–442.

Michaels, S., and Cazden, Courtney B. (1986). Teacher-child collaboration as oral preparation for literacy. In Bambi B. Schieffelin and Perry Gilmore, eds. *The Acquisition of literacy: ethnographic perspectives* (132–154). Norwood, N.J.: Ablex.

Milroy, Lesley (1980). *Language and social networks*. Oxford: Basil Blackwell.

Milroy, Lesley, & Milroy, James (1992). Social network and social class: Toward an integrated sociolinguistic model. *Language in Society, 21,* 1–26.

Morgan, Marcyliena (1991). Indirectness and interpretation in African American women's discourse. *Pragmatics, 1,* 421–451.

Moskowitz, Breyne Arlene (1985). The acquisition of language. In Virginia P. Clark, Paul A. Eschholz, & Alfred F. Rosa (Eds.), *Language: Introductory readings*. (pp. 45–73). New York: St. Martin's Press.

Partridge, Eric (1984). *A dictionary of slang and unconventional English* (8th ed.). London: Routledge and Kegan Paul.

Petyt, K. M. (1985). *Dialect and accent in industrial West Yorkshire*. Amsterdam: John Benjamins.

Pickford, Glenna Ruth (1956). American linguistic geography: A sociological appraisal. *Word, 12,* 211–233.

Poplack, Shana, & Sankoff, David (1987). The Philadelphia story in the Spanish Caribbean. *American Speech, 62*(4), 291–314.

Poplack, Shana, & Tagliamonte, Sali (1991). African American English in the diaspora: Evidence from old-line Nova Scotians. *Language Variation and Change, 3,* 301–339.

Reed, Carroll E. (1977). *Dialects of American English*. Amherst: The University of Massachusetts Press.

Rickford, John R. (1974). The insights of the mesolect. In David DeCamp & Ian F. Hancock (Eds.), *Pidgins and creoles: Current trends and prospects* (pp. 92–117). Washington, DC: Georgetown University Press.

Rickford, John R. (1975). Carrying the new wave into syntax: The case of Black English BIN. In Ralph W. Fasold & Roger W. Shuy (Eds.), *Analyzing variation in language* (pp. 162–183). Washington, DC: Georgetown University Press.

Rickford, John R. (1977). The question of prior creolization in Black English. In Albert Valdman (Ed.), *Pidgin and creole linguistics* (pp. 190–221). Bloomington: Indiana University Press.

Rickford, John R. (1979). *Variation in a creole continuum: Quantitative and implicational approaches.* Doctoral dissertation. Philadelphia: University of Pennsylvania.

Rickford, John R. (1986). The need for new approaches to social class analysis in sociolinguistics. *Language and Communication,* 6(3), 215–221.

Rickford, John R. (1987). The haves and have nots: Sociolinguistic surveys and the assessment of speaker competence. *Language in Society, 16*(2), 149–177.

Rickford, John R. (1991). Grammatical variation and divergence in vernacular Black English. In Marinel Gerritsen & Dieter Stein (Eds.), *Internal and external factors in syntactic change* (pp. 175–200). Berlin and New York: Mouton.

Rickford, John R., Ball, Arnetha, Blake, Renee, Jackson, Raina & Nomi Martin (1991). Rappin on the copula coffin: Theoretical and methodological issues in the analysis of copula variation in African American Vernacular English. *Language Variation and Change, 3*(1), 103–132.

Rickford, John R., & Blake, Renee (1990). Copula contraction and absence in Barbadian English, Samaná English and Vernacular Black English. In Kira Hall, Jean-Pierre Koenig, Michael Meacham, Sondra Reinman, & Laurel A. Sutton (Eds.), *BLS 16: Proceedings of the sixteenth annual meeting of the Berkeley Linguistics Society, February 16–19, 1990.* (pp. 257–268). Berkeley, CA: Berkeley Linguistics Society.

Rickford, John R., & McNair-Knox, Faye (1993). Addressee and topic-influenced style shift: A quantitative sociolinguistic study. In Douglas Biber & Edward Finegan (Eds.), *Perspectives on register: Situating register variation within sociolinguistics* (pp. 235–276). Oxford: Oxford University Press.

Rickford, John R., & Rickford, Angela E. (in press). Dialect readers revisited. *Linguistics and Education.*

Rosenthal, Robert & Jacobson, Lenore (1968). *Pygmalion in the classroom: Teacher expectations and pupils' intellectual achievement.* New York: Holt, Rinehart and Winston.

Sankoff, David (1988). Variable rules. In Ulrich Ammon, Norbert Dittmar, & Klaus J. Mattheier (Eds.), *Sociolinguistics: An international handbook of the science of language and society* (pp. 984–987). Berlin: Walter de Gruyter.

Sells, Peter, Rickford, John R., & Wasow, Thomas A. (1995). An optimality theoretic approach to variation in negative inversion in AAVE. In Jennifer Arnold, Renee Blake, Brad Davidson, Julie Solomon, and Scott Schwenter (Eds.), *Proceedings of the twenty-third annual meeting on new ways of analyzing variation* (*NWAV-23*). Stanford: Center for the Study of Language and Information.

Shuy, Roger W., Wolfram, Walt, & Riley, William K. (1967). *Linguistic correlates of social stratification in Detroit speech.* USOE Final Report No. 6-1347.

Simpkins, Gary A., Holt, G. & Simpkins, Charlesetta (1977). *Bridge: A cross-cultural reading program.* Boston: Houghton-Mifflin.

Simpkins, Gary A., & Simpkins, Charlesetta (1981). Cross cultural approach to curriculum development. Black English and the education of Black children and youth. In Geneva Smitherman (Ed.), *Proceedings of the national invitational symposium on the King decision* (pp. 221–240). Detroit: Center for Black Studies, Wayne State University.

Sledd, James (1969). Bi-dialectalism: The linguistics of white supremacy. *English Journal,* December, pp. 1307–1329.

Smitherman, Geneva (Ed.). (1981). Introduction: Black English and the education of black children and youth. *Proceedings of the national invitational symposium on the King decision* (pp. 11–31). Detroit: Center for Black Studies, Wayne State University.

Smitherman, Geneva (1986). *Talkin and testifyin: The language of black America.* Detroit: Wayne State University Press.

Spears, Arthur K. (1982). The black English semi-auxiliary *come. Language, 58*(4), 850–872.

Starks, Judith A. (1983). The black English controversy and its implications for addressing the educational needs of black children: The cultural linguistic approach. John Chambers, Jr. (Ed.), *Black English: Educational equity and the law* (pp. 97–132). Ann Arbor: Karoma.

Stewart, William A. (1964). Foreign language teaching methods in quasi-foreign language situations. In William A. Stewart (Ed.) *Non-standard speech and the teaching of English.* Washington, DC: Center for Applied Linguistics.

Stewart, William A. (1969). On the use of negro dialect in the teaching of reading. In Joan C. Baratz & Roger W. Shuy (Eds.), *Teaching black children to read* (pp. 156–219). Washington, DC: Center for Applied Linguistics.

Stewart, William A. (1970). Toward a history of American negro dialect. In Frederick Williams (Ed.), *Language and poverty* (pp. 351–379). Chicago: Markham.

Sutcliffe, David (1982). *British black English.* Oxford: Basil Blackwell.

Sutcliffe, David, & Wong, Ansel (Eds.). (1986). *The language of the black experience.* Oxford: Basil Blackwell.

Sutcliffe, David, with Figueroa, John (1992). *System in black language.* Clevedon: Multilingual Matters.

Tagliamonte, Sali, & Poplack, Shana (1988). How black English *past* got to the present. *Language in Society, 17*(4), 513–533.

Taylor, Hanni U. (1989). *Standard English, black English, and bidialectalism.* New York: Peter Lang.

Taylor, Orlando L. (1973). Teachers' attitudes toward black and nonstandard English as measured by the language attitude scale. In Roger W. Shuy & Ralph W. Fasold (Eds.), *Language attitudes: Current trends and prospects* (pp. 174–201). Washington, DC: Georgetown University Press.

Taylor, Orlando L., & Matsuda, Maryon M. (1988). Storytelling and classroom discrimination. In Geneva Smitherman-Donaldson & Teun A. van Dijk (Eds.), *Discourse and discrimination* (pp. 206–220). Detroit: Wayne State University Press.

Terrell, Sandra L., & Terrell, Francis (1983, January). Effects of speaking Black English upon employment opportunities. *ASHA* [Journal of the American Speech-Language-Hearing Association].

Theberge, Christine, & Rickford, John R. (1989). *Preterit* had *in the BEV of elementary school children.* Paper presented at the eighteenth annual conference on new ways of analyzing variation (NWAVE-18). Durham, NC: Duke University.

Trudgill, Peter (1974). *Sociolinguistics: An introduction to language and society.* Middlesex, England: Penguin Books.

Trudgill, Peter (1983). *On dialect.* Oxford: Basil Blackwell.

Valdés, Guadalupe (1988). The language situation of Mexican Americans. In Sandra Lee McKay & Sau-ling Cynthia Wong (Eds.), *Language diversity: Problem or resource?* (pp. 111–139). Cambridge and New York: Newbury House.

Vaughn-Cooke, Fay (1983, June). Improving language assessment in minority children. *ASHA* [Journal of the American Speech and Hearing Association]. *25,* 29–34.

Williams, Frederick (1970). Language, attitude, and social change. In Frederick Williams (Ed.), *Language and poverty* (pp. 380–399). Chicago: Markham.

Williams, Glyn (1992). *Sociolinguistics: A sociological critique.* London: Routledge.

Winford, Donald (1992). Back to the past: The BEV/creole connection revisited. *Language Variation and Change, 4*(3), 311–357.

Wolfram, Walt (1969). *A linguistic description of Detroit Negro speech.* Washington, DC: Center for Applied Linguistics.

Wolfram, Walt (1976). Levels of sociolinguistic bias in testing. In Deborah S. Harrison & Tom Trabasso (Eds.), *Black English: A Seminar* (pp. 263–287). Hillsdale, NJ: Erlbaum.

Wolfram, Walt (1986). Black-White dimensions in sociolinguistic test bias. In Michael B. Montgomery & Guy Bailey (Eds.), *Language variety in the south.* (pp. 373–385). University, AL: University of Alabama Press.

Wolfram, Walt (1991). *Dialects and American English.* Englewood Cliffs, NJ: Prentice Hall and Center for Applied Linguistics.

Wolfram, Walt A., & Fasold, Ralph W. (1969). Toward reading materials for speakers of black English: Three linguistically appropriate passages. In Joan C. Baratz & Roger W. Shuy (Eds.), *Teaching Black children to read* (pp. 138–155). Washington, DC: Center for Applied Linguistics.

Woolard, K. (1985). Language variation and cultural hegemony: Toward an integration of linguistic and sociolinguistic theory. *American Ethnologist, 12,* 738–748.

# 6 *Pidgins and creoles*

Patricia C. Nichols

He gon catch we back!
Huh?
He gon catch us again!

This striking exchange took place some twenty years ago, between an 11-year-old African-American boy and me as we were driving down a four-lane highway along Waccamaw Neck in coastal South Carolina. I was passing a big four-wheeler as it was gathering speed on a straight road, and my young passenger was commenting on the futility of that attempt – first in his native creole and then in a variety closer to mine. Born about 20 miles and 20 years apart along this coast, we had learned very different language varieties in our home communities. Now, working together daily in his newly integrated local school and goofing off that day on a fishing trip, we were learning to accommodate to each other's language patterns. But, as this brief exchange makes clear, the child was doing the major share of the accommodating. When my "Huh?" indicated a lack of understanding, he could make substitutions for two words in his native creole, known as *Gullah,* that moved his variety closer to my standard English. Having worked for 2 months as a classroom aide and researcher in his school, I was able to understand his use of *gon* as an auxiliary marker for *future* and his extension of the standard meaning of *catch,* so that I could then translate his observation to something like: "He [the truck driver] is going to pass us again." But *his* relatively greater understanding of *my* speech, and of how it differed from his, was all too typical for the school setting he was in.

Integrated just 2 years previously, the small elementary school that this child attended (grades 1 to 6 for children ranging in age from 6 to 12) now had a European-American principal and a faculty equally divided between African-Americans and European-Americans, while the student population remained about 90 percent African-American. Most students entering school spoke Gullah at home and with their

I am grateful to Nancy Hornberger, Sandy McKay, and Bill Pollitzer for their careful reading and comments on earlier drafts of this chapter. Frank H. Nichols, Jr., provided invaluable help with the map of pidgin and creole languages.

playmates. The teachers born outside the area received no in-service training in the creole's distinctive structural and functional differences from English. Indeed, some teachers new to the area reported using a designated child as "translator" for nearly a year until they and the children had learned how to accommodate each other's distinctive patterns. After about 4 years in school, many African-American children (particularly the girls) were able to switch between both varieties with ease. Some boys, however, rejected both the standard English of the classroom and the reading activities associated with it (Nichols, 1977b). Most schools in the county had five or six boys at the sixth-grade level who were nonreaders, not because of any "deficiency" on their part but rather because of their rejection of the language variety used in their formal schooling. (See Edwards, 1985, for description of a parallel rejection by creole-speaking adolescents in British schools.) When their own stories were tape-recorded and given back to them in printed versions for the reading lesson, the boys' participation in this activity improved markedly. These transcribed stories used conventional English spelling but preserved the boys' distinctive creole grammatical markers. (See Nichols, 1977b, for a full discussion of these "language experience" lessons.) An interesting indication that these children had at least passive knowledge of standard English grammar came as they read their original stories aloud: Without fail, each child changed at least some of the original creole markers to standard English forms for oral reading. This code switching was probably related to their awareness that English was considered the appropriate language for this activity in the school setting.

The consequences of teachers' and school administrators' ignorance of pidgin and creole language varieties can be enormous for children who enter school speaking them. This chapter will discuss attitudes toward pidgins and creoles in general, as well as structural and functional features of specific creoles that twentieth-century educators are likely to encounter. Attitudes, structures, and functions are equally significant for educational settings, interwoven as these aspects of pidgin and creoles are in daily language use. The origin and development of these languages will also be discussed, along with problems associated with studying them.

## Attitudes toward pidgin and creole languages

Pidgins and creoles, which are essentially new language varieties created out of old cloth, allow us to observe the birth and evolution of a language within a highly compressed time frame. Often coexisting with a more prestigious variety, they present educators with special challenges: (1) they are typically spoken, not written, and (2) they are often viewed with disdain by both their users and by society at large – in part because they do not yet have a respected body of written literature. The most common error made about these language varieties, however, is related to the "old cloth" from which they are created. Because the donor language from which they take their vocabulary is often one with great prestige, pidgins and creoles are mistakenly believed to be merely an inaccurate or incomplete version of that prestige language.

Children who speak a creole as their native language are affected by these factors simply because attitudes toward language and speakers are often conflated (see McGroarty, this volume). In school settings, students' potential at any age will often be evaluated by the variety of language they speak. The low prestige of pidgin or creole language varieties in most school settings can inhibit, and even prevent, educational success. In Britain during the 1960s, large numbers of creole-speaking West Indian immigrant children ended up in remedial classes and schools for the "educational subnormal" (sometimes making up 90 percent of classes for the retarded), whereas their East Indian and Pakistani counterparts were placed in English as a second language classes (Nichols, 1977a). West Indian immigrant children sounded as if they were speaking English, although most were speaking Jamaican-Creole, whereas East Indian immigrant children were obviously speaking something else. (Sridhar, this volume, and Pratt-Johnson, 1993, point to similar problems faced by recent Jamaican immigrants to New York City.) Because recent educational reform efforts have moved the learner, as opposed to the body of knowledge being taught, to the center of attention, teachers have become increasingly aware of the central role that language plays in education. Perhaps the single most important action that might be taken to enhance the educational prospects of children all over the world would be for educational institutions to value and use children's' languages as resources in the classroom rather than as obstacles to learning (see McKay & Wong, 1988; Murray, 1992, for development of this thesis). If teachers and educational policymakers understand pidgins and creoles as the unique language varieties they are, with systematic rules for structure and use, educators in conjunction with community leaders can develop some means of incorporating them into school settings in ways that celebrate both the languages and the learners.

## Origins and development of pidgins and creoles

Pidgins and creoles are linked in a continuum of language development. *Pidgins* come into being because they are needed during times of population upheaval, when normal mechanisms of language transmission are disrupted. No one sits down and decides to create a pidgin. It comes into being through the interaction of large numbers of people who speak several different languages and who have little reason or opportunity to learn another one of the many languages spoken in the contact situation. Typically, pidgins arise when people of many language backgrounds engage in extensive trading or forced labor, often in coastal areas near major seaports. They appear when massive population dislocation and movement take place. In these dynamic situations, there is too much going on for the small number of interpreters to cope with. Harris (1986) summarizes the three conditions needed for emergence of a pidgin language: (1) lack of effective bilingualism, (2) need to communicate, and (3) restricted access to the target language.

In situations like the ones just described, the sheer number of bilingual interpreters required for the many languages spoken prohibits all but a few remarkable individuals from learning all the languages in play. Instead, a compromise is reached that almost always entails using the vocabulary of the language of the more powerful population and the grammars of the less powerful. Typically, the less powerful speakers outnumber the powerful ones and thus comprise the greatest number of speakers of the new pidgin. Since the powerful group controls the goods and human labor being traded, the lexicon of the language they speak is used to name both the goods and the laborers being sold or indentured. Often the new language will be referred to as some modified version of the language spoken by the powerful. Indeed, the names of many of these languages codify relationships of social power and prestige in a given time and place: "bamboo English" in Korea and Japan, "babu English" in India, the "broken English" of the Torres Strait near Australia, "broken Portuguese" in Angola, "français nègre" in Louisiana, and "black English" in colonial South Carolina.

As in most situations of inequality, however, those with great power are few in number. The direction the language takes is determined largely by those who speak it most: the less powerful in the contact situation (see Janeway, 1980, for a general theory of the "powers of the weak" in a variety of situations). If these large numbers of politically weak speakers share grammatically related languages, their impact on how the language develops will be very great. The new contact language will be used more widely, simply because of the large number of users. They and their children will stabilize its word order, the inflectional morphemes that develop over time, and the expanded or constricted meanings of those words adopted from the prestige language. The early speakers of the new pidgin will do this in ways that "fit" the linguistic patterns most familiar to them in the grammars of their native languages, as well as the universal patterns underlying all human language.

Linguists refer to the native languages that make the greatest contributions to the grammar of the new language as its *substratum,* and the language contributing the bulk of the vocabulary of the new language as its *superstratum,* or *lexifier language.*

The resulting pidgin is no one's native language. It is always spoken in addition to a native language. And because it seems like a specific prestige language because of its predominant vocabulary but has a grammar that is very different, the pidgin often is characterized as "broken" or "fractured" ________. The blank can be filled in with almost any of the world's widely spoken world languages, particularly those associated with the slave trade and with colonization on a large scale. In reality, the language born in the contact zone is a new language, similar to, yet quite distinct from, any of the several languages contributing to its structure. In situations of massive population upheaval all over the world, in playgrounds and in marketplaces, pidgins bridge the gaps between speakers thrown together from several disparate language backgrounds and allow basic face-to-face communication for play and trade.

A *creole* can develop from a pidgin language if certain social conditions come into play. When playmates or trading partners, slaves or indentured servants, begin their own families in circumstances where their first language is not spoken, a pidgin that they both know may become the language they use at home. Since the mates do not speak each other's native language, and if (an important *if*) they continue to live in an area where the pidgin is widely used, their children will hear the pidgin as the most important language in their environment. Adult women will speak it at the marketplace, in the fields, and in communal kitchens. Adult men will talk in pidgin on labor gangs, on journeys to nearby villages, and with outsiders who visit their living quarters. Children growing up in these communities will express their primary experiences of love, fear, and interaction with the physical world through this language. It will link them to the human community of which they are a part, in the same way that touch and sight and sound link them to their physical world. For children living in these special conditions, the pidgin language spoken by adults and older youth in their community is the primary language of home and family. As they grow into adulthood and use it with others of their age and those slightly older, the pidgin develops into a creole language with expanded grammar, vocabulary, and a range of functions fully adequate for a native language.

Today, creoles with a French vocabulary have the most speakers, estimated to be more than 4 million in number (DeCamp, 1971, p. 17), with major population centers in the Caribbean and neighboring southern Louisiana, as well as some islands in the Indian Ocean. Creoles with an English vocabulary are also found in the Caribbean and nearby coastal regions of Georgia and South Carolina on the North American mainland, in West Africa, and in Hawaii and other islands of the Pacific. Those with Spanish or Portuguese vocabulary are located chiefly in Asia and on islands off the West African coast; those with Dutch vocabulary have a few speakers in the Virgin Islands; and those with non-European vocabulary can be found in Africa, the South Pacific, and New Guinea (Romaine, 1988). About 100 to 200 pidgin and creole languages are spoken worldwide, depending on the definitions used to identify them. (The map in Figure 1 on page 206 shows the location of many of these languages; Holm [1989] provides comprehensive maps and background information.)

Structurally, the formal distinction between a pidgin and a creole language is difficult to draw. Most often, linguists distinguish between them by the historical and social conditions that have given rise to them and by the relatively greater stability of creole structures. Traditionally, linguists have pointed to a more elaborate grammar and to an expanded vocabulary for creoles, although speakers of these languages may refer to them as *pidgin* while linguists view them as having evolved to *creole* status. Speakers of a creole typically use it as a first language, whereas speakers of a pidgin use it as a second, third, or even fourth language.

## *The study of pidgins and creoles*

For over a century there has been considerable controversy about the specific processes by which these languages originate and, most recently, about precisely how creoles develop from pidgins. Some of this controversy stems from the methods by which they have been studied. Most early accounts consist of travelers' reports of how these languages were used, with some sample phrases as examples of their structures. Knowledge of how pidgin and creole speakers use these languages among themselves, in all the many dimensions of human interaction, has been sparse until very recently (see Rickford's 1987 volume on Guyanese creole for an exceptional study by one who knows this particular creole from the inside). Early comparative studies of these languages were undertaken in the 1880s by the German linguist Hugo Schuchardt, whose essays on English-based pidgins and creoles were translated by Gilbert (1980) a century after Schuchardt wrote them. Although he relied on incomplete and often inadequate descriptions of these languages, Schuchardt was one of the first to note similarities between English-based creoles in the Caribbean and on the North American mainland.

Most pidgins and creoles, however, were studied in isolation rather than comparatively until the 1950s, with the data collected by linguists or missionaries from a few isolated "informants" who responded to questions about their language. Obviously, little information was obtained about how the language was actually used across a range of social contexts and classes. Linguists recorded the answers to their questions in phonemic transcription at the time of utterance, certainly an improvement on relying on memory, but it was not possible to validate the reliability of these transcriptions until mechanical recording became possible in the 1930s. The earliest recording equipment was bulky, ranging from 200 to 500 pounds, and was complicated to operate. Recording sessions were by necessity prearranged and relatively formal social events. (See Brewer, 1991, for a vivid description of the social and associated logistical problems experienced by one early interviewer.). Even though the recording quality was poor by today's standards, the recordings made possible the analysis of longer segments of texts after an interview was concluded; this in turn permitted closer examination of the grammars of these languages. With the benefit of such recorded data, the African-American linguist Lorenzo Dow Turner (1949) made significant comparisons between the creole Gullah spoken along the coasts of South Carolina and Georgia and some languages of West Africa that have contributed to its substratum. Turner studied five of these West African languages in preparation for his analysis of Gullah.

The subsequent development of portable tape recorders, easily transported into remote communities and simple to operate, contributed directly to the recent development of *comparative creolistics,* as the field has come to be known. With the collection of language data far easier and with a growing interest in comparative analysis, the first international conference devoted exclusively to creoles was held in 1959, signaling the birth of a new academic field of inquiry (LePage, 1961). A decade later, another such conference was held (Hymes, 1971), and in 1969 the Modern Language Association began devoting a separate section of its yearly bibliography to the field (Romaine, 1988) – an indication of its established place in general language studies.

The decades of the 1970s and 1980s saw the publication of numerous studies of individual pidgins and creoles, as well as attempts to synthesize information about them and formulate adequate theoretical models that would account for their origin and development. Reinecke and coauthors (1975) provide an annotated bibliography of studies done on these languages prior to the mid-1970s; Mühlhäusler (1986), Romaine (1988), and Holm (1989) provide surveys that include more recent research and discussion of theoretical models. LePage and Tabouret-Keller (1985) contribute their synthesis of several decades of research on creoles of the former British Empire and conclude that both language and community come into being through "acts of identity which people make within themselves and with each other" (p. 2). In 1989 the International Society for Pidgin and Creole Linguistics was formed, associated with the respected *Journal of Pidgin and Creole Languages,* whose publisher (John Benjamins) also sponsors a Creole Language Library, now consisting of more than eleven volumes. The combination of the accumulating data on the world's pidgin and creole languages and these new channels for sharing research has had an impact on other areas of language study. Specifically, the fields of language acquisition (Andersen, 1983) and of historical linguistics (Thomason & Kaufman, 1988) have incorporated new insights from creolistics about the disruption of "normal" language transmission and the processes of language mixing.

## *Theoretical and methodological issues*

The decade of the 1990s has confronted several theoretical issues arising from this outpouring of work, as well as an important methodological one. First, the ambitious and controversial bioprogram theory constructed by Derek Bickerton (1981, 1984, 1990), whose early research on individual creoles was undertaken in Guyana and Hawaii, makes far-reaching claims about the universal processes that underlie the development of creole languages. He maintains that creoles develop from pidgins according to the demands of an innate human bioprogram, one that is little affected by conditions of contact between speakers or by either the superstratum or substratum languages. His claims have spurred considerable research on the structures of pidgins and creoles that are different from the limited number on which he bases his claims. More systematic analyses of sociohistorical conditions of contact and more comparative research on substratum languages within a given contact situation have begun to cast serious doubt on the validity of Bickerton's hypothesis as the sole explanation for creole genesis (Mufwene, 1993; Muysken & Smith, 1986; Singler, 1990). As the 1990s progress, a consensus seems to be forming that, although universal tendencies may have a role in feature selection, they are by no means the only explanation for how these languages develop. In the evolving consensus, contributing factors like universal tendencies, conditions of contact and frequency of speaker interaction, and structures of the superstratum and substratum languages at the time of initial contact are seen to be of differential importance in specific language contact settings.

A second theoretical model, with the potential to encompass issues of pidgin and creole development, comes from work on code switching by Carol Myers-Scotton (1993a, 1993b, in press). Her research was initially conducted in multilingual settings in East Africa, and only recently has she begun to extend the model known as the *matrix language frame model* to pidgins and creoles. This model designates one language in a mixed-language situation as the main, or *matrix,* language; it is used as the morphosyntactic frame for either the code switching or the new contact language that becomes a pidgin. The matrix language contributes the grammatical or system morphemes: quantifiers, specifiers, and inflectional morphemes – including those for tense. Time adverbs and aspectual markers can also come from the matrix language. The model designates another language in the contact situation as the secondary, or *embedded,* language: it contributes the vocabulary or content morphemes. The relationship between the two languages can "turn over" in the process of time, so that the embedded becomes the matrix, and the matrix the embedded. Myers-Scotton cites a wide range of cases where this has occurred for code switching in bilingual situations and argues that this process also occurs among pidgins and creoles. By the time a language has evolved to creole stage, the turnover has happened more than once, thus accounting for the grammatical "mix" creoles typically exhibit. Working within such a model, creolists will need to consider social and historical factors that have precipitated such turnovers and to examine carefully all the relevant matrix languages that may have contributed system morphemes. Without denying the influence of universal tendencies, the matrix language frame model highlights the importance of the social context in determining how specific pidgins and creoles develop and may well usher in a new focus for the field.

A recent collaborative analysis of recordings of African-American former slaves, interviewed as part of the U.S. Federal Writers' Project initiated in the 1930s, raises a serious methodological issue that must be addressed (Bailey, Maynor, & Cukor-Avila, 1991). For this project, copies of about eleven tapes held in the Library of Congress were analyzed over a period of 4 years by twelve linguists, who worked separately and made widely different interpretations of some of the tapes. Linguists who had an extensive background working with creole texts were more likely to recognize creole structures in passages that were doubtful or difficult to hear. A fundamental question arising from these different findings about the same body of data can be stated as follows: If there is substantial disagreement among established scholars transcribing identical texts, how much credence can be given to claims based upon single transcriptions of recorded speech? This collaborative study is likely to affect the way data on language varieties like pidgins and creoles are analyzed in the future. Awareness of the possibility of turnover, as described by Myers-Scotton's model, as well as of the transcriber's familiarity with the language itself, seems relevant to the collection of accurate information about these languages.

## Structures and functions of a creole

With the increasing mobility of the world's population, at some point in their careers many educators in English-speaking countries are likely to encounter students speaking a creole as their first language. Three are indigenous to the United States: *Gullah* or *Geechee,* along the coasts of South Carolina and Georgia, spoken within African-American communities; a French creole known as *Louisiana Créole French* in southern Louisiana, spoken primarily by African-Americans (although this is changing, according to Brown, 1993); *Hawaiian Creole English* among the multiethnic population of the Hawaiian Islands (see Kawamoto, 1993; Sato, 1985, for recent descriptions of the status of this language in the islands). Nichols (1981) provides an overview of these American creoles. In addition to these home-grown languages, recent immigrants to urban centers ranging from the Gulf Coast to New York City enter school speaking Haitain Creole French, Jamaican Creole English, and other creoles of the Caribbean. In the southwestern part of the United States, language contact is generally characterized by code switching between Spanish and English, rather than by creolization.

In other English-speaking countries, both immigrant and indigenous creoles can be found. Speakers of Jamaican Creole and other English creoles of the Caribbean entered Britain in large numbers during the 1950s and 1960s (Edwards, 1985), and travel to and from the islands is frequent. (See Cassidy, 1961, for an introduction to the creole spoken in Jamaica; Lalla & D'Costa, 1990, for a collection of Jamaican Creole texts; Winer, 1990, on English creole in Trinidad and Tobago.) In Australia, an indigenous English creole known as *Kriol* is spoken in the Northern Territory and some urban centers. Other related English creoles are spoken on nearby islands in the southwest Pacific. (See Keesing, 1988, for a discussion of the connections between early pidgins of the Pacific; see Shnukal, 1988, for a detailed description of a contemporary creole spoken by Torres Strait islanders.) Information on these languages has become widely available only within the last decade, and Romaine's 1991 collection of essays on language in Australia helps to place them in the broader sociohistorical context of a multilingual society.

These creoles represent only some of the ones likely to be encountered in contemporary English-speaking classrooms. The map in Figure 1 includes a representation of the world's pidgins and creoles, showing their locations, listing their commonly used names, and indicating about twenty that use English vocabulary.

## *An English creole of South Carolina*

Samples of speech collected from children ranging in age from 8 to 12 in a Gullah-speaking area of coastal South Carolina in the 1970s will serve to illustrate the difference between the system (grammatical) morphemes and the content (lexical) morphemes that typically characterize creoles as language types:

1. Ee hard, John? (Boy, 10 years old, in reference to a football)
2. My stomach ee roll. (Girl, 9 years old, after viewing the underside of a starfish)
3. That lady look to the bottom – ee money all down there. (Boy, 10 years old)
4. They might rub two rock together and ee come fire. (Boy, 10 years old)
5. Everytime John L ________ kill a bird, he scared fuh go in the bush fuh get um. (Girl, 9 years old)

In these five brief utterances, the content words are all clearly English vocabulary, used with conventional meanings for the most part:

Adjectives: hard, scared
Nouns: stomach, lady, bottom, money, rock, fire, bird, bush
Verbs: roll, look, rub, come, kill, go, get

What is not conventional English are the pronominal system for referring to persons and things, the prepositional system for indicating location, and the inflectional system for indicating number and tense. Like most creoles, Gullah omits the copula *be* in many environments.

Pronominal system: *ee* is used for all genders in both nominative and possessive case, and *um* is used for all genders in objective case.

Prepositional system: *to* is used to indicate both position at and movement toward an object. Earlier Gullah texts collected by Turner (1949) show virtually no use of *at*.

Inflectional system: (a) nouns are not inflected for plural or possessive; (b) verbs are not inflected for simple past tense. Aspect (indication of ongoing or completed or habitual and/or repeated action) is indicated by a particle placed *before* the verb, as in the following examples:

6. She duh hit me. (Girl, 9 years old. Translation given by a friend: "She *always* hitting me.")
7. See, that boy duh cheat. (Boy, 10 years old)
8. Gregg duh hide. (Girl, 9 years old, pointing to a friend ducking up and down behind a car)

*Figure 1.* *Selected pidgin and creole languages (not all listed). (Adapted from Holm, 1989; Todd, 1990.)*

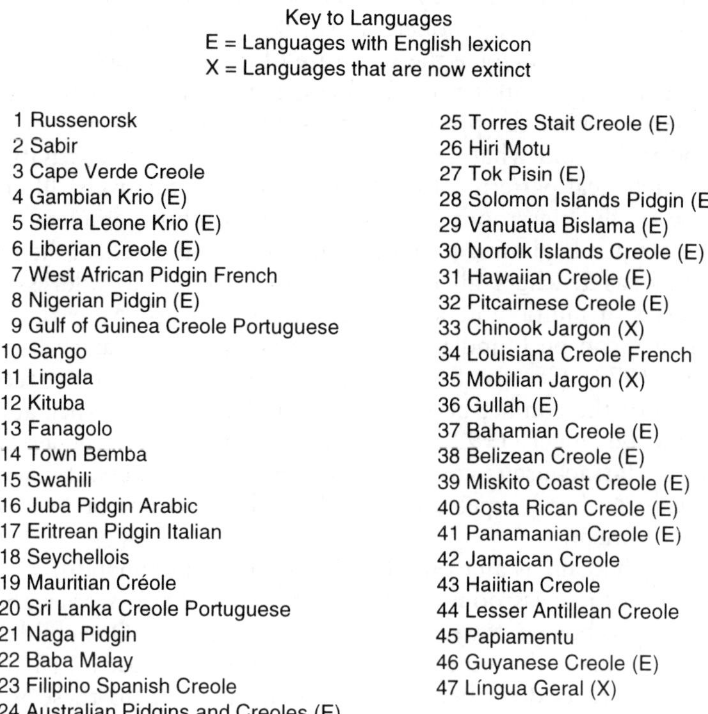


*Figure 1. (Continued)*

Gullah is typical of many creoles in its omission of the copula, as in examples 1 and 5 above, and in its lack of a passive transformation:

9. Chris paper tear. (Boy, 9 years old, referring to a friend's paper that was previously torn)

Although these examples give a far from complete account of the differences between the structures of Gullah and English, the system-content morpheme distinction shown is a useful one. Once this principal distinction is grasped, teachers can understand why a child's language "sounds" like English – but isn't. This principle is applicable across creoles and should enable teachers to discover the salient differences between their students' languages and their own, just as students have been so adept at doing over the years.

Even more important for educational concerns than these structural linguistic differences are the functional differences in the use of language that children may bring from their home communities. These differences are important because they are so much more difficult to observe, a difficulty that obtains for noncreole speakers as well as creole. The functions of language involve the structure of discourse, how the audience is addressed, if an audience is addressed at all on a particular topic (uses of silence), what the presuppositions and shared information are understood to be, and what genre is appropriate for which activity. In short, the rhetorical patterns of the home may be distinctively different from those of the classroom in ways that we cannot completely describe. We are just beginning to understand these differences in the rules for discourse as teachers all over the globe attempt to address the learning styles of multiethnic and multilingual students. An early look at these issues can be found in the influential work of Cazden, John, and Hymes (1972). (See also Saville-Troike, this volume.) A more recent examination of the conflict between home and classroom expectations can be found Ballenger (1992), who worked with Haitian teachers and parents in a Massachusetts community to uncover the roots of disjunction between teachers' expectations and children's behavior in a preschool environment.

Using Gullah again as an example of how such functional differences may operate in the classroom environment, here are two stories about dogs told by two boys in the same fifth-grade classroom. One child was European-American, the other African-American. Obvious structural differences occur, as described earlier. But in addition to these word and sentence-level differences, the organization of the stories themselves is based upon different principles:

> I have this dog and we have a bunch of chickens back at my uncle's and at my house. And this dog, he went after the chickens the other day, and he killed two roosters and four hens and went after some more. And when he did, my uncle shot him in the leg and made him go on. And he came back yesterday and almost got some more. We ran him off again. And when we did we had to go take him to town and put him to sleep 'cause he was real badly hurt. So we had him pretty well fixed up, so we could bury him.
>
> (Boy, 10 years old, European-American, coastal South Carolina)

> Oh, I got one! [Overlapping previous story] One day, yesterday, me and Darryl, we were going in the yard. Me and Darryl hear a car say, "Bump, bump." And then Teria dog – and he say, Darryl said, "Teria dog done get hit." Then me and Darryl run up there and the dog bleed all over. Then Bubba bring um in the yard. Then Bubba gone get ee gun and shoot um.
>
> [Questions from his audience about the dog.] He been dead.
>
> (Boy, 10 years old, African-American, coastal South Carolina)

The story told by the African-American child includes many of the structural features of Gullah: lack of verbal inflections for tense, lack of nominal inflections for possessive, and preverbal markers of aspect, to note just a few:

10. Me and Darryl hear a car say . . .
11. And then Teria dog . . .
12. Teria dog done get hit.

This child's relationship with his audience, however, is quite different from that of the first child. His story is an interactive one, entering as it does on the heels of the other, using first names of the characters in his story under the assumption that his listeners will know them, and ending without summarizing the meaning for his audience but assuming that the listeners will supply any relevant moral from their shared experience of dogs (or people) who get into trouble through being where they are not supposed to be. He uses sound effects and direct quotations in this brief piece, and the general delivery is a lively, animated one that contrasts with the story told by the European-American boy. The first child uses no personal names, no sound effects or direct quotations, and ends with an implied moral for his audience. (See Nichols, 1989, for a fuller comparison of these and other children's stories in a biracial classroom.)

When such differences in oral rhetorical styles are transmitted into written form, the patterns of the European-American child will be "privileged" in the typical classroom environment. His distanced, public discourse, which relies on less interaction and less prior knowledge of persons and places known to the storyteller, is topic-centered and thus in the style preferred for most formal classroom writing. He will have an easier time transferring his oral style to the preferred written style than will the African-American boy, whose approach to his story is more personal and requires greater audience participation and knowledge of the characters involved. Most important, the African-American boy reflects a preference for narrative discourse that leaves the audience to draw its own conclusions about the meaning of the narrative – a strategy in direct conflict with the conclusion expected in much formal classroom writing. Even if this child decides to use the system morphemes of English (which he, like most other children of his age, already understands), his written compositions may continue to reflect the oral rhetorical strategies of his home community and will be judged less than satisfactory by the teachers from the dominant culture who make up half the staff at his small school.

## Pidgins and creoles as resources in the classroom

How are these languages to be honored in today's classrooms? First, it is necessary for teachers to understand students as quickly and as well as possible. Without that understanding, the teaching and learning loop cannot be completed. The teacher cannot know whether the lesson has been understood, and its implications developed. This understanding includes both the words and the intent of an utterance, a tall order for teachers whose classrooms include children from many different backgrounds and cultures. But a basic understanding of what children are saying is the first order of business, and this takes time dedicated to listening to children talk and to hearing what they have to say, using structures and functions most familiar to them. In the early grades, language experience activities for reading lessons can serve to help the teacher learn, as well as the child (Nichols, 1977b). In later years, writing activities that draw on students' own language and family experiences can offer insights for both teacher and student (Nichols, 1992). As Ball (1992) has demonstrated, adolescents of specific ethnic backgrounds are likely to have decided preferences for certain organizational patterns in their spoken and written language – patterns that are all too often neither recognized nor honored in academic settings. Curricula that recognize and incorporate these preferences can enhance the learning of children who demonstrate them and can expand the linguistic repertoires of children who do not.

In some contexts, written pidgin and creole languages are used as the actual language of instruction, particularly in the initial years of schooling, when this practice is reported to enhance acquisition of literacy. There is great resistance to this practice, however, in situations where the prestige superstratum (or lexifier) language coexists with the pidgin or creole language. This resistance is related more to the negative attitudes held toward these varieties than to any systematic evaluation of their effectiveness as languages of instruction. Jeff Siegel (1993) reports on the uses of pidgins and creoles in educational settings of Australia and the southwest Pacific and urges that educators and policymakers undertake a more extensive evaluation of the effectiveness of their use in a variety of settings. Siegel reports that even when teachers agree that using a pidgin or creole would greatly enhance learning and community understanding, they often believe strongly that only the prestige language should be used in the classroom. Since 1991 Siegel has been publishing a newsletter, *Pidgins and Creoles in Education,* to publicize variations on their classroom use and efforts toward evaluation of their effectiveness as languages of educations.[1]

Those who argue for the use of pidgins and creoles in the classroom maintain that early education succeeds best if conducted in the child's native language. To support this position, recent research indicates that second language learning is facilitated when the first language is fully

1 Jeff Siegel, Department of Linguistics, University of New England, Armidale, NSW 2351, Australia.

developed and the child is able to listen, speak, read, and write in the first language (Cummins, 1986; Vasquez, Pease-Alvarez, & Shannon, 1994). In other words, to best help children learn a second language variety, the school and community should help them develop the one they know as a native language. Those who argue against the use of pidgins and creoles in education point out that a child who wishes to obtain higher education or to move beyond his or her local community must learn a language of wider communication; time spent on learning to read and write in the pidgin or creole of the local community is time wasted, they argue. In other words, if the goal is for the child to become a fully participating member of a wider community, where the pidgin or creole is seldom used or valued, then the school's primary task should be to provide access to the language of wider use. Educators on both sides of this argument often agree on end goals; their division comes on the means to get there.

Even if pidgins and creoles are not officially used in the classroom, teachers of students who speak them need to understand more about them. Few beginning teachers can predict which specific pidgins and creoles they are likely to encounter in the course of a lifetime. Sometimes they themselves move to a creole-speaking area, as was the case for military wives in the coastal South Carolina school described at the beginning of this chapter. Sometimes the children immigrate to urban centers, as in the case of many Jamaicans in Britain during the 1950s and 1960s and of Haitians in the United States in recent years. Political upheavals, economic opportunities, and sometimes national policy changes can result in population movement that will affect the makeup of an individual teacher's classroom (see Wiley, this volume). Awareness of the possibility that students using unfamiliar languages may appear in one's classroom can make a teacher alert to information about the languages in professional journals, electronic databases, and electronic media.

As Vasquez, Pease-Alvarez, and Shannon (1994) have so eloquently argued, teachers must know something about the language and cultures of their students in order to develop relevant curricula. To help teachers learn about their students' homes and communities, these researchers recommend a variety of school and community undertakings: collaborative ethnographic studies by school and university-based collaborators; afterschool literacy programs conducted by supervised college students; home and community visits by teachers and school visits by parents and community members; interactive journals between teachers and parents; and community-based research conducted by teachers and students (pp. 188–196).

In situations of widespread population displacement, there is no reason why videotaped exchanges cannot take place between rural and urban centers, with children of the same ages learning about and hearing the voices of their peers in different geographic settings. One can imagine that a videotaped exchange between a school of a child's homeland and that of an urban center would go a long way toward educating both the children and the teacher of the urban classroom, as well as validating the memories of the incoming child and making important links with the classroom of the country or region of origin. As teachers (and their students) become more comfortable with electronic communication, conversations between students worldwide become feasible. Through such activities, students will learn to accommodate their language use to that best understood by their electronic partners – exhibiting once again the rich resources and creativity available to human beings engaged in language contact and change.

In this endeavor to reach across and between language differences, perspective is everything. Children who speak language varieties that are different from "school language" are much more aware of the structures and functions of their own varieties than their teachers typically are, and they have their own evaluation of them. My favorite peek into this level of awareness comes from an 8-year-old boy I interviewed, along with several of his friends. After I left, their teacher asked the boys how things had gone. The leader of the group replied that things had gone well enough and that the "lady" (referring to me) was nice – but –

That lady talk so funny I just hafa turn my head and laugh.

## Conclusion

Thanks to the focused linguistic research of the past several decades, these languages, formerly considered "marginal," are now far better understood by linguists. How they come to life under specific social conditions, how they incorporate structures and vocabulary from several languages, and how they stabilize, disappear, or continue to evolve have provided windows on the nature of language itself. Many teacher-training programs already incorporate information about such language varieties, and practicing teachers who keep abreast of the pedagogical literature read about how their colleagues have applied such findings to curricular design and methodology. More understanding of how creole-speaking and creole-influenced communities view and use these languages is needed, however (Morgan, 1994). Linguistic and pedagogical inquiry alone will not enable children from these communities to achieve educational parity.

The next stage of inquiry into the nature and influence of these languages will require the active participation of teachers, community leaders, and parents, from the initial design of research to its execution and application. This stage will require discourse-level inquiry into the ways in which speech communities organize and use their linguistic resources beyond the word and sentence – what aspects of human experiences they value and how they present these values to interlocutors. Recent studies by Ball (1992) on organizational patterns preferred by African-American adolescents in the United States and by Malcolm (1994; in press), on narrative structures preferred by aboriginal children in Australia point to mismatches between the patterns of discourse of the school and of the home. These studies, conducted in very different settings – an urban area of California and a remote area of Western Australia – have revealed patterns of disjunction between home and school language that go far beyond the levels of phonology, morphology, word order, and phrase structure that have claimed scholars' attention for the better part of the twentieth century. The mismatches described by Ball and by Malcolm are not unique to children from a creole-speaking (or creole-influenced) community, as Heath (1983) has demonstrated for English-speaking children of both European and African backgrounds in the southern United States. However, when there are such dramatic word- and sentence-level differences as we have seen between creoles and their lexifier languages, discourse-level differences are likely to go unrecognized and unaddressed in the classroom setting.

Our attention must focus next on the discourse-level differences between home and school for two reasons: (1) There is as yet very little known about this level, and (2) speakers whose organizational patterns are different from those of their conversational partners are apt to judge the other as "confused" or "spouting nonsense," even though the words and grammatical structures are identical to the ones they are using. Children who use the same linguistic structures as their teachers but organize their discourse in different patterns are all too often judged "inadequate"; these judgments can have serious consequences. Even though the children studied by Ball (1992) and Malcolm (1994; in press), were monolingual or bilingual speakers of English, their preferred discourse patterns were different enough from school discourse patterns to affect their performance in school. Ball's urban African-American students preferred patterns for academic expository writing that are described as *circular* (gets off the point, goes around in circles) and *narrative inside* (has a personal story in the report). Non-African American students in the same school preferred patterns described as *matrix* (compares two or three things) and *web clustering* (each paragraph describes another point about the main topic) – patterns that will be needed in future academic settings. In a nonschool setting, Malcolm's aboriginal children told narratives in a genre that does not exist in nonaboriginal communities. Accompanied by sand drawings made simultaneously with speaking, children told "traveling narratives," organized into moving and stopping activities. Citing other research in the Australian setting, Malcolm characterizes these narratives as being structured by recurrent sequences of travel and event; he reports that this discourse organization can be found in the school writing of these children.

The limited but accumulating research available on discourse structures suggests that old organizational patterns will persist in speech communities long after speakers have shifted to new languages. Teachers who are alert to such possibilities in their students' discourse can make room within the curriculum for expression through the discourse patterns of home and community, even as they are teaching students the new patterns of the school. If we are open to learning from our students and their communities, we can expand our linguistic repertories simultaneously – as teachers and students have long done, the world over.

## Suggestions for further reading

Burling, R. (1992). Pidgin and creole languages. In R. Burling (Ed.), *Patterns of Language: Structure, variation, change* (pp. 323–339). San Diego, CA: Academic Press and Harcourt Brace Jovanovich.
This chapter is the most accessible introduction to pidgins and creoles. It is especially valuable for individuals with little linguistic background.

Holm, J. (1988, 1989). *Pidgins and creoles.* (2 vols.). Cambridge: Cambridge University Press.
This is a comprehensive survey of pidgin and creole languages of the world. Volume 1 deals with theory and structure, providing a historical framework for theoretical approaches and comparative data on specific structures. Volume 2 is a reference survey of about one hundred pidgins, creoles, and semicreoles. Texts from many of these languages are included, as are world and area maps indicating their locations.

Romaine, S. (1988). *Pidgin and creole languages.* London and New York: Longman.
An overview of pidgins and creoles as linguistic phenomena, this volume provides a valuable discussion of theoretical controversies about the origin and development of pidgins and creoles. Romaine gives valuable criticism of claims that have been made about the relationship between children's language acquisition and creole development. This book is not accessible to those who do not have some background in linguistics.

Siegel, J. (1993). Pidgins and creoles in education. In F. Byrne & J. Holm (Eds.), *Atlantic meets Pacific: A global view of pidginization and creolization* (pp. 299–308). Amsterdam and Philadelphia: John Benjamins.
Focusing primarily on Australia and the South Pacific, Siegel has been involved since 1988 in a research project to collect information about where and how these languages are being used and to promote evaluation

of their effectiveness in the classroom. This chapter is an accessible account of that work.

Todd, L. (1990). *Pidgins and creoles* (2nd ed.). London and New York: Routledge.

This slim volume provides a good general introduction to pidgin and creole languages. Todd's maps are especially helpful, and she provides a valuable discussion on how these languages acquire their names.

## References

Andersen, R. (Ed.). (1983). *Pidginization and creolization as language acquisition.* Rowley, MA: Newbury House.

Bailey, G., Maynor, N., & Cukor-Avila, P. (1991). *The emergence of black English: Text and commentary.* Amsterdam and Philadelphia: John Benjamins.

Ball, A. F. (1992). Cultural preference and the expository writing of African-American adolescents. *Written Communication, 9,* 501–532.

Ballenger, C. (1992). Because you like us: The language of control. *Harvard Educational Review, 62,* 199–208.

Bickerton, D. (1981). *Roots of language.* Ann Arbor: Karoma.

Bickerton, D. (1984). The language bioprogram hypothesis. *Behavioral and Brain Sciences, 7,* 173–221.

Bickerton, D. (1990). *Language and species.* Chicago: University of Chicago Press.

Brewer, J. (1991). Songs, sermons, and life stories: The legacy of the ex-slave narratives. In G. Bailey, N. Maynor, & P. Cukor-Avila (Eds.), *The emergence of black English: Text and commentary* (pp. 155–171). Amsterdam and Philadelphia: John Benjamins.

Brown, B. (1993). The social consequences of writing Louisiana French. *Language in Society, 22,* 67–102.

Burling, R. (1992). *Patterns of language: Structure, variation, change.* San Diego, CA: Academic Press and Harcourt Brace Jovanovich.

Byrne, F., & Holm, J. (Eds.). (1993). *Atlantic meets Pacific: A global view of pidginization and creolization.* Amsterdam and Philadelphia: John Benjamins.

Cassidy, F. G. (1961). *Jamaica talk: Three hundred years of the English language in Jamaica.* London: Macmillan.

Cazden, C., John, V. P., & Hymes, D. (Eds.). (1972). *Functions of language in the classroom.* New York: Teachers College Press.

Cummins, J. (1986). Empowering minority students: A framework for intervention. *Harvard Educational Review, 56,* 18–36.

DeCamp, D. (1971). Introduction: The study of pidgin and creole languages. In D. Hymes (Ed.), *Pidginization and creolization of languages* (pp. 12–39). Cambridge: Cambridge University Press.

Edwards, V. (1985). Expressing alienation: Creole in the classroom. In N. Wolfson & J. Manes (Eds.), *Language of inequality* (pp. 325–334). Berlin: Mouton Publishers.

Gilbert, G. G. (Ed. and Trans.). (1980). *Pidgin and creole languages: Selected essays by Hugo Schuchardt.* Cambridge: Cambridge University Press.

Harris, John W. (1986). *Northern Territory pidgins and the origin of Kriol.* Canberra, Australia: Department of Linguistics, Research School of Pacific Studies, Australian National University.

Heath, S. B. (1983). *Ways with words: Language, life and work in communities and classrooms.* Cambridge: Cambridge University Press.

Holm, J. (1988, 1989). *Pidgins and creoles.* (2 vols.). Cambridge: Cambridge University Press.

Hymes, D. (1971). *Pidginization and creolization of languages.* Cambridge: Cambridge University Press.

Janeway, E. (1980). *Powers of the weak.* New York: Knopf.

Kawamoto, K. Y. (1993). Hegemony and language politics in Hawaii. *World Englishes, 12,* 193–208.

Keesing, R. M. (1988). *Melanesian pidgin and the oceanic substrate.* Stanford, CA: Stanford University Press.

Lalla, B., & D'Costa, J. (1990). *Language in exile: Three hundred years of Jamaican creole.* Tuscaloosa and London: University of Alabama Press.

LePage, R. B. (Ed.). (1961). *Proceedings of the conference on creole language studies.* London: Macmillan.

LePage, R. B., & Tabouret-Keller, A. (1985). *Acts of identity: Creole-based approaches to language and ethnicity.* Cambridge: Cambridge University Press.

Malcolm, I. (in press). Aboriginal English inside and outside the classroom. *Australian Review of Applied Linguistics, 17*(1).

Malcolm, I. (1994). Discourse and discourse strategies in Australian Aboriginal English. *World Englishes, 13*(2). 289–306.

McKay, S. L., & Wong, S. C. (Eds.). (1988). *Language diversity: Resource or problem?* New York: Newbury House.

Morgan, M. (Ed.). (1994). *Language and the social construction of identity in creole situations.* Center for Afro-American Studies Publications. Los Angeles: University of California.

Mufwene, S. (Ed.). (1993). *Africanisms in Afro-American language varieties.* Athens, GA: University of Georgia Press.

Mühlhäusler, P. (1986). *Pidgin and creole linguistics.* Oxford: Blackwell.

Murray, D. E. (Ed.). (1992). *Diversity as resource: Redefining cultural literacy.* Alexandria, VA: Teachers of English to Speakers of Other Languages.

Muysken, P., & Smith, N. (Eds.) (1986). *Substrata versus universals in creole genesis.* Amsterdam and Philadelphia: John Benjamins.

Myers-Scotton, C. (1993a). *Social motivations for codeswitching: Evidence from Africa.* Oxford: Oxford University Press.

Myers-Scotton, C. (1993b). *Duelling languages: Grammatical structure in code-switching.* Oxford: Oxford University Press.

Myers-Scotton, C. (in press). Possible structural strategies in pidgin/creole formation. In A. Spears and D. Winford (Eds.), *Pidgin and creoles: Structure and status.* Amsterdam and Philadelphia: John Benjamins.

Nichols, P. C. (1977a). Ethnic consciousness in the British Isles: Questions for language planning. *Language Problems and Language Planning, 1,* 10–31.

Nichols, P. C. (1977b). A sociolinguistic perspective on reading and black children. *Language Arts, 54,* 150–157.

Nichols, P. C. (1981). Creoles in the USA. In C. Ferguson and S. Heath (Eds.),

*Language in the USA* (pp. 69–91). Cambridge: Cambridge University Press.
Nichols, P. C. (1989). Storytelling in Carolina: Continuities and contrasts. *Anthropology and Education Quarterly, 20,* 232–245.
Nichols, P. C. (1992). Language in the attic: Claiming our linguistic heritage. In D. Murray (Ed.), *Diversity as Resource. Redefining cultural literacy* (pp. 275–294). Alexandria, VA: Teachers of English to Speakers of Other Languages.
Pratt-Johnson, Y. (1993). Curriculum for Jamaican Creole-speaking students in New York City. *World Englishes, 12,* 257–264.
Reinecke, J. E., Tsuzaki, S. M., DeCamp, D., Hancock, I. F., & Wood, R. E. (Eds.). (1975). *A bibliography of pidgin and creole languages.* Honolulu: University of Hawaii Press.
Rickford, J. (1987). *Dimensions of a creole continuum.* Stanford, CA: Stanford University Press.
Romaine, S. (1988). *Pidgin and creole languages.* London and New York: Longman.
Romaine, S. (Ed.). (1991). *Language in Australia.* Cambridge: Cambridge University Press.
Sato, C. J. (1985). Linguistic inequality in Hawaii: The post-creole dilemma. In N. Wolfson and J. Manes (Eds.), *Language of inequality* (pp. 255–272). Berlin: Mouton Publishers.
Shnukal, A. (1988). *Broken.* Canberra, Australia: Department of Linguistics, Research School of Pacific Studies, Australian National University.
Siegel, J. (1993). Pidgins and creoles in education. In F. Byrne & J. Holm (Eds.), *Atlantic meets Pacific: A global view of pidginization and creolization* (pp. 299–308). Amsterdam and Philadelphia: John Benjamins.
Singler, J. V. (Ed.). (1990). *Pidgin and creole tense-mood-aspect systems.* Amsterdam and Philadelphia: John Benjamins.
Thomason, S. G., & Kaufman, T. (1988). *Language contact, creolization, and genetic linguistics.* Berkeley: University of California Press.
Todd, L. (1990). *Pidgins and creoles* (2nd ed.). London and New York: Routledge.
Turner, L. D. (1949). *Africanisms in the Gullah dialect.* Chicago: University of Chicago Press.
Vasquez, O. A., Pease-Alvarez, L., & Shannon, S. M. (1994). *Pushing boundaries: Language and culture in a Mexicano community.* Cambridge: Cambridge University Press.
Winer, L. (1990). Orthographic standardization for Trinidad and Tobago: Linguistic and sociopolitical considerations in an English Creole community. *Language Problems and Language Planning, 14,* 237–268.

# 7 *Language and gender*

Rebecca Freeman
and Bonnie McElhinny

## Introduction

In the United States during the late 1960s and early 1970s, women began to examine and critique societal practices that supported gender discrimination in consciousness-raising groups, in feminist cells, in rallies and media events (see Echols, 1989, for a history of the women's movement in the United States). In the academy, women and a few sympathetic men started to examine the practices and methods of their disciplines, subjecting them to similar critique for similar ends: the elimination of societal inequities based upon gender. The study of language and gender was initiated in 1975 by three books, the latter two of which have continued to significantly influence sociolinguistic work: *Male/Female Language* (Mary Ritchie Key), *Language and Women's Place* (Robin Lakoff), and *Language and Sex: Difference and Dominance* (Barrie Thorne and Nancy Henley, Eds.). The study of language and gender, then, like sociolinguistics in general (see Rickford, this volume), has always been grounded in eliminating disadvantage. Nonetheless, it has not always been immediately clear which strategy to adopt in doing so. As Riley writes, "both a concentration on and a refusal of the identity of 'women' are essential to feminism" (1988, p. 1). Like antiracist scholars, antisexist scholars must sometimes challenge false assumptions about both difference and similarity that result in discrimination. Overly dichotomous ideas of gender pervade Western society in ways that must be challenged. Because, however, it is important that challenging exaggerated notions of difference does not simply result in women assimilating to male, or mainstream, norms, feminist scholars must simultaneously document and describe the value of attitudes and behaviors long considered "feminine." In doing so,

The authors wish to note that they contributed equally to this chapter; their names appear in alphabetical order. They wish to thank John Rickford and Elysa Vinson, for early comments about this chapter, and Sandra McKay and Nancy Hornberger, for their comments and suggestions throughout the process. Bonnie McElhinny's work on this chapter was supported by the National Science Foundation, the Mellon Fellowship in the Humanities, Stanford University, and a Mellon Fellowship in Cultural Studies at Washington University.

feminist scholars challenge their exclusive association with women and point out their value for all people.

An important goal of this chapter is to raise awareness of how our language use shapes our understanding of the social world, our relationships to each other, and our social identities, that is, to raise awareness of the constitutive nature of discourse. As is demonstrated throughout the chapter, there are many ways that gender-differentiated language use can reflect and help perpetuate the subordinate status of women in society. However, recognizing the constitutive nature of discourse means that our language choices can challenge and potentially transform discriminatory practices (Fairclough, 1989, 1992). Because making gender-based ideologies explicit is a prerequisite to changing sexist language use, the chapter starts with a brief discussion of language and ideology. Taking English as an example, we illustrate some of the obvious and more subtle ways that women have been negatively positioned by dominant naming and representation practices, and we discuss alternatives that position women more favorably. We then move to a critical review of studies of men's and women's interactional styles. We review, and critique, two models used in such studies (dominance and difference) and point to a series of recent theoretical statements that revise assumptions about how language and gender should be studied. These recommendations are exemplified in a review of the variability in the linguistic expression of gender in cultures around the world and in a survey of differences in language and gender within a single national context, the United States. We conclude with a discussion of language and gender in the classroom that ties together the issues raised throughout the chapter.

## Making gender-based ideologies explicit: Prerequisite to change

Investigating and understanding language use are crucial in eliminating disadvantage because it is through language that relationships with others are negotiated and social identities constructed (e.g., Davies & Harre, 1990; Fairclough, 1989, 1992; Harre, 1984; Ochs, 1993; Swann, 1993). Our notion of language here is dynamic and includes actual spoken and written texts as well as the underlying discourses or social practices that these texts both reflect and shape. Fairclough (1989) provides the diagram in Figure 1 to illustrate discourse as text, interaction, and context.

It is important to emphasize that people do not come to interactions as blank slates; their prior experiences, assumptions, and expectations influence the process of production as well as the process of interpreta-

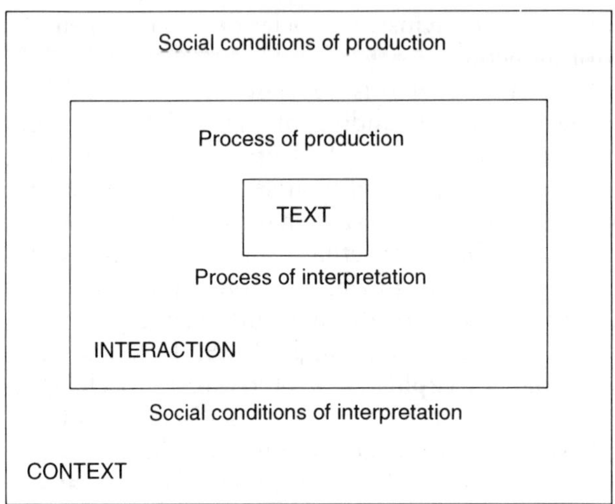


*Figure 1. Discourse as text, interaction, and context (Reprinted with permission from N. Fairclaugh,* Language and power, *p. 25, Longman, 1989).*

tion of spoken and written texts (see also Tannen, 1993a). These texts leave linguistic traces of the underlying discourses that they instantiate, discourses that are structured by ideologies. Because people develop their assumptions and expectations about people, places, events, and objects in the world through their prior experiences in culturally contextualized activities, these interpretive and productive processes are also structured by ideologies. Intertextual analyses that demonstrate coherence in how meaning is linguistically realized within and across spoken and written texts from a particular cultural context or discourse community enable us to make that community's ideologies explicit (see also Fairclough, 1989, 1992; Freeman, 1993; Lemke, 1989, 1990).

Although ideology is often talked about as if it were a static thing, it can be better understood as a dynamic process of creating the patterns of meaning or commonsense assumptions that guide people's behavior within a particular society (see Fairclough, 1989; Gee, 1991; Poynton, 1989, for further discussions). Ideologies, or cultural values and belief systems, are closely linked to power. Gal (1992), drawing on the work of Michel Foucault, Antonio Gramsci, Raymond Williams, and other social theorists associated with the "linguistic turn in social theory," defines *power* as symbolic domination and argues that power and symbolic domination rarely go without resistance. She writes:

[T]he notions of domination and resistance alert us to the idea that the strongest form of power may well be the ability to define social reality, to impose visions of the world. Such visions are inscribed in language and, most importantly, enacted in interaction. (p. 160)

The review of naming and representation practices in the following section illustrates some of the ways that dominant gender-based ideologies are reflected in English, ideologies that may function to constrain women's and men's choices about their gender identities and gender relationships. We also illustrate various ways that resistance to these representations has been linguistically realized. This review is intended to illustrate the concept of gender as a cultural construct, a structure of relationships that is often reproduced, sometimes challenged, and potentially transformed in everyday linguistic practices. As Gal emphasizes, viewing power as symbolic domination and analyzing how forms of resistance can be linguistically realized in different cultural contexts suggest some promising directions for future research – and, as is suggested at the end of the chapter, some promising directions for educational practices as well.

## Naming and representation: Sexist practices and alternatives

Feminist linguists have documented sexism in linguistic representations and offered alternatives, some of which are described later. Wiley (this volume) describes these efforts as examples of *corpus language planning,* which he defines as efforts to change the body or corpus of the language by creating new forms, modifying old forms, or selecting alternative forms, for example, in spelling, pronunciation, vocabulary, and grammar. Note that feminist language planning differs significantly from most of the cases mentioned by Wiley in that the impetus for change originated in a grassroots political movement rather than with the state and is an attempt to contest current power arrangements rather than reinforce the power of the elite. In this section, we attempt to go beyond a traditional feminist critique of titles, surnaming practices, and obviously sexist lexical choices to illustrate more subtle ways that dominant gender-based ideologies are reflected in English. Our discussion of linguistic realizations of forms of resistance to these dominant discursive practices may therefore suggest ways by which other kinds of linguistic minorities can challenge hegemonic discursive practices which disadvantage them.

As with any issue, feminists do not speak with a single voice on the need for sexist language reform. Some feminists believe that sexist language will disappear when other societal inequities are redressed (Lakoff, 1975); others argue (as indeed we do here) that language both creates and reflects societal inequities, so that the use of nonsexist language is itself one step toward redressing societal inequities (see Cameron, 1992; Henley, 1987; Martyna, 1983, for further descriptions of theoretical differences in feminist linguistic reform).

## *Naming conventions and forms of address*

An obvious way that gender-differentiated language use reflects social hierarchies is through *naming conventions,* which are often simultaneously ways of referring to people and addressing them in interaction. Naming conventions have therefore been targeted by feminists for change. For example, there is only one form of address for men, *Mr.,* regardless of marital status. Until recently, however, the marital status of women was distinguished by *Miss* and *Mrs.,* reflecting the notion that whether or not a woman is in a heterosexual marriage is her defining characteristic. Feminists coined another address form, *Ms.,* for women who believed that their marital status should be irrelevant, as it is for men. Some women use *Ms.* with their own surname, and some use it along with their husband's surname, which they may have taken after marriage.

Surnaming practices also mark an area of conflict and change in how women are named. There is currently considerable variability as to which surname American women choose after marriage: some retain their own surname, others adopt their husband's surname, some adopt a last name which is a hyphenated hybrid of their own surname and their husband's, and yet others use their own surname in professional settings and their husband's in community, church, and leisure settings.[1] Although some native English speakers object that the whole issue is too confusing to straighten out, such speakers usually prefer a traditional (most feminists would call it "conservative") naming practice, with the woman addressed as *Mrs.* plus husband's surname after marriage. The situation is no more confusing, however, than being introduced to a man whom one has heard variously called *Richard, Dick, Richie,* and *Rich;* one must ask him what he prefers. To address a man as *Richie* when he would prefer *Richard* is to be deliberately insulting – just as ignoring a woman's preference about her form of address would also be insulting.

1 See Penfield, 1987, for a history of women's surnaming practices in the United States and the legal struggles that took place during the 1970s and 1980s to make women's retention of their own name after marriage legal and uncomplicated. Penfield also mentions some current issues in surnaming practices which are not yet settled legally, for example, a mother's right to give a child a surname different from that of the child's father.

When men and women in similar positions are addressed differently, for example, in the workplace, the effect can be discriminatory. Wolfson (1989) describes a study in which her sociolinguistics students gathered data on the way male and female professors were referred to by secretaries and other staff in a large northeastern university and found that all females and the younger male faculty tended to be referred to by first name whereas older male faculty were referred to by title and last name. She argues:

> [W]here secretaries did use first name for women while reserving title and last name for male faculty, this usage appeared to be a manifestation of a combination of female solidarity with a sense that female professors were in lower-status positions than their male colleagues, even where age and rank were similar. (p. 168)

We prefer to point out the ways that different kinds of hierarchies interact here. Note that younger men, here and elsewhere, are often placed in the same position as women in ways that may disadvantage both, though in slightly different ways. A more positive interpretation of these two groups being addressed in the same way could be that a cultural change is in progress about the kinds of hierarchies that are appropriate between university staff and university faculty, with faculty of a younger generation (women in many universities fall into this group) encouraging more informality.

## *Gender differentiation in lexical choice: Potentially constraining choice*

Discussions of sexist language have often been reduced to what Martyna (1983, p. 25) calls the *he/man* approach to language, that is, the use of male terms to refer both to males in particular and to human beings in general. Such forms designate men as the "unmarked" and women as the "marked" human category. Of the words which serve as "generic" referents, the ones which have received the most attention in English are the masculine pronouns *he, him,* and *his* in such sentences as "The average student is worried about his grades." "We will hire the best-qualified person regardless of his sex." "Each student can select his own topic." "Everyone should do his best." "Each student will do better if he has a voice in the decision." "When everyone contributes his own ideas, the discussion will be a success." Some examples of generic masculine terms are *man, man-to-man, prehistoric man, brotherhood, chairman,* and *policeman.*

Although the discussion of the uses and effects of the generic masculine should be understood as only one part of the study of (non)sexist representational practices, it is one with some quite concrete effects. For instance, Bem and Bem (1973) found that gender-biased job advertisements for positions in traditionally masculine jobs attracted fewer female applicants than unbiased ads. In a series of psychological experiments, Martyna (1978a, b) found that men had an easier time than women imagining themselves as members of the category referenced by generic *he*. Not surprisingly, Martyna (1983, p. 31) also found that women used the generic *he* less often than men and more frequently turned to alternatives like *he or she* or *they* (see further discussion later in this chapter). The fact that the generic *he* can be used to refer to human beings in general, and men in particular, has led to a number of legal disputes in the United States about what is intended, for example, by *a reasonable man,* whether a scholarship fund established for "worthy and ambitious young men" can also be used for women, and whether juries should judge an altercation according to the objective standards that would be applied to a dispute among men or to a dispute among men or women (Martyna, 1983, p. 32). Ritchie (1975, cited in Martyna, 1983) reports that in Canada the ambiguity of the generic masculine has been used to include or to exclude women depending upon the climate of the times and personal biases. Finally, several studies have found that in educational materials the gender-specific *he* appears five to six times for every single generic *he* (Graham, 1973, cited in Martyna, 1983, p. 32; Tittle et al., 1974). Such evidence makes it increasingly unlikely that a "generic" masculine will be so interpreted by readers or hearers.

Many academic journals, newspapers, and magazines now require that submissions be written in more inclusionary language (see, for example, the Linguistic Society of America [LSA] guidelines for nonsexist language, published each December in the LSA bulletin, and "Guidelines for Nonsexist Use of Language" in the National Council of Teachers of English [NCTE] publications). Such changes in linguistic prescriptions, as Cameron (1990) points out, clearly demonstrate that conventions of representation can be deconstructed and reconstructed if they are found to disadvantage groups. Several strategies suggested for avoiding the use of the generic masculine pronoun are:

1. Drop the masculine pronoun.

   *The average student is worried about grades.*

   *We will hire the best person regardless of sex.*

2. Rewrite the sentence in the plural rather than the singular.

   *Students can select their own topics.*

3. Substitute the pronouns *one* or *one's* for *he* or *his.*

   *One should do one's best.*

4. Use *he or she, his or her* (in speech or writing) or *s/he* (in writing).

   *Each student will do better if he or she [s/he] has a voice in the decision.*

5. Use *their* when the subject is an indefinite pronoun.

   *When everyone contributes their own ideas, the discussion will be a success.*

The fifth strategy is often adopted in conversation by native speakers. Some prescriptive grammarians or editors will still mark it as grammatically incorrect, saying that there is number disagreement between pronoun and referent (one singular and one plural). Feminist linguists will note that there is gender disagreement if one retains the generic masculine. Given the widespread use of *they* or *their* as a singular pronoun, many sociolinguists have taken to calling this usage *singular they or their* – a usage no more contradictory than using *you* as both singular and plural. More inclusive terms of reference can generally also be found for other nouns: *firefighter* for *fireman, chair* for *chairman, prehistoric people* for *prehistoric man,* and so forth.

The notion of *man* as the unmarked category and *woman* as the marked category is also reflected in pairs of words that are distinguished by gender. As Graddol and Swann (1989) mention, the masculine terms *dog* and *lion* in pairs are considered the "neutral" terms whereas the feminine counterparts, *bitch* and *lioness* are semantically marked. The term *lioness* is also formally marked with the addition of the suffix *-ess.* When a word referring to a person is distinguished by gender, the feminine form is often marked with a suffix, which at times carries the sense of a diminutive. Examples of words in current use are *actress, hostess, waitress, goddess, princess.* However, using suffixes to mark gender seems to be declining (Graddol & Swann, 1989; Poynton, 1989). So, for example, some women refer to themselves as *actors* rather than *actresses,* and gender-marked terms like *stewardess* are being replaced with gender-neutral terms like *flight attendant.*

Sometimes a word explicitly marking the referent as female or male is added. It is revealing to note which professions are marked for which gender. For example, the unmarked term *nurse* is often marked when the nurse is a man (*male nurse*), reflecting a cultural assumption that nurses are women. Other examples include *doctor* (*lady doctor*), *family man* (but not *family woman*), and *career woman* (but not *career man*). The same pattern plays out in the following textual fragments (Lee, 1992, pp. 111–112):

1. The 'documentary' delightfully explores the rivalries between different orchestral sections, as well as some of the personal ones, like the feud between a

woman cellist who takes nips from a whiskey bottle and a violinist she accuses of molesting little girls. (*Minneapolis Tribune,* 14.11.79)

2. A woman Sandinista guards wounded guerrillas fleeing a clash with Somoza forces. (*Time,* 2.7.79)

These lexical choices reflect the dominant cultural assumptions that cellists, violinists, and Sandinista guards, like doctors and career-oriented people, are all men. Systematically marking certain professions or fields of activity as masculine (e.g., science, technology, math, business, government, religion) and others as feminine (e.g., primary education, nursing, child care) may unnecessarily limit boys' and girls', men's and women's choices. Although there is currently considerable feminist activity that encourages naming and representation of women's contributions, experiences, perspectives, and "voices" in all the fields traditionally dominated by men, a considerable imbalance remains. We will return to this point in the discussion of language, gender, and the classroom later in this chapter.

Asymmetry in the lexicon also reflects gender differentiation. Because the dictionary is considered a cultural authority for meaning and usage, it has been a target for feminist analysis and critique. In response to the absence in traditional dictionaries of words to represent women's experiences, as well as a bias in dictionary entries that reflects and preserves stereotypes about women, Kramarae and Treichler (1985) wrote *A Feminist Dictionary: In Our Own Words.* They explain their goal as follows:

> [T]o document words, definitions, and conceptualizations that illustrate women's linguistic contributions; to illuminate forms of expression through which women have sought to describe, reflect upon, and theorize about women, language, and the world; to identify issues of language theory, research, usage, and institutionalized practice that bear on the relationship between women and language; to demonstrate ways in which women are seizing the language; to broaden knowledge of the feminist lexicon; and to stimulate research on women and language. (Kramarae & Treichler, 1990, p. 148)

Although feminist linguists have regularly needed to find words to describe many of women's experiences, they have found no lack of words to describe a woman's promiscuity. In a study of North American English, Stanley (1977, cited by Graddol & Swann, 1989, p. 110) identified 220 words for a sexually promiscuous woman but only 20 for a sexually promiscuous man. Schulz (1990), reviewing the history of the many terms used to refer to women, argues that the "analysis of the language used by men to discuss and describe women reveals something about male attributes, fears and prejudices concerning the female sex" (p. 135). Words which began with either neutral or positive connotations over time acquired negative implications and finally ended up as "sexual slurs" (p. 135). For example, the term *hussy* derives from Old English *huswif* ("housewife"), which meant "the female head of the house". The term gradually deteriorated to "a rustic rude woman," and finally came to mean "a lewd, brazen woman or prostitute" (p. 137). The term *doll,* "a small-scale figure of a human being," referred first to "a young woman with a pretty babyish face," then became an insulting epithet for women generally, and finally acquired the meaning of "a paramour" (p. 138). Although Schulz's study found no similar derogation of the meanings of terms used to refer to men, Risch's (1987, cited by Graddol & Swann, 1989) study of North American college students found a wide variety of "dirty" words to refer to men, including *bitch, whore,* and *slut,* which have traditionally been used to refer to women. It may, however, be misleading to look for slurs against men which work in the same way as those against women. The current gender order is not maintained by exercising the same pressures on all members of a given culture but, instead, by creating and reinforcing norms for a hegemonic femininity and a hegemonic masculinity. The construction of a hegemonic femininity focusing on women's appearance and sexual passivity immediately implies subordinate femininities – linked to being an active sexual subject, an older women (cf. *biddy*), or a lesbian (cf. *dyke,* when used in a pejorative sense) – and spawns the construction of subversive femininities which actively resist the hegemonic feminine norms. The construction of a hegemonic masculinity based on strength and sexual prowess (cf. *hunk, stud, jock*) implies subordinate masculinities linked to sexual inactivity or lack of strength (cf. *wimp*), "excessive" mental activity (cf. *nerd, geek*), being gay (cf. *faggot*), or older and sexually active (*old goat*). These in turn lead to the construction of subversive masculinities (e.g., *sensitive new-age guys* and positive connotations of *queer*). These cases provide only a few examples of ideological struggles over gender-related meanings in the lexicon.

## *Analyzing gender-based ideologies: Much more than lexical analysis*

Cameron (1990) writes that she, along with many other feminists, questions the traditional feminist focus on "naming" practices because simply analyzing the ways that women and men are named and addressed does not reveal enough about deep-rooted sexist ideologies. To illustrate this point, she provides the following example of two newspaper reports of the same incident; the first from the *Daily Telegraph,* which she referred to as a "quality" paper and the second from the *Sun,* a "popular" tabloid.

1. A man who suffered head injuries when attacked by two men who broke into his home in Beckenham, Kent, early yesterday, was pinned down on the bed by intruders who took it in turns to rape his wife. (*Daily Telegraph*)

2. A terrified 19-stone husband was forced to lie next to his wife as two men raped her yesterday. (*Sun*)

Cameron interprets these news reports as representing rape as a crime against a man rather than against a woman, based on an analysis of how a number of linguistic features function together. First, the experience of the man is foregrounded: he is the first person to be mentioned, the grammatical subject of the main clause, and the subject of the verbs *suffered* and *was forced*. As Cameron points out, a feminist would want to ask *who* is forced and *who* suffers in a rape. The woman, in each case referred to not by her own name or by her profession but as *his wife*, is mentioned third in the *Daily Telegraph* report, which suggests that the rape is less important than the man's head injuries and the violation of his home. The *Sun* provides a similar ordering of events, giving the impression that the rape was less important than the husband being forced to witness it. Cameron argues that linguistic analyses that are limited to identifying sexist naming practices would not reveal the sexist stance taken in these newspaper accounts (see Cameron, 1990, pp. 16–18, for further discussion). Linguists who are interested in analyzing how gender identities and gender relations are discursively constituted need to look beyond lexical choice to analyze who is represented as doing what, to whom, under what circumstances, and with what consequences.

Analyses of metaphor provide a powerful means of understanding how language use shapes experience (see Lakoff & Johnson, 1980, for further discussion). Martin (1987), for example, moves beyond an analysis of the lexicon to explore how metaphors about women's experiences can reflect gender-based ideologies. She compares the way that medical textbooks represent menstruation, childbirth, and menopause with the way that women from racially and socioeconomically diverse backgrounds talk about these experiences to emphasize that women have choices in the ways that they think and talk about their bodies. Her intertextual analyses demonstrate how medical texts use metaphors of production to represent women's reproductive processes, which she argues contribute to the alienation of a woman from her bodily experiences. Because implanting a fertilized egg is represented as the goal of the process, menstruation is represented as failed production (rather than, for example, as the goal of the menstrual process except for when the woman intends to become pregnant), and menopause, which marks the end of a woman's *productivity,* is negatively evaluated (rather than being represented, for example, as a natural part of every woman's life cycle). Childbirth is described using the metaphors of woman as *laborer,* uterus as *machine,* baby as *product,* and doctors as the *management team.* Interviews with middle-class women demonstrated that they used the dominant medical text metaphors. However, Martin's interviews with working-class women revealed alternative constructions which did not reflect the separation of a woman and her body because, she argues, these women derive their view of experience not from medical texts and other instantiations of dominant ideologies but "from their bodily processes as they occur in society" (1987, p. 200).

Of central concern to many feminists is the question of agency (cf. Butler, 1992, p. 13; Collins, 1990, p. 237); however, there has been little work done on investigating how agency is linguistically realized in discursive practices (see Poynton, 1989, pp. 63–65, for a brief discussion). Drawing on contemporary feminist theory, Davies (1990) describes an agentive individual as one who speaks for himself or herself, accepts responsibilities for his or her thoughts, speech, and actions, and is recognizably separate from any particular collective. Davies argues that agency, like any speaking position and role, is contingent upon discursive practices made available to the individual, and not automatically attributed to all human beings in the way that more traditional sociological theory assumes (e.g., Parsons, 1937, cited by Davies, 1990, p. 4). Poynton (1989) argues that the issue of power and powerlessness emerges clearly at the clause level in relation to the question of agency if the analyst investigates patterns in who causes actions and who is being acted upon. Poynton lists the following as the most obvious issues to investigate: the frequency of women compared to men in the role of agent, the nature of the processes involved, what is at the receiving end of the agents' actions, and which kinds of agents in which kinds of processes get deleted (1989, p. 62). Freeman (1993) provides an example of competing representations of agency and power on the clause level. Her analysis of one "successful" bilingual school's discursive practices illustrates the rejection of dominant metaphors that represent language minority students as *forced to abandon their native language and culture, isolated in transitional bilingual programs,* and *required to forget the old country.* Notice that, in these constructions, the language minority students are represented as having no choice and no agency in the assimilation process; instead, some unidentified agent is causing them to be *forced, isolated,* and *required.* In opposition to this dominant discourse, the language minority teachers emphasize how, as adults, they *returned to their culture* and *realized there was nothing wrong with the native language and culture;* thus they encourage the students in the bilingual school to *maintain their native languages and cultures* in a two-way bilingual program. Although Freeman's analysis does not explicitly focus on gender, its utility for gender studies is clear. It demonstrates how the language minority adult and child can be represented as agents who choose and cause acts in the world. Understanding which women and men are linguistically represented as having control over and responsibility for what processes at the clause level in spoken and written texts within particular discourse communities, and relating those cultural images to sociolinguistic analyses of situated activities, promises to be revealing of gender relations and issues of domination and resistance within those discourse communities.

Stereotypes about differences between men's and women's speech provide a clear example of how cultural ideologies and instances of situated interaction are inextricably intertwined, and as such provide a transition from the discussion of naming and representation practices to a review of women and men in interaction. Coates (1986, pp. 15–34) provides the following list of proverbs articulating stereotypes about women's speech that reflect long-standing Western folk beliefs about differences in the ways that women should and do speak:

A woman's tongue wags like a lamb's tail (England)
Foxes are all tail and women are all tongue (England)
Où femme y a, silence n'y a ("Where woman is, silence is not"; France)
The North Seas will sooner be found wanting in water than a woman at a loss for a word (Jutland)
A whistling sailor, a crowing hen, and a swearing woman ought all three to go to hell together (United States)
Many women, many words; many geese, many turds (English)
All the Daddies on the bus go read, read, read. . . . All the Mummies on the bus go chatter, chatter, chatter (British children's song)

A common theme here is that women talk, or gossip, too much. However, feminists using stereotypes as a launching pad for academic inquiry have consistently found that men talk more than women in meetings, television talk shows, and classrooms (see Coates, 1986, p. 103; Graddol & Swann, 1989, pp. 70–71, for a review of this evidence). The question then becomes: If men actually talk more than women, why are women stereotyped as the talkative sex? One explanation put forth by Spender (1985) is that there is a double standard in operation: Society prescribes that girls and women talk very little, so even if girls and women talk less than men but go beyond the prescribed limits, they are seen as talking too much. In addition, women's speech may be negatively evaluated because the topics women have traditionally been preoccupied with (children, relationships, household tasks) were dismissed as trivial or mere gossip (Borker & Maltz, 1989; Goodwin, 1990; Harding, 1975; Spacks, 1985).

Although the spoken and written text representations of women and men reviewed in this section are clearly important for seeing how women and men come to understand what these categories mean relative to each other, this is certainly not the whole story. Perhaps more important than *what* people say about each other is *how* they say it to each other. We turn now to an investigation of interactional studies to see how important everyday interactions are to the social construction of our gendered identities.

## The dominance and difference models

In the introduction to her book *The Feminist Critique of Language*, Cameron (1990) points out that, although many feminist linguists acknowledge some truth in stereotypes about differences in women's and men's interactional style, the stereotyped behavior has often been reinterpreted from a feminist perspective. Reinterpretations of gender-differentiated language use have generally either stressed men's dominance over women or men's and women's cultural differences as explanations for gender-differentiated language use. The "dominance approach" retains a traditional, negative evaluation of women's speech but attributes women's linguistic inadequacies to their political and cultural subordination to men. Under this interpretation, men's conversational dominance reflects their political and cultural domination of women. In contrast, the difference, or dual-culture, approach acknowledges that women use language differently from the way men do but interprets women's speech more positively, that is, as a reflection of women's culture.

### *Documenting male dominance*

One of the earliest and most influential scholars to write about language and gender was Robin Lakoff. Subsequent linguists have been fairly critical of her theoretical orientation and empirical claims, but it is important to place her work in historical context. She was not responding to ongoing developments in the field of linguistics – before her work, there was virtually no work on language and gender within sociolinguistics (other than in large social surveys where sociolinguists asked which languages or dialects men and women used). Furthermore, her theoretical framework was shared by many early feminists of the period. Lakoff argues that a female speaker faces a double bind. If she does not learn to speak like a lady, she will be criticized, ostracized, or scolded. If, on the other hand, she does learn to speak like a lady, she will be systematically denied access to power on the ground that she is not capable of holding it, with her linguistic behavior as partial evidence for that claim. She will be criticized or marginalized for speaking tentatively and for being unable to take part in a serious discussion. Lakoff relied upon her training as a formal linguist in writing *Language and Woman's Place* (1975). Her claims about women's interactional style, though more linguistically precise than the stereotypes examined earlier in this chapter, are based solely on her own intuitions. Her description of "women's language" thus can be understood as a bridge between stereotypes about women's speech and empirical studies of it. Her ideas about women's language can be divided into three categories: (1) It lacks the resources that would enable women to express themselves strongly, (2) it encourages women to talk about trivial subjects, and (3) it requires women to speak tentatively. The following is a complete list of Lakoff's claims (the citations following some of the items are subsequent studies which critically examined the particular claim about women's language):

1. Stronger expletives are reserved for men; weaker expletives are reserved for women (Gomm, 1981).
2. Women's speech is more polite than men's.
3. Topics that are considered trivial or unimportant are women's domain (e.g., women discriminate among colors more than men do).
4. Women use "empty" adjectives (*adorable, charming, divine, nice*).
5. Women use tag questions more than men (e.g., "The weather is really nice today, *isn't it?*") (Cameron, McAlinden, & O'Leary 1988; Dubois & Crouch, 1975; Holmes, 1986).
6. Women use question intonation in statements to express uncertainty ("My name is Tammy?") (Guy et al., 1986; McLemore, 1991).
7. Women speak in "italics" (use intensifiers more than men; (e.g., "I feel *so* happy").
8. Women use hedges more than men do ("It's *kinda* nice") (Holmes, 1984; O'Barr & Atkins, 1980).
9. Women use (hyper-)correct grammar. (Cameron & Coates, 1988; Eckert, 1989a; Labov, 1972b).
10. Women don't tell jokes. (Jenkins, 1986; Painter, 1980).

Other writers who were focusing on male dominance in interaction added different kinds of features to this list. For instance, Zimmerman and West (1975) and West and Zimmerman (1983) argued that interruptions are used to silence others, and that men interrupt women more than women interrupt men.

Throughout the 1970s and the 1980s, scholars testing these empirical claims illustrated several kinds of problems with the assumptions underlying them. The first problem was in postulating a one-to-one mapping between linguistic forms and their interactional functions. Given the polysemy of most linguistic forms, interactants in the same interaction could interpret the use of a given form differently, in ways shaped by previous experiences with or expectations about a speaker, or about speech in a given situation, and so on. Understanding the meaning of a given linguistic form often requires careful attention to the range of possible meanings a form can have as well as to its social context of use and to the relationships among speakers (see Tannen, 1993b).

For instance, Holmes (1986) examined the use of the hedge *you know* to determine whether it is more frequently used by women, as Lakoff would claim. Although *you know* can be used to express speaker uncertainty, as Lakoff might suggest, there are a variety of different kinds of uncertainty it can express, ranging from one associated with linguistic imprecision ("The money seems to be going for basics rather than for things like *you know* extra equipment"), to indicate a false start ("I mean look what Travolta as a as *you know* he's not a pretty face or anything"), to clarify the content of a previous utterance ("We've got quite a big track *you know* relatively speaking"), as well as the appeal for validation that Lakoff focuses on ("It was all very embarrassing, *you know?*"). Holmes also isolates at least three different ways that *you know* can be used to express certainty: for emphasis ("I'm the boss around here, *you know*"), to attribute knowledge about a general situation to another speaker whether or not one knows they have it ("We'd get rid of exploitation of man by man. *You know,* you've heard it before."), and to refer to conjoint knowledge that one is certain an interactant shares (Woman to her domestic partner: "*You know* we went to Sally's that night."). In the database that she has compiled, Holmes finds men using *you know* slightly more often to express linguistic imprecision, women using *you know* slightly more to express emphasis or attribute knowledge to another speaker, and men and women using *you know* at approximately the same rates to express appeals and conjoint knowledge.

The study of interruptions also turned out to be considerably more complicated than was originally thought. West and Zimmerman (1983) had argued that an interruption was "a device for exercising power and control in conversation" (p. 103). But, as Tannen points out (1989), although one can easily identify a *conversational overlap* (as any two voices sounding at once), "to claim that a speaker interrupts another is an interpretive, not a descriptive act" (p. 268). To understand any overlap as an interruption is to argue that the conversational norm is one speaker at a time. However, not all cultures or subcultures have this as a norm, and even in those which do, in some contexts overlapping speech will be understood as supportive rather than dominating. Interruptions must also be examined in ethnographic context.

Just as Lakoff's account of the linguistic meaning of forms was too simple in asserting that a given form had a single meaning such as tentativeness or domination, so did her understanding of how language constituted social identity turn out to be insufficiently elaborated. Lakoff's account of the relationship between language and gender postulated a direct relationship between women and the use of linguistic forms. She treated the use of certain forms as exclusively marking female identity. An early challenge to this view came from O'Barr and Atkins in their study of the believability of witnesses giving courtroom testimony (1980). They looked for the features Lakoff called *women's language* in the speech of male and female expert and nonexpert witnesses. Although it was unfortunate that they did not question Lakoff's understanding of many of these forms as markers of hesitancy or tentativeness, they still made an important contribution toward the understanding of how linguistic forms might be linked with the construction of social identity. They found that the professional witnesses, whether male or female, manifested few features of "women's language," whereas the lower-status witnesses manifested far more of these features. They concluded that

> [I]nstead of being primarily sex-linked, a high incidence of some or all of these features appears to be more closely related to social position in the larger society and/or the specific context of the courtroom. . . . What has previously been referred to as "women's language" is perhaps better thought of as a composite of features of powerless language (which can but need not be a characteristic of the speech of either women or men) and of some other features. (1980, p. 109)

A further contribution to the understanding of how language is used to constitute social identities comes from a recent article by Ochs (1992). Although Lakoff seemed to suggest that all the forms she listed were referential markers of gender, Ochs argues that, in any community, there is a fairly small set of linguistic forms that referentially index gender (examples of such forms in English include third-person pronouns – *he* or *she, him* or her – and some address forms like *Mrs., Mr.,* and *Ms.*). Much more often, gender is nonreferentially (or indirectly) indexed with language. Nonreferential indexes are *nonexclusive* (that is, a given form is not used *only* by a single group like women) and *constitutive* (that is, the relationship between a linguistic form and a social identity is not direct but mediated). With this view, instead of saying that *X* means *Y;* one says that *X* can mean *Y,* which can mean *Z.* That is, instead of suggesting that the use of tag questions means that you are a female speaker, the use of a tag question is sometimes understood as a way of softening a harsh utterance, which may be a strategy more often adopted by women because of cultural or ideological expectations about femininity. With this contribution we come to yet another understanding of how language communicates meaning: a given form might express a variety of meanings (helpfulness, tentativeness, caution), some of which are more likely to be linked with certain social identities than others. This argument suggests that one should not claim, then, that a certain set of forms is better associated with powerlessness than gender (as O'Barr and Atkins argued) but rather that cultural understandings of certain social identities might be more likely to lead to an interpretation of powerlessness when a given form is used by a woman or a child, say, rather than by a man or an adult.

Learning the range of social stances and speech acts that linguistic forms perform, and the social identities that these social stances and speech acts are normatively and actually associated with, is an important part of acquiring communicative competence in a language. Also, and crucially, the notion of index indicates how social and linguistic change can take place. It suggests the ways in which language is a constitutive activity, rather than simply a tool taken up by individuals when they have something to communicate (Williams, 1977, p. 32). With more rigid perceptions of the semiotic nature of language the possibility of human agency is strongly denied. Understanding the construction of social identity in terms of an index leads one to conclude that language is a form of continuing social activity capable of modification and development (Williams, 1977, p. 39).

Language is not simply constitutive of social identity, however. Because language is used dialogically, social identities are negotiated and constructed in interaction. This brings us to the third crucial flaw in Lakoff's description of language and gender. She focused on linguistic forms that seemed to be used as signals, rather than looking at the ways gender is constructed in interaction. One exemplary study which shows how power is expressed in intimate relationships is that by Fishman (1983). Fishman looked at differences in how pairs of professional, heterosexual couples used and responded to language at home. She found that women used 2.5 times as many questions as men, and men used twice as many statements as women (pp. 94–96). Questions and statements have different interactional force. Questions are used to demand a response and often can ensure a minimal interaction of at least a question-and-answer sequence. The use of questions allowed women to strengthen the possibility of a response to what they had to say. Statements, by contrast, do nothing to ensure a continuing interaction. They may also display an assumption that they will be attended to and responded to in their own right (without the need of a more powerful interactional insurance).

A strategy related to the use of questions by women was their use of the preface "Do you know what?" This preface, often used by children, guarantees a slightly longer exchange, since the standard response is "What?" followed by a long answer. Unlike a straightforward question, these question-question-answer sequences are a way of getting oneself invited to take the conversational floor in order to offer a comment instead of soliciting one. Women used these strategies twice as often as men did (Fishman, 1983, p. 95).

Finally, there were marked differences in whether conversational topics initiated by women and men succeeded (adapted from Fishman, 1983, p. 97):

| | *Success* | *Failure* |
|---|---|---|
| Women | 17 | 28 |
| Men | 28 | 0 |
| Total | 45 | 28 |

Fishman's findings show marked gender differences. All the topics initiated by men succeed, and all the failures at initiating a topic are women's. Fishman also found that men's statements were more likely to get responses than women's (p. 96).

Although Lakoff argued that "women's language" was responsible for men's dominance over women, Fishman's work suggests otherwise. As Wolfson (1989) argues:

> Lakoff's (1973) argument that speaking like a lady keeps a lady in her place seems to miss the point. What we see in these analyses of speech behavior to women is that the way a woman is spoken to is, no matter what her status, a subtle and powerful way of perpetuating her subordinate role in society. (p. 173)

Fishman's study offers some important insights into how to investigate the construction of gender in a dialogic way. Nonetheless, her emphasis, like that of Lakoff, is on how women are dominated. In the next section, we explore a series of studies that have a different epistemological and political approach: how to change traditionally negative evaluations of women's speech.

## *Celebrating difference*

Lakoff's strategy, and that of some of the other studies described in this chapter, is typical of other early feminist studies: they tend to portray women as helpless victims of a patriarchy that forces them to act in weak, passive, irrational, or ineffective ways or that evaluates their actions as weak, passive, irrational, or ineffective. By portraying women as victims, such studies attempt to save them from being blamed for their behavior. By overemphasizing the power that men have over women, however, and by failing to acknowledge that women have any sources of resistance, including the possibilities of developing alternative interpretations of the ways in which they interact or of adopting "men's" (or powerful) language in strategic ways, Lakoff and some of these other linguists accord to existing patriarchal institutions more power than they may have. They thus reinscribe patriarchal norms. Overemphasizing the power men have not only distorts reality but also depreciates the amount of power that women have succeeded in winning and minimizes the chances of further resistance (Jaggar, 1983, p. 115). It also fails to take into account the ways that some women benefit from the power of hegemonic men and the ways that some subordinate men are disadvantaged by hegemonic masculine norms (Cornwall & Lindisfarne, 1994). The fact that Lakoff's approach can disempower students is particularly evident in the ways in which students react to her work and the work of others similar to hers. "Oppression is everywhere," they say. "How can we possibly fight that?" Partly as a response to Lakoff's influential work, and partly as a response to the negative stereotypes of women's interaction that exist throughout Western culture (described earlier in this chapter), another prominent strand of linguistic feminism developed which focused on challenging negative stereotypes by celebrating women's interactional styles.

One theme developed in this sort of linguistic work is that women are more nurturing, supportive, and cooperative than men are. This theme was struck early in Kalcik's account (1975) of the interactional practices of consciousness-raising groups. She reported that women in these groups elicited participation from marginalized members, didn't interrupt each other, and presented themselves as sympathetic with facial expressions, gestures, and back-channeling devices while others were telling stories. Women's stories were collaboratively structured, appearing "to support another woman's story, to help achieve a tone of harmony in the group, or to fit the topic under discussion or develop that topic with related ideas" (1975, p. 8). She argued that women's stories were structured in ways which paralleled "the rhythm of many women's lives, filled as they are with small tasks and constant interruptions from children, husbands, telephones, repairmen" (p. 11). In her analysis, Kalcik extends her description of a particular kind of all-female interaction (consciousness-raising) to women in general, though interaction in these groups is better understood as interaction already shaped by a particular kind of feminist ideology. Johnstone's work (1993) on midwestern women and men's storytelling styles similarly argues that, whereas men's stories are about physical and social contests, women's stories revolve around the norms of the community and joint action by groups of people.

Other research which has concentrated on highlighting cooperative interactional styles among women includes Coates (1991, 1992) and Troemel-Ploetz (1992). Troemel-Ploetz believes that the characteristics of women's talk are collaboration, cooperation, balancing of speaking rights, symmetry, and mutual support. She argues that women are fair, honest, clear, modest, respectful, and generous and concludes that women handle power differently from the way men do: they undo hierarchies rather than reaffirm them. In most recent work on language and gender, however, a subtler way of celebrating women's linguistic productions is more typical. For instance, Sheldon (1992) challenges polarized views of gender difference which associate competition and hierarchy with men and boys and cooperation and egalitarianism with women and girls by analyzing the management of conflictual talk by preschool girls. Her description of girls' conflict talk suggests that they "do" conflict talk better than boys do. Boys use "direct, unmitigated, confrontational speech acts" in order to succeed at "their single orientation of pursuing their own self-interest without orienting to the perspective of their partner or tempering their self-interest with mitigation" (Sheldon, 1992, p. 530). On the other hand, girls manifest "elaborate linguistic and interactional skills" and do "difficult and artful work" in order to mediate opposition (p. 531). Girls "resist without being confrontational, justify themselves rather than give in, and use linguistic mitigators while trying to get what they want" (p. 535). In this view, girls come out as more sophisticated verbal actors than boys, but their skill is extended to nonstereotypical verbal activities.

Work which celebrates interactional styles that have traditionally been devalued serves an important purpose in highlighting who defines success and in offering alternative definitions of *success*. However, work that celebrates women tends to offer explanations for differences between women and men that reify and overgeneralize such differences rather than challenging dichotomous notions of gender. Furthermore, such work rarely attends to how issues of language and gender are relevant to broader issues of political economy. It is surely relevant, for example, that a competitive, direct style is normatively valued in the late capitalist economy of the United States – and is normatively associated with men. Placing a positive value on cooperative styles represents a challenge not only to gender stereotypes but to many prevailing economic norms which disadvantage women in a variety of ways (see Jaggar, 1983). That so many different kinds of power hierarchies are intertwined explains why gaining recognition for alternative interactional styles and why challenging stereotypes is so difficult – and so important. However, explanations of interactional styles which refer to people's social roles, activities, or work are rare in language and gender studies; more often, explanations of women's and men's behavior are based solely on the fact that they are women and men. The paradox of this approach is that it does not go far enough in its challenge to current power structures. By glorifying women precisely for the reasons that women have been traditionally scorned, feared, or devalued, cultural feminism engages with conservative thought on its own ground: a ground dominated by sex differences that appear biologically given or socially unalterable (Jaggar, 1983, p. 98). This is most tellingly illustrated in the ways that the arguments of this kind of feminist work can be co-opted to work against women. In a court case now famous for the conflict between opposing feminist views that it exemplified, the Sears Roebuck company was sued for sex discrimination because so few of its female employees were promoted to higher-paying sales jobs. One feminist scholar testified that this was due to gender inequities in hiring and promotion practices. Another feminist scholar testified that female employees often value caretaking and noncompetitiveness more than opportunities for maximizing economic gain. This scholar, and Sears, claimed that the low numbers of women in the higher-paying positions were the results of women's unwillingness to accept the irregular hours (because they wished to be with their families) and the competitive pressures that commissioned sales work required (Rhode, 1989, p. 180). A federal court accepted this account; the case against Sears was dismissed.

Many of the works already mentioned that celebrate women's and girls' interactional styles have as a corollary a sharp criticism of men's and boys' interactional styles (as noted in Sheldon's work). However, there is another important strand of linguistic work, initiated by Maltz and Borker (1982), that accords value to women's interactional styles without condemning men's styles and has come to be called the *dual-culture model* of cross-sex communication. Maltz and Borker suggest that there should be less emphasis on power and gender psychology and more on

> [C]ultural differences between men and women in their conceptions of friendly conversation, their rules for engaging in it, and probably most important, their rules for interpreting it. . . . American men and women come from different sociolinguistic subcultures, having learned to do different things with words in a conversation, so that when they attempt to carry on conversations with one another, even if both parties are attempting to treat one another as equals, cultural miscommunication results. (p. 200)

Maltz and Borker, working in the sociolinguistic tradition of cross-cultural communication pioneered by John Gumperz, argue that each sex interprets the responses of the other in light of their own cultural roles and that, when communicative breakdowns occur, each sex interprets the other's actions in terms of personality clashes or gender stereotypes. Maltz and Borker offer an example of how such differences might work (note that they do not offer empirical support for these claims), with respect to the use of minimal responses. *Minimal responses* are the nods and brief comments like *umhm* and *yes* that occur frequently in English conversation. Maltz and Borker (pp. 201–202) hypothesize that minimal responses mean "I agree with you" for men, and they mean "I'm listening to you – please continue" for women. If these differences exist, one can imagine a woman producing a string of minimal responses to a male interactant; he may think that she is very amiable, always agreeing with him. Conversely, if a woman is speaking and a man is producing very few minimal responses, she may believe that he is not listening to her.[2] Maltz and Borker argue that the strength of Gumperz's model is that it "does not assume that problems are the result of bad faith, but rather sees them as the result of individuals wrongly interpreting cues according to their own rules" (p. 201).

In her 1990 international best-seller *You Just Don't Understand: Women and Men in Conversation,* Tannen adopted and considerably expanded upon the dual-culture model. Tannen argues that many men approach the world as individuals in a hierarchical social order in which they are either one up or one down. In this world:

> [C]onversations are negotiations in which people try to achieve and maintain the upper hand if they can, and protect themselves from others' attempts to put them down and push them around. Life, then, is a contest, a struggle to preserve independence and avoid failure. (pp. 24–25)

She argues that many women, on the other hand, approach the world as individuals in a network of connections:

> In this world, conversations are negotiations for closeness in which people try to seek and give confirmation and support, and to reach consensus. They try to protect themselves from others' attempts to push them away. Life, then, is a community, a struggle to preserve intimacy and avoid isolation. (p. 25)

Using this model, Tannen investigates a wide range of speech actions in which she claims that men and women display these different ways of understanding the social world. Among the kinds of interactional events she analyzes are advice giving, storytelling, reactions to another's account of problems, asking for and giving information, compliments, and gossip.

Where do these gender subcultures come from? It might seem difficult to argue for the creation and perpetuation of such differences in the light of the frequent interactions between the sexes in Western culture.

2 Maltz and Borker (1982, pp. 197–198) provide an extended list of the interactional features which they ascribe to men and women.

Dual-culture theorists argue that, by adulthood, most men and most women have established their interpretive and interactional rules. They believe that the differences are forged in childhood when, they claim, boys and girls tend to play in sex-segregated groups which have different sets of rules; that is, girls play almost exclusively in small cooperative groups, and boys play almost exclusively in larger, more hierarchically organized groups. In effect, dual-culture theorists are arguing that gender differences are created in the same ways that regional and social differences in language use are (see Rickford, this volume), that is, through physical and social separation. Thorne (1990) points out, however, that "the occasions when girls and boys are together are as theoretically and socially significant as when they are apart, yet the literature on children's gender relations has largely ignored interaction between them." Her ethnography of an elementary school demonstrates that "gender separation among children is not so total as the separate world rendering suggests, and the amount of separation varies by situation" (p. 103).

The dual-culture model has also been widely critiqued by academic feminists and linguists (see e.g., Eckert & McConnell-Ginet, 1992; Freed, 1992a; Henley & Kramarae, 1991) for its dismissal of power and dominance relations as an important element in understanding men's and women's interactional styles. According to the dual-culture model, conversations between men and women break down because of cross-cultural misunderstandings, rather than because men are more powerful than women. It is a "no-fault" linguistic model – the negative effects of these "cross-cultural gender differences" (including the many instances when the effect of men's style is to control the interaction) are often not intentional (Tannen, 1990, p. 18). Eckert and McConnell-Ginet believe, however, that

> [T]o deny agency and assume interactional difficulties arise simply from insufficient knowledge of differences is to preclude the possibility that people sometimes use differences (and beliefs about differences) strategically in constructing their social relations. (1992, p. 467)

They offer the example of a man arguing that he knew that a woman's saying no to sexual relations actually meant yes:

> His reading is possible not because his subculture taught him to encourage and welcome sexual advances by feigning their rejection; rather, he tells himself that such coyness is part of "femininity," a mode of being he views as significantly different from his own. . . . Gender relations in many actual communities of practice . . . are often founded on (possibly mistaken) presuppositions not of sameness but of difference. (1992, p. 467)

Many feminist scholars would argue, contra the dual-culture theorists, that one should focus less on intent to discriminate (see Rhode, 1989) and more on the effects of (intentional and unintentional) discrimination.

Tannen's contribution is in many ways similar to Lakoff's. Both unproblematically take men and women to be their analytic categories without questioning when gender is relevant and without questioning how gender interacts with other aspects of social identity in shaping interactional style (see the next section). In both cases, the analyses of women's and men's speech were isolated from its interactional context (where *interactional context* is defined simultaneously as the communities within which the speakers are interacting, the particular situations and activities in which they are involved, and the interactional histories of the speakers). Nonetheless, Lakoff identified a number of linguistic forms that are central for marking certain kinds of social identities and stances in English – even if she mapped the use of these forms in an overly simplistic way onto women. Likewise, Tannen has identified a number of interactional events in which the negotiations of power and intimacy are potentially problematic in mainstream American conversation.

Although the debate has been framed here (and elsewhere in the sociolinguistic literature) as a choice between dominance or difference, this opposition is actually a false one. Difference is more accurately understood as opposed to equality. Focusing on difference can sometimes lead to inequities, as we saw earlier in our description of the Sears case (see also the discussion by Eckert & McConnell-Ginet, 1992, on the compatibility of the dual-culture and dominance models). Likewise, a focus on similarity can lead to inequities where differences exist (as Rickford, this volume, demonstrates). In order to determine whether highlighting difference or similarity is the best strategy for arriving at equity in a given situation, linguists must turn to much more highly contextualized and localized studies of interaction. Next, several innovative suggestions about how this might be done are discussed, and then a series of studies that embody these fruitful new approaches to the study of language and gender are described.

## *Contextualizing language and gender: Recent theoretical insights*

Although notions of how linguistic forms expressed meaning became increasingly sophisticated during the late 1970s and 1980s as scholars tested Lakoff's empirical claims, and although ideas about which linguistic situations were particularly saturated with issues of power were enriched by the research of dual-culture theorists, few sociolinguists critically examined the fundamental analytic categories – man, woman, community – used in this research. Many studies by sociolinguists, like so many early feminist studies, considered populations of white middle-class women and generalized the findings of behavior in this group to all women. Linguistic anthropologists, as we will demonstrate later, have fallen less frequently into such traps, in part because of the close attention to local context that the ethnographic method requires. At the beginning of the 1990s a series of theoretical statements about how to further nuance studies of language and gender appeared. Thus far, only a small number of studies which have taken these insights into account have been completed, although a number of others are currently being planned or the fieldwork for them is being carried out. In this section, some of these new theoretical insights, and the recommendations they provide for new directions in studies of language and gender, are described. These insights also suggest new directions in the applications of language and gender research, which will be briefly pointed out, although a fuller understanding of the uses of this new research must await the completion of more empirical studies.

This new theoretical work addresses two common, but mistaken, assumptions about how gender should be best studied. The first assumption is that gender is always relevant. The second is that gender is best studied when it is maximally contrastive. Together, these two assumptions have led to a number of "get-your-data-and-run studies," in which a researcher tapes an interaction or two, assumes that differences evident in the interaction are due to gender, and too quickly overgeneralizes findings to all men and boys and all women and girls. As Thorne (1990) points out, the assumption that gender is best studied when it is maximally contrastive has led to opposed assumptions about how gender is best studied in child and adult populations, each of which distorts our understanding of the construction of gender in those groups. It has been assumed that gender in children should be studied by comparing the interactions of girls and boys in separate, same-gender groups (p. 104). The inverse assumption has been made for adults: gender was assumed to be most relevant when men and women were together, not when they were separate (p. 279). These ways of studying gender reflect a complicated intertwining of assumptions about age and heterosexuality in our society:

> These inverse ways of locating gender – defined by the genders separating for children and by their being together for adults – may reflect age-biased assumptions. In our culture, adult gender is defined by heterosexuality, but children are (ambivalently) defined as asexual. We load the interaction of adult men and women with heterosexual meaning, but we resist defining children's mixed-gender interaction in those terms. (Thorne, 1990, pp. 279–280)

Sometimes studies which point out the problems with one of these assumptions will leave the other unquestioned. For example, Coates

(1988), among others, focuses on same-sex interactions among adults but does not question the idea that gender is always relevant. On the other hand, Brown and Levinson (1983) critique the assumption that gender is always relevant in interactions but do not question the assumption that gender may be most salient in heterosexually oriented cross-sex interactions or asexual same-sex interactions. In fact, they recommend that gender may be best studied, because it is most salient, in "cross-sex interaction between potentially sexually accessible interlocutors, or same-sex interaction in gender-specific tasks" (p. 53). The current challenge facing language and gender scholars is how to discern when gender is relevant, without reinscribing heterosexist assumptions about gender in ever-smaller domains (i.e., moving from saying that gender is relevant for a whole interaction to saying that gender is relevant at the moment in an interaction when the participants seem to be flirting, say). Two recent theoretical statements (Eckert & McConnell-Ginet, 1992; Goodwin, 1990) offer some suggestions.

In the introduction to her book *He-Said-She-Said* (the only book yet published which is devoted to an ethnographic study of language and gender in a single community),[3] Goodwin argues that activities, rather than cultures or gender or groups or individuals, should be the basic unit of analysis. There are a number of technical definitions of *activity,* including this one, by Levinson (1992, p. 69):

> The notion of an activity type [refers] to a fuzzy category whose focal members are goal-defined, socially constituted, bounded, events with *constraints* on participants, setting, and so on, but above all on the kinds of allowable contributions. Paradigm examples would be teaching, a job interview, a jural interrogation, a football game, a task in a workshop, a dinner party, and so on.

The everyday, commonsensical notion of *activity* is nearly as useful here, however. Goodwin points out that scholars in a number of different disciplines (including anthropology, psychology, sociology, and linguistics) have independently arrived at the idea that activities should be the basic unit of analysis, because of the ways that "the [social and cognitive] structures members of a society use to build appropriate events change in different activities" (1990, pp. 8–9). Individuals thus have access to an array of different cultures – and an array of different social identities. Goodwin argues:

> [S]tereotypes about women's speech . . . fall apart when talk in a range of activities is examined; in order to construct social personae appropriate to the events of the moment, the same *individuals articulate talk and gender differently* as they move from one activity to another. (1990, p. 9, emphasis added)

3 Most of the book-length studies of language and gender are theoretical surveys (see Cameron, 1992; Kramarae, 1981), textbooks (Coates, 1986; Graddol & Swann, 1989; Smith, 1985), summaries of other studies (Tannen, 1990), or unpublished dissertations (McElhinny, 1993; McLemore, 1991; Morgan, 1989).

A crucial point here is that it is not just talk which varies across context but also the kind of gender identity portrayed by individuals. Talk and gender *covary.*

In her book, Goodwin examines the different social structures created by African-American boys and girls in a range of speech activities (directives, argument, gossip-dispute, instigating, and stories) and in a range of play activities (playing house [girls], making slingshots [boys], making glass rings [girls], arguments [girls and boys]). In some activities, she finds girls and boys building systematically different social organizations through their use of talk, and in others, they build similar structures. Edelsky's work (1981) on the construction of conversational floors in mixed-gender committee meetings at a southwestern university supports a similar conclusion.[4] In interactions characterized by monologues, single-speaker control, and interactional hierarchies, some men took much longer turns. In these interactions, turn takers stood out from non – turn takers, with the turn takers controlling the floor. In more collaboratively organized interactions, men talked less than they did in the single-speaker interactions and, occasionally, even less than women did. In these interactions, women's contributions to certain kinds of speech acts (joking, arguing, suggesting, soliciting answers, validating, directing) outstripped those of men.

The notion of language as a form of activity is a way of resolving the long-standing debates in anthropological and Marxist circles about the relationship between language and reality by arguing that they should not be understood as distinct and separate entities but, rather, that language should be understood as constituting reality. It also challenges a model of interaction which suggests that a social structure controls individual acts of will and intelligence (Williams, 1977, p. 28). As a continuing social activity, the use of language allows modification and development. The particular contribution a focus on activities as a basic unit of analysis makes to linguistic research on gender is that it changes the research question from what the differences are between men's and women's speech (an approach which serves to perpetuate and exaggerate the dichotomous gender categories we have already critiqued) to when, whether, and how men's and women's speech are similar and different. It moves, that is, from understanding how sex or gender shapes language use to understanding how and when language use constructs gender difference as a social category.

If Goodwin contributes the idea that language use must always be considered as, and alongside, activity, Eckert and McConnell-Ginet (1992, pp. 471–472) emphasize the importance of studying gender alongside other aspects of social identity. They argue that this means

4 Note, however, that Edelsky focuses more on the ways that language use varies according to the organization of conversational floors than on the variable construction of gender.

studying how gender is constructed in communities of practice. A *community of practice* "is an aggregate of people who come together around mutual engagement in an endeavour. Ways of doing things, ways of talking, beliefs, values, power relations – in short, practices – emerge in the course of this mutual endeavour" (p. 464). Like traditional sociolinguistic definitions of *speech community, community of practice* is defined by its membership (as, for instance, New York City is defined by New Yorkers or the Kaluli speech community is defined by Kaluli speakers), but it is defined less by shared space and more by shared practices (see Saville-Troike, this volume). Focusing on communities of practice means focusing on the continual mutual construction, contestation, and reinforcement of social meaning, social identity, and community membership, rather than on social identity as something fixed and given.

A community of practice identifies a somewhat larger analytic domain than does *activity*. If, for instance, one were studying a particular workplace (say, the police force), the workplace itself would be a community of practice, and different tasks within that workplace (making a traffic stop, taking a burglary report, quelling a bar disturbance) would be activities. The notion of community of practice thus "points to a mediating region between local and global analysis" (Bucholtz, 1994, p. 7). Studying communities of practice also allows us to investigate how gender interacts with other aspects of identity because

> [P]eople's access and exposure to, need for, and interest in different communities of practice are related to such things as their class, age, and ethnicity as well as to their sex. Working-class people are more likely than middle-class people to be members of unions, bowling teams, and close-knit neighborhoods. . . . Men are more likely than women to be members of football teams, armies and boards of directors. Women are more likely to be members of secretarial pools, aerobics classes, and consciousness raising groups. (Eckert & McConnell-Ginet, 1992, p. 472)

In addition to investigating which communities speakers belong to, one can investigate how they manage memberships in different communities or different (perhaps hierarchical) positionings within communities of practice and how communities of practice are linked within larger communities of practice, and so on. In the next section, some of the studies of language and gender which we believe come closest to exemplifying the studies called for by these theoretical statements are discussed. Many of these studies have been done by linguistic anthropologists whose focus on cultural differences has allowed them to avoid the pitfalls of overly rapid generalizations about gender. Some studies have also been done by sociolinguists studying American minority cultures (often themselves members of those cultures) who found that mainstream notions about gender differences did not accurately describe these communities. Although many of these studies use some variant of a notion of community of practice (particularly to the extent that some cultures can be so construed), not all provide the further detail of how gender is coarticulated with activity. We invite you to consider how such a focus might have further nuanced each cultural description as you review the next section. Note also how these studies use the notion of indexicality elaborated by Ochs (1972) and exemplify Gal's (1991) ideas about power and resistance.

## Language and gender around the world

Our review of the early contributions of sociolinguistics revealed an emphasis on attempts to understand instances of dominance and miscommunication in heterosexual intimate relationships, with most of the research conducted by white middle-class women about white middle-class heterosexual couples. ESL/EFL teachers will find it useful to know how gender shapes interactions in the cultures of their students, and they will find it profitable to discuss the way gender interacts with ethnicity, race, and culture in the United States or in other English-speaking countries when they are describing social variation to their students. This section contains a brief overview of some of the findings of scholars who have investigated cross-cultural and intracultural differences in language and gender. Space constraints require that we select only a few cultures to illustrate the range of ways that language use reflects and continually reconstructs gender.[5]

### *Gender and genre*

In societies that traditionally have been called egalitarian by anthropologists (i.e., nonstratified societies in which nevertheless adults can dominate children and men may dominate women), men and women often have their own distinct social spheres. Participation in culturally central rituals, and concomitant verbal genres, is often linked to (though not necessarily absolutely determined by) gender. Sherzer (1987) describes the linguistic practices of the Kuna Indians of Panama. Although he notes that there are relatively few gender differences in phonological variation and intonation, an important difference in the speech of Kuna men and women is linked to differences in ritual and everyday dis-

5 For more extended descriptions, readers may consult Freed (1992b, a bibliography of works written in English about language and gender in languages other than English), Philips, Steele, and Tanz (1987, a collection of articles on language and gender in a variety of cultural contexts), and Borker and Maltz (1989, a partial survey of anthropological work on language and gender, with a selected annotated bibliography).

course. Kuna ritual verbal genres (the chanting of chiefs, the speech making of political leaders, the curing chants of healers, and the chants of puberty rites directors) in which men, and the very occasional woman, participate have specific linguistic properties distinguishing them from everyday speech, as do the two verbal genres which are unique to women (lullabies and tuneful weeping).[6] The relationship between gender and discourse is indirectly indexical: "[T]he linguistic properties of the Kuna ritual verbal genres are not defined or viewed in terms of gender. Rather they are associated with the verbal genres themselves" (Sherzer, 1987, p. 104). The genres in turn are generally linked with certain tasks which are gender differentiated.

Schieffelin (1987) describes a similar situation among the Kaluli, a small nonstratified society in Papua New Guinea. She points out that in everyday conversation there are no marked male or female registers. There is some distinction, though, in other verbal genres: men tend to tell the two major genres of stories (trickster stories and bird or animal stories), and women perform song-texted weeping at funerals and on other occasions of profound loss. Both men and women compose songs and dances for exchange and ceremonial contexts, although women compose a more limited number of song types. Finally, women and girls engage in an interactional routine (known as ElEma which means "say like that") used in the linguistic socialization of children under the age of 3.

## *Gender and multilingualism*

In bilingual or multilingual societies, in postcolonial contexts, and in diglossic linguistic situations, it may be use of, or access to, certain languages which differentiates the speech of men and women (see also Sridhar, this volume). Each of these situations presents its challenges in ways that can only be briefly touched upon here (though see Cameron, 1992, p. 200). Gal's work (1978) on the use of Hungarian and German in Austria focuses on the effects of urbanization and industrialization on the speech patterns of women and men. Because the urban settings associated with use of German have different meanings and present different opportunities for young women and men, they use German

6 Sherzer (1987, p. 106) treats the women's verbal genres as everyday verbal genres, and the men's verbal genres as ritual ones, a distinction which he bases on linguistic and contextual criteria (whether the events are public or private), as well as on who performs the genres. To the extent that it is based on whether women or men are the speakers, and even to the extent that the distinction between public and private is itself often another ideological distinction used to establish separate gender spheres (see Collier & Yanagisako, 1990; Sedgwick, 1990), this distinction may be understood as tautological.

and Hungarian differently. Gal finds that young women are leading in the shift to German because for them German is associated with urban opportunity, having husbands who are workers, and having less strenuous and less time-consuming household responsibilities, whereas Hungarian is associated with having peasant husbands and having physically taxing household and farm responsibilities. Younger men, for whom the peasant lifestyle retains the attraction of self-employment and some measure of personal autonomy, use Hungarian more than young women. Understanding this situation is significant both in undertaking any attempts at the promotion or preservation of Hungarian use in Austria and in understanding the different kinds of incentives and everyday speech situations in which men and women might be learning or using German.

Hill (1987) investigates gender differences in the use of a former colonial language (Spanish) and an indigenous language (Mexicano) in Mexican communities undergoing *proletarianization* (a shift from a base of subsistence agriculture to integration into a regional and national system of industrial wage labor; p. 123). In these communities, use of Spanish is believed to be crucial for access to wage labor, but Mexicano is understood as crucial for expressing solidarity with traditional norms. Women engage in a wide variety of nonwage economic activity, but most do not participate in regular wage labor. One might therefore expect, and indeed Mexicano speakers believe, that women are more likely to use Mexicano (or at least certain salient features of Mexicano) more than men do and that women would use Spanish less (or at least certain salient features of Spanish less), but Hill finds that women's speech is at once less Mexicano and less Spanish than men's speech is. She argues that women are barred from using the full range of code variation in the way that men do because of the constraints of the local political economy. Local men contest their integration into a capitalist system by emphasizing their Mexicano identity and at the same time manipulate Spanish to be able to participate in that capitalist system (p. 158). Understanding the complex politics of such postcolonial situations is crucial for understanding the resistance that both men and women might have to the teaching of Spanish to women in such situations (the kinds of economic advantages and mobility it might give women might be outweighed by the loss of some parts of the traditional culture that both men and women value).[7] When speakers from such a

7 See Harvey (1991) for a description of gender differences in the use of Spanish and Quechua in Peru. She also finds that women are less likely to have access to Spanish than men and are more likely to be monolingual in Quechua. Women who abandon tradition by changing their style of dress and/or acquiring Spanish risk slurs on their reputations, social ostracism, and even violence. As in Mexico, ignorance of Spanish and ability to speak Spanish both count against women. Women become living sym-

linguistic situation choose to migrate to a country where yet another language (say, English in the United States) predominates, there will be different challenges associated with teaching English to men (who might be fluent in another "world" language with which at least some instructors are familiar) and women (who may not be fluent in a "world" language).

In diglossic situations, men and women may have differential access to, different attitudes toward, or different incentives for using the high variety. Haeri (1987) points out that, although education is directly and positively correlated with the use of classical Arabic among men (with the more highly educated men using salient features of classical Arabic more than the less highly educated men), highly educated women in Amman use salient variants of the local urban Arabic standard, which is associated with modernity, progress, and change of the status quo. Haeri argues that it is not surprising that highly educated women might choose not to adopt all aspects of the use of classical Arabic, which symbolizes the norms of the dominant culture and is associated with the "old world of Quranic schools which had and still does have its doors closed to women, and with a world which did not allow them to participate in public life" (pp. 176–177).[8] The quantitative differences in the use by men and women of classical Arabic and the urban standard are important factors to consider in the teaching of Arabic. In general, American students receive instruction in classical Arabic, and only advanced students gain some familiarity with urban standards. The language varieties used by such students also carry certain sociopolitical connotations for native speakers (just as, for instance, the use of British vs. American vs. Australian vs. Irish English carries certain affective value for native English speakers; see Kachru & Nelson, this volume; McGroarty, this volume).

bols of tradition, but their economic mobility is limited and in some instances they become more dependent upon men than in traditional societies (see also Cameron, 1992, pp. 200–202, for further analysis of the significance of Harvey's study for understanding gender and postcolonial linguistic situations).

8 Haeri's account is particularly important in combating Western notions of Middle Eastern women. Accounts of the quantitative differences in the use of classical Arabic by men and women had been understood by some Western and some male Middle Eastern scholars as an artifact of women's sheltered lives and segregation in the private domain in Middle Eastern societies. Haeri (1987) points out that these explanations result from a mistaken analytic assumption which equates classical Arabic (the H variety in a diglossic situation) with the standard language. She argues for a redefinition of *standard* in the Arabic context to mean the *urban standard* and for understanding classical Arabic as the literary norm. Women's, and younger men's, quantitatively greater use of urban standards should then be understood as a more favorable response to modernization and as a result of the way they are participating in public life.

## *Gender and politeness*

The discussion in this section thus far has focused on gender differences in the use of languages, codes, or verbal genres. Pragmatic stances, discourse markers, and morphology also vary according to gender. Politeness is one pragmatic domain in which many kinds of social differentiations are manifest. Politeness is

> [A] special way of treating people, saying and doing things in such a way as to take into account the other person's feelings. On the whole that means that what one says politely will be less straightforward or more complicated than what one would say if one wasn't taking the other's feelings into account. (Brown, 1980, p. 114)

As Brown and Levinson (1983) note and as Brown (1980) exemplifies, there is no straightforward way to operationalize and quantify politeness. Part of the challenge is identifying all devices and strategies which constitute politeness in a given culture (particles, intonation, irony, address forms, discourse strategies, etc.) Another part of the challenge is identifying whether a particular strategy which may sometimes be used for politeness' sake is in fact being so used in the interaction under investigation. One clear finding which has emerged, however, is that in societies where politeness is normatively valued or seen as a skill, or where acquisition of politeness is not an automatic part of language learning but requires additional training, men tend to be understood as more polite, and women are understood as impolite (Keenan, 1974) or too polite (Smith-Hefner, 1988).[9] In societies where directness is valued, and politeness is seen as a form of deference rather than a skill, women tend to be more polite, or at least are perceived as more polite (see the discussion of mainstream culture in the United States, Lakoff, 1975; the discussion of Mayan women's speech, Brown, 1980, 1993). These ideological understandings are not, of course, necessarily descriptions of actual interactional behaviors but cultural ideologies which tend to focus on certain kinds of politeness as central while ignoring other kinds. Several descriptions of how politeness and ideologies about politeness reflect, construct, and reinforce gender distinctions follow.

Keenan (1974) studied a village in Malagasy where the people (male and female alike) believe that men are more skillful polite speakers. She notes that men and women actually share this politeness system, which includes long winding speeches associated with the traditional values

9 In particular, men are more likely to be polite in a way that honors the wishes of others not to be imposed upon (negative politeness – see Brown & Levinson, 1983) rather than polite in a way that recognizes the desire of others to be liked, admired, and ratified (positive politeness).

placed on personal relationships, the use of traditional metaphoric sayings, positive politeness markers such as *we* and *let's,* use of stand-ins to make requests, off-the-record requests, indirect ways of giving orders, and avoidance of outright expressions of anger or criticism. Women do not, however, engage in the ritually oriented interactions that have to do with village-to-village negotiations, dispute resolution, and marriage requests. This is part of the reason why they are perceived as less skilled at politeness. However, another reason women are perceived as less polite is that there are *two* politeness systems in this village – one perceived as traditional, the other perceived as European – and only the traditional politeness system is culturally valued. The devalued European system is largely consigned to women (men use it only when ordering around cows), and it is used in the marketplace in transactions associated with bargaining about and selling food and at times when a village member has behaved in an unacceptable way and must be more directly approached. Men deputize their wives to handle such situations. This specialization in kinds of politeness is like the specialization in verbal genres described by Sherzer (1987) and Schieffelin (1987). Because each group "specializes" in a certain style, and the styles are complementary, each has a certain kind of power within certain situations.

Among the Javanese, the politeness system is quite complicated and elaborate, with every utterance being marked for respect, so that properly "mastering" (we use this verb advisedly!) how to be deferential is understood as a skill that allows one to control others and express authority (Smith-Hefner, 1988). Men are seen in this society, too, as being more adept and skillful at using politeness forms. By producing polite forms for an inferior, a speaker can force the interactant to respond politely in turn – or lose face. The coerciveness of the act is hidden, and thus difficult to challenge. Because people must be explicitly drilled in the more intricate politeness forms (they are not learned along with the rest of the language), an educated man who uses politeness forms can reduce a man not so educated to silence – or at least agreement (disagreement would require explanation and skillful use of politeness forms). Javanese women are understood by men as less skillful in using politeness – not because they are not polite enough, but because they are *too* polite. Women who are mothers are often more polite than befits their status because they are modeling the production of politeness forms for their children to learn and are using forms which are appropriate for children to use toward their elders. Furthermore, in situations in which it is unclear which politeness forms to choose, women tend to speak (choosing the more polite forms to be on the safe side) and men remain silent. Here again, is a complementary system similar to that in Malagasy, where men can use women's actions to preserve their own status. Women interpret their own actions differently than men interpret women's actions. However, they do so in ways that point out the importance of considering how all members of a culture interpret a given act. Women take advantage of the polysemy of politeness to understand their kinds of politeness not as subservient but as refined.[10]

## *Gender and ESL contexts*

In this section, we have offered a brief picture of the ways gender and language can covary in different cultural contexts. Understanding the linguistic and social backgrounds of speakers in ESL classrooms can help instructors understand the strategies students adopt in learning – and where differences might pose particular challenges for instruction. As most experienced ESL instructors are well aware, however, there is no simple, direct transference of experiences – of language, gender, social attitude – from one culture to another. Instructors must continually discover the ways that students' cultural experiences interact with the matrix culture in order to be able to assist them most effectively.

Goldstein's sociolinguistic study of Portuguese-speaking women in Canada (1992) offers a useful cautionary tale. Most ESL curricula for immigrant workers, as Goldstein points out (p. 171), currently center "around the need to learn English to carry out work tasks and assume greater responsibility at work." However, she finds that, at least for these Portuguese-speaking women, the use of English at work is associated with significant social costs. The company she studied adopted a deliberate policy of using Portuguese friendship networks and churches to recruit employees, since non-English-speaking immigrants would work for lower wages. These family and friend networks, which had been central to economic and emotional security in Portugual's peasant economy, were put to different use by Portuguese immigrants and companies in a Canadian industrial context. Hiring family and friend clusters led to the establishment of a Portuguese family-community in parts of the company. The company was able to use this friendship network in industrial relations (problems with bosses were understood as family disputes) and in improving worker efficiency (workers who were friends would help each other meet production quotas when they finished their own work). Non-English-speaking workers reported feel-

10 Space constraints limit the number of examples of gender, culture, and politeness strategies which can be offered here. Another extensively studied case of particular interest to many American ESL and EFL teachers is gender and politeness in Japan. For details see Ide and McGloin (1991), Inoue (1994, in press), Okamoto and Sato (1992), and Shibamoto (1985, 1987). The politeness system these studies describe shares many similarities with that of Java (described in this chapter).

ing insulted or slighted when other workers spoke English. Although workers could obtain better-paying jobs in other contexts, men (83.3 percent of whom had some English competence before being hired by the company) rather than women (only 10 percent of whom had some command of English before being hired) were more likely to get these jobs. Portuguese men had more access to English-speaking ties and better-paying jobs because of the familiarity with English they had gained in Portugual (in contacts with American soldiers at bases or when they themselves were soldiers) and in Canada (where some men took all-day English language classes upon arriving in Canada). Many Portuguese women reported that they were unable to get formal language training because their fathers did not permit them to attend coed classes, because of responsibilities for children or younger siblings, or because they were scared to go out alone in the evenings to classes. Goldstein concludes that:

> [T]he language choices the line workers made on the basis of the linguistic resources to which they have access can be linked to the gendered structure and dynamics of the Portuguese family and the class positions the workers hold within the Canadian political economy. (p. 180)

This example of the effects of transnational labor migration on women's incentive to learn English leads directly to the topic of cultural differences in gender and language use within a single country. The United States is chosen as the case study.

## Gender diversity across cultures in the United States

As has already been mentioned, there has been shockingly little research done on the interactional styles of minority women in the United States. Medicine (1987, p. 159) points out that there are at least 206 distinct languages spoken by Native Americans – which suggests the enormity of the task to be undertaken. Medicine also points out, however, that the experience tribal communities have in common as a result of the policies of the federal government means that many are facing similar tasks with respect to revitalizing languages which were targeted for suppression and eradication and to challenging the power of linguistic domination through the imposition of English. She notes that American Indian women perform three distinctive social roles with respect to language in their communities:

> [T]hey maintain cultural values through the socialization of children; they serve as evaluators of language use by setting the normative standards of the native or ancestral tongue and English; and they are effective as agents of change through mediation strategies with the White society. (p. 160)

With a focus on Lakota women, Medicine mentions some of the kinds of difficulties American Indian women currently face with respect to language use and socialization. For instance, they must make decisions about whether to bring up their children as bilingual or monolingual (in English or the native language) and are often held responsible for the lack of knowledge of a native language by the younger members of the community. In addition, they also often serve as mediators between their own communities and white society, as represented by Bureau of Indian Affairs bureaucrats, county welfare workers, police officers, judges, and so on. This role is crucial but frequently criticized, since it requires knowledge of English and, in the eyes of some community members, getting "too close" to white society. Medicine points out, however, that in some communities women continue to be treated, as they were traditionally, as equals, with the skill of public speaking available to both men and women, and that in other communities, older women, especially those who did not go to government schools, are particularly valued for their knowledge of oral history or traditional ways of doing things.

Americans or American immigrants who speak Spanish natively also reflect considerable cultural variability according to whether they were born in the United States, according to their national or regional origin if they were not born in the United States, according to their social class, and so on. As with Native Americans, the language of many of these different groups remains unstudied, let alone the social variations within these communities along the lines of gender, age, class, and so on. Zentella (1987, p. 168) provides a picture of some of the linguistic issues that Puerto Rican women face. She points out that lower-working-class Puerto Rican speakers, in addition to having the problems that all lower-working-class people do, are faced with a number of identity conflicts triggered by the colonial status of Puerto Rico, racism, and feelings of linguistic inferiority. Puerto Rican speakers ask themselves whether they are Puerto Rican or American, whether they are white or black, and whether they should speak Puerto Rican or Castilian Spanish, or African-American Vernacular English or standard English. Given the diversity of codes and identities that New York Puerto Rican speakers have to choose from, Zentella was interested in how children decided what to speak and to whom. She found that children used three criteria:

> [T]he physical characteristics that distinguish Puerto Ricans and other Latin Americans from North Americans, the age-related classification that assumes infants and the elderly speak only Spanish and all others know English, and the gender-related patterns that link women with speaking Spanish and men with speaking English. (p. 172)

Zentella notes that girls have more exposure to and opportunities to use Spanish than boys because of their greater restriction to the house and/or their mothers, play and friendship with other females, infant caretaking, attendance at Spanish-language religious services, and inclusion in female discussions and activities such as cooking, cleaning, and watching the *novela* (1987, p. 173). Girls use different amounts of English and Spanish at different life stages. Early in their lives they may speak largely Spanish, but as they go to school, English often becomes their dominant language. Female teens alternate between Spanish and English in conversations that deal with education, employment, social services, and friendship. As young women have children, they are reintegrated into older women's networks and tend to use more Spanish to talk about childbearing and household management (p. 173). Perhaps not surprisingly therefore, female speakers are more likely to believe in the importance of speaking Spanish in marking and maintaining Puerto Rican identity and the Puerto Rican nation, although this in no way precludes their appreciation of the importance of bilingualism and their significant community advocacy for bilingual education (pp. 175–177).

Gonzales Velasquez (1992) summarizes studies demonstrating that in northern New Mexico communities, women are using English more than vernacular Spanish, and men are using vernacular Spanish more than English. She finds women are both the conservators of Spanish and the innovators in English (this is a role comparable to that of the men in the community described by Hill), although there are important differences in the three generations of women she studied (unlike Zentella, Gonzales Velasquez does not point out whether this is the result of age grading or a language shift in progress). Among other studies of Spanish-speaking women and language are Chavez (1984), Galindo (1992), Hartford (1978), Patella and Kuvulesky (1973), Redlinger (1979), Valdes-Faltis (1978), and Yanez (1990).

In describing the discourse of African-American women, Morgan (1991), like Medicine, emphasizes the importance of understanding the communication styles of women because of their responsibility for language socialization in children, and thus language maintenance in the community (p. 422). She further points out that because African-American women have often had to function as heads of households in financial, political, or social conditions which caused the absence of their men, they have developed "a collective survival wisdom which has shaped the community's character" (p. 422). This wisdom, developed partly as resistance to "slave reality" and partly as a challenge to the little-changed social and political circumstances after slavery's end, constructed an alternative reality which "allowed them to express a positive self-view as men and women capable of responsibility and control" even in situations in which grown men and women were treated like children (p. 423). She points out that a communication style was imposed on slaves arising from the enslavers' interpretation that direct expression of feelings, questions, and eye contact were acts of aggression. As a result, slaves developed a "counterlanguage," an in-group communication system that was unfamiliar to the enslaver and drew upon ways of speaking inherited from Africa and reshaped by the American context. A distinctive aspect of this system was that speaker meaning and responsibility were determined as much by overhearers as by the individual speaker's "intentions," so that:

> [M]isunderstandings of message content between senders and receivers are seldom recognized as such and what is said, and all reasonable interpretations, is viewed as what is meant. Speakers therefore are rarely viewed as innocent in terms of intent; and what a speaker may argue is a misunderstanding is largely viewed as the hearers' understanding of what the speaker really means. (p. 425)

In Hausa and Akan societies, in the Caribbean and in the United States, indirect speaking strategies, figurative language, and ways of using spokespersons or go-betweens arose partly as a way of avoiding responsibility for the audience's assignment of intentionality (Morgan, 1991, p. 424). Morgan's experimental study, in which she had groups of African-American and white women offer their interpretations of several stories in which speakers offered insults to audience members, clearly demonstrates different cultural perceptions of what is intended, and therefore of speaker responsibility. Classroom instructors could replicate this experiment for themselves and their students by using the same stories. The dialogic evaluation of knowledge claims, the ethic of accountability, and the use of concrete experience as criteria for knowledge claims that Morgan's experimental study describes are also evident in other studies of the speech of African-American women in classrooms (Foster, 1989, 1992), on radio talk shows (Bucholtz, 1992, 1994), and in "everyday" conversations (Morgan, 1989).[11]

Although, as was noted earlier, many early studies of language and gender in the United States focused on white speakers, the inattentiveness to the ways in which gender was articulated with ethnicity means that researchers must return to white, as well as to ethnically mixed, communities to look at the construction of class, race, sexuality, and age alongside gender. Studies by Eckert on Detroit high school students, McLemore (1991) on college students in Texas, and McElhinny on African-American and white women in a working-class work-

11 Bucholtz (1994) is a useful synthetic review of research on African-American women's speech which makes explicit some of the links between more generalized accounts of African American feminist ethics and epistemology and African-American women's speech strategies.

place (the Pittsburgh police department) have begun to remedy these faults. Because of space constraints, two such studies will be described in detail. Eckert (1988, 1989a, 1989b) investigated the linguistic behavior of jocks and burnouts in a suburban high school outside Detroit. *Jocks* and *burnouts* are the expression of class differences within the adolescent culture of a white American high school. Jocks are primarily middle-class students, or students with middle-class aspirations and affinities, and burnouts are primarily working-class students, or students with working-class aspirations and affinities. Jocks tend to be college-preparatory students, bound for white-collar jobs, and burnouts are preparing to take jobs immediately after high school graduation in blue- or pink-collar workplaces. The occupational trajectories these social groups are organized around reflect the options open to white suburban communities. High schools located in predominantly minority communities, in predominantly working-class communities, or in predominantly urban communities will be organized around quite different social categories. The orientation of each group toward school, and the community around the school, reflects the group's sense of how best to prepare for their lives after high school (Eckert, 1988, pp. 190–191). Jocks' communities are largely defined by school district boundaries, and they aim to learn how to control school resources (space, information, freedom, visibility, rights, and materials to organize social events) within the hierarchical corporate structure of the school. Burnouts establish elaborate social networks that bridge school districts and age groups that can, among other things, be utilized for finding jobs once they graduate. Within each group there are important gender differences (Eckert, 1989a, p. 259). Burnout boys can mark their social identity by frequent trips into urban Detroit and by displays of physical prowess in fights, but the restrictions on burnout girls' physical activity means that they must display their social identity with other symbolic means (especially by developing a tough, urban, "experienced" persona). Jock boys can participate in varsity sports; jock girls aggressively develop a friendly, outgoing, active, clean-cut, all-American image.

Eckert finds corresponding gender and social group differences in phonological changes in progress in Detroit.[12] The changes are part of the Northern Cities Chain Shift, a pattern of vowel shifting that involves the fronting of low vowels and the backing and lowering of midvowels (see Eckert, 1988, 1989a, pp. 259–260, for further details). Changes in the use of the vowels spread outward from the urban center. The most recent changes are used to distinguish burnouts and jocks, with burn-

12 A body of scholarship on the significance of sex and gender in variationist (a.k.a Labovian) sociolinguistic studies exists that cannot be addressed here. For reviews, see Eckert (1989a), McElhinny (1993), and Milroy (1992).

outs using the innovative urban variants more. Older changes, which are perhaps less effective as carriers of counteradult meaning, display marked gender differences. Burnout girls display the most frequent use of the innovative urban variants.

In a series of studies on male and female police officers, McElhinny (1993, 1994a, 1994b) has asked whether, when, and how female police officers adopt masculine interactional norms to adapt to their workplace, and whether and how their workplace has redefined what it means to be a police officer in reaction to their presence. She demonstrates that in some situations in which it might be assumed that men and women would react differently (e.g., in responding to domestic violence), in fact male and female police officers share an interactional style (McElhinny, 1993, pp. 186–205). This style, characterized by long strings of questions, long silences in response to complainants' remarks, and interruptions of complainants when they are producing "irrelevant" information, is understood by the police officers as objective, rational, and professional and seems to be perceived by complainants as cold and unsympathetic. It is important to note, however, that this "bureaucratic style" of interaction is only one of several models of interaction available to police officers in Pittsburgh. Another, which focuses on displays of anger and the implicit threat of the use of physical force in order to elicit respect for policing rather than displays of rationality and calmness, might be called a *street warrior style.* McElhinny argues that the hiring of women as police officers reflects, and accelerates, a process of bureaucratization of the police force in Pittsburgh. Given contrasting definitions of masculinity and effective policing on their job, the decision to orient toward a "professional" rather than a "physical" norm must be understood simultaneously as adaptation to one kind of masculinity and as a challenge to another. By resisting the definition of policing as an occupation centered around the exertion of physical force and aggressiveness (which they do not on the whole choose to emphasize in themselves and which many male officers do not believe them capable of), and by offering an alternative definition of policing which centers instead around mental ability, emotional control, and cool efficiency, female police officers create a space for themselves in a formerly all-male and still largely masculine occupation. They do not, however, radically redefine what policing is by introducing interactional norms that focus more on individuals than criminal justice procedures. They do not, that is, introduce the kinds of interactional norms associated with, among other things, mothering or social work. McElhinny concludes that such large-scale redefinitions of policing must come instead from communities determined to change the meaning of policing (by, for instance, adopting community policing programs) rather than simply the composition of the police force.

An important axis of diversity in the United States and elsewhere which has only begun to be explored in linguistics is sexual identity. The ways that gender and sexuality will interact are by no means obvious. Some studies hypothesize a gender-inversion model, in which lesbian women and heterosexual men, and gay men and heterosexual women, are assumed to share linguistic and other traits. Gender-separatist models suggest, on the other hand, that the woman-loving woman and the man-loving man respectively embody what it means to be a "real woman" and a "real man" (see Sedgwick, 1990, p. 88, for further discussion of these two models). Yet other models suggest that the linguistic performances of speakers who display marginalized sexualities can be used to deconstruct prevailing notions of the "naturalness" of gender, sex, and sexuality (Butler, 1990; Sedgwick, 1990). In an exploratory experiment on the intonational patterns of lesbian and heterosexual women based on a very small sample, Moonwomon (1986) found that there was a greater tendency for heterosexual women to use intonational features associated with high affect (high pitch levels, a wider pitch range, and large glides on monosyllables) than lesbian women. In another experimental study on gay and straight men's speech, Gaudio (1992, 1994) found that experimental subjects could reliably distinguish the speech of straight men from that of gay men, yet he did not find any intonational differences between them. He offers suggestions for other aspects of speech that investigators might further examine. As yet no detailed ethnographic study of gay and lesbian speech exists that attends carefully to nuances of situation and identity while simultaneously taking into account many of the insights that gender-focused research has arrived at about the polysemy and indexicality of linguistic forms. Ongoing linguistic research projects in the United States and other cultures by Birch Moonwomon (on the discourse of lesbian women in the San Francisco Bay Area), Rudi Gaudio (on the 'yan daudu of Nigeria), William Leap (on gay American men's discourse patterns), Kira Hall (on hejiras in India), Niko Besnier (on transvestites in Tonga), and others will soon yield increasing insights into this neglected aspect of social identity.

We have attempted to draw attention in this section to some of the cultural diversity within the United States in the ways that language and gender covary. Clearly, there are important gaps in the knowledge about the ways that ethnicity, language, and gender interact. In addition to some of the gaps noted, there is, as far as we are aware, no sociolinguistic study of language and gender among any Asian-American, Amerasian, or Pacific-American group. There are also gender differences in other regional and ethnic groups which have only begun to be studied (see Schiffrin, 1984, on Jewish-Americans; Tannen, 1982, on Greek-Americans).

## Language and gender in the classroom

Many of the issues reviewed in this chapter have far-reaching implications in classrooms. Classrooms and schools are among society's primary socializing institutions. In them, children come to understand their social identity relative to each other and relative to the institution. Although schools are certainly not responsible for teaching students their gender-differentiated social roles, they often reinforce the subordinate role of girls and women through curricular choices and classroom organizations that exclude, denigrate, and/or stereotype them. However, as discussed earlier in this chapter, recent theoretical insights suggest that identity is not fixed, that language use is not static, and that it is possible to negotiate social identities through alternative language use. It follows, then, that schools are sites in which inequities (based on gender, race, ethnicity, language background, age, sexuality, etc.) can be challenged and potentially transformed by selecting materials that represent identity groups more equally, by reorganizing classroom interaction so that all students have the opportunity to talk and demonstrate achievement, and by encouraging students to critically analyze the ways they use language in their everyday lives.

Based on a review of 2 decades of research on gender and classroom interaction, Clarricoates concludes that interaction between teachers and students and among students themselves is "suffused with gender" (1983, p. 46; cited by Swann, 1993). Studies reviewed by Swann (1993) describe a range of ways in which gender differentiation is maintained in mainstream English-speaking classrooms, including the following:

- While there are quiet pupils of both sexes, the more outspoken pupils tend to be boys.
- Boys also tend to 'stand out' more than girls. Michelle Stanworth (1983) notes that in her study teachers initially found some girls 'hard to place'. Boys also referred to a 'faceless' bunch of girls.
- Boys tend to be generally more assertive than girls. For instance, a US study of whole-class talk (Sadker and Sadker, 1985) found boys were eight times more likely than girls to call out.
- Girls and boys tend to sit separately; in group work, pupils usually elect to work in single-sex rather than mixed-sex groups.
- When they have the choice, girls and boys often discuss or write about gender-typed topics.
- Boys are often openly disparaging towards girls.
- In practical subjects, such as science, boys hog the resources.
- In practical subjects, girls 'fetch and carry' for boys, doing much of the cleaning up, and collecting books and so on.

- Boys occupy, and are allowed to occupy, more space, both in class and outside—for example, in play areas.
- Teachers often make distinctions between girls and boys – for disciplinary or administrative reasons or to motivate pupils to do things.
- Teachers give more attention to boys than to girls.
- Topics and materials for discussion are often chosen to maintain boys' interests.
- Teachers tend not to perceive disparities between the numbers of contributions from girls and boys. Sadker and Sadker (1985) showed US teachers a video of classroom talk in which boys made three times as many contributions as girls – but teachers believed the girls had talked more.
- Teachers accept certain behaviour (such as calling out) from boys but not from girls.
- Female teachers may themselves be subject to harrassment from male pupils.
- 'Disaffected' girls tend to opt out quietly at the back of the class, whereas disaffected boys make trouble.

(Swann, 1993, pp. 51–52)

A 10-year research project by Sadker and Sadker (1993; including participant observation, audio and video recordings, interviews with students and teachers, and large-scale surveys) in elementary, junior high, and high school, and in university classes in the United States, and the review of research on language and gender in the classroom by Sommers and Lawrence (1992), both support these general findings. It is interesting to note the parallel between research on girls and boys in schools on the one hand, and on minority and majority students in schools on the other. Just as boys and men (generally with no attention to factors like race and ethnicity) seem to be advantaged at the expense of girls and women in mainstream schools in Britain, Australia, and the United States, white middle-class standard English speakers (generally with no attention to gender) seem to be advantaged at the expense of nonwhite middle-class standard English speakers (see Nieto, 1992, for further discussion).

However, as Swann (1993) points out, these findings need to be interpreted with some caution. The differences between sexes are always average ones, and boys and girls behave differently in different contexts. In other words, these are tendencies, not absolutes, that have been documented in mainstream English-speaking classes. It should be emphasized that there is considerable variation that can be exploited by teachers in their own classes. As discussed earlier, for the variation in how girls and boys use language to be understood, research needs to begin not with boys and girls as fixed categories that behave or are treated the same in all contexts, but with a particular community of practice, in this case a class or a school. The analysis, then, needs to focus on the activity and on how boys' and girls' rights and obligations are constructed within that activity within that community of practice.

Once the class and the activities to be analyzed have been identified, the teacher or researcher can begin by asking how girls and boys, women and men, are represented, for example, in the texts selected for use in the class as well as in the work that the students produce. Researchers have found that women, like other minority groups, tend to be excluded, marginalized, or stereotyped within the mainstream curriculum content (see Nieto, 1992; Sadker & Sadker, 1993; Swann, 1993, for further discussion). Although we are not aware of any studies that have documented short-term and longer-term effects of mainstream curriculum content versus curriculum content that is gender balanced, Swann summarizes the concerns of teachers and researchers about gender imbalances in the curriculum as follows:

> Teachers and researchers have been concerned about imbalances in children's reading materials because of their potential immediate and local effects: they may affect the way pupils respond to a particular book and the subject with which it is associated; they may also affect the pupils' performance on assessment tasks. There is further concern that, in the longer term, such imbalances may help to reinforce gender differences and inequalities: they may influence children's perceptions of what are appropriate attributes, activities, occupations, and so forth for males and females. Introducing alternative images may redress the balance, and also have a disruptive effect, causing pupils to question accepted views of girls and boys and women and men. (p. 113)

Swann (pp. 190–197) provides a variety of checklists that teachers and researchers can use to investigate how girls and boys, women and men, are represented and evaluated in the texts they choose and the activities they organize within their classrooms. When teachers find that their curricular choices are not balanced with respect to gender, for example, that the science text includes few contributions by women, that the literature anthology includes stories primarily by white males about white males, or that the women included in the texts are portrayed only in traditional roles, they can adopt texts that offer images of women and men in less traditional roles. If the goal is to encourage students to question traditional notions, simply providing alternative images in the curriculum content may not be sufficient. Teachers may want to encourage students to talk about traditional and alternative images, perhaps by critically reading and responding to sexist materials, by emphasizing choice in women's and men's roles, and by challenging representations of women and men (and other groups) in the students' own work. We will return to these points later in this chapter.

As has been discussed throughout this chapter, it is not only *what* is talked about, in this case through the curriculum content, that helps shape gender roles; equally or more important is an understanding of *how* girls and boys, women and men, position themselves and each other through their interactions. With respect to the organization of classroom interaction, research suggests that participation frameworks, or groupings of students and teachers for classroom activities (e.g., as individuals, in pairs, in small groups, or as a teacher-fronted classes), can strongly influence the students' opportunities to talk and demonstrate achievement (see Erickson, this volume; Saville-Troike, this volume). For example, mainstream U.S. classrooms are generally characterized by the transmission model of teaching and learning (Cummins, 1989) and the initiation-response-evaluation (IRE) participation structure (Holmes, 1978). In these teacher-centered classes, the teacher talks for most of the time as he or she transmits the curriculum content to the student population in a relatively competitive atmosphere, and initiates the students' participation. The students are encouraged to bid for the opportunity to respond to what Cazden (1988) describes as the "known-answer" question, and the teacher then evaluates the students' responses as right or wrong. It is in this traditional competitive classroom that boys seem to be advantaged (Sadker & Sadker, 1993; Tannen, 1992). However, just as women participated more in more collaboratively organized meetings than in traditional hierarchically organized meetings (see earlier discussions of Edelsky, 1981; Goodwin, 1990), some research suggests that girls, as well as students from linguistically and culturally diverse backgrounds, participate more in cooperative learning organizations than in traditional teacher-centered classes (Kramarae & Treichler, 1990; Tannen, 1992; see also Kessler, 1990, for a general review of benefits of cooperative learning).

However, the picture is much more complicated; simply organizing students into smaller groups is not the answer. In fact, some research suggests that mixed-sex groupings can reproduce boys' dominant role and girls' supportive role. For example, in a study by Sommers and Lawrence (1992) of mixed-sex peer response groups of college students in writing classes, it was found that males took far more turns than females, produced greater quantities of talk, at times appropriated females' ideas as their own, and tended to interrupt and/or silence their female counterparts. Females tended to wait, listen, acknowledge, and confirm other students' contributions. When Sommers and Lawrence compared male and female participation in the peer response groups with their participation in the teacher-fronted participation framework, they found that boys and girls tended to participate more or less equally in the teacher-fronted organization because the teachers could exert more control over how the participation opportunities were distributed. It is important to mention that the teachers in these teacher-fronted classes were Lawrence and Sommers themselves, and that they were aware of and concerned about equal participation opportunities for males and females in their classes. In a study by Rennie and Parker (1987, cited by Swann, 1993) of primary school students in science classes in Australia, it was also found that boys tended to talk more in mixed-sex groupings, and girls tended to watch and listen. However, in single-sex groups, and in classes in which the teachers had participated in a "gender awareness" course, girls tended to participate more actively. Both these examples suggest that when teachers are aware of gender-differentiated language use, they can change the dynamics in their classes so that girls and women are not subordinated, at least in the short run. Swann (1993) provides some useful suggestions for teachers and researchers who are interested in systematically observing and analyzing the dynamics within their own classes to understand how girls and boys are positioned relative to each other (Chap. 8), as well as suggestions for changing discriminatory practices (Chap. 9).

The research discussed thus far has been concerned with gender-differentiated language use in mainstream, white, standard English-speaking contexts in the United States, Britain, and Australia. Even in these relatively homogeneous contexts, it is evident that factors other than gender (e.g., participation framework and activity type) may affect the way people behave. Although there has been relatively little detailed research to date on the ways in which boys and girls from linguistically and culturally diverse backgrounds interact in the classroom, an area of particular concern to ESL and bilingual teachers, it is likely that factors such as culture, race, ethnicity, and socioeconomic status interact with gender to shape students' participation opportunities. For example, Swann (1993) discusses a series of analyses of gender and ethnic imbalances in classroom discussions in four nursery and primary schools in Ealing, England. Swann points out that in the original analysis, Claire and Redpath (1989) found that boys averaged three times as many turns as girls, and that some boys were more talkative than others; this finding is consistent with much of the research on girls' and boys' participation in classes. Their follow-up analysis of the same data, however, suggests an interaction between gender and ethnic group. They found that the boys who dominated the discussion group were white and black Afro-Caribbean; the Asian boys participated much less frequently. White and black Afro-Caribbean girls participated about equally; Asian girls participated the least of any group. They speculate that the topics of discussion and teachers' attitudes and behaviors in the lesson might contribute to these classroom dynamics (see Swann, 1993, p. 65, for further discussion). Consistent with Claire and Redpath's first analysis, research by Sadker and Sadker (1993) found no systematic differences between black and white students, students from different age groups, or students from different socioeconomic backgrounds. Much more work is needed on the interaction between gender and other social factors such as ethnicity, race, and class in the classroom, as well as on how different curricular choices and classroom organizations affect students' opportunities to participate and demonstrate their achievement.

In the meantime, some strategies can be offered to teachers of linguistically and culturally diverse student populations who want to address some of these gaps and to help their language students develop their communicative competences at the same time. It was mentioned earlier that feminist linguists often begin their inquiry by identifying and investigating stereotypes about the language use and social roles of men and women. Their subsequent empirical studies have often refuted these stereotypes, encouraged the development of sociopolitical explanations for gender-differentiated language use, and/or suggested areas to target for change. Teachers might consider following the same procedure with their students. Students can be encouraged to make explicit some of the stereotypes they hold about women and men from different cultural groups, to look for alternative representations, and to discuss the implications of such stereotypes for student behavior. For example, Claire and Redpath's study (1989), discussed earlier, provided an example of the manifestation of a commonly held stereotype that Asians are quiet and passive. It is important to emphasize that *Asian,* like *girl* or *boy, woman* or *man,* is not a homogeneous, static category. There is considerable variation in what it means to be Asian, and stereotypical attitudes can influence behavior. To begin to understand some of this variation, teachers can turn to literary works currently being produced by women in minority communities as well as to literary criticisms of these works, and then they can discuss and challenge such stereotypes with their students. For instance, Sau-ling Cynthia Wong (1993) explores the complexities of the term *Asian-American,* and King-kok Cheung's analysis (1993) of three woman writers (one Japanese-American, one Chinese-American, one Japanese-Canadian) points out how the silence stereotypically associated with Asian-American speakers is often understood as timidity, shrewdness, and femininity, in ways that has important implications for the understanding of Asian-American men and women (see Aguilar-San Juan, 1994, pp. 17–18, for further discussion of these works). Students might be encouraged to compare representations of Asians or Asian-Americans in a variety of texts and to critically evaluate their responses to these texts together (see Fairclough, 1989, pp. 233–247, 1992, Chaps. 3 and 5, for examples of how teachers have encouraged their students to critically analyze discourse and to recognize and challenge discriminatory representations).

A stated goal of all communicative language teaching is students' development of communicative competence. Gee (1991) provides the following description of what is involved in a "successful" social practice. Note that it parallels Eckert's and McConnell-Ginet's notion of a community of practice discussed earlier. He also makes it easy to see the link between recent theoretical insights in language and gender and communicative language teaching and learning approaches. Gee writes:

> What is important [in a 'successful' social practice] is not language, and surely not grammar, *but saying-(writing)-doing-being-valuing-believing combinations in the "right" places at the "right" times with the "right" people and the "right" props (dress and objects)*. p. 7; (emphasis in original)

This statement also reflects trends in second language pedagogy away from the traditional teaching of grammar to the communicative approach, which in practice tends to emphasize sociolinguistic appropriateness. There are currently several unresolved problems with teaching students to be sociolinguistically appropriate.

One problem is simply the question of what we can teach. As Cohen (this volume) points out, to date we do not have enough empirical data to know which speech acts are used by whom in what ways and in which contexts, although research does suggest that when we have this information, students can learn it – at least in the short term (Billmyer, 1990). The field of ethnography of communication has great potential to fill this gap in information, although, as Saville-Troike (this volume) mentions:

> Such potential instructional applications of the ethnography of communication have been proposed for communicative approaches to language teaching since early in the history of the field (e.g., see Paulston, 1974), but implementation has fallen well short of potential in both second and foreign language contexts. In part, this is because commercial concerns in publishing language texts require assumptions about the homogeneity of students' second/foreign language opportunities and needs which are quite unrealistic. Application to instruction in English for specific purposes (ESP) has been more viable (e.g., Munby, 1978), but the ethnography of communication may be a domain in which the *methods* of analysis are even more applicable than its product. (emphasis in original)

Saville-Troike's suggestion, that teacher-researchers themselves determine which communicative situations are relevant for student experiences and needs, and that teacher-researchers then analyze typical events in those situations as a basis for curriculum content and assessment, is one way that teachers can use ethnography of communication methods themselves. Another possibility for L1 students or for more advanced L2 students in a second language context is to have the students conduct their own ethnography of communication studies in the communities of practice in which they participate or are preparing to participate. This suggestion could simultaneously fulfill several goals.

First of all, teaching students to incorporate methodologies from the ethnography of communication themselves would enable the students to learn firsthand what an individual needs to know about language use to be a functional member of the community in which they need to participate. Beginning with a community of practice in which they participate or are preparing to participate, students could investigate many of the issues raised throughout this chapter. For example, they could investigate stereotypes that members of the community hold about men and women and then conduct empirical studies to explain and/or refute them. They could investigate how men and women are named and represented in the texts used in the community, how men and women talk to each other, and how issues of dominance and resistance play out in situated activities throughout the community.

But perhaps more important than providing the student with information about how to be communicatively competent in a particular community of practice, the experience of learning how to conduct an ethnography of communication study would help students develop strategic competence, an aspect of Canale's and Swain's (1980) now-classic model of communicative competence that has been relatively neglected in L2 pedagogy. If students learn how to look, how to ask questions, and how to listen in order to account for when, where, by whom, to whom, in what manner, and in what particular circumstances particular speech acts are used (Saville-Troike, this volume) in one context, they can transfer those strategies to other interactional contexts in which they will participate at other times.

In addition, the L2 classroom itself can provide a forum for critical discourse analysis in which students can question issues of language and power that they observe through their ethnography of communication studies. Fairclough (1992) has argued that language teachers need to adopt a more critical stance toward traditional sociolinguistic studies which tend to describe what happens in a particular speech community as appropriate. As an example, he critiques the unquestioned acceptance of standard English as the goal of ESL/EFL instruction. Returning to issues of language and gender, suppose the students observed a particular context, say, a traditionally organized meeting such as the one Edelsky (1981) described, in which the men dominate and the women rarely contribute. The classroom can provide a forum for students and teachers together to question such practices, to discuss strategies for resisting practices that, for example, position women in a voiceless role. They could suggest creative alternatives and discuss the implications of their choices (cf. Chick, this volume). In brief, having students conduct ethnography of communication studies and discuss their findings from a critical discourse perspective could teach students firsthand about the power of our language choices to shape particular contexts, our notions of ourselves, and our relationships with each other in those contexts. Students learning language can simultaneously learn to challenge and to construct alternative notions of what gender is and should be.

## Suggestions for further reading

Cameron, Deborah (1992). *Feminism and linguistic theory* (2nd ed.). New York: St. Martin's.

A critical review of studies of gender in empirical sociolinguistics, of feminist efforts at linguistic reform of sexist language, and of approaches to language in French feminism (J. Kristeva, L. Irigaray). Focuses on epistemological assumptions.

Coates, Jennifer (1993). *Women, men and language.* London: Longman.

A comprehensive review of studies of language and gender done in dialectology, variationist (a.k.a. *Labovian*) sociolinguistics, language acquisition, and discourse analysis. A solid introduction to the topic, often used as a textbook for undergraduates. The final chapter considers the social consequences of linguistic sex differences, with particular attention to educational applications in British classrooms.

Eckert, Penelope, & McConnell-Ginet, Sally (1992). Think practically and look locally: Language and gender as community-based practice. *Annual Review of Anthropology, 21,* 461–490.

A comprehensive and critical review of language and gender research by two linguists. Rapidly becoming one of the most widely cited articles in language and gender scholarship.

Gal, Susan (1991). Between speech and silence: The problematics of research on language and gender. In Micaela DiLeonardo (Ed.), *Gender at the crossroads of knowledge: Feminist anthropology in the postmodern era* (pp. 175–203). Berkeley: University of California Press.

A comprehensive and critical review of language and gender research, with a focus on what constitutes power, oppression, resistance, and domination.

Goodwin, Marjorie Harness (1990). *He-said-she-said: Talk as social organization among black children.* Bloomington: Indiana University Press.

Investigates similarities and differences in the use of directives (commands), arguments, gossip activities, and stories by African-American boys and girls in Philadelphia. Although the analysis may contain details that are not necessarily relevant to nonspecialists, this remains the only published book-length ethnographic study of language and gender available. It may therefore serve as a model for students on how to conduct a comprehensive ethnography of communicative events in one's own social world.

Hall, Kira, Bucholtz, Mary, & Moonwomon, Birch (Eds.). (1993). *Locating power: Proceedings of the second Berkeley women and language Conference.* (2 Vols.). Berkeley: Berkeley Women and Language Group, Department of Linguistics, University of California at Berkeley.

A collection of fifty-six articles that show the depth and breadth of current studies of language and gender. Includes contributions by many scholars currently working on language and gender.

Hume, Elizabeth, & McElhinny, Bonnie (Eds.). (1993). The Committee on the Status of Women in Linguistics (COSWL) Language and Gender Syllabus Project. Washington, DC: Linguistic Society of America.

This collection is an invaluable resource for those teaching undergraduate or graduate courses on language and gender. It contains twenty-seven syllabi for courses on language and gender taught in an array of departments (linguistics, anthropology, folklore, English, education, French, German). Special features of the collection include syllabi for undergraduate and graduate courses, ideas for paper topics, examples of exam questions, instructions for fieldwork exercises in gathering and/or analyzing gender differences in language use, bibliographies of work on language and gender, and comments from instructors about particularly successful techniques for teaching that have been implemented in the course. For information on ordering hard copies, write to COSWL Language and Gender Syllabus Project, Linguistic Society of America, 1325 18th Street NW, Suite 211, Washington D.C. 20036

Philips, Susan, Steele, Susan, & Tanz, Christine (Eds.). (1986). *Language, gender and sex in comparative perspective.* Cambridge: Cambridge University Press.

Contains chapters investigating language and gender in Japan, Western Samoa, Mexico, Panama, and the United States. Some chapters consider whether there are biological effects on linguistic aptitudes of boys and girls.

Swann, Joan (1993). *Girls, boys and language.* Oxford: Basil Blackwell.

An excellent resource for teachers. In very accessible language, this book summarizes issues relating to language, gender, and education, and provides teachers with a variety of ways to investigate and reform as necessary their curricular choices and classroom practices.

Thorne, Barrie, Kramerae, Cheris, & Henley, Nancy (Eds.) (1983). *Language, gender and society.* Cambridge: Newbury House.

A collection of classic essays that represent a variety of topics and approaches to the study of language and gender, as well as an extensive annotated bibliography of the literature to that date.

## References

Aguilar-San Juan, Karin (1994). [Review of *Reading Asian American literature: From necessity to extravagance,* by Sau-ling Cynthia Wong, and *Articulate silences: Hisaye Yamamoto, Maxine Hong Kingston, Joy Kogawa,* by King-kok Cheung.] *Women's Review of Books, 11*(7), 17–18.

Bem, Sandra, & Bem, Daryl (1973). Does sex-biased job advertising "aid and abet" sex discrimination? *Journal of Applied Social Psychology, 3*(1), 6–18.

Billmyer, Kristine (1990). "I really like your lifestyle": ESL learners learning how to compliment. *Penn Working Papers in Educational Linguistics,* 6(2), 31–48.

Borker, Ruth, & Maltz, Daniel (1989). Anthropological perspectives on gender and language. In S. Morgan (Ed.), *Gender and anthropology* (pp. 411–437). Washington, DC: American Anthropology Association.

Brown, Penelope (1980). How and why are women more polite: Some evidence from a Mayan community. In Sally McConnell-Ginet, Ruth Borker, & Nelly Furman (Eds.), *Women and language in literature and society* (pp. 111–149). New York: Praeger.

Brown, Penelope (1993). Gender, politeness and confrontation in Tenejapa. In Deborah Tannen (Ed.), *Gender and conversational interaction* (pp. 144–164). Oxford: Oxford University Press.

Brown, Penelope, & Stephen Levinson (1983). *Politeness: Some universals in language usage*. Cambridge: Cambridge University Press. (original work published 1979)

Bucholtz, Mary (1993). The mixed discourse genre as a social resource for participants. In Joshua Guenter, Barbara Kaiser, & Cheryl Zoll (Eds.). *Proceedings of the nineteenth annual meeting of the Berkeley Linguistics Society*. (pp. 40–51) Berkeley, CA: Department of Linguistics.

Bucholtz, Mary (1994). *Theorizing African-American women's linguistic practices*. Unpublished manuscript.

Butler, Judith (1990). *Gender trouble: Feminism and the subversion of identity*. New York: Routledge.

Butler, Judith (1992). Contingent foundations: Feminism and the question of 'postmodernism'. In Judith Butler & Joan Scott (Eds.), *Feminists theorize the political* (pp. 3–21). New York: Routledge.

Cameron, Deborah (1990). *The feminist critique of language: A reader*. New York: Routledge.

Cameron, Deborah (1992). *Feminism and linguistic theory* (2nd ed.). New York: St. Martin's.

Cameron, Deborah, & Coates, Jennifer (1988). Some problems in the sociolinguistic explanation of sex differences. In Jennifer Coates & Deborah Cameron (Eds.), *Women in their speech communities* (pp. 13–26). London: Longman.

Cameron, Deborah, McAlinden, Fiona & O'Leary, Kathy (1988). Lakoff in context: The social and linguistic functions of tag questions. In Jennifer Coates & Deborah Cameron (Eds.), *Women in their speech communities* (pp. 74–930). London: Longman.

Canale, Michael, & Swain, Merrill (1980). Theoretical bases of communicative approaches to second language teaching and testing. *Applied Linguistics, 1*(1), 1–47.

Cazden, Courtney (1988). *Classroom discourse: The language of teaching and earning*. Portsmouth, NH: Heineman.

Chavez, Eliverio (1984). *Sexual differentiation in bilingual language proficiency*. Unpublished doctoral dissertation. Albuquerque: University of New Mexico.

Cheung, King-kok (1993). *Articulate silences: Hisaye Yamamoto, Maxine Hong Kingston, Joy Kogawa*. Ithaca, NY: Cornell University Press.

Coates, Jennifer (1988). Gossip revisited: Language in all-female groups. In Jennifer Coates & Deborah Cameron (Eds.), *Women in their speech communities* (pp. 94–121). London: Longman.

Coates, Jennifer (1991). Women's cooperative talk: A new kind of conversational duet? In Claus Uhlig & Rudiger Zimmerman (Eds.), *Anglistentag 1990 Marburg proceedings* (pp. 296–311). Tübingen, Germany: Max Niemeyer.

Coates, Jennifer (1992). The language of the professions: Discourse and career. In Julia Evetts (Ed.), *Women and career: Themes and issues.* London: Longman.

Coates, Jennifer (1993). *Women, men and language.* (2nd ed.) London: Longman.

Collier, Jane & Yanagisako, Sylvia (1990). The mode of reproduction in anthropology. In Deborah Rhode (Ed.), *Theoretical perspectives on sexual difference* (pp. 131–144). New Haven, CT: Yale University Press.

Collins, Patricia Hill (1990). *Black feminist thought.* New York: Routledge.

Cornwall, Andrea, & Lindisfarne, Nancy (1994). Dislocating masculinity: Gender, power and anthropology. In Andrea Cornwall & Nancy Lindisfarne (Eds.), *Dislocating masculinity: Comparative ethnographies* (pp. 11–47). London: Routledge.

Cummins, Jim (1989). The sanitized curriculum: Educational disempowerment in a nation at risk. In Donna Johnson & Duane Roen (Eds.), *Richness in writing: Empowering ESL students* (pp. 19–38). New York: Longman.

Davies, Bronwyn (1990). Agency as a form of discursive practice: A classroom scene observed. *British Journal of Sociology of Education, 11*(3), 341–361.

Davies, Bronwyn, & Harre, Rom (1990). Positioning: The discursive production of selves. *Journal for the Theory of Social Behavior, 20*(1), 43–63.

Dubois, Betty Lou, & Crouch, Isabel (1975). The question of tag questions in women's speech: They don't really use more of them, do they? *Language in Society, 4*(2), 89–94.

Echols, Alice (1989). *Daring to be bad: Radical feminism in America 1967–1975.* Minneapolis: University of Minnesota Press.

Eckert, Penelope (1988). Adolescent social structure and the spread of linguistic change. *Language in Society, 17,* 183–207.

Eckert, Penelope (1989a). The whole woman: Sex and gender differences in Variation. *Language Variation and Change, 1*(3), 245–268.

Eckert, Penelope (1989b). *Jocks and burnouts: Social categories and identities in the high school.* New York: Teachers College Press.

Eckert, Penelope, & McConnell-Ginet, Sally (1992). Think practically and look locally: Language and gender as community-based practice. *Annual Review of Anthropology, 21,* 461–490.

Edelsky, Carol (1981). Who's got the floor? *Language in Society, 10,* 383–421.

Ehrlich, Susan & King, Ruth (1992). Feminist meanings and sexist speech communities. In Kira Hall, Mary Bucholtz, and Birch Moonwomon (Eds.), *Locating power: Proceedings of the second Berkeley women and language conference* (pp. 100–107). Berkeley: Berkeley Women and Language Group, Department of Linguistics, University of California at Berkeley.

Etter-Lewis, Gwendolyn (1991). Standing up and speaking out: African American women's narrative legacy. *Discourse and Society, 2*(4), 425–438.

Fairclough, Norman (1989). *Language and power*. New York: Longman.
Fairclough, Norman (Ed.). (1992). *Critical language awareness*. New York: Longman.
Fishman, Pamela (1983). Interaction: The work women do. In B. Thorne, C. Kramarae, & N. Henley (Eds.), *Language, Gender and Society* (pp. 89–102). Cambridge, MA: Newbury House.
Foster, Michele (1989). It's cookin' now: A performance analysis of the speech events of a black teacher in an urban community college. *Language in Society, 18*(1), 1–29.
Foster, Michele (1992). Are you with me?: Power, solidarity and community in the discourse of African-American women. In Kira Hall, Mary Bucholtz, & Birch Moonwomon (Eds.), *Locating power: Proceedings of the second Berkeley women and language conference* (pp. 132–143). Berkeley: Berkeley Women and Language Group, Department of Linguistics, University of California at Berkeley.
Freed, Alice (1992a). We understand perfectly: A critique of Tannen's view of cross-sex communication. In Kira Hall, Mary Bucholtz, & Birch Moonwomon (Eds.), *Locating power: Proceedings of the second Berkeley women and language conference* (pp. 144–152). Berkeley: Berkeley Women and Language Group, Department of Linguistics, University of California at Berkeley.
Freed, Alice (1992b). A global perspective of language and gender research: A bibliography. *Women and Language, 25*(2), 1–7.
Freeman, Rebecca (1993). *Language planning and identity planning for social change: Gaining the ability and the right to participate*. Unpublished doctoral dissertation. Washington, DC: Georgetown University.
Gal, Susan (1978). Peasant men don't get wives: Language and sex roles in a bilingual community. *Language in Society, 7*(1), 1–17.
Gal, Susan (1991). Between speech and silence: The problematics of research on language and gender. In M. di Leonardo (Ed.), *Gender at the crossroads of knowledge* (pp. 175–203). Berkeley: University of California Press.
Gal, Susan (1992). Language, gender, and power: An anthropological view. In Kira Hall, Mary Bucholtz, & Birch Moonwomon (Eds.), *Locating power: Proceedings of the second Berkeley women and language conference* (pp. 153–161). Berkeley: Berkeley Women and Language Group, Department of Linguistics, University of California at Berkeley.
Galindo, D. Letticia (1992). Dispeling the male-only myth: Chicanas and Calo. *The Bilingual Review/La Revista Bilingue, 17*(1), 3–35.
Galindo, D. Letticia, & Gonzales Vesasquez, Maria Dolores (1992). A sociolinguistic description of linguistic self-expression, innovation and power among Chicanas in Texas and New Mexico. In Kira Hall, Mary Bucholtz, & Birch Moonwomon (Eds.), *Locating power: Proceedings of the second Berkeley women and language conference* (pp. 162–170). Berkeley: Berkeley Women and Language Group, Department of Linguistics, University of California at Berkeley.
Gaudio, Rudolph (1992). Talking gay, freeing speech. Paper presented at the Annual Meeting of the American Anthropology Association, Chicago, Illinois.

Gaudio, Rudolph (1994). Sounding gay: Pitch properties in the speech of gay and straight men. *American Speech* 69(1), 30–57.

Gee, James (1991). What is applied linguistics? Paper presented at the Second Language Research Forum, University of Southern California, Los Angeles.

Goldstein, Tara (1992). Language choice and women learners of English as a Second Language. In Kira Hall, Mary Bucholtz, & Birch Moonwomon (Eds.), *Locating power: Proceedings of the second Berkeley women and language conference* (pp. 171–181). Berkeley: Berkeley Women and Language Group, Department of Linguistics, University of California at Berkeley.

Gomm, I. (1981). A study of the inferior image of the female use of the English language as compared to that of the male. Unpublished bachelor's degree thesis. Edge Hill College, Ormskirk, UK.

Gonzales Velasquez, Maria Dolores (1992). *The role of women in linguistic tradition and innovation in a Chicano community in New Mexico.* Unpublished doctoral dissertation. Albuquerque: University of New Mexico.

Goodwin, Marjorie Harness (1990). *He-said-she-said: Talk as social organization among black children.* Bloomington: Indiana University Press.

Goodwin, Marjorie Harness (1992). Orchestrating participation in events: powerful talk among African American girls. In Kira Hall, Mary Bucholtz, & Birch Moonwomon (Eds.), *Locating power: Proceedings of the second Berkeley women and language conference* (pp. 182–196). Berkeley: Berkeley Women and Language Group, Department of Linguistics, University of California at Berkeley.

Graddol, David, & Swann, Joan (1989). *Gender Voices.* Oxford: Basil Blackwell.

Guy, Gregory, Horvath, Barbara, Vonwiller, Julia, Daisley, Elaine, & Rogers, Inge (1986). An intonational change in progress in Australian English. *Language in Society, 15,* 23–52.

Haeri, Niloofaer (1987). Male/female difference in speech: An alternative interpretation. In Keith Denning, Sharon Inkelas, Faye McNair-Knox, & John Rickford (Eds.), *Variation in language: Proceedings of the fifteenth annual conference on new ways of analyzing variation* (pp. 173–182). Stanford, CA: Stanford University, Department of Linguistics.

Hall, Kira, Bucholtz, Mary, & Moonwomon, Birch (Eds.). (1992). *Locating power: Proceedings of the second Berkeley women and language conference.* (2 Vols.). Berkeley: Berkeley Women and Language Group, Department of Linguistics, University of California at Berkeley.

Harding, Susan (1975). Women and words in a Spanish village. In R. Reiter (Ed.), *Toward an anthropology of women* (pp. 283–308). New York: Monthly Review Press.

Harre, Rom (1984). *Personal being: A theory for individual psychology.* Cambridge: Harvard University Press.

Hartford, Beverly (1978). Phonological differences in the English of adolescent female and male Mexican-Americans. *International Journal of the Sociology of Language, 17,* 55–64.

Harvey, Penelope (1991). Women who won't speak Spanish: Gender, power and bilingualism in an Andean village. In Pauline Wilkings (Ed.), *Women and second language use.* Oxford, England: Berg Publishers.

Henley, Nancy (1987). This new species that seeks a new language: On sexism in language and language change. In Joyce Penfield (Ed.), *Women and language in transition* (pp. 3–27). Albany: SUNY Press.

Henley, Nancy, & Kramarae, Cheris (1991). Gender, power and miscommunication. In N. Coupland, H. Giles, & J. Wiemann, *Problem talk and problem contexts* (pp. 18–43). Newbury Park, CA: Sage.

Hill, Jane (1987). Women's speech in modern Mexicano. In S. Philips, S. Steele, & C. Tanz (Eds.), *Language, gender and sex in comparative perspective* (pp. 121–162). Cambridge: Cambridge University Press.

Holmes, Janet (1978). Sociolinguistic competence in the classroom. In Jack C. Richards (Ed.), *Understanding second and foreign language learning* (pp. 134–162). Rowley, MA: Newbury House.

Holmes, Janet (1984). Hedging your bets and sitting on the fence: Some evidence for hedges as support structures. *Te Reo, 27*, 47–62.

Holmes, Janet (1986). Functions of 'you know' in women's and men's speech. *Language in Society, 15*(1), 1–22.

Hume, Elizabeth, & McElhinny, Bonnie (Eds.). (1993). The Committee on the Status of Women in Linguistics (COSWL) Language and Gender Syllabus Project. Washington, DC: Linguistic Society of America.

Ide, Sachiko, & McGloin, Naomi (1991). *Aspects of Japanese women's Language*. Tokyo: Kuroshio.

Inoue, Miyako (1994, April). Gender and linguistic modernization: A historical account of the birth of Japanese women's language. Paper presented at 3rd Berkeley conference on women and language, Berkeley, California.

Inoue, Miyako (in press). *Language and gender in Japan: Men and women in the workplace*. Doctoral dissertation. St. Louis, MO: Washington University.

Jaggar, Alison (1983). *Feminist politics and human nature*. Totowa, NJ: Rowman and Allanheld.

Jenkins, Mercilee (1986). What's so funny?: Joking among women. *Proceedings of the first Berkeley women and language conference 1985* (pp. 135–151). Berkeley: Berkeley Women and Language Group, Department of Linguistics, University of California at Berkeley.

Johnstone, Barbara (1993). Community and contest: Midwestern men and women creating their worlds in conversational storytelling." In Deborah Tannen (Ed.), *Gender and conversational interaction* (pp. 62–82). Oxford: Oxford University Press.

Kalcik, Susan (1975). . . . like Ann's gynecologist or the time I was almost raped. In Claire R. Farrer (Ed.), *Women and folklore* (pp. 3–11). Austin: University of Texas Press.

Keenan, Elinor Ochs (1974). Norm-makers, norm-breakers: Uses of speech by men and women in a Malagasy community. In Richard Bauman & J. Sherzer (Eds.), *Explorations in the Ethnography of Speaking* (pp. 125–143). Cambridge: Cambridge University Press.

Kessler, Carolyn (Ed.). (1990). *Cooperative language learning: A teacher's resource book*. Englewood Cliffs, NJ: Prentice Hall Regents.

Key, Mary Ritchie (1975). *Male/female language*. Metuchen, NJ: The Scarecrow Press.

Kramarae, Cheris (1981). *Women and men speaking*. Rowley, MA: Newbury House.

Kramarae, Cheris, & Treichler, Paula. (1985). *A Feminist dictionary: In our own words.* London: Pandora Press.

Kramarae, Cheris, & Treichler, Paula (1990). Words on a feminist dictionary. In Deborah Cameron (Ed.), *The feminist critique of language: A reader* (pp. 148–159). London: Routledge.

Labov, W. (1972a). *Language in the inner city.* Philadelphia: University of Pennsylvania Press.

Labov, W. (1972b). *Sociolinguistic patterns.* Philadelphia: University of Pennsylvania Press.

Lakoff, George, & Johnson, Mark (1980). *Metaphors we live by.* Chicago: The University of Chicago Press.

Lakoff, Robin (1975). *Language and woman's place.* New York: Harper and Row.

Lee, David (1992). *Competing discourses: Perspective and ideology in language.* London: Longman.

Lemke, Jay (1989). Semantics and social values. *Word, 40*(1), 37–50.

Lemke, Jay (1990). *Talking science: Language, learning, and values.* Norwood, NJ: Ablex.

Levinson, Stephen (1992) Activity types and language. In P. Drew & J. Heritage (Eds.), *Talk at work* (pp. 66–100). Cambridge: Cambridge University Press. (original work published 1978)

Maltz, Daniel, & Borker, Ruth (1982). A cultural approach to male-female miscommunication. In J. Gumperz (Ed.), *Language and social identity* (pp. 195–216). Cambridge: Cambridge University Press.

Martin, Emily (1987). *The woman in the body: A cultural analysis of reproduction.* Boston: Beacon Press.

Martyna, Wendy (1978a). What does 'he' mean? Use of the generic masculine. *Journal of Communication, 28*(1), 131–138.

Martyna, Wendy (1978b). *Using and understanding the generic masculine: A social psychological approach to language and the Sexes.* Doctoral dissertation. Stanford, CA: Stanford University.

Martyna, Wendy (1983). Beyond the he/man approach: The case for nonsexist language. In Barrie Thorne, Cheris Kramarae and, & Nancy Henley (Eds.), *Language, gender and society* (pp. 25–37). Cambridge, MA: Newbury House.

McElhinny, Bonnie (1993). *We all wear the blue: Language, gender and police work.* Unpublished doctoral dissertation. Stanford, CA: Stanford University.

McElhinny, Bonnie (1994a). An economy of affect: Objectivity, masculinity and the gendering of police work. In Andrea Cornwall & Nancy Lindisfarne (Eds.), *Dislocating masculinity: Comparative ethnographies* (pp. 159–171). London: Routledge.

McElhinny, Bonnie (1994b). Negotiations over the meaning of assault in police officer-citizen interactions: Implications for studies of discourse in linguistics and cultural Studies. Unpublished manuscript.

McLemore, Cynthia (1991). *The pragmatic interpretation of English intonation: Sorority speech.* Unpublished doctoral dissertation. Austin: University of Texas.

Medicine, Bea (1987). The role of American Indian women in cultural continuity and transition. In Joyce Penfield (Ed.), *Women and language in transition* (pp. 159–166). Albany: SUNY Press.

Milroy, Leslie (1992). New perspectives in the analysis of sex differentiation in language. In Kingsley Bolton & Helen Kwok (Eds.), *Sociolinguistics today: International perspectives* (pp. 163–179). London: Routledge.

Mitchell-Kernan, Claudia (1972). Signifying and marking: Two Afro-American speech acts. In John Gumperz & Dell Hymes (Eds.), *Directions in sociolinguistics: The ethnography of communication* (pp. 161–179). New York: Holt, Rinehart and Winston.

Moonwomon, Birch (1986). Towards the study of lesbian speech. In Sue Bremner, Noelle Caskey, & Birch Moonwomon (Eds.), *Proceedings of the first Berkeley women and language conference 1985* (pp. 96–107). Berkeley: Berkeley Women and Language Group, Department of Linguistics, University of California at Berkeley.

Morgan, Marcyliena (1989). *From down south to up south: The language behavior of three generations of black women residing in Chicago*. Unpublished doctoral dissertation. Philadelphia: University of Pennsylvania.

Morgan, Marcyliena (1991). Indirectness and interpretation in African American women's discourse. *Pragmatics, 1*(4), 421–451.

Nelson, Linda Williamson (1990). Code-switching in the oral life narratives of African-American women: Challenges to linguistic hegemony. *Journal of Education, 172*(3), 142–155.

Nichols, P. (1983). Linguistic options and choices for black women in the rural south. In B. Thorne, C. Kramarae, & N. Henley (Eds.), *Language, gender and society* (pp. 54–68). Rowley, MA: Newbury House.

Nieto, Sonia (1992). *Affirming diversity: The sociopolitical context of multicultural education*. New York: Longman.

Nilsen, Alleen Pace (1987). Guidelines against sexist language: A case history. In Joyce Penfield (Ed.), *Women and language in transition* (pp. 37–53). Albany: SUNY Press.

O'Barr, William, & Atkins, Bowman (1980). "Women's language" or "powerless language"? In S. McConnell-Ginet, R. Borker, & N. Furman (Eds.), *Women and language in literature and society* (pp. 93–110). New York: Praeger.

Ochs, Elinor (1992). Indexing gender. In A. Duranti & C. Goodwin (Eds.), *Rethinking Context* (pp. 335–358). Cambridge: Cambridge University Press.

Ochs, Elinor (1993). Constructing social identity: A language socialization perspective. *Research on Language and Social Interaction, 26*(3), 287–306.

Okamoto, Shigeko, & Sato, Shie (1992). Less feminine speech among young Japanese females. In Kira Hall, Mary Bucholtz, & Birch Moonwomon (Eds.), *Locating power: Proceedings of the second Berkeley women and language conference* (pp. 478–488). Berkeley: Berkeley Women and Language Group, Department of Linguistics, University of California at Berkeley.

Painter, Dorothy (1980). Lesbian humor as a normalization device. In C. Berryman and V. Eman (Eds.), *Communication, language and sex* (pp. 132–148). Rowley, MA: Newbury House.

Patella, V., & Kuvulesky, W. P. (1973). Situational variation in language patterns of Mexican-American boys and girls. *Social Science Quarterly, 53,* 855–864.

Penfield, Joyce (Ed.). (1987). *Women and language in transition.* Albany: SUNY Press.

Penfield, Joyce (1987). Surnaming: The struggle for personal identity. In Joyce Penfield (Ed.), *Women and language in transition* (pp. 117–129). Albany: SUNY Press.

Philips, Susan, Steele, Susan, & Tanz, Christine (Eds.). (1987). *Language, gender and sex in comparative perspective.* Cambridge: Cambridge University Press.

Poynton, Cate (1989). *Language and gender: Making the difference.* Oxford: Oxford University Press.

Radway, Janice (1984). *Reading the romance: Women, patriarchy and popular literature.* Chapel Hill: University of North Carolina Press.

Redlinger, Wendy (1979). Mothers' Speech to Children in Bilingual Mexican American Homes. In Betty Lou Dubois and Isabel Crouch (Eds.) *The sociology of the language of American women* (pp. 119–130) San Antonio, TX. Trinity University Press.

Rhode, Deborah (1989). *Justice and gender.* Cambridge MA: Harvard University Press.

Rickford, John, & McNair-Knox, Faye (1994). Addressee- and topic-influenced style shift: A quantitative sociolinguistic study. In D. Biber & E. Finegan (Eds.), *Sociolinguistic perspectives on register* (pp. 235–276). Oxford: Oxford University Press.

Riley, Denise (1988). *Am I that name'? Feminism and the category of 'women' in history.* Minneapolis: University of Minnesota.

Sadker, Myra, & Sadker, David (1993). *Failing at fairness: How America's schools cheat girls.* New York: Scribner's.

Schieffelin, Bambi (1987). Do different worlds mean different words? An example from Papua New Guinea. In Susan Philips, Susan Steele, and Christine Tanz (Eds.), *Language, gender and sex in comparative perspective* (pp. 249–262). Cambridge: Cambridge University Press.

Schiffrin, Deborah (1984). Jewish argument as sociability. *Language in Society, 13,* 311–335.

Schulz, Muriel (1990). The semantic derogation of women. In Deborah Cameron (Ed.), *The feminist critique of language: A reader* (pp. 134–147). London: Routledge.

Sedgwick, Eve Kosofsky (1990). *Epistemology of the closet.* Berkeley: University of California Press.

Sheldon, Amy (1992). Preschool girls' discourse competence: Managing conflict. In Kira Hall, Mary Bucholtz, & Birch Moonwomon (Eds.), *Locating power: Proceedings of the second Berkeley conference on women and language* (pp. 528–539). Berkeley: Berkeley Women and Language Group, Department of Linguistics, University of California at Berkeley.

Sherzer, Joel (1987). A diversity of voices: Men's and women's speech in ethnographic perspective. In S. Philips, S. Steele, & C. Tanz (Eds.), *Language, gender and sex in comparative perspective* (pp. 95–120). Cambridge: Cambridge University Press.

Shibamoto, Janet (1985). *Japanese women's language*. New York: Academic Press.

Shibamoto, Janet (1987). The womanly woman: Manipulation of stereotypical and nonstereotypical features of Japanese female speech. In Susan Philips, Susan Steele, & Christine Tanz (Eds.), *Language, gender and sex in comparative perspective* (pp. 26–49). Cambridge: Cambridge University Press.

Smith, Philip (1985). *Language, the sexes and society*. Oxford: Basil Blackwell.

Smith-Hefner, Nancy (1988). Women and politeness: The Javanese example. *Language in Society, 17*, 535–554.

Sommers, Elizabeth, & Lawrence, Sandra (1992). Women's ways of talking in teacher-directed and student-directed peer response groups. *Linguistics and Education, 4*, 1–36.

Spacks, Patricia Meyer (1985). *Gossip*. New York: Knopf.

Spender, Dale (1985). *Man made language*. London: Routledge.

Swann, Joan (1993). *Girls, boys and language*. Oxford: Basil Blackwell.

Tannen, Deborah (1982). Ethnic style in male-female conversation. In John Gumperz (Ed.), *Language and social identity* (pp. 195–216). Cambridge: Cambridge University Press.

Tannen, Deborah (1984). *Conversational style: Analyzing talk among friends*. Norwood, NJ: Ablex.

Tannen, Deborah (1989). Interpreting interruption in conversation. In B. Music, R. Graczyk, & C. Wittshire, *CLS 25: Papers from the 25th annual regional meeting of the Chicago linguistic society (Pt. 2: Parasession on language in context)* (pp. 266–287). Chicago: Chicago Linguistic Society.

Tannen, Deborah (1990). *You just don't understand: Women and men in conversation*. New York: William Morrow.

Tannen, Deborah (1991, June). How men and women use language differently in their lives and in the classroom. *Chronicle of Higher Education*, pp. B1–B3.

Tannen, Deborah (Ed.). (1993a). *Framing in discourse*. New York: Oxford University Press.

Tannen, Deborah (1993b). The relativity of linguistic strategies: Rethinking power and solidarity in gender and dominance. In D. Tannen (Ed.), *Gender and conversational interaction* (pp. 165–185). New York: Oxford University Press.

Thorne, Barrie (1990). Children and gender: Constructions of difference. In Deborah Rhode (Ed.), *Theoretical perspectives on sexual difference* (pp. 100–113). New Haven: Yale University Press.

Thorne, Barrie, & Henley, Nancy (1975). *Language and sex: Difference and dominance*. Rowley, MA: Newbury House.

Thorne, Barrie, Kramerae, Cheris, & Henley, Nancy, (Eds.). (1983). *Language, gender and society*. Cambridge: Newbury House.

Troemel-Ploetz, Senta (1992). The construction of conversational equality by women. In Kira Hall, Mary Bucholtz, & Birch Moonwomon (Eds.), *Locating Power: Proceedings of the second Berkeley conference on women and language* (pp. 581–589). Berkeley: Berkeley Women and Language Group, Department of Linguistics, University of California at Berkeley.

Valdes-Faltis, Guadalupe (1978). Code-switching among bilingual Mexican-

American women: Toward an understanding of sex-related language alteration. *International Journal of the Sociology of Language, 17*, 65–72.

West, Candace, & Zimmerman, Don (1983). Small insults: A study of interruptions in cross-sex conversations between unacquainted persons. In B. Thorne, C. Kramarae, & N. Henley (Eds.), *Language, gender and society* (pp. 102–117). Rowley MA: Newbury House.

Williams, Raymond (1977). *Marxism and Literature*. Oxford: Oxford University Press.

Wolfson, Nessa (1989). *Perspectives: Sociolinguistics and TESOL*. Cambridge: Newbury House.

Wong, Sau-ling Cynthia (1993). *Reading Asian-American literature: From necessity to extravagance*. Princeton, NJ: Princeton University Press.

Yanez, Rosa (1990). The complimenting speech act among Chicano women. In John Bergen (Ed.), *Spanish in the United States: Sociolinguistic issues* (pp. 79–85). Washington, DC: Georgetown University Press.

Zentella, Ana Celia (1987). Language and female identity in the Puerto Rican community. In J. Penfield (Ed.), *Women and language in transition* (pp. 167–179). New York: SUNY Press.

Zimmerman, Don, & West, Candace (1975). Sex roles, interruptions and silences in conversations. In Barrie Thorne & Nancy Henley (Eds.), *Language and sex: Difference and dominance* (pp. 105–209). Rowley, MA: Newbury House.

# PART III:
# LANGUAGE AND INTERACTION

In their discussion of language and gender, Freeman and McElhinny presaged our move from the macrolevel to the microlevel of social analysis as they traced research and theory in a field that spans both the view that the subordinate status of women is reflected in and partly perpetuated by gender-differentiated language use and a view of discourse as constitutive of social identities which are negotiated and constructed in interaction. Here, in Part 3 of our exploration of language, society, and education, we move to the microlevel of both social and linguistic analysis for a closer look, as we learn about the role and linguistic realizations of such phenomena as situated comembership, contextualization cues, sociolinguistic transfer, interpretative mismatch, and oppositional discourse in face-to-face interaction. As discussed in the other three parts of this book and shown in Figure a in the front matter, the macro-micro distinction here connotes emphasis, rather than exclusion; the authors of the three chapters in this part take care to point out that the larger social and cultural context is both reflected in and affected by the microlevel interactions they explore in depth.

Frederick Erickson, in "Ethnographic Microanalysis," opens the part with an overview of the perspective, methods, and salient findings of the ethnographic microanalysis of social interaction, also known as *microethnography,* the research approach which he is primarily responsible for developing. Erickson begins by briefly tracing the intellectual roots of microethnography (ethnographic microanalysis) and goes on to differentiate between microethnography, the ethnography of communication, and interactional sociolinguistics (all of which are represented in this volume). He highlights the emphases in microethnography on the nonverbal as well as the verbal aspects of interaction, on the importance of audience activity in relation to the activity of speakers, on the improvisational and situationally strategic aspects of interaction as well as its cultural and linguistic patterning, and on the importance of power and politics in immediate social encounters. Through sections focusing on both research in educational settings and implications for pedagogy, he brings alive for the classroom teacher such microethnographic findings as the importance of listening activity in relation to speaking, the role of rhythmic organization of conversation in interaction, the ways in which situated social identity and comembership are enacted in interaction, and the importance of participants' framing of cultural difference in communication style as boundary or as border.

In the next chapter, "Interactional Sociolinguistics," Deborah Schiffrin provides a complement to Erickson's chapter by reviewing the intellectual underpinnings of the interactional sociolinguistic approach. She shows what is at the core of interactional sociolinguistics: sociologist Erving Goffman's ideas about the importance of everyday social interaction in maintaining both self and society and linguistic anthropologist John Gumperz's view of language as a socially and culturally constructed symbol system that can be used in ways that reflect macrolevel social meanings and create microlevel social meanings. She goes on to explore key concepts of interactional sociolinguistics, including those contributed by Goffman, such as frame and footing, as well as those developed by Gumperz, such as contextualization cue, contextual presupposition, and situated inference. The chapter concludes with a brief look at how interactional sociolinguistics might both define the goal of language teaching and guide lesson plans and interactions for the language teacher.

Chapter 10, "Intercultural Communication," by Keith Chick, provides a bridge between the foregoing two chapters, on ethnographic microanalysis and interactional sociolinguistics, and the subsequent two chapters, on the ethnography of communication and speech acts. Chick asks what the sociolinguistics associated with these four approaches have contributed to our understanding of the sources and effects of intercultural miscommunication and, especially, to our potential for improving intercultural communication. He contrasts the approach of speech act studies, which abstract particular linguistic features from a large number of interactions for subsequent categorization and/or counting, with that of interactional sociolinguistic studies, which analyze, in fine detail, a limited number of whole interactions in an attempt to uncover the interpretative or inferential processes of the interlocutors. Drawing from his research in South Africa for illustration, he shows how sociolinguistic transfer and various kinds of interpretative mismatch (e.g., mismatches in interpreting frames of reference, contextualization cues, or face needs), produce intercultural miscommunication. He ends with a call for awareness training and, in particular, critical awareness training, so that language learners can make informed and reflective choices, one of those choices being to opt for or against features marking compliant or oppositional discourse in their interactions with others; thus Chick harks back to the point made by Freeman and McElhinny, that our language choices can challenge and potentially transform discriminatory practices.

# 8 *Ethnographic microanalysis*

Frederick Erickson

## Introduction

### *The perspective of ethnographic microanalysis*

The central concern of ethnographic microanalysis is with the immediate ecology and micropolitics of social relations between persons engaged in situations of face-to-face interaction. Ethnographic microanalysis (which has also been called the *microethnography of social interaction*) is both a method and a point of view. Using videotapes or films of naturally occurring interaction, the microanalyst looks very closely and repeatedly at what people do in real time as they interact. From this approach to analysis comes a particular perspective on how people use language and other forms of communication in doing the work of daily life.

Two emphases in this perspective are especially important for language teaching. One concerns the situated character of communication in social interaction. Goffman (1964) observed that the social situation is the basic unit or scene in which everyday life takes place. The situation is influenced by the wider world, but in important ways what happens in an ordinary social situation has a life of its own; that is, the situation is a partially bounded social setting. What happens in a given situation may be powerfully influenced by general societal processes – the economy, the labor market, and the class position of participants in the situation; race, ethnic, and gender relations; religious identification and beliefs; broad patterns of language and culture in the society at large. But these factors do not totally determine what happens when particular people interact in a social situation. When we look very closely at what people actually do in situations, we realize that there is some "wiggle room" there, some room for improvisation.

Interaction in a social situation, then, although not totally independent from societal rules, patterns, and interests, can be seen as not so much rule governed as rule influenced. This is a subtle but extremely important difference from the ways linguists have tended to think of rules – as determining (or predicting) performance. The sense derived from microethnography of the relation between rules (culturally learned competence) and performance is looser and fuzzier than the sense of this relation that is held in usual linguistics. This has implications for how we think of intelligibility, appropriateness, and effectiveness in language use. It also has implications for social theory and for pedagogy. These implications will be discussed later in this chapter.

How people react to and make sense of each others' communication is, in part, a matter of local framing. We can call this framing an aspect of the "micropolitics" of interaction in a situation. Differences in communication style, including cultural definitions of correctness or appropriateness in speech, can be handled very differently by participants depending on the micropolitics by which the situation is being framed. For example, in one situation a cultural style difference can be treated as troublesome, and in another situation – even among the same participants – the cultural style difference can be treated as no trouble at all. This is not a matter of language or language style per se; it is a matter of the local social construction of situation and of situational framing that shapes the conditions of language use.

A second emphasis in the microethnographic perspective concerns the immediate ecology of relations between participants in a situation. How we communicate – what kinds of language we use and how much, how fluent or eloquent we are, how coherent our speech, how attentive or encouraging our listening may be – is very much a matter of what others are doing in the situation while we are doing what we are doing. Listeners influence speakers and vice versa. When someone seems not able to say something clearly, or persuasively, or appropriately, it may not only be a matter of that individual's linguistic or communicative knowledge (competence) but of how that individual is being influenced by others' actions in the scene at that moment. McDermott (1976, p. 33) puts this ecological perspective very succinctly when he says, "people in interaction constitute environments for each other's activities."

The next sections will explore especially the implications for pedagogy that come from what microethnography and its perspectives can tell us about social situations and their framing and about the immediate ecology of relations among participants as they interact in communicative situations. This perspective can help us think in new ways about how people use language to communicate in daily life inside and outside school.

## *Intellectual roots*

Ethnographic microanalysis is eclectic in its origins, combining five streams of work. These are context analysis, the ethnography of communication and interactional sociolinguistics, Goffman's approach to interaction, conversation analysis, and continental discourse analysis. The first four approaches are more closely related historically to one another than the fifth is to any of the others. (For a more complete discussion of the intellectual antecedents of microethnography, see Erickson, 1992.)

The first approach was called *context analysis* by its originators. It was influenced strongly by Gregory Bateson and Margaret Mead and developed through interdisciplinary collaboration among anthropologists, linguists, and psychiatrists (see Kendon, 1990, for discussion). Context analysis took an ecological, or systems, approach to the study of interaction. This was a perspective akin to that of family systems theory in family therapy, and some of the psychiatrists associated with the context analysts helped to develop family therapy as a field of clinical practice. The emphasis in context analysis was on taking account of the organization of verbal and nonverbal behavior as it occurs simultaneously during interaction. Initially, the context analysts did slow-motion analysis of film, which enables very precise observation and coding. Videotape later replaced film because it was more economical, although some observational precision was sacrificed.

The second influence comes from the ethnography of communication and interactional sociolinguistics. This approach was developed by linguistic anthropologists (see Gumperz & Hymes, 1964, 1972; Hymes, 1974; Saville-Troike, this volume). Here the emphasis was on variation, within and across speech communities or networks, in culturally stylized ways of speaking – and not only on variation in language form (as in dialect studies) but on variation in language function (the purposes of speaking and the implicit meanings of stylistic choices of alternatives). Initially, participant observation was the main research method, with field-workers doing year-long community studies. Gumperz became interested in the moment-by-moment conduct of speech, and he began to use audio recordings centrally in his data collection and analysis (Blom & Gumperz, 1972; Gumperz, 1982; Schiffrin, this volume).

The third influence comes from the work of Goffman, who was a colleague of Hymes and Gumperz. Goffman viewed interaction in terms of strategy and ritual and emphasized the importance of situation – the encounter as an attentionally focused gathering in which some aspects of the presentation of self are salient and others are downplayed or concealed (see Goffman, 1959, 1961, 1981; the review essays in Drew & Wooton, 1988). In his work, Goffman combined participant observation with a review of still photographs and of descriptive accounts of interaction found in literature.

The fourth influence comes from conversation analysis in sociology. This developed within a movement in American sociology, called *ethnomethodology,* that criticized the theoretical assumptions of structural-functionalism – the reigning social theory of the time. Structural-functionalism emphasized, among other things, the stability of cultural patterns within human groups and across generations within those groups. In the study of interaction, this idea leads to an interest in the regularity of cultural patterning, in fairly formal and ritualized situations of communication. Conversation analysis, on the other hand, emphasized the emergent aspects of interaction over the institutionalized ones – the contribution of improvisatory activity of moment-by-moment sense making of participants in extremely informal situations of communication, for example, telephone calls and small talk at the dinner table (see Sacks, et al., 1974; Schenkein, 1978; West & Zimmerman, 1982). Much of the early work in conversation analysis was done by the preparation of detailed transcripts of speech from audiotapes. Currently, videotape is used, but with few exceptions (e.g., Goodwin, 1981), central research attention continues to focus on speech rather than on nonverbal behavior in interaction.

The fifth influence comes from continental discourse analysis, notably carried out by Habermas (1979) and Foucault (1979), among others. Using *discourse* to mean patterns of habitual practice in everyday life (not just *verbal discourse,* as the term is used by linguists), scholars in this stream of work emphasize the importance of power relations. They see the relations of power asymmetry in the wider society played out in microcosm at the level of face-to-face interaction. The research approach of continental discourse analysis is primarily conceptual and literary rather than empirical.

From these various sources come the emphases in ethnographic microanalysis on the nonverbal as well as the verbal aspects of interaction, on the importance of audience activity in relation to the activity of speakers, on the improvisational and situationally strategic aspects of interaction as well as its cultural and linguistic patterning, and on the importance of power and politics in immediate social encounters.

Although ethnographic microanalysis derives in part from two other approaches that are reviewed in this book, the ethnography of communication and interactional sociolinguistics, it differs from those approaches in a few important respects. Ethnographic microanalysis differs somewhat from the ethnography of communication in both research method and theory. The research method of the ethnography of communication is primarily firsthand participant observation. Ethnographic microanalysis uses both participant observation and the detailed analysis of audiovisual recordings of interaction. This enables not only a more precise look at behavioral details than direct observation does, it also forces the analyst to consider subtle variations in performance that often get overlooked in the participant observer's field notes and recollections. These variations are also emphasized in ethnographic microanalysis for theoretical reasons. Because of the influence of ethnomethodology and conversation analysis, ethnographic microanalysis is concerned to show that, in communication, people are not just following cultural rules for style but are actively constructing what they do. Those constructions differ in each concrete circumstance of their enactment. In microethnography, there is an emphasis on communication as practical activity – practice – that is not so centrally considered in the more general focus of the ethnography of communication. In ethnographic microanalysis, there is also more concern for the more mundane and less ritually stylized kinds of interaction than there is in the ethnography of communication, which tends to focus on the culturally stylized speech event rather than on the more casual speaking activities that are at the center of research attention for both ethnographic microanalysis and interactional sociolinguistics.

Interactional sociolinguistics shares with ethnographic microanalysis a constructivist perspective, a focus on very ordinary speech situations, and attention to fine behavioral detail. Both have been influenced strongly by ethnomethodology. However, in interactional sociolinguistics there is more emphasis on speech phenomena per se and less emphasis on nonverbal listening behavior and listener-speaker coordination than in ethnographic microanalysis. This is due in part to the research procedures – much interactional sociolinguistic work has been based on audio recording, whereas ethnographic microanalysis has used cinema film or video in an attempt to analyze nonverbal and verbal phenomena together (and in that respect it is also distinguished from the ethnography of communication, which has tended to focus on what speakers do rather than on what listeners and speakers do together). But these distinctions blur somewhat in the actual conduct of research – some ethnographic microanalysis has been quite speaker-focused, some interactional sociolinguistic work has considered speaker-listener coordination, and some ethnography of communication has considered audience reactions in relation to speech. The crucial issue is not what a stream of work is called but what the work does. Accordingly, let us turn to a more detailed look at the research of ethnographic microanalysis, with emphasis on topics that have special relevance for language teaching.

## Topics in ethnographic microanalysis

This section will consider the behavioral organization of verbal and nonverbal activity in interaction and the symbolic or political construction of the situation in which interaction occurs. Four issues or themes will be treated. Two aspects of the behavioral organization of interaction, listening activity in relation to speaking and the rhythmic organization of conversation in interaction, will be discussed. Then, two facets of the symbolism and politics of situational framing, the notion of situated social identity and the notion of participants' framing of cultural difference in communication style as a boundary or border within a situation of intercultural communication, will be discussed.

## *Listening in relation to speaking*

The holistic emphasis of context analysis in the study of film (and then videotape) led researchers to look analytically at verbal and nonverbal behavior together. This is a corrective to the "linguocentric" tendencies of talk-focused discourse analysis in sociolinguistics. That kind of analysis of speech makes it seem as if in ordinary conversation it is each individual's successive turn at speaking that drives the action in the scene. But that tells only part of the story. When we engage in conversation, we do not just utter little speeches one after another, as in a debate. Much more is going on interactionally in the situation, considered as a whole. A very important component in what is going on is listening, considered not just as passive reception of information but as communicative action that is itself informative to participants in the event.

When one views an audiovisual record of interaction carefully, especially in slow motion, one is impressed by the mutuality of participation by all the interactional partners. While a speaker speaks, those who are listening are not just doing nothing; they do not "switch off" when they are not speaking. Rather, listeners are very active in the scene – they may be gazing at the speaker or at some object in the scene to which the speaker is referring, they are usually posturally oriented to the speaker, they may be nodding or changing facial expression while listening. Listeners may be speaking while the primary speaker is talking – uttering brief "back channel" comments that show attention (e.g., in American English, "mhm" "yeah") or even speaking in full clauses that overlap the talk of the primary speaker.

There are significant cultural differences across different speech communities in the organization of speaker-audience relationships and other aspects of what can be called the *social participation structure* or *social participation framework of conversation*. In a study of first-grade native Hawaiian students in school classrooms, for example, Au and Mason (1983) showed that the cultural organization of turn taking in conversation influenced the students' understanding of what was being discussed. When students and the teacher discussed the students' silent reading, if the students were able to use a culturally familiar participation framework in which more than one speaker narrated, called *talk story* in the speech community, they made fewer errors and recalled more than if they discussed their silent reading in a strict one-speaker-at-a-time participation framework.

Shultz, Florio, and Erickson (1982) found that Italian-American students switched back and forth in discussion at home with their families and in whole-group lessons in the classroom between a one-speaker-at-a-time participation framework and a framework in which there were not only multiple simultaneous speakers but multiple audiences. In these conversations, there was more than one conversational "floor" at a time in which to take turns. Speaker-audience relations were not unitary but multiple. The cultural organization of participation frameworks in conversation, then, is an issue of pedagogical significance, since some classroom participation frameworks may be more or less familiar to students, depending upon the frameworks they are accustomed to in daily life outside school.

Regardless of participation framework, however, the listening activity of auditors is always available to the speaker of the moment as potential information; feedback about how what is being said is coming across to the listeners while the speaker's talk is being produced. Thus audience feedback and the production of coherent discourse by speakers are both "on-line" processes. They take place in real time, and they influence one another continually as speaking and listening are being produced jointly in conversation.

Listening activity by the audience is one of the main ways in which, to recall McDermott's phrase, people in interaction form environments for one another. This mutual influence is both simultaneous and successive. In the immediate moment of speaking, the speaker can see and hear what the auditors are doing – looking away, nodding, uttering a back-channel fragment. This kind of auditor influence is simultaneous with what the speaker is doing; it occurs during the present moment of the speaker's uttering. There is also a retrospective-prospective aspect to the mutual influence of speakers and auditors. The speaker, in making a substantive point, in uttering an informationally crucial word in a strip of speech, or in changing the emotional "key" (e.g., from irony to seriousness, from off the record to on the record) may be anticipating a signal of comprehension or recognition from the listener at a next moment in time. Then the next moment comes. As experienced, it is no longer a future moment but a present one. If the signal of auditor comprehension or recognition occurs in that moment, the speaker can prepare to utter a next word or clause. Then, in the next moment, the speaker produces the next utterance. At that point the auditor's signal of comprehension is no longer an occurrence in the present moment but in the immediately past one.

Thus the mutual influence of speaker and auditor in conversation is both simultaneous and sequential. What holds together the mutuality within which the speaker and listener are able to complete one another's actions rather than stumbling over one another is a shared framework of timing that the speaker and auditor together create and sustain in their verbal and nonverbal behavior.

## *Rhythm and cadence in interaction*

It has already been stated that ethnographic microanalysis points in an especially clear way to the on-line character of the conduct of speech and nonverbal behavior in interaction. Close analysis of an audiovisual record enables one to see what the listener is doing while the speaker is speaking. From infancy, before we learn to speak a language, through childhood and maturity and on through the entire life cycle, when we converse with others, we do so by interacting at similar rates of speed with our interlocutors. Not only has the phenomenon of shared timing been observed developmentally from birth onward, it has also been observed cross-culturally. Thus we can say that shared timing in the performance of interaction is as universal an organizing device in the conduct of speech as are a grammar and a sound system (see the discussion in Erickson & Schultz, 1982; Fiksdal, 1990).

There is a cadential aspect to the organization of timing in interaction. Across various languages it can be observed that volume and pitch emphasis marking certain syllables in the speech stream and points of kinesic (body motion) emphasis in the behavior stream of gesture, posture, and gaze often mark a cadence. In other words, there is a regular time interval between the occurrence of these verbally and kinesically emphasized points in such a way that an underlying "beat" can be detected in the behavior stream. Despite differences in syllable rhythm in various languages that differ in syntactic and phonological organization (e.g., English, French, Chinese, Navaho), an underlying cadence of stressed syllables and body motions can be identified that provides a rhythmic foundation for utterance at the level of the clause. This cadence also helps to mark discourse units, for example, the completion of a turn at speaking, the point at which crucial information is being introduced, the point of a change in "key."

Fluency in verbal performance, then, can be thought of as a matter of participating adequately with interlocutors in a shared framework of mutual interactional timing – literally "going with the flow" of interaction. One needs to know phonology, grammar, vocabulary, and discourse conventions in order not only to be able to produce an utterance in conversation but to do so in the right time. But individual linguistic and sociolinguistic competence is not enough. In order to perform fluently, a speaker must be in an ecology with auditors in which the auditors and speakers complete one another's activity adequately; that is, they must act in ways that meet one another's expectations for shared timing and for listening cues that can be "read" by the speaker. If the timing of listening and speaking activity is off, or if the speaker or listener does not know how to read the other's implicit signals in mutually congruent ways, the speaker cannot speak fluently and interaction will fall apart.

Individual knowledge of language, then, is not enough for a speaker to perform speech fluently. Nor is individual knowledge of sociolinguistic conventions concerning politeness or discourse coherence enough. The fluent speaker must also know how to read listeners successfully, during the on-line production of talk, and – equally important – the listeners must also know how to read the speaker. Without such mutual reading ability, neither speaker nor auditor can act in ways that form an articulated interactional environment for one another. (This last proposition holds unless special framing conditions apply, as will be seen later in this chapter). The individual speaker can be blamed for an apparent lack of *fluency,* considered as an individual trait or skill. But that is to overlook the insight of microethnography that fluency is in part an ecological phenomenon, interactionally produced.

How can we teach second language learners to be rhythmically fluent in conversation, and to be so when they are acting as listeners as well as when they are acting as speakers? From the point of view of microethnography, this is a crucial issue for second language instruction and for bilingual education.

## *Situated social identity*

Much work in sociolinguistics has sought to identify relationships between the social background of speakers and their speech style. Comparisons of speech style (dialect, register, politeness formulas, indirectness) are made in terms of ethnicity or race, social class, geographic region, gender, age, professional or workplace specialization, and the relative superordination and subordination of the speaker and the addressee. It has been assumed that distinct speech communities or networks run along the lines of social division and affiliation listed in the previous sentence. Considerable evidence from correlational sociolinguistics and from the ethnography of speaking supports this position. This evidence validates current approaches to teaching "practical speech," for example, business-negotiation English, ethnic differences in narrative conventions, gender differences in politeness expression. These kinds of social variation in language style are increasingly included in the simulated conversation dialogues found at the beginning of textbook language lessons.

Yet those dialogues still come across as stilted; even sometimes as stereotypical. What may be intended by curriculum developers as "high-fidelity" simulation is in fact a "low-fidelity" simulation. People do not really learn to converse by memorizing written dialogues and speaking them aloud in practice sessions, even if the dialogue text comes from a detailed transcription of naturally occurring speech. Part of what is missing in the prepared dialogue is the on-line mutual influence that we experience in naturally occurring conversation, the dynamic ebb and flow of listening and speaking relations that was discussed earlier. Another part of what is missing in the textbook dialogues is the fluidity of social identification that can occur as real people converse face to face. Who we display ourselves to be, as relevant to the conduct of the interaction at hand, can change from moment to moment in the interaction itself. We are not just typecast by a single category of social identity throughout an entire encounter. Our social identity of the moment is situated in the interaction at hand; we perform it as we go along and we do so conjointly with the other interactional partners.

One reason our situated, or performed, social identity is so labile, capable of shifting like a will-o'-the-wisp from moment to moment, is that our social identity in an encounter is always potentially multidimensional. This is another insight that derives from Goffman. He observed that we bring many potential identities to a given encounter. Which aspects of identity we reveal is optional and strategic, yet not necessarily the result of conscious deliberation.

Barth (1969) also observes that social identity is not a unitary phenomenon; there are badges or diacritical markings of identity that we can display which point to the relevance of certain attributes over others for the purposes of the encounter at hand. For example, in a first conference between a supervisor and a new employee, the person just hired may be Puerto Rican with African facial features and dark skin color, a woman, a speaker of working-class Puerto Rican Spanish as well as middle-class English, a college graduate with an M.B.A. in finance from the Wharton School, a mother of small children, active in a Protestant church, a former track star in high school and college, currently working out at a gym, an active member of the Republican party who does not believe in affirmative action programs, a lesbian, and one whose younger brother just died. Depending on the job and the company, the woman may or may not point to her ethnicity or knowledge of a certain kind of Spanish as salient. She might put more or less emphasis on the M.B.A. and the Wharton connection, depending upon the educational background of her supervisor. Through cues of dress and small talk, she might or not reveal her past and current status as an athlete and a church member. (She could reveal these attributes of identity, together with the M.B.A., as a way of showing that she is hardworking and committed to achievement.)

If the interviewer were a male and had a photograph of himself in his office as a college student jumping hurdles, the applicant might be more likely to reveal – through speech style as well as through anecdote – her shared affiliation with track and field athletics rather than her church or political party membership. Conceivably, although perhaps unlikely in a first encounter, if the supervisor were a woman who displayed implicit badges of identity as a lesbian, the new employee might allude to her own sexual orientation, if not reveal it outright. Any of these attributes of identity could be revealed directly or pointed to indirectly in various aspects of speech, as well as in dress, overall demeanor, and in the written self-presentation of a résumé. Different badges for attributes of identity could be made more salient at one moment in the encounter than at other moments. Thus, which attributes of identity would be emphasized as central to the conduct of interaction might vary for a given individual, not from one social situation to the next but within a given situation.

This kind of variation was shown in a seminal study by Blom & Gumperz (1972). They audiotaped conversations in a post office in a small Norwegian fishing village. During the conversations, the postmaster and the other villagers switched back and forth between the local dialect and a dialect that more closely resembled the national standard. It was not that the postmaster, representing the government, always spoke the national standard and the villagers spoke the local dialect. Both switched back and forth, depending upon the topic and upon the social identity they were projecting at that point in the conversation.

The lay public, and some sociolinguists and language educators, presume certain co-occurrence patterns with regard to social status and identity. This is not just blind prejudice; it is done on the basis of one's cultural knowledge of actuarial probabilities, which can be accurate up to a point. If someone is Puerto Rican, we may tend to assume that this person is a Roman Catholic who is also in favor of affirmative action. If someone is a mother, we may tend to assume that this person is not a lesbian or a serious athlete. But actual people may surprise us, and in actual situations of daily life, certain attributes of our overall identity may or may not be revealed, given the exigencies of the situation at hand. For example, if we work in a company where information about our family life and feelings is officially declared to be irrelevant, it may be quite appropriate or quite inappropriate to reveal to a supervisor that one's brother died recently. It is almost inconceivable that even the most highly conventionalized cultural patterns for speech style, such as the use of Japanese honorifics in politeness relations among employees in a Japanese business firm, are not variable in their use in actual situations.

There is a real danger in language education that, as we become more sophisticated about social and cultural variation in language use, we will take the cultural conventions too literally, not realizing that there is also considerable situational variation in actual use. The question is: How far as variationists are we willing to go in considering the kinds and conditions of variation that may obtain? The audiovisual records of naturally occurring interaction that are used in ethnographic microanalysis help make it clear how labile our social identity, as well as our speech style, is in the actual conduct of interaction.

Just because the microanalyst emphasizes how we conduct actual interaction improvisationally, "playing it by ear" as it were, this does not mean that we do not draw at all on broad cultural patterns as resources for the production of our performance, or that our performance is not constrained by the weight of social forces beyond the span of the immediate situation and beyond the ken of the social actors within it. What is meant is that microethnography tends to emphasize the lability of situated performance, just as the more usual kinds of sociolinguistics tend to emphasize the stability of relations between social status, conceived as a unitary phenomenon, and communicative style. Each approach emphasizes what the other might be said to underemphasize.

## *Culture difference as boundary or as border*

Barth (1969) pointed out that culture (or language) is not the ultimate defining characteristic of an ethnic group. Ethnicity, he argued, was an identification of a distinct political interest group based on descent. In interethnic relations, cultural or linguistic differences between members of differing ethnic groups can be treated as more or less problematic. When a cultural difference obtains between the two groups and it is treated as a boundary, the difference is recognized as an identifying marker but is not politicized; it has no relationship to differences in the distribution of power or advantage between the two groups. When a cultural difference obtains, and those who possess the culture trait are relegated to a position of disadvantage in power relative to those who do not possess the trait, then cultural difference is being politicized; it is being treated as a border, according to Barth's analysis. As an example, consider the relative social advantage or disadvantage of the ability to speak Spanish, English, and French on either side of the national borders between Mexico, the United States, and Canada. On the Mexican side of the U.S. border, no one is stopped and frisked for knowing Spanish. But on the U.S. side of the border, being a native speaker of Spanish or of English is politicized – much more so than is the knowledge of Spanish or English at the border between the United States and Canada. Knowledge of French, however, does not lead to particular social advantages or disadvantages on either side of the border between Mexico and the United States. In contrast, in Quebec Province, whether a native speaker of English also speaks French has become highly consequential. Yet when a native speaker of English crosses the border into Vermont, the political weighting of that person's knowledge of French changes drastically.

McDermott (in McDermott & Gospodinoff, 1981) extended Barth's boundary-border contrast in the political framing of cultural difference to a consideration of how cultural and linguistic difference is treated in school classrooms. He noted that differences in language and culture did not necessarily lead to misunderstanding and conflict in a classroom, nor did cultural and linguistic similarity necessarily lead to understanding and harmony. The issue was how the culture difference was framed in the micropolitics of classroom life – as a boundary matter or as a border matter.

McDermott and Gospodinoff reported a series of incidents of difficulty in a first-grade classroom between an Anglo teacher and a Puerto Rican boy. The difficulty, they claimed, had nothing to do with the language or ethnicity of the child. Rather it had to do with the way the child's language and culture were framed by the situation. They noted my own work (Erickson, 1975), among that of others. I had reported a study of interethnic relations in junior college academic advising sessions in which I found that sometimes cultural difference in communication style had been associated with misunderstanding and negative emotions in the interviews. That was what I had expected to see. Yet there was a more interesting and significant finding: in certain interviews the same kind of communication style difference that had led to misunderstanding and discomfort in other interviews did not seem to lead to trouble – even when the interviewer was the same in all cases. Culture and language style difference, in other words, sometimes made a big difference for the way the interaction happened, and sometimes it did not. What was varying was not the presence of the culture difference but its political framing as a border issue or as a boundary issue in the encounter.

This is very different from the usual assumption in applied sociolinguistics that the greater the linguistic and cultural difference there is between two interlocutors, the greater the misunderstanding and conflict that will result in their interaction. What McDermott, Shultz, and I found was that sometimes cultural difference and trouble co-occurred but sometimes not. In a book-length treatment of these issues (Erickson & Shultz, 1982), Shultz and I showed that what differed in the interviews we studied was the presence or absence of a relationship we called *situational comembership*. We defined *comembership* as the sharing of attitudes of social identity that were distinctive as commonalities relevant in the situation at hand. Examples of situational comembership are both parties having been athletes, or churchgoers, or alumni of the same school or having had a close relative die recently. Unlike ethnicity, race, gender, or class, which tend to be relevant identities in many situations, comembership is a commonality that is fortuitously (and sometimes strategically) made relevant in a given encounter. Ethnicity or class or gender sharing may increase the likelihood of possessing similar attributes that can be invoked as comembership (e.g., church affiliation or motherhood) but comembership is not the same as the more generally relevant aspects of social position and identification.

The crucial point here is that the presence of comembership in the academic advising interviews I studied seemed to change the framing of culture difference from that of a border issue to that of a boundary issue. When comembership was present, the interviewer and interviewee seemed willing to overlook the momentary difficulties in understanding and negative impression that may have been due to cultural differences in communication style. In the absence of comembership, communication style difference often became more and more troublesome as the interview progressed.

This suggests that in classrooms the crucial issue is not the presence or absence of diversity in language and culture between and among the teacher and students. Rather, the issue is how culture difference will be framed, as boundary or as border. McDermott and Gospodinoff (1981) cited a classroom study that is very pertinent here. Piestrup (1973) found that in racially integrated first-grade classrooms in Berkeley, California, the speech style of African-American children was treated differently by teachers. In those classrooms in which African-American vernacular English was treated as a border issue, with the teacher correcting the syntax and phonology of the speech of the African-American students, by the end of the school year the students tended to speak a broader form of the dialect than they had done at the beginning of the year. This was the case whether the teacher was African-American or white. Conversely, in those classrooms in which the teachers did not constantly correct the African-American Vernacular English of the African-American students, by the end of the school year the speech style of those students was shifting in the direction of standard English. This recalls the findings of Labov, that the dialect of Martha's Vineyard islanders diverged from the mainland American English of summer tourists across a generation. As contact with mainlanders increased in the somewhat stressful situation of tourism, so did the divergence of the Martha's Vineyard dialect from the mainlanders' ways of speaking. It was not the dialect that caused the trouble but the ambivalence of relations with tourists that led the islanders to diverge stylistically as a political symbol of their own identity (Labov, 1963).

Piestrup's findings also recall those of Giles and Powesland (1975). They showed that in half-hour conversations between speakers of differing regional dialects in England, if conflict was experimentally introduced into the conversation, by the end of the half-hour the two speakers had diverged in speech style, speaking ever more broad versions of their regional dialects phonologically. The opposite was true in conversations in which conflict was not experimentally introduced. In those conversations, by the end of the half-hour the speech style of the culturally differing partners was converging phonologically. Again, the fundamental issue does not seem to have been the language style difference itself but the politics of relations between those whose styles differed.

Bateson describes this process of progressive divergence of related systems across time as *complementary schismogenesis* (Bateson, et al., 1956). Stylistic divergence in speech style can thus be seen as a manifestation of social conflict between competing groups rather than as a cause of the conflict. If relations of conflict in the larger society make it in the interest of those who are "different" on some dimension to fight and resist one another – ethnicity, class, gender – the cultural or linguistic difference becomes an excellent reason for starting a fight. The implication for language instruction is that, when a student's native language or dialect is one that is stigmatized in the society at large (indicating that the language difference runs along a fault line of power asymmetry and conflict in that society), classroom teachers must take care to frame the student's cultural ways of speaking as a boundary rather than as a border in the classroom. The examples from Piestrup, from Erickson and Shultz, and from Giles and Powesland provide evidence that teachers can frame cultural difference positively so as to minimize the border conflicts that otherwise might be rife in a classroom. In that sense, to return to the initial point from Goffman on the partial boundedness of immediate social situations, the classroom can be a partially bounded setting in which what teachers do can influence the language learning environment to depoliticize differences in cultural ways of speaking. This is an optimistic note on which to end this discussion – conflict over language difference may not totally be eliminated in a classroom when it is a major resource for intergroup conflict in the wider society in which the school is located; but teachers can have considerable influence over the ways in which language and cultural difference is politically framed in the daily conduct of classroom life.

## Issues for pedagogy and curriculum

As with all social research, the connections between microethnographic research findings and educational practice are indirect. There is no straight line between the study of what is and prescription for what ought to be. Yet there are some implications for language teaching practice that can be drawn from the work described here. These implications will be reviewed, and suggestions offered, in the discussion that follows.

Ethnographic microanalysis of interaction reveals that language practices are more fluid than the more usual kinds of sociolinguistics might suggest. This does not mean that nothing can be learned from general reports about culturally customary speech style and the typical participation structures or frameworks that obtain in certain kinds of social situations. Microethnographic research suggests, however, that what actual speakers do is much more subtle than can be represented in general accounts of their practice. Consequently, the language learner and teacher should treat the general accounts gingerly and seek firsthand participatory experience where possible.

Thus a major implication of the microethnographic study of language in interaction underscores a point that is increasingly well understood in language education – students' firsthand participation in conversation in the second language has fundamental importance in language instruction. What ethnographic microanalysis suggests is that, not only does such participation provide practice for students in uttering the second language, it also provides experience with the ecology of listening in relation to speaking. No textbook study or simulation can fully replicate that interactional ecology. Curriculum in language instruction needs to take account of this. Moreover, if native speakers are invited to language classrooms as an instructional resource, the teacher might do well to invite two or three speakers at a time, so that they can demonstrate listening activity as well as speaking. Ethnographic microanalysis, in sum, is not only a means to show us that "speaking a language" is more than just solo uttering, it is a research approach that helps us understand how speaking and listening are socially organized as a collective activity.

Although reflection within firsthand experience may be the most preferable way to learn about listening-speaking ecology and to develop performance skill in participation in conversation, it can be logistically difficult in language instruction. If that is the case, then audiovisual records of naturally occurring conversation that show listeners together with speakers can be a valuable instructional resource. Indeed, one can argue that some vicarious experience is generally beneficial in education, and so video material can play a significant role in instruction even when students have ready access to conversational experience in a second language.

Students in language classrooms can be taught to pay close attention to instructional videotapes of naturally occurring speech situations that show the listener's nonverbal and verbal reactions at the same time as the speaker's activity is shown. Short segments of tape can be viewed by students and replayed repeatedly, so that the students can pay attention to what the listener does as well as to what the speaker is doing. This requires acquiring new cultural "eyes" as a viewer as well as gaining the ability to interact with the audiovisual media display, either through the students' controlling a video cassette playback deck directly or by playing QuickTime(TM) video segments on a personal computer using a hypermedia software package. Conventional camera work, in cinema and on television talk shows, documents speech by cutting back and forth between close-ups of talking heads, without the listener being shown in the same visual frame as the speaker. Instructional video and film can be shot differently, however, and this permits students to learn to watch the audiovisual image analytically, interact with the display medium, and reflect on how the listener listens while the speaker is speaking. In the absence of prepared video materials, a teacher can use a camcorder to make homemade videos of actual people in actual conversations, keeping all (or most) of the participants in the visual frame.

Videos of naturally occurring speech can also be used to study the rhythmic organization of speech and nonverbal behavior in interaction. Through repeated viewing of tape segments, students can become more aware of cadential stress patterns. This can also become an experiential exercise if the students were to speak aloud the "lines" of one of the main participants in the video as a way of experiencing the flow of naturally occurring interaction rhythm. A slightly more artificial simulation is for a student to read aloud oral passages in unison with the teacher or a native speaker of the language being learned. Material from public speeches can be used, as well as more informal oral material. The teacher reads a passage aloud as a model. Then the student, singly or in choral fashion as a member of a group, reads the same passage aloud in unison with the teacher. This demonstrates the customary prosody and cadence patterns in speaking in that language. Consider even so simple an example as Churchill's line in the speech requesting lend-lease aid from the United States:

| *Stressed* | *Unstressed* |
|---|---|
| Give | us the |
| tools | and |
| we | will |
| do | the |
| job. | |

(repeat in unison three times, swinging hands to keep the beat)

Longer passages give a student an even more vivid sense of what it feels like to stay with the flow of cadence in speech performance in a second language.

Video can give students a sense of how multiply floored conversations are organized, and how to participate in them. By watching videotapes of naturally occurring conversation at the dinner table or of conversation that occurs in other routine scenes of small group conversation in which speakers participate in more than one conversation at a time, students can gain an insight about how speaking and listening are done in such participation frameworks. It may be that the best practice in this, however, involves firsthand participation.

Awareness of the importance of situations and of situational style switching can be fostered by having students research their own experience in the use of their mother tongue. Students can be given a pack of 3 × 5 inch cards and be told to carry the cards for a day or half-day, jotting down the place and time and the activity that occurs as they get an intuitive sense that they are in a new social situation. (Usually about fifty cards will be used in this way for a half-day.) The cards can be prenumbered in sequence. After a set of cards is prepared, the student studies their sequence, looking for contrasts in degree of formality, closeness of acquaintance, and cultural and linguistic familiarity in the various situations on the cards. The student can recall topics, speech style, and speech intentions as they vary across the cards. If the student were to carry a small tape recorder and record his or her own speech while writing the cards (or write the cards later, while listening to the tape recording), then the student can study in considerable detail his within and between situation switching in speech style. The tapes and cards can stimulate powerful reflection on the student's own language practices. If the classroom includes students of differing native languages who are studying one another's languages, these tapes, and the transcripts from them, can become curriculum materials for second language learning.

The situational frame cards can be used as well to reflect on the multiplicity of dimensions of social identity that become relevant in social situations. Videos of individuals moving through a series of naturally occurring social situations in their daily round can also give students insight into how the social identity of participants can shift slightly from moment to moment in interaction, and how multiple dimensions of identity can become salient. If the subject of the film is moving back and forth between more and less culturally familiar scenes (with language switching between and within scenes), this kind of footage can also provide insight into code switching and shifts in language function as well as language form.

Again using situational frames cards and audiotape and videotape, students can consider the political framing of culture and language difference within and across differing social situations. Students can learn to seek and reveal comembership with "ethnic others" in daily conversation and to see whether changes in emotional tone and in the severity and frequency of misunderstanding result from the revelation of comembership.

In general, the work of ethnographic microanalysis suggests that, because communication style and social identity are so locally situated and fluid, it is good advice for students to study their own communicative experience reflectively rather than to learn generalizations about the cultural speaking style of ethnic others (see the discussion in Erickson & Shultz, 1982, pp. 198–209). The former produces an insight into the development of one's own second language and second culture capacities. The latter can lead to "neostereotyping" of ethnic others and to clumsy attempts at the use of generic patterns that could be taken by ethnic others as silly, or even as mockery. Imitation may be the sincerest form of flattery, but when done crudely, it can be taken as disrespect. If students participate in naturally occurring second language experiences, and learn to monitor their own experience, that can develop a more true-to-the-self fluency. When something feels a bit uncomfortable in interaction, students can learn to recall the immediately prior moment. They can ask the following questions for reflection: "What was going on in my (the other's) speaking? What was going on in the other's (my) listening? Does the difficulty seem to be more that of listening activity or of speaking activity?"

Finally, teachers can learn not to treat cultural and linguistic difference in the classroom as a border issue but as a boundary one. Diversity in a language classroom can be a tremendous resource for learning. (The kinds of self-study of diversity in dialect and in ways of speaking that Heath [1983] describes in the appendix to *Ways with Words* can be seen as depoliticizing cultural difference, turning what might potentially be treated invidiously as a border issue into a boundary issue.) Attention to diversity – native language and local speech community – when done respectfully is anything but invidious. Reflective awareness by individuals and within and across groups whose speech styles differ need not be disrespectful of difference. Legitimating awareness of and talk about language variation in the language classroom makes "difference" something other than a dirty family secret that cannot be named. There is no direct evidence for this supposition, but it might be assumed that the difficulty native speakers of a stigmatized dialect have had with instruction in a standard version of a language (e.g., Chicanos in high school Spanish classes) is due in part to resistance that is sparked by the teacher's not treating the students' native language with the interest that dignifies and respects. Correcting one's native language seems to be a sure way to alienate the speaker of a stigmatized version of the language that is being taught. Making the differences between the standard and the nonstandard version of the language an object of study can both clarify the differences in language form and function between the two ways of speaking and can show respect for the nonstandard ways of the students and their parents.

As a further way of depoliticizing culture difference in language instruction, the teacher can share his or her second language learning experience with the students. This can be a means for students and the teacher to identify comemberships that change the frame of the classroom situation.

## Summary

From interaction rhythm to comembership, this discussion has ranged over considerable breadth; depth is inevitably sacrificed in such a review. The reader is encouraged to pursue issues further through reading works cited in reference lists in this chapter.

I have said that ethnographic microanalysis helps us see and understand social interaction as an ecosystem. It follows for language instruction that listening needs to be treated as a communicative activity in its own right, and that listener influence over speakers' performance needs to be considered together with more conventional conceptions of sociolinguistic competence in the educator's notion of fluency. Another major point is the importance of timing and interactional rhythm in the conjoint articulation of speaking and listening in interaction. This too has educational implications. Yet another emphasis in microethnography is the notion of situation and its framing: the relation between speech style, audience relationships, and participation structure within the situation, and the political framing of culture difference within the situation. Students in language education can profit from learning more about the nature and characteristics of social situations as the local sites within which speaking is done.

A final educational implication of microethnographic work is that societal influences on the micropolitics of language and culture in situations of interaction need to be taken seriously in language instruction. In this essay I have not elaborated on that point because of limitations of space, but I want to treat it briefly in closing.

Ethnographic microanalysis of interaction, with its awareness of the situatedness and partial flexibility of social identity (especially with regard to the phenomenon of situational comembership), can help in understanding how the usual border conditions for culture difference can be locally reframed to some extent as boundary conditions within an immediate situation. But the need for such local reframing comes from the inequities in power relationship that are prestructured into situations of immediate interaction by the workings of the larger society within which such encounters take place. Counterhegemonic local practice would not be necessary as resistance if hegemony were not the general circumstance within which human communication takes place (see also Chick, this volume).

This is to say that participants in face-to-face interaction conduct their communicative practice within a universe that includes social gravity – their actions are borne upon by the weight of history. What the formal study of history, economics, political science, social theory, and general cultural studies (including ethnography and literary studies) can tell us about the power relations within which scenes of immediate interaction take place is also relevant and legitimate curricular content in language study, in concert with insights from sociolinguistics and ethnographic microanalysis, interactional sociolinguistics, and speech act theory. Knowledge of general social and cultural processes should also inform curriculum and pedagogy in language education, for whenever one touches human language, one confronts issues of power in relation to knowledge and to knowers.

The interests of microethnography, in sum, are not micro at all but are macro in their scope. Close study of what people actually do in the real-time conduct of interaction can help us understand how such interaction is organized in subtle ways and can also lead us to consider how local occasions of interaction both influence and are influenced by the wider society in which they occur. I believe that both of these kinds of insights – into the workings of interaction face to face and into the workings of society in relation to local situations of interaction – can inform fresh approaches in language education.

## Suggestions for further reading

Erickson, F., & Shultz, J. (1982). *The counselor as gatekeeper: Social interaction in interviews*. New York: Academic Press.

A study of interracial and interethnic relations in academic advising sessions in junior colleges, this is perhaps the most complete examination of participation structure, listener-speaker relationships, and interactional rhythm in the literature. In addition, the study shows how social mobility decisions and advice by counselors are deeply influenced by the cultural and social organization of the ways in which conversation takes place.

Erickson, F. (1992). Ethnographic microanalysis of interaction. In M. D. LeCompte, Wendy Millroy, & Judith Preissle (Eds.), *The handbook of qualitative research in education* (pp. 201–225). New York: Academic Press.

This essay on the method and theory of ethnographic microanalysis reviews examples of the use of this approach in educational research. It also provides a comprehensive discussion of how to make and analyze videotapes of interaction, in classrooms and other settings.

McDermott, R. P. (1977). School relations as contexts for learning in school. *Harvard Educational Review*, 47, 298–313.

A classroom study of interaction in reading groups that shows how listening postures and turn taking influence students' reading aloud and teachers' impressions of students' academic ability and motivation.

McDermott, R. P. et al. (1978). Criteria for an ethnographically adequate description of concerted activities and their contexts. *Semiotica*, 24(3/4), 245–275.

This is a discussion of the research methods used in ethnographic microanalysis and the theory on which those methods are based. The discussion emphasizes close behavioral analysis, with special concern for how postural positions organize the conduct of conversation.

Shultz, J., & Florio, S. (1979). Stop and freeze: The negotiation of social and physical space in a kindergarten/first grade classroom. *Anthropology and Education Quarterly*, 10(3), 166–181.

A study of the ways in which social territories of the teacher and of students were marked out by routine nonverbal and verbal behavior, without the conscious awareness of either the teacher or the students. The study shows how much of classroom life is organized in patterns that are beyond the awareness of participants.

Shultz, J., Florio, S., & Erickson, F. (1982). Where's the floor?: Aspects of the cultural organization of social relationships in communication at home and at school. In P. Gilmore and A. Glatthorn (Eds.), *Ethnography and education: Children in and out of school* (pp. 88–123). Washington, DC: Center for Applied Linguistics.

This study investigated the organization of conversation at home and at school, emphasizing speaker-audience relationships in which more than one conversation, or set of audiences, is going on at the same time. The analysis shows that different social participation structures for conversation were used at different times in the classroom, some resembling the children's customary interaction at home and some differing from the way children conversed at home.

## References

Au, K. H., & Mason, J. M. (1983). Cultural congruence in classroom participation structures: Achieving a balance of rights. *Discourse Processes*, 6(2), 145–167.

Barth, F. (1969). *Ethnic groups and boundaries: The social organization of culture difference*. Boston, MA: Little, Brown.

Bateson, G. et al. (1956). Toward a theory of schizophrenia. *Behavioral Science*, 1(4). Also in G. Bateson (1972). *Steps to an ecology of mind* (pp. 201–227). New York: Ballantine.

Blom, J., & Gumperz, J. J. (1972). Social meaning in linguistic structure: Code switching in Norway. In J. J. Gumperz & D. H. Hymes (Eds.), *Directions in sociolinguistics.* (pp. 407–434). New York: Holt, Rinehart and Winston.

Drew, P., & Wooton, A. (Eds.). (1988). *Erving Goffman: Exploring the interactional order.* Cambridge and Oxford: Polity Press.

Erickson, F. (1975). Gatekeeping and the melting pot: Interaction in counseling encounters. *Harvard Educational Review,* 45(1), 44–70.

Erickson, F. (1992). Ethnographic microanalysis of interaction. In M. D. LeCompte, Wendy Millroy, & Judith Preissle (Eds.), *The handbook of qualitative research in education* (pp. 201–225). New York: Academic Press.

Erickson, F., & Shultz, J. (1982). *The counselor as gatekeeper: Social interaction in interviews.* New York: Academic Press.

Fiksdal, S. (1990). *The right time and pace: A microanalysis of cross-cultural gatekeeping interviews.* Norwood, NJ: Ablex.

Foucault, M. (1979). *Discipline and punish: The birth of the prison.* New York: Random House/Vintage Books.

Giles, H., & Powesland, P. F. (1975). *Speech style and social evaluation.* London: Academic Press.

Goffman, E. (1959). *The presentation of self in everyday life.* Garden City, NY: Doubleday.

Goffman, E. (1961). *Encounters: Two studies in the sociology of interaction.* Indianapolis, IN: Bobbs-Merrill.

Goffman, E. (1964). The neglected situation. In J. Gumperz & D. Hymes (Eds.), The ethnography of communication. *American Anthropologist,* 66(2), 133–136.

Goffman, E. (1981). *Forms of talk.* Philadelphia: University of Pennsylvania Press.

Goodwin, C. (1981). *Conversational organization: Interaction between speakers and hearers.* New York: Academic Press.

Gumperz, J. J. (1982). *Discourse processes.* New York: Cambridge University Press.

Gumperz, J., & Hymes, D. (1964). The ethnography of communication. *American Anthropologist,* 66(6), pt. 2.

Gumperz, J., & Hymes, D. (1972). *Directions in sociolinguistics: The ethnography of speaking.* New York: Holt, Rinehart and Winston.

Habermas, J. (1979). *Communication and the evolution of society.* Boston: Beacon Press.

Heath, S. B. (1983). *Ways with words: Language, life and work in communities and classrooms.* Cambridge: Cambridge University Press.

Hymes, D. (1974). *Foundations in sociolinguistics: An ethnographic approach.* Philadelphia: University of Pennsylvania Press.

Kendon, A. (1990). *Conducting interaction: Patterns of behavior in focused encounters.* Cambridge and New York: Cambridge University Press.

Labov, W. (1963). The social motivation of a sound change. *Word,* 19, 273–309.

McDermott, R. P. (1976). Kids make sense: An ethnographic account of the interactional management of success and failure in one first grade classroom. Unpublished doctoral dissertation, Stanford University.

McDermott, R. P., & Gospodinoff, K. (1981). Social contexts for ethnic borders and school failure. In H. T. Trueba, G. P. Guthrie, & K. H. Au (Eds.), *Culture and the bilingual classroom.* Rowley, MA: Newbury House.

Piestrup, A. (1973). *Black dialect interference and accommodation of reading instruction in first grade.* Berkeley, CA: Language-Behavior Research Laboratory.

Sacks, H., et al. (1974). A simplest systematics for the organization of turn-taking in conversation. *Language,* 50, 696–735.

Schenkein, J. (1978). *Studies in the organization of conversational interaction.* New York: Academic Press.

Shultz, J., Florio, S., & Erickson, F. (1982). Where's the floor?: Aspects of the cultural organization of social relationships in communication at home and at school. In P. Gilmore & A. Glatthorn (Eds.), *Ethnography and education: Children in and out of school* (pp. 88–123). Washington, DC: Center for Applied Linguistics.

West, C., & Zimmerman, D. (1982). Conversation analysis. In K. Scherer & P. Ekman (Eds.). *Handbook of methods in nonverbal behavior research.* New York: Cambridge University Press.

# 9 *Interactional sociolinguistics*

Deborah Schiffrin

## Introduction

Interactional sociolinguistics is a theoretical and methodological perspective on language use that is based in linguistics, sociology, and anthropology. Because of these disciplinary roots, it shares the concerns of all three fields with language, society, and culture. Although speech act theory (Cohen, this volume), the ethnography of communication (Saville-Troike, this volume) and microethnography (Erickson, this volume) are also concerned with language, society, and culture, the approach discussed in this chapter is somewhat different in theory, method, origin, and focus (see Schiffrin, 1992, 1994, Chaps. 3 to 5).[1]

The discussion in this chapter begins with the contributions of the sociologist Erving Goffman (see Erickson, this volume). Goffman's analysis of face-to-face interaction provide an understanding of how language is situated in particular circumstances of social life and how it both reflects and adds meaning and structure to those circumstances. Next, the contributions of the linguistic anthropologist John Gumperz are discussed (see Chick, this volume). Gumperz's analyses of verbal communication help us understand how people may share grammatical knowledge of a language but differently contextualize what is said, in such a way that very different messages are produced and understood. The ideas of these two scholars are highlighted because so many contemporary analyses of the language of social interaction are guided by the underlying assumptions, theories, and methods provided by their work.[2] After several basic beliefs about language, context, and social interaction that provide unity to interactional sociolinguistics are reviewed, the discussion turns to the methods used to study the language

1 Although interactional sociolinguists sometimes rely upon the construct of the speech act (as do speech act theorists), analyze nonverbal as well as verbal behavior (as do microethnographers), and consider language as cultural behavior (as do ethnographers of communication), they add to these interests a concern with language structure and function, as well as with the consequences of the methods and findings of interactional studies for linguistic theory.

2 The discussion of Goffman and Gumperz is adapted from Chapter 4 of Schiffrin (1994).

of social interaction. Finally, although earlier sections include examples highlighting the relevance of interactional sociolinguistics to language in the classroom, the final section more explicitly suggests some pedagogical applications of this approach.

## The study of face-to-face interaction

The sociological framework associated with Erving Goffman develops the ideas of several classic sociological theorists and applies them to a domain of social life – face-to-face interaction – whose organization had gone largely unnoticed prior to Goffman's work. Goffman's theoretical perspective builds upon the ideas of two classic sociological theorists. Emile Durkheim (the "father" of modern sociology) was among the first scholars to argue that society could be analyzed not just as the sum of its individual parts (i.e., individual people) but as an entity *sui generis*. Society influences peoples' behavior because they internalize "social facts" (Durkheim, 1895), that is, the values, beliefs, and norms underlying its organization. Durkheim's specific analyses focused on different types of social organization and solidarity, as well as on the meanings of primitive religions. The other major influence on Goffman was Georg Simmel (1950), in particular, his analyses of form and meaning in small social groups, for example, the different social relationships possible in two- versus three-person groups, the social value of telling secrets, the form and meaning of sociability. Goffman combined theories about the material and symbolic organization of society and social life with a sociopsychological interest in the social processes involved in the development of the self (e.g., Mead, 1935) and an ethnographic methodology developed by sociologists interested in everyday social life and culture in urban neighborhoods and establishments.

The unique focus of Goffman's scholarship was to locate the relationship between *self* (our sense of who we are, both personally and socially) and society at a microlevel of analysis, that is, within the everyday encounters, interactions, and activities in which we routinely engage. To oversimplify a bit, what we are (or believe ourselves to be) is a product not only of social processes that operate at the level of social institutions (e.g., family, school, work) but of social processes that are embedded in the situations, occasions, encounters, and rituals of everyday life. These microlevel processes help organize and give meaning to our everyday behaviors and help provide us with a sense of self. Our use of certain mannerisms, styles, and behaviors (both verbal and nonverbal) are not only ways by which we construct and maintain social interactions but also ways of expressing our sense of who we are and who our interactants are. Our everyday behaviors and interactions with each other thus play a crucial role in creating and maintaining the roles we fill, the statuses we occupy (our social identities), and the personalities we feel ourselves and others to have (our personal identities). The identities that we adopt also help produce social order and stability and, hence, actually help to give social institutions their meanings and foundational structures. To take a simple example, when teachers and students learn the expectations and obligations of classroom interactions, they are acquiring social identities; their attachments to these identities, and the behaviors through which those identities are displayed, also reinforce the social structure of classrooms and schools.

Goffman (1967a, p. 5) suggests that one way of viewing the self as a social construction is through the notion of *face,* "the positive social value a person effectively claims for himself by the line others assume he has taken during a particular contact." Rather than locating face in the human psyche, Goffman (1967a, p. 7) states that face is "diffusely located in the flow of events in the encounter and becomes manifest only when these events are read and interpreted for the appraisals expressed in them." The maintenance of both self and face is thus built into the fabric of social interaction (Goffman, 1967a, pp. 11–12, 39–40) and the complementary needs of self and other (Goffman, 1963, p. 16, 1967b, p. 85).

One contribution to the maintenance of face is interpersonal ritual. Goffman identifies two types. *Presentational rituals* are those "acts through which the individual makes specific attestations to recipients concerning how he regards them" (Goffman, 1967b, p. 71). *Avoidance rituals* are "those forms of deference which lead the actor to keep at a distance from the recipient" (Goffman, 1967b, p. 62). Goffman's ideas about presentational and avoidance rituals are revised and expanded in Brown and Levinson's work (1987) on politeness and how different face wants or desires are reflected and negotiated in linguistic form and communicative strategy. Brown and Levinson propose two universal wants: the desire that others want the same thing that self wants (positive face) and the desire that one's own wants and needs be unimpeded and unintruded upon (negative face).

The way we use language is adapted to balancing either one or both of these two different aspects of face. Asking a person to do something, for example, may threaten the asker's negative face because it may require that the person asked alter his or her plans or go out of his or her way. It is because of this threat that such requests are often issued through what speech act theorists (e.g., Searle, 1969, 1975; see also Cohen, this volume) call *indirect speech acts*. The prevalence of indirect speech acts in the classroom suggests the importance of maintaining face in educational settings. For example, rather than say "Give out these papers for me," a teacher might say "Let's give out these papers" (a positive-face strategy because of its appeal to common wants), or "If it's not too much trouble, I was wondering if you might give out these papers," (a negative-face strategy because it avoids imposing upon the addressee). Student strategies for avoiding wrong answers or reprimands (e.g., through silence, Gilmore, 1985) also point out the prevalence of face-saving strategies in the classroom. The organization of some classroom encounters into servicelike encounters (business transactions in which a customer requests a good or service from a server; Merritt, 1984, 1982) suggests that ritualized interchanges and formulaic moves can provide a framework for the preservation of face.

Another contribution not just to the maintenance of face but to the presentation of self more generally is the material and symbolic resources made available through the social establishments and institutions in which people interact. Such resources are useful in several ways: They can display certain favored aspects of self (Goffman, 1959), physically facilitate the division of self into a public character and private performer (Goffman, 1959; Chap. 3), or show performers either embracing or distancing themselves from institutionally allocated characters (Goffman, 1963). Like all institutions and establishments, schools and classrooms contain a wide array of resources that allow people to occupy the different social roles associated with education (e.g., teacher, student, administrator) and to engage in, and coordinate, the activities that sustain those roles. Such resources are both material (e.g., the physical design of classrooms, the arrangement of seats and desks, educational materials and supplies) and symbolic (e.g., explicit codes of dress, implicit codes of verbal behavior, procedures for evaluation, discipline).

Seating arrangements provide a simple example of the relationship of identity to material and symbolic resources in the classroom. Teachers from grade school to graduate school often arrange the seats and desks of their classrooms so that students are facing one another as well as (or instead of) the teacher at the front of the room. Such physical realignments alter the participation framework (Goffman, 1981; Philips, 1983) of the classroom, so that students can talk to one another as well as to the teacher (an adjustment of speaking rights that is believed to allow cooperative learning). Such realignments also alter the division of educational labor in the classroom, blurring the boundaries between more traditional views of the roles of teachers and students. Thus, they are both a material and a symbolic resource for the creation of social identities. (See Eckert, 1989, on the resources used by students to display different social identities in high school.)

It was noted earlier that everyday social interaction plays a crucial role in maintaining our sense of social order and stability. Social interaction – and the maintenance of face – also facilitates linguistic meaning. As Goffman (1967b, p. 85) points out, we share responsibility for the maintenance of one another's face: "[I]ndividuals must hold hands in a chain of ceremony, each giving deferentially with proper demeanor to the one on the right what will be received deferentially from the one on the left." This interpersonal dependency can also be applied to the construction of meaning during verbal interaction: Each utterance receives part of its meaning from another's prior utterance and gives part of its meaning back to the other to use in a next utterance. Such meanings can often be segmented and labeled as particular interactive moves that both respond to and elicit other moves. This dependency helps to create patterned sequences that are more or less appropriate to different social circumstances or occasions.[3] Thus, it is not just the self and the meaning of utterances that owe much to the process of social interaction; our knowledge of what to do with language, and how and when to do it, is also based on the give and take of everyday social interaction.

Although Goffman does not provide detailed analyses of the role of language in social interaction, his focus on interaction provides an important complement to John Gumperz's theory of verbal communication and his study of how situated inferences arise from (and guide) language use. After Gumperz's ideas are reviewed in the next section, several basic beliefs about language, context, and social interaction that provide unity to interactional sociolinguistics are proposed.

## The study of verbal communication

In the introduction to a collection of his essays, Gumperz (1982a, p. vii) states that he "seeks to develop interpretive sociolinguistic approaches to the analysis of real time processes in face to face encounters." After some of Gumperz's work prior to the 1982a collection is described, the concepts and methods that Gumperz has developed for the achievement of his goal are discussed.

Gumperz (1971, edited by Dil) is a collection of Gumperz's essays through 1971. The dual focus of this volume, dialect diversity and language and social interaction, reflects the themes that continue (and become even more unified) in the later collection (1982a). The research reported in the 1971 work is grounded in an assumption that is basic

3 The analysis of such sequences often depends upon ethnographic observations and insights (Saville-Troike, this volume). Compare analyses by the Birmingham group on exchange structure (Sinclair & Coulthard, 1975) and ethnomethodologists on classroom interactions (e.g., Mehan, 1979.)

to social and cultural anthropology: The meaning, structure, and use of language are socially and culturally relative. The importance of this assumption is illustrated through studies focusing on a variety of different issues. For example, Gumperz's work in India – on regional and social language difference, on Hindi-Punjabi code switching, and on linguistic convergence – all focus not just on linguistic structure but on how those structures become part of the verbal repertoires of interacting social groups.

Despite the social and cultural emphasis of Gumperz's early work, individual expression also finds a place in this research. In his studies of code switching, for example, Gumperz defines two types of switching from one language variety to another. First is *situational code switching:* People may switch in accord with "clear changes in . . . participants' definition of each others' rights and obligation" (1971, p. 294). Second is *metaphorical code switching:* People may switch varieties within a single situation just to convey a different view of that situation and their relationship. In such cases, the language switch "relates to particular kinds of topics or subject matters" and is used "in the enactment of two or more different relationships among the same set of individuals" (1971, p. 295; see also Sridhar, this volume).

Connections between culture, society, individual, and code are developed in Gumperz (1982a), essays which seek to develop interpretive sociolinguistic approaches to the analysis of ongoing processes in face-to-face interactions. In the first article of this collection, Gumperz (p. 12) points out that the anthropological and linguistic study of speakers of other languages has had a tremendous impact on our understanding of culture and cognition, by providing "empirical evidence for the contention that human cognition is significantly affected by historical forces." The discovery of different grammatical systems, including different phonemic (sound) and semantic (meaning) systems, showed that "what we perceive and retain in our mind is a function of our *culturally* determined predisposition to perceive and assimilate" (Gumperz, 1982a, p. 12, emphasis added). Put another way, our verbal behavior, as well as the structure of the linguistic code underlying that behavior, is open to external (social, cultural) influences. Gumperz suggests that, in order to understand these influences, we need to integrate what we know about grammar, culture, and interactive conventions into a general theory of verbal communication. Such a theory would be built upon a single overall framework of concepts and analytical procedures.

The framework developed by Gumperz builds upon his earlier ideas about culture, society, language, and the self. The three central concepts discussed here – contextualization cue, contextual presupposition, situated inference – are part of Gumperz's integrated program for the analysis of verbal communication. Before these concepts are discussed, it is important to make some background observations.

Recall, first, Gumperz's observation that our perceptions and memories are an outcome of culturally determined predispositions. One feature of modern urban societies is their social and cultural heterogeneity: People from very different social and cultural backgrounds come into contact with one another. Such contacts can lead to communicative difficulties precisely because of the point noted earlier: People's perceptions of similarities and differences in the world, including their predispositions about language and the way it is used, are culturally bound. To further complicate matters, it is not just the core grammar of a language (i.e., syntax, phonology, semantics) that is open to cultural influence and is a source of communicative difficulty. An equally pervasive source of misunderstanding lies in the marginal features of language: "signalling mechanisms such as intonation, speech rhythm, and choice among lexical, phonetic, and syntactic options" (Gumperz, 1982a, p. 16). Since we are typically unaware that we are using these features, it is all the more difficult for us to realize that they have communicative significance. Gumperz's studies of both interracial (blacks and whites in the United States) and enterethnic (Indians and British in England) settings show how differences in the marginal features of language can cause misunderstandings, lead to the formation of racial and ethnic stereotypes, and contribute to inequalities in power and status (see also Auer & DiLuzio, 1992; Cook-Gumperz, 1986; Gumperz, 1981; Gumperz & Roberts, 1991).

The signaling mechanisms just described are what Gumperz calls *contextualization cues:* aspects of language and behavior (verbal and nonverbal signs) that relate what is said to *contextual presuppositions,* that is background knowledge that allows *situated inferences* about what one's interlocutor intends to convey. The following example (from Gumperz, 1982a, p. 147) illustrates the use of rising intonation as a contextualiation cue.

Teacher: James, what does this word say?
James: I don't know.
Teacher: Well, if you don't want to try, someone else will. Freddy?
Freddy: Is that a p or a b?
Teacher: (*encouragingly*) It's a p.
Freddy: Pen.

The teacher's response ("Well, if you don't want to try, someone else will") indicates her interpretation of James's "I don't know," not only in terms of its literal meaning but as an indication that James did not wish to try to answer the question. Gumperz notes, however, that "I don't know" had final rising intonation, understood in the African-

American community of which James was a member as conveying a desire for encouragement (cf. "I need some encouragement").[4] Thus, we might say that the teacher did not retrieve the contextual presuppositions needed to accurately interpret James's message (his speech act) from his use of rising intonation.

As illustrated in the example, Gumperz's studies show that contextualization cues can affect the basic meaning of a message. Although such cues are used habitually and automatically by members of a particular social group, they are almost never consciously noted or assigned conventional meanings. Rather, they signal the speaker's implicit definition of the situation and more important, how the propositional content of talk is to be understood. It is because contextualization cues are learned through long periods of close, face-to-face contact that many people in modern, culturally diverse, socially heterogeneous societies are likely to interact without benefit of shared cues.

When listeners share speakers' contextualization cues, subsequent interactions proceed smoothly. The methodological consequence of this is that one can discover shared meaning by investigating the process of interaction itself, that is, by using the reaction that an utterance evokes as evidence of whether interpretive conventions were shared (Gumperz, 1981a, p. 5). Especially revealing are analyses of misunderstandings between people from different groups who do not share contextualization cues and thus cannot retrieve the contextual presuppositions necessary to situated inferences about meaning. White teachers' negative reactions to black students' "sharing-time" stories, for example, show that cultural conventions for the telling and interpretation of coherent stories are not shared by the two communities (Michaels, 1981); whereas the white community builds stories upon temporal coherence, the black community depends upon topical coherence. The studies collected in Gumperz (1981b, 1982b), as well as analyses by Tannen (1984, 1990) and Young (1994), also show that misunderstandings can provide telling evidence that contextualization cues are at work. Such misunderstandings can have devastating social consequences for members of minority groups who are denied access to valued resources, based partly (but not totally) on the inability of those in control of crucial gatekeeping transactions to accurately use others' contextualization cues as a basis from which to infer intended meanings (see Erickson & Shultz, 1982; see also Erickson, this volume).

Before this section is summarized, it is important to note that although some of Gumperz's concepts (inference, involvement) seem rooted in the individual, they are actually grounded in a view of the self

4 Gumperz's more recent transcriptions of this utterance would capture its final rising intonation (see Gumperz & Berenz, 1993).

and what it does (e.g., make inferences, become involved) as a member of a social and cultural group and as a participant in the social construction of meaning. For example, Gumperz (1982a, p. 209) reformulates Hymes's concept of communicative competence (1974) in interactional terms, to include "the knowledge of linguistic and related communicative conventions that speakers must have to create and sustain conversational cooperation" (see also Gumperz, 1985; Saville-Troike, this volume). And even in the complex question of speakers' internal differentiation of two linguistic systems, Gumperz (1982a, p. 99) argues that "effective speaking presupposed *sociolinguistically* based inferences about where systemic boundaries lie" and that "members have their own *socially defined* notions of code or grammatical system" (emphasis added).

In sum, the key to Gumperz's sociolinguistics of verbal communication is a view of language as a socially and culturally constructed symbol system that is used in ways that reflect macrolevel social meanings (e.g., group identity, status differences) but also create microlevel social meanings (i.e., what one is saying and doing at a particular moment in time). Speakers are members of social and cultural groups: The way we use language not only reflects our group-based identity but also provides situated indexes as to who we are, what we want to communicate, and how we know how to do so. The ability to produce and understand these indexical processes as they occur in, and are influenced by, local contexts is part of our communicative competence. As described in the previous section, the work of Erving Goffman also focuses upon situated knowledge, the self, and social context. The next section brings together the work of these two scholars as the basis for proposing some overall themes of interactional sociolinguistics and some further suggestions of the relevance of this approach to language in the classroom.

## Language, culture, and society as situated processes

Two different sets of interests have been reviewed, one stemming from concerns about the self and society (Goffman), and the other from concerns about language and culture (Gumperz). As mentioned, Goffman's work focused on how the organization of social life (in institution's, interactions, etc.) provides contexts in which both the conduct of self and the communication with another can be made sense of (both by those present in an interaction and by outside analysts). It was noted that Gumperz's work focuses on how interpretations of context are critical to the communication of information and to another's understanding of a speaker's intention.

Despite these different starting points and analytic foci, several shared themes and perspectives underlie interactional sociolinguistics. Most generally put, *interactional sociolinguistics* is the study of the linguistic and social construction of interaction. It provides a framework within which to analyze social context and to incorporate participants' own understanding of context into the inferencing of meaning. Goffman's sociological research focused attention on the interactional order underlying social occasions, situations, and encounters. Knowledge of the interactional order can lead to analysis of the socially constituted moves that help create a sense of reality in a particular interaction and a set of expectations about what will come next. These expectations are similar to contextual presuppositions and, thus, are critical to the way situated inferences are drawn from contextualization cues. If participants do not have some sense of what is going on during an interaction (e.g., What kind of occasion is this? What kind of activity are we engaged in?), they cannot use contextualization cues to draw inferences about others' meanings. Thus, the richly textured analyses of social situations, social interactions, participant roles, and statuses offered by interactional sociolinguistics all contribute to our understanding of the contextual presuppositions that help us use contextualization cues to draw situated inferences about what others say, mean, and do.[5]

It may help at this point to give an example of how knowledge of *interpersonal meanings* (the symbolic values of what is said and done) and *social structure* (abstract forms of social life) can allow us to more fully understand the contextual presuppositions that figure in hearers' inferences of speakers' meaning. The example also suggests a connection between contextualization cues and the face-saving strategies discussed in the earlier section on Goffman.

The situation described (from Gumperz, 1982a, p. 30) took place after an informal graduate-level seminar. A black student, about to leave the room with several other black and white students, approached the instructor. (Gumperz's presentation of the sequence has been modified.)

5 Contextual presuppositions are similar to the sociological notion of *definition of a situation* (Cooley, 1902): What we know about, and what we expect to find, in a particular activity (or situation) provides information by which we characterize and define that activity (or situation). Our perceptions of social circumstance also have real consequences: "[I]f men define situations as real, they are real in their consequences" (Cooley, 1902). The fact that we draw situated inferences about another's message through the use of contextualization cues that signal our definition of the situation has an important impact on the interactional sociolinguistic perspective on communication. In contrast to some other perspectives (Schiffrin, 1994, Chap. 11), communication requires two sources of intersubjectivity (i.e., shared knowledge and metaknowledge; Schiffrin, 1990; Taylor & Cameron, 1987): a shared definition of the situation in which interaction takes place and the use of strategies dependent on the same repertoire of contextualization cues.

Student: Could I talk to you for a minute? I'm gonna apply for a fellowship and I was wondering if I could get a recommendation?
Instructor: Okay. Come along to the office and tell me what you want to do.
Student: (*As the instructor and other students leave the room, turns his head slightly to the other students*) Ahma git me a gig! (*rough gloss: I'm going to get myself some support*)

Gumperz's analysis of the utterance "Ahma git me a gig!" focuses on how interpretations of the speaker's intent are related to the different linguistic (specifically, phonological and lexical) qualities of the utterance serving as contextualization cues. These cues signal a shift from one variety of English to another: The student asks the instructor for a recommendation in European-American standard English but speaks to the other students in African-American Vernacular English (see Rickford, this volume). Because the student's addressee has changed (from instructor to other students), this is an example of situational code switching which also has metaphorical significance.[6] Gumperz (1982a, pp. 31–32) explains that the lexical and phonological features functioning as contextualization cues evoke a number of contextual presuppositions, which provide for an interpretation of its meaning. Gumperz suggests that the student, by using a method known as *playback* (discussed later), is positioning himself in relation to conflicting norms about what blacks must do if they "are to get along in a White dominated world." "Ahma git me a gig!" thus has a clear face-saving function: It is a positive-face strategy linking together the black students in the classroom. Notice how this interpretation depends upon social and cultural knowledge at a macrolevel (i.e., the social and economic relationships between blacks and whites) and a microlevel (the utterance follows the instructor's exit from the room, and thus he is not an addressed recipient of the remark [Goffman, 1974], and is directed to the black students remaining in the room). Social information at both macrolevels and microlevels thus forms part of the contextual presuppositions underlying the inferred meaning of the utterance.

This example is useful for still another reason. Both code switching and the use of vernacular varieties have often been regarded negatively by teachers (see Sridhar, this volume). These negative views overlook the fact that linguistic alternations may serve not only instructional,

6 The distinction between situational and metaphorical code switching is difficult to maintain in this (and probably other) cases. The student's switch seems situational because of the change in addressee; that is, the teacher left the room. (Note the importance of observation and accurate note taking.) However, the speaker is displaying a changed relationship with people who were already present in the setting, a characteristic of metaphorical code switches: The black students in the classroom switch their participation status from unaddressed to addressed recipients, a switch which also precedes (and allows) the display of solidarity. Heller (1988) presents further studies of code switching in the interactional sociolinguistic perspective.

social, and cultural functions in the classroom but also important interactional face-saving functions (see Gumperz & Hernandez-Chavez, 1972). These functions may be identified by an interactional sociolinguistic analysis.

The connection between contextualization cues and face portrayed through this example reveals an important interdependence between Goffman's and Gumperz's work. Both scholars allow language to have a relatively active role in creating a sense of social order and in altering participants' sense of what is going on from moment to moment. As the example showed, contextualization cues can alter not only the meaning of a message but also the participation framework of talk: Different intentions, and different aspects of self and other, can be displayed through subtle changes in the way utterances are presented. Goffman's later work on the self (1981) builds upon his earlier (1959) division (between character and performer) to locate the self within a participation framework – a set of positions which individuals within the perceptual range of an utterance may take in relation to that utterance. The kinds of devices identified by Gumperz as contextualization cues are exactly what indicate shifts in participation statuses. This means that socialinguists "can be looked to for help in the study of footing [participation status]" (Goffman, 1981, p. 128). But sociolinguists can also get help from the sociological analyses of footing: "[I]f [sociolinguists] are to compete in this heretofore literary and psychological area, then presumably they must find a structural means of doing so . . . the structural underpinnings of changes in footing" (p. 128). Thus, what Gumperz's linguistic analyses add to Goffman's dissection of the self are a knowledge of some of the devices that convey changes in participant status (i.e., footing) and a view of how the way an utterance is produced allows the situated inference of a new participant alignment.

The analysis of involvement also illustrates an interdependence between the ideas of Goffman and Gumperz that may be useful for our understanding of the classroom. Earlier it was noted that contextual presuppositions and contextualization cues are critical to the situated inference of meaning. Also necessary to this process is the maintenance of involvement: We cannot understand each other (i.e., achieve intersubjectivity, shared knowledge) if we cannot attract and sustain each others' attention (Gumperz, 1982a, p. 4). Although understanding thus requires involvement, the process also works in the opposite direction: Maintaining involvement also requires sharing linguistic and sociocultural knowledge (Gumperz, 1982a, p. 3).

Goffman's study (1963) of behavior in public places is relevant to Gumperz's concern with the creation and effects of involvement. Goffman focuses on the social organization of involvement: He describes the way different social occasions (and different phases of occasions) can create a wide array of expectations for the display of involvement. Access rituals such as greetings, for example, require heightened involvement (Goffman, 1971; Schiffrin, 1977). Thus, the processes of both being involved and showing involvement are themselves socially situated. The situated nature of involvement has a bearing on the communicative value of involvement (Gumperz's concern): Since interactions impose their own rules of involvement, inferences that are based on involvement are also subject to broader rules of social engagement.

The relationship between involvement and shared knowledge is clearly relevant to classroom settings. We know from Gumperz's work that involvement both requires and creates shared knowledge. Multicultural classrooms present special challenges in this regard: lack of student involvement in lessons in classrooms in which students' cultures differ from that of the teacher (or differ among themselves) may be due to a lack of shared social and cultural knowledge. Such gaps may, in turn, hinder learning, that is, the acquisition of more shared knowledge. Foster (1989) describes, for example, the communicative strategies and styles that create involvement and facilitate learning for African-Americans in a college classroom, both of which differ from the strategies and styles in classrooms following European-American norms. Other studies reveal the communicative differences between Japanese and American students in student-led discussion groups (Watanbe, 1993) and between Greek and American students during discussion and disagreement with their teachers (Kakava, 1993). It is important for educators to be aware of the different styles through which people from different cultures create and display involvement. Otherwise, it can be difficult to differentiate between behaviors which display a lack of involvement and behaviors which stem from the use of different cultural norms for displaying engagement in an activity.

Goffman's work on involvement is also relevant to the classroom. Goffman demonstrated that involvement is socially structured: Social situations, occasions, and encounters impose their own constraints on the amount, type, and display of involvement. A typical day at school, or a typical classroom period, requires many different kinds of involvement from students: The involvement required during discussion groups, for example, is clearly different from that required during lectures. Norms for displaying involvement also underlie the classroom practices by which students signal shifts in their participation status. Hand raising, for example, is a common contextualization cue used by students to signal that they want to take a turn at talk. Norms for engaging in such practices differ according to classroom type and/or activity: Students in small graduate-level seminars, for example, are often encouraged to speak without raising their hands. Despite the pervasiveness of such contextualization cues in the classroom, neither teachers nor students are always aware of their own reliance on, and interpretation of, such cues. I recently noticed my own tendency to look more at students who looked at me and nodded their heads during my lectures. Not only did I assume that they were more interested and appreciative but also that their nonverbal behavior could help me gauge whether my remarks were being attended to and understood. Recent studies by Sadker and Sadker (1994) show equally subtle interpretations at work in the organization of turn-taking behavior in elementary school classrooms. Whereas boys were likely to start speaking – and be allowed to continue speaking – without raising their hands, girls often raised their hands and did not speak until the teacher called on them; the result was fewer opportunities for girls to contribute to classroom discussion (see Freeman and McElhinny, this volume).

It has been suggested in this section that Goffman's focus on social interaction complements Gumperz's focus on verbal communication: Goffman describes the social and interpersonal contexts that provide the presuppositions that Gumperz finds so crucial to the inferencing of meaning. Thus interactional sociolinguistics can be used to identify different kinds and levels of contexts, to conceptualize the organizational and interpretive role of contexts, and to describe how linguistic aspects of utterances allow us to draw situated inferences about what others say, mean, and do. In brief, interactional sociolinguistics, provides analyses of how language works along with participants' understanding of social context to allow the inferencing of meaning.

## How to study the language of social interaction

Learning how to do interactional sociolinguistic analyses typically requires training in linguistics and in either anthropology or sociology. This section offers some fundamental points about such analyses that might guide teachers who want to adopt some insights of this approach for use in their classrooms.

Detailed analyses of the language of social interaction require high-quality tape (or video) recordings of naturalistic (rather than experimentally elicited) social interactions. Recordings are important for several reasons. First, one cannot discover the structure of interactions without repeatedly viewing and/or listening to what was said and done during those interactions. (By the same token, discovering the regularities in verbal interaction usually requires more than one example of a specific type of interaction; the exact number depends on the length and complexity of the interaction.) Second, since contextualization cues are often relatively subtle aspects of spoken language or gesture, identifying contextualization cues requires a recording of verbal and nonverbal behavior that is accurate enough to allow the analyst to hear (and/or see) the same behaviors to which participants are attending.

Once the interactions of interest have been recorded, it is critical to transcribe the recording. This provides a written record of what has happened that is essential to analysis (it is easier to compare different sections of an interaction by turning pages than by pressing the buttons of a tape recorder). Transcription is a long and tedious process; depending on the number of speakers, their degree of overlapping talk, the quality of the recoding, and so on, a single hour of interaction may take anywhere from 5 to 15 hours to transcribe. Also influencing the amount of time needed for transcription is the transcription system one decides to use. Such systems vary from relatively broad (undetailed) to relatively narrow (detailed); different systems are summarized in Schiffrin (1994, App. 2). Interactional sociolinguists often use transcription conventions that capture some prosodic information (since intonation, stress, and rhythm frequently function as contextualization cues).

The analysis of one's interaction – identifying the way language both structures and is structured by the interaction – requires a process of immersion in the details of the interaction. One must listen to (and/or watch) what happened and review the transcript numerous times before one can understand how the interaction falls into different phases and actions and how different contextual presuppositions guide what is said and done. Earlier the need for tape- and/or video-recorded interactions for this task was noted, as was the considerable investment of time and experience required for producing a usable transcript. Students can, however, become familiar with interactional sociolinguistic methods without recorded data. Some interchanges occur frequently enough, and are regular enough, that students can write down details of what happened after the fact and, after a few observations, develop a coding system for keeping track of what was said and done. A collection of service encounters, greetings, and directions to public places, for example, is relatively easy to assemble and can provide a quick entry into some of the methods and ideas of interactional sociolinguistics. I often introduce students to interactional sociolinguistics by having them ask twenty people for directions to a public place; they write down what happened afterward. Sometimes they do the exercise in pairs, so that one person takes a primarily speaking role (acts as a participant), and the other more of a listening role (acts as an observer who can contribute more to the written record of the interaction). Students then analyze the directions they received by breaking them down into different phases (e.g., opening, request, provision of instructions, information checks, appreciation, closing), identifying the linguistic and behavior cues that differentiate, and are associated with, those phases, and describing the background knowledge that facilitates understanding of the directions.

In addition to identifying the phases of interactions, interactional sociolinguists try to discover interlocutors' inferences about each other's meanings and the communicative strategies that underlie particular utterances. Both these tasks require close attention to what is said by one party and how it is responded to by another. In fact, it is often the response to an utterance (rather than the utterance itself) that provides the most reliable clue to the interactional importance (as well as the situated inferences) of an utterance. Interactional sociolinguists sometimes check their interpretations of actions and meanings with the participants themselves (Tannen, 1984) or with other people who have varying degrees of familiarity with the ways of speaking used in the interaction. This playback method allowed Gumperz to identify the interactional function of "Ahma git me a gig!" for the black students to whom it was directed. As noted in the earlier discussion, this utterance positioned the speaker in relation to conflicting norms about what blacks must do if they "are to get along in a White dominated world." Gumperz also found that people less familiar with ways of speaking in the black community interpreted "Ahma git me a gig!" quite differently. When different interpretations lead to misunderstandings of speaker intentions, playback with the original participants in the interaction is all the more valuable a route toward discovery of contextual presuppositions.

Although interactional sociolinguistic analyses do require technical training, it is important to remember that one of the main goals of interactional sociolinguistics is to understand the language of social interaction. We are all able to use language in our everyday lives and our everyday interactions with other people. One reason that we can do so is through our own implicit analyses of what we (and others) are seeking to do with language and of how what we say and do follows from (and leads to) what others say and do. In a sense, then, what interactional sociolinguistics is trying to do is uncover the knowledge that all of us already have. Thus, even though novices might not be able to do the same kind of interactional sociolinguistic analyses as scholars, they can still try to make explicit the knowledge that they use so automatically in everyday interactions with one another.

## Pedagogical applications

Thus far in this chapter, it has become evident that interactional sociolinguistics provides a way to analyze social context and to incorporate participants' own understanding of context into the inferencing of meaning. This perspective can be applied not only to our understanding of classroom interactions (as suggested through examples in earlier sections) but also to the way we teach a language. It can be said that interactional sociolinguistics has a very general application (in defining the goal of language teaching), as well as more specific applications (in guiding lesson plans and interactions) in the classroom.

Learning a language in a way that enables one to use that language for a range of social and expressive purposes requires more than learning lists of vocabulary items, syntactic paradigms, and nativelike pronunciations. Rather, as ethnographers of communication have made so clear (see Saville-Troike, this volume), language is a system of use whose rules and norms are an intergral part of culture. Thus, learning a language is more like developing communicative competence. What one acquires is knowledge that governs appropriate use of language in concrete situations of everyday life; one learns how to engage in conversation, shop in a store, be interviewed for a job, pray, joke, argue, tease, and warn, and even when to be silent.

Once we see that the focus of language teaching is to help students develop communicative competence, it is easy to find a place for interactional sociolinguistics within the curriculum. Recall that interactional sociolinguistics provides ways of describing and analyzing social events and situations – the contexts that help define particular utterances as socially and culturally appropriate. Thus, when teaching students how to make requests, for example, teachers could incorporate into lessons that cover the use of different forms (e.g., modals, questions, commands) information about to whom, when, why, and where such forms are considered appropriate. A valuable part of such lessons would be discussion of the possible social meanings of using a form that is inappropriate. Imperatives, for example, are often used in situations of asymmetric power, as, for example, when an employer issues a directive to an employee by saying "Type these letters by tomorrow morning." Using a form that implies a higher social position than one usually holds, then, might be interpreted as arrogant or presumptuous (e.g., as if an employee asked for vacation time by saying "Give me a vacation by tomorrow morning").

Such lessons could include not only contextual descriptions of interpersonal and institutional settings but also very specific discussions of how different ways of making requests work as contextualization cues for participants – how different words, intonations, syntactic forms, and so on, structure participants' definitions of what is going on in the interaction. It would be especially useful in an ESL classroom for students to participate in such lessons by actually collecting data from different situations in which they either make or receive requests. They could learn how to analyze such situations (e.g., by identifying the social status and role of participants, the degree to which their request imposed upon the their party) and observe for themselves which forms seem to be used by whom and for what purpose. Similarly, students could tape-record some of their own interactions or role-play interactions that they have found problematic or that differ markedly from those with which they are familiar. Such tape recordings and role-plays could be analyzed by students in both participant and observer capacities: They could comment on the meanings and interpretations of what went on and try to identify what was responsible for their own inferences and their own responses. Finally, students' native experiences could also provide a valuable cross-cultural perspective. By discussing the forms that would be appropriate in comparable situations in their own cultures, they could become aware of the pervasiveness and cultural relativity of contextualization cues.

In addition to guiding specific areas of the language curriculum, interactional sociolinguistics can help both students and teachers understand the social and interactional dynamics of their classrooms. In an earlier section, some of the ways that contextualization cues pervade the classroom were pointed out: Gumperz's example with James's "I don't know" showed their relevance in student-teacher interactions, and his example with the black student's "Ahma git me a gig!" showed their relevance in student-student interactions (see also Gumperz, 1981). Contextualization cues are routinely used in other kinds of classroom interactions, for example, to help organize transitions from one speaker to another (McHoul, 1978) or to signal transitions between different activities (Dorr-Bremme, 1990). Teachers can increase both their own and their students' awareness of the use and interpretation of such cues by video recordings and analyses of classroom interactions. Recordings of student behavior during different classroom activities, for example, might reveal the subtle ways that students indicate shifting interest in a topic, readiness and willingness to ask a question or make a comment, and lack of understanding of a point. Analyses of such recordings could help students (especially in multicultural classrooms) become aware of the behaviors associated with different participation statuses in the classroom – relatively passive roles such as listener to a lecture or more active roles such as participant in group discussions. Likewise, recordings of teacher talk could reveal the verbal and nonverbal behaviors that teachers use to signal transitions from one activity to another, for example, the use of discourse markers such as *now* or *OK* (Schiffrin, 1987) or shifts in physical position or stance to indicate upcoming summaries, introduction of a new topic, or change from lecture to discussion. Thus, both students and teachers could benefit from increased awareness of how contextualization cues can guide classroom interactions.

In sum, interactional sociolinguistics can help teachers and students identify how different kinds and levels of social and cultural contexts guide the use and interpretation of language. By understanding how context is interwoven with what we say, mean, and do through language – and by incorporating that understanding into the goals, curriculum design, lessons, and everyday practices of their classrooms – teachers may be able to help students become more communicatively competent in the language that they are trying to learn.

## Suggestions for further reading

Auer, P., & Di Luzio, A. (Eds.). (1992). *The contextualization of language.* Amsterdam and Philadelphia: John Benjamins.
This is a collection of papers discussing and updating Gumperz's theoretical concepts, as well as recent empirical studies focusing on interactional meanings (with special emphasis on the role of prosody in contextualizing meaning).

Brown, P., & Levinson, S. (1987). *Politeness.* Cambridge: Cambridge University Press.
Brown and Levinson present a theory of politeness in social interaction that has a potentially wide application to different languages, cultures, and social situations. The book also contains a rich set of examples of different communicative strategies that are considered polite.

Goffman, E. (1959). *The presentation of self in everyday life.* New York: Anchor Books.
This is Goffman's earliest book and a classic in sociology. It presents his basic theory of the self and introduces the study of social interaction. The book is rich with examples and insights about self-presentation and social life.

Goffman, E. (1981). *Forms of talk.* Philadelphia: University of Pennsylvania Press.
This collection of Goffman's articles has the most direct relevance to sociolinguistics. Among the chapters are "Footing" (a discussion of participation status, with a mention of contextualization cues) and "Replies and Responses" (a discussion of coherence relations in discourse).

Gumperz, J. (1982a). *Discourse strategies.* Cambridge: Cambridge University Press.
This collection of Gumperz's articles provides a succinct theoretical and methodological introduction to the crucial concepts in this framework. The book also applies the framework in a range of different social and cultural settings.

Gumperz, J. (1982b). *Language and social identity.* Cambridge: Cambridge University Press.
This collection of articles by Gumperz, his students, and colleagues applies the interactional sociolinguistic framework in different social and cultural settings.

Schiffrin, D. (1987). *Discourse markers.* Cambridge: Cambridge University Press.
Schiffrin provides an empirical analysis of different words and expressions

(e.g., *and, I mean, y'know*) in English conversation using insights from interactional sociolinguistics. The book provides an understanding of patterns of language use which are difficult to capture in standard language teaching texts.

Tannen, D. (1984). *Conversational style*. Norwood, NJ: Ablex.

Tannen presents an analysis of conversations between friends, with special attention to misunderstandings based on cultural and subcultural differences in communicative style.

## References


Auer, P., & Di Luzio, A. (Eds.). (1992). *The contextualization of language*. Amsterdam and Philadelphia: John Benjamins.

Brown, P., & Levinson, S. (1987). *Politeness*. Cambridge: Cambridge University Press.

Cook-Gumperz, J. (1986). *The social construction of literacy*. Cambridge: Cambridge University Press.

Cooley, C. H. (1902). *Human nature and the social order*. New York: Scribner.

Dorr-Bremme, D. W. (1990). Contextualization cues in the classroom. *Language in Society, 19*(3), 379–402.

Durkheim, E. (1895). *The rules of sociological method*. New York: Free Press.

Eckert, P. (1989). *Jocks and burnouts: Social identity in the high school*. New York: Teachers College Press.

Erickson, F., and Shultz, J. (1982). *The counselor as gatekeeper*. New York: Academic Press.

Foster, M. (1989). "It's cookin' now": A performance analysis of the speech events of a black teacher in an urban community college. *Language in Society, 18*(1), 1–31.

Gilmore, P. (1985). Silence and sulking: Emotional displays in the classroom. In D. Tannen & M. Saville-Troike (Eds.). *Perspectives on silence* (pp. 139–164). Norwood, NJ: Ablex Press.

Goffman, E. (1959). *The presentation of self in everyday life*. New York: Anchor Books.

Goffman, E. (1963). *Behavior in public places*. New York: Free Press.

Goffman, E. (1967a). On face work. In E. Goffman (Ed.), *Interaction ritual* (pp. 5–46). New York: Anchor Books.

Goffman, E. (1967b). The nature of deference and demeanor. In E. Goffman (Ed.), *Interaction ritual* (pp. 49–95). New York: Anchor Books.

Goffman, E. (1971). Supportive interchanges. In E. Goffman (Ed.), *Relations in public* (pp. 62–94). New York: Basic Books.

Goffman, E. (1974). *Frame analysis*. New York: Harper and Row.

Goffman, E. (1981). *Forms of talk*. Philadelphia: University of Pennsylvania Press.

Gumperz, J. (1971). *Language in social groups* (A. Dil, Ed.). Stanford, CA: Stanford University Press.

Gumperz, J. (1981). Conversational inference and classroom learning. In J. Green & C. Wallat (Eds.), *Ethnography and language in educational settings* (pp. 3–23). Norwood, NJ: Ablex.

Gumperz, J. (1982a). *Discourse strategies*. Cambridge: Cambridge University Press.

Gumperz, J. (1982b). *Language and social identity.* Cambridge: Cambridge University Press.

Gumperz, J. (1985). Communicative competence revisited. In D. Schiffrin (Ed.), *Meaning, form and use: Linguistic applications* (pp. 278–279). Washington, DC: Georgetown University Press.

Gumperz, J., & Berenz, N. (1993). Transcribing conversational exchanges. In J. Edwards & M. Lampert (Eds.), *Transcription and coding methods for language research.* Hillsdale, NJ: Lawrence Erlbaum.

Gumperz, J., & Roberts, C. (1991). Understanding in intercultural encounters. In J. Blommaert & J. Verschueren (Eds.), *The pragmatics of intercultural and international communication* (pp. 51–90). Amsterdam and Philadelphia: John Benjamin.

Hymes, D. (1974). Toward ethnographies of communication. In D. Hymes (Ed.), *Foundations of sociolinguistics* (pp. 3–28). Philadelphia: University of Pennsylvania Press.

Kakava, C. (1993). Negotiation of disagreement by Greeks in conversational and classroom discourse. Unpublished doctoral dissertation, Georgetown University, Washington, DC.

McHoul, A. (1978). The organization of turns at formal talk in the classroom. *Language in Society, 7,* 182–213.

Mead, G. (1935). *Mind, self and society.* Chicago: University of Chicago Press.

Mehan, H. (1979). *Learning lessons.* Cambridge, MA: Harvard University Press.

Merritt, M. (1982). Distributing and directing attention in primary classrooms. In L. Cherry-Wilkinson (Ed.), *Communicating in the classroom* (pp. 223–244). New York: Academic Press.

Merritt, M. (1984). On the use of OK in service encounters. In J. Baugh & J. Sherzer (Eds.), *Language in use* (pp. 139–147). Englewood, NJ: Prentice Hall.

Michaels, S. (1981). "Sharing time": Children's narrative styles and differential access to literacy. *Language in Society, 10,* 423–442.

Philips, S. (1983). *The invisible culture: Communication in classrooms and communities on the Warm Springs Indian reservation.* New York: Longman.

Schiffrin, D. (1977). Opening encounters. *American Sociological Review, 42*(4), 671–691.

Schiffrin, D. (1987). *Discourse markers.* Cambridge: Cambridge University Press.

Schiffrin, D. (1990). The principle of intersubjectivity in conversation and communication. *Semiotica, 80,* 121–151.

Schiffrin, D. (1990). Conversation analysis. In *Annual Review of Applied Linguistics. 11,* 3–16.

Schiffrin, D. (1994). *Approaches to discourse.* Oxford: Basil Blackwell Press.

Searle, J. (1969). *Speech acts.* Cambridge: Cambridge University Press.

Searle, J. (1975). Indirect speech acts. In P. Cole and J. Morgan (Eds.), *Syntax and semantics* (Vol. 3, *Speech acts,* pp. 59–82). New York: Academic Press.

Simmel, G. (1950). *The sociology of Georg Simmel* (K. Wolff, ed.). New York: Free Press (original work published in 1911).

Sinclair, J., & Coulthard, R. (1975). *Toward an analysis of discourse.* New York: Oxford University Press.

Tannen, D. (1984). *Conversational style.* Norwood, NJ: Ablex.

Tannen, D. (1990). *You just don't understand!* New York: William Morrow.

Watanbe, S. (1993). Cultural differences in framing: American and Japanese group discussion. In D. Tannen (Ed.), *Framing in discourse* (pp. 176–209). Oxford: Oxford University Press.

Young, L. (1994). *Crosstalk and culture in Sino-American communication.* Cambridge: Cambridge University Press.

# 10 *Intercultural communication*

J. Keith Chick

## Introduction

This chapter is distinguished from those that immediately precede and follow it because it does not present another approach to the study of language use. Rather it examines answers that sociolinguists associated with the approaches outlined in the chapters on ethnography of communication, ethnographic microanalysis, and, especially, interactional sociolinguistics and speech act theory have given to questions concerning the miscommunication that often occurs when people with different life experiences and different cultural patterns of communication interact with one another. The chapter is concerned, in particular, with the answers that have been given to these research questions:

What are the sources of intercultural miscommunication?
What are the social effects of such miscommunication?
What can be done to improve intercultural communication?

Sociolinguists have traced the sources of intercultural miscommunication to the distinctive nature of the value systems, pervasive configurations of social relations, and dominant ideologies of cultural groups. Such dimensions of the social context shape communicative conventions, thereby giving them their culturally specific character. Thus, for example, Wolfson (1992, p. 205) points out that what members of particular cultural groups thank or apologize for, or compliment on, usually reflects values because, in performing these speech acts, people are often implicitly assessing the behavior, possessions, accomplishments, character, or appearance of others. She also traces the high frequency of complimenting that she found amongst status-equal friends, coworkers, and acquaintances in middle-class urban American society to the configuration of social relations in that society. She explains that they compliment frequently because they "live in a complex and open society in which individuals are members not of a single

The author gratefully acknowledges support in the form of a Fulbright Senior African Research Fellowship and the Centre for Science Development Grant, which made it possible for him to have uninterrupted time to complete this paper.

network in which their own place is well-defined, but rather belong to a number of networks, both overlapping and non-overlapping, in which they must continually negotiate their roles and relationships with one another." Herbert (1985, 1989, 1990) traces differences in the patterns of compliment responses given by white middle-class Americans and white middle-class South Africans to different configurations of social relations and pervasive ideologies in these two societies. He argues that Americans compliment frequently in order to negotiate social relations and frequently reject compliments to avoid the implication that they are superior to their interlocutors. He sees this pattern as consistent with the structure of a society in which social relations are open to negotiation and consistent with the ideology of an egalitarian democracy that most Americans publicly espouse. He argues that, by contrast, South Africans give few compliments but accept most of the ones they receive in order to keep subordinates at distance, by allowing the compliments to imply that they are superior to their interlocutors. He sees this pattern as consistent with a society in which social relations, and especially social relations of power, are, to a large extent, predetermined and also consistent with the ideology of "institutionalized social inequality publicly enunciated in South Africa" (1989, p. 43).

Sociolinguists have also shown that the effects of intercultural miscommunication generated in the microcontexts of talk, in turn, have an impact upon the structural circumstances of society. Thus, for example, interactional sociolinguists (see, e.g., Gumperz, 1982a, b) and microethnographers[1] (see, e.g., Erickson & Shultz, 1982) have demonstrated, through fine-grained analyses of intercultural gatekeeping encounters (interviews for jobs, loan applications, promotions, and licenses, consultations with health care providers, etc.), that misevaluation of the motives and abilities of members of minority groups is frequent in such encounters. They explain that this often results in members of such groups not securing their fair share of resources and opportunities and not being able to realize their potential or attain positions of authority in societal institutions. The outcomes of the encounters, therefore, gen-

1 Erickson (this volume) points out that ethnographic microanalysis (microethnography) has been strongly influenced by interactional sociolinguistics. The relationship, though, has not been unidirectional. Interactional sociolinguistics has been equally strongly influenced by microethnography. Moreover, interactional sociolinguistics has been influenced by all the approaches named by Erickson as having influenced microethnography, with the possible exception of what he terms *continental discourse analysis*. Indeed, so close is the relationship between microethnography and interactional sociolinguistics that some scholars treat them as synonymous. Amongst notable differences is that microethnography, having been more strongly influenced by context analysis, focuses to a greater extent than interactional sociolinguistics does on the nonverbal aspects of communication. Interactional sociolinguistics has, in addition, been more strongly influenced than microethnography by the philosophical tradition of pragmatics (see Schiffrin, this volume).

erate and maintain the inequities in the institutions and societies in which they occur.

Sociolinguists, however, have been slow to address the third research question, namely, how insights from their studies of intercultural communication can be used to improve the practice of intercultural communication. Hornberger (1993) attributes this slowness to the tendency of sociolinguists to take a stance as outsiders and in their recognition of the integrity and equality of all cultures, to be reluctant to "meddle" with the cultures they study. She argues, nevertheless, that, "given our increasingly interdependent and intercultural world, and the rapidly accumulating evidence of the damage caused by poor intercultural communication" (1993, p. 304), it is essential that those who know so much about intercultural communication contribute to its improvement.

My purpose in this chapter is to provide examples of sociolinguistic research that, amongst other things, addresses the three questions listed above, drawing principally on my own research. I will distinguish between the contributions of studies of speech acts (see Cohen, this volume) and interactional sociolinguistics (see Schiffrin, this volume) and show how the findings of each complement the other.[2] I will deal with the first two research questions together and, before addressing the third question, examine the controversial issue of whether sociolinguistic studies of intercultural communication contribute to change or merely reinforce the status quo.

## Speech act studies and intercultural communication

Studies of speech acts constitute a subset of what Carbaugh (1990, p. 292) – to distinguish them from intercultural communication studies – terms *cross-cultural communication studies,* that is studies that focus on a particular feature of communication within and across cultures (e.g., speech act performance, choice of address terms and turn-taking conventions). Intercultural communication studies, by contrast, Carbaugh explains, are concerned with a number of features of two cultural systems as they are used in a particular intercultural encounter. My concern in this section of the chapter is to examine selected speech act

2 Note that Saville-Troike, this volume, sees speech act studies as falling outside the domain of ethnography of communication, and interactional sociolinguistic studies of intercultural communication (she refers to them as *cross-cultural*) as falling within it. My own position is that both fall within the domain of ethnography of communication, although my concern in this chapter is to distinguish not between disciplinary boundaries but between two sociolinguistic approaches to the study of intercultural communication.

studies in which the researchers have used their findings as a basis for addressing the questions about the sources and consequences of intercultural miscommunication referred to in the introduction of this chapter.

A source of intercultural miscommunication highlighted by the findings of cross-cultural studies is sociolinguistic transfer. *Sociolinguistic transfer* refers to the use of the rules of speaking of one's own speech community or cultural group when interacting with members of another community or group. This can occur in interactions in which one or more of the interlocutors is using a foreign or second language but employing the rules of speaking of his or her native language. It can even occur in interactions between individuals who have the same native language but belong to speech communities that have different rules of speaking, as would be the case, for example, with British and American English speakers.

To illustrate how sociolinguistic transfer can be a source of intercultural miscommunication, we turn to some studies of compliment giving and responding behavior. (Other examples of intercultural miscommunication arising from sociolinguistic transfer are provided by Saville-Troike, this volume.) Wolfson (1983) points out that differences in the distribution of compliments in different communities are potential sources of intercultural miscommunication; that is, there is frequently interactional trouble when members of one cultural group compliment in situations in which compliments are inappropriate for members of other groups. She cites the time when former President Carter, during an official visit to France, complimented a French official on the fine job he was doing. Editorial comment in the French press the next day revealed that Carter's remarks had been interpreted as interference in the internal politics of France. The frequency of complimenting is also a potential source of miscommunication, according to Wolfson. She points out that the high frequency with which Americans compliment leads to their being perceived by members of other cultures as "effusive, insincere, and possibly motivated by ulterior considerations" (1989, p. 23).

My own study of compliment responding behavior (see Chick, 1991) suggests that, quite apart from differences in the overall or gross frequencies of performance of particular speech acts by different cultural groups, different frequencies of choices of different strategies for realizing such speech acts are potential sources of intercultural miscommunication.

My principal objectives in this study were to establish whether Herbert's findings about the responses of white middle-class South Africans (referred to in the introduction to this chapter) are generalizable beyond the University of the Witwatersrand campus where his data were collected, and whether the changed structural conditions, associated with desegregation in South Africa, that have taken place since Herbert collected his data have affected speech act performance. Accordingly, I attempted to replicate Herbert's methods of data collection and analysis as far as possible. I asked field-workers to record (on audiotape or, as soon as possible after an encounter had occurred, from memory) compliment giving and responding sequences as they occurred naturally on the campus of another South African university, the University of Natal, Durban campus. They were permitted to initiate sequences themselves but only in circumstances in which they would normally give compliments. They were also asked to record such basic ethnographic information as location of the encounter, identity of interlocutors, and their relationships (if known). I subsequently coded the responses in terms of a typology of twelve response types devised by Pomerantz (1978) and refined by Herbert. Table 1 lists the twelve response types or strategies and gives examples of each. Pomerantz explains that both acceptance and rejection of compliments are problematic, for they violate one or other of two putative universal conversational principles – agree with the speaker and avoid self-praise – and that many of the response types she identified are strategies for resolving this conflict (they exhibit features of both acceptance and rejection). Finally, I counted and aggregated tokens of each response type. One departure from the methods employed by Herbert was in the coding of what he terms *compound responses,* such as:

A: Nice coat.
B: Thanks. Katherine gave it to me.

Herbert (1985, p. 80) reports that he coded such responses on the basis of "perceived intention." Thus, for example, in the preceding exchange, he would have coded B's responses as type 3 (reassignment), even though the first part of the response, if it had occurred on its own, would have been coded type 1 (appreciation token). My misgiving about this way of proceeding is that it increases, to what I consider an unacceptable degree, the subjectivity involved in coding responses. Accordingly, when compound responses occurred, I adopted the policy of coding all the types involved. For example, I coded the above response as 1+3.

The results revealed, amongst other things, significant differences in the frequency of use of response strategies by different panethnic groups (so-called white, Indian, and black South Africans). Table 2 shows the distribution of compliment response types for each panethnic group when interacting intraculturally. Compliment responses produced in

TABLE 1. COMPLIMENT RESPONSE TYPES

| Response type | Example |
| --- | --- |
| *Accepting* | |
| 1. Appreciation token | C: That's a great cake.<br>R: Thank you. |
| 2. Comment acceptance | C: You have such a nice house.<br>R: It's given us a lot of pleasure. |
| *Deflating, deflecting, rejecting* | |
| 3. Reassignment | C: You're really a skilled sailor.<br>R: This boat virtually sails itself. |
| 4. Return | C: You sound really good today.<br>R: I'm just following your lead. |
| 5. Qualification (agreeing) | C: Your report came out very well.<br>R: But I need to redo some figures. |
| 6. Praise downgrade (disagreeing) | C: Super chip shot.<br>R: It's gone rather high of the pin. |
| 7. Disagreement | C: Your shirt is smashing.<br>R: Oh, it's far too loud. |
| *Questioning, ignoring, reinterpreting* | |
| 8. Question (query or challenge) | C: That's a pretty sweater.<br>R: Do you really think so? |
| 9. Praise upgrade (often sarcastic) | C: I really like this soup.<br>R: I'm a great cook. |
| 10. Comment history | C: I love that suit.<br>R: I got it at Boscov's. |
| 11. No acknowledgement | C: You're the nicest person.<br>R: Have you finished that essay yet? |
| 12. Request interpretation | C: I like those pants.<br>R: You can borrow them anytime. |

intercultural encounters were not included because counting revealed that the patterns of choice differed considerably from those in intracultural encounters.

The differences in patterns of response reflected in Table 2 suggest that, on the Durban campus of the University of Natal, there is considerable potential for intercultural miscommunication arising from sociolinguistic transfer. For example, there were marked differences in the frequencies of choice of "disagreement." Whereas, in my data, as much as 10.4 percent of the total responses of Indian students falls into this category, only 3.6 percent of the total white responses and 3.1 percent of the total black responses do so. Moreover, what is distinctive about the Indian disagreements is that many are very direct, such as in the following example:

TABLE 2. DISTRIBUTION OF COMPLIMENT RESPONSES ACROSS PANETHNIC GROUPS AT THE UNIVERSITY OF NATAL, DURBAN

| | *Blacks* | | *Indians* | | *Whites* | |
|---|---|---|---|---|---|---|
| | No. | % | No. | % | No. | % |
| *Accepting* | | | | | | |
| 1. Appreciation token | 8 | 12.5 | 29 | 33.3 | 62 | 36.9 |
| 2. Comment acceptance | 9 | 14.1 | 7 | 8.1 | 10 | 6.0 |
| | | 26.6 | | 41.4 | | 42.9 |
| *Deflating, deflecting, rejecting* | | | | | | |
| 3. Reassignment | 3 | 4.7 | 3 | 3.5 | 4 | 2.4 |
| 4. Return | 1 | 1.6 | 1 | 1.2 | 0 | 0.0 |
| 5. Qualification (agreeing) | 2 | 3.1 | 4 | 4.6 | 8 | 4.8 |
| 6. Praise downgrade (disagreeing) | 3 | 4.7 | 5 | 5.8 | 15 | 8.9 |
| 7. Disagreement | 2 | 3.1 | 9 | 10.4 | 6 | 3.6 |
| | | 17.2 | | 25.5 | | 19.7 |
| *Questioning, ignoring, reinterpreting* | | | | | | |
| 8. Question (query or challenge) | 7 | 10.9 | 9 | 10.4 | 23 | 13.7 |
| 9. Praise upgrade (often sarcastic) | 5 | 7.8 | 6 | 6.9 | 5 | 4.2 |
| 10. Comment history | 2 | 3.1 | 2 | 2.4 | 13 | 7.7 |
| 11. No acknowledgment | 21 | 32.8 | 10 | 11.5 | 18 | 10.7 |
| 12. Request interpretation | 1 | 1.6 | 1 | 1.2 | 2 | 1.2 |
| | | 56.2 | | 32.4 | | 37.5 |
| Totals | 64 | 100.0 | 87 | 99.3 | 168 | 100.1 |

A: Your hair looks nice today.
B: It's a mess.
A: No, it's not.

This suggests that this group gives priority to the principle "avoid self-praise" over the principle "agree with the speaker."

By contrast, the disagreements of whites, in my data, tend to have a hedged quality:

A: You look very bright today.
B: Well, I don't feel very bright.

This suggests that, for this group, disagreements are particularly face-threatening and that devices such as hedges are used as a means of redress or of resolving the conflict between the two principles. In this way, they attend to the face of their interlocutor by marking their response as dispreferred.[3] It follows that this group would probably interpret the overt disagreements of Indian students as rude, even when no offense is intended.

Another potential source of intercultural miscommunication suggested by the results is a difference in the frequency of choice of the compliment response strategy of no acknowledgment. Whereas as little as 10.7 percent of white and 11.5 percent of Indian responses fall into this category, as much as 32.8 percent of black responses do so. Conversation analysts (see, e.g., Schegloff, 1968) have shown that when the first parts of what they term *adjacency pairs* (sequences of two related utterances by different speakers) occur (in this case, a compliment), appropriate second pair parts (in this case, a response) become conditionally relevant; that is, if the relevant second part occurs, the first part will be regarded as having been relevantly responded to, but if it does not occur, its absence will be noticeable or conspicuous. Although *no acknowledgment* is listed as a compliment response type, strictly speaking, it represents the absence of a response. Such conspicuous absence might easily be interpreted, by someone expecting a response, as an unwillingness to engage and, therefore, as face-threatening. Initially, I hypothesized that the preference of blacks for this strategy could be accounted for in terms of their using a second language as the medium. Most people are intuitively aware that, because compliment giving and responding behavior is used to negotiate social identities and relations, inappropriate choice of response can lead to face loss. It seems reasonable to assume, therefore, that people faced with the difficult task of responding in a second language in a socially acceptable way might choose the option that makes the least demands on their linguistic resources. However, I found that Zulus show a preference for the strategy of no acknowledgment even when interacting in Zulu. A case in point is the next example (followed by a translation into English), which is part of a conversation between two male Zulu students in B's university dorm room:

A: *(Knocks)*
B: Come in.
A: Haitor Bheki.
B: Eit kunjani mfowethu.
A: Ei grand man. *(Moves towards the table)* Hawis mfowethu, yaze yayinhle. le radio eyakho?

3 *Preference* is used here in its technical rather than psychological sense. Preference organization, as Blimes (1988) explains, provides for a number of ordered options as second parts of adjacency pairs. *Adjacency pairs* are sequences of two related utterances by different speakers, for example, question-answer or invitation-acceptance / refusal. Preference organization leads the respondent to a first part of an adjacency

B: Yebo.
A: Yaze yayinhle futhi inkulu wayithenga kuphi? Ngamalini?
B: Edrophini ngo R399.
A: Ngizofika ngizodlala ama cassette la kwaklo.

A: *(Knocks)*
B: Come in.
A: Hi Bheki.
B: Sit. How are you brother?
A: I'm fine, thanks. *(moves to the table)* Hey, brother, your radio is so beautiful.
B: Yes.
A: It is so beautiful and big. How much did you pay for it? Where did you buy it?
B: In town. It was R399.
A: I'll come and play my cassettes here one day.

This example is interesting because it suggests why the choice of no acknowledgment is not interpreted by Zulu interlocutors as unwillingness to engage and, therefore, face-threatening. The complimenter frequently makes a response to the compliment less conspicuously absent by adding another speech act immediately after the compliment. Thus, for example, A, after recycling and embellishing his compliment ("It is so beautiful and big." – line 8), asks two questions ("How much did you pay for it?" "Where did you buy it?"). B is thus able to avoid responding to the compliments, by answering the questions ("In town. It was R399." – line 10). It is possible, however, that members of other groups who are unfamiliar with this strategy might not see the conditional relevance of the compliment as having been aborted. In other words, they might not see B as having been released from his obligation to provide a response.

Other parts of this exchange that might be problematic in intercultural encounters are A's very direct enquiry about the cost of the radio (line 8) and his declaration (line 11) that he will play his cassettes on B's radio some day. Many native speakers would see the enquiry as an invasion of privacy and the declaration as interference with B's freedom of action, even if said jocularly or used in an exchange between intimates. In other words, they would experience them as face-threatening.

pair to provide the first of the options (unless she or he has reason not to) or, if not, the next in the list, and so on. Incidentally, Blimes sees what he calls *reluctance markers* (of which the hedges referred to in the text are an example) and preference organization as different, partly independent phenomena. He points out that it is possible to find instances of dispreferred options having been provided without reluctance markers, and preferred options having been provided with them.

## Interactional sociolinguistics and intercultural communication

The cross-cultural studies illustrated in the previous section allow researchers to identify general trends or patterns in sociolinguistic behavior over a great number of encounters and to make generalizations about how such behavior varies across societies, institutions, and cultural groups. These studies allow sociolinguists to trace connections on the one hand, between patterns of sociolinguistic behavior and ideologies and societal structures and, on the other hand, between these patterns and negative cultural stereotypes that may arise from intercultural miscommunication. However, such studies, for the most part, allow researchers to identify only what might be a source of intercultural communication; they do not usually allow researchers to identify what actually are the sources of such miscommunication in any one intercultural encounter. They do not show the cumulative effect of multiple sources of intercultural miscommunication. This is where interactional sociolinguistic studies of intercultural communication play a useful complementary role.

Rather than abstract particular linguistic features from a large number of interactions for subsequent categorization and/or counting, interactional sociolinguistics attempt to reduce idealization of data as much as possible. They analyze, in fine detail, a limited number of entire conversations or substantial episodes within conversations. These conversations are audiotaped or videotaped and transcribed. Rather than impose their own categories, researchers attempt to uncover the interpretative or inferential processes of the interlocutors by playing the recordings to the interlocutors and to informants who share the cultural background of the interlocutors and then eliciting their interpretations about progressively finer details of the discourse. (For a fuller account of these methods, see Tannen, 1984.)

An example is my investigation of the sources and consequences of miscommunication in postexamination interviews between a native South African English-speaking (SAE) professor and his ethnically diverse students. One source of miscommunication was a mismatch of interpretative frames of reference. Whereas some students shared the professor's interpretative frame for the interviews, namely, that the activity they were engaged in was a review of their preparation for and performance in the examination, others did not. In the case of a Zulu student, whose expectation was that the activity was one in which he had to account for his poor performance, the mismatch of frames led to serious cross-purposes. The student and the professor failed to build on one another's contributions, because they could not see their relevance.

It was evident, too, that a further source of miscommunication in these encounters was the systematic difference in the contextualization cues the SAE and Zulu English-speaking (ZE) interlocutors made use of. According to Gumperz (1982a), contextualization cues are constellations of surface features of the verbal and nonverbal message form (lexical, syntactic, phonological, prosodic, and paralinguistic choices; use of formulaic expressions, code switching and style switching; and changes in postural configurations, gestures, and facial expressions) which, as a consequence of previous experience and monitoring of ongoing discourse, interlocutors recognize as *marked usage* (i.e., departing from the established pattern). Together the cues constitute a metamessage (a message about the message) that channels the interlocutors' interpretations of what speech activity they consider themselves to be engaged in (chatting about the weather, telling a joke, negotiating a salary increase, etc.) and what their social relationships are in that activity (professional-client, teacher-student, etc.). It also helps them to predict what will come next, to fill in information not explicitly conveyed in the message, to infer the illocutionary force of what is uttered, and to establish the relationship between what is being uttered and the developing argument or theme. (See also Schiffrin, this volume, for a fuller discussion of context and how it is related in interactional sociolinguistics to two other concepts: contextual presupposition and situated inference.)

Another source of miscommunication is that, probably because Zulu is a tone language, ZE speakers exploit intonation in different ways than SAE speakers do. To illustrate, at one point in the interview, the professor asked the ZE student to reconsider his judgment about which of the questions he chose was more difficult:

Student: I think one and two are which was equally difficult.
Professor: *Equally* difficult
Student: Yah . . .
Professor: And . . .
Student: And not actually difficult but I think er not prepared . . .

Italic = accentuation (nucleus or accent placement)

In line 2 the professor places the accent – a rise-fall pitch movement – on *equally*. In terms of the norms of SAE, this serves as a signal that *equally* is the part of the message that the professor would like the student to build on. However, in his reply (line 5), the student addresses whether the questions were difficult rather than which of the two questions was the more difficult. This suggests that he does not perceive the accentuation on *equally* as salient.

A further source of miscommunication in intracultural as well as intercultural encounters was the mismatch of "readings" by the professor and some students of their relations, and how this mismatch affected their attempts to redress the face loss arising from poor performance in the examination. In arriving at this understanding, I found the account of face-saving and face-repairing or politeness behavior offered by Brown and Levinson (1987) particularly helpful. Building on the explanation provided by Goffman (1967), Brown and Levinson argue that, universally, people have the need, on the one hand, to have freedom of action (negative face needs) and, on the other hand, to be approved of by others (positive face needs). They explain that these needs are often difficult to reconcile since, for example, in attending to one's own negative face needs, as a professor does when she or he evaluates the performance of students, one may threaten the face of one's interlocutor, who may then feel the need to engage in face-repair work that, in turn, may threaten one's own face. Politeness strategies are the resources available to interlocutors for attempting to balance their own face needs against those of others. Brown and Levinson explain further that interlocutors' moment-to-moment choices of strategies from the range available are based on their intuitive calculation of the relative closeness or distance of their relations with their interlocutor(s), of the relative difference in their status, and of how much of an imposition what they are doing (evaluating, requesting, offering, complaining, apologizing) is in their culture.

When interactions involving students (one of whom was a ZE male, and the other an SAE male) who fared relatively poorly in the examination were compared, it was found that they both engaged in considerable face-repair work. However, they tended to use very different strategies to repair face. The ZE student tended to use deference politeness. For example, as the encounter became more stressful, he used the address term *sir* (line 3 in the next example), which contrasts with the absence of any address term earlier in the interaction and which represents an attempt to deal with the increasing stress by implying that he does not wish to challenge the professor:

Professor: You mean you . . . you didn't have the reading . . .
[Or you didn't know what the reading was . . .
Student: [*(starts to speak)* Yes sir

[ = overlapping speech

By contrast, the SAE student tended to use what Scollon and Scollon (1981) categorize as a form of solidarity politeness, namely, *bald-on-record*,[4] without redressive action. For example, he (see line 6 in the

4 Bald-on-record strategies are those used when performing face-threatening acts in direct, clear and unambiguous ways (in ways consistent with Gricean maxims) i.e., without attempting to minimize or off-set the face threat involved. An example would be a direct imperative such as: "Shut the door!"

next example) resisted the professor's attempts to get the floor, and put words in his mouth:

Student: Now I don't think I did this in this essay um answered that question entirely in that frame of reference.
Professor: Ya.
Student: I think that is what you're going to say.
Professor: Well, well, I'm I'm wanting to see.
Student: You're you're going to say I didn't actually um answer the essay in relation . . .

(See Chick (1985) for the full transcripts.)

The systematic nature of the choices made throughout these encounters suggests an orientation towards distinctive interactional styles. As Brown and Levinson (1987, pp. 243–255) explain, to the extent that particular types of social relationships predominate in a particular society, or culture, those who belong to it will typically use or prefer certain types of politeness strategies. Such consistent choices contribute to predominant, targeted interactional styles which give interactions in those societies or cultures a particular affective quality or ethos. I hypothesize that the predominant interactional styles in this setting for SAE speakers are reciprocal solidarity politeness, and for ZE speakers they are nonreciprocal solidarity "down" by the higher-status interlocutor and deference "up" by the interlocutor of lower status.

Significantly, the interactional consequences of the choices of strategies for repairing face by the SAE- and ZE-speaking students were different. In using bald-on-record solidarity strategies, the SAE student challenged the assumptions implicit in the professor's discourse that their relationship was a friendly one but not the professor's assumption that the context they were in was one in which status and distance are minimized. In other words, he did not challenge the professor's assumption that reciprocal solidarity styles are appropriate in this context. By contrast, in using nonreciprocal deference politeness "up," the ZE student more severely challenged the professor's assumptions about equitable relations with his students and was, accordingly, probably more negatively evaluated.

Turning to the consequences of such intercultural miscommunication, I argue that it has serious consequences for members of subordinate groups in South Africa, whose access to jobs, social welfare, educational opportunities, and so on, depends vitally on successful communication with power holders. I suggest that the widespread misevaluation of the abilities of members of subordinate groups that occurs in gatekeeping encounters contributes directly to discrimination and the reinforcement of the inequity of the socioeconomic and political system. I suggest, further, that repeated miscommunication generates and re-enforces negative cultural stereotypes that constitute further barriers to intercultural communication and contribute to the forces which maintain the social barriers and inequities that made it difficult for people to learn one another's conventions in the first place.

## Critique of sociolinguistic studies of intercultural communication

Before addressing the question of how the findings of sociolinguistic studies of intercultural miscommunication might be used to improve intercultural communication and overcome the negative social consequences outlined earlier, I must point out that there is some controversy about whether, on balance, such research contributes to positive social change or whether it re-enforces the status quo.

Fairclough, for example, comments on the "general insensitivity of sociolinguistics towards its own relationship to the sociolinguistic orders it seeks to describe" (1989, p. 8) and the danger that such description may serve to legitimize the facts and the social relations of power associated with them. What presumably makes this danger particularly real is that the "objective" stance taken by sociolinguists imparts authority to their observations. Singh, Lele, and Martohardjono (1988) note that nearly all sociolinguistic studies of intercultural communication focus on minority speakers being misunderstood by majority hearers, and they argue that "the fact that the construals of the dominated minority are almost entirely left out of their accounts suggests quite strongly that they are not only tolerant of the expectations of the powerful but are also willing to oblige them by justifying them with what they call linguistic evidence" (1988, p. 51). They are also critical of overly deterministic interpretations offered by sociolinguists and of the failure of sociolinguists to take economic and political factors sufficiently into account. While not denying that mismatches of sociolinguistic conventions can be sources of miscommunication, they point out that even when the differences are great, miscommunication can be repaired if there is sufficient payoff for the parties concerned. They see interactional sociolinguists, for example, as erring in not highlighting the fact that the institutional framework of gatekeeping encounters discourages dominant speakers from effecting repairs. They suggest that the "repairability threshold" of members of dominant groups who interact with culturally different others increases in proportion to the wealth and status of the culturally different other. McDermott and Gospodinoff (1981) point out, moreover, that, even when differences between the sociolinguistic conventions of groups are small, members of dominant and subordinate groups in societies in which social relations tend to be predetermined may do interactional work, not to overcome barriers but to turn cultural differences into cultural borders. The dominant group, instead of accommodating the conventions of the subordinate group, may become even more insistent that competency in terms of their own conventions is a prerequisite for elevation to positions of power and influence. Subordinate groups, recognizing that the prospects of profiting from accommodating the conventions of the dominant group are poor, may seek refuge in ethnic solidarity by, instead, emphasizing what is culturally distinctive about their communication conventions. (See Erickson, this volume, for further discussion of the issue of communication style as cultural boundary or border.)

These criticisms suggest that, if sociolinguists wish their studies of intercultural communication to be used for emancipatory rather than hegemonic purposes, they need to emphasize, more than they have tended to do in the past, the relationships between sociolinguistic conventions and the social order (especially social relations of power), and how each serves to maintain or change the other. This was the focus of the study of compliment-responding behavior outlined earlier. The principal finding was that the pattern of compliment responding by whites on the Natal campus resembles more closely that evident in Herbert's American work than that in his Witwatersrand work collected 10 years earlier, that is, that whites on the Natal campus overwhelmingly reject compliments given. While acknowledging the possibility that simply regional variation is at work here, I suggest that the difference in the pattern of responses on the Witwatersrand and Natal campuses reflects, instead, the great uncertainty about social relations which is a consequence of the rapid desegregation occurring in the South African university recently and the concern by whites to avoid the implication associated with acceptance, namely, that they are superior to their interlocutors. Drawing on insights provided by critical linguists (see, for example, Fairclough, 1989, 1992), I suggest, further, that changes in the pattern of choices of response types reflect the process or outcome of an ideological struggle between dominant and dominated types of discourse on these campuses. Fairclough (1989, p. 91) explains that in any institution there are a number of competing discourse types, each with its own distinctive discourse conventions (e.g., compliment response strategies), that reflect, amongst other things, different assumptions (ideologies) about the social relations of power. He explains, further, that a dominated discourse type may take on the status of "oppositional discourse" when, as part of an ideological struggle to have a particular discourse type and the social relations of power associated with it accepted as legitimate, it is consciously used as an alternative to the dominant type. These insights form part of the basis of the next section of this chapter.

## Towards more effective intercultural communication

Finally, we turn to how insights from studies of the sort described in this chapter can be used to improve the practice of intercultural communication. Although, as observed earlier, sociolinguists have been slow to address this question, they have provided some useful guidelines, which will be addressed first; then some observations will be added.

There is general consensus amongst sociolinguists who have concerned themselves with applications of their research that, although teachers and learners would benefit from having access to accurate information about the sociolinguistic conventions of different groups, and especially of dominant groups, what is required is not the straightforward teaching of sociolinguistic conventions as a body of knowledge. (Note, though, Cohen's reference, this volume, to studies by Olshtain & Cohen [1990] and Billmyer [1990] that suggest that points of speech act behavior can be taught.) Gumperz and Roberts (1980, p. 3) explain that:

> [T]he conventions of language use operate within such a great range of situations and have to take into account so many variables. There is no neat equation between type of interaction and the conventions which an individual might use. Every piece of good communication depends upon the response and feedback which participants elicit from each other in the course of the conversation itself and so every speaker has to develop his own strategies for interpreting and responding appropriately.

However, while ruling out the teaching of the sociolinguistic rules, they argue that these rules can be learnt. As an example of a process that will facilitate such learning, they suggest involving both learners and native speakers (particularly gatekeepers) in evaluative discussions of interethnic encounters in which they have participated, in order to raise their awareness of their own contributions to miscommunication. Along similar lines, Wolfson (1989, p. 31) argues that "the acquisition of sociolinguistic rules can be greatly facilitated by teachers who have the necessary information at their command and who have the sensitivity to use their knowledge in order to guide students and help them to interpret values and patterns which they would otherwise have difficulty in interpreting." She explains that she sees the goal of such teacher intervention not as imposing the value system or norms of behavior of dominant groups but as helping learners to avoid being unintentionally misunderstood by native speakers. Bardovi-Harlig, et al. (1991, p. 5) argue that teachers need to know about speech acts and their component parts in order to determine what is naturalistic input for learners "even though it would be impossible to impart this knowledge concerning each speech act explicitly." They also express the belief that if students are encouraged to think for themselves about culturally appropriate ways to compliment a friend or say good-bye to a teacher, they may awaken their own lay abilities for pragmatic analysis.

Awareness training is advocated also by Erickson (1979). He dismisses the direct teaching of culturally specific contextualization cues, arguing that such behavior changes are too mechanical and too categorical to be effective. He suggests that learners be encouraged, as they engage in discourse, to focus on the processes of interpretation rather than on the surface message form, although he acknowledges that it may be difficult to sustain this focus for any length of time. A more realistic goal, he suggests, is to develop the capacity for retrospective analysis of what happened when one recognizes that something went wrong, that is, to learn to substitute this scanning for what he terms the "knee-jerk reaction of conversational inference." More recently, Erickson (1985) develops the notion of retrospective scanning further, pointing out that this learning represents a refining of a capacity that learners possess as part of their total communicative competence. He suggests that the insight that interactional "trouble" develops interactionally rather than unilaterally is itself liberating and allows learners to avoid unhelpful repair strategies based on blaming the other participant or oneself. He suggests, further, that repair strategies that seem to work are direct rather than indirect ones, for example, "I'm sorry, but I'm not sure that you understand the point I'm trying to make." (See Erickson, this volume.)

To move beyond the suggestions provided by sociolinguists and to profit from the critique of sociolinguistic studies referred to earlier, I believe that it is necessary to foster not merely awareness but also critical awareness (see Fairclough, 1992). It is important, moreover, not to present sociolinguistic conventions as neutral practices. Learners need to be aware that such conventions reflect assumptions about social relations and values, and that one of the ways in which groups establish and maintain their dominance is through getting their sociolinguistic conventions (and so, too, the social relations and values associated with them) accepted as "appropriate" in particular domains. In other words, learners require information not only about sociolinguistic variation but also about what is at stake. They need to know that, although they may be able to avoid being misevaluated by gatekeepers by making accommodations to their sociolinguistic norms, there is a cost. Not only is there the risk that these conventions will assign to them social identities with which they are uncomfortable, but their compliance will further legitimize the conventions. Only when they are aware of the risks will they be equipped to choose, in the case of each encounter, between the short-term gains of compliance and the possible long-term gains from using "oppositional discourse."

It follows from what has been said that critical awareness should extend also to helping learners to distinguish between interactional trouble arising from unconscious sociolinguistic transfer and that arising from the conscious employment of oppositional discourse. It should also extend to helping learners distinguish between successful intercultural communication arising from considerable overlap in the conventions of the interlocutors and that arising from the cultural sensitivity of the interlocutors and their willingness to effect repairs.

## Suggestions for further reading

Carbaugh, D. (Ed.). (1990). *Cultural communication and intercultural contact.* Hillsdale, NJ: Erlbaum.

This book provides a fairly comprehensive account of the contribution of the ethnography of communication to the understanding of intercultural communication. It includes a selection of ethnographic studies that focus, in turn, on how cultural communication creates and affirms a shared cultural identity, on the phenomenon of asynchrony in intercultural communication, and on cultural relativity in specific communication phenomena. Drawing on these studies, the editor develops an intercultural communication model as a first step in the development of a theory of intercultural communication.

Kramsch, C. (1993). *Context and culture in language teaching.* Oxford, Oxford University Press.

The major assumption of this book is that foreign language teaching is not the teaching of four skills with the teaching of culture tacked on. Rather, it assumes that cultural context is at the core of foreign language teaching. The challenge for foreign language teachers is to teach language as context. In helping teachers meet this challenge, the text deals with speech and social interaction, stories and discourses, literary texts, and authentic texts.

Roberts, C., Davies, E., & Jupp, T. (1992). *Language and discrimination.* London and New York: Longman.

This book, which is based on work carried out by the Industrial Language Training Service (ILTS) in multiethnic workplaces in Britain, provides an illuminating account of how, in the context of intercultural encounters in the workplace, discrimination and disadvantage in employment are generated and maintained. It provides an account of the theories of interaction that informed the ethnographic and linguistic analyses of workplace settings carried out under the auspices of the ILTS. Possibly its most valuable contribution is the account it provides of how these analyses informed the design of language training for ethnic minority workers and awareness training for gatekeepers. This should be a useful resource to teachers and writers of educational materials looking for ways to help learners improve the quality of their intercultural communication.

## References


Bardovi-Harlig, K., Hartford, B., Mahan-Taylor, R., Morgan, M., & Reynolds, D. (1991). Developing pragmatic awareness: Closing the conversation. *ELT Journal, 45*(1), 4–15.

Blimes, J. (1988). The concept of preference in conversational analysis. *Language in Society, 17,* 161–181.

Brown, P., & Levinson, S. (1987). *Politeness: Some universals in language usage* (rev. ed.). (*Studies in interactional sociolinguistics,* Vol. 4). Cambridge: Cambridge University Press.

Carbaugh, D. (Ed.). (1990). *Cultural communication and intercultural contact.* Hillsdale, NJ: Erlbaum.

Chick, J. K. (1985). The interactional accomplishment of discrimination in South Africa. *Language in Society, 14*(3), 299–326.

Chick, J. K. (1991). An ethnography of a desegregating institution: Research in progress. *South African Journal of Linguistics, 9*(4), 110–115.

Erickson, F. (1979). Talking down: Some cultural sources of miscommunication in interracial interviews. In A. Wolfgang (Ed.), *Non-verbal behavior* (pp. 99–126). New York: Academic Press.

Erickson, F. (1985). Listening and speaking. In D. Tannen & J. Alatis (Eds.), *Languages and linguistics: The interdependence of theory, data and application.* Georgetown University Roundtable on Languages and Linguistics (pp. 294–319). Washington, DC: Georgetown University Press.

Erickson, F., & Shultz, J. (1982). *The counselor as gatekeeper.* New York: Academic Press.

Fairclough, N. (1989). *Language and power.* London and New York: Longman.

Fairclough, N. (Ed.). (1992). *Critical language awareness.* London and New York: Longmans.

Goffman, E. (1967). *Interaction ritual: Essays on face to face behavior.* Garden City, NY: Doubleday.

Gumperz, J. (1982a). *Discourse strategies.* Cambridge: Cambridge University Press.

Gumperz, J. (1982b). *Language and social identity.* Cambridge: Cambridge University Press.

Gumperz, J., & Roberts, C. (1980). *Developing awareness skills for interethnic communication.* Occasional papers no. 12. Singapore: Seamo Regional Language Centre.

Herbert, R. K. (1985). Say 'thank you' – or something. *American Speech., 61*(1), 76–88.

Herbert, R. K. (1989). The ethnography of English compliments and compliment responses: A contrastive sketch. In W. Olesky (Ed.), *Contrastive pragmatics.* Amsterdam and Philadelphia: John Benjamins.

Herbert, R. K. (1990). Sex based differences in complimenting behavior. *Language in Society, 19,* 201–224.

Herbert, R. K., & Straight, H. S. (1989). Compliment-rejection versus compliment-avoidance: Listener-based versus speaker-based pragmatic strategies. *Language and Communication, 9,* 35–47.

Hornberger, N. (1993). Review of *Cultural communication and intercultural contact* (D. Carbaugh, Ed.). *Language in Society, 22,* 300–304.

McDermott, R. P., & Gospodinoff, K. (1981). Social contexts for ethnic borders and school failure. In H. T. Trueba, G. Guthrie, & K. H. Au (Eds.), *Culture and the bilingual classroom: Studies in classroom ethnography* (pp. 212–230). Rowley, MA: Newbury House.

Pomerantz, A. (1978). Compliment responses: Notes on the co-operation of multiple constaints. In J. Schenken (Ed.), *Studies in the organization of conversational interaction* (pp. 79–109). Cambridge: Cambridge University Press.

Schegloff, E. A. (1968). Sequencing in conversational openings. *American Anthropologist, 7,* 1075–1095.

Scollon, R, & Scollon, S. (1981). *Narrative, literacy and face in interethnic communication.* Norwood, NJ: Ablex.

Singh, R., Lele, J., & Martohardjono, G. (1988). Communication in a multilingual society: Some missed opportunities. *Language in Society, 17,* 43–79.

Tannen, D. (1984). *Conversational style: Analysing talk amongst friends.* Norwood, NJ: Ablex.

Wolfson, N. (1983). An empirically based analysis of complimenting in American English. In N. Wolfson & E. Judd (Eds.), *Sociolinguistics and language acquisition* (pp. 82–95). Rowley, MA: Newbury House.

Wolfson, N. (1989). *Perspectives: sociolinguistics and TESOL.* New York: Newbury House.

Wolfson, N. (1992). Intercultural communication and the analysis of conversation. In R. K. Herbert (Ed.), *Language and society in Africa* (pp. 197–214). Johannesburg: University of the Witwatersrand Press.

# PART IV: LANGUAGE AND CULTURE

The foregoing three chapters emphasize the emergent and socially and culturally situated nature of interaction and the role that specific features of communication play therein. Throughout all three chapters, the theme of the individual as a communicative actor drawing on a range of linguistic resources in specific social situations stands out. We will turn now to a consideration of larger units of communicative interaction and how participants' social and cultural identities are played out there.

Muriel Saville-Troike, in "The Ethnography of Communication," opens this part with an overview of the basic concepts, methods, and language teaching applications of the ethnography of communication, a research approach which was inaugurated in 1962 by Dell Hymes and which undergirds all the approaches and areas of study covered in Parts 3 and 4 of this volume. Saville-Troike begins by identifying the principal concerns of this approach as being the relationship of language form and use to patterns and functions of communication, to world view and social organization, and to linguistic and social universals and inequalities. She goes on to review such basic sociolinguistic concepts as speech community, communicative repertoire, and communicative competence as they evolved and came to be defined in the ethnography of communication, as well as the characteristic methods and the units of analysis of ethnographic research into communication – communicative (or speech) situation, communicative (or speech) event, and communicative (or speech) act. She concludes with a discussion of the ways in which analysis of communicative events might be used in the preparation of instructional activities for language classes, in determining what aspects of the language need to be taught or learned, in the assessment of communicative skills, in encouraging students to engage in their own reflection and inquiry on language use, and in cultivating a difference rather than a deficit view toward student performance.

In the following chapter, "Speech Acts," Andrew Cohen presents a research approach which takes its cue from the ethnography of communication focusing on the identification and cross-cultural comparison of speech acts. Building on the work of philosophers Austin and Searle, who define the *speech act* as a functional unit in communication, speech act research seeks to define the preconditions and interactional goals of particular speech acts, to identify the performative and semantic prerequisites for the realization of those speech acts, and to explore situational and cross-cultural variation in performance of them. Cohen reviews methods used to investigate the production and reception of specific speech acts – observation of naturally occurring data, role plays, discourse completion tasks, verbal report interviews, and questionnaires. He then reviews the findings of research on apologies, refusals, rejections, compliments, complaints, requests, and other speech acts. Cohen closes with words of both encouragement and caution for language teachers: To the degree that speech acts represent routinized and predictable language behavior, he believes that they can be taught, but to the degree that the speaker's choice of speech act strategy varies according to sociocultural context, the question arises as to whether speech acts can really be taught.

The next chapter, "Literacy and Literacies," by Sandra McKay, continues the theme of language form and use – in this case, the forms and uses of literacy – as being integrally tied to culture and social context. The opening section emphasizes the need to approach literacy as both individual skill and social practice and to study literacy using a variety of research methods, including survey, ethnographic research, and text analysis. Drawing on a wide array of studies in language minority communities and language learning classrooms in the United States for illustration, McKay then goes on to examine four aspects of literacy as they relate to sociocultural context: literacy as collaborative practice, literacy as a reflection of community values and traditions about how to approach texts, literacy as a reflection of cultural values and traditions about text and topic development, and literacy as a reflection of social relationships as well as a vehicle for changing the status quo. She concludes by suggesting that recognizing that literacy is a social practice as well as an individual endeavor means that we as language teachers need to foster collaborative literacy practices, encourage students to read texts critically, value alternative literacy traditions, and be aware and wary of the gatekeeping function of Western academic literacy traditions.

# 11 *The ethnography of communication*

Muriel Saville-Troike

Dell Hymes's call for an ethnography of speaking (1962; later to become more broadly the ethnography of communication) resulted in the advent of a distinctive new subdiscipline, derived from anthropology and linguistics, which has revolutionized the study of the interpenetration of language and culture. This new field focuses on the patterning of communicative behavior as it constitutes one of the systems of culture, as it functions within the holistic context of culture, and as it relates to patterns in other cultural systems. A primary aim of the ethnographic approach to the study of communicative activity is to provide a framework for the collection and analysis of descriptive data about the ways in which social meaning is conveyed, constructed, and negotiated. Its goals are, at least in the first instance, descriptive, guided by the conviction that information about diverse "ways of speaking" in different human societies is a legitimate contribution to knowledge in its own right. Nevertheless, the potential significance of the ethnography of communication goes far beyond a mere cataloging of facts about communicative behavior. Ultimately, its approach and findings are essential for the formulation of a truly adequate universal theory of language and human behavior.

As a blend of scientific and humanistic approaches, the ethnography of communication has two foci: particularistic and generalizing. On the one hand, it is directed at the description and understanding of communicative behavior in specific cultural settings, but it is also directed toward the formulation of concepts and theories upon which to build a general theory of language development and use.

The basic approach taken in the ethnography of communication does not involve a list of descriptive details so much as questions to be asked and means for finding out answers. Its subject matter is best illustrated by one of its most general questions: What does a speaker need to know in order to communicate appropriately and to make sense of communicative situations within a particular speech community, and how does he or she learn this? The ethnography of communication thus seeks to account not merely for what can be said but for when, where, by whom, to whom, in what manner, and in what particular circumstances, and, perhaps more important for language educational professionals, it seeks to account for the processes of acquiring such knowledge.

The potential relevance of this approach to language and teaching includes both its particular and its generalizing aspects. Particular findings concerning the nature of a variety of speech events which occur within target speech communities can guide curricular content for language programs, provide analytic bases for the study of cross-cultural communication and comparative rhetoric, and validate norms and priorities for assessment. General findings concerning the development of communicative competence, the relationship of language learning to enculturation or acculturation, and the social functions of communicative processes can contribute in important ways to the development of language acquisition theory and teaching practices. Further, the methodology which is characteristic of the ethnography of communication is itself applicable to teaching students both their own language and others and to the education of teachers.

Several key concepts will be discussed in this chapter, along with issues which arise in extending the ethnography of communication from first to second and foreign language contexts and in the procedures for data collection and analysis which are characteristic of the approach. The discussion of applications to language learning and teaching will be idealistic in some respects; this stance seems to be appropriate for the exploration of the potential intersection of relatively new and dynamic fields, but limitations on implementation and questions of feasibility will also be addressed.

## Basic terms, concepts, and issues

### *Patterns and functions of communication*

The principal concerns in the ethnography of communication include the relationship of language form and use to patterns and functions of communication, to world view and social organization, as well as to linguistic and social universals and inequalities. The concern for pattern has long been basic in anthropology (e.g., Benedict, 1934), with interpretations of underlying meaning dependent on the discovery and description of normative structure or design. More recent emphasis on the role of the process of interaction in generating behavioral patterns (e.g., Barth, 1966) extends this concern to explanation as well as description. Regularity in observed behavior among members of a group (performance) is recognized as an external manifestation of a deeper cognitive level of knowledge (competence). The task of ethnography in this framework is seen as the discovery and explication of the shared knowledge base for contextually appropriate behavior in a community or group, in other words, what the individual needs to know about language use to be a functional member of the community.

The concern for pattern has also been basic for linguistics in that it has long been recognized that much of linguistic behavior is rule governed; that is, it follows regular patterns and constraints which can be formulated descriptively as rules (see Dittmar, 1983). One of the most important contributions of sociolinguistics, in fact, has been the demonstration that what earlier linguists had considered irregularity or "free variation" in linguistic performance can be seen to follow regular and predictable patterns. Although other sociolinguists have focused on variability in pronunciation and grammatical form, ethnographers of communication are concerned with how communicative situations and events are organized and with how patterns in communication interrelate in a systematic way with – and derive meaning from – other aspects of culture.

A central goal is thus discovering and formulating rules for appropriate language use in specific contexts. The term *rule* is used here with multiple meanings which correspond to subcategories of descriptive and prescriptive statements (see Shimanoff, 1980, for a critical survey). *Descriptive rules* are statements of recurring regularity in actual or real performance or of typical behaviors within a particular speech community and in a specified context. *Prescriptive rules* are metacognitive statements of how people "should" act. These rules are tied to the shared values of the speech community and typically reflect an ideal cultural perception. They are often discoverable in reactions to the violation of the ideal by others and in statements that contrary behavior is "wrong," "impolite," or "odd" in some respect.

*Expectations* constitute a standard shared by members of a speech community. They are likely to be related to both descriptive and prescriptive rules, but neither statistical frequency nor positive or negative valuation is a necessary criterion. This meaning of expectations is closest to the definition of rules used by Cushman and Whiting (1972) – "sets of common expectations about the appropriate responses to particular symbols in particular contexts" (p. 225).

In communicative interactions, some expectations are so strong (some patterns so regular, so predictable) that a very low information load is carried even by a relatively long utterance or interchange, even though the social meaning involved can be significant. For instance, one greeting sequence in English, "How are you?" followed by the expected response "Fine, how are you?" has little if any reference to factual conditions. However, a response of silence, or a long tale of woe about one's health, would be strongly marked communicative behavior and would carry a very high potential load of social meaning. Many nonnative English speakers conclude from the fact that when we ask "How are you?" we do not really want to know, that native speakers of this language are cold and uncaring or hypocritical, or both. For ethnographers it is essential to differentiate the referential and social components of language use; the social component receives the most emphasis. Both language learners and language and educational professionals also need to understand the role of predictability and expectation (i.e., social and linguistic convention) in communication, as well as to be able to distinguish conventional meaning from referential meaning (i.e., meaning that refers to things or actions) in specific contexts.

Research on rules for language use within sociology and sociolinguistics, known as *ethnomethodology,* has generally focused on relatively small units of communication (see Erickson, this volume). Important examples include sequencing in conversational openings (Schegloff, 1968), telephone conversations (Goddard, 1977), and service encounters (Merritt, 1976) or rules for the use of terms of address as they relate to cultural context or sociopolitical sentiments (Bates & Benigni, 1975; Brown & Gilman, 1960; Fang & Heng, 1983; Paulston, 1976). Strategies for conversational interaction have also been the foci of ethnomethodological research; interesting contracts have been found in such phenomena as turn taking, including timing factors (e.g., Crown & Feldstein, 1985), and conventions for talking one at a time (e.g., Sacks, Schegloff, & Jefferson, 1974) versus contrapuntal conversation (Reisman, 1974).

In contrast to the ethnomethodological approach, an ethnography of communication approach typically, though not exclusively, looks for strategies and conventions governing larger units of communication and involves more holistic interpretation. An excellent example can be found in the work of Gumperz in the analysis of cross-cultural conversational events. In analyzing one interview session between a British counselor and a Pakistani mathmematics teacher, for instance, Gumperz (1979) illustrates how the different sociocultural conventions for appropriate language use each participant brings to the encounter yield different interpretive frames. The types of conventions highlighted in this study include those in what might be called the *grammar of expectations* and which Gumperz himself (e.g., 1977) calls the process of *conversational inferencing.* The analytic procedure developed by Gumperz makes an important contribution to the dynamic description of interaction and is of particular importance in language learning and teaching in its applicability to the investigation and explanation of cross-cultural miscommunication (see Schiffrin, this volume).

The ethnography of communication is concerned with communicative conventions which operate at a societal level, for example, with regular patterns and constraints that occur in relation to communicative functions, categories of talk, and attitudes about languages and their speakers and with the use of these rules to affect social and cultural outcomes. Good examples of analysis at this level in the educational domain are provided by Hornberger (1987) and Guthrie (1985), who illustrate how larger societal factors have an impact on language selection and program outcomes in bilingual projects (Quechua-Spanish and Chinese-English, respectively). Communication may also pattern according to particular role, status, and group identity within a society, educational level, rural or urban residence, geographic region, and other features of social organization. Anyon (1981), for instance, documents differences in classroom interaction patterns when schools are situated in upper- versus lower-class neighborhoods, as does Leacock (1969) for urban versus suburban contexts.

Communicative functions also operate at different levels. Areas of sociolinguistics which are most concerned with interactional analysis generally focus on the functions of smaller units of language, such as single utterances or brief exchanges, including requests and greetings (see Cohen, this volume). The ethnography of communication is most concerned with the functions of language at a societal level, such as its function in creating or reinforcing boundaries which unify members of one speech community while excluding outsiders from intragroup communication. The language of a community may be withheld from others, for instance, as in the case of the refusal of early Spanish settlers in Mexico to teach the Castilian language to the indigenous population (Heath, 1972); or members of a community may discourage second language learners by holding the attitude that their language is too difficult, or is inappropriate, for others to use.

Even within a society where speakers share linguistic rules of phonology, grammar, and vocabulary, strategies of language use may establish or maintain differential power relationships between members of different socioeconomic or occupational strata (see Freeman & McElhinny, this volume; Chick, this volume). Strategies of such power relationships are the focus of Erickson and Shultz's study (1982) "The Counselor as Gatekeeper," for instance. The social implications in an educational domain are especially significant because gatekeeping encounters between students and school officials often determine access to career paths, and thus to future power. Gatekeeping is directly related to the process of segregating students for socialization and thus limiting transmission of knowledge in some areas to a chosen few. Segregated socialization may also involve exclusive access to learning the language of transmission so that others cannot understand the content, as described by Philips (1982) for the training of lawyers.

Different languages and language varieties often also serve a social identification function within a society by providing linguistic indicators which can be used to reinforce social stratification. Negative decisions on hiring based on applicants' use of nonstandard pronunciation or verb forms would be an example. Among nonnative varieties of a language, there are often social distinctions depending on which foreign accent is involved. In the United States, for instance, English spoken with a French or German accent may be viewed as prestigious, whereas a Spanish accent may be considered a handicap to educational and economic success. The functions which language differences in a society are assigned may thus include systematic discrimination or empowerment, as well as the maintenance and manipulation of individual social relationships and networks; that is, they are various means of effecting social control. The use of language to create and maintain power is part of the concern of the ethnography of communication with linguistic and social inequalities (Hymes, 1992) and its application to critical discourse analysis (e.g., see Van Dijk, 1993; Chick, this volume).

The functions of language (rather than the forms) generally provide the primary dimension for characterizing and organizing communicative processes and products in a society from an ethnography of communication perspective; without understanding why a language is being used as it is, and the consequences of such use, one cannot understand the meaning of its use in the context of social interaction. To claim primacy of function over form in analysis is not to deny or neglect the formal structures of language; rather, it is to require that words and sentences and even longer strings of discourse not be dealt with as autonomous units but as they are situated in communicative settings and patterns and as they function in society.

## *Speech community*

The immediate universe for the ethnography of communication is traditionally the speech community and the way communication is patterned and organized within that unit. Being a member of a speech community has been defined as sharing the same language (Lyons, 1970), sharing rules of speaking and interpretation of speech performance (Hymes, 1972), and sharing sociocultural understandings and presuppositions with regard to speech (Sherzer, 1975). The focus is on shared rules for contextually appropriate use and interpretation of language (indeed, the term *community* is derived from Latin *communitae,* "held in common"). As will be seen, the degree to which these criteria must necessarily apply to nonnative as well as to native community membership may be somewhat problematic.

Depending on the questions and issues to be addressed and the level of abstraction that is sought, virtually any community in a complex society might be viewed as part of a larger one or, conversely, subdivided into smaller groups. Although small-scale research employing the ethnography of communication model has often focused on a single school, a neighborhood, a factory, or a limited segment of a population, an integrated ethnographic approach would require relating such subgroups to the social and cultural whole, with its full complement of roles and structural units. Small-scale studies (dubbed *microethnography*) are common in research on classroom communication, but from an ethnography of communication perspective, these studies run the risk of providing detail of interactional analysis at the expense of contextual or ecological validity (see Schiffrin, this volume).

There is no expectation that a community will be linguistically homogeneous; as a collectivity, it will include a *communicative repertoire,* or range of languages, language varieties, and registers, that will pattern in relation to the salient social and cultural dimensions of communication. Any one speaker also has a variety of codes, styles, and registers from which to choose. The term *codes* is used here to mean different languages or significantly different varieties of a single language; *styles,* to mean varieties associated with such social and cultural dimensions as age, sex, social class, and relationship between speakers; and *registers,* to mean varieties of language which are more closely associated with the setting or scene in which they are used than they are with the people who are using them. It is very unlikely in a complex community that any single individual can produce the full range of the community's repertoire. Different subgroups within the community may understand and use different subsets of its available codes. Speakers' communicative competence includes knowing the alternatives and the rules for appropriate choice from among the alternatives or for switching between them. Defining the system for such decision making is part of the task of describing communication within any group, and of explaining communication more generally.

Individuals may belong to several speech communities (which may be discrete or overlapping), just as they may participate in a variety of social settings. Which one or ones individuals orient themselves to at any given moment – which set of social and communicative rules they use – is part of the strategy of communication. To understand this phenomenon, one must recognize that each member of a community has a repertoire of social identities and that each identity in a given context is associated with a number of appropriate verbal and nonverbal forms of expression. Although an individual's repertoire of social identities may be within the bounds of a single complex speech community, for bilingual-bicultural individuals, membership in unrelated speech communities is common. Examples include second-generation immigrant children of Greek families who can function appropriately and comfortably both with peers in Chicago, Illinois, and with grandparents and cousins when they visit Athens, and the Navajo leader who is an effective communicator both in the context of a tribal council meeting in Window Rock, Arizona, and in a congressional hearing in Washington, D.C. Such individuals change not only language codes but rules for speaking, nonverbal behaviors, and other strategies for interaction, as well as their social roles and identities.

Extending the identification of speech community from first to second language situations raises complex issues, and these issues are relevant to considering the learning and teaching processes which are involved. Thus far the term *language learning* has been used in the broadest possible sense, but it is important at this point to make a distinction between learning a standard language (for speakers of nonstandard varieties of their first language) and learning a foreign language, second language, or auxiliary language (for native speakers of other languages) – in relation to opportunities and motivation for acquisition, as well as in relation to speech community membership.

For speakers of nonstandard varieties of their first (native) language, learning the standard language typically involves adding a schooled variety to their communicative repertoire for use in social contexts where that variety is more appropriate. This learning process differs significantly from foreign or second language learning since nonstandard speakers normally already have receptive competence in a much wider range of varieties and registers than they actively produce. (This differential distribution of receptive and productive competence is a general principle which is true of standard speakers as well.) Nonstandard and standard varieties have in common the vast majority of the lexical and grammatical structures of a language, and speakers are normally exposed to many varieties which differ from their own through widespread media contact, even when there are not opportunities for personal interactional experiences. Further, even though nonstandard and standard varieties of a language typically differ somewhat in sociolinguistic rules for language performance, speakers of different varieties of a language may have in common many attitudes and values concerning language use, as well as much of the social knowledge which is required for its interpretation (see Labov, 1965). Although speakers of nonstandard and standard varieties of a language may be defined as members of different subgroups within the community according to linguistic as well as social criteria, in important respects they may be defined as part of the same speech community when it is considered as a complex whole.

Students learning a foreign language within the context of their native culture generally have little opportunity even to interact with members of the speech community that speaks the foreign language natively, and they have little opportunity (or need) to become part of it. They may learn about different norms of interaction, different values and beliefs related to ways of speaking, but their learning remains largely an academic exercise.

Students learning a second language within the context of the speech community whose members speak it natively will not be acquiring it automatically as part of *enculturation,* or first culture learning, but of *acculturation,* or second culture learning and adaptation. Except for those who begin learning as children, few of these second language learners are likely to become full-fledged members of the second language speech community, at least if all of the shared language use and interpretation criteria determining speech community membership are applied. In this second language context, it is useful to distinguish between participating in a speech community and being a member of it; speaking the same language is sufficient for some degree of participation but perhaps not for full membership. Immigrants often experience ambivalent feelings about their own group membership during the process of acculturation; such feelings may result in the rejection of one group or the other, dual community membership (perhaps switching between the two according to setting or domain; see Fishman, 1972), or some degree of synthesis of the two. The resolution of such ambivalence must always be seen as a dynamic state, influenced by a host of social factors. For instance, degree of identification and participation in the second language speech community is likely to vary tremendously depending on the age of entry, the attitudes and expectations of extant community members toward assimilation, and educational and employment opportunities or limitations; in other words, functioning effectively within a speech community does not depend merely on language.

Other students learn a language in a context in which it will function as an auxiliary language for political or technological purposes. Examples can be found in India and Africa, for instance, where English or French is required as an official language of government or where access to current technological development and interaction with peers in other countries requires knowledge of a common linguistic code. No membership or even participation in native British, American, or French speech communities is required to use English or French for indigenous Indian and African sociocultural purposes, and very little participation in British, American, or French speech communities is required for technological communication (see Kachru and Nelson, this volume). Further, the role of English, French, and German as international languages means that they are often used for communication in situations where none of the participants are native speakers. This fact, too, adds complexity to the construct of speech community and has major import for the content and processes of language learning and teaching.

## *Language and culture*

The intrinsic relationship of language and culture is widely recognized, and the ways in which the patterning of communicative behavior and that of other cultural systems interrelate are of interest both to the development of general theories of communication and to the description and analysis of communication within specific speech communities. Although there is some controversy regarding the extent to which language shapes and controls the thinking of its speakers or merely reflects their world view, there is little doubt that there is a correlation between at least the vocabulary of a language and the beliefs, values, and needs present in the culture of its native speakers (see Whorf, 1940; Witherspoon, 1977; overviews in Hill, 1988; Hill & Mannheim, 1992).

The vocabulary of a language provides an interesting reflection of the culture of the people who speak it, since it is a catalog of things of import to a society, an index of the way speakers categorize experience, and often a record of past contacts and cultural borrowings. Except in scientific and technological domains, many words do not mean the same thing as their translation equivalents in other languages. Students of English may find color terms included in their elementary-level lessons and quickly memorize (blue, yellow, red, and so on), but apply them to slightly different segments of the color spectrum than do native speakers. Further, they are unlikely to learn what psychoaesthetic values Anglo-American (-Canadian, -Australian, etc.) culture attributes to colors (yellow is cheerful, black is depressing, white represents purity).

A great deal of cross-cultural misunderstanding occurs when the meanings of words being used by people who are speaking the same language are interpreted in radically different ways. Some may seem humorous, as when a Turkish visitor to the United States refused to consume a hot dog because he inferred that it was made of dog meat, which it was against his religious beliefs to eat, or when students from the Dominican Republic precipitated an argument on a Texas college campus by referring to the Texas students as Yankees. Some misunderstandings are much more serious, as when Navajo parents gave up their children for adoption, not realizing that this meant that the children would not return to their families at the end of the school year.

The grammar of a language may reveal the way time and space are segmented and organized, convey beliefs about animacy and the relative power of beings, and imply a great deal of other information by conventional presupposition. Classical Greek and some varieties of Quechua treat the future tense as referring to events behind the speaker and the past tense as referring to events that are ahead, for instance, the reverse of the way they are thought of in English. According to Nida (1975), Quechua speakers point out that we can see the past, since it has happened, but not the future. Therefore, the past must be in front of our eyes, whereas the future that we cannot see must be behind us. To give another example related to grammar, speakers of a variety of Asian languages, despite their unrelatedness, share an interpretation of the passive formation in sentences which could cause serious misunderstanding in English. The passive is used in English for a number of purposes, including emphasizing the object, de-emphasizing the agent, focusing on the completed state of the action, or merely stylistic variation. For example:

John baked that cake.
That cake was baked by John.

To speakers of many Asian languages, however, the two sentences have different meanings, since the subject of a passive sentence is understood to be the "victim" of the action. Thus, the first sentence would be merely a statement of fact, whereas the second would imply that the agent did a bad job. Even fluent English speakers from Chinese and Japanese backgrounds may continue to make this interpretation.

The potential for interaction among language, culture, and cognitive patterning is also realized in conventional discourse organization (i.e., patterning beyond the domain of a single sentence). In Quechua, for instance, "Semantic parallelism [used in the conventional organization of verbal lore] constrains the variability of word meanings by ensuring that they are learned relationally, rather than individually" (Hill & Mannheim, 1992, p. 399, citing research reported in Mannheim, 1986; see also Sherzer, 1987). Comparative study of the discourse organization of individuals from different language backgrounds who are retelling the same story illustrates how cultural differences in experiences and values may be reflected in such patterned elements as sequences of events, forwarding or background of information, and narrative perspective (see, e.g., Chafe, 1980).

It can thus be seen that the meaning of lexical, grammatical, or discourse structures is largely arbitrary and depends upon the agreement of a group of speakers (the speech community) as to their symbolic value. Nonnative speakers of a language may become quite skilled in the use of verbal forms without sharing all the cultural aspects of meaning those forms convey to native speakers. The extent to which they come to share cultural meaning with native speakers depends in large measure on the social contexts of their language acquisition and on the opportunity and motivation for language use. Learners in a second language context (i.e., a situation which includes extensive interaction with members of the speech community for whom the target language is native) are likely to have the opportunity and need to learn much of the cultural meaning that the language forms convey in that community. Learners in a foreign language classroom will have much more limited opportunity to develop shared cultural meanings with native speakers and are also likely to have much more limited need for them. Part of the potential application of the ethnography of communication to language teaching comes in understanding the nature and content of the language-culture relationship in both the specific contexts of communication in which students are likely to want or need to participate and their contexts of learning – and in determining what aspects of culture need to be, can be, and should be taught.

In the discussion of the function of language learning and use in different types of speech communities, reference was made to auxiliary language contexts, in contrast to the second versus foreign contexts just mentioned. Auxiliary languages best illustrate the arbitrary relationship of language and culture because they are generally instances of a colonial language being developed and used creatively in the enactment of different cultural values and beliefs (e.g., see Kachru's and Nelson's discussion of world Englishes, this volume). The use of English, French, or other languages for the indigenous purposes of former colonies is, of course, the legacy of empire building, but these languages have ceased to serve those original functions and have been adapted to the postcolonial needs of groups that have adopted them. In such contexts, it should be recognized that there is no necessary reason why the structures and vocabulary of one language cannot be used by diverse speech communities to express the different cultures of those communities, and in ways in keeping with their own rules of appropriate interaction. When a language is being learned for auxiliary functions in another speech community, as a *lingua franca* for international communication, or merely for access to information in a technological domain (i.e., as a library language), the culture of its native speech community is largely irrelevant and is likely to be unwanted as well. Failure to recognize this fact can foster cultural imperialism and mask important issues of ethnic identity.

## *Communicative competence*

Several references have been made to a central construct within the ethnography of communication: that is the notion of *communicative competence,* introduced by Hymes (1966), which may be broadly defined as what a speaker needs to know to communicate appropriately within a particular speech community. A critical observation by Hymes was that speakers who could produce any and all of the grammatical sentences of a language (per Chomsky's 1965 definition of linguistic competence) would be institutionalized if they indiscriminately went about trying to do so without consideration of the appropriate contexts of use. Communicative competence involves knowing not only the language code but also what to say to whom, and how to say it appropriately in any given situation. Further, it involves the social and cultural knowledge speakers are presumed to have which enables them to use and interpret linguistic forms. Hymes (1974, 1987) augmented Chomsky's notion of *linguistic competence* (knowledge of systematic potential, or whether or not an utterance is a possible grammatical structure in a language) with knowledge of appropriateness (whether and to what extent something is suitable), occurrence (whether and to what extent something is done), and feasibility (whether and to what extent something is possible under particular circumstances). Communicative competence extends to both knowledge and expectation of who may or may not speak in certain settings, when to speak and when to remain silent, whom one may speak to, how one may talk to persons of different statuses and roles, what nonverbal behaviors are appropriate in various contexts, what the routines for turn taking are in conversation, how to ask for and give information, how to request, how to offer or decline assistance or cooperation, how to give commands, how to enforce discipline, and the like – in short, everything involving the use of language and other communicative dimensions in particular social settings.

The concept of communicative competence has important implications for selection and sequencing in language teaching curricula, but there are significant limitations on the extent to which the construct can (or should) transfer from first to second or foreign language contexts, particularly because of the different relationships that hold between first and second or foreign languages and culture. Within the definition of communicative competence, for instance, the content of what a speaker needs to know depends on the social context in which he or she is or will be using the language and the purposes he or she will have for doing so. From this perspective, native language norms in many cases constitute an inappropriate target for instruction, even for learners of a second language who will function within the native language speech community. For what may constitute more reasonable targets of instruction, the next sections will focus in turn on linguistic, interactional, and cultural components of communicative competence.

## LINGUISTIC KNOWLEDGE

Traditional linguistic description generally targets the phonology, grammar, and lexicon of a language, but these elements constitute only a part of the elements in a code used for communication. Paralinguistic and nonverbal phenomena which have conventional meaning in each speech community should also be included, as should knowledge of the full range of variants in all elements of the linguistic code which function to transmit social, as well as referential, information. The ability to discriminate between variants which carry social meaning by serving as markers of social categories and those which are socially insignificant and the knowledge of what the social meaning of a variant is in a particular situation are components of communicative competence.

Recognizing the patterning and significance of variation in language is of central concern to sociolinguists, since it plays such a large part in conveying social, as distinguished from referential, meaning. Paulston (1974) was among the first to call for the extension of this distinction to language instruction, saying that even so-called communicative approaches to teaching were largely limited to referential meaning. Rather, social meaning involves "the social values implied when an utterance is used in a certain context" (Gumperz, 1971, p. 285).

Children learn variation and its social meaning as part of their native speaker intuition, although it is not known exactly how they do this. In contrast, even second language and foreign language speakers who become very proficient in using the linguistic code of a language seldom develop native intuitions for the social meaning of linguistic variation. For instance, foreign students in the United States who hear a native English speaker say "I ain't got none" recognize the utterance as grammatically different but often cannot tell whether it means that the speaker is uneducated, in a jocular mood, or using an alternative grammar to establish solidarity. Also, although foreign students of English tend to be fascinated by slang, they rarely learn to use it appropriately, even when they reside for several years in an English-speaking setting. A case in point is that of a very proper young Japanese woman who attended a class I taught several years ago. In her term paper, she used the phrase "and all that crap" in place of *etc.*, although the tone of the paper was otherwise serious and scholarly. (This example also illustrates the fact that the social meaning of a variable for a hearer or reader is not the same when it is used by a nonnative speaker as it is when it is used by a native speaker. My response in this case was amusement, although I would not have been amused at all with the same usage by an American unless it was clear that it was being used for special effect.) Even when advanced students of English as a foreign language do perceive variable features which mark differences in regional origin, social class, and style, their interpretation of the social meaning which the features convey commonly differs from that of native English speakers.

It must be concluded that this dimension of communicative competence is very difficult to teach and that it is not feasible to teach it in many situations. For one thing, variation and its social meanings cannot be taught apart from social context and understanding of the social structure of the community, and even when there is significant interaction with the target language speech community, it is very difficult for beginning students (at least) to manage multiple varieties of the language.

Because of this limitation on learnability, the selection of regional variety and register becomes an important issue when curricular priorities are established. One factor to consider is the attitude of the speech community, including what communicative behavior its members believe is appropriate for a nonnative speaker of the language. Particularly for individuals who have had experience interacting with people from different language and cultural backgrounds, the same expectations or interpretive frames are not in force; again, native communicative norms do not generally apply. My position on this point is that learners are probably well served to aim for a relatively formal variety of the second or foreign language first, whether primary contact with native speakers is likely to be face to face or through written texts. This is typically the style expected from foreign speakers and is thus less likely to carry the unintended informational load of a more marked variety.

### INTERACTION SKILLS

The second dimension of communicative competence involves interaction skills. Among these skills both knowledge and expectation of who may or may not speak in certain settings, to whom they may speak, when they should remain silent, how they should talk to people of different statuses and roles, what nonverbal behaviors are appropriate for them to use in various contexts, what routines they should use for turn taking in conversation, how they should ask for and give information, how they should request, how they should offer or decline assistance or cooperation, how they should give commands, and how they should enforce discipline. In other words, interactional skills consist of social conventions which regulate the use of language and other communicative devices in particular settings.

Referential meaning may be ascribed to many of the elements in the linguistic code in a static manner, but the description or understanding of language as it occurs in its social context must be seen as an emergent and dynamic process. Describing and understanding speakers' interaction in their native language requires accounting for the perception, selection, and interpretation of salient features of the code used in actual communicative contexts, integrating these features with other cultural knowledge and skills, and implementing appropriate strategies for achieving communicative goals.

Interacting in a second or foreign language often involves the transfer of these elements from first language competence even after considerable proficiency in the target linguistic code has been acquired, as language teachers have long recognized. The English speaker learning

Chinese may respond to a compliment with *xie-xie* ("thank you") instead of the appropriate *nali* ("where"), for instance, and the native Chinese speaker may respond "Where? Where?" to a compliment in English. Similarly, there are reports by Americans that soon after meeting a Turkish speaker at a cocktail party they may be asked, "How much money do you make?" Such examples have already had significant impact on foreign language curricula, influencing the content of communicative activities.

More general differences in interaction patterns between native and target language communities can and do result in more serious communicative conflicts, or they may inhibit communication. For example, members of some American Indian speech communities wait several minutes in silence before taking a turn in conversation or responding to a question; the native English speakers they may be talking to find silences of that length embarrassing because they expect short time frames for responses or conversational turn taking. In addition, important differences can be found not only with the forms and patterns that interaction takes but with how interaction functions in the establishment of social relations and status and in the identification of individuals and groups for themselves and others – in Goffman's (1967) terms, the establishment of face (see Chick, this volume).

In the case of a second or foreign language, learning interaction skills is essentially quite different from learning new linguistic features of grammar, vocabulary, and pronunciation. In some situations, expecting or requiring productive use of second language interaction patterns may in fact have very negative effects on learners. Paulston (1974) suggested that this negative effect could be the consequence of even attempting to teach such skills in second language contexts where minority language students are being acculturated to the dominant language and culture. In her words, "It is the process of trying to eradicate an existing set of social interactional rules in order to substitute another which is so counterproductive" (p. 354). She goes on to speculate that the reason why children of middle and upper socioeconomic classes generally do not suffer ill effects from initial schooling in a second language (as children of lower socioeconomic classes often do) "may well be that there is no attempt to interfere with the rules of communicative competence of the upper-class children . . . [while] with the lower-class children one insists that they adopt the social interactional rules of the target language" (p. 354).

One study which tends to corroborate Paulston's speculation relating the "need" to change interaction style with learners of lower social prestige involved an analysis of nonverbal behavior in French and English storytelling by Canadian bilingual children who were either Francophone or Anglophone (Von Raffler Engle, 1972). When paired with a bilingual Anglophone addressee, Francophone children switched to English nonverbal behaviors, whether they were speaking English or French, although they did not switch with a Francophone addressee even when he or she was speaking English. The socially dominant Anglophone children, on the other hand, made no such accommodation (see also McGroarty, this volume).

Such phenomena suggest that when we leave the surface linguistic structures in language teaching and approach the deeper levels of communicative competence which interaction skills appear to tap, we need to be sensitive to the sociopsychological, as well as the sociolinguistic, factors that might be involved. These factors add very important considerations to issues of what should be taught in a second language, even beyond those of feasibility. Making a distinction between receptive and productive competence is essential here; students who are interacting with native speakers should be helped to understand those speakers' communicative intentions, but they need not be necessarily expected or required to behave likewise.

### CULTURAL KNOWLEDGE

Finally, for reasons already suggested, the concept of communicative competence requires reference to the notion of *cultural competence,* or the total set of knowledge and skills which speakers bring into a situation. As defined by such anthropologists as Geertz (1973) and Douglas (1970), *cultures* are systems of symbols, and language is only one of the symbolic systems in this network. This definition entails that interpreting the meaning of linguistic behavior requires knowing the cultural meaning in which it is embedded.

Ultimately, all aspects of culture are relevant to communication, but the ones that have the most immediate importance for those learning communicative forms and processes in a second or foreign language are the social structure of its speech community and the values and attitudes held about language and ways of speaking. An understanding of social structure is needed in order to use the patterns of address in a language properly, for instance, as well as to know whom to avoid and when to remain silent. This involves determining what subgroups are accorded differential status and prestige and understanding what criteria are applied. Values and attitudes about language use may also relate to social structure, and notions such as what constitutes "speaking well" may vary within a speech community for males versus females or for members of different occupations or social classes. Attitudes toward language considered taboo are extremely strong, and violations may be sanctioned by imputations of immorality or social ostracism. No topic is universally forbidden; linguistic taboos relate integrally to culture-specific beliefs and practices.

Shared knowledge is essential to explain the shared presuppositions and judgments of truth value which are the essential undergirdings of language structures as well as of contextually appropriate usage and interpretation, and much of this is also culture-specific. For instance (to give a somewhat sexist example), to interpret the *but* in the English statement "Bill's a secretary, but he's a man at heart" requires knowledge that men do not typically work as secretaries in U.S. society. Among the domains of language use, understanding humor and interpreting literature perhaps demand the most culture-specific information, whereas the shared knowledge needed for technical and scientific communication is likely to cross cultural boundaries. That is not to say, however, that the latter type of communication is culture-free.

For reasons discussed in the earlier section on language and culture, what aspects of culture need to be, can be, or should be taught in conjunction with a second, foreign, or auxiliary language also depend on the social context in which that language is being learned and in which it will be used. An important application of the ethnography of communication is in making that determination.

## Doing the ethnography of communication

Doing ethnography research in speech community other than one's own involves first and foremost fieldwork, including observing, asking questions, participating in group activities, and testing the validity of one's own perceptions against the intuitions of natives. It is crucial that the ethnographic description of other groups not be approached in terms of preconceived categories and processes but with an openness to discover the ways that native speakers perceive and structure their communicative experiences. Research design must allow for modes of thought and behavior which may not have been anticipated by the investigator. The unique event and the recurrent pattern must be seen both from the perspective of their native participants and from the vantage point afforded by cross-cultural knowledge and comparison.

Even in the study of their own speech communities, ethnographers profit from a comparative orientation, for one of the best means by which to gain understanding of one's own ways of speaking is to compare and contrast these ways with others. This process can reveal that many of the communicative practices assumed to be natural or logical are in fact as culturally unique and conventional as the language code itself.

Other characteristics of most ethnographic approaches to the study of communicative phenomena are that data are normally collected in naturalistic settings rather than with clinical or experimental controls, that the study is in-depth and involves a significant period of time, and that analyses are primarily qualitative (as opposed to quantitative) in nature. The naturalistic orientation is well suited to process research in language learning and teaching situations, since the ethnographer is essentially committed to noninterference with classroom instructional activities, as well as with nonacademic interaction. Although depth and time commitments are sometimes violated – yielding what Rist (1980) calls *blitzkrieg ethnography* – these factors are important to the establishment of reliability in the absence of experimental control. Various modes of qualitative analyses contribute most to claims of validity in interpretation, although the subsequent incorporation of quantitative data collection and analyses may be very useful in establishing the reliability and the typicality of findings.

No single mode of data collection is required in ethnographic approaches to communication, although observation-participation is considered basic. Other modes include library research for background information, archaeological and sociological surveys, artistic and folkloric analyses, and a full range of linguistic and sociolinguistic research. Indeed, the essential element for an ethnography of communication perspective is that multiple databases will be incorporated in description and analysis, with an idealistic goal of holistic explication.

Most developments within the ethnography of communication for data collection and analysis have targeted communicative events within a fairly well defined speech community. This focus is generally appropriate for purposes of applying ethnography of communication findings to teaching about specific events in target second languages, but it needs considerable adjustment before a high level of relevance for description and analysis can be claimed for learning and teaching in foreign and auxiliary language contexts.

## *Units of analysis*

The communicative units (i.e., communicative activities with recognizable boundaries) that are frequently used in ethnographic studies (following Hymes, 1972) are situation, event, and act.

The *communicative situation* is the context within which communication occurs. Typically, terms exist in the language by which to label situations, such as (in English) a *church service,* a *trial,* a *cocktail party,* or a *class in school.* A single situation maintains a consistent general configuration of activities and the same overall ecology within which communication takes place, although there may be great diversity in the kinds of interaction that occur there. For example, I observed and videotaped a group of limited-English-speaking elementary school students each week over the course of an entire school year in a single communicative situation that occurred when these children left their regular English-medium classrooms for 30 minutes each day for a common class in English as a second language (ESL) (Saville-Troike, 1984; Saville-Troike, McClure, & Fritz, 1984). Although the composition of the group changed as the result of student illness or family trips and the appointment of a new teacher at midyear, and the specific activities changed with seasonal interests and the students' developing English language proficiency, the overall structure and purpose of the sessions remained the same. Selecting a single communicative situation such as this in longitudinal and/or or comparative research provides a consistent frame wherein the effects of minimal variation in components of communication (e.g., setting, participants, goal) can be observed and interpreted.

The *communicative event* is the basic unit for descriptive purposes. A *single event* is defined by a unified set of components throughout, beginning with the same general purpose of communication, the same general topic, and the same participants, generally using the same language variety, maintaining the same tone or key, and using the same rules for interaction, in the same setting. An event terminates whenever there is a change in the major participants, their role relationships, or the focus of attention. If there is no change in major participants and setting, the boundary between events is often marked by a period of silence and, perhaps, a change of body position.

In the ESL situation I referred to above, for instance, the class periods were found to divide into a regular sequence of recurring events:

1. Unstructured play
2. Claiming a seat at the large table where the lesson was conducted
3. Opening routines (e.g., "What day is it today?")
4. Teacher-directed lesson on a targeted language form
5. Follow-up activity (usually involving arts and crafts or a game)
6. Closing routines (e.g., "Time to clean up," "See you tomorrow," etc.)

The event as a unit for analysis is important in part so that observations made at different times will be comparable, and so that generalizations can be made about patterns of communication within a constant context. In the situation just described, for instance, patterns and forms for communication varied greatly from event to event, and yet they stayed relatively constant for each type of event throughout the year. It was possible, therefore, to analyze the development of students' competence in English and the strategies that they used to achieve different communicative functions within each event; any comparison of student or teacher language forms and rules for language use at different points of the lesson (or in other situations) would have been quite misleading without taking this unit into account.

For example, the word *is* in such sentences as "Today is Monday" or "This is a table," which was used consistently in the ESL opening routines and teacher-directed lessons beginning during the first week of school, was still absent in the speech of several students in all other events (and in the other situations) after weeks and even months of English instruction. Without reference to different event structures, it might appear that this grammatical form occurred randomly, rather than as part of memorized patterns that were used only during teacher-student interaction when the focus was on the form, rather than the content, of communication. Students and teachers also (unconsciously) recognized that organizational rules, such as raising hands and talking one at a time, operated only during certain segments (events) of the class.

The *communicative act* is generally coterminous with a single interactional function, such as a referential statement, a request, or a command, and may be either verbal or nonverbal. For example, not only may a request take several verbal forms ("I'd like a piece of candy," "Do you have a piece of candy?" or "May I please have a piece of candy?"), but it may be expressed by raised eyebrows and a questioning look or by a longing sigh. In the context of a communicative event, even silence may be an intentional and conventional communicative act used to question, promise, deny, warn, insult, request, or command (see Tannen & Saville-Troike, 1985, for discussions of the functions of silence).

The unit of communicative act is also applicable in second language research for comparative purposes. In the longitudinal study of the ESL class mentioned earlier, for instance, analysis at this level made it possible to determine the relative frequency of different communicative functions for students in different events and across time (e.g., warnings and threats to other students declined significantly, and requests for clarification increased) and to compare the linguistic form that was selected by event across time for each type of act (e.g., from gestures and nonspeech sound used for warnings and threats at the beginning of the year, to holistic routines, to increasing syntactic complexity in the second language).

In applying the analysis of these units to second language teaching, the teacher or researcher might determine what communicative situations are relevant for student experiences and needs and might analyze typical events in that situation as a basis for curriculum content and for assessment. If the application were to be for teaching in an intensive English program for international students who had recently arrived in the United States, for instance, the situation selected might be eating at a fast food restaurant such as McDonalds. A typical recurring event which might be selected for analysis and instruction could be ordering from the menu board, including anticipating and interpreting what is likely to be said by the employee and what the customer should say in reply (including relevant options), along with event-specific vocabulary and routines. Other communicative situations which might merit analysis and instruction in this context could be renting an apartment, extending or responding to a social invitation, finding a book in the library, or dealing with a health or legal emergency.

Such potential instructional applications of the ethnography of communication have been proposed for communicative approaches to language teaching since early in the history of the field (e.g., see Paulston, 1974), but implementation has fallen well short of potential in both second and foreign language contexts. In part, this is because business reasons lead publishers of language texts to make assumptions about the homogeneity of students' second and foreign language opportunities and needs which are quite unrealistic. Application to instruction in English for special purposes (ESP) has been more viable (e.g., Munby, 1978), but the ethnography of communication may be a domain in which the methods of analysis are even more applicable than its product.

## *The act of analysis*

Even very detailed descriptions of classroom situations and events may be static in nature, if they fall short of accounting for the dynamic processes involved in communication. Utterances by teachers and students cannot be analyzed in isolation, for instance; they are part of discourse, or connected units which interact in patterned and rule-governed ways. Furthermore, in naturally occurring communication, meaning is not derived just from speech forms and observable nonverbal cues but also from such factors as the information or presuppositions communicants bring to the task and their expectations and inferences. Understanding what the speakers' frames are, and what processes they are using to relate their expectations to the production and interpretation of language, requires second-level inferencing by the researcher unless more direct evidence is available. Analyzing communication does ultimately require inferences to be made about the intentions and effects of interactions, although such inferences should be grounded wherever possible in an understanding of the perceptions of those who are participants in an event.

An important cautionary word is that researchers should never delude themselves into thinking that they are completely objective – nor should they be. The validity of a researcher's interpretation of interaction is often enhanced by interviewing students and teachers or by asking them to interpret aspects of videotaped interaction they engaged in and the social situation within which it occurred. Teachers who collaborate in these playback (Fanshel & Moss, 1971) and debriefing procedures generally report that the experience is of benefit to them as well as to the researcher, by giving them greater insights into their own teaching strategies and by affording a heightened awareness of their students' behaviors and experiences. In second language research, even 2- and 3-year-old children have contributed important insights about their communicative problems and strategies when they have been asked (in their native language) to describe their participation in videotaped events. It seems ironic that many inferences are made in research without the subjects being asked what they think.

A final characterization that can be made of most ethnographic research in classrooms is that it is open to new questions that may arise in the course of data collection and analysis and that it attempts to account for the full range of communicative phenomena which occur in the social context of interaction. The scope and depth of analysis attempted are admittedly ambitious. Although individual studies have therefore typically been limited to one or, at most, a few classrooms each, they collectively are contributing to the understanding of the way language actually works in classroom settings.

## Findings and applications to language learning and teaching

A strong call for the application of the ethnography of communication to educational issues was voiced by Hymes in his introduction to *Functions of Language in the Classroom* (Cazden, John, & Hymes, 1972). For Hymes, research and application involve a two-way sharing of knowledge – the investigator contributing scientific modes of inquiry and participants providing the requisite knowledge and perspective of the particular community contexts. Within this 1972 volume, very important contributions are made to the understanding of differential rules for classroom language use with respect to ability level (e.g., Gumperz & Hernández-Chavez, 1972) and to culture (e.g., Boggs, Dumont, and Philips, 1972). The findings of Philips that cultural differences relate to different structures of classroom interaction and control have subsequently been extended by research in a variety of situations, including that of Au (1980) and Erickson and Mohatt (1982). The findings of these studies show that certain types of classroom practices may have a negative effect on teaching and learning for students from different cultural backgrounds, as follows:

Required public performance or testing (teachers controlling performance style and calling attention to individual students in front of an audience)
Tempo of teaching (how fast students and teachers interact, and how quickly one activity shifts to the next; wait time between solicitation and response)
Directiveness (how much and what kinds of control teachers can appropriately exercise over students) and use of space (positions in class, pattern of movement, distance between individuals, touching)

Responsive pedagogy might include such adaptations as seating students in table groups instead of rows, calling on groups rather than individual students, and privatizing contact with students (Erickson & Mohatt, 1982).

One of the most influential descriptions of classroom verbal organization is Mehan (1979), which provided an important basis for subsequent analysis of differential home-school continuity in the interactional strategies that children encounter with teachers, depending on cultural and economic background. Cazden, a close collaborator of Mehan in this research, continued interpretation of that experience, including publication of a book (1988) which analyzes structures of classroom interaction in terms of student-teacher rights and responsibilities and analyzes different speaking styles or registers in terms of instructional and learning consequences. The results of such ethnographic research are now widely included in teacher-education curricula of various institutions, particularly as they relate to issues in multicultural education.

To understand classroom interaction processes and content, we must continually bear in mind that teachers are operating within a culturally defined system of educational knowledge and ideology. As emphasized by Gumperz (1981), "What is *communicated* in the classroom is a result of complex processes of interaction among educational goals, background knowledge, and what various participants perceive over time as taking place" (p. 5). The methods of the ethnography of communication can be profitably applied by teachers in observing and analyzing the situation in their own classroom and in heightening their awareness of their own interaction patterns with students (and of how their point of view might differ from students' achievements or expectation level or sociocultural identity).

Ideally, all language in classrooms would be used cooperatively by students and teachers to construct mutually satisfying exchanges that further educational goals. Realistically, however, instances of conflict or subversion occur in classrooms. Most instances of conflict in school settings are charged with emotion, and understanding the culturally different ways in which emotions may be expressed and interpreted is vital to providing a climate for learning in the classroom. Gilmore (1985), for instance, focuses on the displays of "stylized silent sulking" that characterize clashes of will between teachers and students in a low-income, black urban community which she studied. Teachers label students exhibiting such behaviors as having a "bad attitude," and this label often results in tracking them out of academic programs. Close examination of the behavior, however, reveals a great deal of variation in its form and meaning and relates the mode of expression to community norms of appropriate demeanor. In this case, better mutual understanding of different patterns of communication might well contribute to improvement in the quality of learning and teaching.

Ethnographic modes of investigation are also of particular value in the study of both first and second language acquisition and development or the acquisition of communicative competence. One of the most complete ethnographic studies of language development yet conducted was done by Heath (1983), who describes how children from two culturally different communities in the Piedmont Carolinas learn to use language. Their differential socialization experiences yield differential readiness for school, even though both groups acquire full competence in the language patterns of their home and community. Heath goes beyond description to suggest ways in which educators can make use of knowledge from the ethnographies of communication to build bridges between communities and schools and develop ways to accommodate group differences in language and culture.

Ethnographic research on children's second language development has increased the understanding of strategies they use to communicate with one another in spite of limited language skills (e.g., Ventriglia, 1979; Wong Fillmore, 1976, 1979), to resolve social conflicts (e.g., Adger, 1986; Emihovich, 1986), and to make sense of school (e.g., Kleifgen, 1986; Saville-Troike & Kleifgen, 1986). Kleifgen (1986), in particular, demonstrates the value of playback and debriefing procedures which were described earlier, in which both students (in their native languages) and teachers interpreted their own communicative behaviors and experiences as they viewed videotapes of events in which they were participants.

The ways in which analysis of communicative events might be used in the preparation of instructional activities for language classes have been discussed, as has the subject of how research on the functions and contexts of present or prospective language use might be used in determining what aspects of the language need to be learned and/or taught. Another important application of the ethnography of communication is to the assessment of communicative skills, especially as they relate to requirements of the educative process. Traditional language proficiency tests that measure pronunciation, grammar, and vocabulary do not reveal all the communicative requirements necessary for success in school (Troike, 1983). Although the full potential in this area of application has not yet been realized, much progress has been made (e.g., see Rivera, 1983). Such efforts are vital to questions of entry and exit in special educational programs designed for speakers of other languages, such as bilingual education and English as a second language, and to questions regarding the identification and remediation of abnormal speech. The first factor to consider is that testing is itself a socially situated communicative event and that students may perform differentially in differing testing conditions because of their language and cultural background. Evaluation instruments can seldom be considered neutral in these respects, no matter how objective their format.

Finally, for teaching reading and writing skills in a first language or a second or foreign language, methods used in the ethnography of communication can profitably be brought into the classroom for the study of texts. Teachers employing this approach emphasize the necessity of taking situational context into account in interpreting the meaning of texts. Specifically, in studying authentic readings or recordings, teachers can lead students to integrate textual or linguistic analysis with inquiry about related social and cultural phenomena. They can do this by encouraging students to ask relevant background questions and to investigate contextual issues in a variety of ways. Particularly for second or foreign language learners, this does not mean that students must develop encyclopedic cultural knowledge but that both teachers and students might develop an increased sensitivity to the importance of context in interpreting texts and to the range of questions which should be asked. Even teachers working with students at advanced levels where the primary focus is on literature or rhetoric can effectively make use of the ethnography of communication by teaching students to apply its techniques in their interpretation and analysis (see Saville-Troike & Johnson, 1994).

Perhaps most important, an ethnography of communication perspective contributes to the cultivation of a difference rather than a deficit view toward student performance. Knowledge of the ways in which communicative structures and strategies differ across cultures will help teachers better understand the reasons for students' deviations from standard and native language norms. Understanding why students might make certain choices in language use can lead to more tolerant and appreciative attitudes toward students' full range of communicative resources while, at the same time, recognizing and supporting students' needs and desires to operate effectively within certain target speech communities and situations. Although training in language or linguistics is an essential component of teacher preparation, it is not sufficient for understanding the nature of communication. The ethnography of communication provides an important additional set of tools for achieving an understanding of the patterns of language use in the communication systems of different cultures, particularly as they relate to the goals and practices of classroom instruction.

## Suggestions for further reading

Cook-Gumperz, J. (Ed.). (1986). *The social construction of literacy.* Cambridge: Cambridge University Press.

The focus of this book is on the institution of schooling, from the perspective of literacy learning as social transmission. Particularly important is Chapter 2 (by Cook-Gumperz), which relates literacy to societal values, educational ideology, and social order. The value-laden nature of literacy is reflected in selective access and outcomes and is presented as being basic to the issue of equal educational opportunity.

Gumperz, J. J., & Hymes, D. (Eds.). (1986). *Directions in sociolinguistics: The ethnography of communication.* Oxford: Basil Blackwell.

This is a reprinting of a classic collection of articles (first published by Holt, Rinehart and Winston in 1972) which largely defined the field in its emergent stages. It remains valuable for information on how diverse languages relate to dimensions of culture, as well as for the insights it provides on how languages function in socially constructed communicative processes.

Hatch, E. (1992). *Discourse and language education.* Cambridge: Cambridge University Press.

This book consists of an overview of methods for discourse analysis. It particularly targets teachers and graduate students in language-related fields by providing a wealth of examples drawn from Hatch's own experiences in applied linguistics as well as related literature, interesting practice activities, and worthwhile suggestions for research and application. The entire book is relevant to sociolinguistics, with the first four chapters of particular interest to those concerned with the ethnography of communication.

Heath, S. B. (1983). *Ways with words: Language, life, and work in communities and classrooms.* Cambridge: Cambridge University Press.

This book provides an exemplary model for the comparative study of communicative patterns of families within different social groups, particularly as they relate to the socialization of children. Heath shows that, when preschool linguistic experiences are different from those traditionally expected by the schools, they do not necessarily constitute barriers – as long as the school makes appropriate curricular adaptations in order to build on them as a positive foundation for continued learning. She includes descriptions of practical applications of the methods and principles from the ethnography of communication for the accomplishment of this goal.

Saville-Troike, M. (1989). *The ethnography of communication* (2nd ed.). Oxford: Basil Blackwell.

This book is a general introduction to the topic, including a discussion of basic terms, concepts, and issues, as well as a description of methods for analysis of communicative events. It supplements the chapter in this volume with examples of different ways of speaking drawn from a variety of languages and cultures, reviews of research (carried out from the ethnography of communication perspective) on language acquisition and attitudes toward language use, and discussion of additional applications and implications.

## References

Adger, C. T. (1986). When difference does not conflict: Successful arguments between black and Vietnamese classmates. *Text, 6*, 223–237.

Anyon, J. (1981). Social class and school knowledge. *Curriculum Inquiry, 11*, 3–42.

Au, K. H. (1980). On participation structures in reading lessons. *Anthropology and Education Quarterly, 11*, 91–115.

Barth, F. (1966). Models of social organization. *Occasional Papers of the Royal Anthropological Institute of Great Britain and Ireland, 23*.

Bates, E., & Benigni, L. (1975). Rules of address in Italy: A sociological survey. *Language in Society, 4*, 271–288.

Benedict, R. (1934). *Patterns of culture*. Boston: Houghton Mifflin.

Boggs, S. T. (1972). The meaning of questions and narratives to Hawaiian children. In C. Cazden, V. P. John, & D. Hymes (Eds.), *Functions of language in the classroom* (pp. 299–327). New York: Teachers College.

Brown, R., & Gilman, A. (1960). The pronouns of power and solidarity. In T. Sebeok (Ed.), *Style in language* (pp. 253–276). Cambridge, MA: Massachusetts Institute of Technology.

Cazden, C. B. (1988). *Classroom discourse: The language of teaching and learning*. Portsmouth, NH: Heinemann.

Cazden, C. B., John, V. T., & Hymes, D. (Eds.). (1972). *Functions of language in the classroom*. New York: Teachers College.

Chafe, W. L. (Ed.). (1980). *The pear stories: Cognitive, cultural and linguistic aspects of narrative production*. Norwood, NJ: Ablex.

Chomsky, N. (1965). *Aspects of the theory of syntax*. Cambridge, MA: Massachusetts Institute of Technology.

Crown, C. L., & Feldstein, S. (1985). Psychological correlates of silence and sound in conversational interaction. In D. Tannen & M. Saville-Troike (Eds.), *Perspectives on silence* (pp. 31–54). Norwood, NJ: Ablex.

Cushman, D. P., & Whiting, G. C. (1972). An approach to communication theory: Towards consensus on rules. *Journal of Communication, 22*, 217–238.

Dittmar, N. (1983). Descriptive and explanatory power of rules in sociolinguistics. In B. Bain (Ed.), *The sociogenesis of language and human conduct* (pp. 225–255). New York: Plenum.

Douglas, M. (1970). *Natural symbols: Explorations in cosmology*. New York: Random House.

Dumont, R. V., Jr. (1972). Learning English and how to be silent: Studies in Sioux and Cherokee classrooms. In C. Cazden, V. P. John, & D. Hymes

(Eds.), *Functions of language in the classroom* (pp. 344–369). New York: Teachers College.

Emihovich, C. (1986). Argument as status assertion: Contextual variations in children's disputes. *Language in Society, 4*, 485–500.

Erickson, F., & Mohatt, G. (1982). Cultural organization of participation structures in two classrooms of Indian students. In G. Spindler (Ed.), *Doing the ethnography of schooling* (pp. 132–174). New York: Holt, Rinehart and Winston.

Erickson, F., & Shultz, J. (1982). *The counselor as gatekeeper: Social interactions in interviews*. New York: Academic.

Fang, H., & Heng, J. H. (1983). Social changes and changing address norms in China. *Language in Society, 12*, 495–507.

Fanshel, D., & Moss, F. (1971). *Playback: A marriage in jeopardy examined.* New York: Columbia University Press.

Fishman, J. A. (1972). Domains and the relationship between micro and macro-sociolinguistics. In J. J. Gumperz & D. Hymes (Eds.), *Directions in sociolinguistics: The ethnography of communication* (pp. 435–453). New York: Holt, Rinehart and Winston.

Geertz, C. (1973). *The interpretation of cultures*. New York: Basic Books.

Gilmore, P. (1985). Silence and sulking: Emotional displays in the classroom. In D. Tannen & M. Saville-Troike (Eds.), *Perspectives on silence* (pp. 139–162). Norwood, NJ: Ablex.

Goddard, D. (1977). Same setting, different norms: Phone-call beginnings in France and the United States. *Language in Society, 6*, 209–219.

Goffman, E. (1967). *Interaction ritual: Essays on face-to-face behavior.* Garden City, NY: Doubleday.

Gumperz, J. J. (1971). *Language in social groups*. Stanford: Stanford University Press.

Gumperz, J. J. (1977). Sociocultural knowledge in conversational inference. In M. Saville-Troike (Ed.), *Linguistics and anthropology* (pp. 191–212). Washington, DC: Georgetown University.

Gumperz, J. J. (1979). The retrieval of sociocultural knowledge in conversation. *Poetics Today, 1*, 273–286.

Gumperz, J. J. (1981). Conversational inference and classroom learning. In J. Green & C. Wallat (Eds.), *Ethnography and language in educational settings* (pp. 3–23). Norwood, NJ: Ablex.

Gumperz, J. J., & Hernández-Chavez, E. (1972). Bilingualism, bidialectalism, and classroom interaction. In C. Cazden, V. P. John, & D. Hymes (Eds.), *Functions of language in the classroom* (pp. 84–108). New York: Teachers College.

Guthrie, G. P. (1985). *A school divided: An ethnography of bilingual education in a Chinese community*. Hillsdale, NJ: Erlbaum.

Heath, S. B. (1972). *Telling tongues: Language policy in Mexico, colony to nation*. New York: Teachers College.

Heath, S. B. (1983). *Ways with words: Language, life and work in communities and classrooms*. Cambridge: Cambridge University Press.

Hill, J. A. (1988). Language, culture, and world view. In F. J. Newmeyer (Ed.), *Linguistics: the Cambridge survey*. Vol. 4: *Language: The socio-cultural context* (pp. 14–36). Cambridge: Cambridge University Press.

Hill, J. A., & Mannheim, B. (1992). Language and world view. *Annual Review of Anthropology, 21*, 381–406.

Hornberger, N. H. (1987). Bilingual education success, but policy failure. *Language in Society, 16*, 205–226.

Hymes, D. (1962). The ethnography of speaking. In T. Gladwin & W. C. Sturtevant (Eds.), *Anthropology and human behavior* (pp. 13–53). Washington, DC: Anthropological Society of Washington.

Hymes, D. (1966). *On communicative competence.* Paper presented at the Research Planning Conference on Language Development among Disadvantaged Children. New York: Yeshiva University.

Hymes, D. (1972). Models of the interaction of language and social life. In J. J. Gumperz & D. Hymes (Eds.), *Directions in sociolinguistics: Ethnography of communication* (pp. 35–71). New York: Holt, Rinehart and Winston.

Hymes, D. (1974). *Foundations in sociolinguistics: An ethnographic approach.* Philadelphia: University of Pennsylvania Press.

Hymes, D. (1987). Communicative competence. in U. Ammon, N. Dittmar, & K. J. Mattheier (Eds.), *Sociolinguistics: An international handbook of the science of language and society* (pp. 219–229). Berlin: Walter de Gruyter.

Hymes, D. (1992). Inequality in language: Taking for granted. *Working Papers in Educational Linguistics, 8*(1), 1–30.

Kleifgen, J. (1986). Communicative accommodation of teachers to second language children. Doctoral dissertation. Urbana: University of Illinois.

Labov, W. (1965). On the mechanisms of linguistic change. *Georgetown University Monograph Series on Languages and Linguistics, 18*, 91–114, 131–132.

Leacock, E. (1969). *Teaching and learning in city schools: A comparative study*. New York: Basic Books.

Lyons, J. (Ed.). (1970). *New horizons in linguistics*. Harmondsworth: Penguin.

Mannheim, B. (1986). Popular song and popular grammar, poetry and metalanguage. *Word, 37*, 45–75.

Mehan, H. (1979). *Learning lessons.* Cambridge, MA: Harvard University Press.

Merritt, M. (1976). On questions following questions in service encounters. *Language in Society, 5*, 315–357.

Munby, J. (1978). *Communicative syllabus design.* Cambridge: Cambridge University Press.

Nida, E. A. (1975). Principles of translation as exemplified by Bible translation. *Language structure and translation: Essays by Eugene A. Nida.* Stanford, CA: Stanford University Press.

Paulston, C. B. (1974). Linguistic and communicative competence. *TESOL Quarterly, 8*, 347–362.

Paulston, C. B. (1976). Pronouns of address in Swedish: Social class semantics and a changing system. *Language in Society, 5*, 359–386.

Philips, S. U. (1972). Participant structures and communicative competence: Warm Springs children in community and classroom. In C. Cazden, V. P. John, & D. Hymes (Eds.), *Functions of language in the classroom* (pp. 370–394). New York: Teachers College.

Philips, S. U. (1982). The language socialization of lawyers: Acquiring the 'cant.' In G. Spindler (Ed.), *Doing the ethnography of schooling* (pp. 176–209). New York: Holt, Rinehart and Winston.

Reisman, K.(1974). Contrapuntal conversations in an Antiguan village. In R. Bauman & J. Sherzer (Eds.), *Explorations in the ethnography of speaking* (pp. 110–124). Cambridge: Cambridge University Press.

Rist, R. C. (1980). Blitzkrieg ethnography: On the transformation of method into a movement. *Educational Researcher, 9*(2), 8–10.

Rivera, C. (Ed.). (1983). *An ethnographic/sociolinguistic approach to language proficiency assessment.* Clevedon, Avon: Multilingual Matters.

Sacks, H., Schegloff, M., & Jefferson, G. (1974). A simplest systematics for the organization of turntaking for conversation. *Language, 50,* 696–735.

Saville-Troike, M. (1984). What *really* matters in second language learning for academic achievement? *TESOL Quarterly, 17,* 199–219.

Saville-Troike, M. (1989). *The ethnography of communication* (2nd ed.). Oxford: Basil Blackwell.

Saville-Troike, M., & Johnson, D. M. (1994). Comparative rhetoric: An integration of perspectives. In L. F. Bouton & Y. Kachru (Eds.), *Pragmatics and language learning, 5,* 231–246. Urbana: Division of English as an International Language, University of Illinois.

Saville-Troike, M., & Kleifgen, J. (1986). Scripts for school: Cross-cultural communication in elementary classrooms. *Text, 2,* 207–221.

Saville-Troike, M., McClure, E., & Fritz, M. (1984). Communicative tactics in children's second language acquisition. In F. R. Eckman, L. H. Bell, & D. Nelson (Eds.), *Universals of second language acquisition* (pp. 60–71). Rowley, MA: Newbury House.

Schegloff, E. A. (1968). Sequencing in conversational openings. *American Anthropologist, 70,* 1075–1095.

Sherzer, J. (1975). *Ethnography of speaking.* Unpublished manuscript.

Sherzer, J. (1987). A discourse-centered approach to language and culture. *American Anthropologist, 89,* 295–309.

Shimanoff, S. B. (1980). *Communication rules: Theory and research.* Beverly Hills, CA: Sage.

Tannen, D., & Saville-Troike, M. (Eds.). (1985). *Perspectives on silence.* Norwood, NJ: Ablex.

Troike, R. C. (1983). Can language be tested? *Journal of Education, 165,* 209–216.

Van Dijk, T. A. (1993). Principles of critical discourse analysis. *Discourse & Society, 4,* 249–283.

Ventriglia, L. (1979). *Conversations of Miguel and Maria.* Reading, MA: Addison-Wesley.

Von Raffler Engle, W. (1972). Paper presented at the International Conference on Methods in Dialectology, Charlottestown, Prince Edward Island.

Whorf, B. L. (1940). Science and linguistics. *Technological Review, 42,* 229–231, 247–248. Reprinted in J. B. Carroll (Ed.). (1956). *Language, thought, and reality: Selected writings of Benjamin Lee Whorf* (pp. 207–219). New York: Wiley.

Witherspoon, G. (1977). *Language and art in the Navajo universe.* Ann Arbor: University of Michigan Press.

Wong Fillmore, L. (1976). The second time around: Cognitive and social strategies in second language acquisition. Doctoral dissertation. Stanford, CA: Stanford University.

Wong Fillmore, L. (1979). Individual differences in second language acquisition. In C. J. Fillmore, D. Kempler, & W. S-Y. Wang (Eds.), *Individual differences in language ability and language behavior* (pp. 203–228). New York: Academic.

# 12 *Speech acts*

Andrew D. Cohen

"Sorry about that!" may serve as an adequate apology in some situations. In others it may be perceived as a rude, even arrogant, nonapology. In yet other situations, it may not even be intended as an apology in the first place. Hence, it has become increasingly clear that the teaching of second language words and phrases isolated from their sociocultural context may lead to the production of linguistic curiosities which do not achieve their communicative purposes. Given this reality, second language teachers may well find that an understanding of speech act theory and practice will improve their ability to prepare their learners to meet the challenge of producing more contextually appropriate speech in the target language.

Speech act behavior constitutes an area of continual concern for language learners since they are repeatedly faced with the need to utilize speech acts such as complaints, apologies, requests, and refusals, each of which can be realized by means of a host of potential strategies. Although no course of instruction could possibly furnish all the insights that a foreign language learner would need in order to successfully fine-tune each and every speech act utterance, there is some evidence that furnishing learners with selected insights regarding the comprehension and production of speech acts may provide them with valuable information that they would probably not acquire on their own.

This chapter will first define speech acts and provide a brief overview of how this field of discourse has been applied to second language acquisition (SLA). Next, research methodologies used in studying speech acts will be examined, and selected empirical studies that have appeared in recent years will be considered. Finally, the available studies on the teaching of speech act behavior to nonnative speakers will be reviewed, and the pedagogical implications of the findings to date will be described.

I gratefully acknowledge Nancy Hornberger, Sandra McKay, and three anonymous reviewers, as well as Elaine Tarone and Leslie Beebe, for their helpful input at various stages. A special thanks is due to Lee Searles for substantive and editorial assistance in preparing the final draft.

## A definition of *speech act* and a brief historical overview

A *speech act* is a functional unit in communication. According to Austin's theory of speech acts (1962), utterances have three kinds of meaning. The first kind is the *propositional* or *locutionary* meaning, namely, the literal meaning of the utterance. If a pupil says to a teacher or sends a note, "It is hot in here," the locutionary meaning would concern the warm temperature of the classroom. The second kind of meaning is *illocutionary,* namely, the social function that the utterance or written text has. The illocutionary meaning or function of "It's hot in here" may be a request to turn down the heat.[1] If the utterance is expressed emphatically or if it is repeated, perhaps it would also function as a complaint. Austin adds the notion of *perlocutionary force,* that is, the result or effect that is produced by the utterance in that given context. Thus, if the utterance leads to the action of turning down the thermostat in the room, the perlocutionary force of that utterance would be greater than if the request were ignored.[2]

Although such definitions may make theoretical sense, assigning functions to sentences is actually somewhat problematic in that the apparent sentence meaning does not necessarily coincide with the speaker's pragmatic intention, as when a person utters an apology sarcastically,[3] or when a speech act is indirect,[4] as in the request "It's hot in here". Despite problems in interpreting the true intentions of the speaker, efforts have been made to assign functions to speech acts according to a series of categories delineated by philosophers such as Austin (1962) and Searle (1969). Speech acts have been classified according to five categories: representatives (assertions, claims, reports),

1 This would also make the statement an *implicit performative,* in which the request is made by nonverbal features, for example, context and voice modulation (Austin, 1962, in Levinson, 1983, 231–233).

2 A more detailed summary of Austin's theory of speech acts, including the concepts presented here, appears in Levinson (1983, Chap. 5). Levinson also discusses a problem in making the distinction between illocutionary and perlocutionary force.

3 See Hatch (1992) for more on the possible lack of fit between presumed utterance meaning and the speaker's intention. Rundquist (1991) also notes the ironic uses of indirect apologies, particularly on a gender-differentiated basis. When speech acts are taught to nonnative speakers, the focus usually is on learners' comprehension of the explicit, literal significance of a given speech act and not on the more complicated nuances of ironic intention.

4 This chapter will not elaborate on the directness or indirectness of speech acts. For those interested in a detailed treatment of indirect speech acts, one good source is the recent book by Boxer (1993) on indirect complaints. Suffice it to say that numerous speech acts are indirect, in order to mitigate or soften the act somewhat. For example, the imperative is rarely used to issue requests in English; instead, sentences that only indirectly do requesting are usually used (Levinson, 1983).

directives (suggestion, request, command), expressives (apology, complaint, thanks), commissives (promise, threat), and declaratives (decree, declaration).[5]

Although the process of defining and identifying speech acts has been going on since the 1960s, the last 15 years have marked a shift from an intuitively based anecdotal approach to speech act description to an empirical one. Such empirically based research, encompassing both quantitative and qualitative approaches, has focused on the perception and production of speech acts by learners of a second or foreign language (in most cases, English as a second or foreign language, i.e., ESL and EFL) at varying stages of language proficiency and in different social interactions. This work has included efforts to establish both cross-language and language-specific norms of speech act behavior, norms without which it would be impossible to understand and evaluate interlanguage behavior.

Early empirical research on speech act sets (e.g., Cohen & Olshtain, 1981) was in part prompted by a realization that although transfer[6] occurs at the sociocultural level, few if any contrastive studies were systematically undertaken in order to characterize such phenomena (Loveday, 1982; Riley, 1981; Schmidt & Richards, 1981). Research in second language acquisition (SLA) has helped to provide empirical descriptions of speech acts such as requests, compliments, apologies, complaints, refusals, and expressions of gratitude (see Wolfson, 1989; Wolfson & Judd, 1983). Empirical studies concerning the nature of various speech acts in a variety of languages and cultures have been steadily accumulating over the last few years. As a result, there is a growing source of empirical data on the strategies for performing these acts.

## *Empirical validation of speech act sets*

Given a speech act such as apologizing, requesting, complimenting, or complaining, the first concern of SLA researchers has been to arrive at the set of realization patterns typically used by native speakers of the target language, any one of which would be recognized as the speech act in question, when uttered in the appropriate context. This set of strategies is referred to as the *speech act set* of the specific speech act (Olshtain & Cohen, 1983). It has become increasingly clear to researchers that learners of a language may lack even partial mastery of such

5 These categories are further elaborated in Hatch (1992, Chap. 4).

6 See also Chick (this volume) on miscommunication due to transfer, in particular, when there are cultural differences in selecting among the potential strategies for realizing a given speech act.

speech act sets and that this lack of mastery may hinder or even cause breakdowns in communication.

In order to determine what constitutes a speech act set, it is necessary to define the preconditions and interactional goals of the speech act in question[7] and to identify performative and semantic prerequisites for the realization of these goals. If the act of apologizing is considered, for example, one could stipulate that an apology is called for when there is some behavior that violates social norms. When an action or an utterance (or the lack of either) results in one or more persons perceiving themselves as deserving an apology, the culpable person(s) is (are) expected to apologize. According to Searle (1969, p. 4), a person who apologizes for doing *A* expresses regret at having done *A*. Thus, the apology act takes place only if the speaker believes that some act *A* has been performed prior to the time of speaking and that this precondition has resulted in an infraction which affected another person who is now deserving of an apology. Furthermore, the apologizer believes that he or she was at least partly responsible for the offense (Fraser, 1980) and has, as an interactional goal, to make amends.

In the case of the apology, it is necessary to separate the performative verbs (i.e., verbs which name the speech act or illocutionary force of the sentence, e.g., "I apologize" or "I'm sorry") from other semantic formulas that could result in acceptable apology realizations, such as an explanation and justification for the offense (e.g., "The bus was late and so I couldn't possibly get here on time") or an offer of repair (e.g., "I'll do it tomorrow"). The speech act set of apologizing has been found to consist of at least the following main strategies or semantic formulas (Cohen, Olshtain, & Rosenstein, 1986):

1. An expression of an apology, whereby the speaker uses a word, expression, or sentence which contains a relevant performative verb such as *apologize, forgive, excuse, be sorry.*
2. An explanation or account of the situation which indirectly caused the apologizer to commit the offense and which is used by the speaker as an indirect speech act of apologizing.
3. Acknowledgment of responsibility, whereby the offender recognizes his or her fault in causing the infraction.
4. An offer of repair, whereby the apologizer makes a bid to carry out an action or provide payment for some kind of damage which resulted from the infraction.

7 My goal is to address the features of speech acts at the level of discourse. Schiffrin (this volume) suggests an approach that examines more fine-grained grammatical and lexical aspects of language in context.

5. A promise of nonrecurrence, whereby the apologizer commits himself or herself not to have the offense happen again.[8]

In order to investigate the speech act of requesting, it has been necessary to validate empirically a scale of imposition – from the most direct and imposing request to the most indirect and least imposing one (Blum-Kulka, 1989; Olshtain & Blum-Kulka, 1984; Weizman, 1989). An early empirical SLA study on requests involved having native and nonnative speakers of English assign a rank to the degree of politeness of a series of request strategies in the context of making a purchase (Carrell & Konneker, 1981). The ranking of the request strategies came from a theoretical claim that, when requests are made, imperatives are less polite than declaratives, which are in turn less polite than questions (Lakoff, 1977, p. 100). For the native speakers, five levels of politeness were empirically validated, from the elliptical imperative ("Steak and fries") and the imperative ("Give me steak and fries"), on the lower or least polite end, to the interrogative modal ("Could you give me steak and fries?"), on the upper or most polite end. The nonnative speakers generally agreed with these rankings, although they reversed the order of two lower-level requests (the native speakers ranked the declarative with no modal "I want steak and fries" lower than the declarative using a modal, "I'll have steak and fries," whereas the nonnative speakers reversed this ordering).

Two important developments in speech act research are worthy of note at this point. First, one of the most comprehensive empirical studies of speech act behavior, for both its breadth and its depth, has been that of the Cross-Cultural Speech Act Research Project (CCSARP) (Blum-Kulka, House, & Kasper, 1989), which compared speech act behavior of native speakers of a number of different languages with the behavior of learners of those languages. The CCSARP project has also produced useful instruments for data collection and a coding scheme that has been widely replicated in other speech act studies. Second, several excellent surveys of the research literature have appeared which help to define and shape the field of investigation with respect to speech act research (e.g., Kasper & Dahl, 1991; Wolfson, 1989).

8 As more quantitative investigation on apologies is conducted, suggestions are being made as to the addition of main strategies for the speech act set. Whereas Cohen, Olshtain, and Rosenstein (1986) categorized comments such as "How could I?" and "Are you OK?" as modifications of apology strategies, Frescura (1993) would include these with a main strategy which she labels appeals. There are problems with this categorization, such as whether an appeal standing alone would constitute an apology. The point here is that empirical work keeps adding refinements to the categorizations in use.

## Sociocultural and sociolinguistic abilities

What has emerged from the large-scale empirical studies and from the comprehensive reviews of the literature is that successful planning and production of speech act utterances depend on certain sociocultural and sociolinguistic abilities. *Sociocultural ability* refers to the respondents' skill at selecting speech act strategies which are appropriate given (1) the culture involved, (2) the age and sex of the speakers, (3) their social class and occupations, and (4) their roles and status in the interaction. For example, in some cultures (e.g., in the United States) it may be appropriate for speakers who have missed a meeting with their boss through their own negligence to use a repair strategy by suggesting to the boss when to reschedule the meeting. In other cultures (such as Israel), however, such a repair strategy might be considered out of place in that it would most likely be the boss who determines what happens next. Thus, sociocultural knowledge is called for in determining whether a speech act set is appropriate to use and, if so, which members of the set are selected for us.

*Sociolinguistic ability* refers to the respondents' skill at selecting appropriate linguistic forms in order to express the particular strategy used to realize the speech act (e.g., expression of regret in an apology, registration of a grievance in a complaint, specification of the objective of a request, or refusal of an invitation).[9] Sociolinguistic ability constitutes the speakers' control over the actual language forms used to realize the speech act (e.g., "sorry" vs. "excuse me," "really sorry" vs. "very sorry"), as well as their control over register of formality of the utterance, from most intimate to most formal language. For example, if a student is asked to dinner by his or her professor and cannot accept the invitation, although it may well be socioculturally appropriate to decline the invitation, the reply "No way!" would probably constitute an inappropriate choice of form for realizing the speech act set of refusal. The problem is that, sociolinguistically, this phrase would be interpreted as rude and insulting, unless the student had an especially close relationship with the professor and the utterance was made in jest. A more appropriate response might be: "I would love to, but I have a prior engagement I can't get out of."

9 Note that this is a more narrow use of the term *sociolinguistic* than that used by Schiffrin and by Saville-Troike in this volume. The use of the term in this chapter reflects the need for a unit of measure to be contrasted with the term *sociocultural*. Both *sociolinguistic ability* and *sociocultural ability*, as used here, fall within communicative competence as defined by Hymes (1972) and discussed by Saville-Troike (this volume). As with other terms, *sociolinguistic* is seen as having more specific and more general meanings according to the context of use.

### *Selecting the appropriate speech act strategy and the forms for realizing it*

The process of selecting the socioculturally appropriate strategy and the appropriate sociolinguistic forms for that strategy is complex since it is conditioned by the social, cultural, situational, and personal factors described earlier. Strategy selection and selection of forms often depend on the social status of the speaker and the hearer since, in most societies, deference toward higher status, for instance, is realized via linguistic features (e.g., using *vous* rather than *tu* in French) or via modification of the main speech act strategies (e.g., adding intensity to the apology or purposely refraining from cursing). Thus, a person arriving late for a meeting might offer a more intensified and possibly invective-free apology when the apologizee is the boss, rather than a friend. Other factors such as age and social distance are part of the social set of factors that might play a significant role in strategy selection.

It has been found that situational factors also play an important role in strategy selection. Some situations generalize across cultures and hence will elicit similar strategies in different languages, and other situations are more culture-specific and are likely to provoke cross-cultural clashes. In one situation that was used in the CCSARP project for apologies, a waiter brought the customer the wrong order. In all the investigated languages, the native respondents in the role of waiter avoided the expression of personal responsibility, perhaps because admitting such a mistake might cost them their job. In contrast, a cross-cultural study of complaints showed that noise made by neighbors is perceived in some cultures as a serious offense which deserves a complaint but is viewed in other cultures as a less significant offense.

## Methods for collecting speech act data

We will now turn to the various research methods that have been used to investigate speech acts. Later in the chapter, we will review some of the findings obtained from using one or more of these research methods. With regard to the production of speech acts, investigators have used observation of naturally occurring data, role play, discourse completion tasks, and verbal report interviews. With regard to the perception of speech acts, recent research has looked at group reactions to videotaped role play or screen play (from TV series) using questionnaires and verbal report interviews based on review of naturally occurring data. The complexity of speech act realization and of strategy selection requires careful development of research methods for describing speech act production. In the field of language assessment, there is a current emphasis on the multimethod approach. The consensus is that any one method would not assess the entirety of the behavior in question. In speech act investigations, the challenge is to find some means of combining different approaches to the description of the same speech act among both native and nonnative speakers of a language. The ideal cycle of data collection has been perceived as one which encompasses several collection techniques (Olshtain & Blum-Kulka, 1985).

Investigators might start with the generation of initial hypotheses based on observation of naturally occurring data in L1 and L2, whether those data were collected initially in L1 or simultaneously in both languages. Then one could elicit simulated speech (e.g., through using role plays) which can serve to test the initial hypotheses. For example:

> This is not the first time your neighbor has played loud music late at night, and you have to get up early the next morning. Role-play the part of the irate person who knocks on the door of the noisemaker. I will play the role of the neighbor, an avid music lover who is also partly deaf.

Next, a discourse completion task, consisting of a prompt and space for a response, might be used, for example:

> You promised to return a textbook to your classmate within a day or two, after photocopying a chapter. You kept it for almost 2 weeks.
>
> *Classmate:* I'm really upset about the book because I needed it to prepare for last week's class.
>
> *You:* ______________________________

Or, a prompt, a space for a reply, and then one or more rejoinders which the respondent needs to take into consideration might be used (Blum-Kulka, 1982):

> You arranged to meet a friend in order to study together for an exam. You arrive half an hour late for the meeting.
>
> *Friend (annoyed):* I've been waiting at least half an hour for you!
>
> *You:* ______________________________
>
> *Friend:* Well, I was standing here waiting. I could have been doing something else.
>
> *You:* ______________________________
>
> *Friend:* Still, it's pretty annoying. Try to come on time next time.

Such tasks allow investigators to focus on specific speech act realizations and manipulate the social and situational variables. Then, if the concern is with the perlocutionary aspect of speech acts, questionnaires might be used to record perceptions of videotaped speech act interactions. Finally, to follow up, an interview might take place in order to provide further insights regarding the production or perception

TABLE 1. METHODOLOGICAL OPTIONS FOR SPEECH ACT RESEARCH

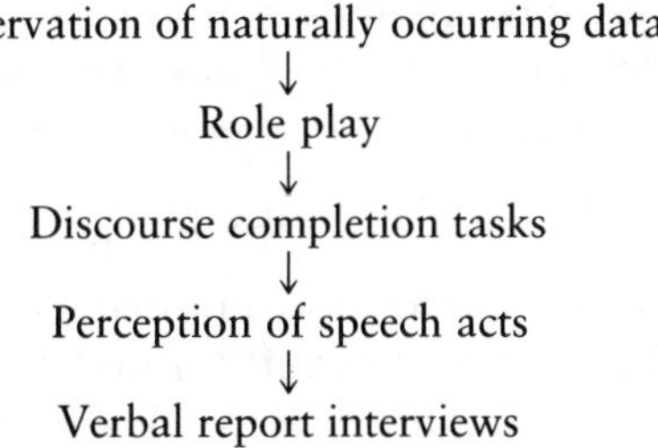

Observation of naturally occurring data
↓
Role play
↓
Discourse completion tasks
↓
Perception of speech acts
↓
Verbal report interviews

of naturally occurring, role-play, or discourse completion data (see Table 1).

Discussions of the relative strengths and weakness of each of these research methods have already begun to appear in the research literature (Beebe & Takahashi, 1989a; Blum-Kulka, House, & Kasper, 1989; Hartford & Bardovi-Harlig, 1992; Kasper & Dahl, 1991; Wolfson, Marmor, & Jones, 1989). In one of the first extensive literature reviews regarding speech act research methodology, for example, Kasper and Dahl (1991) reviewed the methods of data collection employed in thirty-nine studies of interlanguage pragmatics[10] and the acquisition of second language speech act knowledge. Data collection instruments were distinguished according to (1) the degree to which they constrain the informants' responses and (2) whether they tap speech act comprehension or production. The authors questioned the validity of each type of data collection method in terms of its adequacy in approximating authentic performance of linguistic ability.

## *Naturally occurring data*

The case has been made repeatedly for the collection of naturally occurring data. It is pointed out that a broader range of respondents can be studied than is usually the case with studies using predetermined respondents. Furthermore, in principle, one can obtain a sense of the frequency with which particular types of speech acts occur. Other advantages that have been noted include the following (Bardovi-Harlig & Hartford, 1993b):

1. The data are spontaneous
2. The data reflect what the speakers say rather than what they think they would say

10 Here the term is defined narrowly as the investigation of nonnative speakers' comprehension and production of speech acts.

3. The speakers are reacting to a natural situation rather than to a contrived and possibly unfamiliar situation
4. The communicative event has real-world consequences
5. The event may be a source of rich pragmatic structures[11]

The following difficulties of data collection have also been noted:

1. The speech act being studied may not occur naturally very often
2. Proficiency and gender may be difficult to control
3. Collecting and analyzing the data are time-consuming
4. The data may not yield enough or any examples of target items
5. The use of recording equipment may be intrusive
6. The use of note taking as a complement to or in lieu of taping relies on memory

Hence, there are problems with the collection of natural data. Holmes (1989), for example, collected a corpus of 183 remedial interchanges, that is, apologies and apology responses. The research assistants in this study reported difficulty in obtaining the data. Another study attempted to capture on videotape a series of induced apology situations, but the investigators encountered numerous difficulties (Murillo, Aguilar, & Meditz, 1991). In this study, students crouched just outside faculty members' doors; when the professors emerged from their office, they would inadvertently bump into the student and would need to apologize. The method was time-consuming because it could not be predicted when the targeted faculty members would emerge from their offices, and too often there was either no audible apology or a mumbled apology that was not captured on the videotape.

## *Naturally occurring data versus discourse completion data*

Hartford and Bardovi-Harlig (1992) compared naturally occurring data from native-speaker and nonnative-speaker[12] rejections of advice collected from spontaneous conversation in thirty-nine academic advising sessions (eighteen with native speakers and twenty-one with nonnative speakers) with data collected from a discourse completion task (thirteen native speakers and eleven nonnative speakers). They found that the discourse completion task elicited a narrower range of semantic formulas, fewer status-preserving strategies, and none of the extended negotiations found in the natural data. Their explanation was that the dis-

11 That is, structures as they are used in communicative functions in the real world.

12 Unless stated otherwise, the terms *native speaker* and *nonnative speaker* are used in this chapter in reference to the English language; and American refers to citizens and residents of the United States.

course completion task did not promote the turn-taking and negotiation strategies found in natural conversations. Furthermore, the discourse completion task allowed the students to be less polite (i.e., to use fewer status-preserving strategies) and to employ more outlandish statements than did the natural situation because of the absence of face-to-face interaction and despite the respondents' lower status in the discourse task. Finally, the respondents were able to opt out with the discourse completion task, which was not the case in the natural situation.[13]

On the positive side, however, the discourse completion task allowed the testing of hypotheses derived from instances when there were insufficient data from the natural conversations (e.g., testing of the hypothesis that nonnative speakers made a greater use of unacceptable content in their rejections). It was found that the discourse completion task provided data to help explain and interpret the natural data. The more difficult the situation to negotiate in real life (e.g., "You dropped a required course last semester and find out now that it won't be offered until after you graduate"), the greater the difference between natural and elicited data. The researchers concluded that, although there was a need for more observational data, the discourse completion task had an important role to play.

Beebe and Takahashi (1989b) have also pointed out the limitations of using naturally occurring data. They conducted a study assessing American and Japanese performance on two face-threatening acts – disagreement and giving embarrassing information – and combined an ethnographic approach (i.e., keeping a notebook of naturally occurring instances of face-threatening acts) with discourse completion tasks on a written role-play questionnaire (twelve situations, allowing the fifteen American and fifteen Japanese respondents to opt out). They found that the naturally occurring notebook data were biased toward the linguistic preferences of friends, relatives, and associates – since these were the people with whom they tended to interact. They also found a bias in favor of short exchanges because the investigators were not able to record long exchanges in their notebook. Finally, the researchers tended to record utterances with atypical or nonnative-sounding elements because these stood out from more routine utterances.

In another study which, among other things, compared refusals in spontaneous speech and in written discourse completion tasks, Beebe and Cumming (in press) found that the written discourse completion

13 Sometimes in real life, respondents may actually be able to opt out more easily. In fact, Bonikowska (1988) sees instructions in tasks such as discourse completion as a potential hindrance because they force subjects to perform linguistically, whereas in real life they might choose to opt out – for example, in a highly face-threatening act.

task was an effective means for gathering a large amount of data quickly, for creating an initial classification of semantic formulas, and for ascertaining the structure of refusals. However, the discourse completion task did not elicit natural speech with respect to actual wording, range of formulas and strategies, length of responses,[14] or number of conversational turns necessary to fulfill a function.[15] Nor did such discourse completion tasks adequately represent the depth of emotion and general psychosocial dynamics of naturally occurring speech.

## *Multiple comparisons of data collection methods*

Research has also been conducted comparing the open-ended discourse completion task with the version which includes a rejoinder so as to close or structure the response. A study by Bardovi-Harlig and Hartford (1993b) compared the influence of the two forms of discourse completion tasks on the elicitation of rejections of advice. Responses from nineteen native and thirteen nonnative speakers to an open questionnaire which provided scenarios alone were compared with those from a classic dialogue completion task in which a conversational turn was provided. The dialogue completion task was based on authentic language from earlier pilot tests. The researchers concluded that in the case of reactive speech acts (i.e., those which never stand alone) such as rejections, the inclusion of conversational turns is the preferred format. The specificity of the dialogue completion task vis-à-vis the open questionnaire was found to be particularly helpful for the nonnative respondents. It seemed that the native speakers were more adept at imagining a plausible conversational turn in a given scenario than the nonnative speakers, and so for them the inclusion of a written conversational rejoinder made less difference.

A study by Bodman and Eisenstein (1988) used three methodologies to collect data on expressions of gratitude. Speakers of various languages provided written open-ended discourse tasks. Then the researchers collected role-play data from thirty-four native-speaking pairs, forty nonnative-speaking pairs, and twenty-four sets of nonnative speakers paired with native speakers. They also tape-recorded naturally occurring conversations containing expressions of gratitude. Their finding was that all three methods produced similar results in terms of the words and expressions used. The written questionnaires were found to be representative but limited with regard to the quantity and range of response, a finding similar to that of Beebe and Cumming (in press)

14 For example, there were four times fewer words and sentences in the written task than over the phone.

15 That is, there were fewer in written discourse.

with regard to refusals. Role play was also found to be somewhat artificial. Bodman and Eisenstein's recommendation was that all three methodological approaches be integrated into the same study.

## *Verbal report interviews*

### THE PRODUCTION OF SPEECH ACTS

The use of verbal report interviews is a relatively new means of collecting data on speech act behavior and has potential for providing insights into the production and perception of speech acts. There have been only a few studies of speech act production to date that have used verbal report. Perhaps the earliest study was by Motti (1987); it involved ten intermediate EFL university students in Brazil. After filling out a discourse completion task calling for apologies in English, the students were asked to provide a retrospective verbal report in Portuguese with regard to a series of variables, including their depth of analysis of the situation before response and the extent to which they thought through their response in the foreign language (English) or in Portuguese (their native language) while preparing and writing their responses.[16]

In another study, Robinson (1991) asked twelve native Japanese-speaking women to respond to six written discourse completion items calling for refusals of requests and invitations in English. The respondents were asked to think aloud as they filled out the items, and their verbal reports were tape-recorded. Immediately after completing the task, the researcher interviewed the subjects individually for 20 to 30 minutes regarding the content of their utterances from the think-aloud session, playing back the tape recording to remind the respondents of specific thoughts.

Another study which called for role playing and then verbal report after all the tasks had been completed was that of Frescura (1993). Role-play data on apologies were tape-recorded from native Italian speakers in Italy, native English speakers in Canada, Italians residing in Canada, and English-Canadian learners of Italian (a total of 83 respondents). After being tape-recorded in six role-play interactions, the respondents were asked to listen to all six recordings and to provide a retrospective verbal report on(1) how close to real life they felt their performance to be, (2) how dominant they felt their interlocutor was, (3) how sensitive they were to the severity of the offense and to the tone of the complaint, and (4) for Italians in Canada and learners of Italian, what their linguistic difficulties were.

16 Motti found that respondents thought slightly more in English than in Portuguese in the planning and execution of their utterances and were preoccupied with correctness. Respondents also reported paying more attention to the interlocutors' status than to their age.

A study by Cohen and Olshtain (1993) sought to describe ways in which nonnative speakers plan and execute speech act utterances. The fifteen advanced foreign language learners of English who served as subjects in the study were given six speech act situations in which they played a role with a native speaker. The interactions were videotaped, and after each set of two situations of the same type, the tape was played back and the respondents were asked both fixed questions and open-ended probes regarding the factors contributing to the production of their response to that situation.

In the administration of the role-play interview, the interlocutor gave the respondents an opportunity to read the descriptions of two brief role-play situations at a time (two apologies, two complaints, and two requests in all). Then she read each situation slowly out loud, gave the respondent time to think of a response, gave her opener, and had the respondent role-play with her. The interaction was videotaped and audiotaped as well. The probing interviews conducted after each set of two speech act situations had the intent of employing retrospective self-observation in order to obtain verbal report data about the cognitive processes that went into the production of speech act realizations. The interviewer's probes were conducted in what was the native language for eleven of the respondents and a language of greater proficiency than English for the other four respondents.

Effort was made to have the respondents be precise and to give examples where possible. The subjects were interviewed in three sessions – after the apology, complaint, and request situations, respectively – instead of waiting until after all six speech act situations, in order to obtain more accurate retrospective reports of behavior. It was feared that the delaying of the verbal report would reduce the reliability of the retrospective data, even though the videotape was used as a memory aid. When the respondents were not sure about what they did and why, the interviewers played the relevant portion of the videotaped session a second or even a third time. This usually helped to jog the respondent's memory.

### THE PERCEPTION OF SPEECH ACTS

With regard to the perception of speech acts, Benander (1990) underscored the value of direct interview data as a complement for data obtained through discourse completion tasks. She pointed out that the interviewer needs to ask the right kinds of questions, but that a well-designed interview has the potential of eliciting explanations from the respondents regarding their interpretation of the prompt and the reasons for what they say or do not say. In her study on the interpretation of speech acts, Benander gave the example of obtaining from eight native speakers of American English and from eight native Japanese speakers their respective interpretations of compliments in English. The following dialogue was used to illustrate differences in interpretation between native and nonnative speakers of English:

A: What school are you in?
B: Wharton.
A: Oh, you're really smart.
B: Thank you. That is a really tough school.

Interview data showed that the Japanese respondents judged this conversation to be acceptable if it were between friends. If it were between acquaintances, they believed that B would be rude for being too proud but A would be fine. The Americans judged both speakers very harshly even if they were friends, describing A as "stupid" or "an airhead" and B as "arrogant," "conceited," or "a jerk" (Benander 1990, p. 27).

In another study which used verbal report interviews to elucidate findings based on naturally occurring data, Creese (1991) interviewed eight American and four British respondents in order to elicit their perceptions concerning speech act differences between the two cultures. All the Americans either had been to Britain or had had extensive contact with British people outside of the United States, and the British respondents had been living in the United States for various periods of time. The respondents were given a list of speech acts and asked whether they observed any differences in the way the speech acts were expressed in the two cultures. With regard to requests, the Americans perceived the English as being more polite and generally more indirect than Americans. With respect to complimenting, seven of the respondents believed that Americans complimented more than British people. Of these, one believed that Americans used much stronger adjectives (e.g., *great*).

Finally, several recent studies have used videotaped material as a stimulus for obtaining speech act perceptions through questionnaire response. Zuskin (1993) looked at the perception of speech acts by investigating the interpretation of videotaped role plays in twelve vignettes involving apologies, requests, refusals, and complaints. Using a somewhat similar methodology, Edmundson (1992) examined the ways that the semantic formulas in apologies from TV dramas are interpreted and the processes used in arriving at the interpretations. (Details of these two studies are presented later in this chapter.)

## A review of some recent empirical studies

This section will provide a brief review of some of the recent empirical studies of second language speech act behavior. For an earlier and much more extensive review, see Wolfson (1989), which deals with the sociolinguistic behavior of English speakers and, especially, with forms of address, apologies, requests, disapproval, refusals, and the expression of gratitude. The book serves as a compendium for what had and had not been studied by the late 1980s.

## *Apologies*

With regard to more recent studies on the speech act of apology, three studies described in this section involved the production of apologies, and two the perception of apologies. With respect to production, an extensive study by Holmes (1989) presented the range of strategies serving as apologies in a New Zealand corpus of 183 naturally occurring remedial exchanges and the linguistic formulas used in these exchanges. The distribution of apologies was analyzed according to the type of offense needing remedy, the gender of the subjects, and the social relationship between the participants. Holmes found a number of differences based on gender; for example, women used apologies more than men overall, women apologized to other women more than to men, and men apologized to women more than to other men. Men's apologies often alluded to the offender, and women's apologies focused more on the offended person. Other gender differences were found with respect to seriousness of the offense, status difference, social distance, and frequency of acceptance of apologies by the offended party.

Another apology production study, already mentioned earlier, was that of Frescura (1993). Data from role plays were coded according to a taxonomy comprising seven semantic formulas in two categories: *hearer-supportive* formulas and *self-supportive* formulas. The hearer-supportive formulas were used when complainees chose to support the face of the complainer by admitting their own guilt, by recognizing the complainer's rights, or by offering compensation. The self-supportive formulas were used when complainees chose to support their own face by denying guilt, by appealing to the complainer's leniency, or by providing an explanation for the offense. Performance was measured according to the total output of formulas, the types of formulas used, and the intensity of the formulas produced.

Frescura found that native speakers of Italian in Italy preferred the self-supportive formulas overall, whereas native speakers of English preferred the hearer-supportive ones. Learners of Italian did not indicate any preference, whereas native Italian speakers in Canada appeared to maintain some native Italian formulas.

In the final study of production treated here, Linnell, Porter, Stone, and Chen (1992) used the verbal discourse completion situations designed by Cohen and Olshtain (1981) in assessing oral apologies among twenty native and twenty nonnative speakers of English. No significant differences were found between the two groups in six of the eight situations which included situations such as forgetting a meeting with a boss, forgetting a meeting with a friend, and bumping into an elderly lady in a department store. However, the explicit expression of an apology, acknowledgment of responsibility, and intensification of the expression of apology were used significantly less by nonnative speakers in two of the situations. Nonnative speakers also used an explicit apology and an intensifier in an unintentional insult situation significantly less than native speakers and undersupplied an acknowledgment of responsibility for forgetting a meeting with a boss. In addition, performance on the speech act task was not found to correlate significantly with TOEFL scores.

With regard to the perception of apologies, Edmundson (1992) looked specifically at the perception of the semantic formulas in apologies. The study attempted to determine (1) the ways in which semantic formulas are interpreted by native speakers, (2) the cues that subjects use to interpret the sincerity of an apology and the likelihood that it would be accepted, and (3) the rules needed to account for variety in interpretations of semantic formulas. Her study demonstrated one problematic aspect of research which examines strategies in realizing a speech act – namely, that often, one element can be placed in more than one category. In her study, 161 native speakers of English from Introduction to Language classes at Indiana University were asked to view one of two videos containing six apologies from several popular TV programs and to answer several questions concerning each apology.

There were some general patterns of interpretation but much variation in the responses. Subjects used mostly prosodic cues (i.e., intonation and word stress) to judge the sincerity of an apology. Women relied on lexical cues to judge the acceptability of an apology, and men (one-third of the sample) relied on lexical, paralinguistic (nonverbal), and prosodic cues equally. Two interpretations of what accepting an apology means were found. Some thought that it means "acknowledging the offense and forgiving the offender." Others thought that it means "acknowledging that the social balance was fine" (either because the social balance had been restored or because, according to their perception of the situation, there had never been anything wrong in the first place). The appropriateness of an apology was rated according to its level of sincerity. Edmundson also found that the semantic formula justification, explanation, or excuse, which she had posited as one category, was interpreted by the subjects as two or three different categories. Hence, her research paradigm allowed for a validation of the semantic formulas themselves.

Zuskin (1993) supplemented a discourse completion task with audiovisual prompts that were given via video as a means for assessing second language sociocultural and sociolinguistic knowledge. In this study, 103 nonnative and 63 native speakers of American English were asked to interpret the messages contained in twelve vignettes involving apologies, requests, refusals, and complaints. Subjects rated each vignette according to three criteria: (1) the degree of status inequality between the two main characters in the scene, (2) the degree of formality designated by the situation, and (3) the degree of imposition on the interlocutor who was expected to produce a specific speech act. The study examined the overlap between grammatical and sociolinguistic proficiency and the extent to which male-female subcultural norms influenced perceptions about politeness.

Zuskin found few general differences either between native English and linguistically heterogeneous nonnative interpretations of the vignettes or between the interpretations made by the various subgroups of nonnative speakers.[17] However, for three of the twelve vignettes, the gender of the subjects was a significant factor in interpreting the speech acts, contributing more to the variance than either subjects' proficiency level or the interaction between gender and proficiency level. The more grammatically skilled foreign language subjects did not prove to be more sociolinguistically skilled.

## *Refusals*

A refusal study conducted in 1985 (Beebe and Cumming, in press) compared refusals in spontaneous speech and written discourse completion tasks. Twenty-two female native English-speaking ESL teachers were asked whether they could assist the local team in organizing an upcoming national TESOL conference, eleven by questionnaire and eleven by phone. As noted in the preceding discussion of research methodology, the findings demonstrated that the discourse completion task worked well for gathering a large amount of data quickly in order to create an initial classification of semantic formulas and to ascertain the structure of refusals. In only five of twenty-seven semantic formulas or subformulas was there a difference of three or more tokens[18] between the oral and written data. However, the discourse completion task did not elicit the actual wording, the full range of formulas and strategies, the length of responses, or the number of turns necessary to fulfill a function, all of which normally occur in natural speech.

In a follow-up study, Takahashi and Beebe (1987) investigated writ-

17 The scale which was the most sensitive to differences between the native and nonnative groups was that of degree of imposition on the interlocutor.

18 *Tokens* are realizations of the given semantic formula.

ten refusals by native speakers of English, native speakers of Japanese, Japanese ESL students in the United States, and Japanese EFL students in Japan (twenty in each group). They found evidence that transfer existed in both the EFL and ESL contexts and at both lower and higher proficiency levels, with native language influence generally stronger in the EFL context and with negative transfer of native language speech act behavior occurring more at the more advanced levels of ESL (but not EFL). The interpretation that the researchers gave for this negative transfer was that the greater facility of the advanced students at speaking English allowed them to express notions that seemed typically Japanese (e.g., being "deeply honored" to receive a simple invitation).

In another follow-up study, Beebe, Takahashi, and Uliss-Weltz (1990) asked subjects to fill out a discourse completion task; there were twenty subjects in each category: Japanese L1, English L1, and Japanese ESL. Twelve situations and four types of refusals (required because of the rejoinder) comprised the discourse completion task: three requests, three invitations, three offers,and three suggestions – one of each type to persons of higher, equal, and lower status. They found that pragmatic transfer influenced the English of Japanese speakers in the United States in terms of order, frequency, and intrinsic content (or tone) of the semantic formulas they selected for their refusals. Although excuses were common for subjects from both languages, native Japanese excuses in Japanese were less specific than American ones in English (e.g., in refusing an invitation, they just said that they were busy, whereas Americans specified what prevented them from accepting). Also, native Japanese speakers' responses in Japanese sounded more formal in tone than the Americans' English responses.

In Robinson's multimethod study (1991), described earlier, twelve native Japanese-speaking women responded to a written discourse completion task that called for refusals of requests and invitations in English. The respondents were asked to think aloud as they completed the task, and their verbal reports were tape-recorded. Although given the option of responding in Japanese, all respondents reported in English, which the investigator attributed to her inability to speak Japanese. The use of verbal report in this case helped to reveal a sociocultural problem which these respondents had with the refusal task. Since Japanese women are brought up to say yes, or at least not to say no, the task of refusing was difficult for them to perform.

A final refusal study looked at pragmatic transfer in ESL refusals by Japanese speakers and provided material for cross-cultural programs which train American businesspeople to deal more effectively with Japanese clients (Tickle, 1991). The subjects were thirty-one Japanese men who had a minimum of 5 years of business experience, all in the United States for about a year. The results of a discourse completion task showed that turf (the customer's vs. the businessperson's), relationship (positive or negative), status (higher or lower), and function (i.e., a refusal to an invitation vs. a refusal to a request) affected the frequency, content, and order of semantic formulas used in Japanese L1 refusals. Directness was used more often in refusals on a customer's turf but also with more gratitude and regret. There was also more directness in refusals when no prior relationship existed between the interlocutors. More regret was expressed from the lower-status interlocutor to the higher-status one, as it was in refusals to invitations (e.g., to go drinking). More negative willingness/ability (e.g., "I can't") and empathy (rather than regret) occurred in refusals to requests (e.g., of co-workers).

## *Rejections*

Bardovi-Harlig and Hartford conducted a series of studies investigating rejections used by native and proficient nonnative speakers of English during audiotaped academic advising sessions (Bardovi-Harlig & Hartford, 1991, 1993a). They found that, whereas native speakers are able to reject an adviser's suggestion while maintaining the status balance, nonnative speakers are less predictably able to do so.

The Hartford and Bardovi-Harlig study (1992) discussed in detail earlier compared data on rejections of advice by native and nonnative English speakers from naturally occurring conversations in academic advising sessions with data collected from a discourse completion task. It was found that nonnative speakers used more semantic formulas to realize each rejection and made more rejections altogether than did native speakers, and native speakers made suggestions more than twice as often as they rejected advice. Three semantic formulas predominated in the speech act of rejection: explanations, alternatives, and rejections. Also, numerous less common semantic formulas were found in the data.

## *Compliments*

In the second of two studies, Creese (1991) collected naturally occurring compliments from a teachers' lounge at the University of Pennsylvania and from a teachers' lounge at a school in London. Her in-depth analysis of this cross-cultural data looked at lexical predictability, compliment response, syntactic categories, and compliment topic. She found overall similarity between the two groups in the first two areas, although the British speakers tended to deflect compliments slightly more. However, with regard to syntactic preference, British speakers preferred the syntactic pattern *NP is/looks (intensification) ADJ* (40 percent of the cases) (e.g., "That shirt looks really neat"), while Americans preferred *I (intensification) like/love NP* (42 percent of the cases) (e.g., "I really like your shirt"). Although Americans used the preferred British pattern 34 percent of the time, the British used the Americans' preferred pattern only 12 percent of the time. With respect to compliment topic, Americans complimented more on someone's appearance than on their ability (66 percent vs. 33 percent), but for the British speakers this was reversed (54 percent for ability vs. 39 percent for appearance).

Benander's study of speech act perception(1990), discussed in detail earlier, used ten short dialogue situations in which six respondents (three Japanese and three Americans) described the nature of each situation in writing and stated whether what people said to each other was "nice." Another ten subjects (five Japanese and five Americans) responded through oral interview. Benander found that native speakers were more likely to identify inappropriate compliment behavior, as in "fishing for a compliment" or in showing conceit in response to a compliment. On the other hand, native speakers were more likely to justify being rude if the compliment was not interpreted as a positive assessment but rather as a joke or a come-on. Native speakers tended to point out how apparent compliments could be interpreted as either inappropriate or unpleasant.[19]

Finally, Olshtain and Weinbach (1988) looked at 330 Israeli and 330 American responses to compliments through the use of a discourse completion task and found five forms of response: reinforcing the compliment, simply thanking the complimenter, agreeing with it, justifying it, or expressing surprise. They concluded that Israelis accepted a compliment with greater difficulty than Americans. Although the American subjects were likely to say "thank-you," Israelis tended to apologize, to justify the compliment, or to be surprised.

## *Complaints*

A study by Piotrowska (1987) used a discourse completion task to collect written complaints from two groups: EFL respondents in their final year in the English department of the English-medium University of Hong Kong and native English speakers. She used categories from Schaefer (1982): an opener, an orientation statement, an act statement, a justification of the speaker or addressee, a remedy or threat, a closing,

19 This observation about native speakers suggests the difficulties faced by second language teachers in providing a "complete" understanding of all the communicative functions of a given speech act. Ironic uses – such as facetiousness and sarcasm – tend to complicate the burden of teaching considerably. One study of speech acts, that of Rundquist (1991), has examined how apologies are used differently by men and women in regard to implied intent. The problem is that, if nonnative speakers are to acquire communicative competence, they may need to master such alternative meanings. It would be difficult, to say the least, to set up realistic classroom situations that imitate the natural settings in which speech acts are ironically performed.

and a valuation statement about the addressee or the wrong committed. She also added eight categories: societal justification, a request for an explanation, blame, resignation, conciliation, persuasion, indirect disagreement, and a request for agreement. The original categories from Schaefer accounted for 94 percent of native realizations and 86 percent of nonnative-speaker data. The study also elicited several other strategies – an expression of gratitude, an appeal for understanding, an apology, a counter to denial by the complainee, and a request for an opinion.

In another study using discourse completion, DeCapua (1988) looked at complaints in English by fifty native speakers of German (American Field Service students in the United States for a year of high school) and fifty American college students. The semantic formulas used repeatedly by the German respondents were a statement of the problem (the act statement) and a request or demand for repair. Threats were also used for more serious problems. Female respondents made more requests for repairs than males, and there were also more requests for repair in German than in English. Transfer errors from German into English sometimes produced overly adamant complaints, as in "You *must* pay for a new one" (a translation of *müssen* from German) rather than *should*.

In order to examine responses to complaints, Boxer (1989) conducted a participant observation study of naturally occurring data involving university personnel in 70 complaint sequences. Six types of responses to the complaints emerged from the data: (1) zero response or change of topic – a response to chronic complainers, (2) a request for an elaboration of the complaint – possibly a delaying tactic, (3) a response in the form of joking or teasing, (4) a contradiction or explanation, (5) advice or a lecture, and (6) commiseration. The last type appeared in 52 percent of the cases, and most of these cases were in the "bulge" (Wolfson, 1989), that is, occurred among status equals who were neither at minimal nor at maximal social distance (thus excluding both intimates and strangers). The other types appeared in fewer than 15 percent of the cases.

Boxer (1993) conducted a study of indirect complaints, involving 295 interlocutors producing 533 such complaints. She defined an *indirect complaint* as a negative evaluation wherein the addressee is not held responsible for the perceived offense (i.e., griping) – the expression of dissatisfaction to an interlocutor about a speaker himself/herself or someone or something not present. She found that indirect complaints were frequently employed in an attempt to establish rapport or solidarity between interlocutors. She also identified six types of responses to them: none or a topic switch, a question, a contradiction, a joke or teasing, advice or a lecture, or commiseration. She found that the native speaker's reaction to complaints was often that of commiserating and indicated that nonnative speakers need to know this if they wish to build solidarity with the speaker. With respect to gender differences, women were mostly found to commiserate with indirect complaints, and men were more prone to contradict them or to give advice.

## *Requests*

Fukushima and Iwata (1987) compared strategies used in requesting and offering among eighteen native Japanese and fourteen native English speakers in the United States and among fourteen native English speakers in Japan. The study found that the sequence of semantic formulas in request utterances was generally similar in Japanese and English: apology→reason→request, address term→request→reason, or address term and/or apology→reason (where the reason functioned as a request). In addition, similar strategies were used in the two languages with regard to understaters, grounders (the reason for the request), cost minimization, and address terms (attention getters). However, Japanese respondents made distinctions between sociocultural strategies and sociolinguistic expressions depending on the closeness of friendship, whereas American English-speaking respondents did not.

Goldschmidt (1989) examined the favor as a form of request. Data on favor asking was collected ethnographically and analyzed according to the status, gender, age, and social relationships of the participants. Among the strategies were being minimally offensive, showing the importance of the need for a favor, hinting at reciprocation, and building solidarity. Three types of favors were identified: veiled obligation, a veiled favor, and a true favor.

In addition, the Cohen and Olshtain verbal report study of speech act production (1993) produced an interesting finding with regard to requesting. The study gave empirical backing to the fact that not all speaking tasks are created equal – that there are tasks which make far greater demands on learners than do others. The seemingly simple task of requesting a lift home from a teacher, for example, was the task which called for the most mental logistics in terms of selecting the language of thought and monitoring for pronunciation and grammar. Verbal report revealed that for the French-Hebrew-English trilingual, the request itself was the result of mental processing in three languages and of repeated internal debate as to which lexical word or phrase to choose. Respondents also reported doing more monitoring for pronunciation and grammar because they were speaking to their teacher.

## *Other speech acts*

Bodman and Eisenstein (1988), cited earlier, investigated expressions of gratitude with speakers of various languages. Their corpus consisted of ninety-eight role plays: thirty-four performed by native pairs, forty by nonnative pairs, and twenty-four by native speakers paired with nonnative speakers. They found thanking to be a speech act that was mutually developed by the two interlocutors. The giver (i.e., the person being thanked) was seen to be as active during the speech act as the thanker in commenting, prompting, and reacting, as well as in providing needed reassurance and approval. The thanker asked for favors, gifts, or services indirectly and, once these were offered, made ritual refusals and downplayed the giver's obligation. The investigators found that even advanced learners of English still had considerable difficulty in such thanking situations, requiring information on what to say or needing experience in attending to what native speakers said.

Beebe and Takahashi (1989a, 1989b) looked at the performance of American and advanced Japanese ESL speakers in three face-threatening acts: disagreement, giving embarrassing information, and chastisement. The researchers made notes about naturally occurring instances of face-threatening acts and asked fifteen American and fifteen Japanese respondents to do a discourse completion task in English with twelve situations and a choice of opting out. They found that, contrary to popular belief, the American respondents were not always more direct or more explicit than the Japanese respondents, nor did the Japanese always avoid disagreement or critical remarks.[20] Although both Japanese and American respondents used questions to warn, correct, disagree, chastise, or signal embarrassing information, the questions asked differed significantly in tone and content from one group to the other. In general, the Americans used positive remarks more frequently and in more places than did the Japanese.

Finally, the style of both the Japanese and the American respondents shifted in English according to the status of the interlocutor. The Japanese subjects were more outspoken if they did not like the boss's plan. To explain this, the investigators speculated that this candidness may have resulted from the context of second language learning – that is, their ESL guise influenced their behavior. Another explanation would be overcompensation in the efforts of the subjects to conform to their perception of the more direct speech patterns of American English.

Takahashi and Beebe (1993 in press) examined American and Japanese performance in the speech act of correction in language classrooms – a situation of status inequality in which a higher-status person, the teacher, corrects the error of a lower-status person, the student. The investigators gave a twelve-situation discourse completion task to fifteen native English speakers and fifteen Japanese speakers in the United States – all of whom responded in English – and to fifteen Japanese

20 They were most critical when talking to lower-status persons.

speakers in Japan who responded in Japanese. They found that positive remarks were an important adjunct to face-threatening acts in English – "I agree with you, but . . ." Although 64 percent of Americans did this, only 13 percent of the Japanese speaking in Japanese did so. All groups used softeners such as "I believe" and "I think" and questions like "Did you say . . . ?" In addition, they used expressions that played down the gravity of the mistake (e.g., "You made one small error in the date") or that defended the interlocutor. The Japanese respondents used softeners less frequently in the ESL context than did native English speakers. Both groups used more verbal softeners than did the Japanese respondents in Japanese, although paralinguistic means such as facial expressions, tone of voice, sighs, and hesitancy served that function among the last group. Although the Japanese were more overtly conscious of status and did not cover it up in their use of language, the Americans were found to harbor a polite fiction that they and their interlocutors were equals.

## The acquisition of speech acts

To date, there appear to be only a few studies of the untutored acquisition of oral speech act behavior among nonnative speakers. One such study was conducted with elementary school children, and another study was conducted with college students.

Ellis (1992) looked at the extent to which communication in an ESL classroom in London resulted in the acquisition of requests by a 10-year-old Portuguese speaker and an 11-year-old Punjabi speaker. The latter had had little formal education in Pakistan. Ellis recorded 108 requests over 16 months for the former and 302 requests over 21 months for the latter. The researcher made a written record of everything the subjects said and had an audio recording as a backup. He found that both learners failed to develop a full range of request types and also lacked a broad linguistic repertoire for performing the types of requests that they were able to acquire. They also failed to develop the sociolinguistic competence needed to vary their choice of request to take account of different addressees. The researcher's interpretation was that the classroom lacked the conditions for the whole range of sociolinguistic needs even though it fostered interpersonal and expressive needs. There were no data, however, as to the kinds of requests the two boys were exposed to.

In the study with college students, Bardovi-Harlig and Hartford (1993a) conducted longitudinal research on the acquisition of pragmatic competence, specifically on the speech acts of suggestion and rejection. Ten advanced adult nonnative speakers of English were taped in two advising sessions over the course of a semester – an early and a later session. The speech acts of suggestion and rejection were analyzed according to their frequency, form, and successfulness and compared with similar data gathered from six native speakers. The nonnative speakers showed a change toward the native speaker norms in their ability to employ appropriate speech acts, moving toward using more suggestions and fewer rejections, and they became more successful negotiators. However, they changed less in their ability to employ appropriate forms of the two speech acts, continuing to use fewer mitigators than the native speakers. Furthermore, unlike native speakers, they also used aggravators. The investigators claimed that these results may be explained by the nature of the input: learners received positive and negative feedback from the adviser regarding the desirability and outcome of particular speech acts, but they did not receive such feedback regarding the appropriateness of the sociolinguistic forms that they used to realize those speech acts.

## The teaching of speech acts

The fact that speech acts reflect, for the most part, routinized language behavior helps learning in the sense that much of what is said is predictable. For example, almost half the time an adjective is used in a compliment, it is either *nice* or *good* (e.g., "That's a nice shirt you're wearing" or "It was a good talk you gave"), with *beautiful, pretty,* and *great* making up another 15 percent (Wolfson & Manes, 1980). Yet despite the routinized nature of speech acts, there are still various strategies to choose from – depending on the sociocultural context – and often a variety of possible language forms for realizing these strategies, especially in the case of speech acts with four or more possible semantic formulas such as apologies and complaints. Target language learners may tend to respond the way they would in their native language and culture and find that their utterances are not at all appropriate for the target language and cultural situation.

The findings from a cross-cultural study by Cohen, Olshtain, and Rosenstein (1986) can serve as an example of gaps between native and advanced nonnative apology behavior in English. The 180 respondents for this study included 84 native Hebrew-speaking advanced learners of English studying at one of five Israeli universities and a comparison group of 96 native speakers of American English studying at one of six U.S. universities. The basic finding was that nonnative speakers lacked sensitivity to certain sociolinguistic distinctions that native speakers make, such as between forms for realizing the semantic formula of expressing an apology, for example, *excuse me* and *sorry.* At least one of every five times a native speaker offered an expression of apology, it was with *excuse me,* whereas few nonnative speakers used this form. Nonnative speakers limited themselves to the use of *sorry* in contexts where *excuse me* would also be acceptable and possibly preferable.

Although native speakers and nonnative speakers did not seem to differ markedly in the use of main strategies for apologizing, striking differences emerged in the various modifications of such apologies, especially in the use of intensifiers such as *very* and *really.* Nonnative speakers intensified their expression of apology significantly more in one situation (forgetting to help a friend buy a bike) than did native speakers. This extra intensity on the part of the nonnative speakers was not necessarily warranted, given the generally low or moderate severity of the offense in that situation.

Non only did nonnative speakers tend to intensify more, but they also used a wider and more indiscriminate set of forms. Actually, the nonnative pattern was either to overgeneralize one of the forms (*very* and *sorry*) or to use a variety of forms (*terribly, awfully, truly*). The nonnative speakers did not use *really* in the way that the native speakers did. They attributed to the intensifier *very* the same semantic properties as to *really,* whereas the native speakers tended to make a distinction whereby *really* expressed a greater depth of apology, regret, and concern and *very* was used more for matters of social etiquette. For example, in a situation of scalding a friend with coffee in a cafeteria, the native speakers tended to use *really sorry* and nonnative speakers used *very sorry,* which sounded less intensified.

There is evidence that acquisition of nativelike production by nonnative speakers may take many years (Olshtain & Blum-Kulka, 1984) because the sociocultural strategies and the sociolinguistic forms are not always "picked up" easily. Hence, the question has arisen as to whether speech act strategies can be taught effectively. The research question is whether teachers would be contributing to the learners by explicitly teaching them some of the finely tuned speech act behavior that is not simply acquired over time. The rationale for doing this would be that learners do not necessarily have an adequate awareness of what is involved in complex speech behavior. The purpose of research would be to gather information that could then be used to prepare a course of instruction to teach gaps in speech act behavior.

At present, there are only a few published studies dealing with explicit teaching or tutoring of speech act behavior, but the findings seem promising. For example, Olshtain and Cohen (1990) conducted a study with advanced EFL learners in Israel, ten of whom were studying in private language schools and eight in a teachers college. Native speakers of American English provided baseline data for comparative purposes. The learners were pretested to determine gaps in their apologizing behavior. Then they were taught a set of three 20-minute lessons aimed at filling in the gaps – information about the strategies within the apology speech act set and about modifications of apologies through the use of intensification and emotionals. Finally, they were posttested to determine what was learned.

The findings suggested that the fine points of speech act behavior, such as (1) types of intensification and downgrading, (2) subtle differences between speech act strategy realizations, and (3) consideration of situational features, can be taught in the foreign language classroom. Whereas before the instruction, the nonnative speakers' apologies differed noticeably from those of the native speakers, after instruction, advanced learners were somewhat more likely to select apology strategies similar to those used by native speakers in that situation. For example, in a situation of forgetting to buy medicine for a neighbor's sick child, the response of one nonnative before training was a weak expression of responsibility ("Unfortunately not yet . . .") and an offer of repair (". . . but I'll be happy to do it right now."). After training, it was an intensified expression of apology ("I'm deeply sorry.") and an offer of repair ("I can do it right now."). Furthermore, after training, nonnative speakers produced shorter utterances, also more in keeping with native behavior.

Prior to instruction, one learner responded verbosely to a situation of forgetting to meet a friend with "Did you wait for me? You must forgive me. I could not come because of problems and I tried to warn you by phone but . . ." This response was typical of learners at the advanced-intermediate stage of language acquisition who, when uncertain about how to say something, would overcompensate by using too many words (Blum-Kulka & Olshtain, 1986). After training, the utterance was shorter: "Oh, I'm so sorry. It dropped out of my mind." Perhaps the area that met with most success was that of the use of intensifiers. Before training, intensifiers were generally absent in situations like forgetting to buy medicine for a neighbor's sick child (only 20 percent use). After training, intensifiers (e.g., "I'm really sorry I forgot . . .") were used in almost all cases (90 percent).

In another study involving the teaching of speech acts, Billmyer (1990) compared nine female Japanese ESL learners tutored in complimenting and responding to compliments with nine similar learners who were untutored in complimenting. The study assessed not just the speech act but the reply – that is, whether the respondent accepted, deflected, or rejected the compliment – and the types of deflecting moves (a comment, a shift of credit, a downgrade, a request for reassurance, or a return). It was found that learners who were tutored in complimenting produced a greater number of norm-appropriate compliments, produced spontaneous compliments (which the untutored group did not), used a more extensive repertoire of semantically positive adjectives, and deflected many more compliments in their reply. The researcher concluded that formal classroom instruction concerning the social rules of language use can assist learners in communicating more appropriately with native speakers outside the classroom.

In a small-scale instructional study, a group of three intermediate ESL students received 70 minutes of training in refusal strategies in a conversation class (which the researchers admit may have been too little), and three others just received conversation on getting to know Americans (King & Silver, 1993). Pretests and posttests consisted of a written discourse questionnaire on refusals – without rejoinders. In addition, to elicit a spoken refusal, 2 weeks after instruction, participants were telephoned and asked to perform a burdensome activity known to conflict with their schedule (to give a talk when they had a class and to set up an information booth on exam day).

Results from the questionnaire indicated that instruction had had little effect, and the telephone interview indicated no effect. A large disparity between the written and the spoken refusal strategies was found. Although the study did not describe the responses in any detail, they apparently included saying something to make the person feel good before refusing, using a starter ("Let me see . . ."), using "That's too bad" instead of "I'm sorry" (which nonnative speakers overuse), and using specific rather than general excuses. The researchers were surprised to find that the telephone conversation prompted many fewer strategies than did the discourse completion task.

Finally, Dunham (1992) describes an informal study of 45 Southeast Asian high school students, employing the complimenting strategy as outlined by Wolfson. The students in the study were instructed on how to connect, that is, to maintain or continue the conversation based on the response of the addressee. Feedback from the students concerning their use of complimenting and connecting was encouraging and often resulted in increased confidence in initiating and maintaining conversations with native speakers.

The author then describes a series of ten techniques for teaching complimenting behavior (Dunham, 1992, pp. 82–83): reviewing how it is done in the native culture, reviewing how it is done in the United States, vocabulary phrase lists, student practice, role playing in pairs, teacher role play with students in front of the class, projects in which learners must compliment native speakers, students' oral reports to the class following their field experiences with native speakers, connecting techniques to lengthen conversation, and paired interaction with complimenting and connecting techniques.

## Implications for the language teacher, the learner, and the language classroom

Undoubtedly, a review of this nature leaves many questions unanswered. The field of sociolinguistics deals with variation and looks as much at how people differ in their speech behaviors as it does at how they are similar. Hence, it is somewhat risky to make assertions about the way that native speakers say *X, Y*, or *Z*. All the same, it is evident that there are somewhat predictable alternatives for how native speakers perform certain routinized speech acts, and these patterns can be and have been described and can be passed on to nonnative speakers as useful insights into how the language functions in communicative situations.

The role of the teacher-researcher can be to obtain some information on how native speakers perform certain important speech acts, such as requesting, complaining, and apologizing. This sounds like a tall order, but information is already available in some of the more empirically based textbooks. Other sources of information are available in the research literature (e.g., works cited in this chapter). If information is not available, a valid means for obtaining it is through observing speech acts as they occur naturally. As noted in this chapter, however, this may not be a very efficient means of obtaining data, especially if fine-tuned distinctions are desired. So, there is a need to turn to more contrived means whereby data are elicited in a more or less structured way.

Actually, if learners have access to native-speaking informants (more likely in a second language than in a foreign language learning experience), they could elicit speech act samples from the native speakers. In fact, this approach may enhance the learning process more than if the teacher were simply to lay out the possible alternatives in class.

Once descriptions of the speech acts are made available, the next task is to determine the degree of control that learners have over those speech acts through the multiple measures already suggested – role play, discourse completion tasks, verbal report interviews, and acceptability ratings. Ideally, this information could then be used to prepare a course of instruction that would fill in the gaps in language knowledge and also give tips on strategies that might be useful for producing utterances. The role of the learners is to notice similarities and differences between the way that native speakers perform such speech acts and the way that they do – which is often influenced to some extent by the way they would perform such communicative functions in their native language.

The following is a brief review of techniques for teaching speech acts. There are various means for presenting and rehearsing the use of speech acts. Whatever approach is used, it is always necessary to specify the situation (e.g., student making request of professor, patron complaining to waiter) and to indicate the social factors involved (age, sex, social class and occupation, roles in the interaction, status of the participants) and then to match the situation and the social factors with the most common realizations of the speech act. It is important for learners to realize, for example, that in English, neglecting to intensify an expression of apology dilutes the apology, and hence the apology might not be adequate when interacting with friends or interlocutors who have a higher status than they do. Unintensified apologies are more common with strangers and are appropriate when the infraction is not severe. Continuing with the example of apologizing, learners need to become aware that intensification with the word *very* is not always perceived as true intensification, since *really* is more common as an intensifier in colloquial American English. In order for learners to become aware of the preferred sociolinguistic forms for apologies, they need to be given the chance to compare apologies in a variety of contexts, carefully considering the similarities and differences.

The planning and implementation of lessons on speech acts could involve, among other things, the following five steps (adapted from Olshtain & Cohen, 1991):

1. Diagnostic assessment is often the first step which helps the teacher determine the students' level of awareness of speech acts in general and of the particular speech act to be taught. Such assessment can be done through acceptability ratings, to reveal perception of speech acts, or through discourse completion tasks or role play, to assess the ability to produce the speech acts. Such assessment can be done orally, in writing, or through a combination of the two. For example, in a task of speech act perception of acceptability, the student can be presented with a situation followed by a number of possible responses. For instance, suppose that one accidentally bumps into an older person in a department store, causing her to drop some packages. Which of the following apologies would be most appropriate? (1) "Forgive me, please." (2) "I'm really sorry. Are you okay?" (3) "Lady, such things happen." (4) "Hey, watch where you're going."

   If the students choose item 1, it may be a translation from what they would say in their native language. If they choose item 3 or 4, they may not see the event as constituting an infraction. In some cultures, bumping goes on so often in crowded places that apologizing would seem superfluous. If students choose item 2, they would be considered to have some grasp of what is appropriate in this instance. Production tasks could also be used; in this case, the learners are not given choices but instead provide their own responses. Once results have been obtained on such assessment measures, it becomes easier for the teacher to plan teaching goals and procedures.

2. Model dialogues are a useful way to present students with examples of the speech act in use. These dialogues should be short and natural sounding. At the first stage, the students listen and identify the speech act(s) of concern. Then they are given the dialogues without the information concerning the particular situation, and they must guess whether the people speaking know each other, if they are of the same age, and, in the case of an apology or complaint, for example, whether the matter of concern constituted a serious offense. These considerations, which can be discussed in groups, help sensitize students to the sociocultural factors that affect speech acts. These model dialogues can be used to focus attention on key distinctions, such as between different intensifiers of apologies like *very* and *really*.
3. The evaluation of a situation is a useful technique to further reinforce the learners' awareness of the factors affecting the choice of semantic formulas. In this activity they are given a set of complaint or apology situations, for example, and for each they must decide, in pairs or small groups, whether the violation requiring the complaint or apology is mild or severe, whether the complainer or apologizer needs to intensify the complaint or apology, whether the hearer is likely to accept to accept the apology or provide a remedy to the complaint without further ado, and whether a certain situation-specific strategy is called for.
4. Role-play activities are particularly suitable for practicing the use of speech acts. Here it is important to supply the learners with ample information about the interlocutors who are going to interact in the conversation and about the situation. Thus, for a complaint situation, the students may receive a card or see a video clip of a situation in which one role is that of a neighbor who is having a party and playing loud music late at night and the other is that of the person in an adjacent apartment who needs to get to sleep because she or he must take an important exam the next morning. The learners provide the details of the violation and then act out, in role-play fashion, the conversation which is likely to take place between the two interlocutors.
5. Feedback and discussion are useful activities for speech act teaching because students need to talk about their perceptions, expectations, and awareness of similarities and differences between speech act behavior in the target language and in their first culture. Such feed-

back relating to the role plays, for example, and further discussion with a larger group of learners help participants become more aware of speech act behavior and help them recognize areas of negative transfer where communication failure may occur.

These five steps or techniques are but some examples of the kind of activities that might be appropriate for speech act teaching, but they reflect the need to expose students first to the common realization patterns, then to gradually make them understand some of the factors involved, and finally to enable them to practice the use of the speech act set. Even if, as a result of such carefully planned activities, learners do not necessarily begin to behave like native speakers, they have a good chance of becoming better listeners and of reacting more appropriately to what native speakers say to them. Needless to say, it is imperative for the sake of language instruction to continue the research efforts necessary to provide accurate information regarding the way speech acts actually work in communicative situations within differing languages and cultures.

## Suggestions for further reading

Bardovi-Harlig, K. (1992). Pragmatics as part of teacher education. *TESOL Journal, 1*(3), 8–32.

This article asserts that learning appropriate forms of English is necessary for language fluency. The author believes, however, that many teachers are unaware of what comprises pragmatic competence in English. She describes a way to develop ESOL teachers' pragmatic awareness so that they can better teach the rules of language appropriateness to their students. The project was designed as part of in-service teacher training at Indiana University and was intended to increase awareness of pragmatics through direct observation of speech acts in context (e.g., expressions of gratitude and replies, apologies, commands, greetings, complaints, polite requests for action, invitations). The course involved background reading, data collection from native speakers through observation and elicitation for 3 to 6 weeks, discussion, evaluation of approximately fifteen textbooks, and development of pragmatically appropriate materials (with the scope varying from discrete lessons to larger units).

Blum-Kulka, S. (1991). Interlanguage pragmatics: The case of requests. In R. Phillipson, E. Kellerman, L. Selinker, M. Sharwood Smith, & M. Swain (Eds.), *Foreign/second language pedagogy research* (pp. 255–272). Clevedon, UK: Multilingual Matters.

The author presents a model for the study of interlanguage pragmatics which expands interlanguage to embrace intercultural dimensions. She focuses on the pragmatics of requests and discusses constraints (level of proficiency, transfer from $L_1$, perception of target language norms, and length of stay in the target community). She presents data from bilingual English-Hebrew immigrant speech acts, showing that the behavior is different from Israeli and from American patterns – authentically intercultural. The author claims that native Israeli norms are defied because learners do not wish to identify with such native speaker norms.

Blum-Kulka, S., House, J., & Kasper, G. (1989). Investigating cross-cultural pragmatics: An introductory overview. In S. Blum-Kulka, J. House, & G. Kasper (Eds.), *Cross-cultural pragmatics: Requests and apologies* (pp. 1–34). Norwood, NJ: Ablex.

The authors examine why it is important to study speech acts – their cultural specificity and contrastive pragmatics. They describe the Cross-Cultural Speech Act Realization Project (CCSARP) – looking at requests and apologies across languages and within speech communities with different social variables operating. They discuss the use of the *discourse completion task,* that is, an incomplete dialogue with a section to be filled in (in writing) by the respondent. They then present some data from requests and apologies in their various studies using the discourse completion task. They list the nine request types they found (i.e., performatives to hints). They close with implications for foreign language teaching.

Wolfson, N. (1989). *Perspectives: Sociolinguistics and TESOL.* Cambridge: Newbury House/HarperCollins.

This books examines the impact of sociolinguistics on the TESOL profession, reviews new material and current issues, and provides a historical overview and critical discussion of research methods. Chapter 4 deals with the sociolinguistic behavior of English speakers and, especially, with forms of address, apologies, requests, disapproval, refusals, the expression of gratitude, and so forth.

## References

Austin, J. L. (1962). *How to do things with words.* Cambridge, MA: Harvard University Press.

Bardovi-Harlig, K., & Hartford, B. S. (1991). Saying "no" in English: Native and nonnative rejections. *Pragmatics and Language Learning, 2,* 41–57.

Bardovi-Harlig, K., & Hartford, B. S. (1993a). Learning the rules of academic talk: A longitudinal study of pragmatic change. *Studies in Second Language Acquisition, 15,* 279–304.

Bardovi-Harlig, K., & Hartford, B. S. (1993b). Natural conversations, institutional talk, and interlanguage pragmatics. Unpublished manuscript. Bloomington: Indiana University, Program in Applied Linguistics.

Bardovi-Harlig, K., & Hartford, B. S. (1993c). Refining the DCT: Comparing open questionnaires and dialogue completion tasks. *Pragmatics and Language Learning, 4,* 143–165.

Beebe, L. M., & Cumming, M. C. (In press). Natural speech act data vs written questionnaire data: How data collection method affects speech act performance. In J. Neu & S. M. Gass (Eds.), *Speech acts across cultures.* Berlin: Mouton de Gruyter.

Beebe, L. M., & Takahashi, T. (1989a). Do you have a bag?: Social status and pattern variation in second language acquisition. In S. Gass et al (Eds.),

*Variation in second language acquisition: Discourse, pragmatics and communication* (pp. 103–125). Clevedon, UK: Multilingual Matters.

Beebe, L. M., & Takahashi, T. (1989b). Sociolinguistic variation in face-threatening speech acts: Chastisement and disagreement. In M. R. Eisenstein (Ed.), *The dynamic interlanguage: Empirical studies in second language variation* (pp. 199–218). New York: Plenum.

Beebe, L. M., Takahashi, T., & Uliss-Weltz, R. (1990). Pragmatic transfer in ESL refusals. In R. C. Scarcella et al. (Eds.), *Developing communicative competence in a second language* (pp. 55–73). New York: Newbury House.

Benander, R. (1990). Cultural expression in speech behavior, Methods of inquiry. *Penn Working Papers in Educational Linguistics, 6*(2), 21–19.

Billmyer, K. (1990). "I really like your lifestyle": ESL learners learning how to compliment. *Penn Working Papers in Educational Linguistics, 6*(2), 31–48.

Blum-Kulka, S. (1982). Learning to say what you mean in a second language: A study of the speech act performance of learners of Hebrew as a second language. *Applied Linguistics, 3*, 29–59.

Blum-Kulka, S. (1989). Playing it safe: The role of conventionality in indirectness. In S. Blum-Kulka, J. House-Edmondson, & G. Kasper (Eds.), *Cross-cultural pragmatics: Requests and apologies* (pp. 37–70). Norwood, NJ: Ablex.

Blum-Kulka, S., House, J., & Kasper, G. (Eds.). (1989). *Cross-cultural pragmatics: Requests and apologies*. Norwood, NJ: Ablex.

Blum-Kulka, S., & Olshtain, E. (1986). Too many words: Length of utterance and pragmatic failure. *Studies in Second Language Acquisition, 8*(2), 165–179.

Bodman, J., & Eisenstein, M. (1988). May God increase your bounty: The expression of gratitude in English by native and non-native speakers. *Cross Currents, 15*(1), 1–21.

Bonikowska, M. P. (1988). The choice of opting out. *Applied Linguistics, 9*(2), 169–181.

Boxer, D. (1989). Building rapport through indirect complaints: Implications for language learning. *Penn Working Papers in Educational Linguistics, 5*(2), 28–42.

Boxer, D. (1993). *Complaining and commiserating: A speech act view of solidarity in spoken American English*. New York: Peter Lang.

Carrell, P. L., & Konneker, B. H. (1981). Politeness: Comparing native and nonnative judgments. *Language Learning, 31*, 17–30.

Cohen, A. D., & Olshtain, E. (1981). Developing a measure of sociocultural competence: The case of apology. *Language Learning, 31*, 113–134.

Cohen, A. D., & Olshtain, E. (1993). The production of speech acts by ESL learners. *TESOL Quarterly, 27*(1), 33–56.

Cohen, A. D., Olshtain, E., & Rosenstein, D. S. (1986). Advanced EFL apologies: What remains to be learned. *International Journal of the Sociology of Language, 62*, 51–74.

Creese, A. (1991). Speech act variation in British and American English. *Penn Working Papers in Educational Linguistics, 7*(2), 37–58.

DeCapua, A. (1988). *Complaints: A comparison between German and English.*

Unpublished manuscript. Bronxville, NY: Concordia College, English Language Center.

Dunham, P. (1992). Using compliments in the ESL classroom: An analysis of culture and gender. *MinneTESOL Journal, 10,* 75–85.

Edmundson, R. J. (1992). *Evidence for native speaker notions of apologizing and accepting apologies in American English.* Unpublished doctoral dissertation. Bloomington: Indiana University.

Eisenstein, M., Bodman, J., & Carpenter, M. (In press). Greetings. In J. Neu & S. Gass (Eds.), *Speech acts across cultures.* Berlin: Mouton de Gruyter.

Ellis, R. (1992). Learning to communicate: A study of two language learners' requests. *Studies in Second Language Acquisition, 14*(1), 1–23.

Fescura, M. A. (1993). *A sociolinguistic comparison of "reactions to complaints": Italian $L_1$ vs. English $L_1$, Italian $L_2$, and Italian as a community language.* Unpublished doctoral dissertation. Toronto: University of Toronto, Graduate Department of Education.

Fraser, B. (1980). On apologizing. In F. Coulmas (Ed.), *Conversational routines* (pp. 259–271). The Hague: Mouton.

Fukushima, S., & Iwata, Y. (1987). Politeness strategies in requesting and offering. *JACET Bulletin, 18,* 31–48.

Goldschmidt, M. (1989). For the favor of asking: An analysis of the favor as a speech act. *Penn Working Papers in Educational Linguistics, 5*(1), 35–49.

Hartford, B. S., & Bardovi-Harlig, K. (1992). Experimental and observational data in the study of interlanguage pragmatics. *Pragmatics and Language Learning, 3,* 33–52.

Hatch, E. (1992). *Discourse and language education.* Cambridge: Cambridge University Press.

Holmes, J. (1989). Women's and men's apologies: Reflectors of cultural values. *Applied Linguistics, 10*(2), 194–213.

Hymes, D. (1972). On communicative competence. In J. B. Pride & J. Holmes (Eds.), *Sociolinguistics* (pp. 269–293). Harmondsworth, England: Penguin.

Kasper, G., & Dahl, M. (1991). Research methods in interlanguage pragmatics. *Studies in Second Language Acquisition, 13*(2), 215–247.

King, K., A., & Silver, R. E. (1993). "Sticking points": Effects of instruction on NNS refusal strategies. *Penn Working Papers in Educational Linguistics, 9*(1), 47–82.

Lakoff, R. (1977). What you can do with words: Politeness, pragmatics and performatives. In A. Rogers, B. Wall, & J. Murphy (Eds.), *Proceedings of the Texas conference on performatives, presuppositions, and implicatures* (pp. 79–105). Arlington, VA: Center for Applied Linguistics.

Levinson, S. C. (1983). *Pragmatics.* Cambridge: Cambridge University Press.

Linnell, J., Porter, F. L., Stone, H., & Chen, Wan-Lai (1992). Can you apologize me? An investigation of speech act performance among non-native speakers of English. *Penn Working Papers in Educational Linguistics, 8*(2), 33–53.

Loveday, L. (1982). *The sociolinguistics of learning and using a non-native language.* Oxford: Pergamon.

Motti, S. T. (1987). *Competência comunicativa em lingua estrangeira: O uso de pedido de disculpas*. Unpublished manuscript. São Paulo, Brazil: Pontificia Universidade Católica de São Paulo, Program in Applied Linguistics.

Murillo, E. A., Aguilar, H., & Meditz, A. (1991). *Teaching speech act behavior through video: Apologies.* Paper presented at the Ohio TESOL Fall Conference, Athens, OH: Ohio University.

Olshtain, E., & Blum-Kulka, S. (1984). Cross-linguistic speech act studies: Theoretical and empirical issues. In L. Mac Mathuna & D. Singleton (Eds.), *Language across cultures* (pp. 235–248). Dublin: Irish Association for Applied Linguistics.

Olshtain, E., & Blum-Kulka, S. (1985). Crosscultural pragmatics and the testing of communicative competence. *Language Testing, 2,* 16–30.

Olshtain, E., & Cohen, A. D. (1983). Apology: A speech act set. In N. Wolfson & E. Judd (Eds.), *Sociolinguistics and language acquisition* (pp. 18–35). Rowley, MA: Newbury House.

Olshtain, E., & Cohen, A. D. (1990). The learning of complex speech act behavior. *TESL Canada Journal, 7*(2), 45–65.

Olshtain, E., & Cohen, A. D. (1991). Teaching speech act behavior to nonnative speakers. In M. Celce-Murcia (Ed.), *Teaching English as a second or foreign language* (pp. 154–169). New York: Newbury House/HarperCollins.

Olshtain, E., & Weinbach, L. (1988). Giving and responding to compliments – characterizing compliments in Israeli society (In Hebrew). *Hed Haulpan, 53,* 35–39.

Olshtain, E., & Weinbach, L. (1993). Interlanguage features of the speech act of complaining. In S. Blum-Kulka & G. Kasper (Eds.), *Interlanguage pragmatics* (pp. 108–122). New York: Oxford University Press.

Piotrowska, M. (1987). *An investigation into the sociolinguistic competence of Hong Kong University students with specific reference to "making complaints."* Unpublished manuscript. Hong Kong: University of Hong Kong, Language Centre.

Riley, P. (1981). Towards a contrastive pragmalinguistics. In J. Fisiak (Ed.), *Contrastive linguistics and the language teacher* (pp. 121–146). Oxford: Pergamon.

Robinson, M. (1991). Introspective methodology in interlanguage pragmatics research. In G. Kasper (Ed.), *Pragmatics of Japanese as native and target language* (pp. 29–84). (Technical Report; Vol 3). Honolulu: Second Language Teaching and Curriculum Center, University of Hawaii.

Rundquist, S. M. (1991). *Flouting Grice's maxims: A study of gender-differentiated speech.* Unpublished doctoral dissertation. Minneapolis: University of Minnesota, Department of Linguistics.

Schaefer, E. J. (1982). An analysis of the discourse and syntax of oral complaints in English. Unpublished Master's thesis. Los Angeles: ESL Section, Department of English, University of California.

Schmidt, R. W., & Richards, J. C. (1981). Speech acts and second language learning. *Applied Linguistics, 1*(2), 129–157.

Searle, J. R. (1969). *Speech acts: An essay in the philosophy of language.* Cambridge: Cambridge University Press.

Takahashi, T., and Beebe, L. M. (1987). The development of pragmatic competence by Japanese learners of English. *JALT Journal, 8*(2), 131–155.

Takahashi, T., & Beebe, L. M. (1993). Cross-linguistic influence in the speech act of correction. In S. Blum-Kulka & G. Kasper (Eds.), *Interlanguage pragmatics* (pp. 138–157). New York: Oxford University Press.

Tickle, A. L. (1991). Japanese refusals in a business setting. *Papers in Applied Linguistics – Michigan, 6*(2), 84–108.

Weizman, E. (1989). Requestive hints. In S. Blum-Kulka, J. House-Edmondson, & G. Kasper (Eds.), *Cross-cultural pragmatics: Requests and apologies* (pp. 71–95). Norwood, NJ: Ablex.

Wolfson, N. (1989). *Perspectives: Sociolinguistics and TESOL*. Cambridge: Newbury House/HarperCollins.

Wolfson, N., & Judd, E. (1983). *Sociolinguistics and language acquisition*. Rowley, MA: Newbury House.

Wolfson, N., & Manes, J. (1980). The compliment as a social strategy. *Papers in Linguistics, 13*(3), 391–410.

Wolfson, N., Marmor, R., & Jones, S. (1989). Problems in the comparison of speech acts across cultures. In S. Blum-Kulka, J. House, & G. Kasper (Eds.), *Cross-cultural pragmatics: Requests and apologies* (pp. 174–196). Norwood, NJ: Ablex.

Zuskin, R. (1993). *$L_2$ Learner interpretations of the DCT prompt: Sociolinguistic inference generated from context*. Unpublished doctoral dissertation. Albuquerque: University of New Mexico.

# 13 *Literacy and literacies*

Sandra Lee McKay

To those who view literacy as an individual skill, it may be surprising to see a chapter on literacy in a sociolinguistics text. Yet, for those who view literacy as a social practice, literacy is an essential component of the study of sociolinguistics. One purpose of this chapter is to illuminate the debate between those who view literacy as an individual skill and those who see it as a social practice and to point out the dangers of ignoring the social aspect of literacy. This chapter supports the notion that literacy is a complex interplay between both individual skills and social knowledge. However, since the focus of this book is on the interaction between language and society, the chapter will emphasize the ways in which literate behavior is dependent on the social context. The chapter will examine four aspects of literacy as it relates to the social context – (1) as a collaborative practice, (2) as a reflection of community values and traditions about how to approach texts, (3) as a reflection of cultural values and traditions about text and topic development, and (4) as a reflection of social relationships as well as a vehicle for changing the status quo. The chapter will conclude with a discussion of the pedagogical implications of viewing literacy as a social practice for language classrooms in Anglophone countries. Throughout the chapter, the term *text* will be used to refer to any printed material, ranging from signs and forms to extended academic prose.

As the title suggests, it is assumed in this chapter that literacy is multidimensional. Different contexts demand different types of literacy expertise. The ability to fill out an employment application calls for very different kinds of literacy expertise than does writing an academic paper. Speech communities can encourage individuals to interact with texts in different ways. Reading a story out loud in a speech community which encourages listeners to participate in storytelling is a different experience from reading a story in a speech community in which listeners are discouraged from participating. Finally, cultures can foster specific rhetorical traditions. A business letter written in English for a Western audience rests on different assumptions about the appropriate organizational pattern and the writer-audience relationship than does a business letter written in Japanese for a Japanese audience.

Frequently, those who view literacy as an individual skill ignore or minimize the social components of literacy. It is this lack of attention to the social parameters of literacy that have led some people to argue for a more inclusive view of literacy in which the social aspects of literate behavior are recognized. In order to understand the assumptions made by both groups, the chapter begins by examining these two perspectives on literacy.

## Literacy: Definitions and methods of investigation

### *An individual skill perspective*

For those who approach literacy as an individual accomplishment, *literacy* is taken to be a skill that is acquired by an individual, generally within an educational context, utilizing oral language as a basis and ultimately affecting cognitive development. Street (1984) terms this view an *autonomous model of literacy.* Viewed from this perspective, discussions of literacy often involve a delineation of skill level and an examination of the relationship between oral and written language as well as between literacy and cognitive development. The focus is on the individual rather than on the larger social context in which the individual operates.

#### LEVELS OF LITERACY

Those who view literacy as a skill often posit various levels of literacy. Wells (1987), for example, delineates four levels of literacy: the *performative,* which involves an individual's ability to decode a written message into speech in order to ascertain its meaning; the *functional,* which entails the ability to deal with the demands of everyday life that are expressed in the written word; the *informational,* which involves the ability to process the written word in order to attain information; and, finally, the *epistemic,* which entails the ability to act upon and transform knowledge and experience that are not available to those who are not literate (pp. 110–111).

In examining biliteracy, Read and Mackay (1984) define literacy in terms of the level of skill one attains in the second language. These levels include *initial literacy,* or "the ability to write one's own name"; *basic literacy,* or the ability to "read and write a short simple sentence on . . . everyday life"; *survival literacy,* or the "ability to read, write and comprehend texts on familiar subjects and to understand whatever signs, labels and instructions and directions are necessary to get along within one's environment"; *functional literacy,* or "the possession of skills perceived as necessary by particular persons and groups to fulfill their own self-determined objectives"; and, finally, *technical literacy*, or the "acquisition of a body of theoretical or technical knowledge and the development of problem-solving capacities within that specialized field" (pp. 5–6).

Although both taxonomies are set forth as hierarchical levels of literacy skills, it is important to note that the ability of an individual to attain one of the specified levels is not just a matter of acquiring a specific skill level; rather, the acquisition of a particular level often provides one with a social identity (Street, 1991). The attainment of what Wells terms the *epistemic level* can provide one with the identity of an academically educated individual; the attainment of what Read and Mackay call *technical literacy* can define one as a specialist in a particular field of study. In this way, the level of literacy an individual attains affects that individual's perceived role in the society.

The terms *literate* and *illiterate* are clearly the most highly charged labels in terms of providing one with a social identity. Whereas use of these terms suggests that one is either literate or not, such a view of literacy is a tremendous oversimplification. As Crandall notes (1992):

> Dichotomies such as "literacy-illiteracy" or "functional literacy or functional illiteracy" are simplistic and reductionist, and the statistic of illiteracy which they engender, equally so. The complex notion of literacy cannot be captured by any one definition of skills, functions, or practices. (p. 88)

In discussing literacy, it is important to recognize the dangers of such dichotomies and, in addition, to always qualify literacy in reference to a particular language. Although an individual may not be literate in English, he or she may be highly literate in another language. Labeling such individuals as illiterate is doubly harmful since it marginalizes them without justification. In addition, it is important to recognize that individuals who are biliterate may or may not have developed oral skills in their second language. Some individuals living in non-Anglophone countries have developed high levels of English literacy with little oral fluency in English. Literacy in a language, then, does not presuppose oral fluency.

### WRITTEN AND ORAL LANGUAGE

Those who approach literacy as an isolated individual skill frequently examine the relationship between written and oral language as well as the relationship between literacy and cognitive development. Following in the tradition of Goody (1977) and Ong (1982), some researchers maintain that there are inherent differences between oral and written language. As Wells (1987) puts it:

> [I]n moving from speech to writing, more is involved than simply a change in the channel (oral/aural, manual/visual) through which the linguistic message is

expressed. As a result of the change of mode, the nature of the message itself changes, in response both to the different purposes the two modes usually serve and to the inter- and intrapersonal contexts in which they are typically used. Writing is not simply speech written down. (p. 112)

For Wells (1987), one reason for the significant difference that exists between oral and written language arises from the fact that conversation "is jointly constructed in a shared social context in which the participants can assume a considerable amount of shared information. . . . By contrast, sustained prose is written by a writer who is distant in time and space from his or her potential readers" (p. 113). What Wells fails to note is that both spoken and written discourse contain a wide range of genres which differ in their assumptions about audience involvement and their level of abstraction. A letter to a close friend assumes a considerable amount of shared information; a formal speech is a piece of sustained prose.

Whereas some researchers like Wells emphasize the differences in the audience relationship between written and oral language, other researchers maintain that one of the essential differences between written and oral language is that the permanence of the written word allows language to become an object of awareness. Olson (1990), for example, argues that literacy

[I]s in principle a metalinguistic activity. . . . [L]iteracy turns language into an object of awareness. . . . In the same way that language makes objects and events in the world objects of awareness, so literacy makes language an object of awareness. (p. 20)

By making language an object of awareness and separating the speaker from his or her speech, Olson contends that literacy allows the production of an *autonomous text,* or authorless text exemplified by such things as encyclopedias or school textbooks. What is unique about such texts is that "there is no indication of the fact that each of those statements is in fact an assertion by an author – a speech act" (p. 21).

Although the idea of an autonomous text may be common in English, in some languages the concept of an autonomous text may be nonexistent. (See, for example, Osterloh, 1986, for a discussion of the close identification of an author and a text in many Arabic-speaking cultures; Kachru & Nelson, this volume, for a more general overview of different cultural asssumptions about texts.) Missing, then, from Olson's assertions regarding written texts is an exploration of the ways in which the cultural context frames the way a text is viewed.

## LITERACY AND COGNITIVE DEVELOPMENT

Researchers who view literacy as an individual skill do not limit their examination of literacy to the relationship between written and oral language. Following in the tradition of Goody and Watt (1968) and Olson (1977), they frequently examine the relationship between literacy and cognitive development, contending that the ability to process the written word has a profound impact on cognitive development, transforming the mind and creating the ability to think independently and abstractly. Whereas some concede that cognitive development is possible with oral language, they maintain that the written language allows for greater cognitive benefits. Wells (1987), for example, argues that:

> [C]ertainly, composing in speech may also be an aid to thought just as one may be led to reorganize one's thinking in listening to the speech of others. However, if the skills of transforming thoughts and knowledge are not dependent on having learned to read and write, they are most effectively extended and developed through engaging in these more reflective modes of language use. (p. 113)

Others maintain that the acquisition of literacy, because it requires people to function independently, offers unique benefits to cognitive development. According to Cumming (1990), these unique cognitive benefits include the ability to view texts schematically, to use problem-solving strategies to control thinking while reading and writing, and finally, to transform knowledge gained from reading and writing into new understandings and ideas (p. 37).

The linking of literacy to cognitive development can result in the highly questionable conclusion that those who are not literate are in some ways cognitively less able. For some people, the fact that an individual is not literate suggests that this individual does not have the cognitive development that people with literacy skills, particularly those with the "high" levels of literacy skills outlined earlier, possess. Fingeret (1984), for one, disputes such a view, noting that:

> [I]lliterate adults are seen not only as nonfunctional, but also as unable to take their place in society with the dignity accorded to all human beings. Although literacy educators strive to respect illiterate adults, the larger society still tends to equate illiteracy with more primitive cognitive abilities. (p. 12)

An examination of the relationship between oral and written language, as well as that between literacy and cognition, is often undertaken within a theoretical framework in which literacy is viewed essentially as an individual phenomenon. Questions such as how the uses of literacy differ cross-culturally, how children are socialized into the way they deal with texts, or to what extent literacy is valued by the society are not the major focus. Instead, these questions are examined by those who see literacy as embedded within a sociocultural context. Next, some of the issues raised within this perspective are discussed.

## *A sociocultural perspective*

### LITERACY IN A HISTORICAL CONTEXT

Those who approach literacy from a sociocultural perspective point out that the value a society places on literacy and exactly what is meant by *literacy* changes over time. Graff (1979), for example, points out that in nineteenth-century Canada, many high-level commercial posts could be held by an illiterate person if the bureaucratic record keeping could be done by someone else; the main criteria required for the high posts were the social skills imparted in private education and a middle-class environment. Thus social skills were more valued than literacy.

Both the value a society places on literacy and the standards of literacy in that society can change over time. For example, in the United States during World War II, one had to have a fourth-grade reading level to be admitted into the armed forces. However, by the 1980s, the criterion was a high school diploma (Mikulecky, 1990). Such changes occurred because, as more and more individuals mastered basic literacy, it was easier to communicate information in print. Complex written information became part of the society. In some ways, as Mikulecky points out, rising literacy demands are similar to what happens in a crowd when the front row rises: everyone else has to rise in order to see and participate (p. 27).

Because of rising literacy demands, Christie (1990) contends that the literacy of the twentieth century is a far more complex phenomenon than the literacy of earlier periods. As she puts it:

> Literacy in today's world is a very different thing from what it was either at the turn of the century or even mid-century. The contemporary world demands a level of sophistication in literacy greater than at any time in the past. It demands a people capable not only of handling the awesome range of print materials now a feature of a technologically advanced society, but also of creating and responding to new ones, for we do keep generating new kinds of writing, new kinds of genres, as a necessary part of generating new knowledge and new ways of thinking. (p. 21)

Viewed from a historical perspective, what it means to be literate is dependent on the literacy values and standards of the period. Individuals who do not attain the level of literacy skills valued by a society at a particular time are often viewed as "illiterate" in the sense that they are unable to meet the literacy demands of that time.

### THE IDEOLOGICAL MODEL OF LITERACY

Those who approach literacy from a sociocultural perspective focus primarily "on literacy as a social and cultural phenomenon, something that exists between people and something that connects individuals to a range of experiences and to different points in time" (Schieffelin & Cochran-Smith, 1984, p. 4). One of the main proponents of such a view is Street (1991), who sets forth what he calls an *ideological model of literacy,* which recognizes a multiplicity of literacies in which "the meaning and uses of literacy practices are related to specific cultural contexts" (p. 1). He contrasts this model with what he calls the *autonomous model of literacy,* which:

> [A]ssumes a single direction in which literacy development can be traced, and associates it with "progress," "civilisation," individual liberty and social mobility. . . . It isolates literacy as an independent variable and then claims to be able to study its consequences. These consequences are classically represented in terms of economic "take-off" or in terms of cognitive skills. (Street, 1984, p. 2)

Street criticizes two tenets of the autonomous model that were discussed earlier: first, that oral and written language are very different, and second, that literacy per se is related to cognitive development. Street (1984) contends that, within specific cultural contexts, oral and written language assume certain functions in which "there is an overlap and a 'mix' of modes of communication" (p. 110). He points out, for example, that in nineteenth-century Canada, pictures and decorations were as important in providing directions as were signs bearing words. In light of such examples, Street argues that what he calls the "great divide" between oral and written language has been exaggerated and that, in fact, the uses made of the written language in some societies can be easily handled by oral language in others.

Street (1984) also disputes the claim that literacy per se is beneficial to cognitive development. Street argues that, since the introduction of literacy is generally accompanied by new forms of social organization, differences in cognitive processes may not be due to literacy itself but rather to the new forms of social interaction that arise to foster literacy. He cites the work of Scribner and Cole (1981), who studied the Vai people of Liberia, where certain literacies were taught through individual teaching and not in schools. They found that nonliterates performed as well or better than literates on many tasks. The only tasks that those Vai who were literate without schooling did better on than the nonliterates were tasks closely related to skills they had used in becoming literate. They could, for example, use language as a means of instruction in discussions of grammar or board games. Furthermore, in comparing Vai, Arabic, and English literacy, all of which existed among the Vai, Scribner and Cole found that some cognitive skills were enhanced by practice in specific scripts. For example, people who were literate in Arabic and had learned the language through memorization of the Koran were better at tasks demanding rote memorization. Thus, for Street, the way language is used and the kinds of cognitive skills that are developed are related to social practices surrounding the use of literacy.

### LITERACY AND DISCOURSE

A major tenet of those who support a sociocultural perspective of literacy is that literacy practices, such as evaluating a book or movie, involve particular kinds of thinking which can take place in either written or oral language, so that literacy is not merely reading and writing. Langer (1987), for example, contends that the rapid developments in the mass media and computers have blurred the narrow definition of literacy as an act of reading and writing so that:

> [A] focus on simple reading and writing skills as defining "literate" thinkers, and on uses of oral and written language as involving different intellectual dimensions, are unhelpful distinctions. Uses of oral and written language mix and blur and vary as the language situation changes, and these complexities need to be considered if we are to understand the literacy demands that occur within a technological culture. (p. 4)

Accepting the premise that "oral and written language mix and blur," Gee (1992) contends that literacy practices are "almost always fully integrated with, interwoven into and part of, the very texture of wider practices that involve talk, interaction, values and beliefs" (p. 32). Gee calls such practices *Discourses,* with a capital *D* (p. 32). Gee argues that "literacy is inherently plural (literacies) and that writing, reading, and language are always embedded in and inextricable from Discourses (social practice, cultures, and subcultures, or whatever analogous term is used)" (p. 33). Viewed from this perspective, reading and writing are not private affairs involving a set of discrete skills but, rather, social acts that one engages in within a community. Thus, for example, writing an announcement regarding the sale of Vietnamese handmade crafts entails not just mastering the necessary language but also knowing what should be emphasized in the announcement and where it should be posted. How does one learn the set of social practices that surround the use of the printed word? For Gee, Discourses are not mastered solely by overt instruction but rather by supportive "interaction with people who have already mastered the Discourse" (p. 33). In this way, becoming literate entails social interaction with those who know how to use a text to serve a particular social purpose.

Although the debate between those who view literacy as an individual skill and those who emphasize its social dimensions suggests that literacy is one or the other, clearly both individual literacy skills and social knowledge are involved in any literacy endeavor. One clear example of this interplay is provided by Hornberger and Hardman (1994), who discuss a reading-aloud activity in an ESL class for recent Cambodian refugees taught by a Cambodian nonnative speaker of English. The students were reading a dialogue about a patient at the dentist which began in the following way:

Dr.: Do you have any pain?
Kim: Yes. A little (*pointing*) in this tooth here in back.

In the oral exercise on the dialogue, the teacher and students consistently read *pointing* as if it were a part of the dialogue rather than as a stage direction. Although the class had mastered the literacy skill of decoding the printed word into oral language, they were unfamiliar with the social conventions used to indicate stage directions. In this, as in all cases, successful literate behavior entails the ability not only to decode written symbols but also to interpret these symbols against a backdrop of social convention. It is assumed in this chapter that literate behavior involves a complex interplay between individual skills and knowledge of social practices. However, because in many educational contexts the importance of the latter is ignored, the remainder of the chapter will be devoted to exploring the social dimensions of literacy and its educational implications. Before this discussion begins, it will be useful to consider the methods of analysis available to those who wish to study literacy.

## *Common methods of analysis*

Those who approach literacy as an individual skill often rely on survey methods to determine the extent of literacy or illiteracy in a country. When the results of such surveys are assessed, it is important to examine what measures have been used to determine literacy levels. In some literacy surveys, such as the one currently used in Canada, the completion of a particular grade level in school is used as the basis for determining the overall literacy level of the population. In other surveys, like the U.S. National Assessment of Educational Progress (NAEP) literacy survey of young adults, simulations of literacy tasks are used to assess literacy. The problem with such simulation tasks is that they often contain culture-specific information that puts some groups at a disadvantage. For example, in one literacy survey in Australia, the nonnative English-speaking test takers did poorly on tasks such as writing checks on a charge card and reading a prose passage on Australian technology (see McKay, 1993).

Those who view literacy as a social practice often employ ethnographic research methods. They examine a speech community over an extended period of time, observing the ways in which individuals in these communities interact around a written text. Their goal is to illuminate how literacy is valued in the community and how children are socialized regarding printed material. In evaluating such studies, one must consider to what extent the researcher attempted to attain an *emic,* or insider's, view of the community by interacting with community members in many contexts over a considerable length of time. If this is not done, it is difficult to attain an accurate view of literacy values and traditions in the community. (See Watson-Gegeo, 1988, for an overview of some principles of ethnographic research, particularly as it applies to second language classrooms.)

Those who emphasize the social dimensions of literacy also employ text analysis to determine cross-cultural differences in text development. Studies in contrastive rhetoric are often undertaken by those who are involved in the teaching of writing to nonnative speakers of English. The goal of such research is to characterize cross-cultural differences and to examine to what extent individuals transfer the literacy traditions they have learned in their first language to a second language. (See Sridhar, this volume, for a discussion of language transfer.) In reviewing such studies, one needs to consider whether the differences found are due to cultural differences or to developmental differences on the part of the writer. (For a critical review of the findings of contrastive rhetoric, see Leki, 1991; Mohan & Lo, 1985).

Text analysis is also used by those who wish to discover the assumptions contained in texts regarding power relationships. Such text analysis focuses on how particular groups are positioned in a text by what is said about them and how it is said. The goal is to make readers aware of the manner in which texts can reinforce existing power relationships. (See Freeman & McElhinny, this volume, for a discussion of the manner in which women are positioned through the use of sexist language.) In assessing these studies, one needs to consider how representative the text is before drawing conclusions as to the extent it reflects existing social relationships. Are the views presented in the text regarding particular ethnic or social groups evident in other texts? The discussion turns now to an examination of various studies that employ these methods. The goal will be to demonstrate how literacy is related to the social and cultural context in which it is used.

## Literacies: The social and cultural context

### *Literacy as a collaborative practice*

One way the social context affects literacy is by influencing who reads and writes in what language for what purpose. The literacy history of a community often determines the distribution of literacy skills in the community. Reder (1987), for example, has demonstrated how the literacy history of three communities in the United States influenced the distribution of literacy skills. The three communities he investigated were an Eskimo fishing village in south-central Alaska, a partly migrant, partly settled Hispanic community in the Pacific Northwest, and a community of Hmong immigrants living on the West Coast. In undertaking an ethnographic investigation of these communities, Reder found that, in the Eskimo community since English literacy had been imposed from the outside, the change to English literacy was nearly complete. There was little or no literacy in the native language, and English literacy skills were concentrated in people under 40 years of age. Although literacy skills were becoming more widely distributed, there was still a use of literacy specialists in the community.

In the Hispanic community, the distribution of English literacy and Spanish literacy was much more diverse. Some members of the community used English literacy exclusively, whereas others used Spanish and English. Some were recent immigrants learning English, some were monolingual Spanish speakers with some literacy in Spanish, and some had no literacy in either language. In this community, literacy skills were concentrated among educated residents. Because both English and Spanish literacy had value in this community, there were literacy specialists in both languages.

Finally, in the Hmong community, exposure to literacy had taken place only within the past 20 years, and native literacy was often self-taught. In general, in this community there was little literacy in English or in the native language. What literacy existed was heavily concentrated among the wealthier, better-educated first-wave immigrants and the young. Thus the community relied heavily on literacy specialists. It is important to note that the literacy abilities important for particular community literacy specialists such as a lay minister or owner of a small business may or may not involve the same literacy abilities valued in academic contexts. Hence, individuals who serve important literacy roles in their community may or may not excel in academic contexts.

Since in all three communities literacy specialists were often needed, literacy became a collaborative effort in which different individuals played different roles in enacting a literacy event. For Reder, such collaborative literacy practices entail three possible modes of engagement. The first is *technological engagement,* in which an individual is engaged in the actual technology of writing or reading. The second is *functional engagement,* in which an individual supplies knowledge or expertise necessary for the enactment of the literacy practice. Finally, there is *social engagement* in which individuals may have knowledge of the nature of the practice and its implications for the community, although they may not be technologically or functionally engaged.

Reder gives an example of how these levels of engagement interacted in the case of a town meeting he attended. In this situation, one individual took on the task of writing a formal letter (technological engagement). Another individual, who could not write a formal letter himself, nevertheless had the political savvy to understand how to use the letter to write to the editor of a regional newspaper in order to advance the town's interest (functional engagement). And finally, the third individual, a town elder, had the historical knowledge to provide the relevant background information necessary to compose a persuasive letter (social engagement).

Reder contends that each of these three modes of engagement is learned as a practice. Expertise in one area of engagement does not necessitate expertise in another. For example, some of the adults in Reder's study had the technological skill to sign their name on a document but did not have the functional knowledge to understand the significance of the contents of the document. In another instance, Hmong immigrants had learned of the American practice of sending greeting cards for special occasions, demonstrating functional knowledge of the literacy practice, but they did not have the technical knowledge to sign their name.

The different distribution of literacy skills in a community often results in individuals taking different roles in a literacy event. In many immigrant families, young people take on the role of providing the technological engagement, and other members of the community are involved in a literacy event on a functional or social level. Because individuals participate in a literacy practice in different ways, the "use of oral and written language mix and blur and vary as the language situation changes" (Langer, 1987, p. 4). Vasquez (1992) points out several examples of this variation in the Mexican families she studied. For example, in one family the children read the grocery ads to their father, who could not read English or Spanish. As the children translated the written text, they simultaneously interpreted it and discussed which item to purchase. In her study, Vasquez found that:

> [B]ilingual children frequently acted as language brokers, interpreting the language and cultural norms embodied in the texts, making it possible for monolingual Spanish-speakers who cannot read to enter into deliberations about printed materials. Individuals who did not speak or read English equally contributed background information to contextualize the text in terms of time, space, personal attitudes, and previous associations. Everyone involved could provide descriptive details on use, historical context, and other aspects of the text associated with their personal lives. (p. 126)

Hence, from this study, as from the one by Reder, it is evident that individuals can be intimately involved in a literacy practice without having technological engagement. In such instances, literacy events are collaborative ventures in which various members of a group participate in different capacities. These collaborative ventures often arise because forces in the larger social context have influenced who is literate and in what language. A second way in which literacy practices reflect the social context arises from the fact that different communities socialize their young in different ways regarding these practices. How the values and traditions of a community affect the way in which literacy practices are approached is the topic of the next section.

## *Literacy and the community*

Various studies have examined the ways in which particular communities deal with texts. The seminal work in this area is Heath (1983), who studied the literacy behavior of two communities in the Piedmont Carolinas – Trackton, a working-class African-American community, and Roadville, a working-class white community. Based on extensive ethnographic research, Heath found that Roadville residents tended to use writing only when they had to. In general, they viewed literacy as a necessary tool to aid their memory and to help them buy and sell things. Roadville family members collected reading materials for themselves and children but often did not read them. Parents gave lip service to the value of reading but did not read extensively themselves. Since adults considered reading materials important for their children's development, children in Roadville grew up surrounded by print, with their parents reading to them and asking them to memorize texts.

In Trackton, on the other hand, residents did not have an accumulation of reading materials as they did in Roadville. However, reading permeated the flow of daily social interactions. Residents commonly read aloud to other members of the community, interpreting the meaning of whatever was read jointly and socially. Heath argues that, in Roadville and Trackton, the different ways the children approached literacy were dependent on the way "each community structured their families, defined the roles that community members could assume, and played out their concepts of childhood that guided child socialization." (p. 11)

Trackton and Roadville, however, are not unique in fostering particular literacy practices. As Heath points out, "in communities throughout the world . . . features of the cultural milieu affect the ways in which children learn to use language. The place of language in the cultural life of each social group is interdependent with the habits and values of behaving shared among members of that group" (p. 11). Indeed, other studies of particular communities have found the unique ways these communities deal with literacy practices. (See, e.g., Fishman, 1988, in reference to the Amish community; Nichols, 1989, in regard to storytelling traditions of children of African and European ancestry in South Carolina; Shuman, 1986, regarding white, Hispanic, and African-American youths in Philadelphia). What all these studies demonstrate is that specific communities perpetuate particular ways of approaching and valuing texts. Such differences are even more pronounced when one considers different languages and different cultures.

## *Literacy and culture*

In their discussion of the influence of cultural and intellectual traditions on literacy, Ballard and Clanchy (1991) contend that a culture's attitude toward knowledge can be ranked on a continuum ranging from placing a value on conserving knowledge to placing a value on extending knowledge. Cultures which emphasize conserving knowledge promote reproductive approaches to learning, stressing strategies such as memorization and imitation, dealing with questions of what. Cultures in the middle tend to value analytical thinking, focusing on judging and reconciling ideas, examining questions of why and how. Cultures at the other end focus on deliberately searching for new possibilities and explanations and answering questions of what if. Ballard and Clanchy argue that many Asian countries favor a reproductive mode of learning, whereas many Western countries favor an analytic or speculative mode. These different approaches to "learning spring from different basic attitudes to knowledge and its function in society" (p. 23).

Such divergent attitudes toward knowledge can affect how texts are valued and approached within a culture. Different cultures, for example, can make very different assumptions regarding the development of a written argument. In a Western university context, an argument is typically expected to conform to four criteria reflecting an analytic or speculative mode of learning: It should be clearly focused, be the result of wide and critical reading, present a reasoned argument, and be competently presented (Ballard & Clanchy, 1991, p. 30). The social practices surrounding argumentation, however, can be quite different in other cultures, reflecting a value placed on conserving rather than extending knowledge. For some cultures a written text is to be studied and imitated rather than critically analyzed as part of an argument. (For a discussion of different attitudes toward texts in developing countries, see Osterloh, 1986.) Furthermore, how authority is used in an argument can differ tremendously. Ballard and Clanchy (1991), for example, point out how one Muslim student developed an argument in a reproductive mode by summarizing a position of someone whose work he read and then concluding the paragraph with a direct quotation from the source to which he was referring. This reflected a pattern he used in oral argumentation in his native language – he ended each point with a quotation from the Koran. Such differences illustrate how socially learned practices can affect what writers choose to write, whether they are writing in their first or second language.

Cross-cultural studies on literacy have tended to focus on two ways in which culture influences text development – how a text is organized and how a topic is developed. Studies in contrastive rhetoric have shown that different cultures have different ways of organizing text and different expectations regarding the relationship between the writer and the reader. (See, e.g., Connor & Kaplan, 1987; Hinds, 1990; Norment, 1986.) Kaplan (1966), in a seminal article on contrastive rhetoric, maintains that Eastern writing is marked with indirection in which "things are developed in terms of what they are not, rather than what they are" (as cited in McKay, 1984, p. 49). More recently, Hinds (1987) has distinguished two types of writing: The first, of which English is typical, is writer-responsible, so that the responsibility for effective communication is the writer's; the second, which is typical of many East Asian countries, is reader-responsible, so that the reader is primarily responsible for effective communication.

What might be contributing to both Kaplan's and Hind's characterization of East Asian writing is the fact that several East Asian countries have been influenced by a pattern of rhetorical development which originated in classical Chinese poetry. In this pattern, the first section, called the *ki,* begins an argument and is followed by the *shoo,* which develops the argument. The third section, the *ten,* abruptly changes the direction of the argument to an indirectly related subtheme, and the fourth section, the *ketsu,* reaches a conclusion (Eggington, 1987, & Hinds, 1987). The fact the *ten* introduces a new topic may lead Western readers to see this section as an irrelevant aside, whereas Eastern writers are likely to view this section as introducing an important tangential topic that the reader must relate to the main topic.

What might also be contributing to the characterization of much East Asian writing as indirect and reader-responsible is the fact that the statement of purpose for many East Asian writers may not be initially stated in the discourse. Chutisilp, for example (1985; as cited in Siriphan, 1988), maintains that a typical style for Thai writers is to delay the introduction of purpose. She maintains that, for "Thai English writers, getting to the point too soon does not stimulate the readers' curiosity nor does it create suspense. It is common, therefore, to find an elaborate maze of wordiness before arriving at the topic sentence which is normally placed at the end of a passage" (p. 112). Hinds (1990) maintains that the writing of many East Asian writers has what he calls a "delayed introduction of purpose" which has "the undesirable effect of making the essay appear incoherent to the English-speaking reader, although the style does not have that effect on the native reader" (p. 99).

The cultural context can also affect how a topic is developed. Hu, Brown, and Brown (1982), for example, compared the written responses of two groups of students to the same prompt. One group consisted of Chinese students majoring in English in China, and the other Australian students writing at home. Both groups were writing in English. He found that the Chinese and Australian students approached a given topic with a different set of cultural assumptions and role expectations. For example, in writing on how they would persuade their brother to work hard in school, the Chinese students, in contrast to the Australian students, frequently emphasized the importance of education for the nation as a whole. In writing on why one might catch a cold, most Chinese students wrote that catching a cold is due to neglect of self, and the Australians focused on catching a cold from someone else. Hu, Brown, and Brown (1982) conclude that the diversity of topics introduced in the two groups of essays is "due mainly to differences in the informants' social or cultural backgrounds. Informants in the two countries have their own experience of the real world" (p. 40).

McKay (1989) compared the written responses of Chinese students writing in English in China with nonnative English-speaking students in the United States. Both groups of students were asked to describe a situation in which they were waiting in line for a bus and suddenly it began to rain. The Chinese students tended to describe unruly behavior on the part of the passengers in getting on the bus and to draw a moral from the situation. Students writing in the United States, on the other hand, never drew a moral from the narration. Both studies demonstrate how shared experiences and social values affect the topic development of a text. Another way texts illustrate social values is by reflecting power relationships in the society. It is this area of literacy and its social context on which the discussion now focuses.

## *Literacy and power*

One of the seminal works in exploring the relationship between literacy and power is that of Fairclough. In his book *Language and Power* (1989), Fairclough posits an approach to language termed *critical language study,* which seeks to examine the connections between language, power, and ideology. Fairclough maintains that:

> [L]inguistic phenomena are social in the sense that whenever people speak or listen or write or read, they do so in ways which are determined socially and have social effects. Even when people are most conscious of their own individuality and think themselves to be most cut off from social influences . . . they

> still use language in ways which are subject to social conventions. And the ways in which people use language in their most intimate and private encounters are not only socially determined by the social relationships of the family, they also have social effects in the sense of helping to maintain (or, indeed, change) those relationships. (p. 23)

For Fairclough, all linguistic interactions reflect the social order and can be used to either maintain or change the status quo. Although Fairclough illustrates how both spoken and written texts reflect the social order, here written texts will be discussed.

One way in which texts reflect the social order is by how their subjects are assigned certain social roles. Auerbach (1986), for example, describes one literacy text for second language learners which described language minorities in very limited working-class roles. Furthermore, although it taught students how to accept authority, it never advised them on how to deal with supervisors who abused their authority. The following is one excerpt from the text (Walsh, 1984; as cited in Auerbach, 1986, p. 418):

1. Go to work on time. Don't be late.
2. Work hard. Don't be lazy.
3. Work carefully. Always do your best.
4. Ask questions if you don't understand or are not sure.
5. Be friendly. Get along with everybody. Be nice to other workers. Smile at them. Be clean and neat.

Frequently, gender roles perpetuated by the society at large are reflected in texts (see Freeman & McElhinny, this volume). O'Barr (1982), for example, describes several trial practice manuals that advise lawyers how they should treat female witnesses, urging them to be especially courteous to women and to avoid making them cry. There are more subtle examples of texts positioning people. Fasold, Yamada, Robinson, and Barish (1990), for example, found gender differences in the use of a middle initial in reference to prominent men and women referred to in *The Washington Post*. Although they found significantly fewer gender differences in this usage subsequent to the publication of a style manual on nonsexist usage, the use of a middle initial was still more prevalently used with prominent men than with prominent women. The fact that the implementation of the style manual made a difference, however, illustrates how texts can also be used to alter the status quo.

One major proponent of using literacy to change the social order is Freire (1970), who argues that literacy can empower people to change their lives. For Freire, "learners are sociohistorical, creative, and transformative beings, and literacy is the process through which these learners can come to critically reflect on reality and take actions to change oppressive conditions. The ultimate goal of literacy is thus empowerment and social transformation" (Walsh, 1991, p. 15).

Recently in the United States, the Freirian view of literacy has resulted in what is termed a *critical approach to literacy* (Walsh, 1991). Those who support this approach contend that education should always involve intervention. In essence, the approach depends upon students questioning and challenging the existing social order. For Walsh, an advocate of a critical approach to literacy, critical literacy "entails developing strategies to analyze the multiple ways race, ethnicity, class, gender and language are used in school to serve dominant interests" (p. 18). By using literacy to critically examine the existing social order, this approach, according to Walsh:

> [M]akes possible an expansion of what it means to be literate beyond a functional capacity to read and to write. In other words, it fosters a reading of reality itself which goes beyond merely producing or reproducing the existing social relations and the "legitimate" knowledge which schools frame but instead encourages learners to look at the world around them in critical ways . . . and to know that their actions and involvement can make a difference. (p. 18)

The idea that literacy can provide students with the power to make changes in their lives and in the social order is one that is gaining support from literacy educators. Some of the educational implications of viewing literacy in the social context are the subject of the next section.

## Implications for the literacy classroom

In this chapter we have demonstrated how literacy is a social practice embedded in community and cultural values about literate behavior. We have discussed how literacy is a collaborative endeavor in which different members of the community play different roles in literacy events. We have shown how communities and cultures foster particular approaches to texts, to how they are organized, and to what they say. Finally, we have examined the ways in which the texts are related to issues of power in that they position individuals and groups through what they choose to say or not say about a topic. Texts, however, can also be used to change the social order. What do these findings suggest for classroom language teachers?

First, they suggest that, since literacy activities outside the classroom are often collaborative efforts, language classrooms should foster a similar approach to literacy. Hence, to increase their literacy skills, students need to be encouraged to become involved with texts on all the levels of engagement mentioned by Reder – technological, functional, and social. One way this might be done is to have students assume different roles in different assignments. Classrooms should become communities in which students share the knowledge they have about texts both in determining the meaning of texts they read and in effectively writing their own. As students share their insights about texts, the line between oral and written language will mix and blur as literate behavior permeates both. Viewing literacy as a collaborative effort in which oral and written language overlap also suggests that, for those who come to the language classroom with oral and literacy skills in a language other than English, using their first language to discuss and plan texts in English may be a very productive strategy. (See Auerbach, 1993, for a critique of the English-only classroom; Friedlander, 1990, for the benefits of using the native language in second language writing classes.)

Second, the fact that literacy is related to issues of power suggests that the language classroom needs to help students become more critical readers. Students need to learn to carefully examine the assumptions contained in texts regarding particular gender, economic, racial, and ethnic groups. Furthermore, students need to discuss whether such positioning reflects the kind of social order they wish to promote. If it does not, in the tradition of Freire, students need to be encouraged to choose or create texts to change the power relationships they believe need changing.

The fact that speech communities and cultures foster particular assumptions about texts means that some students will come to school with assumptions regarding texts that are very different from those promoted in mainstream language classrooms. It is this aspect of literacy that raises the most difficult educational issue, for it calls into question the overall goals of language classrooms and how to assess these goals. To the extent that multiple literacies exist, some of which more closely match those of mainstream classrooms than others, the important question is: Whose culture, literacy, and language do we teach, and why? Because of the importance of this question for language teachers, it needs to be carefully examined.

To do this, it is helpful to consider the work of Walters (1992). In an article entitled "Whose Culture? Whose Literacy?" Walters takes issue with Hirsch (1987), who argues that there is a body of cultural literacy that all people must learn. Citing the work of Williams (1989), Walters argues that individuals like Hirsch are promoting a *culture in common,* which belongs only to a privileged minority who hold social and political power. Walters rejects Hirsch's goal of promoting a culture in common and, in its place, advocates the promotion of a *common culture* in which:

[E]ducation is not limited to information gained from canonized texts of a distant past, participation is not mere assent, and democracy is not a completed achievement. A curriculum favoring culture as process, rather than possession, would value highly the insights offered by many groups – especially those represented in the classroom and the community – so as to profit from their many perspectives on the past, present, and future. (p. 9)

Frequently, what Williams terms a *culture in common* becomes the basis for assessment in literacy. Because of this, when students come to the classroom with different ideas about texts arising from expectations fostered in their speech community, they are penalized. (See Kachru & Nelson, this volume, for a discussion of cross-cultural differences and standardized tests.) Basham and Kwachka (1991), for example, point out how the native Alaskan students they studied did poorly in literacy assessment contexts because they employed social practices they had learned in their native language regarding the personalization of knowledge and extensive qualification in their writing. Often the students would include their personal opinions or narrations within summaries and essay examinations, violating the Western tradition of objectivity in such texts. They would also qualify statements, overusing, according to Western standards, adverbs like *probably* or *usually*. These practices differed from the assessment criteria used, which required that knowledge be objectified and directly presented without extensive qualification.

Basham and Kwachka suggest two ways that the negative effects of these cultural differences could be minimized in this testing context. First, prompts could "be phrased in a way that allows student writers to relate personal knowledge to the general" and second, in training readers to evaluate essay tests, readers could be sensitized to their own biases concerning the effective presentation of written texts (pp. 42–43). Whereas the first suggestion is specific to the social practices of native Alaskan students, the second is certainly applicable to all testing situations. In discussing second language writers, Land and Whitley (1989) argue that teachers should become familiar with the literacy traditions that their students bring with them and "acquire the ability to suspend judgment, to allow the piece of writing at hand to develop slowly, like photographic print, shading in detail" (p. 290). Although their suggestion is directed at second language teachers specifically, it is applicable to all teachers whose students have been enriched by ethnic and cultural backgrounds that differ from those of the Western academic context.

Recognizing that literacy is a social practice as well as an individual endeavor means that, as language teachers, we need to foster collaborative literacy practices in the classroom. We need to encourage students to read texts critically in terms of how they position particular social groups. We need to value alternative literacy traditions, encouraging others to do the same. Finally, we need to critically examine the gate-keeping function of Western academic literacy traditions and explore ways in which assessment can be undertaken in a manner that will respect differences without becoming arbitrary. Doing so will unquestionably be the most challenging part of our endeavor to respect diversity in literacy traditions while promoting literacy standards that support a common culture.

## Suggestions for further reading

Ferdman, B., Weber, R. M., & Ramírez, A. (Eds.). (1994). *Literacy across languages and cultures.* Albany: State University of New York Press.

This collection of articles examines the social and cultural context of literacy development among language minorities in a North American context. The first three chapters synthesize different theoretical and research perspectives on the acquisition and development of literacy, and the remaining chapters exemplify the application of a sociocultural perspective of literacy to the investigation of various linguistic minority groups. The closing chapter, by James Cummins, emphasizes the importance of examining existing power relationships in addressing the so-called literacy crisis.

Grabe, William (Ed.). (1992). *Annual review of applied linguistics.* (Vol. 12: *Literacy*). Cambridge: Cambridge University Press.

This special issue of the journal contains valuable articles on sociocultural approaches to literacy as well as literacy and ideology. Of particular value in offering insight into the sociocultural perspective of literacy is James Gee's chapter. The collection also includes case studies of literacy in various countries, including Canada, Australia, and South Africa.

Heath, S. B. (1983). *Ways with words: Language, life and work in communities and classrooms.* Cambridge: Cambridge University Press.

This seminal work is a model of how ethnographic studies can be used to provide an understanding of the relationship between literacy and community. The work documents how children in two different communities in the Piedmont Carolinas of the United States learned to use language; it also demonstrates how teachers can begin to understand and use the diverse literacy traditions of their students in their classrooms.

McKay, S. L. (1993). *Agendas for second language literacy.* Cambridge: Cambridge University Press.

Drawing on case studies of families, countries, and literacy programs, the author examines the manner in which sociopolitical, economic, and educational policies set literacy goals for language minorities that often conflict with an individual's own literacy goals. Throughout the book, the author examines the pedagogical implications of conflicting literacy agendas for second language learners.

Murray, D. (Ed.). (1992). *Diversity as resource.* Washington, DC: Teachers of English to Speakers of Other Languages.

This book is a collection of readings that deals with diversity in literacy traditions. Part 1 examines various definitions of literacy and culture; Part

2 discusses the literacy practices of culturally diverse groups; Part 3 discusses the pedagogical implications of diverse literacy traditions. The chapter by Keith Walters is especially relevant to the discussion in the current chapter in its examination of the challenging question of whose language, culture, and literacy language teachers should be teaching.

Spener, D. (Ed.). (1994). *Adult biliteracy in the United States*. McHenry, IL: Center for Applied Linguistics and Delta Systems.
This book contains the proceedings of a 2-day research symposium on biliteracy. The first three chapters examine issues of linguistic diversity in the United States and its pedagogical implications. The following two chapters focus on the development of literacy within a family context, and the remaining chapters are case studies of individuals becoming literate in differing contexts.

## References

Auerbach, E. (1986). Competency-based ESL: One step forward or two steps back? *TESOL Quarterly, 20*(3), 411–429.

Auerbach, E. (1993). Reexamining English only in the ESL classroom. *TESOL Quarterly, 27*(1), 9–33.

Ballard, B., & Clanchy, J. (1991). Assessment by misconception: Cultural influences and intellectual traditions. In L. Hamp-Lyons (Ed.), *Assessing second language writing in academic contexts* (pp. 19–36). Norwood, NJ: Ablex.

Basham, C., & Kwachka, P. (1991). Reading the world differently: A cross-cultural approach to writing assessment. In L. Hamp-Lyons (Ed.), *Assessing second language writing in academic contexts* (pp. 37–49). Norwood, NJ: Ablex.

Christie, F. (1990). The changing faces of literacy. In F. Christie (Ed.), *Literacy for a changing world* (pp. 1–26). Victoria: The Australian Council for Educational Research.

Connor, U., & Kaplan, R. (Eds.). (1987). *Writing across languages: Analysis of L2 texts*. Reading, MA: Addison-Wesley.

Crandall, J. (1992). Adult literacy development. In W. Grabe (Ed.), *Annual Review of Applied Linguistics* (pp. 86–104). New York: Cambridge University Press.

Cumming, A. (1990). The thinking, interactions, and participation to foster in adult ESL literacy instruction. *TESL Talk, 20*(1), 34–51.

Eggington, W. (1987). Written academic discourse in Korean: Implications for effective communication. In U. Connor & R. Kaplan (Eds.), *Writing across languages: Analysis of L2 texts* (pp. 158–168). Reading, MA: Addison-Wesley.

Fairclough, N. (1989). *Language and power*. London: Longman.

Fasold, R., Hamada, H., Robinson, D., & Barish, S. (1990). The language-planning effect of newspaper editorial policy: Gender differences in *The Washington Post. Language and Society, 19*, 521–539.

Fingeret, A. (1984). *Adult literacy education: Current and future directions*. Washington, DC: ERIC National Clearinghouse on Literacy Education.

Fishman, A. (1988). *Amish literacy: What and how it means.* Portsmouth, NH: Heineman.

Freire, P. (1970). *Pedagogy of the oppressed.* New York: The Seabury Press.

Friedlander, A. (1990). Composition in English: Effects of a first language on writing in English as a second language. In B. Kroll (Ed.), *Second language writing: Research insights for the classroom* (pp. 109–125). Cambridge: Cambridge University Press.

Gee, J. (1992). Socio-cultural approaches to literacy (literacies). In W. Grabe (Ed.), *Annual Review of Applied Linguistics* (pp. 31–48). New York: Cambridge University Press.

Goody, J. (1977). *The domestication of the savage mind.* Cambridge: Cambridge University Press.

Goody, J., & Watt, I. (1968). The consequences of literacy. In J. Goody (Ed.), *Literacy in traditional societies* (pp. 27–69). Cambridge: Cambridge University Press.

Graff, H. J. (1979). *The literacy myth: Literacy and social structure in the 19th century.* New York: Academic Press.

Heath, S. B. (1983). *Ways with words: Language, life and work in communities and classrooms.* Cambridge: Cambridge University Press.

Hinds, J. (1987). Reader versus writer responsibility: A new typology. In U. Connor & R. Kaplan (Eds.), *Writing across languages: Analysis of L2 texts* (pp. 141–152). Reading, MA: Addison-Wesley.

Hinds, J. (1990). Inductive, deductive, quasi-inductive: Expository writing in Japanese, Korean, Chinese and Thai. In U. Connor & A. Johns (Eds.), *Coherence in writing* (pp. 87–110). Alexandria, VA: TESOL.

Hirsch, E. D., Jr. (1987). *Cultural literacy: What every American needs to know.* Boston: Houghton Mifflin.

Hornberger, N., & Hardman, J. (1994). Literacy as cultural practice and cognitive skill: Biliteracy in a Cambodian adult ESL class and a GED program. In D. Spener (Ed.), *Adult biliteracy in the United States.* (pp. 147–170) McHenry, IL: Center for Applied Linguistics and Delta Systems.

Hu, A., Brown, D. F., & Brown, L. B. (1982). Some linguistic differences in the written English of Chinese and Australian students. *Language learning and communication, 1,* 39–49.

Kaplan, R. (1966). Cultural thought patterns in inter-cultural education. *Language Learning, 16,* 1–20.

Land, R. E., & Whitley, C. (1989). Evaluating second language essays in regular composition classes: Toward a pluralistic U.S. rhetoric. In D. Johnson & D. H. Roen (Eds.), *Richness in writing: Empowering ESL students* (pp. 284–293). New York: Longman.

Langer, J. (1987). A sociocognitive perspective on literacy. In J. Langer (Ed.), *Language, literacy and culture: Issues of society and schooling* (pp. 1–20). Norwood, NJ: Ablex.

Leki, I. (1991). Twenty-five years of contrastive rhetoric: Text analysis and writing pedagogies. *TESOL Quarterly, 25,* 123–144.

McKay, S. L. (Ed.). (1984). *Composing in a second language.* Rowley, MA: Newbury House.

McKay, S. L. (1989). Topic development and written discourse accent. In D. Johnson & R. Roen (Eds.), *Richness in writing: Empowering ESL students* (pp. 253–262). New York: Longman.

McKay, S. L. (1993). *Agendas for second language literacy.* Cambridge: Cambridge University Press.

Mikulecky, L. (1990). Literacy for what purpose? In R. Venezky, D. Wagner, & B. Ciliberti (Eds.), *Toward defining literacy* (pp. 24–34). Newark, DE: International Reading Association.

Mohan, B., & Lo, W. (1985). Academic writing and Chinese students: Transfer and developmental factors. *TESOL Quarterly, 19,* 515–534.

Nichols, P. C. (1989). Storytelling in Carolina: Continuities and contrasts. *Anthropology and Education Quarterly, 20,* 232–245.

Norment, N. (1986). Organizational structure of Chinese subjects writing in Chinese and in ESL. *Journal of the Chinese Language Teachers Association, 23,* 49–72.

O'Barr, W. (1982). *Linguistic evidence: Language, power and strategy in the courtroom.* New York: Academic Press.

Olson, D. (1977). From utterance to text: The bias of language in speech and writing. *Harvard Educational Review, 47*(3). 257–281.

Olson, D. (1990). Contribution to the forum: When a learner attempts to become literate in a second language, what is he or she attempting? *TESL Talk, 20*(1), 18–20.

Ong, W. J. (1982). *Orality and literacy: The technologizing of the word.* London: Methuen.

Osterloh, K. (1986). Intercultural differences and communicative approaches to foreign language teaching in the third world. In J. Valdes (Ed.), *Culture bound* (pp. 77–84). Cambridge: Cambridge University Press.

Read, C., & Mackay, R. (1984). *Illiteracy among adult immigrants in Canada.* Montreal: Concordia University (ERIC Document Reproduction Service No. ED 291 875).

Reder, M. (1987). Comparative aspects of functional literacy development: Three ethnic American communities. In D. A. Wagner (Ed.), *The future of literacy in a changing world* (pp. 250–269). Oxford: Pergamon Press.

Schieffelin, B., & Cochran-Smith, M. (1984). Learning to read culturally: Literacy before schooling. In H. Goelman, A. Oberg, & F. Smith (Eds.), *Awakening to literacy* (pp. 3–23). Portsmouth, NH: Heinemann Educational Books.

Scribner, S., & Cole, M. (1981). *The psychology of literacy.* Cambridge: Harvard University Press.

Shuman, A. (1986). *Storytelling rights: The uses of oral and written texts by urban adolescents.* Cambridge: Cambridge University Press.

Siriphan, S. (1988). An investigation of syntax, semantics, and rhetoric in the English writing of fifteen Thai graduate students. Unpublished doctoral dissertation. Texas Women's University.

Street, B. (1984). *Literacy in theory and practice.* Cambridge: Cambridge University Press.

Street, B. (1991). *Cross-cultural literacy.* Paper presented at the Conference on Intergenerational Literacy. New York: Teachers College, Columbia University.

Vasquez, O. (1992). A Mexican perspective: Reading the world in a multicultural setting. In D. Murray (Ed.), *Diversity as resource: Redefining cultural literacy* (pp. 113–134). Alexandria, VA: Teachers of English to Speakers of Other Languages.

Walsh, C. (1991). Literacy as praxis: A framework and an introduction. In C. Walsh (Ed.), *Literacy as praxis* (pp. 1–24). Norwood, NJ: Ablex.
Walters, K. (1992). Whose culture? Whose literacy? In D. Murray (Ed.), *Diversity as resource: Redefining cultural literacy* (pp. 3–29). Alexandria, VA: Teachers of English to Speakers of Other Languages.
Watson-Gegeo, K. (1988). Ethnography in ESL: Defining thc essentials. *TESOL Quarterly, 22,* 575–592.
Wells, B. (1987). Apprenticeship in literacy. *Interchange, 18*(1–2), 109–123.
Williams, R. (1989). The idea of a common culture. In R. Gable (Ed.), *Resources of hope: Culture, democracy, socialism* (pp. 3–18). London: Verso.

# CONCLUSION

# 14 *Language and education*

Nancy H. Hornberger

The foregoing chapters have made it abundantly clear that language in all its societal, variational, interactional, and cultural diversity both influences and is influenced by education. Education is the site where, on the one hand, broad social and political forces are reflected in the kinds of educational opportunities offered to speakers of different language varieties and, on the other, language use mediates the participation of these speakers in those opportunities and, ultimately, their potential contributions to the larger society.

Consider the following narrative vignettes from my own ethnographic research on language and literacy learning among language minorities in the United States and Peru.

*July 13, 1983*
Victoria, now age 33, was born and finished primary school in Kinsachata, a rural Quechua-speaking community of highland Puno, Peru. She then roomed alone in Lampa, about 35 to 40 kilometers away, in order to attend the *colegio* [high school] there, the closest *colegio* to her home. Although many of her teachers were Quechua-speaking, and may have occasionally used Quechua informally with their students, the medium of instruction for both her primary and secondary education was Spanish.

The first vignette, dated July 13, 1983, is adapted from my published work (Hornberger 1988, pp. 67, 70) and draws from research carried out in 1982 and 1983 with the permission and support of the Proyecto Experimental de Educación Bilingüe - Puno in Puno, Peru; the Dirección Departamental de Educación in Puno, Peru; and the Instituto Nacional de Investigación y Desarrollo de la Educación (INIDE) in Lima, Peru. Financial support for this work came from the Inter-American Foundation and the U.S. Department of Education (Fulbright-Hays). Their assistance is gratefully acknowledged.

The second and third vignettes, dated April 18 and 22, 1989 and October 5, 1989, draw from research carried out beginning in 1987 in school and community settings of Philadelphia. I am grateful for a National Academy of Education Spencer Fellowship that enabled me to devote full time to this research in 1989, and to the Dean's Fellowship, the Literacy Research Center, and the Research Fund at the Graduate School of Education, University of Pennsylvania, for providing support for graduate student research assistance.

I am especially grateful to the students, families, teachers, and administrators who made these studies possible.

Upon completing secondary school, she entered and won a competition to go to Spain and receive training at the *Escuela Universitaria de Instructoras Rurales* [University School for Rural Instructors]. Having successfully completed the 5-year course of study, she began work in Spain teaching domestic sciences, and was on the point of marrying and staying there, when her father suffered an accident and her family insistently pleaded with her to return home. She finally did return in 1976, not only because the contract she had was for study only (since that could have been changed), but especially because she did not want to abandon her family.

She has returned to her community and works in adult education out of the district capital, Cabanillas. This adult education program teaches literacy in Spanish. Since returning to her native region, Victoria has reaccustomed herself to speaking Quechua, although she had not used it at all for several years; she has, however, never learned to read and write Quechua. She has recently acquired a traditional outfit, including the *pullira* [full skirt] characteristic of indigenous women in the Andes, and takes pleasure in wearing it, although she continues to wear more "westernized" clothing, including slacks, on regular working days.

*April 18, 1989*

When Chantah (now about 19), arrived in Philadelphia in 1985 as a refugee from Cambodia, she immediately entered tenth grade at University City High School. She knew hardly any English when she came, but after about 3½ months, she managed to get a C on her finals.

The following year, they put her in William Penn High School so that she could attend the Randolph Skills Center, a vocational school which opened in September 1975, operates on a shared-time basis with the student's home school, and offers training in seven clusters – communications, construction, health services, manufacturing and maintenance, personal services, power mechanics, and warehousing. She would go one week to William Penn for math and other subjects and the other week to Randolph Skills Center, where she studied to be a nursing assistant. She finished eleventh and twelfth grades there. She's now in her second year at the Community College of Philadelphia, studying to be a registered nurse. There are no other Cambodians in her class.

She wanted to work after graduating from high school, but her father made her continue to study. Her father wanted her to learn English. He has had great trouble learning it himself; though he has studied it, he can't seem to learn it – he gets the words backward.

Chantah knows how to read and write in Khmer, and uses it once every month or so in writing letters to her relatives in Cambodia. Her younger siblings are not literate in Khmer, and for now her father wants them to learn English. Maybe when they are 10 or 15, they can learn Khmer.

Chantah invites me to go with them this Saturday to the Cambodian New Year celebration at the Civic Center, and brings out a several-page program, printed in Khmer and partly in English, about it. She tells me that some Khmer traditions are very old and have been passed on from one generation to the next, but now, many people are imitating the Americans.

*April 22, 1989*
When I arrive at their home, Chantah is wearing traditional clothes – a long green silk skirt, white blouse, gold necklaces, bracelets, earrings, rings. At the Civic Center, she tells me she feels uncomfortable in these clothes, but that her mother wanted her to "act like Cambodian." Later, after returning from the Civic Center, she changes out of these clothes at the first opportunity, into jeans, a shirt, and jacket. While at the several-hour-long New Year's celebration, she meticulously carries out all the traditional activities – serving the rice, making offerings to the monks, praying, and lighting and carrying incense to the sand mountain.

*October 5, 1989*
At Aspira's *Abriendo Caminos,* [Creating Opportunities] a GED program for high school dropouts in North Philadelphia, the last hour of the morning session on Thursdays is devoted to what the program calls *the reinforcement session.* Today's class is structured around a page of questions the teacher had given the class before their visit yesterday to *Taller Puertorriqueño,* a Puerto Rican cultural arts center in the community. When I enter, about 10 minutes into the period, the students are busy writing the answers on their papers, talking among themselves and with the teacher as they do so.

Then the teacher begins a group discussion based on the questions, going through them one by one, seeking participation by all. The students are very lively in their participation, several often talking at once, and with frequent code switching from English to Spanish and back.

The students, all aged 16 to 21, seem to have been inspired by what was for most of them apparently their first visit to *Taller.* Their discussion reflects their awakening sense of pride in being Puerto Rican. They mention some of the typical Puerto Rican musical instruments, songs, and dances they know, and two students exchange experiences they had at school, performing in *La Plena* and singing *La Borinquen.* Ana says she was proud of being Puerto Rican before, and now, having seen and learned at *Taller,* feels even prouder. Linda says she feels especially proud as a woman because of what was said at *Taller.* Sandra agrees, noting that they said Puerto Rican women treat their men well. One young woman notes that, it's true, her mother really does do everything around the house, and she never thought about the fact that that was a Puerto Rican trait. Robert, who had not gone with the class, comments that he thinks his classmates have learned to "esteem themselves" and affirms that "we are a handsome and a beautiful race."

It becomes clear through the discussion that some of the students have an English version, and some a Spanish version, of the questionnaire. Though the questions are apparently the same, their order of appearance is not. The teacher opts to follow the order on the English version.

After class, one student stays to copy the questions and answers before turning her paper in to the teacher. She had commented during class that she wanted to keep them.

Later, talking to the teacher, I express some surprise that most of these young people had never visited *Taller Puertorriqueño* until yesterday, even though it is just a few blocks away, right in their neighborhood. This leads to a discussion with him about how, growing up here, with the media coverage of their community, and so on, the Puerto Rican young people's Puerto Rican identity in some ways comes to reflect the external rather than the internal point of view. That is, they take on the identity portrayed in the media (drugs, violence, dropping out), rather than the identity within the community, for example, that represented by *Taller.*

Thus, when they first are acquainted with *Taller,* it really is an eye-opening experience, because they begin to realize that many of the things they know and live with are part of their culture and shared history, not just odd stray things.

Each of these vignettes depicts ways in which language and culture interact with policy and program in language minority young peoples' educational experiences. My own research, from which these vignettes are taken, has focused primarily on language minority learners; however, the same issues are relevant for dialect, creole, or pidgin speakers within so-called monolingual settings, as well as for gender-differentiated language use. In order to encompass all kinds of learners, in what follows the term *language* is used in the sense of *language variety;* that is, it simultaneously connotes different language varieties in bilingual or multilingual settings and different dialects, creole varieties, or gender-differentiated language use in monolingual settings. We will return often to the preceding experiences as we consider in detail the ways in which language and language use both shape and mediate young peoples' participation in educational opportunities and, ultimately, their contributions, real and potential, to the larger society.

## Continua of biliteracy

We began the book with a conceptual framework for sociolinguistics – one that distinguishes between societal and linguistic perspectives and macrolevels and microlevels of analysis. We end with another conceptual framework – one that attempts to draw together the various pieces highlighted in the foregoing chapters, the various sociolinguistic dimensions that play into a learner's language and literacy development. I call the framework the *continua of biliteracy* (Hornberger, 1989), where biliteracy is defined as "any and all instances in which communication occurs in two (or more) languages in and around writing" (Hornberger, 1990, p. 213). As such, biliteracy epitomizes the relationship between language and education for first and second language (L1 and L2) learners, and the continua of biliteracy provide a framework in which to explore the dimensions of their education.

In the framework, the notion of *continuum* is intended to convey that, although one can identify (and name) points on any one continuum, those points are not finite, static, or discrete. For an understanding of biliteracy, it is as elucidating to focus on the common features as on the features that distinguish the points of the continuum from one another.

The framework proposes three nested sets of three intersecting continua each, sets which define the development, media, and contexts of biliteracy, respectively (see Figure 1). Each three-dimensional intersection depicts three constituent continua, thereby representing the interrelatedness among them. The nesting of the three sets, in turn, is intended

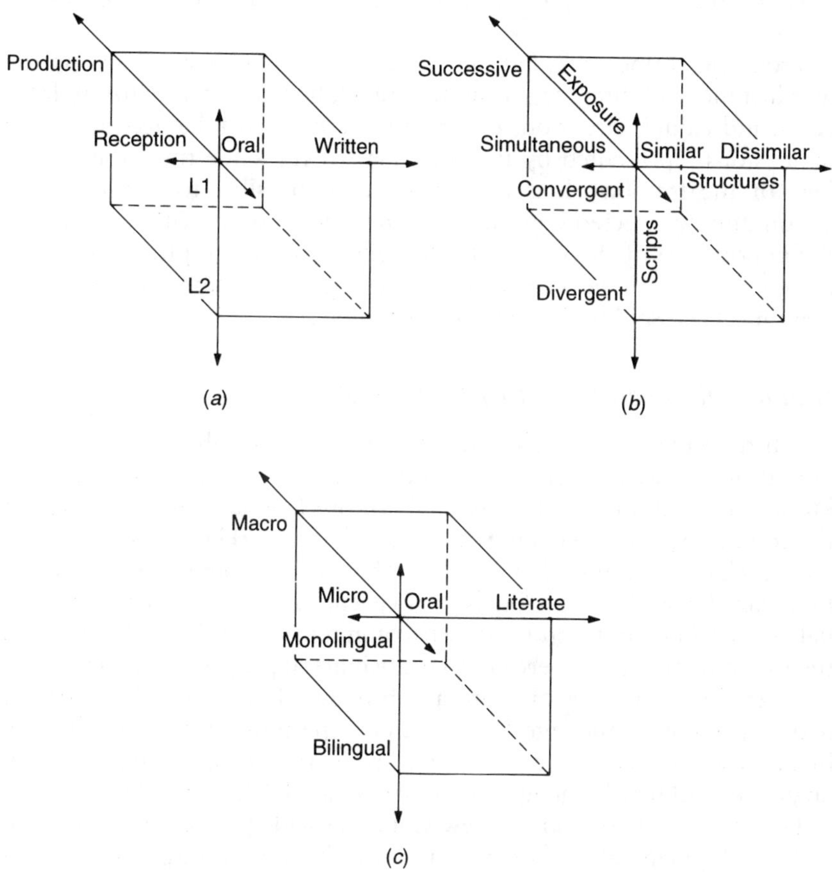


*Figure 1. The continua of biliteracy. (a) the continua of biliterate development in the individual. (b) The continua of biliterate media. (c) the continua of biliterate contexts. (From Hornberger, 1989.)*

to convey that the interrelationships extend across, as well as within, the development, media, and contexts of biliteracy.

Thus, I suggest that the development of biliteracy occurs along intersecting first language-second language, receptive-productive, and oral-written language skills continua; through the medium of two (or more) language varieties and literacies whose linguistic structures vary from similar to dissimilar, whose scripts range from convergent to divergent, and to which the developing biliterate individual's exposure varies from simultaneous to successive; and in contexts which range from microlevels to macrolevels and are characterized by varying mixes along the monolingual-bilingual and oral-literate continua. By extension, the same framework applies to language and literacy in trilingual or multilingual settings as well, all of them here subsumed under the term *biliteracy.*

From this framework, I argue that in order to understand any particular instance of biliteracy (or multiliteracy), be it a biliterate (or multiliterate) individual, situation, or society, we need to take account of all dimensions represented by the continua. At the same time, the advantage of the framework is that it makes it possible to focus on one continuum or selected continua and their dimensions without ignoring the importance of the others. In the following paragraphs, each of the three sets of continua is discussed, as an organizing rubric for reviewing what has been said in the foregoing chapters.

## *Individual development of biliteracy*

As Muriel Saville-Troike shows, within the ethnography of communication framework, the term *communicative competence* designates the knowledge and ability of individuals to use language appropriately in the communicative events in which they find themselves in any particular speech community (Hymes, 1972a, b). This competence is, by definition, variable within individuals (from event to event), from one individual to another, and across speech communities. Individuals draw on their communicative repertoire to participate appropriately in any given context. The continua of biliteracy framework suggests that, for the first and second language learner, that repertoire is crucially defined by at least three continua: reception-production, oral language-written language, and first language-second language (L1-L2) transfer.

Deborah Schiffrin and Andrew Cohen provide perspectives on learners' development along the reception-production continuum, with respect to particular interactions and particular speech acts. Cohen, in particular, asks the question whether reception in the form of instruction in specific speech acts leads to appropriate production of them.

Sandra McKay's chapter explores the ways in which literate behavior is dependent on the social context, demonstrating how individuals' development along the oral language-written language continuum brings with it their induction into the collaborative practices and social relationships, as well as the cultural and community values, in which literacy is embedded. Keith Chick brings out the potential for not only transfer but conflict when culturally specific assumptions and expectations and communicative conventions from one language group are carried over into interaction with another.

It should be noted that the notion of continuum in development is not intended to suggest that development is necessarily continuous or gradual; it may, in fact, occur in spurts and with some backtracking. Rather, the argument is that development within any one continuum draws on features from the entire continuum.

Thus, the reception-production continuum emphasizes the view that language and literacy development does not necessarily proceed in a linear sequence from receptive (listening and reading) to productive (speaking and writing) skills but may begin at any point and proceed, cumulatively or in spurts, in either direction. In highland Puno, Peru, Quechua-speaking children who, unlike Victoria, were taught via their first language as the medium of instruction in primary school showed not only improved oral participation but increased reading and writing performance in school (Hornberger, 1988, pp. 190 – 198). Further, as Saville-Troike suggests in her examples of second language learners who are aware of but prefer not to adopt rules for interaction in the second language when they conflict with their own cultural values and beliefs, development may, by the learners' choice, never proceed from reception to production at all.

Similarly, the oral language-written language continuum suggests that reading and writing (written language skills) are complementary to, rather than sequentially related to, listening and speaking (oral language skills). McKay highlights this complementary relationship in her discussion of Reder's analysis of technological, functional, and social modes of engagement in collaborative literacy practices in his study of three communities and Vasquez's description of the different roles in literacy events taken by individual members of the bilingual U.S. Mexican families she studied.

The first language-second language (L1-L2) transfer continuum reflects research findings that suggest that (1) what appears to be interference from L1 in L2 is often better construed as evidence for learning in that it represents the application of L1 knowledge to L2 and (2) the stronger the foundation and continuing development in L1, the greater the potential for enhanced learning of L2. My ethnographic study of bilingual education for Quechua-speaking children in Peru (1988), Edelsky's study (1986) of Spanish-speaking students' writing development in a bilingual program in the southwestern United States, and McLaughlin's study (1992) of literacy and empowerment of Navajo speakers in the United States provide support for the latter claim. Patricia Nichols and John Rickford appeal to this claim in presenting arguments in favor of the use of pidgins, creoles, and African-American Vernacular English (AAVE) in the classroom. Note that the finding that a stronger first language leads to a stronger second language does not necessarily imply that the first language must be fully developed before the second language is introduced. Rather, the first language must not be abandoned before it is fully developed, whether the second language is introduced simultaneously or successively, early or late, in that process. This point will be addressed again later (simultaneous-successive exposure continuum).

As to the former claim about interference, application, and learning, Cohen's review of studies on the teaching of speech act behavior to nonnative speakers provides examples in which L1 knowledge is applied to L2 learning; Saville-Troike argues that communicative competence entails not only linguistic but also interactional and cultural knowledge and that native cultural values and beliefs have direct impact on second language linguistic performance; and Rebecca Freeman and Bonnie McElhinny, Frederick Erickson, Deborah Schiffrin, and Keith Chick caution against static conceptions of culture and its role in guiding interaction, noting that it is necessary to understand that talk is not only shaped by culture but also socially negotiated.

Implicit in the continua framework, and particularly congruent with the perspectives of interactional sociolinguistics and microethnography, is this notion of social negotiation, the notion that the development of biliteracy in individuals occurs along the continua in direct response to the contextual demands placed on these individuals. "The environmental press that requires the successful interactant to use distinct subsets of linguistic and sociolinguistic knowledge can change from moment to moment in face to face interaction, and from one discourse unit to another in a written text with which ego is confronted. Interaction with these verbal and written texts, and with the text producers, constitutes practice in language use." (Erickson, 1989, p. 5).

The implications of the continua of biliterate development for language teaching and minority education are clear. With respect to the learners' biliterate development, the most favorable context is one that provides opportunities for the learner to practice along all points of the continua, that is, production as well as reception, written as well as oral language, and first as well as second language variety.

## *Media of biliteracy*

Learners pursue this practice through the medium of the language varieties and literacies available to them in any particular context. In the bilingualism field, a distinction is often made between simultaneous and successive bilingual language acquisition (McLaughlin, 1985), or early and late bilingualism (Lambert, 1985, p. 120), both distinctions referring to the sequence and timing in which bilinguals acquire their languages; the same distinctions are relevant to bidialectal or creole speakers' acquisition of their language varieties (cf. Rickford, this volume; Nichols, this volume). The simultaneous-successive exposure continuum draws attention to the fact, made clear in the chapter by Kamal Sridhar, that a number of configurations exist as to the simultaneous or successive development of biliteracy, each one involving varying degrees of development of the first and second languages. Saville-Troike's distinction between second, auxiliary, and foreign languages clearly evokes one dimension of these configurations; Braj Kachru and Cecil Nelson depict a parallel distinction with respect to the use of English worldwide, between Inner Circle, Outer Circle, and Expanding Circle countries. Another dimension of simultaneous versus successive exposure to the media of biliteracy might be the level of L1 literacy upon which L2 literacy is built – minimal, moderate, or highly developed – as exemplified by transitional bilingual education, secondary schooling in a language of wider communication (LWC) in former colonial states (see Wiley, this volume), and foreign language studies at the college level, respectively; or the level of L1 literacy built upon prior L2 literacy – French immersion students in Canada eventually take up English (L1) literacy and continue to develop it throughout their schooling, and immigrants to the United States who are schooled in their second language may subsequently take up or retake up L1 literacy, although probably only for limited uses, as in the case of Chantah.

Some have suggested that biliterate development in two languages with greatly dissimilar structures, such as Khmer and English, or Quechua and Spanish, will be quite different from that in two structurally more related languages, such as Spanish and English, from that in two varieties of the same language, such as standard and nonstandard English, or from that in a pidgin and its superstrate or substrate language such as Haitian creole and French. Yet the complex relationships between these structurally more similar varieties, as demonstrated by Rickford in his discussion of regional and social variation within languages, Freeman and McElhinny in their cross-cultural perspectives on one such type of variation, gender-differentiated language, and Nichols in her description of the structural characteristics of pidgins and creoles and the social contexts in which they arise, belie any easy prognosis as to whether those differences suggest an easier biliterate (bidialectal) development.

As with simultaneous versus successive exposure and similar versus dissimilar language structures, researchers have also argued that convergent versus divergent scripts of the two or (more) language varieties involved have a bearing on an individual's development of biliteracy; however, as in the other cases, research has not clarified which, if either, end of the continuum is the more conducive to positive transfer across languages and literacies. Further research in settings in which there are, for example, two languages with different writing systems (e.g., Khmer and English), one language with two writing systems (e.g., Serbian and Croatian; see Wiley, this volume), or two languages with one writing system (e.g., the varieties of Chinese) is needed to elucidate the role of this continuum in biliterate development.

One of the difficulties in gaining an understanding of the role of particular scripts in literacy acquisition is that the multitude and complexity of contextual factors have a tendency to mask any possible effect of more or less convergence between alternative scripts. For example, Wiley argues in his chapter that standardization, and the orthography planning (i.e., the development, renovation, reform, etc., of a writing system) that often accompanies it, is more often motivated by political goals than by pedagogical criteria or concerns for equal educational access. Mary McGroarty shows how learners' and teachers' attitudes toward languages and their varieties, and in particular toward these languages and varieties in their written form, have direct implications for learners' literate development. McKay demonstrates that the acquisition of literacy entails acquisition of community values and traditions about how to approach texts as well as of cultural values and traditions about text and topic development. The strong role of contextual factors such as these – political motivations, language attitudes, and cultural and community values – on learners' acquisition of reading and writing skills seems to overwhelm considerations of the media through which they are acquired. Thus the discussion turns to context.

## *Contexts of biliteracy*

The continuum of oral-literate contexts has its parallel in the continuum of oral language-written language in biliterate development and, like the latter, suggests that orality and literacy are complementarily, rather than linearly, related. As McKay shows, the view of literacy as an isolated, individual skill linked to cognitive development, and of literate societies as fundamentally different (and more civilized) than oral ones, has been superseded by a recognition that literacy practices are but part of wider sociocultural practices that involve talk, interaction, values, and beliefs (Gee, 1992). In this latter, ideological model (Street, 1984), literacy is seen as a social and cultural phenomenon, and cultures and societies are differentiated not so much by whether they are "literate" or not but, rather, by the variations in their particular mix of oral and literate language channels and functions (cf. Street, 1988). One implication of this view for L1 and L2 language learners is that the ways in which contexts mix oral and literate language use will affect those learners' use and development of language and literacy. McKay provides a number of examples of how this is so for Hmong, Eskimo, and Mexican language minorities, as well as working-class African-American and white communities in the United States; similarly, in the introductory narrative vignettes of this chapter, Victoria's nonuse of Quechua literacy, Chantah's limited use of Khmer literacy, and *Abriendo Caminos* participants' moderate use of Spanish literacy can all be linked to the particular mix of first and second language oral and literate channels and functions in the culture and society of each of them.

The second of the continua of biliterate contexts, the monolingual-bilingual continuum, also finds a parallel in other continua, in particular the L1-L2 transfer continuum and the similar-dissimilar language structures continuum. Here, however, the emphasis is on the contexts in which learning and teaching occur, rather than on the individual's language and literacy development or the media through which that occurs. The monolingual-bilingual continuum underlines that the degree to which particular contexts may involve the use of one or both of the learners' language varieties affects the development of their language and literacy. Sridhar has shown how, in bilingual or multilingual societies, use of the different languages is functionally distributed in terms of domains, social meanings, and prestige or utility configurations. It turns out that the same is true in monolingual societies: Rickford shows how different varieties of a language arise because of regional or social factors (age, social class, race or ethnicity, gender); Freeman and McElhinny review discourse and interactional features of gender-differentiated language and suggest that these differences provide both a reflection of and an opportunity to challenge and transform societal norms; and Nichols explores the acts of identity represented by use of a creole language in home and community and the social meanings associated with use of a standard variety in a formal educational setting. In both monolingual and multilingual contexts, in other words, different language varieties have different functions and social meanings.

The functional specialization of languages and varieties does not, however, preclude use of more than one language or variety within a given context. Sridhar details the code switching and code mixing, as well as borrowing, convergence, and transfer, that characterize language and language use in multilingual societies. Kachru and Nelson's discussion of the nativization and acculturation of English in various settings all across the world provides ample evidence of the ways in which contact between English and other languages over time has led to formal, functional, and attitudinal changes with respect to English. As for monolingual settings, both Rickford and Freeman and McElhinny suggest that monolinguals switch styles according to specific functions and uses in the same way that multilinguals switch languages. Rickford argues for the value of acquainting students with regional and social variation as a resource rather than a problem, and Freeman and McElhinny review selected cross-cultural findings on how women and men may vary their speaking styles according to genre or politeness conventions, for example.

The third continuum of biliterate contexts, and the last of the nine continua of biliteracy in the framework, is the micro-macro continuum, which draws attention to the fact that contexts at every level, from face-to-face interaction to national policy and global politico-economic situations, affect the use and development of language and literacy. This brings us full circle to our introductory premise that an understanding of the role of social context is central to the task of educating L1 and L2 language learners in the classrooms of today's world, and to our framework of the macrolevels and microlevels of sociolinguistics that provides a way of understanding those contexts.

Each of the four preceding parts of this volume discusses the role of social context in L1 and L2 language education. Part 1, "Language and Society," points to the role of language attitudes, societal language use patterns, language prestige, and language policy and planning, and Part 2, "Language and Variation," to the significance of colonial history and economic relations and of social factors like age, class, race or ethnicity, and gender to L1 and L2 language education; all of the chapters in these parts address the macrocontext. Turning to the microcontext, Part 3, "Language and Interaction," takes up face-to-face interaction and the negotiation of social identities as contexts for communicative development, and Part 4, "Language and Culture," emphasizes the influence of situation and event and of participants' cultural attitudes and norms, values, and traditions on L1 and L2 language learners' negotiation of their learning. The point to be emphasized is that each and every one of these aspects of social context is important to our understanding of L1 and L2 language education.

Language and literacy development is a complex phenomenon. The interrelatedness of the nine continua of biliteracy makes it possible to see why there is potential for transfer across languages and literacies, whereas the nested nature of the continua makes it possible to see that there are a myriad of contextual factors that may abet or impede such transfer. Indeed, Street has recently suggested that "[If] you start from the assumption that learning literacy is in fact a process of cultural learning . . . then learning one literacy will not necessarily help in learning another" (1993). One clear implication of the continua model of biliteracy, however, is that the more the contexts of their language and literacy use and development allow learners to draw on all points of all nine continua, the greater are the chances for their learning. We will turn now to a consideration of the educational implications of these insights.

## Sociolinguistics in language teaching and minority education

A central theme of this volume is, as stated in the introduction to this chapter, that education is the site where, on the one hand, larger social and political forces are reflected in the kinds of educational opportunities offered to speakers of different language varieties and, on the other, language use mediates their participation in those opportunities and, ultimately, their potential contributions to the larger society. If that is so, then it is also true that the educational choices we make can have a direct impact on the opportunities, participation, and potential contributions of language and minority learners. We turn now to a direct consideration of educational alternatives that address the sociolinguistic concerns raised throughout this book. In so doing, we will review and build on what has been said in the foregoing chapters. Policy and program options are addressed first, then language, culture, and interaction in the classroom, and finally issues of evaluation and assessment.

### *Policy and program options*

McGroarty, Sridhar, Kachru and Nelson, and Wiley present the many dimensions which define the global and national contexts in which L1 and L2 language education occur, among them, language attitudes, standards, and norms, multilingualism, language prestige, and language in education policy. At the global level, a clear picture of the normalcy of multilingualism and the spread and diversification of English as a world language emerges; yet these trends define only a part of the national context of countries such as India, Nigeria, and the Philippines. Differing histories, attitudes, and policies contribute as well. The contemporary national context in the United States is characterized by strong pressures on nonnative English speakers to accommodate and acculturate and equally strong negative attitudes toward English dialect variation; a series of language-related court decisions frame a national policy context which in essence recognizes the need for tolerance and limited accommodation to languages and varieties other than standard English but stops well short of protecting their maintenance or promotion.

Despite the many differences in such contexts, common questions continually arise around L1 and L2 language education, for example: Which language variety will be the medium of instruction? When should a second language be introduced? When should a foreign language be introduced? Which subjects will be taught in which language variety? For what purpose will this language variety be taught? Will it be introduced as subject of instruction? As medium of instruction? Who will teach this language variety? What qualifications will be required of teachers? Given the variety and complexity of possible contexts for language teaching and minority education around the world, it comes as no surprise that there cannot be any one best answer to these questions for all possible cases. Instead, language educators need to construct the best answers for their own contexts on the basis of a decision-making process involving the community the program is intended to serve (e.g., Delgado-Gaitan, 1990). I have suggested a heuristic for such decision making, in the form of a typology of bilingual education models and programs, which is summarized here (Hornberger, 1991).

The heuristic distinguishes between models and programs, defining *models* in terms of their goals with respect to language, culture, and society and *program types* in terms of characteristics relating to student population, teachers, and program structure (see Table 1 and Figure 2). I suggest that any one type can theoretically be implemented within any of the three models, and any model can be implemented via a wide range of types. Wiley identifies language shift, language maintenance, and language enrichment policies; the three bilingual education models in the heuristic correspond closely to those policy alternatives. A transitional model encompasses programs which aim toward language shift,

TABLE 1. BILINGUAL EDUCATION MODEL TYPES

| *Transitional model* | *Maintenance model* | *Enrichment model* |
|---|---|---|
| Language shift | Language maintenance | Language development |
| Cultural assimilation | Strengthened cultural identity | Cultural pluralism |
| Social incorporation | Civil rights affirmation | Social autonomy |

*Source:* From Hornberger (1991).

**Contextual characteristics**

*Student population*
- Numbers
- Stability (high or low turnover each year)
- Participation (voluntary or involuntary)
- Assessment and placement (advocacy or legitimizing)
- Socioeconomic status
- Minority status (involuntary or immigrant)
- First language background
  - Heterogeneous or homogeneous
  - Minority or majority
  - Degree of bilingualism

*Teachers*
- Ethnic background
- Degree of Bilingualism
- Training
- Roles (classroom or supplementary teacher, aide, tutor, etc.)

**Structural characteristics**

*Program in school*
- School-wide or targeted
- One-way or two-way

*Languages in curriculum*
- Sequencing of languages as mediums of instruction
- Oral and literate development
- Subject allocation

*Classroom language use*
- Patterns
  - Alternate: lessons, teachers, days/weeks/am-pm, rooms
  - Mixed: code switching, concurrent translation, preview-review, new concurrent approach
- Functions: speech acts, interactional structures

*Figure 2. Bilingual education program types. (Adapted from Hornberger, 1991.)*

cultural assimilation, and social incorporation of language minorities in the national society; a maintenance model encompasses programs which aim toward language maintenance, strengthened cultural identity, and the affirmation of ethnic groups' civil rights in the national society; and an enrichment model encompasses programs which aim toward not only maintenance but development and extension of the minority language varieties, cultural pluralism, and an integrated national society based on autonomy of cultural groups.

As already mentioned, each of these models can be implemented via a wide range of program types; these are defined by contextual and structural characteristics (see Figure 2). Contextual characteristics are formulated in terms of student characteristics – including numbers, stability, and language background; and teacher characteristics – such as training, ethnic background, and instructional roles. Structural characteristics include consideration of the program's place in the school – whether it targets all or only a part of the school's population and whether it is a one-way or two-way program with respect to language learning; the treatment of language varieties in the curriculum – which language varieties for which subjects, in which sequence, and to what degree of oral and literate development; and the patterns and functions of language use in the classroom.

We suggest that when program decisions are made through a process involving not only teachers but also the community served, and on the basis of a heuristic such as this, in which both goals and program structure are agreed on by those involved, the likelihood of achieving the optimal context for L1 and L2 language learners' education is greatly improved. What that "optimal context" will look like may differ greatly from context to context. Consider, for example, the cases represented by the opening vignettes: an involuntary indigenous language minority (Victoria), an immigrant-refugee language minority (Chantah), and an involuntary immigrant language minority (the *Abriendo Caminos* participants). Ogbu (1987) suggests that an understanding of the different histories and experiences of involuntary minorities versus those of voluntary immigrant minorities is the only way to account for the variability in their school performance. Although immigrant minorities experience primary cultural differences (of cultural content such as marriage practices), retain their sense of peoplehood from before emigration, accommodate to the discrimination they experience, and accept the dominant group's folk theory of "making it" while keeping as reference point the worse conditions they experienced before immigrating, involuntary minorities experience secondary cultural differences (of style), develop a sense of identity in opposition to the dominant group, maintain a deep distrust toward the dominant group born of the discrimination they experience, and develop their own theory of "making it" while keeping as reference point their former better state (before conquest, colonization, or slavery). An enrichment model of education, designed to maximize learners' biliterate development and educational opportunities, might look very different in each of these contexts.

## *Language, culture, and interaction in the classroom*

Erickson, Schiffrin, Chick, Saville-Troike, Cohen, and McKay have amply demonstrated the important roles of culture and interaction in L1 and L2 language education. Cross-cultural variation in literacy practices was discussed as were communicative competence, ways of speaking, and the culturally specific assumptions, expectations, and conventions these encompass. The potential for miscommunication but equally, for the social negotiation of comembership, in intercultural communication was also brought out.

In each case, implications for education have been clearly indicated. McKay suggests that literacy activities in the classroom should foster the kinds of collaborative approaches to literacy that exist in the community. Saville-Troike points out that findings concerning the cultural norms and meanings of a variety of speech events in particular target speech communities can guide curricular content for language programs, but she simultaneously cautions that some levels of social and cultural meaning (such as the social meaning of linguistic variation) are virtually impossible to teach in foreign language teaching situations and, further, that in auxiliary language teaching situations, the culture of the native speech community may be largely irrelevant to and even unwanted by the learners. Schiffrin notes that an understanding of how contextualization cues (verbal and nonverbal signs such as intonation and code switching) can affect the basic meaning of a message is important for both teachers and learners in intercultural teaching situations.

The hidden message embedded in code switching behavior has emerged recurringly as a significant factor in the distribution of the two languages of instruction in bilingual education and in second and foreign language teaching classrooms. Although some researchers have argued for strictly alternating the use of the two languages, by person, place, time, or topic, on the grounds of preventing possible cognitive confusion from "confusing" the languages, mixed use in the form of code switching, translation, or preview-review persists (see Jacobson & Faltis, 1990; Legarreta-Marcaida, 1981). Studies of code switching in a variety of bilingual classrooms suggest that the significant dimension of language use is not the pattern but, rather, the functions of use (Guthrie, 1985; Hornberger, 1988; Milk, 1981, 1986; Tsang, 1983; Zentella, 1981). For example, as in the case of Victoria, described earlier, if one language (Quechua) is used exclusively for affective, nonacademic communication and classroom control, and the other (Spanish) for all instructional content, it seems likely that students will quickly pick up the hidden message that the second language is more useful and important (cf. Sapiens, 1982, on the uses of Spanish and English in a high school civics class). Just as McKay suggests that collaborative literacy practices from the community can be useful models for classroom instruction, Zentella (1981) notes that "it seems premature to ban code-switching from the classroom when we do not know what we are banning along with it" (p. 130; see also Huerta-Macías & Quintero, 1992).

Incorporating norms and behaviors from the community into the classroom emerges as a common pedagogical implication throughout this volume. Yet, just as Zentella goes on to say, about code switching, "nor is it helpful to say it should be incorporated into the classroom in a mechanistic way" (1981, p. 130), it is also true that the incorporation of the community's culture into the classroom must go beyond simply incorporating culturally compatible pedagogy to culturally responsive (Jacobs & Jordan, 1987) and culturally relevant (Ladson-Billings, 1992) pedagogy.

A special issue of the *Anthropology and Education Quarterly* (Jacobs & Jordan, 1987) explores the strengths and inadequacies of two major anthropological explanations for the school performance of minority students: the cultural difference approach and the secondary cultural discontinuity approach. The cultural difference approach suggests that differences between mainstream and minority cultures in interactional, linguistic, cognitive, communicative, motivational, literate, and writing styles can lead to cultural conflicts that interfere with minority children's ability to perform well in school and that culturally compatible classroom instruction offers a possible route to school success for these children (Vogt, Jordan, & Tharp, 1987). The secondary cultural discontinuity approach, on the other hand, claims that the variability in school performance across and within minority groups and the persistence of problems created by cultural differences for some groups can be explained by differences in relationships between the larger society, school, and minority groups (referring to Ogbu's voluntary and involuntary minorities described earlier) and suggests little remedy for minority student failure short of major societal transformation (Ogbu, 1987). Jacobs and Jordan conclude that, since the cultural difference explanation cannot account for minority student school success in the absence of culturally compatible instruction, and the secondary discontinuity explanation cannot account for those involuntary minorities who do succeed in school, perhaps a synthesis of the two explanations is needed.

In my view, Erickson (1987; this volume) offers such a synthesis, noting that it is only when cultural boundaries (differences) are made into cultural borders that students resist and that culturally responsive pedagogy, that is, adapting instruction in the direction of the student's home cultural communication style, can provide a positive option for schools to use to reduce miscommunication, foster trust, and work toward transformative practice (pp. 345–355). Ladson-Billings (1992) makes a similar point when she advocates culturally relevant pedagogy or "the kind of teaching that is designed not merely to fit the school culture to the students' culture but also to use student culture as the basis for helping students understand themselves and others, structure social interactions, and conceptualize knowledge" (p. 314).

One way in which students can be encouraged in these directions is by becoming critical observers of the language and literacy practices around them. Saville-Troike and Schiffrin suggest classroom use of research methodologies from the ethnography of communication and interactional sociolinguistics, respectively, as a means of involving students in analyzing (and gaining insight into) the content and significance of particular speech events and acts, contextualization cues, inferences, and so on, in interaction. Rickford, Nichols, and Freeman and McElhinny likewise suggest that teachers involve their students in exploration and critical reflection on regional, social, and gender variation in their own and their community's language use.

## *Evaluation and assessment*

Repeatedly throughout this volume, the point is made that language varieties other than the standard are usually evaluated negatively, as are the speakers of those varieties. Wiley argues that the promotion of a standard variety through the schools can be seen as a divisive force, for not all groups are provided equal access to acquiring it. Nichols depicts the effects of society's negative attitudes toward creole languages on language learning in school settings.

Yet, it has also been affirmed that this situation can and should change. Freeman and McElhinny state emphatically that "schools are sites in which inequities (based on gender, race, ethnicity, language background, age, sexuality, etc.) can be challenged and potentially transformed by selecting materials that represent identity groups more equally, by reorganizing classroom interaction so that all students have the opportunity to talk and demonstrate achievement, and by encouraging students to critically analyze the ways they use language in their everyday lives." McGroarty recommends that teachers must develop linguistic awareness in order to distinguish dialectal variation from errors and to separate intelligibility from social preferences and prejudices in assessing students. Rickford urges that teachers be encouraged to assist and empower students to acquire additional dialects which might be useful to them in their social lives, schools, or careers. Kachru and Nelson note that the increasing acceptability of nativized varieties of English around the world has implications for English proficiency assessment, and McKay suggests that teachers and students be encouraged to be critical consumers of literacies and the cultural assumptions implicit in them.

At the same time that it encourages an expanded tolerance and even promotion of social and regional variation in monolingual settings, this volume urges the adopting of an expansive view of language competence in multilingual settings. Sridhar draws attention to the identity functions of accent, the acceptability of code switching, and the appropriateness of functional versus native competence depending on the situation. Saville-Troike distinguishes between second, foreign, and auxiliary language learning situations and the different levels of competence appropriate for each. Chick explores the sources and consequences of intercultural miscommunication in postexamination interviews in a South African university.

The common theme in all these perspectives is the need for language evaluation and assessment to be integrally tied to context. Saville-Troike suggests that particular findings from ethnographies of communication for particular speech communities and events can serve to validate norms and priorities for assessment; such an approach implies that assessment norms and priorities will vary from community to community, from event to event, from context to context. For example, to hold bilingual Spanish-English speakers such as the *Abriendo Caminos* participants to monolingual language proficiency norms for Spanish and English reflects a skewed assessment of each language and a simultaneous failure to recognize the additional resources these speakers may have in their code switching and translation abilities.

Throughout this volume, the constructive, interactive, and negotiative nature of the relationship between language and society is also emphasized. Such processes as language contact (Sridhar), nativization (Kachru & Nelson), acculturation (McGroarty; Kachru & Nelson; Saville-Troike), accommodation (McGroarty), dialect divergence (Rickford), gender differentiation in language (Freeman & McElhinny), language strategizing and language rights advocacy (Wiley), negotiating comembership through talk (Chick; Erickson), constructing social identities through discourse (Freeman & McElhinny), and collaborating in literacy activities (McKay) recurringly evoke an image of language and its users in a dynamic interaction in which the users' language and literacy abilities not only position them in certain ways in their social and cultural milieu but also provide them with the resources to negotiate new positions. Further, these negotiations take place in the context of conflict and social struggle generated by relations of power (see also Martin-Jones, 1989).

Under these conditions, with language use constantly transforming and being transformed, evaluation and assessment must also take on a dynamic aspect, focusing on processes rather than outcomes. In L1 and L2 language education, this means that students' language proficiency and academic achievement are measured more by observing their written and spoken language use in specific situations over time than by standardized decontextualized test measures (e.g., Edelsky, 1986); that a program's success is measured more in terms of language and literacy use and interaction in the classroom than by pretest and posttest score outcomes (e.g., Cazabon, Lambert, & Hall, 1993; Hornberger, 1988, 1990); that a school's success is measured more in terms of ongoing development of parental involvement (Torres-Guzmán, 1991), community funds of knowledge (Gonzalez et al., 1993; Moll, 1992), parental empowerment (Delgado-Gaitan, 1990), and school attendance and completion than by school testing performance criteria.

## Conclusion

In Calexico, in California on the border with Mexico, a school district with a 98 percent Hispanic and 80 percent limited English proficient student population appears to be defying low expectations for Hispanic students in the United States – its annual dropout rate is half the state average for Hispanic students. This success is attributed to a districtwide approach which puts priority on the basic curriculum and accommodates language of instruction to students' needs; as one teacher says, they "take the children where they are at – with the home language that they bring – and build on that." Both the superintendent and the assistant superintendent for instructional services note that they no longer think in terms of bilingual and monolingual programs; rather, they have parallel curricula in Spanish and in sheltered English (English geared to the students' level of proficiency) and focus their efforts on making sure that all their students have the opportunity to learn the curriculum, in whatever language(s) works for them. To implement this program, the district has made a concerted effort to recruit Hispanic bilingual personnel; 70 percent of the elementary teachers hold state certification in bilingual education, and 58 percent of the administrators are Hispanic and bilingual. Their own high school graduates constitute about half the district's bilingual elementary teachers, a matter of pride for the district (Schmidt, 1993).

This is just one example in a bilingual setting, among many possible in monolingual, bilingual, and multilingual settings, of an approach that maximizes the likelihood that the contexts of learners' language and literacy use and development will allow them to draw on all points of all nine continua of biliteracy. In so doing, the approach maximizes the educational opportunities offered to these learners, maximizes their participation in those opportunities, and, ultimately, maximizes their potential contributions to the larger society. In Calexico, as elsewhere, such an approach to L1 and L2 language education can only be to the benefit of everyone involved.

## Suggestions for further reading

The following book-length ethnographies provide in-depth interpretation and analysis of language minority education in five different settings.

Delgado-Gaitan, C. (1990). *Literacy for empowerment: The role of parents in children's education.* New York: Falmer.
This book focuses on twenty Mexican families in a small community of southern California and on their concern with their children's academic success in literacy. It is based on the researcher's involvement with the families over a period of 3 years and her documentation of activities in the context of classroom literacy lessons, home literacy-related experiences including homework, and parental interactions with the school.

Edelsky, C. A. (1986). *Writing in a bilingual program: Había una vez.* Norwood, NJ: Ablex.
This book, according to its author, tells three stories: one about elementary school children's writing as it changed during a school-year-long study, one about the evolution of theory and practice in the areas of writing and reading, and one about the life of a Spanish-English bilingual education program in the southwestern United States.

Guthrie, G. P. (1985). *A school divided: An ethnography of bilingual education in a Chinese community.* Hillsdale, N. J.: Erlbaum.
This book is about bilingual education in a Chinese-American community of northern California. Through ethnographic documentation of attitudes and activities at the classroom, school, and community levels, it clearly shows how what was intended to be a maintenance bilingual program came to be implemented as a transitional bilingual program.

Hornberger, N. H. (1988). *Bilingual education and language maintenance: A southern Peruvian Quechua case.* Berlin: Mouton de Gruyter.
Bilingual education is often associated with language maintenance by both its proponents and its detractors, yet few studies have examined the relationship directly. This book does so by looking at the Experimental Bilingual Education Project (PEEB) of Puno, Peru, in terms of the language and education policies it grew out of, the history of language and education among the Quechuas it served, contemporary patterns of language use in Quechua-speaking communities, and factors involved in Quechua language maintenance.

McLaughlin, D. (1992). *When literacy empowers: Navajo language in print.* Albuquerque: University of New Mexico Press.
This ethnography describes the uses of Navajo and English literacy in one community on the Navajo reservation, situating literacy practices and beliefs in a cultural perspective. Contrary to the prevailing view that the Navajo reject literacy in the vernacular, the study shows how the indigenization of church and school in this community contributes directly

to the indigenization of Navajo literacy and, for many, legitimizes the idea of reading and writing Navajo for an individual's own purposes.

## References


Cazabon, M., Lambert, W. E., & Hall, G. (1993). *Two-way bilingual education: A progress report on the Amigos program.* Research report no. 7. Santa Cruz, CA: Center for Research on Cultural Diversity and Second Language Learning.

Delgado-Gaitan, C. (1990). *Literacy for empowerment: The role of parents in children's education.* New York: Falmer.

Edelsky, C. A. (1986). *Writing in a bilingual program: Había una vez.* Norwood, NJ: Ablex.

Erickson, F. (1987). Transformation and school success: The politics and culture of educational achievement. *Anthropology and Education Quarterly, 18*(4), 335–356.

Erickson, F. (1989). Advantages and disadvantages of qualitative research design on foreign language research. In B. Freed (Ed.), *Foreign language acquisition research and the classroom* (pp. 338–353). Lexington, MA: Heath.

Gee, J. (1992). Socio-cultural approaches to literacy (literacies). In W. Grabe (Ed.), *Annual review of applied linguistics* (pp. 31–48). New York: Cambridge University Press.

Gonzalez, N., et al. (1993). *Teacher research on funds of knowledge: Learning from households.* Educational practice report no. 6. Santa Cruz, CA: Center for Research on Cultural Diversity and Second Language Learning.

Guthrie, G. P. (1985). *A school divided: An ethnography of bilingual education in a Chinese community.* Hillsdale, NJ: Erlbaum.

Hornberger, N. H. (1988). *Bilingual education and language maintenance: A southern Peruvian Quechua case.* Berlin: Mouton de Gruyter.

Hornberger, N. H. (1989). Continua of biliteracy. *Review of Educational Research, 59*(3), 271–296.

Hornberger, N. H. (1990). Creating successful learning contexts for bilingual literacy. *Teachers College Record, 92*(2), 212–229.

Hornberger, N. H. (1991). Extending enrichment bilingual education: Revisiting typologies and redirecting policy. In O. García (Ed.), *Bilingual education: Focusschrift in honor of Joshua A. Fishman on the occasion of his 65th birthday* (Vol. 1, pp. 215–234) Philadelphia: John Benjamins.

Huerta-Macías, A., & Quintero, E. (1992). Code-switching, bilingualism, and biliteracy: A case study. *Bilingual Research Journal, 16*(3&4), 69–90.

Hymes, D. H. (1972a). Models of the interaction of language and social life. In J. J. Gumperz and D. Hymes (Eds.), *Directions in sociolinguistics: The ethnography of communication* (pp. 35–71). New York: Holt, Rinehart and Winston.

Hymes, D. H. (1972b). On communicative competence. In J. B. Pride and J. Holmes (Eds.), *Sociolinguistics* (pp. 269–293). Harmondsworth: Penguin.

Jacobs, E. & Jordan, C. (Eds.). (1987). Explaining the school performance of minority students. *Anthropology and Education Quarterly, 18*(4), 259–382.

Jacobson, R. & Faltis, C. (1990). *Language distribution issues in bilingual schooling*. Clevedon: Multilingual Matters.

Ladson-Billings, G. (1992). Reading between the lines and beyond the pages: A culturally relevant approach to literacy teaching. *Theory into Practice, 31*(4), 312–320.

Lambert, W. E. (1985). Some cognitive and sociocultural consequences of being bilingual. In J. E. Alatis & J. Staczek (Eds.), *Perspectives on bilingualism and bilingual education* (pp. 116–131). Washington DC: Georgetown University Press.

Legarreta-Marcaida, D. (1981). Effective use of the primary language in the classroom. *Schooling and language minority students: A theoretical framework* (pp. 83–116) Los Angeles: Evaluation, Dissemination, and Assessment Center, California State University.

Martin-Jones, M. (1989). Language, power and linguistic minorities: The need for an alternative approach to bilingualism, language maintenance and shift. In R. Grillo (Ed.), *Social anthropology and the politics of language* (pp. 106–125). London: Routledge and Kegan Paul.

McLaughlin, B. (1985). *Second language acquisition in childhood: Vol. 2. School-age children*. Hillsdale, NJ: Erlbaum.

McLaughlin, D. (1992). *When literacy empowers: Navajo language in print.* Albuquerque: University of New Mexico Press.

Milk, R. (1981). Language use in bilingual classrooms: Two case studies. In M. Hines & W. Rutherford (Eds.). *On TESOL.* (pp. 181–191.) Washington DC: TESOL.

Milk, R. (1986). The issue of language separation in bilingual methodology. In E. Garciía and R. Flores (Eds.), *Language and literacy research in bilingual education* (pp. 67–86). Tempe: Arizona State University.

Moll, L. (1992). Bilingual classroom studies and community analysis: Some recent trends. *Educational Researcher, 21*(2), 20–24.

Ogbu, J. (1987). Variability in minority school performance: A problem in search of an explanation. *Anthropology and Education Quarterly, 18*(4), 312–334.

Sapiens, A. (1982). The use of Spanish and English in a high school bilingual civics class. In J. Amastae & L. Elías-Olivares (Eds.), *Spanish in the United States* (pp. 386–412). Cambridge: Cambridge University Press.

Schmidt, P. (1993). Districtwide approach enables border system to defy low expectations for L.E.P. students. *Education Week*. Extra edition, July 14, 6–7.

Street, B. (1984). *Literacy in theory and practice.* Cambridge: Cambridge University Press.

Street, B. (1988). A critical look at Walter Ong and the "Great Divide." *Literacy Research Center, 4*(1), 1, 3, 5.

Street, B. (1993). The implications of the new literacy studies for the new South Africa. *Journal of Literary Studies, 9*(2).

Torres-Guzmán, M. (1991). Recasting frames: Latino parent involvement. In M. McGroarty & C. Faltis (Eds.), *Languages in school and society: Policy and pedagogy* (pp. 529–552). Berlin: Mouton.

Tsang, C. (1983). Code-switching strategies in bilingual instructional settings. In M. Chu-Chang (Ed.), *Asian and Pacific-American perspectives in bilingual education* (pp. 197–215). New York: Teachers College Press.

Vogt, L., Jordan, C., & Tharp, R. (1987). Explaining school failure, producing school success: Two cases. *Anthropology and Education Quarterly, 18*(4), 276–286.

Zentella, A. C. (1981). Tá bien, you could answer me en cualquier idioma: Puerto Rican codeswitching in bilingual classrooms. In R. Durán (Ed.), *Latino language and communicative behavior* (pp. 109–131). Norwood, NJ: Ablex.

# Index

*Note:* Page numbers followed by n indicate footnotes.


accents, 356
  dialects vs., 73–74, 153
accommodation theory, 11–13, 179
accountability, principle of, 167
acculturation, 359
additive bilingualism, 137–138
address, forms of, 223
adjacency pairs, 336, 336n3
African-Americans
  discourse and gender differences among, 256–257, 265–266
  discrimination against, 121
  speech activities of, 166, 245
African-American Vernacular English (AAVE), 172–185, 456
  attitudes toward, 16–18, 131, 132–136, 151–152, 180–184, 296, 316–317
  creole origins of, 173n11, 178–179
  grammatical features of, 174–178
  implications for teachers, 181–183, 296, 316–317
  parent attitudes toward, 20, 180–181
  phonological features of, 174–178
  speaker attitudes and, 13–15
  teacher attitudes toward, 16–18, 131, 132–136, 151–152, 180–184
  use of, in schools, 132–136
age grading, 165–167
Anglo, as term, 80
Angola, pidgins in, 198
apology acts, 386, 395, 398–400, 408–410, 413, 414
Appalachian English, 6–7
appropriateness, 90–91, 104, 363, 389
Arabic, 48, 55, 59, 71, 88, 111, 125, 250, 250n8, 424
Asian-Americans
  concept of, 266
  discourse and gender differences among, 265–266
  *see also specific languages*
assessment, 5–7, 8–11, 390, 467–469
  *see also* psychometric approach
assimilation, 116, 119–121
attitudes toward language, 1, 3–36
  accommodation theory and, 11–13
  African-American Vernacular English and, 16–18, 131, 132–136, 151–152, 180–184, 296, 316–317
  creole, 196–197
  defined, 5
  dialects, 6–7, 73, 91, 105, 118, 154, 180–181
  educational implications of, 15–22, 30–36
  elite groups and, 29–30, 106–107
  gender and, 15
  language policies and, 27–30
  measurement of, 5–7, 8–11
  of native speakers of English, 78–79, 81–82, 94–95
  overemphasizing, 105–106
  of parents, 19–20, 63, 180–181
  pidgin, 196–197
  positive, encouraging, 4
  social identity and, 3–5, 33–35, 87, 89
  speakers and, 13–15
  and status of language in society, 4, 63, 73
  of students, 18–19, 33
  of teachers, 16–18, 33, 62–65
Australia, 72, 126, 429
  and gender differences in the classroom, 261–265
  as Inner Circle English country, 78
  language policy in, 110
autonomous approach, to language planning, 115–121
autonomous model of literacy, 422, 427–428

back channeling, 288, 289
bald-on-record strategies, 340–341
basilects, 81
Bengali, 112
bilingualism
  additive, 137–138
  choice of language and, 1, 21, 51–52

bilingualism *(cont.)*
  creativity of, 84–87, 96–97
  diglossia and, 26, 55–56
  discursive practices in, 229–230
  gender and, 229–230
  language shift and, 123
  models of education, 462–464
  multilingualism vs., 47
  public attitudes toward, 28–30
  student attitudes toward, 21–22
  *see also* multilingualism
biliteracy, 452–461
  *see also* literacy
black English, *see* African-American Vernacular English (AAVE)
blitzkrieg ethnography, 369
borrowing, 460
  code mixing vs., 58
  convergence vs., 61
British English
  accommodation theory in, 11–12
  American English vs., 27, 74–75, 82–83, 159–161, 402–403
  dialects in, 73, 159–161
  Received Pronunciation (RP) in, 73, 160–161

Canada
  attitudes toward English and French in, 5, 366–367
  Canadian-French immersion programs, 28n6
  as Inner Circle English country, 78
  literacy in, 426–427, 429
  measuring language attitudes and motivations in, 5–8
  multilingualism in, 48, 126, 366–367
chain shifts, 163–164, 258–259
China, English use in, 78
Chinese, 59–60, 108, 112, 121, 126, 365–366, 435, 436
code mixing, 57–60, 64, 88n9, 93–94, 460
codes, 357
  defined, 50
code switching, 47, 56–57, 64, 88n9, 460, 465–466
  attitudes toward, 317–318
  creoles and, 195–196, 202–203, 204
  metaphorical, 56, 312, 317n6
  situational, 56, 293, 300, 312, 317n6
cognitive development, literacy and, 116–117, 424–425, 427
cognitive patterning, 361
colonialism, 48, 53, 54, 81–82, 124, 362, 457
common language, 107–108, 125–126
communicative acts, 371–372
  *see also* speech acts
communicative competence, 89–92, 267, 315, 323, 345, 357, 362–368, 454
communicative events, 370–371
communicative repertoire, 357
  verbal, 49–51
communicative situations, 369–370, 372
community
  literacy and, 433–434
  norms and behaviors in, 466
  *see also* speech communities
community of practice, 246–247
comparative creolistics, 201
complaint acts, 403–405, 408, 414
compliments, 332–337, 402–403, 411
compound responses, 332–337
comprehensibility, 93, 94
conflict
  in discourse, 238, 346
  over language in the United States, 130–131
contact hypothesis, 21
context analysis, 285, 288
context of situation, 93
contextualization cues, 313–314, 316, 318, 324, 345, 399, 465
contextual presuppositions, 313
continental discourse analysis, 286, 330n1
contrastive rhetoric, 430, 435
conventions of language, 344
convergence, 12, 60–61, 460
conversation, *see* discourse
conversation analysis, 285–287
conversational floors, 245, 289, 300
conversational inferencing, 354
conversational overlap, 233–234
corpus language planning, 2, 108, 221
creoles, 18–19, 149–150, 199–200, 456
  attitudes toward, 196–197
  code switching and, 195–196, 202–203, 204
  development of, 199–200
  English-based, 195–196, 197, 200, 204, 205–209
  French-based, 199–200, 204
  Gullah, 173n11, 195–196, 201, 204, 205–209
  Haitian, 55, 204, 211, 457
  Jamaican, 64, 178, 197, 204, 211
  origins of, 199
  origins of African-American Vernacular English in, 173n11, 178–179
  pidgins vs., 200
  structures and functions of, 204–209
  study of, 200–203
critical language study, 436–437
cross-cultural communication studies, 331–337, 387, 389
cultural competence, 367–368

cultural transmission, 48
culture
  as boundary vs. border, 294–297, 301
  classroom interaction and, 465–467
  contextualization cues and, 313–314, 316, 318, 324, 345, 399, 465
  cross-cultural studies, 331–337, 387, 389
  defined, 367
  in dual-culture model of cross-sex communication, 239–242
  ethnography of communication and, 360–362
  interactional sociolinguistics and, 316–318, 324
  literacy and, 434–436, 439–440
  and situated social identity, 291–294
  *see also* intercultural communication
curriculum
  and microethnography, 288–289, 297–302
  *see also* language learning

dialect areas, 157–158
dialect maps, 155–157
dialects, 18–19, 149, 151–185
  accents vs., 73–74, 153
  African-American, *see* African-American Vernacular English (AAVE)
  age grading and, 166–167
  attitudes toward use of, 6–7, 73, 91, 105, 118, 154, 180–181
  challenges of, 152–153
  concept of, 105
  languages vs., 92, 105
  parent attitudes toward, 20, 180–181
  reasons for studying, 151–152
  regional, 6–7, 154–164
  social, 164–185
  socioeconomic status and, 16, 73, 160–161, 167–172, 174
  standards and, 24
  stigma attached to, 73, 91, 105, 118, 154
  world Englishes and, 72–73
  writing instruction and, 31–32
diglossia, 26, 54–56
  bilingualism and, 26, 55–56
  code switching vs., 57
  defined, 54
  examples of, 54–55
  gender and, 250
discourse
  cognitive patterning and, 361
  continental discourse analysis, 286, 330n1
  conversational floors, 245, 289, 300
  face-to-face interaction, 307, 308–311, 314, 315–320
  gender and, 229–242, 257–259
  interruptions, 233–234
  literacy and, 428–429
  male vs. female, 230–242
  oppositional, 238, 346
  world English and, 97
discourse completion tasks, 390–391, 392–394, 398–400, 401
discrimination, 119–121, 132
divergent accommodation, 12, 179
domains
  of English, 81, 87–88, 95, 96
  language choice and, 51–52
dual-culture model of cross-sex communication, 239–242

economic goals, of language planning, 126–128
elementary school
  acquisition of speech acts in, 407
  African-American Vernacular English and, 181–183
  classroom behavior in, 320
  foreign language in, 10–11
  gender issues in, 241, 265
  social participation structure in, 288
embedded language, 57, 203
enculturation, 359
English, 294–295, 457
  African-American, *see* African-American Vernacular English (AAVE)
  American vs. British, 27, 74–75, 82–83, 159–161, 402–403
  British, *see* British English
  code mixing in, 60
  creoles based on, 195–196, 197, 200, 204, 205–209
  domains of, 81, 87–88, 95, 96
  identity marking with, 58–59
  as international language, 2, 65, 71–98
  monolingualism in, 84–87, 96–97, 105
  nonnative varieties, 65
  as official language, 74, 75, 77–79, 113, 123, 359
  origins of, 82
  South African vs. Zulu, 78, 339–342
  standard, *see* standard English
  *see also* world Englishes
English as a foreign language (EFL), 79
English as a native language, native speakers of, 78–79, 81–82, 94–95
English as a second language (ESL), 79, 163
  ethnography of communication and, 369–372
  gender and, 253–254
  student attitudes toward, 19–21
  teacher attitudes toward, 16–18, 33, 62–65

English for special purposes (ESP), 96, 372
epistemic literacy, 422, 423
ethnicity
as boundary vs. border, 294–297, 301
and situated social identity, 291–294, 295–297
*see also* African-American Vernacular English (AAVE); *specific ethnic groups*
ethnic revitalization, 124
ethnography of communication, 90, 282, 285, 286, 307, 349, 351–377, 467
approach taken in, 351–352
classroom applications of, 373–377
communicative competence and, 357, 362–368
doing, 368–373
ethnomethodological approach and, 354
functions of communication and, 354–356
instructional applications of, 267–269
intercultural communication and, 329
language and culture in, 360–362
patterns of communication and, 352–354
speech communities and, 356–359
*see also* microethnography
ethnomethodology, 285–287, 354
Expanding Circle countries
defined, 78
expression of power in, 87
importance of English in, 88
standards for English in, 83, 89
teaching English in, 71, 88–89, 95–98
extrinsic motivation, 7–8

face-saving strategies, 308–311, 316, 317–318, 339–341, 407
face-to-face interaction, 307, 308–311, 314, 315–320
fluent English proficient (FEP) designation, 137
foreign language(s), 4
elementary-level learners of, 10–11
ethnography of communication and, 358–359, 362
motivation to learn, 9–11
speech acts and, 395, 409–410, 412
forms of address, 223
free morpheme constraint, 58
French, 28n6, 48, 55, 71, 112, 154, 294–295, 359, 457
creoles based on, 199–200, 204
dialects of, 161–162
identity marking with, 58–59
standards for, 83
functional literacy, 422–423

gender, 218–269
activity and, 244–245, 246
apologies and, 398
attitudes toward language and, 15
in the classroom, 229–230, 241, 261–269
corpus planning and, 108
difference model of, 219, 236–242
diversity across cultures in the United States, 254–260, 265–266
dominance model of, 218, 219, 231–236
and ESL contexts, 253–254
genre and, 247–248
interactional styles and, 219, 231–247
literacy and, 437
and male vs. female discourse, 230–242, 257–259
multilingualism and, 248–250
politeness and, 251–253
schools as feminine setting and, 18
sexist language and, 219–231
and situated social identity, 291–294, 295–297
standards and, 24n4
women's language and, 234, 236–237, 238
world Englishes and, 86
*see also* sexism
German, 55, 126, 131–132, 154, 173, 248–249, 404
dialects of, 162–163
grammar, 360–361
African-American Vernacular English (AAVE), 174–178
of expectations, 354
generative, 48–49
Great Britain
and American vs. British English, 27, 74–75, 82–83, 159–161, 402–403
compliments in, 402–403
creoles in, 197
dialects in, 297
and gender differences in the classroom, 261–265
as Inner Circle English country, 77–78
greeting rituals, 91, 319
guest (embedded) language, 57, 203
Gullah, 173n11, 195–196, 201, 204, 205–209
Guyana, creoles in, 202

Haitian Creole, 55, 204, 211, 457
Hawaii
creoles in, 200, 202, 204
institutional racism in schools, 136–137
social participation structure, 288–289
Hebrew, 54, 108, 408–410
hegemony, defined, 113
Hindi, 52–53, 57, 59, 71, 90, 312

Hispanic-Americans, *see* Mexican-Americans; Puerto Rican Americans
historical-structural approach, to language planning, 111–112, 115, 117, 119–122, 132
Hmong, 129, 431
Hong Kong, 403–404
  code mixing in, 59–60
host (matrix) language, 57, 203
human rights, language rights as, 107

identity marking, 58–59
ideological model of literacy, 426–428
immigrant groups
  language policies and, 117–122
  language shift and, 122–123
  *see also specific groups and languages*
India, 54, 59, 312, 461
  code mixing in, 93–94
  convergence in, 61
  cross-cultural issues in, 91
  English use in, 78, 80, 81, 84–86, 90
  language choice in, 52
  official languages in, 359
  patterns of use in, 52–53
  pidgins in, 198
  verbal repertoire in, 50
indirect complaints, 404–405
indirect speech acts, 309–310
informational literacy, 422
initial literacy, 422
Inner Circle countries
  defined, 77–78
  intelligibility and, 94–95
  interlanguage and, 79–80
  linguistic power of, 88
  multiculturalism and, 96
  native English speakers in, 78–79, 81–82, 94–95
  range of English in, 86–87
  standards for English in, 83–84
input, 81, 88–89, 95–98
instrumental motivation, 7–8
integrative motivation, 7–8
intelligibility, 92–95
interactional context, 242
  *see also* microethnography
interactional sociolinguistics, 282, 285–287, 307–325, 467
  analysis of verbal communication in, 307–308, 311–320
  classroom applications of, 316–320, 322–325
  described, 307–308, 316
  ethnography of communication and, 354
  face-to-face interaction in, 307, 308–311, 314, 315–320
  intercultural communication and, 329, 330, 331, 338–342
  language of social interaction in, 320–322
  pedagogical applications of, 316–320, 322–325
  transcription process in, 320–322
  *see also* intercultural communication
interaction skills, 365–367
intercultural communication, 282, 329–346
  critique of sociolinguistic studies of, 342–344, 345
  improving effectiveness of, 344–346
  interactional sociolinguistics and, 329, 330, 331, 338–342
  microethnography and, 329, 330, 330n1
  in South Africa, 330, 332–342
  speech acts and, 329, 330, 331–337
  *see also* ethnography of communication; interactional sociolinguistics; microethnography; speech acts
interlanguage, 79–80
intrinsic motivation, 7–8
isoglosses, 157, 158–161

Jamaican Creole, 64, 178, 197, 204, 211
Japan, 253n10
  English use in, 78
  pidgins in, 198
Japanese, 10, 90, 121, 126, 393, 395, 396–397, 401–402, 405, 406–407, 410–411
Javanese, 52, 252–253

Khmer, 129, 457, 459

language(s), 360–362
  common, 107–108, 125–126
  dialects vs., 92, 105
  as form of social control, 104–105, 111–112, 113, 121–122, 124–126
  grammar of, 360–361
  nonstandard varieties of, 104
  as social behavior, 104
  social identity and, 3–5, 33–35, 87, 89, 231–247, 257–259, 355–356
  status in society, 4, 63, 73–75, 77–79, 105, 112
  varieties, 65, 74–79, 83, 99, 104, 153–154, 452
  vocabulary of, 360
  *see also specific languages*
language acquisition planning, 2, 109, 130–139
language choice, 1, 21, 51–52, 219–231
language classification, 137
language enrichment policy, 124
language learning
  African-American Vernacular English in, 132–136

language learning *(cont.)*
  attitudes toward language and, 15–22, 30–36
  dialects in, 163–164, 181–184
  ethnography of communication and, 373–377
  gender and, 261–269
  interactional sociolinguistics and, 318–320, 322–325
  literacy and, 438–441
  microethnography and, 288–289, 297–302
  multilingualism and, 62–65, 88–89, 95–98
  pidgins and creoles and, 209–212
  speech acts in, 408–415
  of standard vs. foreign language, 358–359, 362
  *see also* students
language loyalty, 123–124
  gender and, 254–260
language minority, 106n1, 108, 120, 130–131
  discrimination against, 120–121
language planning, 103–140
  conflicts and, 106–107
  corpus, 2, 108, 221
  defined, 108, 109–110
  evolution of, 103–104
  explicit vs. implicit, 104, 111, 113
  goals of, 122–129
  government involvement in, 110–112
  historical-structural and ideological approach to, 111–112, 115, 117, 119–122, 132
  language acquisition, 2, 109, 130–139
  language strategists and, 110–112
  literacy vs., 117, 127–128
  neoclassical-autonomous approach to, 115–121
  orientations toward, 114–115
  status, 2, 108–109
language policies, 4–5, 27–30, 91, 109
  defined, 27
  goals of, 122–129
  government involvement in, 110–112
  immigrant groups and, 117–122
  influencing, 35–36
  in institutional contexts, 136–139
  in language teaching, 461–464
  literacy campaigns and, 34, 34n7, 115, 127
  nature of, 111
  neoclassical-autonomous approach to, 115–121
  public attitudes and, 27–30
language problems, 109–110, 117, 127–128
language rights, 107, 139
language shift, 122–123
  chain shift in, 163–164, 258–259
language strategists, 110–112
*Lau v. Nichols,* 131
lexical choice
  gender-based ideologies and, 227–231
  gender differences in, 223–227
lexical cues, 399
lexifier language, 199
Likert-type scales, for measuring language attitudes, 6
limited English proficient (LEP) designation, 137
lingua franca, 53, 362
linguicide, 124
linguistic anthropology, 243
linguistic autonomy, principle of, 134
linguistic competence, 363
  *see also* communicative competence
linguistic convergence, 60–61
linguistic knowledge, 363–365
linguistic racism, 117
listening
  contextualization cues and, 313–314, 316, 318, 324, 399
  in microethnography, 284, 288–290
literacy, 350, 421–441
  biliteracy, 452–461
  classroom implications of, 438–441
  and cognitive development, 116–117, 424–425, 427
  as collaborative practice, 430–433, 465
  and the community, 433–434
  and culture, 434–436, 439–440
  and discourse, 428–429
  in historical context, 426
  ideological model of, 426–428
  as individual skill, 421, 422–425, 429
  language and development of, 460–461
  language planning vs., 117, 127–128
  levels of, 422–423
  methods of analyzing, 429–430, 435
  in native language, 31–32
  and power, 430, 436–438
  as social practice, 421, 426–438
  social problems and, 127–128
  technical, 423
  in written and oral languages, 423–424, 428–429
literature, new-English, 84–87, 96–97
local framing, 284, 300–301
locutionary meaning, 384

*Martin Luther King Jr. Elementary School Children v. Ann Arbor Board of Education,* 131, 133–136, 152n1
matched guise technique, 6–7
matrix language frame model, 57, 58, 203

metaphorical code switching, 56, 312, 317n6
Mexican-Americans, 16, 120, 121, 173, 469
Mexicano, 249–250
*Meyer v. Nebraska,* 131–132
microethnography, 281–303, 307, 357
  and culture difference as boundary vs. border, 294–297, 301
  curriculum issues and, 288–289, 297–302
  described, 283–284
  intercultural communication and, 329, 330, 330n1
  and listening in relation to speaking, 284, 288–290
  origins of, 284–287
  pedagogy issues and, 288–289, 297–302
  and rhythm and cadence in interaction, 290–291
  and situated social identity, 291–294, 300–301
  videos and, 283, 285, 299–301
  *see also* ethnography of communication
minimal responses, 240
miscommunication, intercultural, *see* intercultural communication
model dialogues, 414
models
  bilingual education, 462–464
  concept of, 77
  gender, 218, 219, 231–242
  literacy, 426–428
  programs vs., 462–464
monolingualism
  attitude to English, 84–87, 96–97, 105
  borrowing in, 58
  code mixing in, 59
  code switching and, 47
  as ideal state, 105
  language shift and, 123
  teaching English from perspective of, 88–89
  verbal repertoire and, 50
motivation, 4
  accommodation theory and, 11–13
  to assimilate into dominant society, 116
  definitions of, 5, 8–9, 30
  measurement of, 7–11
  promoting, 30–32
  relevant language and, 32–33
  types of, 7–8
  to use language in social control, 105
multiculturalism, English as medium of, 95–96
multilingualism, 1–2, 47–65
  asymmetric principle of, 52
  bilingualism vs., 47
  code mixing and, 57–60
  code switching and, 56–57
  convergence and, 60–61
  diglossia and, 26, 54–56
  gender and, 248–250
  implications for teachers, 62–65
  language choice in, 51–52
  language learning and, 62–65, 88–89, 95–98
  language shift and, 123
  patterns in structure, 60–62
  patterns of use and, 52–60
  personality principle of, 48
  reasons for, 48
  speech communities and, 48–52
  territorial principle of, 48
  transfer and, 61–62
  types of, 47–48
  verbal repertoire in, 49–51
  *see also* bilingualism

naming conventions, 222–223
nationalism, language planning in, 124–126
national literacy campaigns, 34, 34n7, 115, 127
Native Americans, 34, 121, 366, 456
  English-only policies and, 113
  gender and language among, 254–255
native language(s), 79
  English as, 78–79, 81–82, 94–95
  promoting literacy skills in, 31–32
  respect for, 301–302, 430–431
  standards and, 24
  *see also* creoles; pidgins
naturally occurring data, 391–394
neoclassical approach, to language planning, 115–121
new-English literatures, 84–87, 96–97
New York City English, 160–161, 167–169
New Zealand, 72, 398
  additive bilingualism in, 137–138
  as Inner Circle English country, 74, 78
  vestigial racism in, 130–131
non-English proficient (NEP), 137
norms, 22–23
  for classroom behavior, 319–320
  descriptive, 22
  influences on choice of, 26–27
  language, 104
  prescriptive, 22, 23, 24, 111
  in speech communities, 49
  for tests of English, 71, 97–98
  world Englishes and, 83–84
Northern Cities Chain Shift, 163–164, 258–259

official language(s), 1, 106
 English as, 74, 75, 77–79, 113, 123, 359
oppositional discourse, 238, 346
orientation, toward language planning, 7, 114–115
Outer Circle countries
 colonial legacy of, 48, 53, 54, 81–82, 124, 362, 457
 defined, 78
 expression of power in, 87
 importance of English in, 84–85, 88, 92–93
 intelligibility in, 94
 interlanguage and, 79–80
 multiculturalism and, 96
 standards for English in, 83, 89
 teaching English in, 71, 88–89, 95–98

Pakistan, English use in, 75–76
paralinguistic cues, 399
parents
 African-American Vernacular English (AAVE) and, 20, 180–181
 attitudes toward language, 19–20, 63, 180–181
 standards and, 24–26
pedagogy
 attitudes of teacher and, 16–18, 33, 62–65
 attitudes toward creoles and pidgins, 197, 209–212
 ethnography of communication and, 373–377
 of interactional sociolinguistics, 316–320, 322–325
 literacy and, 438–441
 and microethnography, 288–289, 297–302
 multiple forms of language and, 33–35
 promoting motivation in, 30–32
 relevant language and, 32–33
 second language, 267–269
 *see also* students
performative literacy, 422
perlocutionary force, 384
phonology
 African-American Vernacular English (AAVE), 174–178
 Received Pronunciation (RP), 73, 160–161
pidgins, 149–150, 197–199, 456
 attitudes toward, 196–197
 creoles vs., 200
 development of, 198–199
 Nigerian, 81
 origins of, 197–198
 study of, 200–202, 202–203
pluralism, of norms and standards, 84
pluricentric languages, 71
politeness, 387
 gender and, 251–253
 strategies for, 341
political goals, of language planning, 124–126
Portuguese, 253–254, 395, 407
 creoles based on, 200
power relationships
 agency and, 229–230
 defined, 220–221
 development of pidgins and, 198–199
 and ethnography of communication, 355–356
 intercultural communication and, 343
 language as instrument of, 104–107, 111–112, 113, 121–122, 124–126
 linguistic, 87–88
 literacy and, 430, 436–438
 in male vs. female discourse, 230–242
 in work situations, 238–239
prescriptive norms, 22, 23, 24, 111
prescriptive rules, 353
propositional meaning, 384
prosodic cues, 399
psychometric approach
 English tests and, 71, 97–98
 to language classification, 137
 limitations of, 8–11
 to measuring language attitudes, 5–7, 8–11
 to measuring motivation, 7–11
Puerto Rican Americans, 121, 255–256, 451–452
Punjabi, 173, 312, 407

Quechua, 20, 249–250n7, 361, 449–451, 455–456, 457, 459, 465
questions, in male vs. female discourse, 235–236

race
 and situated social identity, 291–294, 295–297, 300–301
 *see also* African-American Vernacular English (AAVE); *specific racial groups*
racism, 132
 institutional, 120–121, 136–137
 language classification in, 137
 language policy and, 112
 linguistic, 117
 vestigial, 130–131
reading skills, African-American Vernacular English and, 181–183
Received Pronunciation (RP), 73, 160–161
referential meaning, 364, 365
refusal acts, 393–394, 400–402, 411

regional dialects, 6–7, 154–164
  classroom implications for, 163–164
  combinations of features for, 161–162
  dialect areas for, 157–158
  dialect maps and, 155–157
  isoglosses of, 157, 158–161
  reasons for, 162–163
  surveys in study of, 155
rejection acts, 402, 407–408
request acts, 387, 405, 407
rituals, 91, 309, 319
role playing, 395–396, 398, 414

Samaná English, 179, 179n16
Sanskrit, 53, 54, 59, 88
scripts, 458
second language(s), 4
  defined, 384
  ethnography of communication and, 359, 361–362, 375
  language transfer and, 61–62
  literacy and, 437
  motivation to learn, 9–11
  pedagogy of, 267–269
  speech acts and, 383, 385–387, 401–402, 406–407, 410–411, 412
  standards and, 24
  student attitudes toward learning, 21–22
self, and society, 308–311, 318
sexism, 150
  in forms of address, 223
  and gender-based ideologies, 219–221, 227–231
  language choices and, 219–231
  language policy and, 108, 112
  in lexical choices, 223–227
  in naming conventions, 222
  *see also* gender
silence, 90, 310, 366, 371
Singapore, English use in, 78, 81–82
situated social identity, 291–294, 295–297, 300–301
situational code switching, 56, 293, 300, 312, 317n6
situational comembership, 282, 295–297
situational frame cards, 300–301
social identity
  language and, 3–5, 33–35, 87, 89, 231–247, 257–259, 355–356
  and male vs. female discourse, 230–242, 257–259
  situated, 291–294, 295–297
  situational comembership and, 282, 295–297
socialization, 130, 375, 433–434
social networks, 172, 329–330
social participation structure, 288–289
sociocultural ability, 388, 389, 408
socioeconomic status (SES)
  communicative competence and, 366–367
  dialects and, 16, 73, 160–161, 167–172, 174
  gender and language differences, 257–259
  improving, 128
  and situated social identity, 291–294, 295–297, 300–301
sociolinguistic ability, 388
sociolinguistic transfer, 282, 332–342
South Africa, 282
  English use in, 78, 338–342
  intercultural communication in, 330, 332–342
South African English-speakers (SAE), 338–342
Spanish, 10, 48, 71, 129, 173, 249–250, 294–295, 431, 456, 457, 465
  code mixing in, 60
  creoles based on, 200
  cultural variability among speakers of, 255–256
  language choice and, 52
  norms for, 27
  parental use of, 19–20
  teacher attitudes toward, 16–17
speech acts, 282, 309–310, 349–350, 383–415
  acquisition of, 407–408
  apologies, 386, 395, 398–400, 408–410, 413, 414
  assessment of, 390, 413–414
  awareness of, 413–414
  classroom implications of, 412–415
  complaints, 403–405, 408, 414
  compliments, 332–337, 402–403, 411
  data collection methods, 389–397
  defined, 350
  empirical validation of, 385–387
  historical overview of, 385
  intercultural communication and, 329, 330, 331–337
  refusals, 393–394, 400–402, 411
  requests, 387, 405, 407
  selecting appropriate, 389
  sociocultural ability and, 388, 389, 408
  sociolinguistic ability and, 388
  suggestions, 407–408
  teaching of, 408–411
  types of, 384–385, 397–407
speech act sets, 385–387
speech communities, 48–52, 285, 356–359
  defined, 49, 82
  expectations in, 353
  foreign language, 358–359
  generative grammar in, 48–49
  language choice in, 51–52

speech communities *(cont.)*
membership in multiple, 357–358
nature of, 356–357
second language, 359
verbal repertoire in, 49–51
world English and, 82–83
standard English
accents in, 74
African-American Vernacular English and, 181, 182–183
concept of, 77
defined, 73
world Englishes and, 83–84, 89
standards, 1, 23–26
changes in, 24
common language as, 125–126
concept of, 77
gender and, 24n4
influences on choice of, 26–27
multiplicity of, 25, 32–35
schools and, 24–25, 113, 125–126, 130
status planning and, 108–109
state boards of education, attitudes toward language and, 29–30
status language planning, 2, 108–109
strategists, language, 110–112
Street, B. V., 115–116, 422, 423, 427–428, 459, 461
students
attitudes toward language, 18–21, 33
standards and, 24–26
*see also* elementary school; language learning
substratum language, 199
suggestion acts, 407–408
superstratum language, 199
surnaming practices, 222–223
survival literacy, 422

talk stories, 288–289
teachers
attitudes toward creoles and pidgins, 197, 209–212
attitudes toward language, 16–18, 33, 62–65
dialects and, 163–164, 180–185, *see also* African-American Vernacular English (AAVE)
ethnography of communication and, 373–377
and gender in the classroom, 229–230, 241, 261–269
interactional sociolinguistics and, 316–320, 322–325
language policies and, 35–36, 461–464
language socialization and, 17–18
literacy and, 438–441
microethnography and, 288–289, 297–302
motivation toward language and, 1
professional responsibility of, 134–136
relevant language and, 32–33
speech acts and, 412–415
standards and, 24–26
training programs, 65
and transmission model of teaching, 264
world Englishes and, 71, 88–89, 95–98
*see also* students
technical literacy, 423
technological engagement, 431–432
tests
of English, 71, 97–98
for language classification, 137
*see also* psychometric approach
text analysis, 430
transfer, 61–62, 64, 460
pragmatic, 401–402
sociolinguistic, 282, 332–342
transmission model of teaching, 264
transnationalism, 125
tribal languages, 14

United States
and American vs. British English, 27, 74–75, 82–83, 159–161, 402–403
conflicts over language in, 130–131
dialects in, 154–155
English as official language of, 74, 75, 78, 113, 123
and gender differences in the classroom, 261–265
gender diversity across cultures in, 254–260
as Inner Circle English country, 77–78
language loyalty in, 123–124
language maintenance in, 62–63
language policy in, 110, 111
language shift in, 122–123, 163–164
management styles in, 238–239

variationist paradigm, 13–15
varieties, language, 65, 74–79, 83, 99, 104, 153–154, 452
verbal communication, in interactional sociolinguistics, 307–308, 311–320
verbal discourse, 286
*see also* discourse
verbal repertoire, 49–51
verbal report interviews, 395–397
Virgin Islands, creoles in, 200

West Africa, 84
creoles in, 200, 201
women's language, 234, 236–237, 238
work situations
domains of language in, 51–52, 81, 87–88, 95, 96

work situations *(cont.)*
forms of address and, 223
management styles in, 238–239
medical services, 128–129
police work, 259
street warrior style in, 259
world Englishes, 71–98
bilinguals' creativity and, 84–87, 96–97
characteristics of, 72–77
communicative competence in using, 89–92
depth of use of, 81
dialects and, 72–73
discourse pragmatics for, 97
domains of, 81, 87–88, 95, 96
Expanding Circle users, 78, 83, 87, 88, 89, 95–98
functions of, 81, 87–88, 90, 95, 96
Inner Circle users, 77–78, 79–83, 86, 88, 94–95, 96
intelligibility of, 92–95
interlanguage and, 79–80
multiculturalism and, 95–96
native speakers and, 78–79, 81–82, 94–95
official language status of, 74, 75, 77–79
Outer Circle users, 78, 79–80, 81, 83, 84–87, 88, 89, 92–93, 94, 95, 96
range of use of, 80–81
sociolinguistic considerations for, 89–92, 96
speech communities for, 82–83
spread of, 2, 65, 71–72, 81
standards and, 73, 74, 77, 83–84, 89, 97–98
teaching issues for, 71, 88–89, 95–98
varieties of, 74–79, 83, 153–154
writing skills
African-American Vernacular English and, 183–184
creole vs. European-American approach to, 209, 213–214
world Englishes and, 31–32

Zambia, English use in, 78, 91
Zulu English-speakers (ZE), 339–342